Research Handbook on the Law of Treaties

RESEARCH HANDBOOKS IN INTERNATIONAL LAW

This highly original series offers a unique appraisal of the state-of-the-art of research and thinking in international law. Taking a thematic approach, each volume, edited by a prominent expert, covers a specific aspect of international law or examines the international legal dimension of a particular strand of the law. A wide range of sub-disciplines in the spheres of both public and private law are considered; from international environmental law to international criminal law, from international economic law to the law of international organisations, and from international commercial law to international human rights law. The *Research Handbooks* comprise carefully commissioned chapters from leading academics as well as those with an emerging reputation. Taking a genuinely international approach to the law, and addressing current and sometimes controversial legal issues, as well as affording a clear substantive analysis of the law, these *Handbooks* are designed to inform as well as to contribute to current debates.

Equally useful as reference tools or introductions to specific topics, issues and debates, the *Handbooks* will be used by academic researchers, post-graduate students, practicing lawyers and lawyers in policy circles.

Titles in this series include:

Research Handbook on the Law of International Organizations
Edited by Jan Klabbers and Åsa Wallendahl

Research Handbook on the Theory and History of International Law
Edited by Alexander Orakhelashvili

Research Handbook on International Sports Law
Edited by James A.R. Nafziger and Stephen F. Ross

Research Handbook on International Conflict and Security Law
Jus Ad Bellum, Jus in Bello and Jus Post Bellum
Edited by Nigel D. White and Christian Henderson

Research Handbook on International Law and Migration
Edited by Vincent Chetail and Céline Bauloz

Research Handbook on International Energy Law
Edited by Kim Talus

Research Handbook on International Law and Terrorism
Edited by Ben Saul

Research Handbook on the Law of Treaties
Edited by Christian J. Tams, Antonios Tzanakopoulos and Andreas Zimmermann

Research Handbook on the Law of Treaties

Edited by

Christian J. Tams

Professor of Public International Law, University of Glasgow, UK

Antonios Tzanakopoulos

Associate Professor of Public International Law, University of Oxford, UK

Andreas Zimmermann

Professor of Public International Law, University of Potsdam, Germany

Assistant Editor

Athene E. Richford

Research Assistant, University of Glasgow, UK

RESEARCH HANDBOOKS IN INTERNATIONAL LAW

Edward Elgar

Cheltenham, UK • Northampton, MA, USA

Published by
Edward Elgar Publishing Limited
The Lypiatts
15 Lansdown Road
Cheltenham
Glos GL50 2JA
UK

Edward Elgar Publishing, Inc.
William Pratt House
9 Dewey Court
Northampton
Massachusetts 01060
USA

A catalogue record for this book
is available from the British Library

Library of Congress Control Number: 2014937749

This book is available electronically in the ElgarOnline.com Law Subject Collection, E-ISBN 978 0 85793 478 9

MIX
Paper from responsible sources
FSC www.fsc.org FSC® C013056

ISBN 978 0 85793 477 2

Typeset by Columns Design XML Ltd, Reading
Printed and bound in Great Britain by T.J. International Ltd, Padstow

Contents

Contributors

Enzo Cannizzaro is full Professor of International and European Law at the University of Rome, Italy.

Jean d'Aspremont is Professor of International Law, University of Manchester, UK and Professor of International Legal Theory, University of Amsterdam, The Netherlands.

Katherine Del Mar has a PhD in International Law from the Graduate Institute of International Law and Development in Geneva, Switzerland.

James G. Devaney is PhD researcher at the European University Institute in Florence, Italy.

Jasper Finke is Assistant Professor (Juniorprofessor) of Public, International and European Law at Bucerius Law School, Hamburg, Germany.

Malgosia Fitzmaurice is Professor of Public International Law in the Department of Law, Queen Mary, University of London, UK.

Markos Karavias is Senior Research Fellow at the Amsterdam Center for International Law (ACIL), University of Amsterdam, The Netherlands.

Markus Kotzur is Professor of European and International Law, University of Hamburg, Director of Studies, Europa-Kolleg Hamburg, as well as Managing Director of the Institute for European Integration, Hamburg, Germany.

Sotirios-Ioannis Lekkas is DPhil candidate in International Law at St Anne's College, Oxford, UK.

Vaughan Lowe QC practices from Essex Court Chambers in London. He is Emeritus Chichele Professor of Public International Law at the University of Oxford and a Fellow of All Souls College, UK.

Panos Merkouris is Lecturer in Public International Law in the Faculty of Law of the University of Groningen, The Netherlands.

Marko Milanovic is Associate Professor at the University of Nottingham School of Law, UK as well as Secretary-General of the European Society of International Law, Italy.

André Nollkaemper is Professor of Public International Law at the Faculty of Law of the University of Amsterdam, The Netherlands.

Martins Paparinskis is Lecturer at the Faculty of Laws, University College London, UK.

Ilias Plakokefalos is Senior Research Fellow at the Amsterdam Center for International Law (ACIL), University of Amsterdam, The Netherlands.

Alexander Proelss is Professor for International and European Law, Trier University, Germany.

Surabhi Ranganathan is a Junior Research Fellow at the Lauterpacht Centre for International Law and at King's College, Cambridge, as well as an Affiliate Lecturer at the Cambridge Faculty of Law, UK.

Akbar Rasulov is Lecturer in Public International Law at the University of Glasgow, UK.

Yaël Ronen is Professor of International Law at Sha'arei Mishpat Academic Center, Israel, and a Fellow of the Minerva Center for Human Rights at the Hebrew University in Jerusalem, Israel.

Christian J. Tams is Professor of International Law at the University of Glasgow, UK.

Antonios Tzanakopoulos is Associate Professor of Public International Law at the University of Oxford and a Fellow of St Anne's College, UK.

Michael Waibel is University Lecturer at Jesus College, University of Cambridge and the Lauterpacht Centre for International Law, UK.

Philippa Webb is Lecturer in Public International Law, The Dickson Poon School of Law, King's College London, UK.

Andreas Zimmermann is Professor of International and European Law at the University of Potsdam and Director of the Potsdam Centre of Human Rights, Germany.

Preface

The idea to edit a *Research Handbook on the Law of Treaties* came as a reaction to the resurgence of interest in the subject in the late 2000s and early 2010s, which found expression in the publication of new treaty law handbooks and commentaries on the Vienna Convention(s) on the Law of Treaties ('VCLT'). Yet we did not want to add another such book to the already growing literature on the subject. Rather, we set out to edit a collection of reflective pieces, not necessarily on less-studied aspects of the law of treaties, but on aspects that we wished to see pursued from different angles, less attached to the VCLT. This we explain in more detail in our Introduction.

In our endeavour, we found warm support and a hospitable forum in Edward Elgar Publishing – in particular our editor Ben Booth – and the Research Handbook series. The process was long and arduous but staff at Edward Elgar did their best to make it as painless as possible; for this, and for the quality of production of the volume at hand, we owe them heartfelt thanks.

If the *Research Handbook* would not exist without Edward Elgar, it would certainly not exist without the authors who agreed to contribute to this volume, and who were so accommodating of our sometimes demanding editorial instructions and requests. We thank them warmly for their patience and for their excellent contributions: whatever merit there may be to this book is due to the careful and considered work of the contributing authors.

We must not neglect to thank our Assistant Editor, Athene Richford: her careful and tireless work, including the editing of the chapters and the communication with authors, and her happy demeanour, made the process of editing the *Research Handbook* considerably shorter and more enjoyable than it would otherwise have been.

Finally, thanks are due to our home institutions, the Universities of Glasgow, Oxford, and Potsdam, for providing us with a research environment in which projects like this can be pursued.

Christian J. Tams
Antonios Tzanakopoulos
Andreas Zimmermann
June 2014

Introduction

Christian J. Tams, Antonios Tzanakopoulos and Andreas Zimmermann

Without treaties, international law and international relations are difficult to imagine. From the dramatic to the mundane, so much activity today is regulated by treaties. Where war is waged, we argue about the scope of the Geneva Conventions, human rights treaties and of course the UN Charter. When States make peace or draw boundaries, they do so by treaty. Where individuals suffer, international agreements provide us with a language and a benchmark to characterise atrocities as 'crimes' or 'human rights violations'. When we are about to board a flight, we make use, usually unconsciously, of international rules on standardised passports derived from treaties, and we benefit from international conventions on civil aviation. Some treaties reflect the international community's hope for a more just world order, others entrench grave injustices. Treaties are ubiquitous: since the end of World War I, around 56,500 have been registered with the United Nations and its predecessor, as envisaged in Article 18 of the League's Covenant and Article 102 of the UN Charter.[1] This figure, however, does not reflect the total number of treaties concluded: it includes neither oral agreements nor treaties between non-UN members; and of course it does not capture the considerable number of treaties that, contrary to Article 102, have not been registered. International law is difficult to imagine without treaties indeed.

The contemporary dominance of treaties as the principal instrument for ordering international relations owes a lot to 19th and 20th century phenomena such as the rise of multilateralism, the establishment of

[1] For details about the United Nations practice see the information provided by the UN Treaty Section, at https://treaties.un.org/Pages/DB.aspx?path=DB/UNTS/page1_CIintro_en.xml. The figure of treaties registered with the League of Nations is given as 4834 (https://treaties.un.org/Pages/LONOnline.aspx). More than fifty years ago, AD McNair rightly described this depository of international regulation as 'an indispensable piece of international apparatus' (*The Law of Treaties*, 2nd edn., 1961, at 179).

international organisations, coordinated attempts at codification, and of course to the major increase in the number of international law subjects (States, and others). However, in addition to dominating contemporary international law, treaties were 'present at creation', too. 'Since ancient times, political entities have used treaties as a tool to shape their international or neighbourly relations', states Malgosia Fitzmaurice.[2] Historical treatments rely on early treaties – boundary agreements between Mesopotamian City States, early versions of FCN treaties between Egyptians and Hittites, or alliance and peace treaties between the Greek City States – to determine when international law really began. And according to the Encyclopedia Britannica, '*pacta sunt servanda*', that quintessential treaty law principle,[3] is 'the oldest principle of international law'.[4]

That treaties – foundational then, ubiquitous today – need a legal framework is unsurprising. They would be useless if treaty parties had not, previously, somehow agreed on their binding force. And in order to operate, unless everything is spelled out in minute detail, treaties presuppose an understanding on how, when, where and between whom they should apply; how they can be terminated or suspended (if at all); what happens if they are breached; whether they survive the demise of their parties, and much more. The law of treaties provides this legal framework. We may debate whether it should be viewed as a unitary set of rules (a point taken up in Vaughan Lowe's opening contribution to this book); but the existence of *some framework* governing treaties is a practical necessity. Dominated by treaties, international law needs a law of treaties.

* * *

The legal framework governing treaties draws on, but is not exhausted by, the 1969 Vienna Convention on the Law of Treaties ('VCLT'). That Convention may be canonical, perhaps even a 'bible'.[5] But if it is a bible, it is a rather short one: authoritative, no doubt, but by no means

---

[2] M Fitzmaurice, 'Treaties', in Max Planck *Encyclopedia of Public International Law* (online edition at www.mpepil.com), at para 5.

[3] See ILC, Draft Articles on the Law of Treaties with Commentaries, ILC Yearbook 1966, vol. II, 211, para. 1 ('the fundamental principle of the law of treaties').

[4] See the *Encyclopaedia Britannica*, online edition, at http://www.britannica.com, entry on 'International Law'. (http://www.britannica.com/EBchecked/topic/291011/international-law/233499/Treaties?anchor=ref794916)

[5] A Aust, *Modern Treaty Law and Practice*, 1st edn., CUP 2000, at 4.

comprehensive. To some extent, this flows from its (convention-specific) understanding of the term 'treaty' as set out in Article 2(1)(a).[6] Covering inter-State agreements in writing, the Convention purposefully leaves to a side non-written agreements governed by international law as well as treaties with actors other than States (a limitation partially addressed by the 1986 Vienna Convention). More importantly, even with respect to written inter-State agreements, it addresses only some of the questions raised above. Its focus, as Rosenne notes,[7] is on the treaty as 'an instrument', not primarily on treaty obligations. Hence the convention provides considerable detail on the modalities of concluding treaties, on their scope of application, on reservations, on interpretation, on treaty interaction and contains a very bulky part on the 'invalidity, termination or suspension of the operation of the treaty'. However, core aspects of the legal framework governing treaties are left to a side. This notably applies to the *trias* of reserved matters mentioned in Article 73: treaty breaches are addressed as within the larger framework of responsibility; succession to treaties is outsourced into a separate framework governing State succession (of which succession to treaties is the main part); while the impact of war on treaties, has long been viewed as a discrete topic (which is now being studied in earnest again). As regards other matters, not covered by Article 73, the Vienna Convention rules often remain rudimentary: suffice it to think of the interplay between treaties and domestic law and the regime of reservations; or the VCLT's minimalist provisions on the geographical, temporal, and personal scope of application of treaties.

In the light of all this, the VCLT can hardly be seen as a comprehensive codification of the law of treaties. Its principal historian, Sir Iain Sinclair, noted 'the drafters' unwillingness to venture more than they thought strictly necessary beyond the confines of the law of treaties in the narrower sense – that is to say, as a series of provisions concerning the formation, effects and duration of written agreements between States'.[8] And he went on to observe: 'It is as if the Commission had deliberately decided to paint in the style of Pieter de Hooch rather than Titian or

---

[6] According to that provision, '[f]or the purposes of the present Convention: "treaty" means an international agreement concluded between States in written form and governed by international law, whether embodied in a single instrument or in two or more related instruments and whatever its particular designation'.

[7] S Rosenne, *Breach of Treaty* (Grotius, 1985), 3–4.

[8] IM Sinclair, *The Vienna Convention on the Law of Treaties* (2nd edn, Manchester UP, 1984), 244.

Veronese. They denied the broader canvas in order to concentrate on the domestic minutiae'.[9]

There is nothing wrong with domestic minutiae, or with Pieter de Hooch for that matter. The VCLT illustrates the beneficial effect of inclusive expert debate and regular practice, which over time can distil agreed norms that, largely irrespective of their force as treaty law,[10] come to be seen as binding. But in view of its purposefully limited scope, and its inadvertent limitations, the VCLT should not be equated to the law of treaties.

* * *

All of this is perhaps trite. If it is spelled out here regardless, then it is because the drafters' 'de Hooch' approach has had an impact on scholarly debates on the law of treaties. Many a textbook chapter on treaties focuses on the VCLT and treats other matters in passing; some even fail to look beyond the VCLT. And of course, no one can overlook the surprising resurgence of VCLT-scholarship in the recent literature. This scholarship is valuable, in some instances invaluable. And yet it covers only part of the law of treaties, and leaves to a side essential aspects.

The contributions to the present book address a different law of treaties. This is not yet another VCLT Commentary or treaty law handbook. Questions addressed in the Vienna Convention of course are covered, and to many chapters they are central. However, as editors we have made a serious attempt to look at 'The Law of Treaties beyond the Vienna Convention'.[11] As a consequence, readers will find chapters addressing the VCLT's main substantive gaps – succession, treaty breaches, impact of war, domestic law, etc. The role of non-State actors as parties to treaties, or as actors in the treaty process, is considered. And we have invited a series of reflections on the concept of treaties, and of treaty law, in the contemporary legal order. The resulting 21 chapters are

---

9 Ibid.

10 It is worth noting that even today, almost 50 years after the finalisation of the ILC's text, only 114 have joined the VCLT regime. Prominent outsiders include India, Indonesia, South Africa, Turkey, France and Norway. The United States, Bolivia, Iran and Pakistan are signatories only. In terms of treaty participation, the VCLT remains one of the less successful universal agreements sponsored by the UN. (For details see https://treaties.un.org/pages/ViewDetailsIII.aspx?&src=TREATY&mtdsg_no=XXIII~1&chapter=23&Temp=mtdsg3&lang=en).

11 Cf. the title of the *Gaja Festschrift* (E. Cannizaro (ed.), *The Law of Treaties Beyond The Vienna Convention,* OUP 2011), as well as G Gaja, '*Jus Cogens* Beyond The Vienna Convention', Receuil des Cours, 172 (1981), 271.

organised in five parts – *Principles, Dimensions, Tensions, Interactions & Ruptures,* and *Expansions*. Each of these parts is selective in its coverage, but we believe taken together, the book provides a 'critical mass' of scholarship on salient questions of treaty law – as addressed, scratched upon, or side-stepped by the VCLT's drafters.

In selecting the issues to be covered, we have sought to identify cross-cutting themes or questions. In this respect, too, this is not another VCLT Commentary. Contributors were invited take a step back and write 'think pieces' reflecting on tensions, premises, undercurrents, challenges, and trends in the law of treaties. This approach reflects our own research interests (and preferences), and also a belief that some of the recent scholarship on the law of treaties may have perhaps been a bit too granular. While it is difficult to break radically new ground when writing about the law of treaties (even in the broader sense of the term, as used here), we believe the chapters do offer novel perspectives and original reflections on important questions of practical and theoretical relevance. In keeping with the aims of the Research Handbook series (which is meant to 'inform as well as to contribute to current debates'), we have asked contributors to conclude their chapters with suggestions for further study in 'their' field of expertise. These concluding sections identify dozens of avenues for research, which we hope will be considered worth pursuing.

* * *

Beyond the individual suggestions for further study, in our view, one central question underlies many of the contributions to the present book: should the law of treaties be seen as one general (and presumably uniform) regime, or does it need to make more room for sectoral rules applicable to particular categories of treaties (such as bilateral treaties, human rights treaties, treaties setting up institutions, etc.)? Vaughan Lowe addresses this tension expressly by inquiring whether it makes sense to,

> lump together treaties declaring the course of international boundaries, treaties for the provision of specified sums of foreign aid, status of forces agreements, multilateral conventions on Antarctica or on the Law of the Sea or human rights, treaties establishing the European Union or the UN or the WHO … . [which], as sets of rules establishing legal relations, … have in common little or nothing.[12]

---

[12] AV Lowe, in this volume, p. 4.

As editors, unsurprisingly, we would not hesitate to answer in the affirmative the question he draws from this and which forms the sub-title of his contribution ('Should this book exist?'). Yet that this question is being asked is no doubt useful. It invites serious reflection on whether international law can continue to operate with one legal regime to address treaties in their 'infinite variety'.[13] The Vienna Convention in principle accepts this idea: while admitting certain differentiations between types of treaties and while nearly always allowing parties to opt out of the general regime, the drafters purported to set out general rules. But since 1969, international lawyers have begun to argue about special rules for special classes of treaties, both in relation to matters covered by the VCLT and those left aside.These debates are reflected in the chapters of this book. To name just a few, the two chapters on uniformity versus specialisation take it up directly; as does the one on suspension and termination of treaties. The contributions on treaty breaches, on treaties and armed conflict, and on succession to treaties show how, outside the VCLT, drafters devising general rules embraced differentiations between types of treaties. And the same holds true for the analysis of treaties and domestic law, in which very little depends on whether a rule is found in a treaty, and so much on what type of treaty it is. Of the many questions raised in the subsequent chapters, the tension between general and sectoral rules governing treaties is perhaps the most important. We should be glad if this book was read as an encouragement to pursue it further.

---

[13] Cf. RR Baxter, 'Internationall Law in "Her Infinite Variety"', ICLQ 29 (1980), 549.

PART I

PRINCIPLES

1. The law of treaties; or, should this book exist?

Vaughan Lowe

This short chapter is not about rules of international law applicable to treaties. It is about the concept of 'the law of treaties' as a subject or topic within international law. It takes as its starting point the conception of treaties, which is the paradigm implicit in the 1969 Vienna Convention on the Law of Treaties. That paradigm is of a written instrument negotiated by the States parties to it, where the binding force comes from the *consensus ad idem*. It is a clearly consensualist model, as befits a body of doctrine whose roots lie in consensualist conceptions of international law in general.[1] The main argument of the chapter is that 'the law of treaties' may no longer be the most useful way of approaching legal obligations voluntarily assumed by States.

The law of treaties is a curious phenomenon. It has the appearance of solidity and certainty. Scarcely any piece of international litigation does not include in its overture a reference to the rules on treaty interpretation that are contained in the Vienna Convention. That almost ritualistic reference commonly continues with an assertion that the Vienna Convention is regarded as an accurate statement of customary international law; and in most cases that assertion is accepted without demur. And in many cases the court or tribunal is spared a reading of the relevant provisions of the Vienna Convention on the ground that they are too well known to need repetition. One may argue over the results of the application of the

[1] See the classic discussions by JL Brierly, *The Basis of Obligation in International Law* (OUP, 1958) 1–67, and by Sir H Lauterpacht, *Oppenheim's International Law* (8th edn, vol I, Longmans, 1955) 15–23; and compare the brevity with which the International Law Commission ('ILC') dealt with the definition of a 'treaty' in what became Article 2 of the Vienna Convention on the Law of Treaties ('VCLT'): Sir A Watts, *The International Law Commission 1994–1998* (OUP, 1999), 619–23, reprinting the ILC's Final Draft Articles from the Yearbook of the ILC (1966) vol II, 177. The assumption of the consensual basis of the law of treaties continues: see, eg, the discussions of the VLCT Preamble and Articles 1 and 2 in O Corten and P Klein, *The Vienna Convention on the Law of Treaties: A Commentary* (OUP, 2011).

Vienna Convention rules to whatever treaty is in question in the case: but it is practically unthinkable that the content of the law of treaties should be challenged – and even less likely that the very existence of the law of treaties should be questioned.

That last observation is perhaps explicable by the context. Litigation is not a place where it is considered prudent to raise questions about the very structure of international law. Cases may result in the drawing of structural lines:[2] the relationship between the body of rules on self-determination and the body of rules on the acquisition of territorial sovereignty, which found clear expression in Judge Dillard's separate opinion in the *Western Sahara* case,[3] and the separation of the validity of grants of nationality into different categories in the *Nottebohm* case,[4] are two examples. But the arguments put before the court are much narrower and more tightly focused than the doctrinal implications that may be drawn from the court's judgment. So it is perhaps unsurprising that in the practice of international litigation the existence, and indeed even the content, of the law of treaties should have remained without serious challenge. The 'law of treaties' is, however, a concept that is ripe for reappraisal.

First, the very idea of a 'treaty' is a Procrustean bed: and one must not forget that Procrustes[5] inflicted real pain. To lump together treaties declaring the course of international boundaries, treaties for the provision of specified sums of foreign aid, status of forces agreements, multilateral conventions on Antarctica or on the law of the sea or human rights, treaties establishing the European Union or the United Nations ('UN') or the World Health Organization, has the appearance of making sense only if one first designates them all as treaties. In reality, as sets of rules establishing legal relations, they have in common little or nothing beyond the label that is affixed to them.[6]

---

[2] On the general question of the drawing of lines between concepts, see E Hirsch, *Dividing Reality* (OUP, 1993).

[3] *Western Sahara*, Advisory Opinion, ICJ Rep 1975 (16 October) 12, 121.

[4] *Nottebohm (Liechtenstein v Guatemala)*, Second Phase, Judgment, ICJ Rep 1955 (6 April) 4, para 17.

[5] Six decades ago it would have been assumed that any reader of a book such as this would know who Procrustes was. Three decades ago, editors of law journals (particularly in the USA) would have insisted on copious footnote references to explain who Procrustes was. If you do not know, try Google and Wikipedia. *O tempora, o mores!* (ditto).

[6] The problem was well understood at the time of the preparation of the VCLT, but not resolved: see, eg, Lord McNair, *The Law of Treaties* (OUP, 1961) 5–6.

This is not the place to attempt a comprehensive classification of instruments carrying the label of treaty. One reason is that if one accepts (as the ILC did)[7] that there may be unwritten treaties, and that an unwritten treaty could be counted as an 'instrument,' it is far from obvious where the category of treaties ends and that of unilateral commitments which have some discernible link with each other *ratione materiae* or *ratione temporis* begins. Another reason is that the fineness of dissection has more to do with the sharpness of the knife than distinctions between the constitutive parts that are inherent in the body being dissected; and one of the points I try to make here is that all classifications of treaties are, like the limits of the category of treaties as a whole, essentially arbitrary.

It is sufficient for present purposes to draw attention to some of the main differences between the kinds of legal relations produced by treaties. To be more precise, I should say that the differences lie between treaty provisions, because provisions with different characteristics can and commonly do co-exist in a single instrument – the territorial dispositions, indemnities and obligations regarding future conduct and the terminations of states of war in peace treaties are good examples,[8] as are the distinct provisions on substantive matters and on the procedures for the handling of disputes in a very wide range of treaties.

To begin, some treaties are dispositive, in the sense that their legal effects are wholly realized immediately upon their conclusion. A treaty that establishes an international boundary, or that recognizes a pre-existent boundary, would be an example. The treaty is essentially declaratory, rather than based on an exchange of things, each given in consideration of the other (although any actual boundary treaty may in fact involve swaps of land, or the entire boundary may be seen as an exchange or abandonment of claims in respect of parts of the entire area in dispute). The moment the treaty enters into effect, the boundary is where the treaty says it is; and in the case of a treaty that recognizes a pre-existent boundary, no legal weight will be given to a claim by either of the States parties that the boundary previously lay anywhere else.

Contrast that with the treaties establishing what became the European Union. One of the great mysteries of contemporary legal education in Europe is how students can give confident accounts of the interpretation and application of treaties in public international law one day, and give

---

[7] See the ILC Commentary to Article 2, para (7). The index to McNair, *The Law of Treaties* (n 6) 784, carries the wonderfully terse entry 'Oral agreement, *see* Treaties,' though his discussion of the point (ibid 7–10) is more nuanced.

[8] See, eg, the San Francisco Peace Treaty, 8 September 1951, 136 UNTS 45.

an account of the great cases, such as *Van Gend en Loos*,[9] that laid the foundations of the European legal order the next, as if they were all parts of a seamless tapestry made up of legal orders, national, regional and international. The European Court of Justice's decision in *Van Gend en Loos* that a provision of the treaty concluded between the member States of the European Economic Community ('EEC')[10] created rights for individuals that are directly effective within the national legal orders of member States is a decision that, for all the commonplace status that it has since achieved, was about as radical a departure as can be imagined from the traditional 'treaty-as-contract' analysis that the questions would have received had they been put before the International Court of Justice ('ICJ') at that time. It should not be forgotten that it was a case between a Netherlands national and the Netherlands government, and that two States parties to the treaty (Belgium, the Netherlands) challenged the Court's jurisdiction in the case, on grounds based squarely within the traditional understanding in public international law of the proper way of handling treaties. But the Court rejected the challenges. The Court's reasons for not confining the effect of the treaties to the member States, which were the only legal persons bound by them, and for not confining its own decision to the consequences of the treaty as between the States parties, leaving them to decide how to give effect in their own legal orders to the treaty obligations and to any obligations regarding reparation that might arise, were pegged precisely to the point that a treaty-as-contract analysis was inapposite. And that is my point.

The European Court of Justice had the wisdom to see that the treaties establishing the European Communities ('EC') were not like other treaties.[11] More importantly, the Court had the courage to act on that perception, and to do so boldly and decisively. It imagined into existence an entire, new, legal order, hammering into place the other great beams of that legal order, such as the supremacy of Community law and the

---

[9] Case 26/62, *N V Algemene Transport- en Expeditie Onderneming Van Gend & Loos v Nederlandse administratie der belastingen* [1963] ECR 1. And see the helpful version on the EUR-Lex website, accessed 26 May 2014, at http://eur-lex.europa.eu/legal-content/EN/ALL/?uri=CELEX:61962CJ0026.

[10] The Treaty establishing the European Economic Community, 1957, 298 UNTS 3.

[11] At that time there were three separate 'Communities', each having its own constitutive treaty: the European Economic Community ('EEC'), the European Coal and Steel Community ('ECSC') and the European Atomic Energy Community ('EAEC' or 'Euratom'). Their constitutional relationship evolved by stages, and they were succeeded by the European Union ('EU'). The *Van Gend en Loos* case was concerned with the EEC treaty.

'occupied field' doctrine of Community competences.[12] These were not dispositive treaties, such as boundary treaties. These were treaties establishing a relationship – a little like marriage contracts, where certain basic terms are spelled out but the important thing is not the catalogue of express terms but the underlying relationship which is the object and purpose of the making of the agreement, even though there is barely any attempt to spell out the detailed rules of that relationship. Spouses do not often make express provision for what will happen if they move from rented to owned accommodation, for the clubs and societies of which they may remain members, for where holidays will be taken, and so on. Nor could the position in such eventualities be predicted. We have moved, as Henry Maine[13] might have said, from contract to status. It is not simply that the few express terms in the instrument that signals the inception of the relationship – the marriage contract; the EC treaties – are supplemented by a host of implied terms. In the case of the EEC, there was no body of previous practice from which such terms could be drawn. It was the fact that the treaties establishing the European Communities were, in the eyes of the Court, intended to create a new relationship that warranted its extraordinary approach to the questions before it.

The Court did not scrutinize the treaty text and ask, what did the parties actually agree? It did not even say, what object and purpose can we discern from the treaties, which may guide us in the interpretation of the express treaty terms? In retrospect, at least, one can see the Court staking out its ground not as a passive, neutral adjudicator upon disputes that might arise from time to time over the meaning of a legal instrument, but rather as one of the key organs of the European Communities, with a key, active role to play in the progressive development of the European project. Whatever one may think of the European project, the dashing boldness of the Court in its early cases stands in sharp contrast to the

---

[12] See, eg, B De Witte, 'Direct Effect, Supremacy, and the Nature of the Legal Order', in P Craig and G De Búrca (eds), *The Evolution of EU Law* (OUP, 1999) chp 12.

[13] Author of *Ancient Law* (John Murray, 1861); chapter V of which sets out his brilliant hypothesis that societies move from a condition where personal rights and duties rest on the status of individuals to a condition where they are freely negotiated and have a contractual basis. Maine was a professor at Cambridge, an influential government official in India and vice-chancellor of the University of Calcutta, and a professor at Oxford, before returning to Cambridge as Master of Trinity Hall, and was a doyen of jurists who make grand assertions unsupported by evidence or authority. Sometimes it is better to be interesting than to be correct.

cautious, almost two-dimensional, approach of the ICJ at that time.[14] This view of dispute settlement as an integral part of the process, as a key part of the relationship established by the treaties, is a characteristic of other, more recent multilateral treaties. The 1982 United Nations Convention on the Law of the Sea and the 1994 Agreement establishing the World Trade Organization are fine examples. At a certain point the treaty negotiators decide that there is no need to try to pin down further agreed solutions in express treaty provisions: the parties have agreed the core principles, and if problems arise the parties will discuss them and, if they cannot find a negotiated solution themselves, the parties are content to leave it to a dispute settlement body to decide.

There are several points implicit in what I have said so far. First, approaches to treaty interpretation should differ as between 'dispositive' treaties on the one hand and 'relationship' treaties that create new legal regimes on the other. In the former, but not the latter, case it makes sense to focus upon the question, what did the parties actually agree? In the latter, but not the former, case it makes sense to say that the parties may not have addressed a certain point at all in the express terms of the treaty (as 'direct effect' was not addressed in the EEC treaty) but that the point is one that bears crucially upon the relationship established by the treaty, that the Court has been given the role of responding to important lacunae, and that the Court will accordingly decide upon what are essentially teleological grounds, where the precise goal is fixed by the Court itself.

Second, the reasons for a difference in approach are not confined to treaty interpretation. Take a variant on the boundary treaty example, in which a boundary settlement involves the withdrawal of each party's administration from certain areas and the exchange of certain parcels of land. If one party does not perform its obligations and fails to withdraw from and hand over a parcel of land, a contractual analysis based on breach of material terms in a treaty makes sense. But the imposition of a border tax or duty on a specific product contrary to the express terms of the EEC treaty (or now, the EU treaties) would almost certainly not be thought by other States parties to provide a legal justification for the termination of that treaty. A deal cannot survive the breaking of a material term: a relationship can. So the differences between types of treaties can affect the approach to questions of their validity and termination, as well as questions of their interpretation.

---

[14] This was the era of the judgments in the *Barcelona Traction*, ICJ Rep 1970, 3, *Certain Expenses of the United Nations*, ICJ Rep 1962, 151, and *South West Africa (Second Phase)*, ICJ Rep 1966, 6, cases.

Third, the different perspectives that flow from the different types of treaty are extraneous to the treaties themselves. It was not by staring at the terms of the EEC treaty that the European Court of Justice decided that it should establish the doctrine of direct effect: it was by asking the question, what is our role in relation to the relationship that the States parties have established by this treaty? And the same question can be asked in cases where the scope of the treaty's aims are at the other end of the spectrum, and the court or tribunal decides that its proper role is no more than that of a (perhaps ad hoc) neutral adjudicator on the question, what did the parties actually agree in the treaty?

At this point it may be helpful to refer briefly to some other kinds of treaty (or treaty provision). Boundary treaties were referred to above as dispositive treaties with instantaneous effect, in contrast with the long-term evolving relationship initiated by the EEC treaty. Treaties that declare the location of boundaries can also be contrasted with synallagmatic treaties that consist of an exchange of reciprocal promises regarding the parties' future conduct (even within a fixed and limited framework that is not expected to evolve significantly), such as extradition treaties. For example, the ILC has singled out boundary treaties as not susceptible to unilateral denunciation at the will of one party or terminable on the ground of a fundamental change of circumstances.[15] That might be explained in terms of international law's almost fetishistic respect for boundaries; but I think that it can also be explained in terms of the different distinction between executed and executory treaties.

Then there are treaties that purport to bind only States parties, such as the various treaties on nuclear non-proliferation or on high seas fisheries; and there are those treaties that purport to create an objective state of affairs, such as the treaties declaring the moon and other celestial bodies to be beyond the reach of national claims to sovereignty and of rights to deploy weapons systems there, and the deep sea-bed provisions in Part XI of the United Nations Convention on the Law of the Sea. In terms of the effect that it is intended, or hoped, that the treaty will have upon non-party States, and the legal consequences of denunciation, they are markedly different. The received wisdom seems to be that departure from a high seas fisheries regime can release the departing State from all of its

---

[15] See para 2 of the ILC Commentary to Draft Article 53 (VCLT, Article 56) and para 11 of the ILC Commentary to Draft Article 59 (VCLT, Article 62), in Sir A Watts, *The International Law Commission 1994–1998* (OUP, 1999), 619, reprinting the ILC's Final Draft Articles from the Yearbook of the ILC (1966) vol II, 177.

treaty obligations,[16] whereas the treaties on the 'Moon and Other Celestial Bodies'[17] and the deep sea-bed have some kind of objective status. Similarly,[18] bodies such as the UN are regarded as having an objective legal personality, opposable even to non-party States and other entities; and the agreed boundaries of States are also regarded as having an objective existence. While such purportedly objective statuses might be treated as instances of the emergence of a rule of customary international law alongside the treaty,[19] this would be a remarkable claim when the practice consists precisely in doing nothing – in making no claim to sovereignty or sovereign rights over the area in question that is incompatible with the treaty regime. It stretches the conception of customary international law to describe it thus;[20] and there seems to be no better reason for doing that than there is for adjusting the law of treaties to reflect the fact that not all treaties stand in the same relationship to the *pacta tertiis* principle.

Then there is the category of human rights treaties. It has been persuasively argued that these treaties are instances not of reciprocal exchanges of promises between States, analogous to synallagmatic contracts, but of pledges by each State party individually to uphold the rights set out in the relevant treaty.[21] Cynics (and others) might argue that adherence to multilateral human rights instruments is no less a matter of reciprocal commitments than are treaties on international trade law or competition law. In the same way that trade and competition agreements seek to establish a level playing field for international commerce, they

---

[16] See Articles 8, 17 and 18 of the 1995 UN Agreement for the Implementation of the Provisions of the United Nations Convention on the Law of the Sea of 10 December 1982 relating to the Conservation and Management of Straddling Fish Stocks and Highly Migratory Fish Stocks 2167 UNTS 3.

[17] This is the almost Swiftian designation employed in the 1979 Moon Treaty (the 'Agreement Governing the Activities of States on the Moon and Other Celestial Bodies'): see UNGA Res 34/68 (5 December 1979), and 1363 UNTS 3. The application of the agreement is limited to 'celestial bodies within the solar system, other than the earth': see Article 1.1.

[18] But not identically: there are subtle but important differences in the reasoning.

[19] See *Military and Paramilitary Activities in and against Nicaragua (Nicaragua v United States of America)*, Merits Judgment, ICJ Rep 1986 (27 June), 14, paras 175–79.

[20] See *Jurisdictional Immunities of the State (Germany v Italy: Greece Intervening)*, ICJ Rep 2012 (3 February) paras 55, 101, 106 and *passim*.

[21] See L Brilmayer, 'From "Contract" to "Pledge": The Structure of International Human Rights Agreements,' (2007) 77 BYIL 163.

might say, so human rights agreements seek to ensure that in the promotion of human rights (which may, admittedly, be driven by altruism and moral conviction) no State or economy (or at least, none among a State's significant trading partners) is advantaged by the government maintaining unacceptably low human rights standards. The key to understanding human rights treaties, on this view, is to focus not on the substance of the rights but on the fact that a lot of States can agree to sign up to them and that acceptance of the standards is, through a host of political, cultural and economic mechanisms, made a condition of 'joining the club.'

Even if that view is accepted, so that the key characteristic of a human rights treaty is precisely that it is a 'deal,' a reciprocal exchange of promises, it is undeniable that human rights treaties are different from other treaties in certain respects. The best-known instance is the approach of the European Court of Human Rights to reservations and interpretative declarations in the *Belilos* case,[22] which departs from the more strictly consensualist approach of the Vienna Convention. But one might also point to other subtle differences. For instance, it seems to be a characteristic of human rights treaties, and of other treaties that create dispute settlement procedures providing for the settlement of disputes through the litigation of cases before standing tribunals – the EU treaties are another outstanding example – that the tribunal is prepared to take an approach to treaty interpretation that is not only teleological (see above) but programmatic. The tribunal may say, there was a wrong done in this case and we will give a remedy, but because this is the first time we have explained the law on this point we will not treat cases in future so leniently. It may even say, as the European Court of Justice did in the *Defrenne* case,[23] that though a wrong was done (there, sex discrimination in employment terms) it was so widespread that to allow all those who suffered similarly to initiate claims would cause economic chaos, so the judgment will operate only prospectively, in relation to discrimination occurring after the judgment (and in relation to claims already pending concerning earlier discrimination). One might argue that these are more a matter of the powers or the discretion of the tribunal than of the nature or effect of the treaty. But the point is that this phenomenon is, as far as I can see, largely confined to practice in the application of treaties where there is an understanding that the tribunal will play a continuing and

---

22 *Belilos v Switzerland* (Decision), App no 10328/83, (ECHR 29 April 1988).

23 Case C-43/75, *Defrenne v Sabena (No 2)*, [1976] ECR 455.

active role in developing the law, and that in the case of these treaties (but not others) there is a distinctive approach to the interpretation and application of the terms of the treaty. The same phenomenon can also be seen to a lesser degree in situations where there is an expectation that a series of decisions by ad hoc bodies, or by chambers of a tribunal, will play such a role: the World Trade Organization disputes panels, and perhaps (in time) the various tribunals that operate under Part XV of the Law of the Sea Convention might be given as examples.

Another characteristic of a group of treaties of which human rights treaties are a prominent example is that, as far as many States parties are concerned, the treaty is not a negotiated consensus. It is a text drafted by others to which the State may or may not choose to accede, rather like a *contrat d'adhésion*, but whose existing provisions the State cannot, generally speaking, modify.[24] In the case of such treaties it is impossible to say – in contrast to the position regarding bilateral treaties, where one can and does say – that tasks such as treaty interpretation can be defined in terms of a search for what the parties actually agreed between themselves.

The Vienna Convention itself separates out certain categories of treaty for special treatment. Boundary treaties[25] have been mentioned already; and there is also special treatment for humanitarian treaties[26] and treaties whose limited number of negotiating States makes apparent that the application of the treaty in its entirety between all the parties is an essential condition of the consent of each one to be bound by the treaty.[27]

I could go on: but I hope that enough has been said to make the point that a considerable variety of legal instruments fall under the label of 'treaties.' The class of treaties is by no means a homogenous collection of instruments, even when viewed in the context of the matters that are the traditional concern of the law of treaties, such as interpretation, termination, and the permissibility and effects of reservations and interpretative declarations. This observation in turn leads to the question whether the category of 'treaties' is a useful one. Do all treaties have enough in common to warrant the creation of a distinct law of treaties?

Arguably the most basic characteristic common to all treaties is that they are agreements between two or more States or other international

---

[24] Reservations, in so far as they are permissible, are one exception; but under the VCLT regime reservations operate essentially as consensual amendments of the treaty.

[25] See VCLT, Article 62(2)(a).

[26] See VCLT, Article 60(5).

[27] One wonders how treaty-making practice within the EU, with its various 'opt-out' provisions, sits within this framework.

legal persons governed by international law.[28] But even that characteristic does not really bind the category together. I have argued above that the law of treaties in fact treats in different ways various distinct kinds of instruments that all possess that characteristic – albeit in various forms, such as the paradigms of the bilateral treaty-contract and the multilateral treaty-*contrat d'adhésion*. The law of treaties itself thus accepts that the category is not homogenous. Moreover, it is at least arguable that a more rational, more exact and more useful common characteristic focuses not on the relationship between or among the parties to the treaty but upon the relationship of each individual State party to the text.

One might say that the true uniting characteristic is that each State commits itself to the application to itself of the treaty text by any tribunal that is competent to determine whether or not the State has acted in accordance with its obligations under international law. Forget consensus. Forget attempts to divine the common intention of the parties, which are at best exercises in the construction of a credible story of what the thinking of a wise, honest and near-omniscient hypothetical negotiator of the treaty might have been, while pragmatically ignoring the thoughts and intentions (if any) of the harried human beings who actually negotiated the treaty while trying to interpret their mandates and to keep an array of government departments and other interest groups happy and their own chances of promotion or of a generous pension intact – not to mention the thoughts (again, if any) of the parliament or minister or other body which actually takes the decision to assent to the treaty and ratify it. Like a good detective story, the truth does not matter as long as the story fits the handful of facts that we are given, in the *travaux* and elsewhere.

The one thing that *is* certain is that the State signed up to the treaty, and that should be the starting point for analysing the legal consequences of the State's commitment. This approach would, in effect, invert the dictum, *pacta sunt servanda*: the point is not that treaties are binding (though they are), but rather that a text to which a State assents to be bound is a treaty. *Pacta sunt quod servanda sunt.*

Approached in that way, the law of treaties would be part of a broader body or law applicable to obligations to which a State explicitly commits itself, as distinct from the body of customary international law, which binds a State not because it has expressly assented to it but because State practice in general, in which the State may not have participated, has

[28] Cf VCLT, Article 2.1.

generated a rule from which the State has not excepted itself.[29] If the commitment of the State is the starting point, there is no *a priori* reason to confine it to commitments given in the context of bilateral and multilateral treaties. It could also embrace unilateral statements. Taking the classic *Nuclear Tests* formula,[30] the conclusion or accession of a treaty is an instance – overwhelmingly the most common, and paradigmatic, but still only an instance – of a broader conceptual category of actions by which a State commits itself legally to the application of certain legal rules. Similar commitments might be discerned in classical unilateral statements, or oral commitments such as the 1919 Ihlen Declaration.[31] And unilateral commitments, and perhaps also rules of international law of equivalent effect, such as estoppel, fall within the broader conceptual category along with treaties.

One would then have to divide the broader category, but along different lines from those drawn by the Vienna Convention. A certain common core of principles relating to the validity of a State's assent, the withdrawal or termination of that consent, and so on, would exist; but beyond that core, many other questions such as the approaches to treaty interpretation, the effects of treaties on third States, the effects of reservation and the like would be recognized as differing from one class of treaty or commitment and another.

Why bother? It is not that the result would be a difference in the outcomes of particular cases. The European Court would still blaze its trail and lay the foundations of a distinct Community legal order. Tribunals examining bilateral commercial treaties could still hold the parties to the letter of the treaty with a rigidity that even Shylock might envy. All that would change is the configuration of international law as a scholarly discipline, the taxonomy of international law. While scholars may be unable to make international law, they certainly have the dominant influence over the development of its analytical framework, within which courts and tribunals and governments operate. Where that framework is creaking under the weight of exceptions, or where the

---

29 Eg, by entering into a treaty (in the case of rules of customary law other than rules of *jus cogens*) or according to the doctrine of persistent objection.

30 *Nuclear Tests (Australia v France)*, Judgment, ICJ Rep 1974 (20 December), 253, para 43. This statement was distinguished almost out of existence (as a common lawyer would say) by the decision in *Frontier Dispute (Burkina Faso v Republic of Mali)*, Judgment, ICJ Rep 1986 (22 December), 554, paras 39–40; but not so as to affect the argument here.

31 See the *Legal Status of Eastern Greenland* case (1933), PCIJ Rep, Series A/B, No. 53, 22, at 71.

framework appears to be applied only formally and in a manner that sits awkwardly with the realities of the underlying situation, it is right to review the adequacy of that framework. There are, I think, signs enough that we have already reached that stage, and that the conceptual framework of what we have for generations called the law of treaties is ripe for reconsideration. The work of the International Law Commission on unilateral acts of States,[32] and its work on the identification of customary international law,[33] already addresses neighbouring topics. As the Vienna Convention approaches its half-century one is entitled to ask, given how the law has developed, would we approach the subject in the same way again?

---

[32] See the 'Guiding Principles Applicable to Unilateral Declarations of States Capable of Creating Legal Obligations,' Yearbook of the ILC (2006), vol II, part 2.

[33] See the ILC website, accessed 26 May 2014, at www.un.org/law/ilc/index.htm. The ILC has also been working on a range of other treaty-related topics in recent years.

2. The law of treaties through the interplay of its different sources

Enzo Cannizzaro

I. INTRODUCTION: CODIFICATION, DE-CODIFICATION, RE-CODIFICATION

It is commonly accepted that the 1969 Vienna Convention on the Law of Treaties is one of the most ambitious, and perhaps also among the most successful, endeavours to codify international law ever attempted. It has conceptualized a system of the law of treaties that remains relevant to date. Many of its provisions are routinely mentioned in judicial and diplomatic practice as unequivocally corresponding to customary law. The Vienna Convention has also spread its influence over other branches of international law and has contributed to the general development of international law. Its blend of tradition and innovation now constitutes a model for codification.

At closer look, however, the application of the Vienna Convention also reveals some problematic issues and lays bare the fragile paradigm of codification. Although frequently mentioned in judicial and diplomatic practice as the living codification of the law of treaties, the Vienna Convention has certainly not prevented the further development of this area of law. The interplay between the Vienna Convention and other sources of international law is rather bidirectional. The Convention has certainly exerted a robust influence on international practice. However, evolution in the law of treaties and other areas of international law has also had a major impact on the Vienna Convention and has led to the further development of some of its normative solutions. The precise determination of the current scope and content of the law of treaties is therefore a difficult exercise and requires an assessment of the interplay of multiple sources: custom, general principles of law and institutional law.

On a more general note, this interrelation seems to epitomize the fate of codification treaties in international law. On the one hand, the law of treaties is subject to a creeping process of de-codification by virtue of the impact of other sources of law on the Convention. On the other hand, emerging needs in specific sectors of the law of treaties may trigger a process of re-codification which would update the solutions adopted in the Vienna Convention.[1] The recurrence of de-codification and subsequent re-codification is a prominent feature in the development of the law of treaties and constitutes one of the important threads running through the present study.

II. THE VIENNA CONVENTION AND PRE-EXISTING LAW: THE CLASSICAL SCHEME

From a formal perspective, the relationship between the Vienna Convention and custom is epitomized in the dichotomy between codification and progressive development of the law. Provisions of the Convention embodying previous practice apply to all the members of the international community; innovative provisions of the Convention only apply to its parties. Beyond this simplistic paradigm, however, closer analysis reveals that the interplay between the Vienna Convention and custom is much more varied and multifaceted.

Judicial practice often referred to the Convention as proof of the existence of customary law even before it had entered into force. A few months after its adoption, in its advisory opinion on *Namibia*, the International Court of Justice (ICJ) referred to the Vienna Convention provisions concerning termination of a treaty on account of breach by saying that 'these provisions (adopted without a dissenting vote) may in many respects be considered as a codification of existing customary law on the subject'.[2] In the two *Fisheries* decisions of 25 July 1974, the ICJ

---

[1] The obvious example is given by the recent adoption of the *Guide to Practice on Reservations to Treaties*, adopted by the International Law Commission (ILC) in 2011. The *Guide*, devoid per se of binding effect, takes into account the most recent practice and attempts to fill some of the incoherences of the regime adopted by the Vienna Convention or even to modify it. For example, the *Guide* enlarges the scope of objections to reservations and recognizes that the objecting State has the power to exclude the application of provisions of the treaty other than those to which the reservation relates, in its relations with the reserving State (Rule 3.4.2).

[2] *Legal Consequences for States of the Continued Presence of South Africa in Namibia (South West Africa) Notwithstanding Security Council Resolution 276 (1970)*, ICJ Rep 1971, 16, para 94. See also the case concerning the *Appeal Relating to the ICAO Council (India v Pakistan)*, Judgment, ICJ Rep 1972 (18 August) 46, in which the ICJ applied Article 60 of the Convention, and in particular, the definition of the notion of material breach, *qua* customary law (para 38). In its jurisprudence, the ICJ has quite often referred to provisions of

held that '[t]here can be little doubt, as is implied in the Charter of the United Nations and recognized in Article 52 of the Vienna Convention on the Law of Treaties, that under contemporary international law an agreement concluded under the threat or use of force is void'.[3] More recently, the ICJ has continued this tendency to cite provisions of the Convention as unequivocal proof of the existence of customary rules. In its judgment of 20 July 2012 relating to the *Obligation to Prosecute or Extradite (Belgium v Senegal)*, the Court found that Article 28 of the Convention, which concerns the temporal application of treaties, 'reflects customary law on the matter'.[4]

---

the Vienna Convention as unequivocal evidence of the pre-existence of custom. See the case of the *Aegean Sea Continental Shelf*, Judgment, ICJ Rep 1978 (19 December) 3, para 96, referring to the principle of the freedom of forms expressed in Articles 2, 3 and 11; the case of *Maritime Delimitation and Territorial Questions between Qatar and Bahrain*, Jurisdiction and Admissibility Judgment, ICJ Rep 1994 (1 July) 112, para 23, referring to the principle that 'international agreements may take a number of forms and be given a diversity of names' embodied in Article 2(1)(a); also see the case of the *Territorial Dispute (Libyan Arab Jamahiriya/Chad)*, Judgment, ICJ Rep 1994 (3 February) 21, para 41; the case of the *Kasikili/Sedudu Island (Botswana/Namibia)*, Judgment, ICJ Rep 1999 (II) (13 December) 1059, para 18; the case of *Application of the Convention on the Prevention and Punishment of the Crime of Genocide (Bosnia and Herzegovina v Serbia and Montenegro)*, Judgment, ICJ Rep 2007 (I) (26 February) 109, para 160; the case of the *Dispute Regarding Navigational and Related Rights (Costa Rica v Nicaragua)*, Judgment, ICJ Rep 2009 (13 July 2008) 213, para 47; the case of the *Application of the Interim Accord of 13 September 1995 (The Former Yugoslav Republic of Macedonia v Greece)*, Judgment, ICJ Rep 2011 (5 December) para 91, all referring to Articles 31 and 32 on treaty interpretation as reflecting customary law.

[3] *Fisheries Jurisdiction Case (United Kingdom of Great Britain and Northern Ireland v Iceland)*, Merits, ICJ Rep 1974, 3; *(Germany v Iceland, United Kingdom v Iceland)*, Merits, ICJ Rep 1974, 175.

[4] See para 100. Further on, in para 113, the Court observed that 'under Article 27 of the Vienna Convention on the Law of Treaties, which reflects customary law, Senegal cannot justify its breach of the obligation provided for in Article 7, paragraph 1, of the Convention against Torture by invoking provisions of its internal law …'. See also the case concerning the *Pulp Mills on the River Uruguay (Argentina v Uruguay)*, Judgment, ICJ Rep 2010 (20 April) 14, para 122, where the Court mentioned the 'well-established customary rule reflected in Article 27 of the Vienna Convention on the Law of Treaties, according to which "[a] party may not invoke the provisions of its internal law as justification for its failure to perform a treaty"'.

Only rarely, however, do international courts take care to specifically demonstrate that a certain rule existed *qua custom* before its incorporation in the Convention. Quite the contrary, in some instances one has the impression that the Vienna Convention is referred to not so much as a proof of the existence of custom, but rather as an essential element of the process of formation of customary law.[5]

This observation leads on to one of a different order, in which the Vienna Convention is seen as a factor in the process of law-making.[6] This role tends to reverse the ordinary sequence of the process of codification. Here it is not that the Vienna Convention embodies rules already formed in State practice, but rather that the Convention establishes a new behavioural model toward which practice tends to converge, in a more or less spontaneous manner. In a slightly different scheme, the Convention can be seen to represent the ultimate step in a process of formation of customary law, already underway at the time of the conclusion of the Convention, and which also influenced the drafting of the Convention's provisions.[7] This phenomenon is also of interest from a sociological viewpoint and testifies to the mutual influence of 'factual law' and 'formal law' in the law of treaties.

---

5 In his separate opinion in the case of the *Application of the Interim Accord of 13 September 1995* (n 2) Judge Simma seems to have conceived Article 60 of the Vienna Convention as establishing an all-encompassing legal regime governing reactions to a breach of treaties, including reactions falling within the law of State responsibility (see, infra, n 27). It is noteworthy that the ICJ, the *Gabčíkovo-Nagymaros Project*, Judgment, ICJ Rep 1997 (25 September) 7, pointed out that the correspondence between Article 60 and general law was only partial:

> it is only a material breach of the treaty itself, by a State party to that treaty, which entitles the other party to rely on it as a ground for terminating the treaty. The violation of other treaty rules or of rules of general international law may justify the taking of certain measures, including countermeasures, by the injured State, but it does not constitute a ground for termination under the law of treaties. (para 106)

6 For a recent discussion of the notion of law-making treaties, see C Brölmann, 'Law-Making Treaties: Form and Function in International Law' (2005) 74 Nordic J Intl L 383.

7 See T Treves, 'Customary International Law', in R Wolfrum (ed), *The Max Planck Encyclopedia of Public International Law* ((vol II, OUP, 2012) 937.

III. THE VIENNA CONVENTION AND SUPERVENING CUSTOM

The previous analysis corresponds to the classical legal paradigm of codification. This paradigm is based on a static analysis of the relations between treaties and custom, which tends to fix the legal situation existing at a certain point in time and makes it immaterial in determining their respective temporal sequence. Once ascertained that provisions of the Vienna Convention correspond to customary rules, the establishment of this sequence appears as a purely academic exercise.

However, as is well known, law changes over time. Treaty rules evolve mainly by means of evolutionary or contextual interpretation, and through subsequent practice. Customary law evolves and adapts to the development of social custom more rapidly than treaties. All in all, treaties and custom evolve according to different speeds and their development generally points in different directions.

As a consequence thereof, the identity between 'codificatory' treaties and custom, established at a certain point in time, is doomed, sooner or later, to dissipate. Sometimes the two sets of rules maintain a common bulk, while diverging on matters of detail; in other instances their core contents begin to differ, occasionally even dramatically. This divergence poses the question as to whether the two sources of law still maintain their independence, or rather whether a change in one might have a normative effect on the other.

A formal argument in favour of the respective independence of the two sets of rules is the distinction that can be made between them based on their respective sources. This is a consideration that inspires a number of provisions in the Vienna Convention.[8] The application of this principle of the independent coexistence of customary and treaty rules should lead to the more general conclusion that the vicissitudes of the provisions of the Vienna Convention should not impinge upon the corresponding customary rules on the law of treaties. For example, reservations to the Vienna

---

[8] See, for example, Articles 4 and 43 of the Vienna Convention. According to this latter provision:

> the invalidity, termination or denunciation of a treaty, the withdrawal of a party from it, or the suspension of its operation, as a result of the application of the present Convention or of the provisions of the treaty, shall not in any way impair the duty of any State to fulfil any obligation embodied in the treaty to which it would be subject under international law independently of the treaty.

Convention should not affect the general application of customary rules incorporated into its provisions.[9]

The principle of independent coexistence has been confirmed, albeit in a different setting, by the ICJ in *Nicaragua*. There, the Court found that customary rules do not cease to exist after they have been incorporated in a treaty that reflects customary international law.[10] Rather, custom survives as a source of law and continues to apply even in the relations between parties to that treaty, when and to the extent it is not inconsistent with the new conventional rules.

It can be reasonably assumed that the principle of autonomy applies in the relations between codification treaties and pre-existing practice. It is less reasonable to apply it in the reverse situation, namely to demonstrate that the development of the law has no effect on pre-existing codification treaties. The persistence of a treaty regime could only be justified if that treaty had not just the effect of contracting out of pre-existing custom,

---

[9] See Rule 4.4.2 of the *Guide to Practice* (n 1):

> Absence of effect on rights and obligations under customary international law – A reservation to a treaty provision which reflects a rule of customary international law does not of itself affect the rights and obligations under that rule, which shall continue to apply as such between the reserving State or organization and other States or international organizations which are bound by that rule.

A different view can be based on the idea that reservations to a provision of a codification treaty and acceptance thereto ought to be construed as a convention between the reserving and the accepting parties, aimed at derogating, in their mutual relations, from the customary rule reflected by that provision. This idea echoes, *a contrario*, in the famous passage contained in the Human Rights Committee, 'General Comment No 24: Issues Relating to Reservations Made upon Ratification or Accession to the Covenant or the Optional Protocols thereto, or in Relation to Declarations under Article 41 of the Covenant' (11/04/1994) CCPR/C/21/Rev.1/Add.6, which excludes the possibility of making reservations to provisions of the Covenant 'that represent customary international law (and a fortiori when they have the character of peremptory norms)', because 'human rights treaties are stipulated not in order to exchange reciprocal obligations among the parties, but rather "for the benefit of persons within their jurisdiction"'.

[10] See the case of *Military and Paramilitary Activities in and against Nicaragua (Nicaragua v United States of America)* Merits, ICJ Rep 1986 (27 June) 14, paras 175 *et seq*, especially para 178: 'even if two norms belonging to two sources of international law appear identical in content, and even if the States in question are bound by these rules both on the level of treaty-law and on that of customary international law, these norms retain a separate existence'.

but was also intended to prevent the application of supervening inconsistent custom in the relations between its parties.

Supervening custom interferes with provisions of the Vienna Convention in a number of situations. It may interfere in a relatively limited manner, as for example when it operates in the normative spaces left open by the Convention's provisions, filling the gaps created by ambiguous provisions. But it may also cause significant interference when it purports to establish legal regimes inconsistent with those established by the Convention.

An example of the first type of interference is evident in the tendency to attempt to objectively assess the compatibility of a reservation with the object and purpose of a treaty.[11] This tendency, while still evolving, seems to indicate that the mechanism of individual assessment established by the Vienna Convention is not exclusive and that, at least with regard to treaties protecting collective interests, it must be reconciled with the need to have the compatibility of a reservation determined objectively.

There are, however, situations in which trends in practice seem to be largely inconsistent with the normative system set up by the Vienna Convention. Again with regard to reservations, one cannot but refer to the tendency of States to react to impermissible reservations with objections, which purport to modify the legal effect of provisions other than those to which the reservations relate to. This practice seems at odds with Article 21(3) of the Vienna Convention, which confines the effect of objections to the same provisions the reservations related to.[12]

---

[11] See, for example, the case concerning *Armed Activities on the Territory of the Congo (New Application: 2002, Democratic Republic of Congo v Rwanda)* Jurisdiction of the Court and Admissibility of the Application, ICJ Rep 2006 (3 February) 6, para 66. See G Gaja, 'Il Regime della Convenzione di Vienna concernente le riserve inammissibili', in *Studi in onore di Vincenzo Starace* (Editoriale Scientifica, 2008) 349; A Pellet and D Müller, 'Reservations to Treaties: An Objection Is Definitely Not an Acceptance', in E Cannizzaro (ed), *The Law of Treaties beyond the Vienna Convention* (OUP, 2011) 37; B Simma and GI Hernández, 'Legal Consequences of an Impermissible Reservation to a Human Rights Treaty: Where Do We Stand ?' ibid, 60.

[12] These objections have been labelled as having 'intermediate' effect by the Special Rapporteur A Pellet, *Eighth Report on Reservations to Treaties*, Add 1, Doc A/CN.4/535/Add.1. See D Müller, 'Article 21 – Convention de 1969', in O Corten and P Klein (eds), *Les Conventions de Vienne sur le droit des traités. Commentaire article par article* (Bruylant, 2006) 921. This situation well exemplifies the process of de-codification and re-codification of some provisions of the Vienna Convention (see the *Guide to Practice*, (n 1) Rule 3.4.2).

The question thus arises as to whether subsequent custom also applies to the relations among parties to the Vienna Convention.

This is not an easy issue. It concerns the degree of resistance the Vienna Convention has to the evolution of custom, and, to my knowledge, this issue has never been dealt with by the international judicature. Two considerations seem of some relevance in solving this problem, but they are not entirely coherent with each other. First, the Convention ought to be generally considered as *lex specialis* among the parties, unless there is clear indication to the contrary. Second, nowhere does the Convention express the intent to set up a self-contained regime of the law of treaties, which blocks the evolution of general law in perpetuity. As stated expressly in its preamble, the Vienna Convention purports to codify and further develop the law of treaties, but not to insulate it from the beneficial influence of the general regime.[13]

It seems, therefore, unreasonable to adopt a one-size-fits-all solution, which is applicable to all possible relations between the Vienna Convention and subsequent custom. Rather, these relations ought to be established on a case-by-case basis, taking into account a number of elements, including not only the generality of the new law and the resilience of the provisions of the Vienna Convention, but also other more impalpable factors such as the quest for uniformity at the general level compared with the interest in maintaining a special regime among the parties. Whereas in principle the Vienna Convention should apply in the relations among its parties *qua lex specialis*, a different solution should not be automatically excluded, the more so when parties to the Convention expressly or implicitly show a certain propensity to contribute to the creation of new law.

---

[13] Indeed, the preamble contains a passage devoted to the relations between the Convention and customary law worded as follows: 'the rules of customary international law will continue to govern questions not regulated by the provisions of the present Convention'. This assertion seems to confine the application among the parties of pre-existing customary law to matters not regulated by the Convention. It seems to be a large step to assume that by it the parties also intended to contract out supervening customary law in their mutual relations and, thereby, exclude custom as a source of the law of treaties in matters regulated by the Convention.

IV. CUSTOM AND INNOVATIVE PROVISIONS OF THE CONVENTION

Innovative provisions of the Vienna Convention that prove incapable of serving as a model for future conduct fail to discharge either of the two main purposes of codification. They do not codify pre-existing law and they do not develop new law. Thus, the question arises as to their fate. Will they block the future development of the law and remain in force as a self-contained legal framework applicable to the States parties to the Vienna Convention only, or should their inability to serve as the basis for the creation of new law be considered as grounds for their termination?

This conundrum is not easily solved.

From a formal perspective, the principle of the autonomy of the two sources supports their perpetual coexistence. This solution appears thoroughly reasonable for provisions designed to contract out of custom and create a parallel legal regime applicable in the relations between the parties to the treaty.

This should be the case, for example, where the Vienna Convention prescribes that certain declarations must be made in writing.[14] Arguably, these provisions were laid down to create more legal certainty in the relations among the parties than that required by customary law. The same can be said with regard to provisions establishing other procedural conditions for the exercise of rights and faculties. This might be the case for Article 56(2), for example, which establishes that a party shall give not less than twelve months' notice of its intention to denounce or withdraw from a treaty. In its advisory opinion of 20 December 1989 on the *Interpretation of the Agreement of 25 March 1951 between the WHO and Egypt*,[15] the ICJ did not consider this rule as forming part of

---

[14] See, for example, Articles 35 and 67(1). ME Villiger, *Commentary on the 1969 Vienna Convention on the Law of Treaties* (Martinus Nijhoff, 2009) 479 (section on 'Article 35'), while admitting that 'the requirement of written consent (in Article 35) may appear as innovative when it was introduced at the conference in 1969', nonetheless, concludes that 'in view of the unanimous adoption in Vienna of Article 35, this requirement has most likely come to share the customary basis of the provision as a whole'.

[15] ICJ Rep 1980 73, para 49: the Court said: 'it is for the parties in each case to determine the length of those periods by consultation and negotiation in good faith'. Some indications as to the possible periods involved, as the Court has said, can be seen in provisions of host agreements, including Section 37 of the Agreement of 25 March 1951, as well as in Article 56 of the Vienna Convention on the Law of Treaties and in the corresponding Article of the International Law

customary law, but dealt with it as solely constituting a standard of reference for measuring good faith.[16] The Court appears to conceive Article 56(2) as a rule which has materialized and given a precise content to a pre-existing general rule of good faith.[17] The further development of custom should therefore be, in principle, unable to supersede this established content of the good faith requirement, unless one can demonstrate that the parties to the Convention also contributed to this process of subsequent development of supervening custom.

However, there are situations in which the idea of the persistence of a double legal regime – one customary, which continuously evolves over time, and the other conventional, resisting *in aeternum* the change of social custom – is not convincing. In particular, it seems logical to assume that provisions which have unsuccessfully attempted to create new customary law should, as a consequence of their failure, be set aside even in relations among the parties.

This might be the case in relation to the specific procedural requirements established by Article 65 with respect to invalidity and termination of treaties, designed to reduce the indeterminacy and arbitrariness of unilateral declarations of termination or invalidity of treaties.[18] This procedure has, to my knowledge, never been used. In *Racke*, the ECJ

Commission's Draft Articles on the Law of Treaties between States and International Organizations or between International Organizations.

[16] The ICJ took an analogous stance with regard to some general aspects of Articles 65 to 67. In the aforementioned judgment concerning the *Gabčíkovo-Nagymaros Project* (n 5), the Court said that 'Articles 65 to 67 of the Vienna Convention on the Law of Treaties, if not codifying customary law, at least generally reflect customary international law and contain certain procedural principles which are based on an obligation to act in good faith' (para 109).

[17] See para 47:

> A further general indication as to what those obligations may entail is to be found in the second paragraph of Article 56 of the Vienna Convention on the Law of Treaties and the corresponding provision in the International Law Commission's draft articles on treaties between States and international organizations or between international organizations. Those provisions, as has been mentioned earlier, specifically provide that, when a right of denunciation is implied in a treaty by reason of its nature, the exercise of that right is conditional upon notice, and that of not less than twelve months. Clearly, these provisions also are based on an obligation to act in good faith and have reasonable regard to the interests of the other party to the treaty.

[18] See M Cosnard, 'Article 65 – Convention de 1969', in Corten and Klein, *Les Conventions de Vienne* (n 12) 2353.

found that 'the specific procedural requirements laid down (by Article 65) do not form part of customary international law'.[19]

In and of itself, the non-use of certain provisions of the Vienna Convention can hardly justify their termination.[20] However, a different conclusion could be reached with regard to innovative provisions of the Vienna Convention, namely those which were laid down with a view to progressively developing the law. It is reasonable to presume that they are tacitly quashed by supervening custom due to their failure to fulfil their purpose.

V. THE VIENNA CONVENTION AND GENERAL PRINCIPLES OF LAW

Considerable perplexities surround general principles of law as a source of the law of treaties, due to a plurality of reasons. In contemporary international law, general principles of law enjoy quite a bad reputation. They are commonly regarded as a proof of the incompleteness of the international legal order: allegedly incapable of filling its gaps through its own sources, it must refer to external, heteronomous, sources. Moreover, recourse to general principles of law is clearly at odds with the tendency of legal scholarship to look at the Vienna Convention as a full-fledged set of rules covering virtually all possible aspects of the law of treaties.

In spite of this, a theoretical discourse on general principles of law and on their function in the system of the law of treaties might be very useful. Precisely in this context, this particular source of law has significantly changed its role. Originally conceived of as the transplantation of concepts and institutions of the law of contract into the international order,[21] more recently 'general principles' have also come to be understood as referring

---

[19] Case C-162/96 *A Racke GmbH & Co v Hauptzollamt Mainz* [1998] ECJR I-3655.

[20] See M Kohen, 'Desuetude and Obsolescence of Treaties', in Cannizzaro (ed), *The Law of Treaties* (n 11) 350.

[21] See the famous passage of the dissenting opinion by Judge Anzilotti to the judgment of the *Diversion of Water from the Meuse*, PCIJ 1937 (28 June) Series A/B, No 70, 50, according to whom:

> the principle underlying this submission *(inadimplenti non est adimplendum)* is so just, so equitable, so universally recognized, that it must be applied in international relations also. In any case, it is one of these 'general principles of law recognized by civilized nations' which the Court applies in virtue of Article 38 of its Statute.

to principles of law originating in the structure of international legal relations and in the function of international legal rules.

The best example of the dual role of general principles as exemplified in the law of treaties is probably to be found in the celebrated advisory opinion of the ICJ of 28 May 1951 on the *Reservations to the Convention on the Prevention and Punishment of the Crime of Genocide*.[22]

The Court was asked to decide whether a State which had made a reservation could be regarded as a party to a multilateral treaty in spite of an objection to this reservation by another State party. In its answer, the Court took note that the traditional legal regime, inspired as it was by the notion of integrity of treaties, would have given a negative answer to this question. Further, the ICJ observed that this 'concept, which is directly inspired by the notion of contract, is of undisputed value as a principle'.[23] Nonetheless, the Court went on to refer to a variety of circumstances suggesting more flexibility. Among these circumstances, the Court mentioned the 'clearly universal character of the United Nations under whose auspices the Convention was concluded and the very wide degree of participation envisaged by Art. XI of the Convention'.[24] These elements, which allude to the structure of the legal relations of the new emerging international public order, led the ICJ to establish a different legal regime for reservations based not only on the need to secure the integrity of the treaty, but also on the perceived need to preserve the universal aspiration of the Genocide Convention.

The Court can be taken to have referred to the existence of differing, possibly opposing, general principles of law. The first is the classical scheme, in which a domestic principle, which inspires the legal regime of contracts, is subsumed into international law and is used to determine the legal regime of reservations to treaties in international law. The second is a new scheme, in which the legal regime of reservations is based on the principle of universality of multilateral treaties, a principle that is unknown in domestic law and relates to the rise of a category of collective fundamental interests. It is by balancing these competing principles against each other that the ICJ finally established the new legal regime for reservations to treaties, and objections thereto, in international law.

Nor is the impact of general principles of law on the law of treaties confined to the transitory situations of law change. General principles of

---

22 ICJ Rep 1951, 15.

23 Ibid, 17.

24 Ibid, 21.

law can also be invoked to fill apparent gaps in the legal regime of the law of treaties. An example of such use of general principles can be seen in the context of the dispute concerning the *Gabčíkovo-Nagymaros Project*, decided by the ICJ in 1997.[25] In the course of these proceedings, Slovakia invoked the principle of approximate application in order to justify the unilateral construction and operation of the so-called *Variant C*, namely a water management project on the Danube river designed to replace the original project that had been envisaged in a treaty between Hungary and Czechoslovakia. According to Slovakia, this 'is a principle of international law and a general principle of law'.[26] Reference to its alleged dual nature was clearly intended to enhance the authority of the principle and to facilitate its application. The ICJ did not pronounce on the existence of the principle. It merely held that the principle, if in existence, would not apply in the case at hand due to the profound difference between the conduct performed by Slovakia and that required by the original treaty.

From a different perspective, general principles of law can be invoked as a substitute for custom in order to identify the source of rules considered as necessary and inherent in the logic of the international legal system in situations where there is a relative scarcity of practice. In his separate opinion to the judgment of the ICJ of 5 December 2011, in the case of the *Application of the Interim Accord of 13 September 1995*, Judge Simma pointed to general principles of law as a possible source of the rule *inadimplenti non est adimplendum* in international law. He noted that such a rule corresponds to a rule uniformly present in the contemporary law of contract, as applied by domestic judges. In contrast, this rule in international law does not have the benefit of subsequent 'impartial adjudication' and is therefore more prone to abuse. In Simma's opinion, it is precisely this circumstance that explains the reluctance of States to invoke the principle and makes 'the recognition of the principle's consecration as customary international law very difficult'.[27]

The progressive obsolescence of the normative solutions adopted by the Vienna Convention may even increase the role and importance of general principles of law as a source of the law of treaties, in particular in

---

[25] Note 5.

[26] Paras 67 *et seq*. Slovakia relied on the authority of Sir Hersch Lauterpacht, who devoted to this principle a passage of his separate opinion to the *Admissibility of Hearings of Petitioners by the Committee on South West Africa*, Advisory Opinion, ICJ Rep 1956, 46.

[27] *Application of the Interim Accord of 13 September 1995* (n 2), Simma, Separate Opinion, paras 13–14.

their most fascinating guise as principles emerging from the legal structure of international legal relations.

Among their many virtues, general principles of law have the function of diffusing the changes that have taken place in some of international law's sectoral regimes or canonical areas throughout the entire edifice of international law. In other words, in a decentralized and minimally institutionalized legal order such as international law, general principles of law produce an effect analogous to that of the principle of the communicating vessels. As law evolves, general principles tend to balance out the different branches to the same level of development, which likely constitutes the product of the interplay between the innovative tendencies pioneered in one field and the resistance to innovation experienced in others. In this sense, general principles of law operate more as a source of inspiration for determining the state of the law rather than as a source of law-making in the proper sense of the term.

This premise may help one to understand the development of the law of treaties as applied to certain categories of treaties, such as human rights treaties. It is well known that in this field, treaty bodies have put much emphasis on the special character of the relevant treaties, which in their view justifies the adoption of a special regime in the law of treaties whose legal basis is to be found neither in the Vienna Convention nor in State practice.[28] When the existence of such a special regime is determined on the basis of a purely logical process of deduction, it may be reasonable to assume that general principles of international law have a role to play in this process. This role of general principles, as a tool

---

[28] A well-known example comes from the regime of reservations (see the famous decision of the ECtHR in the cases *Belilos v Switzerland* App no 10328/83, (ECHR, 29 April 1988); *Weber v Switzerland* App no 11034/84 (ECHR, 22 May 1990); *Loizidou v Turkey* App no 15318/89 (ECHR, 23 March 1995); see moreover the 'General Comment No 24 …' (n 9); the joint separate opinion of Judges Higgins, Kooijmans, Elaraby, Owada and Simma, appended to the case of *Armed Activities on the Territory of the Congo* (n 11). A further example comes from the doctrine of the objective nature of human rights, which justified the exercise of jurisdiction by the European Commission of Human Rights in an interstate dispute with regard to conduct performed at a time in which the claimant state was not yet party to the Convention (see the famous decision of the Commission in *Austria v Italy, the Pfunders Case* App no 788/60 (11 January 1961)). This doctrine has been further applied as a legal basis for special regimes in a number of other situations, including the regime of withdrawal from or denunciation of a treaty (see the decision in the case *Baruch Ivcher-Bronstein v Peru*, Inter-American Court of Human Rights (6 February 2001)).

permitting the creation of general law on the basis of a logical process of deduction, is particularly important for the development of the law of human rights treaties. These treaties differ, as to their structure and function, from the vast majority of other treaties, which typically possess reciprocal character.

Finally, recourse to general principles of international law, and in particular the observation of how law develops on the basis of a logical process of deducting new rules from the structure of pre-existing ones, can help to explain the somewhat mysterious process of the evolution of the law of treaties under the pressures coming from other fields of law.

This process can be closely observed in the evolution of the legal regime of *jus cogens*, as laid down in the Vienna Convention and moulded according to the blend of bilateralism and communitarianism which characterizes the Convention's conceptual system. Successively, however, the notion of *jus cogens* has been applied in other areas of the international legal system and, in particular, to the law of State responsibility, where it underwent significant evolution – the particular object and the nature of the interests protected by *jus cogens* account for this development. However, this development did not proceed by linear progression in these two fields, but rather through discontinuous leaps followed by a process of mutual adaptation. Developments in the law of treaties thus prompted analogous developments in the law of international responsibility and vice versa. One of the following paragraphs will be devoted to such a development occurring in the legal regime of *jus cogens* in the law of treaties, one which was possibly inspired by a similar development that had previously occurred in the law of State responsibility.

VI. INSTITUTIONAL LAW-MAKING AND THE LAW OF TREATIES

Albeit quantitatively and qualitatively modest, the contribution of institutional law to the law of treaties is not entirely negligible. It shapes a tendency towards the institutionalization of law-making, which may well acquire more importance in the future.

This contribution is well epitomized in the activities of the United Nations Security Council. Although deprived of normative competences, the Security Council has contributed to the development of the law of treaties in connection with its primary responsibility of maintaining and restoring international peace and security.

This is reflected in the Security Council resolutions which established that accession to certain treaties might be necessary in order to guarantee international peace and security or, conversely, that withdrawal from them amounts to a threat to international peace and security.[29]

At first glance, this is at odds with the function assigned to the Security Council by the UN Charter, which is certainly not to act on the normative plane but rather on the factual plane. It sounds obvious that peace cannot be secured through normative commitments alone, but needs to be ensured through deeds. Nonetheless, States' acceptance of mechanisms of verification set up by treaties might enormously facilitate the Security Council in preventing crises from both arising and escalating. Therefore, it comes as no surprise that the Security Council has promoted widespread accession to the 1968 Non-Proliferation Treaty (NPT) and has encouraged States to accept verifications by the International Atomic Energy Agency (IAEA). The Security Council has even gone beyond this. On the occasion of one State announcing its withdrawal from the NPT, the Security Council issued a declaration in which it seemed to point out, although in quite ambiguous terms, that this withdrawal would be null and void.[30]

This tendency by the Security Council seems to indicate that the need to prevent threats to peace may require States not only to abstain from conduct in breach of fundamental interests of the international community, but also to enter into treaties, or to remain parties to treaties, which impose obligations to respect collective interests and which establish forms of international control over compliance with their provisions. The idea that the institutions set up to protect the collective interests and values of the international community are also entitled to impose a duty to enter into certain conventional engagements or prohibit withdrawal from them is not only fraught with problematic implications; but it also further highlights the public policy dimension of the law of treaties. This is a dimension of the law of treaties that needs to be further considered in order to elaborate some key issues which require in-depth research.

---

29 See, among many, UNSC Res 1540 (2004), UNSC Res 1887 (2009).

30 See UNSC Res 1718 (2006), where the Council stated that 'the international regime on the non-proliferation of nuclear weapons should be maintained', and demanded that 'the DPRK [Democratic People's Republic of Korea] immediately retract its announcement of withdrawal from the Treaty on the Non-Proliferation of Nuclear Weapons'. See also UNSC Res 1695 (2006) and UNSC Res 1874 (2009).

VII. OUTLOOK AND CONCLUSION

1. Contractualism, Objectivism and the Law of Treaties of the Future

If I were called, at the end of this hasty journey, to identify how the law of treaties will develop in the future, I would not be hesitant in pointing to the enduring tension between contractualism and objectivism. By contractualism I mean the tendency to look at treaties as mere international contracts, serving the individual interests of the parties. By objectivism I mean the tendency to look at treaties as normative instruments, serving not only private but also collective interests, and limited by public policy considerations.

The tension between these two tendencies featured in the drafting of the Vienna Convention and re-emerges periodically as one of the main factors prompting the development of the law of treaties.[31] In contemporary international law, treaties serve a plurality of aims. They can be used to set up international organizations, establish common actions and joint enterprises, determine the use of common resources, set up collective mechanisms of compliance and protect collective or universal values.[32] The decentralized structure of the international community and the correspondingly minor role assigned to institutional sources in the international order account for the use of treaties as sources of objective law. Accordingly, the law of treaties seems to be increasingly inspired by public policy considerations, whether pertaining to the community of the parties or to the international community at as a whole.

Many provisions of the Vienna Convention reflect the unsettled tension between antithetical functions assigned to treaties as mere contracts between international subjects or as instruments for creating objective law. This can be observed in the provisions concerning the vicissitudes of multilateral treaties, alternatively conceived of as a unitary normative tool or as a bundle of bilateral relations among the parties.

Article 60(2) is probably the most radical example in which the need for an objective assessment on the existence of a breach, and on the need to terminate or to suspend the treaty in consequence thereof, prevails over

---

[31] For a general account, see J Klabbers, 'The Community Interest in the Law of Treaties: Ambivalent Conceptions', in U Fastenrath, R Geiger, D-E Kahn, A Paulus, S von Schorlemer and C Vedder (eds), (OUP, 2011) 768.

[32] The multifarious nature of international treaties has long been recognized. For an appraisal, see AD McNair, 'The Functions and Differing Legal Character of Treaties' (1930) 11 British Ybk Intl L 100.

the right of unilateral assessment by every single party.[33] Other rules of the Convention, albeit recognizing the existence of collective interests of the parties, rely more heavily on the unilateral power of each party to assess its legal situation vis-à-vis other parties. A notable example can be found in Article 41, which recognizes the power of two or more parties to a multilateral treaty to determine the existence of the conditions allowing them to conclude an agreement to modify the terms of the treaty as between themselves.

In some cases, however, the balance of contractualism and objectivism reflected in the provisions of the Vienna Convention is challenged by the subsequent practice of States.

I have already mentioned the recent vicissitudes of the regime of reservations. Whereas the solutions adopted by the Vienna Convention tend to permit the splitting of the unitary regime of a treaty into a bundle of reciprocal ties among the parties, the most recent practice seems to mark, at least partially, a return towards a regime which can objectively assess the compatibility of reservations and objections with the object and purpose of a treaty.[34]

It is equally interesting to follow the evolving conception of contextual interpretation. According to the terms of Article 31(3) of the Vienna Convention, the context of a treaty for the purpose of interpretation includes both subsequent practice and subsequent treaties that are applicable in the relations between the parties. The purpose of this provision is apparently to contextualize interpretation in the normative background common to the parties. However, this would limit the normative context to be taken into account to the practice and treaties applicable in the relations between *all* the parties. In the case of multilateral treaties this condition will rarely ever be met. The opposite assumption, which would permit the interpretation of a treaty provision in the context of obligations binding on *some* of the parties to the multilateral treaty, would have the effect of splitting the contents of multilateral treaty obligations on a bilateral basis, an effect hardly reconcilable with the objective of contextual interpretation.

Both these antithetical positions are echoed in recent case law. In *Bosphorus,* the European Court of Human Rights interpreted the European Convention on Human Rights (ECHR), a treaty with a broad scope *ratione personae*, in the light of the obligations flowing for some of its

---

[33] See B Simma and CJ Tams, 'Reacting against Treaty Breaches' in DB Hollis (ed), *The Oxford Guide to Treaties* (OUP, 2012) 576.

[34] Supra, n 1 and n 9.

parties by the founding treaties of the European Union, which had more limited personal scope than the ECHR itself.[35] This solution does not appear particularly appropriate as it has the effect of making the protection accorded to individuals by the Convention dependent on international law rules not applicable in the relations between all the State parties. On the other hand, the recent case law of World Trade Organization (WTO) judicial organs points in a different direction: tending to exclude interpretation of WTO provisions in the light of international rules that are not binding on *all* of its parties. This conclusion seems to entail that WTO provisions must be interpreted objectively, in the interest of the community of its parties.[36]

2. Contractualism, Objectivism and the Protection of Fundamental Values

The tendency towards objectivism and the insufficiency of a purely contractualist approach becomes even more evident when the protection of universal values is at stake. Traditionally, the law of treaties was

---

[35] *Bosphorus Hava Yollari Turizm Ve Ticaret Anonim Şirketi v Ireland* App no 45036/98 (ECHR, 30 June 2005).

[36] See the Panel Report on *European Communities – Measures Affecting the Approval and Marketing of Biotech Products*, WT/DS291/R, WT/DS292R, WT/DS293/R, adopted on 29 September 2006, especially para 7.70, where the Panel expressly took the view that Article 31(3)(c) of the Vienna Convention of the Law of Treaties requires 'consideration of those rules of international law which are applicable in the relations between all parties to the treaty which is being interpreted'. However, the scope of this statement was somewhat limited in para 7.72., where the Panel refused to take a position on whether rules of international law which are binding for all the parties to a dispute but not for all the parties to the WTO must be taken into account. In the same Report, the Panel seems to suggest the fascinating idea that other rules of international law, even if not binding for all the parties to the WTO, could nonetheless be considered as evidence of the 'ordinary' meaning to the given to WTO provisions. This assumption seems to pave the way for a wider consideration of international legal rules, regardless of their scope *ratione personae*, as enlightening the lines along which international law develops. The idea that besides international rules binding for all the parties to the WTO, which must be taken into account as part of the WTO context, other rules of international law, even not binding for all the parties to the WTO, can also be equally considered as informative of the state of the law, seems to shape the contours of a technique of global interpretation. It further reinforces the idea that interpretation of multilateral treaties is an objectively logical operation, which cannot be split according to the reciprocal relations among the parties.

neutral in this regard, as it was narrowly conceived of as the set of rules designed to govern the conduct of States in concluding, applying or terminating contractual engagements. In this respect, the existence of agreements to act in violation of fundamental values of the international legal order does not appear particularly relevant as long as these agreements are not implemented.

This approach has significantly changed with the inclusion of the notion of *jus cogens* in the Vienna Convention, a notion which, by nature, points to the existence of a sphere of values and interests that transcend the reciprocal interests of the parties. The inclusion of *jus cogens* among the grounds for invalidating or terminating a treaty expresses the idea that international law does not tolerate the existence of an agreement to violate fundamental values of the international community, regardless of whether this agreement is put into effect or not.

However, the Vienna Convention maintained an ambiguous approach towards *jus cogens*, which were still conceived as a sort of defence at the disposal of the parties to escape compliance with their contractual engagements. Consistent with this conception, Article 65 of the Convention confers the right to invoke *jus cogens* as grounds for invalidating or terminating a treaty to the parties to the treaty only.[37]

---

[37] This conception might have been borne in mind by the ICJ when it failed to entertain the dispute between Portugal and Australia in the case of *East Timor (Portugal v Australia)*, Judgment, ICJ Rep 1995 (30 June) 90. The decision of the Court did not mention *jus cogens*. It rather focused on the troubled relationship between the consensual nature of the jurisdiction of the Court and the *erga omnes* structure of the principle of self-determination. It is common knowledge that the Court declined to exercise its jurisdiction because a decision on the merits would have involved the assessment of the legal situation of Indonesia, a State not a party to the dispute. Indonesia was thus an indispensible party to that dispute, according to the doctrine established in the case of the *Monetary Gold Removed from Rome in 1943 (Italy v France, United Kingdom of Great Britain and Northern Ireland, and the United States)* ICJ Rep 1954, 19. However, one could wonder whether the doctrine of the indispensible party should apply at all when fundamental values of the international community are at stake. Its application would render a judicial determination of the breach of rules which establish the consequences of a serious breach of peremptory norms for third States under Article 41 of the Articles on State Responsibility virtually impossible, in particular when no State is especially affected by the violation. For more in-depth analysis on the impact of peremptory law on the traditional bilateralist conception which inspires the law of treaties, see, infra, para VIII. In its recent judgment on *Questions Relative to the Obligation to Prosecute or Extradite (Belgium v Senegal)*, Judgment, ICJ Rep 2012 (20 July) the ICJ found that:

The notion of *jus cogens* and its legal implications have been further elaborated, in particular in the process of codification of the law of State responsibility. Article 41(1) and (2) of the Articles on State Responsibility, adopted by the ILC in 2001, establish secondary obligations incumbent upon all the States of the international community flowing from a grave breach of a *jus cogens* norm. These include, among others, the obligation to cooperate to put an end to the breach, and the obligation not to recognize as lawful situations created by the breach nor to render aid or assistance in maintaining the breach. One can reasonably assume that a State not directly injured by the breach of a *jus cogens* norm has the right to claim the violation by another State of the secondary obligations incumbent upon all the States of the international community, in accordance with Article 41.[38] The main argument supporting this assumption is of a logical character. Many *jus cogens* rules are established in the interest of individual beneficiaries only, and breach of a *jus cogens* norm does not necessarily entail the existence of an injured State. The contrary assumption that the injured State is the only entity having the power to invoke the violation of the obligations laid down by Article 41 would render the existence of these obligations practically meaningless.

> any State party to the Convention may invoke the responsibility of another State party with a view to ascertaining the alleged failure to comply with its obligations *erga omnes partes*, such as those under Article 6, paragraph 2, and Article 7, paragraph 1, of the Convention, and to bring that failure to an end.

This consideration was sufficient for the Court to recognize a *locus standi* to the claimant. If the obligations enshrined in Article 41 were obligations *erga omnes*, this finding would entail that every State is empowered to invoke the responsibility of another State alleged to have disregarded the consequences of a serious breach of peremptory norms of international law. The doctrine of the indispensible party was not applicable in this case, since the claim directly addressed the State alleged to have breached obligations *erga omnes partes*, and not a third State alleged to have disregarded the consequences of the breach. On the power of third parties to invoke the invalidity of a treaty conflicting with *jus cogens*, see, J Verhoeven, 'Invalidity of Treaties: Anything New in/under the Vienna Convention?', in E Cannizzaro (ed), *The Law of Treaties* (n 11) 297.

[38] For different views on this subject, see S Talmon, 'The Duty Not To Recognize as Lawful a Situation Created by the Illegal Use of Force or Other Serious Breaches of a *Jus Cogens* Obligation: An Obligation without Real Substance?', in C Tomuschat and JM Thouvenin (eds), *The Fundamental Rules of the International Legal Order* (Martinus Nijhoff, 2006) 99; C Tams, *Enforcing Obligations* Erga Omnes *in International Law* (CUP, 2006) especially 184; A Gianelli, 'Absolute Invalidity of Treaties and their Non-Recognition by Third States', in Cannizzaro (ed), *The Law of Treaties* (n 11) 333.

The recognition of the existence of a sphere of special secondary obligations arising out of the breach of a *jus cogens* norm, the violation of which could be invoked by all the members of the international community, can also influence the further development of the law of treaties. There seems to be no reason to deny that the special secondary obligations envisaged by Article 41 can be violated either through unilateral action or through the conclusion of a treaty. In recent practice the question has arisen more than once as to whether the conclusion of a treaty designed to regulate the effect of a *jus cogens* breach amounts to a violation of one or more of these obligations. It seems therefore logical to infer that every State of the international community is entitled to invoke the international responsibility of any State which has breached Article 41 through the conclusion of a treaty.

It is quite obvious that the conclusion of a treaty may constitute a violation of international obligations incumbent upon one or more of its parties and there is no point in dwelling upon it. Nevertheless, the assumption that the conclusion of a treaty may constitute a breach of *erga omnes* obligations laid down by Article 41, designed to prevent a *jus cogens* breach from continuing and from producing its intended effect, is quite striking and may have far-reaching implications. It seems to mark a significant step towards the objective nature of *jus cogens*. One can wonder whether this development might also entail the further implication that treaties concluded in breach of these obligations are void and must be terminated.[39]

All in all, the codification of the law of State responsibility is telling as regards the development of international law which occurred between the adoption of the Vienna Convention and the elaborations of the ILC Articles. Still based on a bilateralist scheme, it is nonetheless inspired by

---

39 The tantalizing but simplistic idea that Article 41 is, by itself, part of *jus cogens* seems to be misguided. It would equate offences against the fundamental values of the international community with conducts of a lesser degree of severity. One can rather suggest that the existence of special consequences flowing from a grave breach of *jus cogens* rules has the effect of enlarging the notion of conflict adopted by Articles 53 and 62 of the Vienna Convention, with the consequence that treaties which purport to regulate unlawful situations arising out of a *jus cogens* breach are, in turn, conflicting with *jus cogens*. This conclusion could be based on the hierarchical nature of the rule of conflict set up by Articles 53 and 64 of the Vienna Convention. Hierarchy expresses the idea that higher values are offended not only by rules which purport to violate them directly, but also by rules which aim to produce effects inconsistent with the *ordre public*. For some discussion of this approach, I refer to my study 'A Higher Law for Treaties', in E Cannizzaro (ed), *The Law of Treaties* (n 11) 425.

a communitarian conception which applies where fundamental interests of the international community are at stake. It seems to point to a road that the law of treaties could follow in the future.

3. Regulating treaties: A comparative perspective

Martins Paparinskis

I. INTRODUCTION

Legal concepts of domestic law profoundly influence the way one approaches and conceptualizes international law. James Crawford has observed that 'it cannot be said too often that our thinking about law is infiltrated, marinated, drenched with the influence of national legal systems, with their characteristic ways of enforcing obligations and vindicating rights. We were all national lawyers first'.[1] That is surely right (although the trend towards specialization that erodes the authority of generalists might also eventually expunge the memory of the domestic origins of the invisible college). The domestic law perspective applies with particular force to international treaties that combine a consensual form, *prima facie* reminiscent of the structure employed in the domestic law of contracts, with a substantive breadth, *prima facie* extending beyond the legal relationships that would be addressed by the law of contracts in domestic law. This chapter will attempt to explore the tension between underlying assumptions about the appropriateness of domestic analogies. A convenient point of departure is the proposition made by Arnold McNair as long ago as in 1930, contrasting the variety of legal forms employed by the domestic legal order with the sparseness of form by which international law addressed substantively comparable legal relationships:

> The internal laws of the modern state provide its members with a variety of legal instruments for the regulation of life within that community: the contract; the conveyance or assignment of immovable or movable property, which may be made for valuable consideration or may be a gift or an exchange; the gratuitous promise clothed in a particular form; the charter or private Act of Parliament creating a corporation; legislation, which may be constituent, such as a written constitution, fragmentary or complete, or may

[1] J Crawford, 'Multilateral Rights and Obligations in International Law' (2006) 319 Recueil des Cours 325, 345.

> be declaratory of existing law, or create new law, or codify existing law with comparatively unimportant changes. Further, though rarely, we may find a constitutional document which closely resembles the international treaty itself, for instance, Magna Carta.[2]

If the debate is put in a historical perspective, it may be said that the appropriateness of domestic analogies has been debated in slightly differing terms by each succeeding generation of international lawyers. In the late 19th century, Heinrich Triepel drew the distinction between treaties analogous to contracts properly so-called (*Verträge*), where the contractual parties pursued opposing interests, and the law-making treaties analogous to agreements (*Vereinbarungen*), where the contractual parties pursued common interests.[3] In the inter-War period, Hersch Lauterpacht dismissed any practical value of this distinction[4] and made a powerful argument of analogy between domestic contract law on the one hand and the law of treaties and particular treaty regimes on the other hand.[5] Conversely, McNair made an equally powerful argument for a broader list of possible analogies from domestic law,[6] shifting the attention to public law,[7] and in particular cases showing scepticism about the value of relying on private law.[8]

---

[2] A McNair, 'The Functions and Differing Legal Character of Treaties' (1930) 11 BYBIL 100, 100. McNair's article has been taken as a point of departure in a number of sophisticated analyses of the law of treaties, see H Lauterpacht, 'Some Observations on the Preparatory Work in the Interpretation of Treaties' (1935) 48 Harvard L Rev 549, 552; CW Jenks, 'Hersch Lauterpacht: The Scholar as Prophet' (1960) 36 BYBIL 1, 6; B Simma, 'From Bilateralism to Community Interest in International Law' (1994) 250 Recueil des Cours 217, 322; J Klabbers, 'How to Defeat a Treaty's Object and Purpose Pending Entry into Force: Towards Manifest Intent' (2001) 34 Vanderbilt J Transnational L 283, 289; R Jennings, 'Book Review: D Bederman, *The Spirit of International Law*' (2003) 97 AJIL 725, 727; K Keith, 'Bilateralism and Community in Treaty Law and Practice: Of Warriors, Workers, and (Hook-)Worms' in U Fastenrath et al (eds), *From Bilateralism to Community Interest: Essays in Honour of Bruno Simma* (OUP, 2011) 754-55.

[3] H Triepel, *Droit International et Droit Interne* (R Brunet tr, Á Pedonne, 1920) 52, generally chp 3.

[4] H Lauterpacht, *Private Law Sources and Analogies of International Law* (Longmans, Green and Co Ltd, 1927) 158–59.

[5] Ibid, chp IV.

[6] McNair, 'Functions and Character ...' (n 2).

[7] A McNair, 'So-Called State Servitudes' (1925) 6 BYBIL 111, 121–25; A McNair, 'International Legislation' (1933–1934) 19 Iowa L Rev 177, 183–88.

[8] A McNair, 'Mandates' (1928) 3 Cambridge L J 149, 150.

The immediate post-World War Two developments in international criminal law, international human rights law, and the law of international organizations, and later developments in the law of non-proliferation and international environmental law clearly demonstrated that rules with substance not easily conceptualized in contractual terms do exist as a matter of positive law. Despite (or perhaps precisely because of) the challenge of providing a theoretical framework for these developments, the analogies with different domestic regimes were largely left unexplored in the law-making process and replaced by sophisticated elaboration of particular rules and regimes directly at the international level. The 1969 Vienna Convention on the Law of Treaties ('VCLT') does not use language explicitly relying on analogies from domestic law,[9] and its structure is not generally based on distinctions between different types of treaties.[10] The development of the law of treaties further influenced the development of the law of State responsibility, with certain ideas regarding termination for material breach taken up in the 2001 ILC Articles on State Responsibility ('2001 ILC Articles'), where primary obligations more generally were distinguished between, on the one hand, bilateral(izable) obligations, and genuinely multilateral – interdependent or *erga omnes* – obligations on the other hand.[11] In contemporary law,

---

[9] The International Law Commission's Draft Articles on the Law of Treaties mention contractual and law-making treaties only to deny the relevance of this distinction for the particular legal issues (of interpretation, separability of provisions, denunciation, and termination), see ILC, 'Draft Articles on the Law of Treaties with Commentaries' in Yearbook of the ILC (1966) vol II (A/CN.4/SER.A/1966/Add.1) 112, respectively 219 para 6; 238 para 2; 251 para 3; 255 para 7.

[10] The Vienna Convention does provide for a few special rules for particular types of treaties in particular circumstances: it excludes treaties between States and other subjects of international law from its scope, Vienna Convention on the Law of Treaties (adopted 23 May 1969, entered into force 27 January 1980) 1155 UNTS 331, Article 3; requires acceptance of a reservation to a constituent instrument of an international organization by a competent organ of that organization, ibid, Article 20(3); nature of treaties affects the right of termination, ibid, Article 60(2)(c); and certain rules on termination are inapplicable to treaties of humanitarian character, ibid, Article 60(5).

[11] J Crawford, 'Responsibility for Breaches of Communitarian Norms: An Appraisal of Article 48 of the Articles of State Responsibility for Wrongful Acts' in Fastenrath et al (eds), *From Bilateralism to Community Interest: Essays in Honour of Bruno Simma* (n 2).

while the nature of treaties has important legal and conceptual implications for the law of treaties and State responsibility,[12] the post-War practice has generated its own terms of art that seem sufficiently sophisticated to no longer depend on or necessarily allude to domestic analogies.[13]

With the VCLT, the 2001 ILC Articles, and the practice and judicial decisions applying them firmly in place, with rare exceptions there would be little added value in going back to domestic analogies to derive general principles that could have direct and significant legal impact.[14] Consequently, the perspective adopted in the chapter has to be necessarily more modest than that adopted by Triepel, Lauterpacht, and McNair in the first third of the last century. It is limited to reflecting upon, rather than deriving legal effects from the comparison of how domestic and international legal orders deal with similar challenges. The admissibility of arguments about analogy depends upon certain assumptions about the nature of domestic and international legal orders.[15] The present chapter is consciously ambivalent about the underlying premises, evaluating the possibilities of comparison of particular rules of the law of treaties and treaty law with particular rules of domestic law from perspectives that are based on different assumptions about the relationship. The chapter will also not define 'contract', 'statute', 'consideration', or other terms denoting particular instruments in domestic law, nor will it engage in any detailed discussion of approaches in particular domestic legal systems. In the contemporary international legal order, positively structured along the lines of the VCLT and the 2001 ILC Articles, it is (no longer) terribly exciting to inquire whether international rules trail the finer print of Roman, English, Soviet, or Chinese law, or Sharia. Such an exercise is in any event unlikely to be very illuminating to a legal

---

[12] In a recent International Court of Justice ('ICJ') judgment, the nature of the particular obligations of the 1984 Convention against Torture and Other Cruel, Inhuman or Degrading Treatment or Punishment determined the admissibility of claims and remedies that could be invoked, *Questions Relating to the Obligation to Prosecute or Extradite (Belgium v Senegal)*, ICJ Rep 2012, paras 67–121.

[13] D Bowett, 'Book Review: E Rafropoulos, *The Inadequacy of the Contractual Analogy in the Law of Treaties*' (1993) 64 BYBIL 439.

[14] Ibid.

[15] AV Lowe, 'The Role of Equity in International Law' (1988–1989) 12 Australian YB Intl L 54, 57 fn 11; Crawford 'Multilateral Rights and Obligations' (n 1) 345; M Koskenniemi, 'Solidarity Measures: State Responsibility as a New International Order?' (2002) 56 BYBIL 337.

inquiry about particular rules and structures.[16] The following debate is instead conducted through loose abstractions of concepts of domestic law, seeking to capture the broadest variety of aspects of international legal reasoning that might be illuminated by typical or even atypical aspects of form and content of domestic legal constructs, without sinking into minutiae of their fine print.

The argument will be made in five steps. The most obvious similarity of treaties with rules of domestic law lies in the consensual form by which both contracts and treaties are made. The limitations and the challenges of consent, both of a technical and conceptual nature, will therefore be dealt with first (II and III respectively). Conclusion of treaties will be dealt with next (IV). The fourth step will deal with reservations, an area of law sitting on the fault lines of assumptions about the consensual nature of treaty form and their possibly multilateral content (V). The conclusion of the chapter will draw preliminary conclusions and identify questions left open for future research (VI). The chapter does not purport to be descriptively exhaustive (in light of the availability of general texts elsewhere),[17] focusing instead on a limited

---

[16] The variety of possible situations where the question of domestic law analogies may arise in international law cautions against generalizations. Still, the preference for specifically *international* law reasoning and criteria suggested above seems to go with the grain of practice more generally, even when domestic analogies are available. A recent example of that tendency is provided by the oral proceedings in the ICJ case regarding *Whaling in the Antarctic*, where standard of review, a topic on which a wealth of domestic practice exists, was one of the issues addressed, *Whaling in the Antarctic (Australia v Japan: New Zealand Intervening)*, ICJ Rep 2014; oral proceedings accessed 4 May 2014 at www.icj-cij.org/docket/index.php?p1=3&p2=3&k=64&case=148&code=aj&p3=2. Vaughan Lowe on behalf of Japan addressed the issue twice (CR 2013/15 17 paras 15–45; CR 2013/22 56 paras 2–22), and James Crawford on behalf of Australia once (CR 2013/19 64 paras 17–24). Domestic law was mentioned only once, when Lowe noted that '[w]e are all familiar with the concepts in domestic law', stated that 'the question is, what is the test in international law?' (CR 2013/15 19 para 28), and proceeded to discuss the position in international law (Crawford did not allude to domestic law at all). For the present purpose, the question is indeed 'what is the test in international law?'. In the sophisticated and normatively dense contemporary international law, the domestic analogy is often likely to be limited to at most illuminating the discussion, rather than providing or necessarily calling for particular answers.

[17] From the recent texts, see ME Villiger, *Commentary on the 1969 Vienna Convention on the Law of Treaties* (Martinus Nijhoff, 2009); O Corten and P Klein (eds), *The Vienna Convention on the Law of Treaties* (OUP, 2010); O Dörr

number of illustrative examples provided by recent practice that serve best to illustrate the normative tensions in the field.

The overall thesis is that a tension may exist between analogies from domestic contractual law, derived chiefly from the consensual form of treaties but also the traditional bilateralism and reciprocity of their content, and analogies from types of public law, derived from the increased multilateralism of obligations in the post-War regimes of international law.[18] To some extent, the tension may be disposed of by drawing a clearer distinction between two types of rules. Secondary rules of recognition and change, expressed largely in the law of treaties, are to a considerable extent influenced by the similarity of the (consensual) form of treaties with domestic contracts. Primary rules, on the other hand, may be analogized to a greater variety of domestic legal regimes, depending on the content, structure, and purpose of the particular rules.[19] At the same time and put into a broader perspective, the tension is also inherent in the structure of international (treaty) law. To that extent, the tension is a necessary aspect of the dynamic of the legal process, providing a spectrum of legal techniques that may capture (or indeed fail to capture) the development of international law in the most appropriate form.

II. CONSENSUAL FORM: TECHNICAL ISSUES

'The autonomous will of the parties is, both in contract and in treaty', as Hersch Lauterpacht put it, 'the constitutive condition of the legal relation',[20] and this perspective provides a convenient starting point for thinking about the comparative argument. Section I of Part 2 of the

---

and K Schmalenbach (eds), *Vienna Convention on the Law of Treaties: A Commentary* (Springer, 2012). A post-VCLT analysis of contractual analogy is available at E Rafropoulos, *The Inadequacy of the Contractual Analogy in the Law of Treaties* (Hellenic Institute of International and Foreign Law, 1990).

[18] Lauterpacht, 'Some Observations' (n 2) 552; J Klabbers, 'The Community Interest in the Law of Treaties: Ambivalent Conceptions' in U Fastenrath et al (eds), *From Bilateralism to Community Interest: Essays in Honour of Bruno Simma* (n 2) 772–6.

[19] In this chapter, the taxonomy of primary and secondary rules is that of Hart, rather than Ago, cf HLA Hart, *The Concept of Law* (3rd edn, OUP, 2012) chp 5; and E David, 'Primary and Secondary Rules' in J Crawford, A Pellet, and S Olleson (eds), *The Law of International Responsibility* (OUP, 2010).

[20] Lauterpacht, *Private Law Sources* (n 4) 156.

VCLT reflects the contractual analogy in its consensual form,[21] with Articles 11–17 using the concept of 'consent to be bound by a treaty' as the normative precondition for the existence of the international obligation. Section III of Part 3 restates the same argument in negative terms, prohibiting in Article 34 a treaty-based creation of obligations or rights for a third State 'without its consent'. The anathema of non-consensual treaty-making is further emphasized by Article 35 that only permits the creation of an obligation for a third State if it 'expressly accepts that obligation in writing'; a formal requirement more stringent than that required for the conclusion of a treaty itself under general customary rules not covered by VCLT.[22] This section will test the limits of technical aspects of the contractual analogy, considering in turn challenges to its consensual underpinning that may be more apparent than real, as well as more serious challenges. The next section will address conceptual challenges to the consensual analogy posed by the role of treaties in the structure of sources of international law.

1. Apparent Challenges

In some cases, treaty obligations appear to emerge without a formalized expression of consent. While they can be explained by reference to other elements of the international law (of treaties), they also demonstrate certain inadequacies of at least a simplistic contractual analogy. One might single out three examples to illustrate the point that even issues that do not raise challenges to the consensual model in a technical sense may still be plausibly presented as raising questions of consent, in light of the unarticulated importance of this perspective for thinking about treaty law.

---

[21] This chapter uses VCLT rules to illustrate the general position in the law of treaties. It should not be taken as a rejection of the basic proposition that the scope of the VCLT is limited, particularly in temporal and personal terms according to Article 4. In technical terms, even in a contemporary dispute VCLT will often not be applicable as a treaty rule. Still, in practice VCLT rules are often (presumed by international courts to be) reflective of customary law and applicable in any event. At the very least, VCLT can be taken as an authoritative, if not universally accurate, statement on the particular issue, with the finer points of treaty/custom left to be canvassed in the general texts on the issue, see n 17.

[22] VCLT 'does not apply' 'to international agreements not in written form', VCLT (n 10), Article 4, confirming, by necessary implication, the existence of such agreements under customary law, C Laly-Chevalier, 'Article 35: Convention of 1969' in Corten and Klein (n 17) 912–13.

For the proverbial man that spends excessive amounts of time commuting through Clapham, innovatory and expansive judicial interpretation of international treaties, most prominently in regional human rights regimes[23] but also more generally, might suggest an imposition of new obligations without consent. For the purposes of such an argument, international courts are perceived as moving beyond the exposition of substantive and procedural obligations, which have been created in an anterior and consensual manner. Instead, courts would be stepping into a role more appropriately analogized with law-makers that provide rules without a prior consent of the persons being bound by them. The shift from a contractual to a law-making analogy may be expressed in at least two related but conceptually distinct ways, building on two views about the precise distinction between contracts and laws: first, consensual perspective is insufficient because the obligation imposed by *res judicata* goes beyond the consent given to relevant primary and secondary (and tertiary) rules in the process of law-making; second, consensual perspective is insufficient because the *inter partes* exercise of interpretation and application by an adjudicator has an impact on all the persons and entities that the particular rule binds, by authoritatively establishing the content of the rule for general purposes.[24] One might take different views about either of these strands of reasoning, inter alia criticizing the inappropriateness of practice,[25] pragmatically accepting judicial law-making as an integral aspect of particularly formulated international

[23] E Bates, *The Evolution of the European Convention on Human Rights: From Its Inception to the Creation of a Permanent Court of Human Rights* (OUP, 2011) chps 7–10.

[24] Of course, these perspectives may overlap in practice, with courts both interpreting and applying the rules in a manner that is perceived as going *ratione materiae* beyond the role of an adjudicator, and treating the judgments as de facto or de jure authoritative statements of the content of the underlying rules with an *erga omnes partes* relevance, as both European Courts may have done.

[25] On the reaction to the European Court of Human Rights ('ECtHR'), AWB Simpson, *Human Rights and the End of Empire: Britain and the Genesis of the European Convention* (OUP, 2001) 13. A not dissimilar view was taken by one of the most authoritative international lawyers on the law of treaties of the last century, ECtHR Judge Gerald Fitzmaurice: Bates *The Evolution* (n 23) chp 9. For more on treaty interpretation, and claims to special *canones* of interpretation of human rights treaties, see Waibel (in this volume).

regimes,[26] or even engaging with the developments in a generally approving manner.[27]

Without entering the broader debate about the role of international adjudicators in the development of international law, the reliance on language taken from domestic law to articulate such arguments demonstrates the power of domestic analogies to shape and structure debates about international law. The power appears even more striking when put in the perspective of the limited helpfulness of the argument for a technical legal inquiry: Articles 31–33 of the VCLT and the analogous customary law on treaty interpretation are perfectly open to purposive and evolutionary interpretation of treaty rules that goes beyond limited textualism;[28] concretization of content of rules of international treaty law through (judicial) interpretation and application is an equally unremarkable and accepted element of development of international law;[29] and, if adjudicators mistakenly move beyond even those rules, it is an error of legal reasoning that is conceivable in any legal regime from which analogy may be drawn.[30]

Secondly, a very different challenge is raised by most-favoured-nation ('MFN') clauses. While differing at the level of fine print between

---

[26] R Steinberg, 'Judicial Lawmaking at the WTO: Discursive, Constitutional, and Political Constraints' (2004) 98 *AJIL* 247; T Ginsburg, 'Bounded Discretion in International Judicial Lawmaking' (2005) 45 *VJIL* 1, particularly 4–6.

[27] For a recent exploration of the argument that puts judicial law-making in a (domestic) public law perspective, see A von Bogdandy and I Venzke, 'Beyond Dispute: International Judicial Institutions as Lawmakers' (2011) 12 *GLJ* 979; A von Bogdandy and I Venzke, 'In Whose Name? An Investigation of International Courts' Public Authority and Its Democratic Justification' (2012) 23 *EJIL* 7; I Venzke, *How Interpretation Makes International Law: On Semantic Changes and Normative Twists* (OUP, 2012) particularly 135–47, 190–96; and generally, A von Bogdandy and I Venzke (eds), *International Judicial Lawmaking* (Springer, 2012).

[28] R Gardiner, *Treaty Interpretation* (OUP, 2008) chps 5.5, 7.1.

[29] See the classic analysis in H Lauterpacht, *The Development of International Law by the International Court* (Stevens and Sons, 1958); and recent reflections in C Tams and J Sloan (eds), *The Development of International Law by the International Court of Justice* (OUP, 2013).

[30] Of course, the approach to legal reasoning and rules of interpretation adopted might in their own turn challenge the limits of contractual analogy, as is implicit in the approval of Judge Fitzmaurice's 'statement of the principles guiding an international as opposed to constitutional lawyer or, so one is tempted to say, a lawyer as opposed to politician', FA Mann, 'Britain's Bill of Rights' (1978) 74 LQR 512, 523, fn 53.

different treaties and different treaty regimes, MFN clauses usually require in an explicit manner the treatment of the treaty party at the level of the most favourable third party.[31] The existence, scope, and content of other international obligations dictate the obligations of States under the MFN clause, and certain readings of the interplay of obligations may conceivably raise consensualist eyebrows. Zachary Douglas, when speaking on the particular question whether MFN clauses can apply to more favourable rules of international dispute settlement in other investment protection treaties,[32] has pointed to 'a domestic contract law analogy [as] probably the root cause of the mistaken approach' of permitting such an application.[33] One might be perfectly justified in agreeing with Douglas' conclusions,[34] but it is less obvious that a contractual analogy is to be blamed for the decisions that he criticizes. Douglas draws a distinction between a reference in a commercial contract to standard trade terms and an MFN clause that is alleged to refer to rules of international dispute settlement, but this contrast is not entirely persuasive.

It is tolerably clear that an MFN clause regarding substantive obligations operates in the manner of elaborating the content of an existing obligation by means of a certain parameter that varies according to other

---

[31] *Rights of Nationals of the United States of America in Morocco (France v US)*, Judgment, ICJ Rep 1952, 176, 191–2. The MFN clause has an ancient pedigree and was widely used in 19th and early last century practice, mostly regarding international economic law, G Schwarzenberger, 'The Most-Favoured-Nation Standard in British State Practice' (1945) 22 BYBIL 96. In contemporary practice, it plays an important role in WTO law and investment protection law, and the latter regime provides the example discussed further.

[32] See generally UNCTAD, 'Most-Favoured-Nation Treatment' in *UNCTAD Series on Issues in International Investment Agreements II* (UN, 2010) accessed 4 May 2014 at http://unctad.org/en/Docs/diaeia20101_en.pdf; M Paparinskis, 'MFN Clauses and International Dispute Settlement: Moving beyond *Maffezini* and *Plama*?' (2011) 26 (2) ICSID Review – Foreign Investment L J 14.

[33] Z Douglas, 'The MFN Clause in Investment Arbitration: Treaty Interpretation off the Rails' (2011) 2 *Journal of International Dispute Settlement* 97, 106.

[34] I have explained my position in Paparinskis 'MFN Clauses and International Dispute Settlement' (n 32), suggesting that the key term in the clause is 'favourable', requiring a possibility for comparison on a spectrum between greater and lesser favourability, and therefore excluding objectively different procedural regimes that cannot be put on this spectrum, see also *ICS Inspection and Control Services Limited (UK) v Argentina*, UNCITRAL Case, Award on Jurisdiction, 10 February 2012 paras 318–25.

undertakings.[35] Questions of application of MFN clauses to rules of international dispute settlement should be dealt with in similar terms, identifying the extent to which the presence of different procedural rules in other treaties triggers the parameter by which the MFN clause elaborates its content. It does not seem that rules on incorporation by reference pose the question in qualitatively different terms.[36] The root of a mistake, if any, lies not in the adoption of a peculiarly contractual analogy but in the failure to carry out the more pedestrian inquiry (equally valid in any legal regime from which the analogy is drawn, whether the law of contracts, statutes, or treaties) of identifying the scope and criteria of application of the particular rule. It is perfectly conceivable both that consent to investment arbitration is achieved through an incorporation of the arbitral clause,[37] and that an MFN clause is explicitly applied to rules of international dispute settlement.[38] In cases where the treaty or contractual language is ambiguous, an answer has to be given by focusing on the scope of the clause, particularly the meaning of such terms as 'favourable' and 'treatment'. A close attention to the scope of the clause would be precisely the lesson to be derived from contractual analogies with commercial arbitration, where the content of the document referred to, and the degree to which it can be transposed to the original document are important.[39] The idea of expressing obligations by reference to future legal changes falls within the contractual analogy,

---

[35] P Reuter, *Introduction au Droit des Traites* [Introduction to the Law of Treaties] (3rd edn, PUF, 1995) 98–9; Paparinskis 'MFN Clauses and International Dispute Settlement' (n 32) 19, 42. Another example of determination of content of a rule of international law by reference to a different rule is the requirement in human rights law for restrictions of human rights to be in accordance with domestic law.

[36] Article 7(6) of the 1985 UNCITRAL Model Law on International Commercial Arbitration (with Amendments as Adopted in 2006), accessed 4 May 2014 at www.uncitral.org/pdf/english/texts/arbitration/ml-arb/07-86998_Ebook.pdf.

[37] *Ceskoslovenska Obchodni Banka, AS v Slovakia*, ICSID Case no ARB/97/4, Decision of the Tribunal on Objections to Jurisdiction, 24 May 1999 paras 51–58.

[38] Eg, Article 3(3) of the 1995 UK-Albania BIT, accessed 4 May 2014 at unctad.org/sections/dite/iia/docs/bits/uk_albania.pdf.

[39] See cases discussed at UNCITRAL, *2012 Digest of Case Law on the Model Law on International Commercial Arbitration* (United Nations, 2012) accessed 4 May 2014 at www.uncitral.org/pdf/english/clout/MAL-digest-2012-e.pdf, 30–31.

whether addressing changes in interest rates or standard terms (re)adopted by one party or an expert institution.

A different kind of challenge to the contractual analogy is raised by law-making in and through international organizations. One scenario relates to obligations imposed by the binding decisions of international organizations, in particular the Security Council of the United Nations acting under Chapter VII of the 1945 United Nations Charter. A more extreme version of the same scenario relates to cases where the resolutions of the Security Council impose internationally binding rules that refer to or are equivalent to such treaty obligations that have not been consented to by the particular State in the traditional treaty-making format.[40] The technical legal response is that parties to the Charter have provided their consent to be bound by the resolutions of the Security Council in consenting to the Charter, and the binding nature of the resolutions is only a particularization of the content of that obligation.[41] The principle of consensual basis, even if removed from the articulation of the particular obligation by several steps of anterior legal reasoning, still fits the substance of the contractual analogy. Even non-consensual conclusion of treaties (ie, imposition in the absence of, or even specific denial of the consent required for the particular treaty) is capable of being explained through the lenses of anterior consent to the Charter.[42]

---

[40] Some of the best-known examples are: the imposition of non-proliferation treaties on Iraq in UNSC Resolution 687 (1991); extension to non-party States of the effects of the International Convention for the Suppression of the Financing of Terrorism in UNSC Resolution 1373 (2001); referral of situations to the International Criminal Court ('ICC') regarding States not parties to the ICC in UNSC Resolutions 1593 (2005) and 1970 (2011); and the imposition of a treaty establishing the Special Tribunal for Lebanon on Lebanon in UNSC Resolution 1757 (2007) after it failed to ratify it, *Prosecutor v Ayyash and Others*, Special Court for Lebanon, Appeals Chamber, Case no STL-11/01/PT/AC/AR90.1, Decision on the Defence Appeals against the Trial Chamber's 'Decision on the Defence Challenges to the Jurisdiction and Legality of the Tribunal', 24 October 2012, paras 27–31. See generally, S Talmon, 'The Security Council as World Legislature' (2005) 99 AJIL 175, 177–8; S Talmon, 'The Security Council as Dispenser of (or with) International Law' (2010) 3 Select Proceedings ESIL 243, 244–9.

[41] H Thirlway, 'Concepts, Principles, Rules and Analogies: International and Municipal Legal Reasoning' (2002) 294 Recueil des Cours 265, 347; P D'Argent, 'Article 35: Convention of 1969' in Corten and Klein (n 17) 908–9.

[42] *Ayyash* (n 40) para 28; D Sarooshi, 'Aspects of the Relationship between the International Criminal Court and the United Nations' (2001) 32 Netherlands YB Intl L 27, 29–35.

In the most general sense, these instances do not challenge the contractual analogy because they may be traced, with lesser or greater artificiality, to anterior consent. To return to the contractual analogy, it is perfectly plausible to imagine that, in complex contractual settings, a framework contract may set out general contours within which changes in rights and obligations are articulated. At most, the right of a pre-agreed institution to adopt or elaborate particular types of new obligations may be more accurately captured by a narrower analogy with domestic corporate law, combining the broader consensual foundation with narrower institutions that have the power of adopting binding decisions. In all of these cases, challenges to the consensual paradigm are only apparent. At the same time, the perfectly natural way of articulating concerns and criticisms in terms of domestic law demonstrates the strong pull that such analogies still have in international legal thought.

2. Real Challenges

There are elements of practice that raise more serious challenges to the contractual analogy, of which one might single out one old and one new challenge (a third challenge relates to the law of reservations and will be dealt with *infra* at V). An old challenge is raised by the so-called objective regimes: treaties dealing with territorial matters that are alleged to be binding not only for the parties but also more generally (eg, treaties on the Suez Canal, Panama Canal, and Antarctic).[43] One might certainly explain these instances of practice in orthodox terms by reference to acquiescence, subsequent practice, waivers of objections, or customary law.[44] However, one might also articulate the general relevance of territorial settlements by reference to private law analogies with servitudes and rights *in rem* or, alternatively, public law analogies with legislative rule-making.[45] While any generalization necessarily simplifies the complexity and nuance of the argument, the general sense is that of explicit uncertainty, with the legal rules sitting somewhat uneasily within the traditional consensual paradigm, yet raising even greater challenges

[43] For details see Proelss (in this volume); and further the exhaustive discussion of doctrine and practice by M Fitzmaurice, 'Third Parties and the Law of Treaties' (2002) 6 Max Planck UN YB 37.

[44] D'Argent, 'Article 35 …' (n 41) 909–10.

[45] Already in 1925, the debate was articulated in terms of appropriateness of analogy with either domestic private law of servitudes or domestic public law, McNair '… Servitudes' (n 7) 121–6.

when analogies with private property or public law are suggested or their criteria evaluated in particular cases.[46]

A recent and very different challenge is raised by the claim of State immunity before international criminal tribunals, where, as it is sometimes suggested, the (traditionally inter-State) rules on immunity cannot be invoked.[47] From the perspective of contractual analogy (and traditional international legal reasoning), to say that a State A can oppose immunity to States B and C but that such immunity cannot be invoked before an international court D created by B and C seems directly incompatible with the consensual structure of treaty-making.[48] However, an argument against immunity that is based on the assumption that 'international criminal tribunals ... are not organs of a state but derive their mandate from the international community'[49] makes more sense for a public law analogy, with (vertical) organs of the international community being inherently free from (horizontal) inter-State restrictions. The very different subject matters of particular territorial settlements and State immunity show both the limits and authority of the contractual analogy: to be

---

[46] B Simma, 'The Antarctic Treaty as a Treaty Providing for an "Objective Regime"' (1986) 19 Cornell J Intl L 189; A Watts, *International Law and the Antarctic Treaty System* (CUP, 1992) 295–8; Fitzmaurice 'Third Parties ...' (n 43) 136–7; M Kohen, *Possession contestée et souveraineté territoriale* (PUF, 1997) 108, fn 118. James Crawford notes the link between the deliberate eschewing of legal certainty and the political success of the Antarctic Treaty, J Crawford, 'The Antarctic Treaty after 50 Years' in D French, M Saul, and N White (eds), *International Law and Dispute Settlement: New Problems and Techniques* (Hart Publishing, 2010) 295–6.

[47] *Prosecutor v Charles Ghankay Taylor*, Special Court for Sierra Leone, Appeals Chamber, Case no SCSL-2003-01-I, Decision on Immunity from Jurisdiction, 31 May 2004 paras 43–51; *Prosecutor v Omar Hassan Ahmad Al Bashir*, International Criminal Court, Pre-Trial Chamber I, Case no ICC-02/05-01/09, Decision Pursuant to Article 87(7) of the Rome Statute on the Failure by the Republic of Malawi to Comply with the Cooperation Requests Issued by the Court with Respect to the Arrest and Surrender of Omar Hassan Ahmad Al Bashir, 12 December 2011 para 18, para 23–36. See generally, H Fox and P Webb, *The Law of State Immunity* (3rd edn, OUP, 2013).

[48] In cases of referrals by the Security Council to the ICC, challenge of immunity might conceivably be disposed of without moving beyond traditional treaty law, by finding a waiver either in the resolution of referral or the ICC statute, see D Akande, 'The Legal Nature of Security Council's Referrals to the ICC and Its Impact on Al Bashir's Immunities' (2009) 7 J Intl Crim Justice 333, 337–42. However, that is not the rationale that the ICC itself adopted, *Al Bashir* (n 47).

[49] *Taylor* (n 47) para 51.

radically innovative, arguments may have to be explicitly articulated by public law analogies; at the same time, the switch of analogies leaves them vulnerable to criticism about legal incompatibility with the basic architecture of positive international law.

III. CONSENSUAL FORM: CONCEPTUAL ISSUES

The distinction between technical and conceptual challenges may be a somewhat arbitrary one: complex technical issues may raise conceptual concerns, and debates about conceptual questions presuppose and are carried out through technical legal arguments. For the purposes of this argument, 'conceptual questions' relate to the role that treaties may play in the international law-making process, particularly regarding the 'law-making' treaties that may affect customary international law. As a matter of positive law of sources, it is clear that, as the ICJ explained in the *North Sea Continental Shelf* cases, treaties may interrelate with custom in three ways: treaties may codify custom; treaties may crystallize custom; and treaties may give rise to custom.[50] Again, in technical terms, it is clear that general customary rules are in principle binding for all States (to the extent that States are not persistent objectors or have not opted out of general custom by way of special custom or treaties). In *Symbolae Verzijl*, Sir Gerald Fitzmaurice famously argued, with what appears to have been a slight sense of annoyance at the excessively enthusiastic attribution of customary law effects to treaties,[51] that treaties were formally sources of obligations (like contracts in domestic law) rather than law (as statutes in domestic law and customary law internationally).[52] One might question the correctness of Sir Gerald's argument on a number of levels[53] but, for the present purpose, the clarity of

---

[50] *North Sea Continental Shelf (Germany/Denmark; Germany/Netherlands)*, ICJ Rep 1969, 3, paras 61–81.

[51] C Warbrick, 'The Theory of International Law: Is there an English Contribution?' in W Butler (ed), *Perestroika and International Law* (Brill, 1990) 41, 46–8.

[52] G Fitzmaurice, 'Some Problems Regarding the Formal Sources of International Law' in JHW Verzijl, *Symbolae Verzijl* (Martinus Nijhoff, 1958) 153–4.

[53] M Mendelson, 'Are Treaties Merely a Source of Obligation?' in WE Butler (ed), *Perestroika and International Law* (Brill, 1990) 82–7; Thirlway, 'Analogies …' (n 41) 321–2. It has recently been suggested that, quite to the contrary, '[m]ultilateral treaties … are the nearest analogy to legislation that a horizontal, decentralised system can achieve', J Crawford, 'Chance, Order, Change: The Course of International Law' (2013) 365 Recueil des Cours 9, 167–8).

his dichotomy permits the formulation of the key question: how can the contractual analogy explain the law-making process by which the content of consensual (opt-in) rules affects the content of generally binding (opt-out) rules?[54]

As a starting point, it has been suggested that the process of codification of customary international law by treaties has no obvious parallels in national systems of law.[55] One might query whether the unqualified form of the statement is accurate: at a greater degree of abstraction, one might see certain parallels with either the process of legislative codification of *jurisprudence constante* in civil law countries or case law in common law countries; or systematization of best practices by particular industry groups or specialized institutions in the form of rules or standards.[56] Still, apart from the situation where contracts draw upon best practices in the field (in many ways peculiar, raising the anterior question about the legal relevance of these practices), the idea of a legal tool aimed at restating generally binding rules in contractual form feels somewhat odd. If dispositive rules are not changed, they will apply in any event; if dispositive rules are changed, the contractual rules will apply; and peremptory rules of domestic law cannot in any event be changed by contract. For the purposes of analogy, the contrast between the plausibility of using contracts and treaties for the purposes of codification illustrates the different functions that they may be employed for: in the domestic legal order, contracts would take the general rules as a given and tailor them for the particular (private) legal relationship; in international law, treaties may be used for the (public) purpose of setting out rules of general relevance with greater clarity.

---

[54] The opt-in/opt-out terminology highlights the difference in formation of treaty law and customary law; for treaty law, a positive expression (opt-in) is required to become bound by an international treaty. For customary law, while a positive expression of will may be important in contributing to the general consensus that creates custom, it is not a necessary precondition for establishing its binding force for the particular State, and a positive expression is rather required to opt out of the general rule (whether as a persistent objector, by joining a special customary law regime, or indeed by concluding a treaty).

[55] Thirlway, 'Analogies ...' (n 41) 328.

[56] KP Berger, *The Creeping Codification of the New Lex Mercatoria* (2nd rev edn, Wolters Kluwer, Law & Business, 2010) chps 4–5; G Cordero-Moss, 'The Transnational Law of Contracts: What It Can and What It Cannot Achieve' in T Weiler and F Baetens (eds), *New Directions in International Economic Law: In Memoriam Thomas Wälde* (Martinus Nijhoff, 2011) 46–9.

One might tackle the same question from the perspective that is opposite to that of mere codification: how does the law-making contribution of treaties to custom fit within the contractual analogy? The immediate answer is that it does not fit at all, with the contractual obligations having no potential for generating generally binding rules in the absence of express or implied consent by particular parties. A narrower analogy, suggested by Thirlway, may be drawn from standard forms and conditions that may contribute to usage or custom in some areas of legal relations, capable of operating as implied conditions in contracts.[57] Perhaps the same argument could be presented in more persuasive terms if treaties were to be presented 'as analogous to "transnational" contracts between entities which acknowledge each other's existence but not the existence of a common superior'.[58] Without entering into the debate about the scope and nomenclature of *lex mercatoria* and transnational commercial law, there is support for the view that commercial and particularly contractual practices may generate usages,[59] sometimes possibly going even further than merely implying terms into contracts so as to impose mandatory rules.[60] If one pulls together the strands of thought that accept the completeness of *lex mercatoria* as a substantive legal order and of international arbitration as an autonomous procedural legal order,[61] the argument by analogy becomes more plausible, with transnational traders both autonomously generating customs and settling their disputes, 'acknowledg[ing] each

---

57 Thirlway, 'Analogies ...' (n 41) 326–7.

58 Crawford, 'Multilateral Rights and Obligations' (n 1) 345. As Roy Goode noted, 'one finds an astonishing correlation between the kinds of issue discussed by the international lawyers and those that have perplexed the scholars of transnational commercial law', and international law was particularly useful regarding 'relationships ... between treaties and customary international law', R Goode, 'Usage and Its Reception in Transnational Commercial Law' (1997) 46 ICLQ 1, 1.

59 Goode, ibid; Berger, *The Creeping Codification* (n 56).

60 JH Dalhuisen, *Dalhuisen on Transnational Comparative, Commercial, Financial and Trade Law* (Volume 1, 5th edn, Hart, 2013) chp 3.25.

61 E Gaillard, 'Transnational Law: A Legal System or a Method of Decision Making?' (2001) 17 Arbitration Intl 59, 65–71; E Gaillard, *Legal Theory of International Arbitration* (Martinus Nijhoff, 2010) chp 1.C. It is not suggested that this perception of international commerce and arbitration is uncontested (for a response to Gaillard's monograph, see J Paulsson, *The Idea of Arbitration* (OUP, 2013) chp 2, and for a scathing criticism of *lex mercatoria*, see Crawford, 'Chance, Order, Change' (n 53) 143–5), merely that it does provide a valid analogy with the operation of this particular aspect of treaty law.

other's existence' and, if one is permitted to paraphrase, 'the existence of [no] common superior'.

Another facet of the same question is raised by the creation of treaty rules with content different from that of customary law. In domestic private law, there is no expectation that contracts reflect the content of (dispositive) domestic law, to the extent that they fulfil the peremptory requirements of form and substance. Thirlway has drawn attention to a passage in the *Rights of Passage over the Indian Territory* case where the ICJ suggested the existence of 'a rule of interpretation', according to which treaties 'must, in principle, be interpreted as producing and as intended to produce effects in accordance with existing law and not in violation of it'.[62] In his view, no such principle exists for contracting out of dispositive rules, and its formulation in such terms suggests an assumption that treaties are sources of law that could therefore not contain internal contradictions.[63] Of course, the ICJ's *dictum* would not apply to customary law binding between the particular parties: there would be no potential violation because a conflict would be resolved by the application of a *lex specialis* principle in favour of the treaty (entirely in line with the contractual analogy of removing residual general rules by party-created special written rules).

If a conflicting treaty rule binds a treaty party regarding a third party, the presumption against conflict indeed has to be considered. There is support in international practice for the existence of the principle of systemic integration or harmonious interpretation, even if not unanimous.[64] The idea of internal coherence of different rules does fit easier within an analogy drawn from domestic public law, based on the assumption of a unitary, if fictional, law-maker and its coherent intent.[65] At the same time, one might question the analogy on a number of levels.

---

[62] *Rights of Passage over the Indian Territory (Portugal v India)*, Merits, ICJ Rep 1960, 6, 142.

[63] Thirlway, 'Analogies …' (n 41) 328–30.

[64] Cf the landmark argument in favour of systemic integration in C McLachlan, 'The Principle of Systemic Integration and Article 31(3)(c) of the Vienna Convention' (2005) 54 ICLQ 279, the explicit approval of the argument in *Nada v Switzerland* (App no 10593/08) [GC] ECHR Reports 2012 para 170, and equally explicit rejection in *Electrabel S.A. v Hungary*, ICSID Case no ARB/07/19, Decision on Jurisdiction, Applicable Law and Liability, 30 November 2012, paras 4.130, 4.173.

[65] R Michaels and Y Pauwelyn, 'Conflict of Norms or Conflict of Laws? Different Techniques in the Fragmentation of International Law' in T Broude and Y Shany (eds), *Multi-Sourced Equivalent Norms in International Law* (Hart, 2011) 23–6.

In domestic law, if sufficiently complex contractual undertakings exist that conflict between or within themselves (say, regarding subcontractors), it would not be implausible to attribute some contextual interpretative value, in whatever technical terms expressed, to other undertakings bearing on the same matters. At the international level, perhaps a further distinction needs to be drawn between different types of analogies. Some international cases may be perceived as analogous to conflicts within a single domestic public law system – like *Rights of Passage over the Indian Territory*, where a conflict within the optional clause system was considered. However, conflicts between different branches of international law may be more similar to conflicts between different domestic (private law) systems, where the proper analogy could be sought in international *private* law.[66] Overall, a simple contractual analogy cannot easily explain the relationship between treaties and generally binding customary rules; however, an appropriately qualified argument that draws on insights into the formation of the *lex mercatoria* (and reads their legal regime in expansive terms) might be more plausible.

The observations about the conceptual challenges faced by fitting the consensualist paradigm into the international legal order do not lead themselves to a natural and clear conclusion. It is a rather trite point that the structure of the international legal order and its sources raises challenges of a character that often seems qualitatively different from that faced by any of the domestic legal arguments. It may be that the main conceptual challenge for the comparative argument lies in the manner in which the differences and similarities between treaty and custom are combined: an obvious difference exists in the opt-in/opt-out manner of creation; but there are equally obvious similarities in the scope, content, structure, subjects, and importance of rules that may be created through these sources. In domestic law, one might expect similarities and differences to be consistently followed through to the processes of rule-making as well, rather than have identical rules created through radically different procedures. McNair's famous argument, cited at the beginning of this chapter, identified the conceptual challenge of expressing in consensualist treaty form the legal relations dealt with by a variety of legal instruments domestically.[67] Even accepting the insight, the challenge is further complicated by the fact that one simultaneously has to address the challenge of expressing the same legal relations in the form of customary law, a rule of considerably less importance in most

[66] Ibid, 26–31, 35–9.
[67] McNair, 'Functions and Character …' (n 2).

domestic systems than contract, and the meta-challenge of coordinating these sources and the legal relations addressed therein. Having said that, while the manner of particular arguments and their broader coordination makes sweeping analogies impossible, a narrower focus on particular aspects of treaties and custom, and particular aspects of domestic law, still permits illuminating analogies.

IV. TREATY CONCLUSION

The consensual form of treaties is expressed through the criteria for their existence. The limits of contractual analogy may therefore be tested by considering the degree to which VCLT rules for conclusion of treaties may be analogized with contracts. In technical terms, for the existence of a contract most domestic legal systems would require the existence of the will of the parties to conclude the contract, often expressed in the form of offer and acceptance; the common law systems may also require the existence of consideration. The next sections will consider in turn the will of the parties, offer and acceptance, and consideration in the law of treaties.

1. Will of the Parties

The will of the parties to conclude a treaty may be further broken down into three separate issues: the authority to express the will, the genuineness of the will expressed, and the willingness to conclude a binding instrument. On all of these issues, the argument for the contractual analogy seems strong. Article 7 of the VCLT deals with full powers, drawing the distinction between certain enumerated authorities that may represent the State *ex officio* (particularly the head of State, head of government, and foreign minister), and representation due to explicit authorization or its implicit waiver. The obvious analogy to be drawn here is with domestic corporate law where a company is represented by its organs *ex officio* and by other persons that have been particularly authorized.[68] (One caveat to be noted is that contemporary international

---

[68] Eg, Directive 2009/101/EC of the European Parliament and of the Council of 16 September 2009 on coordination of safeguards which, for the protection of the interests of members and third parties, are required by Member States of companies within the meaning of the second paragraph of Article 48 of the Treaty, with a view to making such safeguards equivalent, OJ L 258, 1.10.2009 11, Articles 2(d)(i), 9–10.

law may approach the list of organs with the capacity of *ex officio* representation with greater flexibility, in light of the underlying shift in the nature of international cooperation.[69])

The finer points of the international legal rules governing the question of whether will is genuine are drafted almost entirely in terms of private contract and company law. The implications of authority for the validity of obligations is addressed by asking similar questions, whether regarding the manifest nature of an absence of competence[70] or the implications of notification of particular restrictions.[71] The rules of genuineness of will mostly trail the traditional contractual rules: error, fraud, and duress (coercion) (even if addressed in the VCLT as part of termination of treaties, rather than their conclusion).[72] (Indeed, the probable lack of the rule on duress in traditional international law was one of the two chief reasons to question the similarity of contract law to treaty law, and its emergence suggests that such analogy goes with the grain of modern international law.[73]) The formulation of the rules suggests an appreciation of the distinct if necessarily interrelated roles played by a legal entity and its representative in representing the entity to the outside world: sometimes the defects of the will are those of the former (error, fraud, and coercion of the State), and sometimes of the latter (corruption and coercion of the representative).

The final facet of the genuine will is perhaps the most basic one: the will to create rights and obligations *under international law*, a point not

---

69 The ICJ has suggested, albeit in very careful terms, that ministers or other officials 'exercising powers in their field of competence in the area of foreign relations', like a Minister of Justice, may also bind a State, *Armed Activities on the Territory of the Congo (New Application: 2002) (DRC v Congo)*, Jurisdiction and Admissibility, ICJ Rep 2006, 6, paras 46–8. While the Court in the particular instance was dealing with unilateral acts, the tenor of the argument suggested that the scope of *ex officio* powers ran similarly in the law of treaties, ibid, para 46.

70 Cf VCLT, Article 46(2) and Directive 2009/101/EC (n 68), Article 10(1).

71 Cf VCLT, Article 47 and Directive 2009/101/EC (n 68), Article 10(2).

72 VCLT, Articles 48–9, 51–2; Lauterpacht, *Private Law Sources* (n 4) 175–6; see E Wyler and R Samson, 'Article 48: Convention of 1969' in Corten and Klein, (n 17) 1118; G Niyungeko, 'Article 49: Convention of 1969' ibid, 1145; G Distefano, 'Article 51: Convention of 1969' ibid, 1179–80; O Corten, 'Article 52: Convention of 1969' ibid, 1203. The rule on corruption in Article 50 was innovatory, at least as a rule separate from fraud, but was still justified by reference to domestic law, J-P Cot, 'Article 50: Convention of 1969' ibid, 1170–73.

73 Lauterpacht, *Private Law Sources* (n 4) 161–7; Thirlway, 'Analogies …' (n 41) 322–3.

addressed directly in the VCLT but considered implicit in the definition of 'treaty' as an instrument 'governed by international law'.[74] The ICJ in the *Qatar v Bahrain* case found that the enumeration of commitments in the minutes of a meeting created rights and obligations, even though there was some uncertainty about the intention of the parties to conclude a treaty.[75] The post-*Qatar* debate about the correct – or indeed any, for that matter – criteria for distinguishing binding treaties from non-binding instruments has generated some well-known doctrinal heat.[76] For the present purpose, what is important is that neither position rejects the contractual analogy: for those in favour of the distinction, a very traditional analysis of content and circumstances of conclusion would provide answers[77] (that might even benefit from the introduction of contract law techniques);[78] for the sceptical authors, the greatest concern is the absurdity of using the classic contractual principle of *pacta sunt servanda* to create non-binding instruments.[79] Overall, the fine print of the rules on will trails closely the analogies of private law.

2. Offer and Acceptance

The traditional contractual rules on offer and acceptance are not easily discernible when consent to be bound by a treaty is expressed by signature (VCLT, Article 12), ratification, acceptance, approval (Article 14), or accession (Article 15). In these cases, consent is not the acceptance of an offer to be bound by a particular act with particular content that is offered by the other party, but the acceptance of an obligation that has to be accepted in the same manner by the other party

---

[74] VCLT, Article 2(1)(a); see P Gautier, 'Article 2: Convention of 1969' in Corten and Klein (n 17) 43–5.

[75] *Maritime Delimitation and Territorial Questions between Qatar and Bahrain (Qatar v Bahrain)*, Jurisdiction and Admissibility, ICJ Rep 1994, 112, paras 23–30.

[76] The debate between Klabbers and Aust is probably known best; for the most recent version of the argument, see J Klabbers, 'Not Re-Visiting the Concept of Treaty' in A Orakhelashvili and S Williams (eds), *40 Years of the Vienna Convention on the Law of Treaties* (BIICL, 2010); A Aust, *Modern Treaty Law and Practice* (3rd edn, CUP, 2013) 46–9.

[77] Aust, (n 76) 29–39.

[78] Perhaps an international equivalent of the English private law expression 'subject to contract' is what is required, H Thirlway, 'The Law and Procedure of the International Court of Justice 1960–1989: Supplement, 2006: Part Three' (2006) 77 BYBIL 1, 6.

[79] Klabbers, 'Not Re-Visiting the Concept of Treaty' (n 76) 32.

as well. Of course, the offer/acceptance dynamic might very well underlie the negotiations of the treaty rules in question (particularly for bilateral treaties or bilateralizable obligations in multilateral treaties), but the same dynamic might also underlie negotiations of contractual rules, of which only some stages will be formally expressed in terms of offer/acceptance. One is interested here in the formal procedure of conclusion rather than the underlying bargaining positions and strategies, and in formal terms most aspects of treaty conclusion do not obviously rely on offer and acceptance.

It has been suggested that offer and acceptance usually have no role to play in treaty law,[80] and that at least multilateral 'law-making' conventions may better correspond to pre-established contracts ('adhesion contracts') that may be accepted only as a whole.[81] To take the second point first, the analogy may be questioned: in the domestic legal setting, the adhesion contract would still be prepared and (technically) offered by one party; in international law, the immutability of the treaty would not follow from the superior bargaining power of a particular party but from the treaty-making process itself, where drafting of the treaty may be separated from expression of consent. As regards the first point, one might also identify elements of offer and acceptance in treaty law. Most obviously, exchange of instruments constituting a treaty (Article 13) would in technical terms be expressed as offer and acceptance.[82] Acceptance of and objection to (permissible) reservations also reflect the contractual dynamic: a formulated reservation is no more than a unilateral proposition put forward, and only acceptance will produce legal effects.[83] A 'reservation' to a bilateral

---

[80] H Thirlway, 'The Law and Procedure of the International Court of Justice 1960–1989: Part Four' (1993) 63 BYBIL 1, 12; but see the acceptance of the probable background existence of offer and acceptance in the law of conclusion, H Thirlway, 'The Law and Procedure of the International Court of Justice 1960–1989: Supplement, 2007: Parts Four, Five and Six' (2007) 78 BYBIL 17, 25.

[81] Thirlway, 'Analogies …' (n 41) 324–5; Mendelson, 'Are Treaties Merely …' (n 53) 82.

[82] C van Assche, 'Article 13: Convention of 1969' in Corten and Klein (n 17) 247–8.

[83] *Reservations to the Convention on the Prevention and Punishment of the Crime of Genocide*, Advisory Opinion, ICJ Rep 1951, 15, 21; VCLT, Article 20; A Pellet, 'Article 19: Convention of 1969' in Corten and Klein (n 17) 496–8.

treaty would probably have the legal effect of an offer to renegotiate the treaty.[84]

If the legal relationships are expressed in the form of offer and acceptance, certain technical consequences may follow. Clearly, for an acceptance of an offer to have legal effect, it has to comply with the conditions of the offer.[85] In light of possible differences in domestic contractual law regarding the act that produces legal effect (acceptance of the offer, communicating acceptance, its reception, or awareness of acceptance),[86] there is some uncertainty about the position in international law. In the general law of treaties, it might be the case that acceptance has to be received for it to have effect;[87] at the same time, this is clearly not the case regarding the ICJ Optional Clause, interpreted by the ICJ as a standing offer that leads to a consensual bond by the act of acceptance.[88] Overall, offer and acceptance are still lurking behind the

---

[84] ILC, 'Guide to Practice on Reservations to Treaties' in *Report of the ILC (Sixty-Third Session)* UN Doc no A/66/10/Add.1, para 1.6.1, Commentaries, 17–20.

[85] In the *Monetary Gold* case, the UK argued that Italy had not complied with one of the essential conditions of the offer made by the UK, the US and France – a definite and unqualified acceptance by Italy of the Court's jurisdiction – because it had raised preliminary objections. The Court rejected the argument on the facts but appeared to accept the general (contractual) principle underlying the UK position, *Monetary Gold Removed from Rome in 1943 (Italy v France, UK, and US)*, Preliminary Question, ICJ Rep 1954, 19, 28, 29, 31.

[86] van Assche, 'Article 13: Convention of 1969' in Corten and Klein (n 17) 275.

[87] Article 13 of the VCLT that directly deals with exchanges of instruments does not solve the question conclusively, but it may be that the reception theory, by analogy with other modes of providing consent, fits the VCLT framework best, van Assche, ibid, 276–9.

[88] *Land and Maritime Boundary between Cameroon and Nigeria (Cameroon v Nigeria)*, Preliminary Objections, ICJ Rep 1998, 275, paras 21–35. See a criticism of this position from the perspective of domestic contractual law, ibid, Dissenting Opinion of Vice-President Weeramantry 362, 368–73. Perhaps the position is best explained as reflecting a pre-agreed regime that deals with the matter of acceptance in special terms, Thirlway, 'The Law and Procedure …' (2007) (n 80) 24–6, or indeed the peculiar nature of the optional declarations that raises questions about the degree of permissible analogy with the law of treaties, M Fitzmaurice, 'The Optional Clause System and the Law of Treaties: Issues of Interpretation in Recent Jurisprudence of the International Court of Justice' (1999) 20 Australian YB Intl L 127.

treaty-making process, with certain elements reflecting the analogy in particularly clear terms, and international uncertainties echoing the domestic ones.

3. Consideration

Judge Philip Jessup was certain that '[t]he doctrine of "consideration", which plays so large a part in Anglo-American contract law, has not been taken over into the international law of treaties',[89] and indeed the ILC Draft Articles on the Law of Treaties make no mention of it.[90] Still, it may be possible to discern glimpses of consideration (or at least, to press the pun, considerations underpinning consideration), scattered around different legal regimes of international law. Consideration may appear as an interpretative argument: in the 19th and early last century debates about (un)conditionality of MFN clauses, the US maintained that the most favoured treatment could only be granted for consideration or equivalent compensation.[91] It may also appear in relation to the formation and termination of treaties. The doctrine of unequal treaties, unsuccessful as it (probably) was in affecting positive international law of treaties, appears to reflect concerns similar to the doctrine of consideration, that is, the antipathy against arrangements that are entirely one-sided and give nothing of legal value to one party.[92] Despite Judge Jessup's scepticism noted above, in the *Fisheries Jurisdiction* cases the Court accepted, at least in principle, that treaty termination may be based 'on an hypothesis familiar in the law of certain States under the guise of "failure of consideration"',[93] rejecting it in the particular instance because Iceland had already benefited from the agreement, might have still benefited, and

---

[89] *South West Africa Cases (Ethiopia v South Africa; Liberia v South Africa)*, Preliminary Objections, ICJ Rep 1962, 319, Separate Opinion of Judge Jessup 387, 403.

[90] 1966 ILC Draft Articles (n 9).

[91] CC Hyde, 'Concerning the Interpretation of Treaties' (1909) 3 AJIL 46, 57–8. It is not suggested that there is a necessary causal link between domestic legal traditions and the interpretative position taken internationally – after all, the UK position was consistently opposed to that of the US (ibid; SK Hornbeck, 'The Most-Favored-Nation Clause: History' (1909) 3 AJIL 395, 405–21) – but it was articulated in terms of domestic contractual law.

[92] A Peters, 'Treaties, Unequal' in R Wolfrüm (ed), *Max Planck Encyclopedia of Public International Law* (Volume X, OUP, 2012) 38, paras 27–37, 39, accessed 4 May 2014 at http://opil.ouplaw.com/home/EPIL.

[93] *Fisheries Jurisdiction (UK v Iceland)*, Merits, ICJ Rep 1974, 3, para 30.

the agreement was only in part executory.[94] The rationale and scope of the suggested rule are at best unclear[95] but, for the present purpose, *Fisheries Jurisdiction* is important in illustrating the powerful pull of even unrepresentative contractual concepts in reasoning about international treaties.

Finally, at a greater level of abstraction, one might say that considerable parts of the law of treaties are underpinned by an implicit assumption of consideration: something of direct legal value that the other party or parties may be expected to monitor, defend if disagreeing, or approve or acquiesce in changes if agreeing. The creation of genuinely multilateral obligations makes these assumptions less obviously correct (and undercuts the systemic logic of particular rules).[96] The law of reservations, addressed in greater detail below at V, is one example: the operational assumption underlying VCLT rules seems to be that treaties provide something of legal value to their parties, and therefore parties might be expected to monitor whether the reservations affect the legal value of the original bargain and their own particular interests, and to react to the reserving State by denying the legal value of entry into force of a treaty.[97] The law of interpretation, particularly if subsequent practice

---

[94] Ibid, paras 31–4.

[95] The argument was not explicitly raised by Iceland (which in any event did not participate in the proceedings), and appears not to have been at all discussed in the pleadings, *Fisheries Jurisdiction*, ICJ Pleadings, Volumes I–II. The question of consideration was not commented on in the opinions appended to the judgment, even those by judges from common law legal systems (ibid, Declaration of President Zafrulla Khan 66; ibid, Separate Opinion of Judge Fitzmaurice 68 – Fitzmaurice did provide a domestic law example about excessiveness of payment not being a reason to ask for the money back). The idea of analogy may be questioned on a number of levels: the Court's conception of consideration in domestic law might not fit at least the English version of it, Thirlway, 'The Law and Procedure …' 1993 (n 80) 83, fn 295; its transposition on the international level goes entirely against the grain of the law of treaties elaborated by the ILC and the Vienna Conference on the Law of Treaties; and the argument about a change to the benefit to be received is already dealt with by rules on fundamental changes of circumstances, VCLT, Article 62.

[96] The traditionally reciprocal bilateralism of multilateral rules, as opposed to genuinely multilateral obligations, may be said to reflect the consideration at the international level, see generally, Simma, 'From Bilateralism to Community Interest …' (n 2).

[97] J Klabbers, 'On Human Rights Treaties, Contractual Conceptions and Reservations' in I Ziemele (ed), *Reservations to Human Rights Treaties and the Vienna Convention Regime: Conflict, Harmony or Reconciliation* (Martinus Nijhoff, 2004) 155; I Ziemele and L Liede, 'Reservations to Human Rights

under Article 31(3)(b) of the VCLT is read to include acquiescence by one party to the practice of other(s), might also presuppose something of legal value to the particular party that justifies an assumption that disagreement would lead to a protest.[98] Overall, the international law of treaty conclusion demonstrates three facets of the comparative argument: rules on will of the parties closely trail the law of contract and company law; domestic law rules on offer and acceptance may form the broader intellectual background but have been almost entirely replaced by special international law techniques; and the common law of consideration, while not appearing as a formal legal criterion in international law, trails reciprocity – one of the underlying operational principles of large parts of international law.

V. RESERVATIONS

The law of reservations provides a particularly interesting case study of the comparative domestic argument. The practice, judicial decisions, and legal writings regarding the law of reservations present a rich and subtle picture[99] that may for the present purpose be discussed in two steps: first, setting out the elements of the law that fit easily within the contractual framework; second, considering certain more problematic situations, particularly regarding the legal regime of reservations not compatible with the object and purpose of the treaty. The traditional position in pre-World War Two international law was, as the ICJ described it in the *Reservations to the Convention on the Prevention and Punishment of the Crime of Genocide* advisory opinion (albeit rejecting it), 'directly inspired by the notion of contract', and 'involved the proposition that no reservation was valid unless it was accepted by all the contracting parties

---

Treaties: From Draft Guideline 3.1.12 to Guideline 3.1.5.6' (2013) 24 EJIL 1135, 1140, 1144–5.

[98] *EC-Customs Classification of Frozen Boneless Chicken Cuts*, Appellate Body Report, WTO/DS269/AB/R, WTO/DS286/AB, 12 September 2005, paras 271–3; M Paparinskis, *The International Minimum Standard and Fair and Equitable Treatment* (OUP, 2013) 128–9, 136–7.

[99] The ILC recently concluded its work on the Guide to Practice on Reservations to Treaties that contains useful overview and analysis of the practice and literature, (n 84); for an authoritative overview, see A Pellet, 'The ILC Guide to Practice on Reservations to Treaties: A General Presentation by the Special Rapporteur' (2013) 24 EJIL 1061. A select bibliography may be found in A Pellet, 'Article 19: Convention of 1969' in Corten and Klein (n 17) 406–8.

without exception'.[100] The broad contours of the traditional system fit the contractual analogy very well indeed, even though the idea of deriving implied acceptance from the lack of objections to a notified reservation[101] may already raise the first normative eyebrows (and suggest that the pre-*Reservations* golden age of integrity was not as purely contractual as it is sometimes presented). Articles 20 and 21 of the VCLT set out the rules regarding the acceptance of and objections to reservations through a contractual framework, providing the right to contracting States to accept (whether explicitly or implicitly) the formulated reservation or object to it, and in the latter case to object to the entry into force of the treaty between the particular States. While expressed within a framework different from that of conclusion of treaties, it is still the case that the entry into force of a particular treaty with particular content between particular parties depends on the consent of the other contracting party.

The law of reservations illustrates a shift of positions, with (contractual) analogies from domestic law providing support for entirely opposite positions in the spectrum between universality and integrity of treaties.[102] The traditional regime, as suggested above, proceeded from contractual assumptions of consent to ensure the absolute integrity of treaties. The *Reservations* Court rejected the contractual assumptions, emphasizing instead the special nature of the 1948 Convention for the Prevention and Punishment of the Crime of Genocide that required universality of participation; in which 'contracting States do not have any interests of their own; they merely have, one and all, a common interest, namely, the accomplishment of those high purposes which are the *raison d'être* of the convention'.[103] The VCLT regime of acceptance and objections to reservations, sketched above, relies on individualized consent of various forms to ensure universality by fragmenting the content of the treaty. The problematic aspect of the contractual analogy is the apparent assumption that treaties are, in general terms, bilateralizable and therefore can be

---

[100] *Reservations* Advisory Opinion (n 83) 21, see also 24: 'This theory rests essentially on a contractual assumption of the absolute integrity of the convention as adopted.'

[101] HW Malkin, 'Reservations to Multilateral Conventions' (1926) 7 BYBIL 141, 148, 150, 151, 153, 159.

[102] On the perspectives of universality and integrity, see C Redgwell, 'Universality or Integrity? Some Reflections on Reservations to General Multilateral Treaties' (1993) 64 BYBIL 245.

[103] *Reservations* Advisory Opinion (n 83) 23, generally 21–4.

perfectly broken down into a bundle of bilateral obligations with potentially different content.[104] The VCLT is not entirely insensitive to this concern and provides for two special cases where acceptance is required for the treaty to come into force.[105] Still, the rules raise a more general question about the appropriateness of bilateralization of non-bilateral obligations of integral (human rights, environmental law) or interdependent character (non-proliferation treaties). One might suggest that the contractual analogy consisted of two layers: in the traditional law, the top layer of consensual form sufficed to ensure absolute integrity (whatever the content of the rules might be); after *Reservations* removed the first layer, it revealed the second layer of earlier, unarticulated assumptions about the bilateralizable content of the rules, shifting the regime very strongly in the opposite direction of universality.

The same flux of positions within and between arguments by analogy may be seen regarding the more contested issues. The first issue relates to the relationship between Articles 19 and 20 of the VCLT: essentially, can States accept reservations contrary to the object and purpose of the treaty (as *per* the 'opposability school') or is Article 20 acceptance open only to those reservations that are formulated in accordance with Article 19, including its paragraph (c) on object and purpose (as *per* the 'permissibility school')?[106] Whatever position is the right one (probably the latter, with qualifications regarding the effect that explicit acceptance might have for reinterpretation of or amendment to the treaty), they can both be justified in terms of analogies. The opposability school would rely on the contractual framework of offer and acceptance as underlying any treaty-making process; the 'permissibility school' could respond by relying both on the traditional version of the argument in favour of presumptive contractual integrity, and on a faintly public law notion of an immutable core of the treaty that cannot be eroded by bilateral bargains.

---

[104] Klabbers, 'On Human Rights Treaties …' (n 97) 165.

[105] In Article 20(2), acceptance for all parties is required when the application of the treaty in its entirety is an essential condition of consent; in Article 20(3), acceptance by a competent organ of an international organization is required for a reservation to its constituent instrument. Both of these rules reflect the traditional system and are probably customary, D Müller, 'Article 20: 1969 Vienna Convention' in Corten and Klein (n 17) 493.

[106] A Pellet, 'Article 19: Convention of 1969' in Corten and Klein (n 17) 442, 474–82.

The other great debate in the area relates to the consequences of impermissible reservations.[107] One might say, in orthodox contractual terms, that if a party has given a conditional consent and the condition is legally invalid then no consent has been given in a technical sense: the State ceases being the contracting party.[108] Or one might say that the author of the invalid condition should choose whether to be a party without it or cease being a party. The opposite position of severing the reservation without affecting consent may be expressed in different ways. The more radical version of the argument, associated with the Human Rights Committee, may be deriving severability from the nature of the treaty itself, probably moving beyond the contours of consent and operating under law-making assumptions of ensuring the binding effect of substantively benevolent rules.[109] The *prima facie* less radical argument has been presented by the European Court of Human Rights and broadly followed by the ILC, identifying a rebuttable presumption that consent is reflected in conclusion of the treaty rather than in the reservation.[110]

Leaving aside the technical legal position,[111] as a matter of intellectual honesty one might have considerable sympathy with the explicit language of the Human Rights Committee: *but of course* the contractual assumptions of reciprocal benefit of obligations and consideration, where lack of participation is the greatest concern, do not work for non-bilateralizable obligations; *but of course* these are public law assumptions, where the benchmark for binding effect is the benevolence of the rule rather than the will of the addressee. Overall, there is something to be said for the joint dissenting opinion in *Reservations*, left aside as it has been by history. The Court removed the first layer of contractual consent only to bilateralize the 'common will' of the Genocide Convention by contractual reciprocity. Dissenting judges (led, one imagines, by McNair) disagreed:

---

[107] See Guide to Practice on Reservations to Treaties (n 84) para 4.5.3 and its Commentaries for an overview of different approaches.

[108] Ibid, paras 13–18.

[109] Ibid, paras 10–11, 29.

[110] Ibid, paras 19–28, 30–55.

[111] The present author has argued elsewhere that the most accurate description of *lex lata* may be given by relying on special customary law: the non-severability regime still provides the general rule, to the extent that States have not opted into a special (and only *inter se* opposable) customary regime of severability, M Paparinskis, 'Atrunas jēdziens un atbilstība līguma objektam un mērķim' [Concept of Reservations and Compliance with the Object and Purpose of the Treaty] (2010) Jurista Vārds [Lawyer's Word], 22 June 2010, no 25/26, accessed 4 May 2014 at www.juristavards.lv.

even though multilateral treaty-making 'activity is often described as "legislative" or "quasi-legislative", ... the legal basis of these conventions, and the essential thing that brings them into force, is the common consent of the parties'.[112] To consider subsequent developments through these lenses, the trade-off between universality and integrity is inherently insolvable: to move beyond the current tensions, either legislative elements have to honestly manifest themselves in entirely overriding consent, or the framework for dealing with permissible reservations has to apply contractual tools and assumptions to solve non-contractual challenges.[113] The law of reservations is probably an example of clear analogies that do not entirely fit at the international level, with assumptions regarding the creation of rules and content of obligations pulling in opposite directions even within the four corners of a single analogy, leading to odd systemic dynamics.

VI. CONCLUSION AND OUTLOOK

The chapter has looked at three particular elements of the law of treaties – consensual form, conclusion, and reservations – to demonstrate how analogies from domestic law, particularly contractual analogies, may have varying degrees of usefulness in illuminating the rationale and operation of treaties, leading to tensions between different assumptions in domestic and international law. A cursory look at almost all aspects of the law of treaties might demonstrate similar tensions, some of which are highlighted in the concluding paragraph of the chapter. Still, it may be useful to consider the broader implications of the argument. The overall thesis may be expressed as stating that a tension exists between analogies from domestic contractual law, derived chiefly from the consensual form of treaties but also the traditional bilateralism and reciprocity of their content, and analogies from types of public law, derived from the increased multilateralism of obligations in the post-War regimes of international law. Is there something more to it?

---

112 *Reservations* Advisory Opinion (n 83) Dissenting Opinion of Judges Guerrero, McNair, Read, and Hsu Mo, 31, 32.

113 Therefore one might very well conclude that the right solution lies not in the rules and procedures but in the institutional structure through which their formulation and application takes place, where one might again see glimpses of both private law (reservations dialogue) and public law elements (mechanisms of assistance), M Wood, 'Institutional Aspects of the Guide to Practice on Reservations' (2013) 24 EJIL 1099, 1105–12.

One might plausibly answer the question in at least two ways. Perhaps there is, and a clearer distinction should be drawn between two distinct legal issues. On the one hand, there are rules of the law of treaties that are entirely agnostic regarding the content of particular treaties, and are chiefly influenced by the similarity to contractual form. On the other hand, there are particular treaty regimes as well as rules of the law of treaties that do depend upon certain assumptions about the content and structure of treaties, and analogies with a variety of domestic legal regimes may be appropriate, depending on the content. That is what the dissenting judges, including McNair, effectively suggested in the *Reservations* advisory opinion.[114]

Alternatively, perhaps the thesis is banal and there is nothing more to it. The choice of the international legal order, outlined in the opening citation of McNair,[115] to squeeze the universe of all substantive issues into the ball of treaty form[116] necessarily results in a deformation of perspective to the extent that excludes the possibility of a systemically coherent comparison. Or, to put the same point in more positive terms, perhaps the real lesson is that the development of international law more generally is a never-ending battle for the control of analogy.[117] The equal inadequacy of all sources of analogy frees international law of any *a priori* intellectual straightjacket of natural and inevitable development. Instead, the inadequacy permits the articulation of legal arguments to address matters of individual and community interest[118] by choosing from many normative toolboxes, permitting the use of different possible domestic analogies as well as the creation of entirely innovatory technical terms and regimes of international law[119] (as the rules on responsibility

---

[114] *Reservations* Advisory Opinion (n 83) Dissenting Opinion of Judges Guerrero, McNair, Read, and Hsu Mo, 31, 32.

[115] See n 2.

[116] 'Would it have been worth while, … To have squeezed the universe into a ball', TS Eliot, 'The Love Song of J Alfred Prufrock' in P Larkin (ed), *The Oxford Book of Twentieth-Century English Verse* (OUP, 1973) 231.

[117] Lowe, 'Equity' (n 15) 61; AV Lowe, 'Can the European Community Bind the Member States on Questions of Customary International Law?' in M Koskenniemi (ed), *International Law Aspects of the European Union* (Martinus Nijhoff, 1998) 166.

[118] S Villalpando, 'The Legal Dimension of the International Community: How Community Interests are Protected in International Law' (2010) 21 EJIL 387.

[119] Eg, O'Keefe suggests that in territorial disputes the technical terms of international law have proved superior to domestic analogies, R O'Keefe, 'Legal

regarding breaches of multilateral obligations have done).[120] Tension, then, is not only inevitable but also useful. The truth, as it sometimes does, lies probably somewhere in the middle between the two views: many aspects discussed flow from the general structure of the international legal order and could be affected only by its wholescale reformation, yet a more thoughtful and analytical reading of rules, regimes, and their systemic similarities and differences can only improve the quality of the international legal process.[121]

Future research is needed to spell out the spectrum of plausible analogies, identify the systemic assumptions about domestic and international law that underpin them, and sketch the to and fro relationship between analogies, assumptions underlying analogies, and the dynamic of international legal process. Tensions between different analogies may be identified in many treaty rules and regimes.[122] For example, the law of interpretation has been influenced by analogies drawn from both domestic contracts[123] and statutes, particularly of constitutional character.[124] In

---

Title versus *Effectivités*': Prescription and the Promise and Problems of Private Law Analogies' (2011) 13 Intl Community L Rev 147.

[120] See recent analyses of responsibility and multilateral obligations that entirely avoid the contract/legislation dichotomy in favour of sophisticated international law terms of Articles of State Responsibility, *Belgium v Senegal* (n 12); Crawford, 'Responsibility for Breaches of Communitarian Norms ...' (n 11); P-M Dupuy, 'Back to the Future of a Multilateral Dimension of the Law of State Responsibility for Breaches of "Obligations Owed to the International Community as a Whole"' (2012) 23 EJIL 1059.

[121] This conclusion might be similar to the one that Klabbers seems to have reached: the contractual form and possibly law-making content have led to tensions in the VCLT framework, yet the approach itself was probably inevitable and the end result seems to be working reasonably well, 'The Community Interest in the Law of Treaties' (n 18) 779–80.

[122] Eg, Klabbers identifies a tension between contractual and legislative assumptions in the post-VCLT practice regarding the obligation not to defeat the object and purpose of the treaty, Klabbers, 'How to Defeat a Treaty's Object and Purpose' (n 2), and material breach, Klabbers, 'The Community Interest in the Law of Treaties' (n 18) 779–80; and Judge Keith considers the private law analogies to be of limited value for law on armed conflict, labour, and epidemics, (n 2).

[123] Eg, H Lauterpacht, 'Restrictive Interpretation and the Principle of Effectiveness in the Interpretation of Treaties' (1949) 26 BYBIL 48, 56–61, 67–8.

[124] Eg, regarding teleological and evolutionary interpretation in human rights law, Bates *The Evolution* (n 23) chp 8; S Hennette-Vauchez, 'Constitutional v International? When Unified Reformatory Rationales Mismatch the Plural Paths of Legitimacy of ECHR Law' in J Christoffersen and MR Madsen (eds), *The*

the law on termination and invalidity of treaties (already mentioned in the analysis of conclusion of treaties), some rules may be easily analogized to contract law;[125] the rules on fundamental change of circumstances have been narrowed down from earlier suggestions of almost unlimited discretion (that raised considerable questions about the possibility of analogy with contract law at all) into a narrow rule;[126] and Article 53 of the VCLT both introduces a communitarian vision of *jus cogens* into the international legal order more broadly[127] and completes the contractual analogy for treaties by supplementing the private relationship with the peremptory public rules. Particular regimes of treaty law also reflect the tensions. In the law of territory, elements both of private property law and perhaps also public *erga omnes* effects play an important role.[128] The law of international organizations may be viewed from the perspective of domestic constitutional or administrative law[129] or even private law.[130]

European Court of Human Rights between Law and Politics (OUP, 2011) (and see the less charitable description by FA Mann, cited at n 30), or constitutionalist interpretation of international organizations, J Alvarez, *International Organizations as Law-Makers* (OUP, 2006) chp 2.

[125] See n 72 on Articles 46–52. The same applies to termination due to a material breach in Article 60, B Simma and C Tams, 'Article 60: Convention of 1969' in Corten and Klein (n 17) 1135 fn 20; impossibility of performance in Article 61, P Bodeau-Livinec, 'Article 61: Convention of 1969' ibid, 1386.

[126] VCLT, Article 62; Lauterpacht, *Private Law Sources* (n 4) 167–75; Thirlway, 'Analogies …' (n 41) 323–4.

[127] Simma, 'From Bilateralism to Community Interest …' (n 2) 334.

[128] See the discussion at n 43–6.

[129] See in general terms, J Klabbers, A Peters, and G Ulfstein, *The Constitutionalization of International Law* (OUP, 2009) chp 2; regarding the UN, Alvarez, *International Organizations* (n 124) chp 2; B Fassbender, *The United Nations Charter as the Constitution of the International Community* (Martinus Nijhoff, 2009); in the particular context of delegation, D Sarooshi, *The United Nations and the Development of Collective Security: The Delegation by the UN Security Council of Its Chapter VII Powers* (OUP, 2000) 16–17, 21–4; D Sarooshi, *International Organizations and Their Exercise of Sovereign Powers* (OUP, 2005) 14–17; and regarding judicial review, A Tzanakopoulos, *Disobeying the Security Council* (OUP, 2011) 94–110.

[130] The private law of trusts has been used both to explain the Mandates System of the League of Nations, *International Status of South-West Africa*, Advisory Opinion, ICJ Rep 1950, 128, Separate Opinion of Judge McNair 146, 148–53; and analyse more recent developments, I Bantekas, 'The Emergence of Intergovernmental Trust in International Law' (2010) 81 BYBIL 224. In one curious case, domestic courts examined whether an international organization was a charity, AB Lyons, 'Was the League of Nations a Charity' (1950) 27 BYBIL 434, and English courts have famously grappled with the question whether, for

Human rights treaties raise the question in perhaps the clearest terms: it seems counterintuitive to conceptualize obligations under human rights law as bilateralizable,[131] but the alternatives of viewing them either as law-making (perhaps even constitutional) or as a framework within which unilateral pledges can be made create tensions with the contractual underpinnings of the consensual structure.[132] Overall, the post-ontological nature of rules on sources of international law permits leaving aside for the moment the technical part of Lauterpacht's project of analogies in international law[133] – deriving positive international law from consensus in domestic law – and concentrating on what may be a more challenging project – rethinking the nature, underpinnings, and future of international law against the background of the wonderful variety of domestic law.

---

the purposes of personality in English law, international organizations could be analogized to corporations, D Sarooshi and A Tzanakopoulos, 'International Organizations before United Kingdom Courts' in A Reinisch (ed), *Transnational Judicial Conversations on the Personality, Privileges and Immunities of International Organizations* (OUP, 2013).

131 Although not impossible, see regarding labour rights, Klabbers, 'On Human Rights Treaties …' (n 97) 179–80. If structure of the obligations is at least to some extent dictated by the content of the rights in issue, it seems distinctly odd that human rights obligations regarding fair trial and property rights would be multilateral, while substantively very similar investment protection obligations would be perceived as bilateral, M Paparinskis, 'Investment Arbitration and the Law of Countermeasures' (2008) 79 BYBIL 264, 330–31 (on the comparative argument between human rights and investment law, see Paparinskis ibid, 325–30, and Paparinskis, *International Minimum Standard and Fair and Equitable Treatment* (n 98) chps 8–9). If one reasons backwards from the possibility of expressing content of human rights in bilateral(izable) obligations, the intuition of necessary multilateralism of human rights might need to be critically re-examined.

132 L Brilmayer, 'From "Contract" to "Pledge": The Structure of International Human Rights Agreements' (2006) 77 BYBIL 163.

133 Lauterpacht, *Private Law Sources* (n 4).

4. Theorizing treaties: The consequences of the contractual analogy

Akbar Rasulov

Ready-made concepts whose appeal is deceptive lie in wait.[1]

It is characteristic of human experience that the familiar is complex.[2]

I. WHAT PLACE FOR THEORY?

In every branch of social sciences, as JK Galbraith once noted, the ultimate test of truth always lies with the conventional wisdom, especially that part of it which is endorsed by the respective scientific community.[3] Seen from this angle, the single most important thing that one would need to know about international legal theory today, undoubtedly, would be the fact that in the minds of most international lawyers presently the word 'theory' is most commonly associated with the ideas of fanciful gibberish, sophistry, and, depending on what one feels about modern academia more generally, a slightly offensive culture of verbal self-indulgence. A slightly less charitable reading would be to say that in the minds of most international lawyers today the concept of theory would be most accurately defined as: (i) a decidedly unpractical, self-consciously speculative, jargon-heavy intellectual exercise that is (ii) ostensibly aimed at uncovering some form of deeper philosophical truth, the acquisition of which in the end, however, is certain to be of no evident benefit to anyone, save maybe for (iii) those who, following a logic not entirely dissimilar to that identified by Veblen behind the late 19th-century custom of building educational curricula in upper-class institutions around the study of dead languages and athletic pursuits, might see in it a talisman of some kind of hierarchically inspired symbolic status. For, indeed, if one of the best ways to broadcast the fact of one's exclusive social position generally is 'to put in evidence some

[1] E Auerbach, 'Philology and Weltliteratur' (1969) 13 *Centennial Review* 1, 16.

[2] G Gardner, 'An Inquiry into the Principles of the Law of Contracts' (1932) 46 Harv L Rev 1, 2.

[3] See JK Galbraith, *The Affluent Society* (first published 1958, Penguin, 1999) 6–12.

learning which is conventionally recognised as evidence of wasted time', then in international law it would certainly have to be 'theory' that would lend itself most readily to this use.[4]

Predictably enough, the vast majority of those who tend to identify themselves as international legal theorists typically tend to find this set of views fundamentally unsubstantiated. For good or ill, however, theirs is not an unbiased opinion, and inasmuch as most of their protests in this case appear to be directed at the idea that theory is 'completely irrelevant' to the world of 'practice,' their responses against it also seem entirely to miss the point.

The conventional concept of theory to a very large extent stems from the combination of the following three assumptions: (i) that 'theory' is, at its root, a rather uniform type of activity, that is, 'all theorists ultimately do the same kind of thing, discuss the same sets of questions, inquire after the same sets of issues'; (ii) that as a form of social activity 'theory' is fundamentally dissimilar from 'practice'; and (iii) that in the grand scheme of the intra-disciplinary division of labour in modern international law, 'theory' firmly belongs on the list of those activities that are practised exclusively by professional, that is, university-based, academics. Hence, by way of direct logical implication, the highly popular notion that in principle it should always be possible for someone to 'practise' international law without having anything to do with 'theory' and the corollary axiom that only those international lawyers who are employed full-time in legal academia can ever really develop the need for the 'theoretical turn'.

As Wittgenstein noted, in a fundamentally secularized cultural environment the meaning of any given concept in the last instance can only be established through the stabilization of its everyday popular usage. The

---

[4] See T Veblen, *The Theory of the Leisure Class* (first published 1899, Dover, 1994) 242–3:

> Indeed, there can be little doubt that it is their utility as evidence of wasted time and effort, and hence of the pecuniary strength necessary in order to afford this waste, that has secured to the classics their position of prerogative in the scheme of higher learning, and has led to their being esteemed the most honorific of all learning. … In this respect the classics have until lately had scarcely a rival [, though] lately college athletics have won their way into a recognised standing as an accredited form of scholarly accomplishment … in American and English Schools. Athletics have an obvious advantage over the classics for the purpose of leisure-class learning, since success as an athlete presumes, not only a waste of time, but also a waste of money, as well as the possession of certain highly unindustrial archaic traits of character and temperament.

fact that the vast majority of those international lawyers who would normally identify themselves as the practitioners of international legal theory have tended to regard this combination of assumptions as fundamentally unconvincing is not, on this view of things, going to undermine to any meaningful extent its essential validity. If a sufficiently large number of the rest of the international law profession continues to construct its sense of professional identity and coordinate everyday social relations with one another and the world outside the profession on the assumption that this is, in effect, 'what international legal theory is all about,' pointing out the basic unsustainability of its view within the narrow, self-servingly apologist community of international legal theorists is not going to achieve anything.

So far, so bleak. But, of course, there also exists another way of approaching this issue. It starts with the idea that rather than trying to disprove any given set of popular (mis)conceptions, one may attempt to displace it by putting forward (and popularizing) another set of equally calibrated (mis)conceptions. As Fredric Jameson notes in a similar context, if it should be true that 'no interpretation can be effectively disqualified on its own terms by the simple enumeration of inaccuracies or omissions,' then the only effective way to 'overthrow' it would be to produce another, much stronger interpretation that could be put in its place.[5]

The concept of international legal theory that I would like to suggest in these pages follows from this logic of substitutive competition and displacement. In lieu of a concept centred around the idea of a distinctly abstract, jargon-heavy, self-consciously speculative discourse, I would like to propose an alternative definition centred around the notions of tacit knowledge, implicit assumptions, *doxa*, and what Claude Levi-Strauss some time ago called the infrastructure of unconscious beliefs.[6] Each of these notions, to be sure, has its own, frequently highly convoluted history, but the underlying meaning in each case seems to be essentially the same: what we talk about when we talk about 'theory' in this sense of the word is all those aspects of our *knowledge-base* that influence the course of our day-to-day practices of reasoning without our necessarily being consciously aware of them. Call it 'implicit reasoning protocols,' 'standard habits of thought,' or 'default analytical routines' – the precise labels do not matter so much – to study international legal

---

[5] F Jameson, *The Political Unconscious* (first published 1981, Routledge, 2002) xiii.

[6] J Culler, *Structuralist Poetics* (first published 1975, Routledge 2008) 31.

theory *thus conceived* would be to study the 'mechanics of influence' produced by all these various elements on the way in which the community of international lawyers, academics and practitioners alike, work within and through their commonly shared discipline, that is to say, how they speak, reason, and act whenever they speak, reason, and act before one another, in the medium of international law.

Seen from this perspective, the practice of theory could never be regarded as the sole preserve of the professional academic entrepreneur. 'Doing theory,' on this view of things, would then be a feature properly characteristic of all species of international legal space-process – and not just in the simple, naïve-rationalist sense that every action necessarily presupposes some kind of implicit guiding framework that helps to orientate it, but in the broader, much more 'structural' sense that it is, in fact, rather impossible to institute any set of socially meaningful facts that would not automatically reproduce within the conditions of their *practical* possibility the essential formula of their 'animating' *theory*.[7]

II. THE QUESTION OF MUNICIPAL ANALOGIES: GENERAL REMARKS

One of the first questions that confronts every student of international law – today no less urgently than in the days of Lassa Oppenheim and Heinrich Triepel – is to what extent, if at all, the enterprise of international legal studies could be aided by the importation into it of concepts developed originally in the context of the everyday practices typically characteristic of municipal legal systems. Can categories that have proved themselves useful to municipal legal practitioners in what concerns the articulation of their typical professional experiences also prove useful to the practitioners of *international legal knowledge* in what concerns the development of those analytical frameworks by which the learning of international law is supposed to be organized? What kind of benefit – epistemological, ideological, or otherwise – could the discipline of international law gain from transplanting such terms and phrases as 'contract,' 'estoppel,' or 'constitutionalism' into its operative vocabulary? Will it become easier to capture all the different intricacies of the law of territorial sovereignty if they are articulated in the idiom of property law? Will the general logic of the international dispute settlement process be

---

[7] For a further elaboration of this thesis, see E Balibar, 'Althusser's Object' (1994) 39 *Social Text* 157, 172–4.

revealed more effectively if the respective mechanisms are presented as a species of litigation? Would the international legal regime determining the consequences arising out of changes of sovereignty turn out to be less unwieldy if it were reconceptualized in the private law language of inheritance and succession? Will the law of State responsibility become less difficult to summarize if one rewrites it using the vocabulary of tort law?

As in many other fields of international law, the course of the intra-disciplinary debate in this area over the years has hardly evolved in anything approaching a progressive fashion. The same three basic positions which took shape at the start of the last century have by and large persisted to present times, each replete with its own distinctive vision of what ought to constitute the best strategy of disciplinary development for international law.

The first school – whose general argument line was perhaps most famously illustrated in the writings of the great Austro-British jurist (and later a judge on the International Court of Justice (ICJ)), Sir Hersch Lauterpacht[8] – has generally tended to support the strategy of active cross-disciplinary importation, the underlying reasoning behind which being a product of two basic assumptions. The first assumption held that, objectively speaking, international law and municipal law shared so many important features that it was virtually certain they had to be regarded as species of the same common genus, the study of which, appropriately enough, would be called 'general jurisprudence.'[9] The second assumption, in turn, asserted that because of this shared commonality the 'science of international law' not only should not discourage the importation of municipal legal analogies into international legal practice, but that it should also, in fact, elevate such kind of practice to the rank of a *general epistemic policy*. Not only would such an approach help resolve the perennial challenge of normative gaps but it would also increase the general rigour of international legal reasoning, without which it was highly likely that the discipline of international law might eventually collapse into some form of apologist ideology.

---

[8] See, characteristically, H Lauterpacht, *Private Law Sources and Analogies of International Law* (The Lawbook Exchange Ltd, 1927).

[9] For a more recent statement of this position, see W Riphagen, 'Techniques of International Law' (1994-II) 246 Recueil des Cours de l'Académie de Droit International 235.

The second school – whose standard position was exemplified, among others, in the writings of Lauterpacht's English mentor and his predecessor at Cambridge and at the ICJ, Lord McNair[10] – has tended, by contrast, to lean towards a much more cautious, 'pragmatic' approach. The notion that any given set of municipal legal categories, no matter how basic or well established in pedigree, could be expected to fit within the operative fabric of international law 'lock, stock, and barrel,' on this view of things, was simply a grandiose folly.[11] What is more, as a matter of general principle, such kind of operation would also seem quite impossible to reconcile with any reasonable reading of the traditional doctrine of sources,[12] not to mention – as a number of scholars repeatedly pointed out[13] – the customary law principle of the least restrictive interpretation.[14] Naturally, this did not mean that *any* recourse to municipal legal analogies was automatically wrong. That international law could 'seek and find inspiration and guidance' in municipal legal experience and 'usefully borrow' from it in some situations was never to be put in doubt. The point rather was that when it came to determining how wide the range of such borrowings should be, the better approach

---

[10] See, eg, A McNair, 'So-Called State Servitudes' (1925) 6 BYIL 111; A McNair, 'The Functions and Differing Legal Character of Treaties' (1930) 11 BYIL 100. For a more recent example of the second school, see M Shahabuddeen, 'Municipal Law Reasoning in International Law', in V Lowe and M Fitzmaurice (eds), *Fifty Years of the International Court of Justice* (CUP, 1996) 90.

[11] Cf A de Lapradelle, *Les Principes Généraux du Droit International* (Centre Européen de la Dotation Carnegie, 1932), 6–8 (contending that the habit of importing into the study of international law the standard analytical frameworks borrowed from the municipal legal tradition is liable to lead not only to a great deal of methodological confusion but also to many disastrous policy choices and grave errors in the practical application of the law).

[12] *International Status of South-West Africa*, Advisory Opinion, Separate Opinion of Judge McNair, ICJ Rep 1950 (11 July) 146, 148.

[13] See, eg, P Guggenheim, 'Les Principes de droit international public' (1952-I) 80 Recueil des Cours 1, 62. In a similar vein, see also *Reparation for Injuries Suffered in the Service of the United Nations*, Advisory Opinion, Dissenting Opinion of Judge Badawi-Pasha, ICJ Rep 1949 (11 April) 205, 211 (arguing that any use of analogy in international law needs to be constrained due to the principle of State sovereignty).

[14] Often also called the 'Lotus principle,' the principle of the least restrictive interpretation holds that in those cases where the applicable rules leave the resolution of a particular question insufficiently clear, the interpretation that results in the least degree of 'restriction upon the independence of States' will be considered correct.

was to decide each individual case on its own merits, without seeking to establish any general rules or blanket presumptions.

Where the second school criticized the first school for its excessive penchant for sweeping generalizations, the third school, for its part, admonished the former for its glaring lack of long-term epistemic strategy. Seeking to articulate a more ambitious plan of disciplinary development than one that could be simply reduced to 'let us treat each case on its individual merits', its followers have by and large tended to take the position diametrically opposite to Lauterpacht's:[15] if international law wants to become a 'proper' intellectual discipline (and thus to secure itself against stealth colonization by second-rate public lawyers), it must assemble its own, completely 'indigenous' structure of analytical instruments, reasoning protocols, and conceptual apparatuses. And just as Lauterpacht's theory had presupposed as its absolute precondition the implicit acceptance of the classical monist paradigm of legal ontology, an essential prerequisite for the intelligibility of the third school's basic argument was the unqualified endorsement of the classical dualist vision of the relationship between the international and the municipal legal orders.[16] Characteristically, thus, it was only inasmuch as it seemed possible to demonstrate how fundamentally different the general institutional structure and substantive remit of the former seemed compared to those of the latter, that the proponents of the third approach have found it admissible to insist that the discipline's constituent reasoning protocols must likewise be made fundamentally dissimilar from those used in a typical municipal legal context.[17]

---

[15] The standard argument line here has been exemplified most vividly in recent practice in the writings of another Cambridge-ICJ alumnus, Hugh Thirlway. See H Thirlway, 'Concepts, Principles, Rules and Analogies: International and Municipal Legal Reasoning' (2002) 294 Recueil des Cours 265.

[16] For a classical statement of the dualist theory on which this approach relies, see CH Triepel, 'Rapports Entre le Droit Interne et le Droit International' (1923-I) 1 Recueil des Cours 73, 83:

> *le droit international public et le droit interne sont non seulement des parties, des branches du droit distinctes, mais aussi des systèmes juridiques distincts. Ce sont deux cercles qui sont en contact intime, mais qui ne se superposent jamais. Puisque le droit interne et le droit international ne régissent pas les mêmes rapports, il est impossible qu'il y ait jamais une 'concurrence' entre les sources des deux systèmes juridiques.*

[17] In social theory, this way of reasoning is sometimes described in terms of an ontological determinism of knowledge. A classic example of an ontologically determinist theory of knowledge can be found in the traditional Marxist concept of ideology: the structure of social intercourse determines the contents of social

As fashions changed over time, so too did the fortunes of each school. At no point, however, did any of the three camps manage to displace its rivals so definitively as to drive them out of competition completely. At each given moment there could thus be found multiple proponents (and opponents) of each of the three approaches.[18] What is more, the general terms of the debate in which they engaged in the vast majority of cases have similarly continued to remain essentially unchanged. The same basic group of issues that had been considered theoretically dispositive in the 1910s were also recognized as such in the 1930s, the 1960s, and even the 2000s. What might have been the ultimate reason for this remarkable pattern of endurance remains unclear. On the whole, however, it seems highly plausible that, all things considered, the remarkable durability of this three-way division of opinion should be interpreted, in the final analysis, far less as an indication of there being perhaps some genuinely complex theoretical challenge at its heart that for one reason or another has managed to remain unresolved all these years, than as a sign that the apparent theoretical controversy around which it revolves may, as a matter of fact, very well be no such thing at all. That is to say, against the background of such an obvious lack of progression in its resolution over such a long period of time, it seems highly probable that the debate, 'To what extent should the discipline of international legal studies allow the use of municipal legal analogies?', may, in fact, be a product of what in modern analytical philosophy would be called a pseudo-question: whatever answer one gives to it can, in the final analysis, neither be successfully defended nor disproven, but only asserted by way of a self-justifying wager (à la Pascal) or a naked decisionist choice (à la Schmitt).[19]

---

consciousness. Characteristically, thus, it was not only Western international lawyers who have tended to subscribe to this pattern of argument. See, eg, G Tunkin, 'Co-Existence and International Law' (1958-III) 95 Recueil des Cours 1, 76–7.

[18] For an account of the same tripartite division in the general doctrinal debate concerning the 'transferability of the notion of error to international law,' see E Wyler and R Samson, 'Article 48', in O Corten and P Klein (eds), *The Vienna Conventions on the Law of Treaties: A Commentary* (OUP, 2011), 1117, 1121–2.

[19] On decisionism, Pascalian wagers, and what happens when 'the reason runs out' but decisions have to be made nevertheless, one can do far worse than choose as one's starting point D Kennedy, 'A Semiotics of Critique' (2001) 22 Cardozo L Rev 1147, 1158–69, and P Schlag, *The Enchantment of Reason* (Duke UP, 1998).

For, indeed, every time one of us makes a claim about whether or not, say, the law of State responsibility is 'really' just like the law of torts or the law of treaties 'really' follows the same essential logic as the law of contracts, what actually happens, in practice, is that we only put forward an entirely 'naked' guess that, on balance, *perhaps* it is going to be *easier* to find out more about whatever given question we are looking to answer by isolating its core issue through the prism of these metaphors.

But, of course, in the end, there is not really anything 'there' to find out: questions of law, like all institutional facts, have no inherent logic to them beyond the idea that, like the Tinker Bell fairy, they exist only insofar as they are believed to exist; and metaphors, like all linguistic forms, are not a set of cognitively neutral devices which one can use to reach more deeply into whatever pre-existing reality one assumes one is investigating with their help. For, as every trial lawyer knows all too well, the metaphors we use help to construct that very reality rather than just depicting it. A legal relation established on the basis of an international treaty does not in and of itself have an inherently contractual character:[20] as with all discursively constructed phenomena, there simply is no objective essence behind the idea of a treaty (or, for that matter, contract) that inheres within it. Recall the earlier point from Wittgenstein: it is only through the accumulation of repeated usages that meanings (essences) become infused into concepts (words). We may allow ourselves to become unaware of this basic fact, but let there be no mistake about it: whatever 'essences' there exist in law are all entirely conventional constructs, that is to say, they are all, in the last instance, logically arbitrary and historically contingent fictions. Over time we may come to treat some of these fictions as though they were reflective of some factual objective reality.[21] But the only thing that in truth will be objectively real

---

[20] This point is rather obvious, and yet it is striking to note how frequently it tends to be overlooked in modern international law scholarship. The empirically existing legally mediated social relation which is treated by the legal discourse as its *purported* object of reflection is not, in fact, the same 'thing' as the mentally constructed object of that discourse's knowledge on which it focuses in the process of its actually implemented theoretical practice. Cf L Althusser and E Balibar, *Reading Capital* (Verso, 1970) 40 ('the *idea* of the circle, which is the *object* of knowledge must not be confused with the circle, which is the *real object*') (italics in the original).

[21] In the Marxist tradition, this particular trajectory of miscognition is called 'reification.' As Marx explains in the first volume of *Das Kapital*, the archetypal example of reificationist practice is the fetishism of commodities. The emergence of the idea of a single unified theory of contractual transactions has many obvious parallels with commodity fetishism. For a classical introduction to the

about them will be the fact of our collective misrecognition of them as such, that is to say, the purely *historical* event of the adoption within the given discursive community of a certain set of *analytical presumptions* as manifested in the entrenchment of the corresponding *discursive patterns* (tropes).

Seen from this angle, it appears, consequently, that, whether or not we may be fully aware of it, the *real* question behind the question, 'Does it make sense to speak of treaties as contracts?', is not so much, 'To what extent, if at all, should the use of municipal legal analogies be encouraged in the construction of the international legal analytic?', but rather, 'What have been the most common discursive patterns that historically have been used in the law of treaties (LOTR) discourse; which of these patterns can be considered reflective of that discourse's fundamental analytical presumptions (and thus of its operative protocols of knowledge); and to what extent can the same patterns also be traced in the field of the law of contracts (LOC)?'

Put in these terms, what follows below then can be essentially summarized as: (i) an investigation of the *immanent patterns* of the LOTR discourse (ii) as carried out through a close narratological examination of its dominant tropes and (iii) aimed, by and large, at determining the general extent of its regular reliance on the same sets of conceptual resources as have been utilized in the traditional LOC discourse (iv) over the same period of time – late 19th century to the present day – and within the same socio-cultural setting – what the 'three globalizations of law' school[22] calls the 'Western legal tradition' – in which they have historically developed.

III. THE PARADIGMATIC STRUCTURES OF THE TRADITIONAL LOC DISCOURSE: A BRIEF HISTORY

As commonly presented in the literature, the history of the modern LOC regime 'as we know it' – that is to say, that body of norms, ideas, and institutional recipes which in the Western legal tradition over the last

---

Marxist theory of reification, see G Lukacs, *History and Class Consciousness* (R Livingstone tr, Merlin, 1971) 83–110.

[22] For an introduction to the 'three globalizations of law' tradition, see D Kennedy, 'Three Globalizations of Law and Legal Thought: 1850–2000', in D Trubek and A Santos (eds), *The New Law and Economic Development* (CUP, 2006) 19.

several decades has come to be associated with the idea of the legal regulation of contractual transactions – began sometime in the first half of the 19th century.[23] Over the course of the next one and a half centuries it has proceeded through three broadly consecutive stages, each of which gave rise to a relatively distinct way of conceptualizing LOC, that is to say, a relatively distinct pattern of inter-related epistemic presumptions, argument tropes (*topoi*), and analytical protocols deployed by the practitioners of the LOC discourse in their exchanges with one another.[24] For convenience purposes, we can call these three stages as follows: the age of the subjectivist approach; the age of the objectivist approach; and the modernist age.

1. The Subjectivist Approach to LOC

a) General outline

In the main, the age of the subjectivist approach in the history of the modern LOC was characterized by the rise to prominence of two main sets of ideas. The first revolved around the so-called 'will theory of contract'; the second, around the principle of judicial reticence.

The basic concept at the heart of the will theory tradition will be familiar to most students of international law. To use the classical

---

[23] The account of LOC history presented in this section derives in considerable part from the following sources: G Gilmore, *The Death of Contract* (Ohio State UP, 1974); M Horwitz, 'The Historical Foundations of Modern Contract Law' (1974) 87 Harv L Rev 917; PS Atiyah, *The Rise and Fall of Freedom of Contract* (OUP, 1979); B Mensch, 'Freedom of Contract as Ideology' (1981) 33 Stan L Rev 753; M Horwitz, *The Transformation of American Law 1870–1960: The Crisis of Legal Orthodoxy* (Harvard UP, 1992) 9–63; D Kennedy, 'From the Will Theory to the Principle of Private Autonomy: Lon Fuller's "Consideration and Form"' (2000) 100 Col L Rev 94. Due to considerations of space, most of the discussion here focuses on the history of the LOC discourse in a primarily Anglo-American context. Nevertheless, it needs to be noted that the broader paradigmatic shifts described here can also be traced with relative facility across various other Western jurisdictions. See further in this respect F Wieacker, *A History of Private Law in Europe* (T Weir tr, OUP, 1995); A von Mehren, 'The "Battle of Forms": A Comparative View' (1990) 38 AJCL 265.

[24] I trace the trajectory of this transformation from a slightly different vantage point and in a more abridged form in A Rasulov, 'The Life and Times of the Modern Law of Reservations: The Doctrinal Genealogy of General Comment No. 24' (2009) 14 Austrian Rev Intl and Eur L 103, 147–55, and A Rasulov, 'The Doctrine of Sources in the Discourse of the Permanent Court of International Justice', in M Fitzmaurice and C Tams (eds), *Legacies of the Permanent Court of International Justice* (Martinus Nijhoff, 2013) 269, 284–94.

formula, in the eyes of the will theory approach, the legal meaning of the idea of contract was that it embodied an underlying 'meeting of the minds.' A legally binding contractual obligation, in other words, on this view of things, was formed as a result of – and by – the fact of attaining, between the respective contracting parties, a successful convergence of wills.[25] The underlying assumption, mirrored years later in Triepel and Anzilotti's theory of voluntarist positivism, would suggest, thus, that what made a contractual agreement legally binding was the underpinning psychological process whereby a set of previously separate individual wills held by the respective parties were fused into one single 'united will' of the contract (*concorde volontà* in Anzilotti; *Gemeinwille* in Triepel).[26]

As the conventional wisdom suggests, the origins of this way of thinking most probably should be sought in the philosophy of classical 19th-century liberal individualism,[27] one of the central defining tenets of which, along with the doctrine of *laissez-faire*, was the unqualified belief in the idea of contract as the unbridled expression of the free will of the autonomous private actors (*l'autonomie de la volonté*).[28] An obligation

---

25 Further on the will theory of contract, see Kennedy, 'From the Will Theory …' (n 23) 115–6.

26 See Tunkin, 'Co-Existence …' (n 17) 33.

27 C Dalton, 'An Essay in the Deconstruction of Contract Doctrine' (1985) 94 Yale L J 997, 1012.

28 The doctrine of *l'autonomie de la volonté* was a central building block of the late 19th-century Western legal consciousness, or what in the 'three globalizations of law' theory is called the Classical Legal Thought. Broadly speaking, the adherents of Classical Legal Thought conceived of law as a system for the enforcement of various categories of autonomous wills each of which was imagined to be simultaneously perfectly privileged within its specific designated sphere and void outside it. The field of all legal action, thus, was essentially presented as a complex multilayered structure of mutually non-overlapping 'packages of competences' (spheres). Within the limits of its respective sphere each legal subject enjoyed the full liberty of conduct and thus remained the uncontested master of its fate. Outside it, its position was entirely determined by the exercise of the liberty enjoyed by another such subject. The general function of law, on this view of things, was to police the boundaries between the respective spheres and thus, where necessary, decide which of the respective competence holders' will should be given effect. It was from this set of assumptions that the traditional liberal belief that the government should not interfere with private rights, that private interests should yield in the face of the eminent domain, that the federal government should not interfere with the competences of federal subjects, etc, devolved. For further discussion of the operative logic of the Classical Legal Thought, see D Kennedy, *The Rise and Fall*

that could only be created by the free will of autonomous subjects, by logic, required as a necessary precondition for its enforcement the demonstration of the attainment of that will: a legal-political system fundamentally wedded to the idea of law as the guarantor and enabler of personal liberty could not afford to take any other position on this issue.[29] Hence the traditional subjectivist assumption that any bargain achieved between two free legal subjects, so long as it could be shown to have resulted from the genuine convergence of their wills, deserved the unqualified protection of the law. Hence also the corollary conclusion that in the absence of the possibility of demonstrating the attainment of such a convergence any attempt to enforce the proposed bargain in a court of law would be fundamentally illegitimate and inappropriate, since it effectively would be tantamount to imposing on the defendant a burden he or she did not freely consent to – and, of course, the whole point behind making contractual bargains enforceable through the machinery of the legal system was to protect precisely against this sort of infringement on the principle of liberty, for indeed therein lay the logic of one of the most important conceptual foundations of the subjectivist age: the sharp categorical distinction between the coercive order of public law and the non-coercive, freedom-fortifying order of private law.[30]

A classic example traditionally cited in the literature to illustrate the internal logic of the subjectivist approach is the mid-19th-century English case of *Raffles v Wichelhaus*.[31] The facts of the case were as follows: the defendant had agreed to purchase from the plaintiff a consignment of cotton to be shipped from Bombay to Liverpool on a merchant ship named *Peerless*. As it later turned out, there had been, in fact, at least two different ships called *Peerless* which were due to sail from Bombay to Liverpool that year, one of which did so in October, while the other, in December. The plaintiff apparently had had it in mind that the consignment would be sent by the latter, while the defendant believed that it would be sent by the former. When the shipment arrived, the defendant refused to pay the agreed price, arguing, inter alia, that the apparent

---

of Classical Legal Thought (first published 1975, Beard Books, 2006) xiii; Kennedy, 'Three Globalizations …' (n 22) 26–36; Kennedy, 'From the Will Theory …' (n 23) 106–8; Horwitz, *Transformation* (n 23) 9–30.

29 For a modern-day treatment of the question of the subjectivist reliance on liberal individualism, see the discussion in *Kabil Development Corp v Mignot*, 279 Or. 151, 566 P. 2d 505 (1977).

30 Horwitz, *Transformation* (n 23) 10–11; Kennedy, 'From the Will Theory …' (n 23) 108.

31 *Raffles v Wichelhaus*, 159 Eng Rep 375 (1864).

confusion between the parties as to the identity of the 'correct' *Peerless* meant that no valid contract could have been concluded between itself and the plaintiff. The court, after examining the argument, upheld the defendant's contention on the grounds that since there had been no actual agreement as to the principal object of the bargain (*consensus ad idem*), it was impossible to conclude that there was a valid meeting of the minds between the two parties, which meant that no legally binding contract could be said to have come into existence between them and the plaintiff, therefore, was to be given no relief. As striking as this line of reasoning might seem to the modern eye – surely, it would have been a great deal more prudent and in line with good business sense to conclude that the failure to specify which *Peerless* would be engaged for the delivery of the purchased cotton had to be treated as a risk commonly assumed by both parties, and inasmuch as the plaintiff had performed its obligations in perfect good faith, the decision to leave it without any relief seems in this context unduly harsh – in the mid-1800s this way of going about LOC disputes appears to have been rather common – and not just in England, but also in France, Germany, and various other Western countries.[32]

b) Operative tropology

As *Raffles v Wichelhaus* illustrates, from the broader structural point of view, the essential theory at the heart of the subjectivist approach manifested itself through the combination of the following three main sets (clusters) of tropes:

(1) the meeting-of-the-minds doctrine, through which the subjectivist approach articulated both the ultimate *raison d'être* of the LOC as a regulatory enterprise and its central limiting principle, the underlying set of assumptions being that legal enforcement could be given to private agreements only to the extent that they embodied the underpinning 'convergences' of the free autonomous wills of their parties, and that beyond this scenario the legal system had no legitimate business to interfere in the private dealings of the contracting parties;

---

[32] Indeed, as various contract law historians have since pointed out, the great majority of the leading theorists of the subjectivist approach were, in fact, French and German jurists. See further R Pound, 'The Role of Will in Law' (1954) 68 Harv L Rev 1, 4–5; M Cohen, 'The Basis of Contract' (1933) 46 Harv L Rev 553, 575; and Atiyah, *Rise and Fall* (n 23) 407, Kennedy, 'Three Globalizations …' (n 22) 27 (all explicitly identifying Savigny as the key figure in this regard).

(2) the principle of private autonomy, around which the subjectivist approach articulated its basic theory of interpretation, the central assumption behind which being the idea that the parties not only remain the absolute 'masters of their obligations' at the point of their initial creation, that is, at the point where the respective contractual arrangement is supposed to come into existence, but also the primary source for the determination of the meaning of each contractual provision during the life of the contract;

(3) the doctrine of privity, around which the subjectivist approach articulated its general theory of the essential limits of contractual bindingness, the central assumption here being that inasmuch as contractual obligations can only be assumed pursuant to the attainment of a requisite meeting of the minds, the possibility of establishing any kind of legal effects for third parties by means of contractual arrangements (*stipulations pour autrui*) was inadmissible.

2. The Objectivist Approach to LOC

a) General outline

The age of subjectivism did not last very long. By most accounts, already by the last quarter of the 19th century the subjectivist approach had run itself into the sand.[33] Partly under the influence of what the subsequent generation of LOC scholars came to see as the 'misapplication of the principle of estoppel,'[34] partly as a reaction against the notion that to think of 'wills merging' and 'minds meeting' was ultimately a rather silly idea,[35] but mainly, it also seems, because of the rapidly growing recognition that the essential premise of the subjectivist paradigm – *viz.*,

---

[33] See, eg, Horwitz, *Transformation* (n 23) 33 *et seq*; Kennedy, 'From the Will Theory … ' (n 23) 116 *et seq*.

[34] Kennedy, *Rise and Fall* (n 28) 212.

[35] For a typical (if also rather polite) expression of this sentiment, see M Cohen, 'The Basis of Contract' (n 32) 575:

> The metaphysical difficulties of this view have often been pointed out. Minds or wills are not in themselves existing things that we can look at and recognize. We are restricted in our earthly experience to the observation of the changes or actions of more or less animated bodies in time and space; and disembodied minds or wills are beyond the scope and reach of earthly law.

For a somewhat more forceful version of the same argument, see F Cohen, 'Transcendental Nonsense and the Functional Approach' (1935) 35 Col L Rev 809.

that a binding contract can only come into existence where a perfect unity of intention has been achieved – was fundamentally unrealistic, seeing as the great majority of contracts in practice would tend to be drafted in a structurally incomplete form, that is, various otherwise generally quite probable contingencies related to their performance would never be addressed by either party – the operative theoretical apparatus of the LOC discourse increasingly came to be organized less and less around the quasi-psychological tropes of 'wills' and 'minds' and increasingly more around the quasi-sociological tropes of 'standard practices' and 'reasonable man standard.'

A classic early example of the new approach can be found in Oliver Wendell Holmes's *The Common Law*. 'The standards of law', argues Holmes in one of that book's most famous passages, '[are] the standards of general application'; thus, as a matter of principle, the law has no business taking into account any of 'the infinite varieties of temperament, intellect, and education which make the internal character of a given act so different in different men.' Instead it should direct itself only to such 'external phenomena, manifest acts and omissions' as can be verified with sufficient degree of certainty, the interpretation of all such phenomena being decided in practice by the consideration of 'what would be blameworthy in the average man, the man of ordinary intelligence and prudence.'[36] Proceeding from this perspective, it followed, therefore, that in every LOC dispute the task of the legal adjudicator was not so much to determine the actual intentions of the given set of empirical parties, but rather what the 'average man' would normally understand those intentions to have been from observing the externally manifested acts and deeds exchanged between them. Or, as was declared in another English case some seven years after *Raffles v Wichelhaus*:

> If, whatever a man's real intention may be, he so conducts himself that a reasonable man would believe that he was assenting to the terms proposed by the other party, and that other party upon that belief enters into a contract with him, the man thus conducting himself would be equally bound as if he had intended to agree to the other party's terms.[37]

By the start of the new century the transition to the 'objectivist theory of contract', as the new approach would soon come to be known, was essentially completed. For a contract to arise, notes Ashley, 'there must be a mutual assent [between the parties], or, … actions which the law

---

36 See OW Holmes, *The Common Law* (Little, Brown, 1881) 108–110.

37 *Smith v Hughes* [1871] LR 6 QB 597 (per Blackburn J).

will treat as taking the place of such mutual assent,' even if that be 'contrary to the intent of [either] one of them,' so long as for 'a reasonable man ... [such] actions will fairly indicate assent on his part.'[38]

'A contract,' declared Learned Hand in the case of *Hotchkiss v City Bank of New York* in 1911, has, strictly speaking, nothing to do with the personal, or individual, intent of the parties. A contract is an obligation attached by the mere force of law to certain acts of the parties, usually words, which ordinarily accompany and represent a known intent.[39]

Note the assured terseness of Hand's closing formulation: 'words which ordinarily represent a known intent'. A large part of what gave the objectivist sensibility its internal coherence came from the classic Victorian concept of positivist social science: not only is it possible as a matter of fact to establish the objective ('intrinsic') meaning of a given set of acts but it is also possible to do so with a sufficient sense of certainty and precision. In the post-World War I world that came to know Freud and de Saussure – and Lukács too – there would be no place for such kind of naïve confidence.

Note also the rather strong functionalist undertones emerging in the second part of Hand's formula: a contract is an obligation that is created *because* the law attaches a certain kind of force to a certain set of acts. In a later case, decided some eighteen years later, Hand went on to elaborate this view further: not only the *fact* of the existence of a legally binding contractual obligation, but also its substantive content 'depend[s] upon the meaning which the law imputes to [it]' as opposed to 'what the [respective] parties actually intended.'[40]

Having started out from the idea that the old subjectivist hypothesis which reduced the enterprise of contractual dispute settlement to various forms of psychological 'fact-finding' created an excessively cumbersome and often quite unpredictable dynamic of legal practice that would perhaps be best replaced by some new approach that would allow the legal system to achieve a greater degree of analytical rigour, by the early years of the new century the objectivist theory gradually arrived at what in the eyes of the next generation of legal scholars came to be recognized as one of the most significant breakthroughs in the history of the Western legal tradition. The general philosophical label under which this breakthrough would subsequently come to be remembered was 'legal functionalism,' and what lay at its basic core was essentially the 'simple'

---

[38] C Ashley, 'Mutual Assent in Contract' (1903) 3 Col L Rev 71, 72.

[39] *Hotchkiss v National City Bank of New York*, 200 F 287 (SDNY 1911).

[40] *New York Trust Co v Island Oil & Transport Corp*, 34 F2d 655 (2nd Cir, 1929).

realization that, inasmuch as what made a particular set of social facts into a legally enforceable contract, in principle, was nothing more than whether or not it fitted with those patterns the legal system had proven through its past conduct it would lend the power of legal enforcement to, it did not ultimately make much sense to go off on the search for any kind of quasi-Platonic idea of Contract, that is to say, as a matter of LOC practice, there was no actual reason to presume the existence of any kind of conceptual master category that would unite all the different varieties of contractual arrangements under one common heading. The key to the question of what made *something* into a contract was to be sought solely in the standard indicators of the general patterns of legal enforcement, *viz.*, formal legislative pronouncements and judicial custom. Given that the basic policy configuration which stood behind each legislative act could change at any given time, it thus made no sense as a matter of common prudence to expect that the exact same set of criteria which would be relevant for the determination of the existence of a contract of sales would also apply in the case of an employment contract, a lease agreement, or a contract for the purchase of an insurance policy.

Admittedly, what is considered today the most iconic statement of the functionalist creed did not appear until the mid-1930s.[41] And yet the earlier precursors, such as this classical passage from Henry Terry's 1903 article on legal duties, seem as characteristic:

> Much labor and ingenuity have been expended in the attempt to find some general criterion of legal right and wrong [in any given field of law], some general basis of legal liability. But in vain; there is none. Various acts are commanded or forbidden for various reasons, generally on grounds of expediency; and they are different in different places and periods. In this respect the law presents itself as having a purely arbitrary or positive character, and the duties that exist in any particular system of law must simply be separately learned.[42]

In the end, the early generation of the objectivist scholars did not go on to internalize the full ramifications of the functionalist revolution. In part this happened probably because the old Platonic reflexes installed by the late 19th-century education system had proven too strong. Another possible explanation might be that it was probably felt by too many LOC practitioners that were the LOC to accept the general functionalist argument in its full extent, it would become effectively impossible for the legal system to maintain any meaningful distinction between contractual

---

41 See F Cohen, 'Transcendental Nonsense …' (n 35).

42 H Terry, 'Legal Duties and Rights' (1903) 12 Yale L J 185, 187–8.

and tortious liability,[43] and to risk that sort of instability at that point in time was deemed undesirable.[44] In any event, the basic consequence of all this was that instead of mobilizing the full field of theoretical opportunities opened by the rise of the functionalist argument at the earliest possible point, the objectivist school turned its analytical protocols backwards, seeking to work out, against its own best instincts, a new general unified theory of Contract with a capital C – and thus, more generally, the categorical boundary between the coercive order of public law and the non-coercive order of private law[45] – by substituting the old subjectivist formula of the meeting of the minds with the new formula of 'manifested assent' built, in its standard Anglo-American configuration, around three mutually defined conceptual blocks of 'offer', 'acceptance', and 'consideration.'

According to the classical objectivist approach, every legally valid contract was considered essentially an embodiment of this tripartite formula. For a legally binding contract to come into existence, thus, the principal requirement was that the parties in question in each case should follow the same basic procedure, whereby one set of highly formulaic acts (offer) was met with another set of equally formulaic acts (acceptance), the performance of a third related set of equally formulaic action (the assumption of a certain explicitly identified set of detriments by each party in return for a comparably weighty set of detriments to be assumed by the other) being treated as the metonymic stand-in for what in the subjectivist period had been conceptualized as the meeting of the minds.

b) Operative tropology

At the level of its principal discursive features, the classical objectivist approach to LOC was characterized by three main sets of tropes:

(1) The first set of tropes expressed itself in what can be described in aesthetic terms as a deep, structural commitment to the culture of procedural formalism: whether or not a given private transaction would qualify as a legally enforceable contract was determined by

---

43 As indeed was acknowledged by Clarence Ashley already as far back as 1903. See Ashley, 'Mutual Assent … ' (n 38) 78. For the classical thesis about the dissolution of LOC into the law of torts, see, of course, Gilmore, *Death of Contract* (n 23) 95 *et seq.*

44 Ibid, 96.

45 Dalton, '… Deconstruction of Contract Doctrine' (n 27) 1012–3 ('even in this objectified form, [LOC] was equated with the absence of state regulation: The parties governed themselves; better yet, each party governed itself').

simply asking whether or not the given set of procedures for the exchange of offer and acceptance had been duly observed. One of the main hinge points of this new conceptual apparatus was the so-called mirror image theory of contract formation: to form a legally valid contract, the objective scope of the tendered acceptance had to reflect exactly that of the original offer. Any discrepancy between the two automatically converted the putative acceptance into a counter-offer and thus, as it were, reactivated the negotiation.

(2) Closely related to the procedural formalist tropology was the tropology established on the basis of the doctrine of 'bargained for' detriments, the essential logic of which was that as a matter of general rule recovery in contract could be only awarded with respect to those particular detriments which the respective contracting parties had explicitly bargained for, that is, formally specified in advance as part of the 'consideration' exchange.

(3) By far the most important consequence of the objectivist revolution, at least as far as the configuration of the LOC's internal institutional balance was concerned, came, however, at the level of the new interpretative protocols. Where the old subjectivist approach had relied primarily on the logic established under the principle of private autonomy, the new model, grounded as it was in a radical anti-psychologist ethos, consistently gravitated towards the tropology of loosely decontextualized textualism, the dominant operative *topoi* here being the 'ordinary meaning of the words' doctrine and the parol evidence rule.[46]

3. The Modernist Approach to LOC

a) General outline

Unlike its predecessor, the downfall of the objectivist paradigm came by and large as a result of an essentially 'internal' logical process.

Schematically, its trajectory could be summarized as follows. Once it had been accepted that what turned a given set of social interactions into a legally valid contract was not the actual attainment of the meeting of the minds between the respective parties but only the completion of a certain set of highly formalized externally observable rituals that were

---

[46] The standard definition of the parol evidence rule reads: 'where a contract has been reduced to writing, neither party can rely on extrinsic evidence of terms alleged to have been agreed, i.e. on evidence not contained in the document'. C Mitchell, *Interpretation of Contracts* (Routledge, 2007) (quoting from Treitel).

meant to present an irrefutable evidence of such an attainment, it was really only a matter of time before the legal community started to recognize the possibility that a valid contractual relation could be created even in those situations where the parties in question had not, objectively speaking, entered into any kind of practically meaningful pattern of communication – as would be the case, for example, with contracts concluded 'through telephone operators who fail to repeat messages properly'[47] as well as any species of standard-form contracts where the parties, typically, do not even need to be aware of one another's immediate identities to be able to enter into a legally enforceable contractual relation. Since without meaningful communication there could be no expression of consent, it followed then that, despite everything that might be said at the level of the official doctrine, at the level of its actual analytical protocols the LOC practice did not really care that much about the observance of procedural formalities, which gave the lie to the old Holmesean compromise that proposed to regard the execution of such formalities as the standard expression of consent.[48] As soon as that idea began to sink in, it was only a matter of short logical deduction to discover that since in all probability none of those formalized rituals whose completion was initially identified as probatively crucial were, in fact, necessary to make a contract, what made a contract was, in truth, only a function of what the background legal regime indicated it was prepared to recognize as a contract. Put differently, if it was true indeed that 'the making of a contract does not depend on the state of the parties' minds, it depends on their overt acts,'[49] and that a direct implication of this idea would be that, in practice, 'a person is bound not by his real but by his manifested intention, [so that, in effect]

---

[47] G Costigan, 'Implied-in-Fact Contracts and Mutual Assent' (1919) 33 Harv L Rev 376, 379.

[48]

> [The] shift from a subjective to an objective theory [of contract] was part of a broader tendency to create formal, general theories that would provide uniformity, certainty, and predictability of legal arrangements. … In the process of formalizing and generalizing the system of contract law, the legal rules came to bear a more and more tenuous relationship to the actual intent of the parties. What once could be defended and justified as simply a more efficacious way of carrying out the parties' intentions came eventually to be perceived as a system that subordinated and overruled the parties' will. … Objectivism could not be reconciled with individual autonomy or voluntary agreement. (Horwitz, *Transformation* (n 23) 35–6)

[49] Holmes, *Common Law* (n 36) 307.

contracts [can] often arise where there has been no mutual assent, no meeting of the minds of the parties, in fact,'[50] then as a matter of elementary common sense it would appear to be as justified to consider as part of the LOC regime those cases where the law sought to award recovery to those plaintiffs who enjoyed the protection of a formally concluded contractual agreement as those in which it awarded recovery to those who, despite having acted in good faith and discharged their part of the bargain, did not. The moment this realization began to rise to surface, the entire objectivist paradigm was done for.

The first cracks in the edifice had begun to appear already at the turn of the century. By the early 1930s, the writing was fully on the wall: even the previously entirely essentialist doctrine of consideration received its functionalist makeover.[51]

A number of factors combined to deliver the finishing blow: the rapid expansion of the traditional doctrine of equitable estoppel[52] into what increasingly came to be known as promissory estoppel,[53] a doctrine which effectively declared that a plaintiff may recover in contract for a detriment suffered even in the absence of an actual contractual arrangement;[54] the growing recognition of the institutions of 'quasi-contracts'[55] and 'implied contracts';[56] the steady popularization of the concept of unilateral contracts and its close sibling 'option contracts created by part performance';[57] the emergence of the so-called phenomenon of the

---

[50] WW Cook, 'Agency by Estoppel' (1905) 5 Col L Rev 36, 40.

[51] See, eg, Gardner, '... Principles of the Law of Contracts' (n 2) 9: '[consideration] include[s] all acts or omissions on the part of anyone other than the promisor which, taken in connection with the promise, may be thought to afford a reason for granting a legal remedy upon its breach.'

[52] For a standard illustration, see *Ricketts v Scotthorn*, 57 Neb 51, 77 NW 365 (1898).

[53] For a standard illustration, see *Allegheny College v National Chautauqua County Bank*, 246 NY 369, 159 NE 173 (1927); *James Baird Co v Gimbel Bros*, 64 F.2d 344 (1933).

[54] For background on the evolution of the promissory estoppel doctrine, see A Konefsky, 'How to Read, or at Least Not Misread, Cardozo in the *Allegheny College* Case' (1987) 36 Buff L Rev 645.

[55] For a representative period statement on which, see W Keener, *A Treatise on the Law of Quasi-Contracts* (Baker, Voorhis, 1893).

[56] For a representative period statement on which, see Costigan, 'Implied-in-Fact Contracts ...' (n 47). For a brief note on the history of the apparent distinctions in the doctrinal treatment of quasi-contracts and implied contracts, see also Dalton, '... Deconstruction of Contract Doctrine' (n 27) 1011 *et seq.*

[57] For their basic trajectory, see S Henderson and D Baird (eds), *Dawson and Harvey's Contracts* (9th ed, Foundation Press, 2008).

'battle of forms';[58] the spreading practice of the contracts of adhesion[59] and their gradual recognition as a special case requiring the development of a separate legal regime and a much more active culture of judicial interventionism.[60]

The attack on the traditional logic of the objectivist approach proceeded along broadly two different avenues. In the first case, the main charge focused on the fundamental inability of the standard objectivist formula to account for the common realities of contractual practices; in the second, on its inadequacy and failure to protect what would be commonly considered entirely blameless parties acting *in bona fide* against the rampant abuse of their undeservedly better bargaining positions by their manipulative counterparts.

As the students of the battle of forms phenomenon repeatedly remarked:

> One need not observe modern commercial practice for very long before concluding that [many businesses] do not negotiate the details of every transaction. They prefer instead to exchange forms containing the standard terms on which they conduct business. … Consequently, the chances are pretty good that differences will exist between the seller's 'acknowledgement' or 'sales order' and the buyer's 'purchase order'. … Whatever the mechanics of the particular exchange of forms, … it is obvious that this process of achieving assent differs greatly from that presupposed by orthodox formation doctrine.[61]

How should a contract formed in this manner be executed with regard to those of its terms over which the parties' standard forms diverge? One answer that was eventually proposed can be found in the (in)famous §2-207 of the Uniform Commercial Code (UCC) 1952: in interpreting such terms the courts may assume they were never concluded and proceed to fill them in by drawing the necessary material from background law.[62] 'In effect [thus]', observes Arthur von Mehren, 'contracts

---

[58] For a basic background on which, see ibid, 451 *et seq*. See also, generally, von Mehren, '"Battle of Forms" …' (n 23).

[59] For a representative period statement, see F Kessler, 'Contracts of Adhesion: Some Thoughts about Freedom of Contract' (1943) 43 Col L Rev 629.

[60] In Gilmore's version of LOC history, it was mainly the rise of promissory estoppel that 'did it' for objectivism. See Gilmore, *Death of Contract* (n 23) 95 *et seq*. I trace the main thrust of that argument in Rasulov, 'Doctrine of Sources …' (n 24).

[61] Henderson and Baird, *Contracts* (n 57) 451.

[62] For a classical recent illustration of this approach, see *Richardson v Union Carbide*, 347 NJ Super 524 (2002) ('the conflict terms fall out and, if necessary, are replaced by the suitable gap-filler provisions').

resulting from battles of forms are treated as a particular class of indefinite or incomplete contracts.'[63] While this rather 'innovative' (as he calls it) approach has not been adopted with equal enthusiasm in Britain and France, a number of unmistakable parallels since the early 1970s could be traced in German LOC practice.[64] The common threads going through both contexts are the radical revision of the traditional division of roles between the contracting parties and the third party adjudicator in the determination of contractual meaning and the obvious erosion of boundaries between the domains of private and public law.

By contrast, in the case of the contracts of adhesion the standard line of argument proceeded in a considerably more moralist, and thus policy consideration-coloured, key. The central theme here was what Clare Dalton would later call objectivism's 'blatant abdication of responsibility.'[65]

The development of large scale enterprise with its mass production and mass distribution made a new type of contract inevitable – the standardized mass contract. A standardized contract, once its contents have been formulated by a business firm, is used in every bargain dealing with the same product or service. The weaker party, in need of the goods or services, is frequently not in a position to shop around for better terms, either because the author of the standard contract has a monopoly (natural or artificial) or because all competitors use the same clauses. His contractual intention is but a subjection more or less voluntary to terms dictated by the stronger party, terms whose consequences are often understood only in a vague way, if at all. Thus, standardized contracts are frequently contracts of adhesion; they are *à prendre ou à laisser*.[66]

By ignoring such kind of unequal distribution of bargaining power, the classical objectivist approach not only threatened to enshrine as 'freedom' what, in effect, was the most pernicious case of unconscionable coercion, it also surreptitiously assisted the coercers and the abusers in the advancement of their interests:[67]

> Freedom of contract enables enterprisers to legislate by contract and, what is even more important, to legislate in a substantially authoritarian manner

---

63 See von Mehren, '"Battle of Forms" ...' (n 23) 296.

64 Ibid, 290–4.

65 Dalton, '... Deconstruction of Contract Doctrine' (n 27) 1013.

66 Kessler, 'Contracts of Adhesion ...' (n 59) 631–2.

67 For a classical period statement developing this argument, see R Hale, 'Coercion and Distribution in a Supposedly Non-Coercive State' (1923) 38 Political Science Q 470.

> without using the appearance of authoritarian forms. Standard contracts in particular could thus become effective instruments in the hands of powerful industrial and commercial overlords enabling them to impose a new feudal order of their own making upon a vast host of vassals.[68]

The standard assumptions concerning the patterns of contractual behaviour that informed the classical objectivist theory, it followed thus, were quite evidently 'no longer apt.'[69] While this did not mean, of course, continued the argument, that the *whole* of that theory had to be summarily discarded, it certainly could not be doubted now that the classical doctrinal edifice built under its influence should no longer be maintained in its original form: 'the use of the word "contract" does not commit us to an indiscriminate extension of the ordinary contract rules to all contracts,'[70] and 'freedom of contract must mean different things for different types of contracts. Its meaning must change with the social importance of the type of contract and with the degree of monopoly enjoyed by the author of the standardized contract.'[71]

What initially had been experienced by most LOC scholars as little more than a relatively common turn to fragmentation – the explosion of quasi-contractual doctrines and the regime of promissory estoppel had already driven home the idea that instead of one single regime of LOC there should be a series of different sub-regimes many years earlier – in reality masked a much more fundamental transformation: the functionalist revolution, having stalled in its first several decades, was finally getting its homecoming in LOC.[72]

At the level of the scholarly debate, the most iconic moment of this transformation probably came with the publication of the article 'Offer and Acceptance, and Some of the Resulting Legal Relations' by Arthur Corbin, in the 1917 volume of *Yale Law Journal*. 'The rule generally laid down,' observes Corbin, implies:

> that the acts of offer and acceptance must be expressions of assent. This has long been the theory upon which contractual obligations have been enforced. The test question usually put is, what was the intention of the parties? It must not be supposed from this, however, that no contractual relation can exist

---

68 Kessler, 'Contracts of Adhesion …' (n 59) 640.

69 von Mehren, '"Battle of Forms" …' (n 23) 266.

70 Kessler, 'Contracts of Adhesion …' (n 59) 633.

71 Ibid, 642.

72 It is arguable that the beginnings of the functionalist breakthrough can be traced at least as far back as Holmes's seminal essay 'The Path of the Law.' See OW Holmes, 'The Path of the Law' (1897) 10 Harv L Rev 457.

> unless the parties both foresaw and intended it. If two parties have gone through the form of offering and accepting, the law determines the legal relations that follow. Frequently these come with surprise and shock to the parties themselves.[73]

The standard explanation for this state of affairs, observes Corbin, reflects the classical objectivist assumption that the parties will be 'bound by the reasonable meaning of what they said and not by what they thought' because this should enable the courts to 'carry out the intentions of the parties in the great majority of cases.' The actual reality of legal practice, however, does not seem to offer that much support for this conclusion:

> The legal relations consequent upon offer and acceptance are not wholly dependent *even upon the reasonable meaning of the words and acts of the parties*. The law determines these relations in the light of subsequent circumstances, these often being totally unforeseen by the parties. In such cases it is sometimes said that the law will create that relation which the parties would have intended had they foreseen [it]. *The fact is, however, that the decision will depend [solely] upon the notions of the court as to policy, welfare, justice, right and wrong, such notions often being inarticulate and subconscious.*[74]

From the 'intention of the parties' to the 'reasonable meaning of words', to 'not even the reasonable meaning of words', to 'the law determines' and the 'decisions depend on the notions of policy, welfare, justice and morality' – two pages of text, half a century worth of theoretical progress.

The logic of Corbin's closing comment left no room for doubt: as objectivism's foundational fictions of manifest assent and the reasonable man standard lost their analytical purchase, the whole concept of LOC as an inherently distinct legal phenomenon evaporated into thin air. If the decision to enforce a particular set of private expectation under the heading of LOC was effectively really only a question of *public policy*, what reason was there not to accept this fact 'in the open'? And if one accepted it in full, what reason was there then to prevent one from going one more step further and noting that, if only one looked at it closely

---

[73] A Corbin, 'Offer and Acceptance, and Some of the Resulting Legal Relations' (1917) 26 Yale L J 169, 204–5.

[74] Ibid, 206 (emphasis added).

enough, the law of contracts, like the law of property and tort, was, in fact, quite indistinguishable from public law?[75]

'From this point of view,' declared Morris Cohen in one of the most often quoted passages in LOC history, 'the law of contract may be viewed as a subsidiary branch of public law.'[76] For, indeed, in some sense, it can easily be said that it:

> ha[s] a function somewhat parallel to that of the criminal law. Both serve to standardize conduct by penalizing departures from the legal norm. Not only by decrees of specific performance or by awards of damages, but also by treating certain contracts as void or voidable and thus withholding its support from those who do not conform to its prescribed forms, does the law of contract in fact impose penalties.[77]

Speaking about LOC in this way seemed a far cry from the heyday of the will theory approach. And yet the true extent of the paradigmatic rupture brought on by the modernist age was even greater at the level of its underpinning analytical regime.

Operative tropology

There were five main parts to the modernist paradigm. In discursive terms, in the main, they expressed themselves as follows:

(1) Comprehensive displacement of the Platonic analytical vocabulary by one constructed around a nominalist-functionalist outlook grounded in a decidedly positivistic reasoning protocol, the central respective tropes of which being anti-formalism and the arguments that 'a contract is what a contract does' and 'a contract is whatever the law is prepared to recognize as a contract';

(2) Explicit endorsement of the proportionalist aesthetic as an indispensable element of practical legal reasoning, as articulated through the idea that 'everything is balancing' (all forms of legal decision-making, including interpretation, are ultimately nothing but balancing exercises), repeated acknowledgement that 'every legal act is a product of conflicting considerations,' and recurrent references to conceptions of public policy;

---

[75] On which, see, classically, Hale, 'Coercion ...' (n 67); M Cohen, 'The Basis of Contract' (n 32); M Cohen, 'Property and Sovereignty' (1927) 13 Cornell L Q 8; L Green, 'Tort Law Public Law in Disguise' (1959) 38 Tex L Rev 1; (1960) 38 Tex L Rev 257.

[76] Cohen, 'The Basis of Contract' (n 32) 586.

[77] Ibid, 589.

(3) A culture of consistent disregard for 'conceptual purity,' as expressed through endorsement of descriptive eclecticism, opportunistic use of discursive forms lifted from presumably entirely incomparable contexts, and the systematic blurring of the traditional doctrinal categories, as exemplified by the regular importation of the analytical categories and vocabularies from the fields of tort law, the law of unjustified enrichment, property law, and so on, and the elimination of traditional boundaries between the public and the private legal orders, contract and equity, misfeasance and nonfeasance, and so on;

(4) Rejection of the 'single model of contract' approach, as expressed through repeated invocation of such tropes as Llewellyn's 'narrow issue thinking,' depiction of the LOC landscape as potentially endlessly fragmentable, and the decisive replacement at the level of the dominant operative principles of the old Procrustean offer-acceptance-consideration formulaism in favour of the new, considerably more fluid mix comprised of the doctrines of 'injurious reliance,' 'unequal bargaining powers,' 'object and purpose interpretation,' 'contextual interpretation,' and the principle of good faith;

(5) Enthusiastic acceptance of the culture of judicial activism, as expressed through the rise of such doctrinal clusters as UCC §2-207, implied contracts, and quasi-contracts and the progressive displacement of the language of 'donative promises' by that of promissory estoppel and the principle of legitimate expectations.[78]

4. Further Methodological Clarifications

Each of the three models described above represents a certain regime of analytical predispositions, or a system of discursive *habitus*, if you will. In that context each of them finds its 'material expression' not in any particular collection of first-order substantive legal rules, let alone a specific configuration of political or moral positions, but in a certain structure of reasoning patterns, or, if one is willing to use this metaphor, a certain *mode of legal consciousness*.[79] To make an argument about the presence of any such model in the context of the LOTR discourse, on this view of things, would be to claim the discovery of the characteristic giveaway signs of the respective operative tropologies.

---

[78] On this last point, see also Konefsky, 'How to Read …' (n 54).

[79] For further discussion of this concept, see Kennedy, *Rise and Fall* (n 28) 11–14, and Kennedy, 'Three Globalizations …' (n 22) 22–3.

IV. THE LOGIC OF THE CONTRACTUAL ANALOGY: CACOPHONY OR USELESSNESS?

A fundamental contradiction plagues the internal organization of the contemporary LOTR regime. As long as it has been able to remember itself, the classical LOTR doctrine has regularly drawn on various building blocks of the traditional LOC vocabulary, using them to articulate its principal operative concepts, express its central postulates, and fix its most fundamental assumptions about itself. In the course of time, this regime of systematic rhetorical cross-subsidization, one might say, has proved itself essential not just to the simple everyday task of the practical stabilization of its various structural elements but to the emergence of the very idea of LOTR itself. And yet even the briefest glance at the manner in which this regime has been set up in practice suggests the presence of a widespread pattern of fraud behind its otherwise decidedly unremarkable façade.

Historically, the central enabling premise has been the basic silent assumption that somewhere in the background, behind all its various complications, there must exist, somehow, a single, internally unified, universally valid model of 'pure LOC' – a stable analytical benchmark that expresses some kind of objective essential truth about what contracts really are, what it takes for a contract to become a contract, and what and why, therefore, must be the most correct manner to approach contracts in practice. As the discussion in the preceding section shows, all the available historical evidence that we have today about the evolution of LOC unequivocally demonstrates the fundamental indefensibility of this assumption. Neither now nor at any other stage in the past has there existed within the analytical space of the LOC discourse such a thing as a single unified model of 'pure' contract. What is more, at least since the beginning of the interwar period, and quite possibly even before that, the historical archive of the LOC tradition has been populated by at least three, entirely different, and in many ways mutually irreconcilable, competing paradigms, each of which projected its own pattern of operative tropes, giving rise to a correspondingly distinct mode of legal consciousness.

Even the shortest glance at the most salient patterns of the modern LOTR discourse shows that one could easily find traces of each one of these three paradigms in the internal theoretical fabric of the contemporary LOTR discourse. Equally importantly, it should also not be that difficult to demonstrate that not one of these paradigms can, in fact, be adjusted to the existing realities of the LOTR discourse sufficiently closely to make it possible for the latter to be subsumed exclusively under that one paradigm. Each of them, in other words, is structurally indispensable, meaning that it would not be possible even in principle to explain the existing LOTR materials in terms of any one of these paradigms alone; nor would it be possible to 'clean up' the current configuration of these materials in such a way as to allow that, without changing the structure of the existing doctrinal edifice beyond all recognition.

Even more crucially, it should also not be that difficult to show how and why each of these paradigms would in fact be entirely unsuitable for the purposes of such a clean-up/subsumption exercise on the grounds that its animating logic would go squarely against what would be commonly considered the 'fundamental tenets' of the international legal order. The contours of how that argument might be constructed can be summarized as follows:

(1) Historically, the great majority of LOC's main operative doctrines and their enabling analytical protocols have been developed with a view to providing a blueprint for a legal regime designed for the regulation of an essentially bilateral pattern of contractual transactions. For the last one hundred years at least, the principal thrust of the LOTR doctrinal effort has been focused on the production of rules intended for the organization of a decidedly multilateral treaty-making context. A system of analytical dispositions structured by an orientation towards bilateral patterns is by definition extremely ill-suited for the development of a system of dispositions designed for a multilateralist context. Public law theory has discussed this matter at great length, explaining the implications of the radical disjunction between private interest and public interest dynamics. So have welfare economics and the newly emerging 'political science' of the commons.[80]

(2) While it can certainly still be considered one of the main sacred cows of liberal political theory, as the discussion in the preceding section shows, in the historical evolution of LOC the doctrine of *l'autonomie de la volonté* has proved to be neither theoretically essential nor ideologically indispensable. It would be impossible to imagine, however, that the equivalent doctrinal cluster built around

[80] The most relevant strand of the debate here probably would be that which focuses on the so-called 'tragedy of the commons' problem; for the classical introduction to which see G Hardin, 'The Tragedy of the Commons' (1968) 162 Science 1243.

the concept of sovereign consent could be dispensed with equally effortlessly in the LOTR doctrine. The same holds true for the LOTR equivalent of the LOC doctrine of the 'master of the offer,'[81] without the summary displacement of which, of course, the possibility of the emergence of the modernist approach as described earlier becomes distinctly unlikely.

(3) Any attempt to construct what could be considered a LOTR equivalent of the classical objectivist model of LOC would have to contend from the very first step with the virtually insurmountable challenge of developing a 'local' version of the reasonable man standard that would be *sufficiently concretized* to resemble an operable legal doctrine and at the same time not open the road for the revival of the old racist-colonialist doctrine of the 'standard of civilization,' What is more, even if it were possible to resolve this particular challenge successfully, what would one do then about the fact that the reasonable man of modern private law, at his root, is essentially a petty-bourgeois philistine: an 'average man', as Holmes put it, 'of ordinary intelligence and prudence'? What would an 'average State of ordinary intelligence and prudence' look like and how could this concept be meaningfully translated into a legal test? Granted, the 'ordinary prudence' part of the standard could, in principle, be assimilated to the doctrine of 'peace-loving states,' as developed, for instance, in the context of Article 4 of the United Nations Charter (1945).[82] But how exactly is one meant to determine then what ought to count as 'ordinary intelligence' among States?

One can go on adding other strands and sub-strands to the argument, but the basic thrust of it should already be clear, just as it should also be clear that it does not try to suggest *as a matter of descriptive claim* that the modern LOTR regime has *not*, in fact, tried to adopt any of these model solutions, by, for example, enacting a LOC-style objectivist protocol of treaty interpretation or attempting to overcome its deep ideological commitment to the principle of sovereign consent by developing a modernist-style epistemological disposition. Quite on the contrary: what this argument *does* try to suggest, rather, is that the way in which these enactments and adaptations were carried out in practice has

---

[81] See Henderson and Baird, *Contracts* (n 57) 335.

[82] On which see famously, though not perhaps very helpfully, *Conditions of Admission of a State to Membership in the United Nations*, Advisory Opinion, ICJ Reports 1948 (28 May) 57.

at the very best created a completely self-contradictory, randomly syncopated, cacophonous space of ideas and half-aborted sub-regime fragments. One only needs to cast the briefest look at the standard building blocks of the modern LOTR regime to see the sheer scale of this cacophony.

1. The Cacophony of LOTR

Consider, for starters, the standard definition given to the term 'treaty' in modern LOTR: an international agreement regardless of its official designation or form, whether embodied in a single instrument or in two or more related instruments, that is concluded between States or international organizations and governed by international law. The modernist ethos could hardly have been expressed more effectively: to create a legally enforceable treaty relation, the contracting parties can reduce their agreement to any desired form, including, if they so please, a series of exchange of *notes verbales* or any other type of 'separate documents which [are] not jointly signed by the parties.'[83] What is more, even if it is concluded in an oral form, the agreement in question can still qualify as a legally valid treaty. Although it is not clear how relevant this scenario might be in modern diplomatic practice, the official doctrinal position on the matter seems rather unequivocal: the only thing that matters *de lege lata* is the 'existence of a record of an agreement.'[84] A popular example typically offered in illustration of this scenario is the Danish–Norwegian 'exchange' in the *Legal Status of Eastern Greenland* case,[85] a pattern which at first glance may seem a little misleading, but which in fact is actually rather revealing. To be sure, from the rigid taxonomic point of view the *Eastern Greenland* precedent presents one of the most awkward challenges. The Court itself, notoriously, refused to be drawn into any classificatory games,[86] and while in his dissenting opinion Judge Anzilotti did state that on the facts of the case it had been made clear that a binding 'international agreement' was created between the two States

---

83 P Gautier, 'Article 2', in Corten and Klein, *Vienna Conventions* (n 18) 33, 37.

84 Ibid, 38 (quoting from an early report by the Special Rapporteur Hersch Lauterpacht).

85 *Legal Status of Eastern Greenland (Denmark v Norway)*, Judgment, PCIJ 1933 Series A/B, No 53.

86 Although it did consider it 'beyond all dispute' that the Norwegian response gave rise to 'an unconditional and definitive undertaking' on its part (ibid, 71–2).

'by means of purely verbal declarations,'[87] most subsequent commentators have tended to locate the legal basis for Norway's assumption of obligation either under the rubric of something that looks suspiciously like the 1970s-style 'unilateral declarations' doctrine,[88] the principle of good faith, or, as McNair repeatedly proposed, estoppel[89] (in its non-territorial sense).[90] Confusion of this kind, naturally, could rarely be commendable, but for diagnostic purposes, given the earlier observations about the discursive symptomatology of the modernist paradigm, it is priceless. Regardless of what might be the most appropriate classification of the basis of decision in the *Eastern Greenland* case, the very pattern of disagreement between the secondary sources is in itself extremely revealing: even where the doctrinal position would openly disagree that the situation in question resulted in the creation of an international treaty in the classical sense of the word,[91] it still found no difficulty in treating the ensuing 'hybrid' regime as being legally binding in the exact same way as if it had, using, moreover, in justification of this view the exact same set of tropes and doctrinal clusters – unilateral agreements, injurious reliance, good faith, promissory estoppel – that characterize the standard line of modernist reasoning.

An equally strong sense of modernist orientation can also be picked up from the way in which the doctrine has traditionally framed the 'essential legal character' (or as Gautier calls it 'minimum legal content') debate. How should international law distinguish between legally binding treaties and those 'formal international instruments which … are [by their] nature statements of policy'?[92] As a recent authoritative commentary on the 1969 Vienna Convention on the Law of Treaties (VCLT)[93] remarks, the standard position on this question has always been that '[i]n this matter, the decisive criterion is the creation of legal rights and obligations.'[94] The underlying test on which the categorical determination turns, in other

---

87 Ibid, 91.

88 For a discussion of the strengths and weaknesses of this particular classification, see A Rubin, 'The International Legal Effects of Unilateral Declarations' (1977) 71 AJIL 1, 4.

89 Lord McNair, *The Law of Treaties* (OUP, 1961) 486–7.

90 It is one of the peculiarities of international legal usage that the concept of estoppel in international law is typically reserved for the discussion of the law of territorial disputes. For a classic illustration, see I Sinclair, 'Estoppel and Acquiscence', in Lowe and Fitzmaurice, *Fifty Years at the ICJ* (n 10) 104.

91 See MacNair, *Law of Treaties* (n 89) 10.

92 Gautier, 'Article 2' (n 83) 43 (quoting Lauterpacht).

93 Vienna Convention on the Law of Treaties, 1969, 1155 UNTS 331.

94 Gautier, 'Article 2' (n 83) 43–4.

words, is that agreements which 'create neither rights nor obligation for the parties are … of no significance from the point of view of the law of treaties.'[95] Put differently, to resolve a question of status – whether or not a given international agreement qualifies as a treaty – the correct approach is to establish the performance of a specific function – to establish whether or not it creates a set of what in the eyes of LOTR would be considered legally recognizable rights and obligations. The functionalist line – a contract is what a contract does; a contract does what the law says it does – could not have been articulated more vividly.

Turning to the rules relating to the conclusion and entry into force one finds the same basic dynamic. To be sure, one can still easily make the case that with its strong emphasis on proceduralism and rituals the modern LOTR regime appears to retain a distinctly pre-modernist aesthetic on this front. But its two main focal points – the rules encapsulated in terms of the VCLT taxonomy in Articles 11 and 18 – quite unmistakably seem to carry in them a very significant dose of the anti-formalist ethos. The former establishes a fairly broad range of procedural options that are open to the contracting parties when it comes to choosing the means for the expression of consent-to-be-bound; especially when read in conjunction with such provisions as Article 13(b) or 14(1)(b), this approach implies a high measure of disregard not only for the culture of procedural formalism specifically but also for the whole broader idea of procedural uniformity. The latter, long recognized as one of the two principal components of the LOTR version of the principle of good faith,[96] describes a set of obligations which in a weird anachronistic twist, although being established only in consequence, and within the scope, of the given treaty, appear to enter into force even *before* that treaty itself has done so. What is more, even though it may not be immediately clear what specific range of remedies would be available for the violation of these obligations, there does not seem to exist any doubt, as a matter of doctrinal consensus, that such violations 'must be able to trigger the responsibility of the [respective] State.'[97] A doctrine that recognizes the existence of duties arising *ex contractu* that become enforceable even before the respective contractual bond is duly finalized – what could be a more obvious illustration of the idea of quasi-contract and the 'reliance on a promise' approach?[98]

---

95 Ibid, 44 (quoting James Brierly).

96 L Bousson de Chazournes et al, 'Article 18', in Corten and Klein, *Vienna Conventions* (n 18) 369, 371.

97 Ibid, 402–3.

98 See Henderson and Baird, *Contracts* (n 57) 261.

What holds true for the regime relating to the conclusion of treaties appears also, at first glance, to hold true for the regime relating to treaty interpretation. As the conventional wisdom has it, historically, three main schools of thought have dominated the course of the doctrinal debate in this sub-field of LOTR.[99] The 'intentions of the parties' school began from the assumption that all international legal documents must be interpreted in the light of the (presumed) intentions entertained by their drafters at the time of their conclusion. The operative tropology here, predictably enough, has tended to revolve around the will theory model, the principle of private autonomy, and the meeting-of-the-minds doctrine. The textualist school, by contrast, insisted that every legal document had to be interpreted according to the ordinary-meaning-of-the-words approach, the source of which invariably was to be found within the respective document's text. The operative logic here, rather evidently, mirrored that of the classical objectivist model. Finally, the so-called teleological school appeared to propose that every treaty ought to be interpreted with a view to giving force to its underlying objectives and goals, that is, in such a manner as to increase the likelihood of successfully realizing these objectives and goals in practice. Since no meaningful test could be specified for how one was supposed to ascertain all of a given treaty's objectives and goals, the resulting reasoning protocols inevitably turned towards the same rhetorical clusters as 'public policy reasoning,' 'balancing considerations,' and 'contextual interpretation.'

As one would expect, numerous attempts have been made over the years to resolve the question of which of the three approaches ought to be given precedence.[100] None of these attempts, however, have met with any success as a matter of *lex lata*. Neither the State practice before and after it, nor the Vienna Conference itself managed to work out anything approaching a clear resolution. What is more, it seems in neither case had there been any real effort towards that end.

Writing from the height of his illustrious judicial career, in 1961, McNair put the matter most succinctly when stating that the only meaningful conclusion that could be gleaned from the existing practice

---

[99] See GG Fitzmaurice, 'The Law and Procedure of the International Court of Justice: Treaty Interpretation and Certain Other Treaty Points' (1951) 28 BYIL 1, 1–2; I Sinclair, 'Vienna Conference on the Law of Treaties' (1970) 19 ICLQ 47, 61; A Aust, *Modern Treaty Law and Practice* (CUP, 2000) 185; M Shaw, *International Law* (5th ed, CUP, 2003) 839.

[100] For one of the most impressive recent displays of such 'legal mathematics,' see, eg, U Linderfalk, *On the Interpretation of Treaties* (Springer, 2007).

was that the main task of all interpretative work was to give effect to the *manifest intentions* of the parties as 'expressed in the words used by them *in the light of the surrounding circumstances*,' while all the various maxims and canons that have come to abound in textbooks and elsewhere were, ultimately, only so many helpful tools that undoubtedly could provide a source of *useful contextual inspiration*, when one is seeking for the most appropriate *balance*, but could hardly be treated as binding rules to be followed as such.[101] Eight years later the drafters of Part III (3) of the VCLT seemed to echo the same sentiment of anti-doctrinaire eclecticism by deciding to back every horse in the race[102] and lump all three schools of interpretation into one single 'super canon,' without establishing any internal hierarchy among them other than by tentatively relegating the intentions approach to the rank of 'supplementary' methodologies. As if to make sure that the message that eclecticism ought to rule the day was not lost on the reader, the resulting melange was then further sprinkled for good measure by yet another series of references to the notions of contextual equity and good faith.[103]

Stepping outside the Vienna context, one only has to cast the briefest look to find the same sensibility reveal itself over and over across different segments of the literature. A good decade before McNair, another prominent British international lawyer, Sir Gerald Fitzmaurice, at the time the second legal adviser at the UK Foreign Office, had remarked in an article purporting to summarize the general state of the law on the question:

> There has lately been a revolt against the over-elaboration of rules of interpretation [which] in its more extreme form amounts virtually to a rejection of such rules as being confusing and of little practical value in application. According to this view, the rules contradict or cancel each other out, or have to be applied with so many exceptions or variations that the rule itself tends to be lost sight of. It would be better therefore to ... accept the fact that in the last resort all interpretation must consist in the exercise of common sense by the judge, applied in good faith and with intelligence.[104]

---

[101] See McNair, *Law of Treaties* (n 89) 365–6 (emphasis added).

[102] It bears noting in this context that this part of the Convention was adopted without a single dissenting vote at the Vienna Conference. See E Jiménez de Aréchaga, 'International Law in the Past Third of a Century' (1978-I) 159 Recueil des Cours 1, 42.

[103] For background on the debates relating to this question during the Vienna Conference, see Sinclair, 'Vienna Conference ...' (n 99) 62–6.

[104] See Fitzmaurice, 'Law and Procedure ...' (n 99) 2–3.

Note the strongly pronounced functionalist motif and the obvious parallels with Henry Terry's 'there is no single logic' and Corbin's 'it's all down to the judges' preconceived notions.'

Half a century later the same discursive trajectory could also be uncovered in another seminal text on LOTR written by another ex-Foreign Office lawyer, Anthony Aust, subsequently a professor at University College London. Having reviewed the recent trends of international practice, Aust in an easily discernible parallel with McNair and Fitzmaurice notes that the most reasonable view of the matter of treaty interpretation would be that however many good arguments might be made *in abstracto* in support of any given set of interpretative canons, in practice the interpretative process always returns to the same basic solution: the key to any interpretative challenge must be sought partly in the text of the treaty itself,[105] partly in common sense,[106] but mostly in the exercise of holistic contextual analysis,[107] which, if need be, may be defined as including the duty of the interpreting agent to read into the text of the treaty provisions which it does not otherwise contain, under the rubric of the 'implied terms' doctrine.[108] Whatever reasoning protocol may crystallize from this basis, it seems safe to conclude, could never be reduced to any single logical scheme.[109] For even though the theoretical pedigree behind the traditional canons of interpretation may seem unassailable, in the end none of them can do anything more than provide a useful starting point for an enterprise whose logical culmination will always be in the act of contextual balancing. Because no matter how faithfully one may try to apply any of them, it seems invariable that they will 'offer more than one possible result'[110] and so will need to be used 'with special care' and never trusted blindly.[111]

A more typical modernist statement-of-creed would be difficult to imagine; and yet it would be certainly incorrect to conclude at this point that the law of interpretation has all just been one large playfield for the classical modernist paradigm. For, indeed, as soon as one broadens the scope of one's examination beyond the writings of career diplomats and judges, a completely different pattern of tropes starts to emerge. Freed

---

105 Aust, *Treaty Law* (n 99) 187.
106 Ibid, 202.
107 Ibid.
108 Ibid, 201.
109 Ibid, 187.
110 D French, 'Treaty Interpretation and the Incorporation of Extraneous Legal Rules' (2006) 55 ICLQ 281.
111 Aust, *Treaty Law* (n 99) 201.

from the 'inbred professional inhibitions' of the harried practitioner and the unprincipled negotiator, the 'Doctrine of international law,' writes Georg Schwarzenberger on the eve of the 1969 Vienna Conference, overwhelmingly seems to support the view that the object of all treaty interpretation is to give effect to nothing more than the *expressed intentions* of the contracting States *as contained in the actual language used by them*, subject to the implicit requirements of equity and *reasonableness*.[112] Most of the standard canons of interpretation offered in the literature, remarks Ian Brownlie some thirty years later, appear vague, contradictory, and question-begging. Nevertheless, a critical examination of the applicable case law and the relevant segments of State practice quite unambiguously tends to suggest 'that what matters [at all times] is the intention of the parties *as expressed in the text*, which is the best guide to the more recent common intention of the parties'.[113] Even where the interpretative task can only be concluded by adopting a 'systemic integration' approach[114] which rejects the view that any given treaty can be treated as a self-contained regime and requires the interpretative agent to look beyond the four corners of the treaty, the dominant principle, it is regularly asserted, still 'must be the ordinary meaning of the terms,'[115] for just as the 'determination of object and purpose may be deceptive,' 'reference to *travaux préparatoires* … is unlikely to assist' much, if at all.[116]

Even McNair himself before his ascension to the bench seemed to sing from the same hymn sheet, putting the Holmesean tropology of reasonableness at the centre of his theoretical construct: 'all treaties must be interpreted according to their *reasonable* sense,' 'the terms used in a treaty must be interpreted according to their *usual meaning in the language of everyday life*,' 'it is taken for granted that the contracting parties intend something *reasonable* … , if, therefore, the meaning of a stipulation is ambiguous, *the reasonable meaning is to be preferred*';[117] nevertheless, 'in case of a discrepancy between the clear meaning of a

---

[112] See G Schwarzenberger, 'Myths and Realities of Treaty Interpretation' (1968) 9 Va J Intl L 1 (emphasis added).

[113] I Brownlie, *Principles of Public International Law* (5th ed, OUP, 1998) 632 (emphasis added).

[114] C McLachlan, 'Investment Treaties and General International Law' (2008) 57 ICLQ 361, 369.

[115] Ibid, 371, 399.

[116] Ibid, 371–2.

[117] A McNair, *Oppenheim's International Law: Volume 1 (Peace)* (4th ed, Longmans, Green and Company, 1928) (emphasis added).

stipulation and the intentions of the parties as unanimously declared during the negotiations which preceded the signing of the treaty, the meaning which corresponds to the *real intentions* of the parties must prevail over *the meaning of the text*.'[118]

And yet, how does one work out what the 'real intentions of the parties' may have been in situations that involve highly complex legal and economic categories, such as, for example, the concept of 'fair and equitable treatment' in international investment law, which in all likelihood may have never been clearly understood by the respective signatories themselves beyond the vague notion that it might be a good idea to include a reference to them somewhere in the final draft? Should one go back to the subjectivist-style vision of interpretation as a species of forensic inquiry? It seems obvious that 'in relation to [such provisions], there is rarely [found] any linguistic ambiguity latent in their formulation,' which is to say that 'nothing [can be] gained by resorting to dictionary definitions of "fair" and "equitable."'[119] Inevitably, then, one gravitates back to the idea of contextual balancing, which if the patterns of arbitral practice are anything to go by, is going to mean not only drawing on the vague preambular provisions under the rubric of 'transforming policies into principles,'[120] but also grounding the less convincing aspects of the proposed solution in the fiction of the 'demands' imposed by the 'particular circumstances of the case.'[121]

Furthermore, as a recent comprehensive review of the newly emergent International Centre for Settlement of Investment Disputes jurisprudence reveals, even where the operative tropologies used by the arbitral bodies tend to focus around the objectivist language of reasonableness, the real animating dynamic behind them in terms of their narrative-creating effects often turns out to be that which would be typically expected from a more modernist-style theoretical outlook: advancement of the project of judicial activism,[122] infusion of public policy considerations into legal reasoning, reorganization of rules-based analytical tasks into balancing exercises purporting to '[take] into account a much broader legal and

---

118 Ibid, 763.

119 Z Douglas, *The International Law of Investment Claims* (CUP, 2009) 82.

120 Ibid, 83.

121 Ibid, 87.

122 For a more general characterization of the phenomenon of judicial activism in modern international law, see F Zarbiev, 'Judicial Activism in International Law: A Conceptual Framework for Analysis' (2012) 3 J Intl Dispute Settlement 247.

political context' than would otherwise be implied by the treaty in question.[123]

Turning from the law of interpretation to other standard topics of modern LOTR the underlying theoretical cacophony hardly seems any less strongly pronounced. In an earlier essay addressing the history of LOTR I have endeavoured to explore the general discursive organization behind the modern law of reservations. As I argued there, a close scrutiny of the historical trajectory of this segment of LOTR up until the emergence of the Vienna regime quite unequivocally seems to suggest a very strong tilt in favour of the classical objectivist paradigm.[124] Despite an occasional irruption of modernist tropes, coming into the 1990s the essential theoretical foundations of the modern law of reservations thus had remained firmly grounded in the standard reasoning protocols of the objectivist approach. But then came the infamous attempt by the Human Rights Committee in its General Comment No. 24[125] to engineer a new system of centralized appraisal and oversight. And even though that reform initiative almost immediately failed,[126] the usual modernist mixture of tropes – policy balancing, community interests, public regime considerations, and so on – took no time to explode all over the accompanying scholarly discourse, a trend that nearly two decades down the line shows no signs of abatement.[127]

If the 'technical segment' of the LOTR doctrine seems to show few signs of theoretical orderliness, the internal organization of the LOTR discourse relating to the more foundational questions reveals an even more schizophrenic pattern. As any student of the subject will be able to recall, it was not that long ago that one of the most popular schools of thought on the question of what exactly constitutes the legal basis of the treaty-making process was the view that, to quote Tunkin, '[a]greement, as a means of creating norms of contemporary international law, is the

---

123 OK Fauchald, 'The Legal Reasoning of ICSID Tribunals: An Empirical Analysis' (2008) 19 EJIL 301, 353–4.

124 See Rasulov, '… Modern Law of Reservations …' (n 24) 168–99.

125 Human Rights Committee, General Comment No. 24 (52), *General Comment on Issues Relating to Reservations Made upon Ratification or Accession to the Covenant or the Optional Protocols thereto, or in Relation to Declarations under Article 41 of the Covenant*, UN Doc. CCPR/C/21/Rev.1/Add.6 (1994).

126 Rasulov, '… Modern Law of Reservations …' (n 24) 111–20.

127 See, eg, E Baylis, 'General Comment No. 24: Confronting the Problem of Reservations to Human Rights Treaties' (1999) 17 Berkeley J Intl L 277; R Goodman, 'Human Rights Treaties, Invalid Reservations, and State Consent' (2002) 96 AJIL 531; E Swaine, 'Reserving' (2006) 31 Yale J Intl L 307.

result of the *co-ordination of wills* of different States.'[128] Even to this day it remains a commonplace among the LOTR scholars to affirm as a matter of discursive routine that *the principle of sovereign consent* constitutes the sole ground 'for the coming into being of legal obligations by way of treaty,'[129] and that 'in a legal order where restrictions on states are not to be presumed lightly' it is only logical that the *principle of intent*, at the very least, must provide 'one of the main determinants of international legal rights and obligations'[130] and should otherwise be considered 'controlling.'[131] Equally significantly, for the vast majority of international lawyers it still holds true that the one distinguishing factor which separates non-binding international agreements from legally binding treaties is the presence of the requisite meeting of the minds among the parties concerning that very question:

> a treaty ... require[s] an *intention by the parties* to create legal rights and obligations or to establish relations governed by international law. If that *intention* does not exist, an agreement is considered to be without legal effect ('sans portée juridique').[132]

For all its protestations about the extreme impracticality of any theory of interpretation centred on the idea of examining subjective states of mind, taken in such contexts the LOTR doctrine's rhetorical protocols still seem rather heavily engrossed in the conceptual imagery and standard vocabulary[133] of the classical will theory approach.

And yet one may also recall at this point that curious passage in the *Qatar v Bahrain* case,[134] in which the ICJ, having remarked that it did not find it necessary to consider what might have been the actual intentions of the relevant State officials when signing the text, appeared

---

[128] Tunkin, 'Co-Existence ...' (n 17) 34 (emphasis added).

[129] C Tomuschat, 'International Law: Ensuring the Survival of Mankind on the Eve of a New Century' (1999) 281 Recueil des Cours 9, 311.

[130] J Klabbers, *The Concept of Treaty in International Law* (Kluwer Law International, 1996) 68.

[131] de Aréchaga, 'International Law ...' (n 102) 35–7.

[132] O Schachter, 'The Twilight Existence of Nonbinding International Agreements' (1977) 71 AJIL 296, 296–7 (emphasis added).

[133] Note, for instance, the language used to frame the opening statement of the section on the conclusion of treaties in Ian Brownlie's iconic text: 'The manner in which treaties are negotiated and brought into force is *governed by the intention* and *consent* of the parties.' See Brownlie, *Principles* (n 113) 610 (emphasis added).

[134] *Maritime Delimitation and Territorial Questions (Qatar v Bahrain)*, Judgment, ICJ Rep 1994 (1 July) 112.

to imply its readiness to 'find' a treaty where none had apparently been intended as a matter of the underlying sovereign consent, relying solely on the external form of the respective textual record.[135] To be sure, the particular set of circumstances to which the Court had reacted in that case were so unique that the precedential value of that pronouncement in all likelihood should be considered non-existent. But what matters here is not that aspect of the judgment but rather the fact that the Court's argument appears to have been made in terms of a tropology that had already long been put in place, that is, a theoretical model that had already been long internalized as part of the LOTR doctrine's ideational fabric.

To add an even further layer of complexity: if one also looks at the way that judgment has subsequently been received into the disciplinary consciousness, another distinct pattern of theoretical reaction that arose from it in recent years has been the intensification of the broader doctrinal debate about the possibility that, as Jan Klabbers puts it, 'when states enter into commitments,' the only possible reaction which the international community will have to these commitments, unless some magical verbal formula has been used, will be to view them as invariably giving rise to a treaty.[136] Again, it is not so much the correctness of this particular deduction as the terms of the debate in which it is framed that ought to merit critical consideration. The reason why that is the case can be gleaned from the following observation made by Christian Tomuschat in his Hague Academy lectures.

Turning his attention to the problem of the so-called unilateral declarations, Professor Tomuschat remarks:

> particular care is required in assessing the legal connotation of unilateral declarations. ... Above all, it must not be overlooked that when making a unilateral declaration a State receives no consideration. It commits itself without obtaining a corresponding advantage in juridical terms. For this

---

135 Cf Tomuschat, 'International Law ...' (n 129) 310:

> [I]n the case between Qatar and Bahrain dispute arose ... over the interpretation of the minutes of a meeting where recourse to the ICJ had been envisaged for the settlement of a boundary dispute. With exceptional firmness, the ICJ stated that it had to base itself on the plain meaning of the text which had been agreed upon. It did not matter whether both parties had been fully aware of the legal significance of what they had signed. This decision deserves full approval. For the sake of reliability in international relations, what matters is not the will as it may have existed internally, but the will as it was manifested towards the other party involved.

136 See J Klabbers, *International Law* (CUP, 2013) 45.

> reason, the binding character of unilateral declarations cannot have the same strength as the *pacta sunt servanda* rule with regard to treaties. States must be able to repeal their engagement, provided that they take care of the confidence which they have engendered. No denunciation with immediate effect could be considered to be permissible. The addressees of the declaration concerned must be given sufficient time to adapt to the new situation brought about by the revocation of the original pledge. But a possible rule of *promissio est servanda* cannot have the same rigidity as the corresponding rule applying to treaty engagements.[137]

Does the doctrine of consideration really matter so much in modern LOTR as Tomuschat's argument seems to imply? The answer would certainly be: not at all. According to the traditional understanding, the concept of consideration has no place in the ideational landscape of the modern LOTR. The same goes for 'pledge' taken as a juridical category. And yet note the obvious implications of Tomuschat's turn to relative normativity against the background of Klabbers's earlier contention. The only meaningful conclusion which this schizophrenic configuration of the terms of the debate suggests about the state of the theoretical foundations behind this area of the LOTR discourse is that there are, most probably, no such foundations at all. It is not just that there exist two different schools of thought that hold diametrically opposite views on the same subject. The two schools are not really 'schools' in the regular sense of the word at all: the only 'thing' which they share in common with one another is the general vocabulary and a set of descriptive rubrics. In everything else, from analytical procedures to motivating questions to theoretical objects, they speak entirely past one another.

One does not find the same degree of discontinuity in the debate concerning the effects of treaties on third parties. On the contrary, the general thematic pattern there seems to come out very clearly. Although in some highly exceptional circumstances a treaty regime may create legal effects for non-members, the unanimous view both among the practitioners and scholars remains that a treaty can only be operational between the parties to it, and that it cannot by its own force, without the consent of the respective third party, create any rights or obligations for it.[138] Commonly known under the rubrics of *pacta tertiis nec nocent nec prosunt* and *res inter alios acta*, this doctrine is enshrined in Articles 34–36 of the VCLT. The common view suggests that its animating logic

---

137 Tomuschat, 'International Law …' (n 129) 345–6.
138 Aust, *Treaty Law* (n 99) 207; Brownlie, *Principles* (n 113) 628–9.

comes on the one hand from 'the fundamental principles of the sovereignty and independence of states'[139] and on the other hand from the principle of the 'relativity of treaties.'[140] A close narratological examination indicates that its basic theoretical mechanics mirrors that of the classical subjectivist doctrines of *l'autonomie de la volonté* and the privity of contract. Inasmuch as the *pacta tertiis* rule continues to be seen as fundamentally true, then, the spirit of the subjectivist paradigm in LOTR appears to be quite alive and well.

That said, looking at the rest of the 'foundational questions' debate, such a state of affairs certainly seems to be quite an exception.

One finds no similar degree of clarity if one considers, for example, the question to what degree the modern LOTR has moved on from the idea of a single doctrinal field, that is, to what extent it has internalized as part of its operative condition the modernist attitude towards regime fragmentation – that deeply anti-Platonist sensibility which famously drove Corbin to transform the *law of Contract* into the *law of contracts* and convinced Llewellyn of the need to group cases and legal situations into ever narrower sub-headings and categories.[141]

It was, of course, nearly a century ago that McNair had first made the observation that while in all municipal legal orders the legal practice had long come to recognize a wide variety of instruments for the regulation of social relations, from contracts and conveyances, to acts of parliament and constitutional documents, as a result of which no knowledgeable legal professional could ever come to presume that all these different transactions must follow the same operative logic and should therefore be governed by the same set of rules 'of universal or even of general application,' in international law it was precisely this presumption which had been elevated to the level of disciplinary dogma.[142] From the Kellogg–Briand pact to the various treaties of cession to the Anglo-American Liquor Convention to the Treaty of Versailles – how likely was it that 'all these multifarious [instruments] can be effectively governed by the same system of rules'? The answer, ventured McNair, was: not at all, which meant, of course, that the most pressing necessity confronting the modern LOTR regime, if it were to meet the historical challenges presented to it, was to 'free [itself] from the traditional notion that the instrument known as the treaty is governed by a single set of rules' and to

---

139 Shaw, *International Law* (n 99) 834.

140 McNair, *Law of Treaties* (n 89) 309.

141 K Llewellyn, 'Some Realism about Realism: Responding to Dean Pound' (1931) 44 Harv L Rev 1222, 1237.

142 McNair, '... Legal Character of Treaties' (n 10) 100–1.

'set [itself] to study the greatly differing legal character of [the different] kinds of treaties and to frame rules appropriate to the character of each kind.'[143] More than eight decades later that 'traditional notion' which McNair advocated against so passionately still remains firmly in place. One only needs to take a quick look at the most prominent recent scholarly works dealing with the subject,[144] or, indeed, the general structure of the VCLT regime itself, to see how comprehensively the LOTR imaginary continues to be dominated by the belief in 'a single set of rules of universal application.'

And yet it remains beyond doubt that in a whole range of areas the modern LOTR regime regularly tends to carve out all kinds of exceptional sub-regimes, indicating that the modernist dynamic of fragmentation has certainly not been absent from its theoretical organization. Consider, for example, Article 60(5) of the VCLT, which states that the general rule about the entitlement to terminate as a result of a material breach by another party does not apply to humanitarian treaties; Article 62(2)(a), which exempts boundary treaties from the reach of *clausula rebus sic stantibus*; or Article 20(3), which states that a reservation to a treaty that serves as the constituent instrument of an international organization requires the acceptance of the competent organ of that organization.[145]

At the same time, consider also how the principle of the fundamental change of circumstances (*clausula rebuc sic stantibus*) has been configured and articulated in the traditional LOTR doctrine. Article 62(1)(a) of the VCLT speaks of those circumstances which 'constituted an essential basis of the consent of the parties to be bound by the treaty.' The way this language has been framed appears to indicate a fairly clear commitment to the classical subjectivist logic of consent validation. Any inquiry into what it was that the parties had actually consented to, however, would have to be carried out according to the general rules of treaty interpretation, which, as noted earlier, tend to lean quite strongly in the direction of the modernist-functionalist approach. Does this mean then that, contrary to its actual formulation, the scope of applicability for the

[143] Ibid, 118.

[144] See, generally, Aust, *Treaty Law* (n 99); Klabbers, *The Concept of Treaty* (n 130). Note that the same integrationist pattern is present also in Linderfalk, *Interpretation of Treaties* (n 100).

[145] The most basic taxonomic division of treaties in the eyes of the modern LOTR, of course, remains that between bilateral, restricted multilateral, and non-restricted multilateral treaties. Cf L Henkin et al, *International Case Law and Materials* (3rd ed, West Publishing Co, 1993).

principle of *rebus sic stantibus* will have to be established according to the same modernist-functionalist logic? Or does it mean that the question of what forms an essential basis of the parties' consent would have to be resolved according to different analytical protocols depending on whether or not the dispute in question concerns the application of the principle of *rebus sic stantibus*?

2. The Uselessness (and Dangers) of Analogic Reasoning

Looking at the general patterns of the modern LOTR discourse through the prism of an inquiry focused on the question to what extent they rely on the same analytical resources as had been used traditionally in the area of LOC, the images of disorderly confusion and cacophony appear rather difficult to dislodge from one's mind. And yet, like all other metaphors, such images are only a product of our own interpretative prejudices. However well justified these prejudices may be otherwise, the objective reality 'on the ground' (whatever that might be in the present case) has exerted no intrinsic pressure that compelled our adoption of them and thus the production of this particular reading of events. Recalling an earlier point from Jameson, it should not be too difficult, then, to see the need to work out a fundamentally different reading that would allow us to arrive at a fundamentally different set of 'lessons' and 'conclusions' that could be drawn from our preceding inquiry.

One way to achieve this sort of alternative reading would be to start treating the recurrent failures of the LOTR discourse to fit its theoretical patterns within the standard grids of the three classical LOC paradigms as precisely that – a failure to fit rather than a failure to adopt or to execute properly.

It is said that when he first encountered a rhinoceros on one of his legendary journeys, Marco Polo allegedly wrote in his journal that unicorns in reality turned out to be a lot less elegant and graceful than he had expected them to be. Perhaps, the main lesson one should draw from the story related in these pages must be that it does not really make any more sense to approach the existing realities of LOTR from the angle of their 'relationship' to the ideal typology of contract law or the extent of their 'reliance' on the use of the same theoretical frameworks than it would to compare rhinoceroses to unicorns.

Or, perhaps, the main thrust of that story should also not be built around the idea of how all those different and mutually irreconcilable paradigms of contract law outlined earlier have come to be retained simultaneously in the same intellectual space, but rather how badly and imprecisely the LOTR's immanent theoretical structure maps onto the traditional patterns of the LOC imaginary; how inappropriate and misleading, therefore, it would be to perceive behind the recurrent use of the contractualist language by the LOTR practitioners anything more than a simple case of discursive convenience and analytical inertia; how useless and, finally, how intellectually dangerous as a knowledge strategy the whole practice of municipal legal analogies, consequently, might be, and how completely misguided and devoid of value the related enterprise of 'general jurisprudence' ultimately should be considered.

V. BY WAY OF CONCLUSION

Like all intellectual constructs, legal concepts have no stable, fixed meaning. Each of them is invested simultaneously with multiple significational possibilities that tend to become mobilized in different configurations, depending on how the specific discursive conjuncture is structured. Even the most seemingly unproblematic concepts, such as contract, consent, or liability, are not immune to this dynamic. They enter into the general legal imaginary from within highly specific orders of discourse, each of which has its own rules, conventions, and protocols of reasoning. In these 'original contexts' it is the structural conditions of (im)possibility imposed by those rules, conventions, and protocols which ensure that the 'excessive' parts of their significational potentialities remain suppressed to allow their discursive circulation to continue effectively. When they escape these contexts, that suppressive regime is lifted. With this, inevitably come the increase in content indeterminacy and the possibility of these concepts developing new functions and taking on new roles.

The indeterminacy of the contractual analogy in modern LOTR has been thrown into high relief by the previous discussion. The question that remains to be asked now is: what has been its broader role and its function in that context?

What role has been played by the insertion of the concepts of contract and contractuality into the analytical economy of the modern LOTR? What function has been performed by the deployment of the contractual imagery in the LOTR discourse? Now that it appears virtually certain that no valuable knowledge can be drawn from the study of whatever parallels in the use of common theoretical resources may exist between the LOTR and the LOC traditions, such questions remain the only line of inquiry that can be pursued meaningfully. They may not look like the kind one would usually come upon in a work of a legal-theoretic orientation. But it would be ill-advised to deny their profound critical importance. For even in the most rarefied intellectual contexts, one will never find such a thing as an innocent metaphor, and the continuous retention of the contractual analogy in the modern LOTR tradition has certainly not been an innocent enterprise.

In one of the most inspiring studies of the question of municipal legal analogies in modern international law, Anthony Carty famously notes that in the final analysis the problem of municipal legal analogies can only be grasped in full if it is placed in the context of the much broader debate about the foundational goals of international law *as a project*[146] and in particular its long-standing 'commitment to the goal of supranational organisation.'[147] Ever since the days of Lauterpacht and McNair, argues Carty, international lawyers by drawing hasty analogies between various ill-matching international and municipal legal categories have constantly engaged in the enterprise of putting forward and gradually entrenching a 'framework [meant] to replace the politics of international relations with institutions approximating as far as possible to those of a world State.'[148]

Even when the terms of the debate among them unfolded in such a way as to push some of them to protest against a particular case of analogical reasoning, the only aspect to which any attention was paid would be the patterns of apparent institutional discontinuities between the two legal orders. No questions would be asked of the typically extremely self-evident discontinuities in the basic systemic functions of the respective legal concepts, nor of what in the more recent critical international legal writing has come to be recognized as the *problem of the legal form*,[149] that is to say, the specificity of international law *taken as juridical-technical combinatory*, that is, as a system of assumptions determining what would be considered, on the whole, an acceptable rules-to-standards ratio in the structure of the constituent legal materials; what is supposed to be a 'normal' level of the resultant legal regime's practical administrability, that is, what Rudolph von Ihering called

---

[146] On the idea of international law as a project, see further M Koskenniemi, 'The Fate of Public International Law: Between Technique and Politics' (2007) 70 MLR 1; D Kennedy, 'A New World Order: Yesterday, Today, and Tomorrow' (1994) 4 Transnational L and Contemporary Problems 329.

[147] A Carty, *The Decay of International Law? A Reappraisal of the Limits of Legal Imagination in International Affairs* (Palgrave Macmillan, 1986) 80.

[148] Ibid.

[149] For a general explanation of the importance of the problem of the legal form for contemporary international legal theory, see, inter alia, C Mieville, *Between Equal Rights: A Marxist Theory of International Law* (Brill, 2005); U Özsu, 'The Question of Form: Methodological Notes on Dialectics and International Law' (2010) 23 Leiden J Intl L 687.

'formal realisability';[150] what would be the favoured pattern of rights-remedies tie-ins;[151] what causes of action would be preferred and how wide an area of conduct therefore would have to be covered by a *damnum absque injuria* regime; how exactly the boundary between fault and no-fault liability should be drawn, and so on and so forth.

One of the main practical consequences of this recurrent pattern of omissions, remarks Carty, has been the fact that a very substantial part of the international legal reality, in particular, the realities pertaining to the operation of treaties, has tended to escape any form of serious legal analysis. Because its operative analytical protocols have continued to be clogged by false analogisms, the LOTR doctrine has failed not only to attend to the fact that international treaties do not ultimately bind their parties in the same way in which private contracts do theirs. It has also prevented its practitioners from tackling adequately what ought to have long since been recognized as the most important systemic question that besets the modern LOTR, *viz.*: which of its various features can best help achieve 'the maximum stabilising effect on international relations.'[152] The job of all critical thought, suggested Loïc Wacquant once, must be to bring to light the price paid for the perpetuation of conventional wisdoms.[153] One would be hard-pressed to find a more fitting note on which to conclude this chapter than by putting up Carty's comments against the backdrop of this observation.

---

150 For further discussion of administrability, formal realizability, and Ihering's use of the latter concept, see D Kennedy, 'Form and Substance in Private Law Adjudication' (1976) 89 Harv L Rev 1685, 1687–9.

151 For a classical statement on the centrality of the rights-remedies linkage to the determination of the character of the legal form, see KN Llewellyn, *The Bramble Bush: On Our Law and Its Study* (Oceana Publications, 1930) 82–5.

152 Carty, *Decay of International Law* (n 147) 79. The passage continues:

> The municipal law analogy itself, the insistence that treaties be regarded as contracts, focused the attention of jurists on what were supposed to be the original intentions of the parties to the treaty, whenever any dispute arose, to the neglect of the surrounding political-diplomatic context at the moment of the dispute.

153 See L Wacquant, 'Critical Thought as Solvent of Doxa' (2004) 11 *Constellations* 97.

5. The effects of treaties in domestic law

André Nollkaemper

I. INTRODUCTION

Treaties, while operating primarily at international level, by definition require a legal connection to the national level. They cannot stand on their own feet.[1] State organs, whether of the legislative, the executive or the judicial branch, will need to be empowered by national law to perform acts that are required by the treaty. The treaty may also require that (part of) its content is made part of national law. The connection between treaties and domestic law is particularly relevant when treaties regulate matters that are also dealt with by domestic law and determine the position of private individuals who by their very nature are (primarily) subjected to national law.

The question then is how treaties acquire effect at national level. A range of sub-questions follow. What is the influence of international law itself on the effects of a treaty at national level? What properties of a treaty may be conducive to or limiting such national effect? What techniques do States apply to determine the ways and extent in which a treaty acquires legal effect in domestic law? Under what conditions and with what effects do they allow a national court to apply the rules of a treaty?

Obviously, the domestic effect of treaties is not just a matter of technique. It serves important policy objectives and reflects deeply political questions. In the final analysis, determining whether and how a treaty has direct effect requires an answer to the question of who has, or should have, the final authority to determine the contents of the law applicable in any particular society.

This chapter will review various ways (or 'techniques') to moderate the effect treaties acquire in the domestic legal order of a States party to such treaties. The term 'moderate' is used here in a neutral way in the sense of 'regulate'. It will also explore the dilemmas that relevant actors face in choosing whether or not to use such techniques.

---

[1] CH Triepel, 'Les Rapports Entre Le Droit Interne et Le Droit International' (1923) 1 Recueil des Cours de l'Académie de Droit International 73, 106.

To the extent relevant, the chapter will address the various techniques both from the perspective of international law and from the perspective of national (comparative) law. As to the former, while international law is generally silent on its effects in national law, it does have something to say, and variations between the contents of treaties may help explain variations in effect. As to the latter, given the infeasibility of addressing in this chapter the wide variety of conditions under which legal orders across the world allow for domestic effects of treaties, this chapter will identify and systematize relevant patterns that we find in State practice.

To provide proper background and perspective, section II will set out the political context in which the discussion of domestic effects of treaties is to be situated. Section III will review what international law has to say on the matter. Section IV will discuss the main approaches employed by States in their national legal orders. In section V I will make some brief concluding observations and identify questions for research.

II. THE POLITICAL CONTEXT

What effect treaties acquire at the domestic level, and how they acquire such effect, are both deeply political questions. Treaties may affect the law applicable in a particular society and serve political purposes. These purposes may be reflected in the content of a treaty, that is, a treaty may further the realization of particular policy objectives. Treaties may also influence the power of public authorities.

In considering the relevance of the political context for the domestic effects of treaties, we can distinguish two interrelated dimensions: an external and an internal one. The external dimension concerns the relationship between the international and the national legal order (section II.1). The internal dimension concerns the question which actors in a particular national legal order (should) have the power to determine the effect of treaties (section II.2).

1. The External Dimension

The way in which treaties are given effect in national law reflects political decisions on the allocation of power between the international and the national sphere. Blocking domestic effect may lead to an internationally wrongful act if the State does not perform its treaty obligations, but does preserve national policy space.[2] A decision to grant a treaty full effect in national law may facilitate effective performance of international obligations, but comes at the price of national policy space, as it fixes the law at a level where it is beyond the control of individual States.

Decisions on the 'vertical' allocation of power may be taken both at international and at national level. On the one hand, they may be taken (though often somewhat implicitly) by the collectivity of States party to a treaty, for example by including in a treaty particular properties that co-determine the domestic effect of the treaty and thereby shape the allocation of power between the national and the international level.[3]

On the other hand, political decisions on the allocation of power between the international and the national sphere may be taken by individual States. Such decisions may determine the domestic effect of treaties generally, for example by means of constitutional provisions determining the status or hierarchical rank of treaties in national law.[4] They also may relate to a single treaty in particular, for instance by attaching a reservation to a treaty as to the treaty's domestic effect,[5] or by deciding to withhold the direct effect of that treaty.[6]

It may be said that eventually – at both levels – the State is in control of the domestic effect of the treaty. After all, the State that is to perform treaty obligations at national level is itself present at the negotiations and will not be bound by a treaty before it has given its consent to be bound.[7]

However, this argument is vulnerable on three grounds. First, for weaker States, the choice to stay out of a treaty is not a perfectly free one. In particular when a treaty protects the common interests of multiple States, the pressure on States to become a party may be strong.[8] Weiler

---

[2] A von Bogdandy, 'Pluralism, Direct Effect and the Ultimate Say: On the Relationship between International and Domestic Constitutional Law' (2008) 6 Intl J Constitutional L 397 (arguing that it is preferable to retain 'the capacity legally to limit the effect within the domestic legal order of a norm or an act under international law if that norm or act conflicts sharply with constitutional principles').

[3] See section III.

[4] Infra section IV.

[5] Infra section IV.

[6] Infra section IV.

[7] Article 24(2) of the Vienna Convention on the Law of Treaties (entered into force 27 January 1980) 1155 UNTS 331 (VCLT).

[8] M Kumm, 'The Legitimacy of International Law: A Constitutionalist Framework of Analysis' (2004) 15 EJIL 907, 914.

notes: 'The legitimation that comes from sovereignty is increasingly untenable. The ability to choose one's obligations has gone.'[9]

It is to be added that most negotiating parties generally will be more concerned with the substance of a treaty and its supervision at international level, than with the modalities of its implementation domestically. Because of the large diversity in terms of implementation procedures in different States, attempts to lay down precise rules on domestic effect are generally doomed to fail, and negotiating States leave such modalities to the domestic level.[10] But that does not mean that whatever is contained in a treaty does not affect the domestic level – particular international obligations in the sphere of domestic regulation or individual rights may circumscribe the pre-existing liberty of States to shape their domestic policies in these areas, and as such they involve a reallocation of power, even if the implementation of the treaty may be left to States.

Second, treaties evolve over time. The law that is binding on States may evolve in different directions and thus it may become significantly different when compared with the law that they originally signed on to. Treaty interpretation is only marginally controlled by individual States and may evolve in directions unforeseen, and unwanted, at the time of creation. This limits the controlling power of signatory States. States may seek to terminate their obligations under treaties that have developed in unforeseen directions by withdrawing from the relevant treaties.[11] But States do not often do so, and they generally attach more weight to continuing involvement in the treaty.[12]

Third, treaties may grant international institutions powers to interpret and modify the treaty. This holds for intergovernmental organizations that may have been constituted by treaties,[13] for more informal arrangements

---

[9] JHH Weiler, 'The Geology of International Law: Governance, Democracy and Legitimacy' (2004) 64 Heidelberg J Intl L 547, 557.

[10] See also section III.1.

[11] Under Article 54 VCLT (n 7).

[12] LR Helfer, 'Exiting Treaties' (2005) 91 Virginia L R 1579, 1648.

[13] See, eg, on the role of the United Nations (UN) Security Council in developing the meaning of the Charter of the United Nations (1945) provisions, inter alia, B Fassbender, 'Review Essay: Quis Judicabit? The Security Council, Its Powers and Legal Control' (2000) 11 EJIL 219; V Santori, 'The UN Security Council's (Broad) Interpretation of the Notion of the Threat to Peace in Counter-Terrorism' in G Nesi, *International Cooperation in Counter-Terrorism: The United Nations and Regional Organizations in the Fight against Terrorism* (Ashgate, 2006); R Higgins, *Development of International Law through Political Organs of the United Nations* (OUP, 1963). Another example is the World Health

such as meetings of the parties set up by a treaty,[14] and for international courts that have the power to adjudicate claims and in that process will have to interpret the treaty. Such international institutions can exercise interpretative authority quite independently from the States that originally set them up.

As a result of these three points, the fact that a State is not bound by a particular treaty before it consents to it does not at all put it in control over the content of a treaty and its projected effects at domestic level. To mitigate and manage that gap, States will seek to include in the treaty safety valves that allow them to control the effect of treaties at national level.

2. The Internal Dimension

A quite different set of dynamics operates at the domestic level. The domestic application of treaties can affect and shift the power relations between domestic actors. Such shifts are particularly powerful as their effects may extend over time. Any shift in the domestic political spectrum will confront the new majority with international rules consented to by a previous regime. While this is to some extent also true for domestic law, in regard to the latter the process there is at least the possibility that a new majority rescinds or amends laws set up by a previous regime. This is not as easily done for treaties.

Treaties can affect two distinct sets of domestic power constellations: first, the horizontal relation between the government, parliament and courts, and, second, the vertical relation between the central (or federal) government and local government.

In terms of the horizontal separation of powers, treaties are primarily a source of power for the government. The government normally represents

Organization, see SF Halabi, 'The World Health Organization's Framework Convention on Tobacco Control: An Analysis of Guidelines Adopted by the Conference of the Parties' (2011) 39 Georgia J Intl and Comparative L 121.

[14] See, eg, for the role of institutions set up under multilateral environmental agreements, R Churchill and G Ulfstein, 'Autonomous Institutional Arrangements in Multilateral Environmental Agreements: A Little Noticed Phenomenon in International Law' (2000) 94 AJIL 623; A Wiersema, 'The New International Law-Makers? Conferences of the Parties to Multilateral Environmental Agreements' (2009) 31 Michigan J Intl L 231. See on the interpretative powers of human rights bodies H Keller and L Grover, 'General Comments of the Human Rights Committee and Their Legitimacy' in H Keller and G Ulfstein (eds), *UN Human Rights Treaty Bodies: Law and Legitimacy* (CUP, 2012).

the State in the negotiation and conclusion of treaties,[15] and, compared to other domestic actors, has superior power in influencing and shaping the content of the treaty.[16] Although formally the legislative branch may have the last word (at least in those States where parliamentary approval is a precondition for ratification), the text will be fixed, and the possibility for parliament to change anything or even to say 'no' is limited.[17] In States where the executive negotiates and ratifies treaties, the legislative branch will be confronted with a fait accompli, as the treaty will be binding on the State whatever the legislature's own take on it may be. The legislative organ may choose not to transform the treaty into domestic law, but even then it may not be able to preclude (some of) its domestic effects.[18] Where the legislature implements the treaty domestically, it will have no influence over the content, except for the rather limited option of requiring the executive to add reservations at the stage of ratification.

Yet, at the domestic level the government (the executive branch) is only one actor, limited in its powers vis-à-vis parliament and the courts.[19] Other branches of government are in competition with the executive and will naturally seek to curtail the empowering effect of the treaty on the executive branch. In so-called monist States, parliaments may do so by withholding approval of a treaty, which thus, though signed, cannot be ratified. In dualist States they may do so by declining to 'transform' or implement a treaty in national law.

Courts also have a role in this contestation of treaty-based power. Once a treaty is binding on the State, the courts can use it to bolster their powers by interpreting and applying it. This effectively puts the courts in a position of superiority vis-à-vis other organs, as they are in the final analysis the ones to decide on interpretation and application of the treaty in circumstances where challenges are raised. They may thereby also curtail the exercise of powers of other branches of government in the

---

[15] Article 7(2) VCLT (n 7).

[16] See in the context of the US: OA Hathaway, 'Presidential Power over International Law: Restoring the Balance' (2009) 119 Yale L J 140.

[17] Weiler, 'The Geology of International Law ...' (n 9) 547.

[18] See Australia, High Court of Justice, *Baker v The Queen*, Final Appeal Judgment (2004) 223 CLR 513; ILDC 515 (AU 2004); Australia, High Court of Justice, *Minister of State for Immigration and Ethnic Affairs v Teoh* (1995) 183 CLR 273 (7 April 1995).

[19] See generally, D Haljan, *Separating Powers: International Law before National Courts* (TMC Asser Press, 2012) 262.

interest of preservation of democratic values.[20] But here again the courts may find themselves in competition with other organs over these powers – legislatures may reserve for themselves the power to interpret and apply treaties, for instance by declaring a treaty to be non-self-executing.[21]

The effect of a particular treaty on the (separation of) powers between branches of government, and the competition between these branches, is obviously not determined anew for every individual treaty. Every State will have structural (constitutional or other) provisions determining the respective powers of the various branches of government in the implementation of treaties. Doctrines such as 'direct effect' or non-justiciability will serve as parameters within which branches of government can carve out their role. Such moderating techniques fix the relations between the branches of government, but they are themselves not stable and may be reshaped at any point in order to reconfigure the relation between the branches of government in relation to the implementation of treaties.

The second dimension of the effect of treaties on domestic power constellations relates to the vertical division of powers between a central or federal government and the federal States or local levels of government. A government may, by concluding a treaty, accord itself a new power or strengthen an existing power against lower levels of government. Cases from Australia[22] and the United States[23] illustrate the point. Treaty-making power and the power to implement treaties through legislation, then, is a means to influence the vertical allocation of power within States.

---

[20] E Benvenisti and GW Downs, 'National Courts, Domestic Democracy and the Evolution of International Law' (2009) 20 EJIL 59; E Benvenisti, 'Reclaiming Democracy: The Strategic Uses of Foreign and International Law by National Courts' (2008) 102 AJIL 241.

[21] See, eg, the declaration of the US at the time of ratification of the International Covenant on Civil and Political Rights, stating that '[t]hat the United States declares that the provisions of articles 1 through 27 of the Covenant are not self-executing', http://treaties.un.org/doc/Publication/MTDSG/Volume%20I/Chapter%20IV/IV-4.en.pdf, accessed 22 January 2013.

[22] *Commonwealth v Tasmania* (Tasmanian Dam case) [1983] High Court of Australia 21; (1983) 158 CLR 1 (1 July 1983).

[23] *State of Missouri v Holland* 252 US 416, 40 S. Ct. 382 (1920). The question whether the power of Congress to implement treaties through legislation is restricted by this Amendment will be considered by the Supreme Court in *Bond v United States* 564 US (2011).

General techniques that govern the domestic effect of treaties may also influence this vertical contestation for power. For instance, in the US, even though the federal government does not have the power to legislate in order to implement a treaty, it may still rely on a technique such as the declaration of a treaty as self-executing in order to create 'supreme law of the land' (see Article VI clause 2 of the US constitution) that has to be applied by the courts at all levels of government.[24]

III. THE INTERNATIONAL LEVEL

In light of the substantial impact that treaties may have on domestic law, and on the domestic allocation of powers, it is not surprising that States prefer international law to allow them great flexibility in determining how domestic effect is to be given to treaties. We can distinguish between general international law (section III.1), the law of treaties (section III.2) and the content of particular treaties (section III.3).

1. General International Law

International law does not lay claim to supremacy over national law at the national level. International law traditionally also suffers from weak enforcement. These characteristics of the structure of the international legal order are reflected in the retention of power on the part of States to structure the relationship between treaties and domestic law at the domestic level. General international law leaves the domestic effect of treaties to national law.[25]

One of the manifestations of this discretion that is particularly relevant for the domestic effect of treaties is that a treaty that binds a State, as a matter of international law, is binding only on the State and not directly on the organs of the State. International law does not determine the domestic organization of States and cannot directly determine the powers

---

[24] Again this question is to be considered in *Bond v United States* (n 23).

[25] P Reuter, *Introduction to the Law of Treaties* (Kegan Paul International Ltd, 1995) 21; EM Borchard, 'The Relation between International and Municipal Law', Proceedings, 8th American Scientific Congress, Washington, 1940, X (1943) 77, 82; HW Briggs, *The Law of Nations: Cases, Documents and Notes* (2nd edn, Stevens & Sons Ltd, 1952) 63.

of the organs of the State in the national legal order to give effect to treaties.[26]

It may be argued that if a treaty becomes binding upon the State 'it becomes binding upon the State as a whole, and, by derivation, upon each of its several organs and institutions, each of which becomes bound, as part of the State, to play whatever part is necessary in order to make the treaty effective'.[27] Even though, formally, the obligations rest on the State, there is no dispute whatsoever that the legislature, the executive and the courts are the organs of the State and that such organs should give effect to the State's international obligations.[28] However, the powers of each organ will be determined and limited by national law.

2. The 1969 Vienna Convention on the Law of Treaties

The Vienna Convention is mostly silent on the domestic effect of treaties. The two most relevant provisions are Article 26 (*pacta sunt servanda*) and in particular its corollary Article 27,[29] which provides that a State 'may not invoke the provisions of its internal law as justification for its failure to perform the treaty'.[30] These provisions are fundamental to the effective operation of treaties. However, their scope and effect is limited to the international level. They do not take away or alter the right of the State 'to choose the means of implementation it sees fit according to its traditions and to the fundamental principles of its political organization'.[31]

The International Law Commission did consider whether or not more detail should have been added in the eventual Convention. Special Rapporteur Fitzmaurice proposed several principles that intended to

---

[26] ILC, 'Third Report on State Responsibility by Mr Roberto Ago, Special Rapporteur' (5 March–18 May 1971) UN Doc A/CN.4/246, para 114.

[27] ILC, 'Fourth Report on the Law of Treaties by Mr GG Fitzmaurice, Special Rapporteur' (17 March 1959) UN Doc A/CN.4/120, para 143.

[28] S Rosenne, *The Law and Practice of the International Court* (Sijthoff, 1965) 129; CH Schreuer, 'The Implementation of International Judicial Decisions by Domestic Courts' (1975) 24 ICLQ 153, 157.

[29] ME Villiger, *Commentary on the 1969 Vienna Convention on the Law of Treaties* (Martinus Nijhoff Publishers, 2009) 371.

[30] See generally, A Schauw, 'Commentary to Article 27: Internal Law and Observance of Treaties' in O Corten and P Klein (eds), *The Vienna Conventions on the Law of Treaties: A Commentary* (OUP, 2011) 702; Villiger, *Commentary* (n 29) 371.

[31] Reuter, *Law of Treaties* (n 25) 21.

clarify the relevance of the domestic aspects of treaty application. For instance, draft article 29, introduced in his Fourth Report, provided:

> The treaty obligation produces its effects primarily in the international field, it being the duty of the parties to carry it out in that field. The question of its effects in the domestic field is relevant only in so far as it may affect the capacity of the parties to discharge this duty.[32]

It was rather mysterious what the legal import of the second sentence of this provision was, if it was to have any legal effect. Obviously domestic law could be a cause of non-compliance, but it hardly seemed to be the task of the Vienna Convention to spell that out.

Fitzmaurice also proposed a draft article 30, stipulating that it is the basic duty of every State (the commentary added: 'by the term "State" is meant the whole State, including all of its organs') so to conduct itself in relation to its law and constitution that it is in a position to carry out its treaty obligations. It also stated in paragraph 2 that provided the object contemplated by paragraph 1 is attained, it is immaterial by what means this is done, and it is a domestic matter for each State to decide for itself what method shall be employed.[33] Paragraph 3 then added that in those cases where the treaty cannot be carried out without specific legislative, administrative or other action in the domestic field, a party to the treaty which finds itself in this position is under a duty to take such action. None of these provisions made it into the VCLT.

Also, nothing came of the proposals to include provisions on the effects of treaties on private individuals and juridical entities within the State.[34] While the relevant draft article raises interesting questions on the legal personality of individuals, from the perspective of the effects of treaties in domestic law it is again simply an application of the general principle that would apply even without express stipulation: if a treaty seeks to protect rights, or to impose obligations on, individuals, States parties should take the necessary measures in their internal legal order to secure that such rights or obligations will be realized.[35]

---

32 'Fourth Report on the Law of Treaties by Mr GG Fitzmaurice …' (n 27).

33 Ibid, 49 and paras 145–6.

34 Ibid, 49 (discussing Article 32 VCLT).

35 Ibid, para 157. See also ILC, 'Third Report on the Law of Treaties by H Waldock, Special Rapporteur' (3 March–7 July 1964) UN Doc A/CN.4/167 and Addendum 1–3, 45–7 (stating that this provision did 'little more than repeat the *pacta sunt servanda* rule in the particular context of treaties affecting individuals').

All these 'principles' are covered by the common sense principle that States have to do what is necessary to perform a treaty and, implicitly, also by the provision of Article 27, which after all requires States to ensure that these provisions are brought into line with treaty obligations.[36] It is hard to see how these proposals would have made much of a legal difference.

Special Rapporteur Waldock indeed concluded that there was no need to include any of this in the Vienna Convention. He was of the opinion that the principles that a State must take effective measures in its internal law to fulfil its treaty obligations and that a State may not plead the deficiencies of its internal law in justification of a failure to perform its treaty obligations when general principles of State responsibility apply to any form of international obligation and belong to the responsibility of States rather than to the law of treaties. Both principles were implicit in and covered by the *pacta sunt servanda* rule.[37]

Some further suggestions were made to provide more detail on domestic effects of treaties at the Vienna Conference of 1969. Luxemburg suggested that Article 26 should be followed by an article stipulating that 'The Parties shall take any measures of internal law that may be necessary to ensure that treaties are fully applied.'[38] The proposed amendment was to ensure that States would take any measures of internal law which would allow for the full application of treaties.[39] The majority at the Conference, however, opposed it on the ground that it would amount to an encroachment on State sovereignty and that it would add nothing new to the obligation already implicit in Article 26.[40] These two grounds for resistance are not fully compatible, and may indicate that the principle that States shall take any domestic measures that may be necessary to ensure that treaties are fully applied is less of a common sense proposition and not as beyond controversy as may be thought.

Apart from the core provisions of Articles 26 and 27, a few other provisions of the Vienna Convention may be relevant for the domestic effect of treaties.[41]

---

36 Villiger, *Commentary* (n 29) 372.

37 'Third Report on the Law of Treaties by H Waldock …' (n 35).

38 T O Elias, *The Modern Law of Treaties* (Oceana-Sijthoff, 1974) 43–5.

39 Ibid.

40 Ibid.

41 I leave the procedures for conclusion of treaties, including Articles 46 and 47 VCLT aside here.

The provisions on conclusion and ratification[42] are relevant, since these allow States to adjust domestic law to the requirements of a treaty and to ensure that a State is not bound as a matter of international law before it has had the opportunity to bring its national law into conformity with the international obligations to be assumed by means of the treaty to be ratified.[43]

The provision on provisional application[44] is relevant, since the practice of provisional application may bypass internal law regimes, and as such limits whatever control the domestic constitutional order exercises over the domestic effect of treaties.[45]

Furthermore, the provisions on treaty interpretation are relevant, since national organs, notably courts, may draw on them to interpret treaty provisions in a particular way, even if the executive branch may suggest or desire a different interpretation. There is considerable practice of national courts that interpret treaties with express reference to the international principles of interpretation, and further interpret domestic law in conformity with the international obligations of the State.[46]

Finally, the provisions on withdrawal and termination[47] are relevant since, like the conclusion of a treaty, termination of treaties may directly affect domestic law. The question here again is which State organ may avail itself of the power to terminate a treaty. The Vienna Convention is silent, and it falls to domestic actors to invoke the provisions on the termination of a treaty, or abstain from doing so. There is some practice of national courts assuming a power in this regard, in effect changing the law binding on, and possibly binding in, the State.[48]

The VCLT does not address itself to the organs of the State directly. Only in a few places does the Convention touch upon the question of the power of State organs. Beyond that, what particular organ(s) will be burdened with or empowered to implement the treaty domestically is a question left to domestic law. However, it may be required that the State empower specific domestic organs in order to fulfil its obligation to take all measures necessary to give effect to a treaty.[49] Murphy notes: 'in

---

[42] Articles 6–18.

[43] In particular the procedures provided for by Article 14 are relevant here.

[44] Article 25.

[45] Corten and Klein (eds), *The Vienna Conventions* (n 43) 643.

[46] Ibid, 823.

[47] Articles 54–64.

[48] B Conforti and A Labella, 'Invalidity and Termination of Treaties: The Role of National Courts' (1990) 1 EJIL 44.

[49] See AD McNair, *The Law of Treaties* (2nd edn, Clarendon Press, 1961) 78.

some circumstances perhaps the only reasonable way to apply a treaty that protects or benefits individuals is for national courts to be available for individuals to litigate claims arising from the treaty'.[50] And yet, this is not a requirement under the Vienna Convention. International law allows States discretion as to whether they will do so.[51]

3. Individual Treaties

To retain control over the effects of treaties in domestic law, States have at their possession a wide variety of techniques and modalities that they may introduce in particular treaties, including opting for flexibility in treaty provisions and deferential supervision. Conversely, those who seek to use a treaty as a source of power in national law will seek to include provisions that create rights for individuals which may be invoked before the courts, or provisions that allow for immediate (direct) application of the treaty rules by national courts, or even a provision to the effect 'that [the treaty's] rules shall prevail in court over any municipal provision, including subsequent legislation'.[52]

Here I will focus on four properties of treaty regimes that can be relevant for the domestic effect of treaties: the precision of treaty provisions; provisions that require guarantees in national law; provisions that create individual rights; and provisions that allow for provisional application.

First, while the question of direct effect of treaties is a matter of national law,[53] the content of a treaty may have an influence on those cases where domestic law allows for direct effect.[54] In determining whether a treaty should be given direct effect, courts generally accord much weight to interpretation and to the intention of the parties.[55] The US Supreme Court in *Medellin* referred to 'our obligation to interpret

---

[50] SD Murphy, 'Does International Law Obligate States to Open Their National Courts to Persons for the Invocation of Treaty Norms that Protect or Benefit Persons?' in D Sloss (ed), *The Role of Domestic Courts in Treaty Enforcement: A Comparative Study* (CUP, 2009).

[51] McNair, *The Law of Treaties* (n 49) 345.

[52] Reuter, *Law of Treaties* (n 25) 22; Murphy, 'Does International Law Obligate States …' (n 50).

[53] See infra.

[54] T Buergenthal, 'Self-Executing and Non-Self-Executing Treaties in National and International Law' (1992) IV Recueil des Cours 303, 319.

[55] Eg, Belgium, Court of Cassation, *Art Research & Contact Naamloze Vennootschap v BS*, Case No C 00 0391 N; ILDC 44 (BE 2001) paras 30–31.

treaty provisions to determine whether they are self-executing'.[56] In the Netherlands the question of whether a norm has direct effect is determined by whether it is of 'such a kind that the provision can function as an objective rule in the national legal order'.[57] This test is a matter of treaty interpretation: the notion of the self-executing treaty 'rests on a characteristic inherent in the treaty'.[58] If that is the case, then the question of direct effect is to that extent a matter of international law.[59]

Second, treaties may require that States make particular international obligations part of their domestic law. To be precise, international law does not require automatic validity, but a treaty may prescribe that States will have to ensure that the substance of certain treaty obligations is made part of domestic law.[60] The European Court of Human Rights (ECtHR) has held that 'it follows from the Convention, and from Article 1 in particular, that in ratifying the Convention the Contracting States undertake to ensure that their domestic legislation is compatible with it'.[61] The Inter-American Court of Human Rights held in similar vein that

---

[56] *Medellín v Texas,* 552 US 491, ILDC 947 (2008) para 37.

[57] The Netherlands, Supreme Court, *Nederlandse Spoorwegen* (30 May 1986) NJ 1986/688; (1987) NYIL 392. See also the Netherlands, Council of State, *Reinier van Arkel Foundation v Minister of Transport*, LJN AR2181; 200401178/1; AB 2005/12; ILDC 129 (NL 2004) para 2.2.6.

[58] A Bleckman, 'Self-Executing Treaty Provisions' (1984) *Encyclopedia of Public International Law* 414, 414.

[59] Eg, the Netherlands, Supreme Court, *Hansa Chemie v Bechem Chemie* (16 May 1997) NJ 1998/585; [1998] 45 Netherlands International Law Review 129.

[60] *Exchange of Greek and Turkish Populations (Greece v Turkey)*, Advisory Opinion, PCIJ Series B No 10; ICGJ 277 (PCIJ 1925) para 51; see also *Greco-Bulgarian 'Communities'*, Advisory Opinion, PCIJ Series B No 17; ICGJ 284 (PCIJ 1930) para 84. See also in this context Article 33 proposed by Special Rapporteur Fitzmaurice in his 'Fourth Report on the Law of Treaties' (1959) II Yearbook of the ILC 49, providing that:

> where a treaty provides for rights, interests or benefits to be enjoyed by private parties, or where the treaty otherwise redounds to their advantage, it is the duty of the contracting States to place no obstacle in the way of enjoyment of these rights, interests, benefits or advantages by the individuals or juristic entities concerned, and to take all such steps as may be necessary to make them effective on the internal plane.

Special Rapporteur Waldock thought that this provision was superfluous as it was inherent in the principle *pacta sunt servanda*, (n 35) 47.

[61] *Maestri v Italy* App no 39748/98 (European Convention on Human Rights, 17 February 2004 (ECHR)) para 47 (discussing Article 1 of the ECHR).

'[t]he States Parties to the Convention must guarantee compliance with its provisions and its effects (*effet utile*) within their domestic law'.[62]

The question is whether such provisions, or interpretations, make any legal difference. In the final analysis, it is only the result that counts, and non-adoption of domestic implementing legislation will not constitute in principle an internationally wrongful act. However, combined with a strong international court supervising the implementation of the treaty, such provisions may exercise pressure on States to adjust national law and provide a source of authority for those domestic actors seeking such adjustment of national law.

Third, treaties may provide for individual rights, creating a presumption that individuals have standing to rely on such treaties in national court proceedings.[63] States can structure international obligations in such a way as to allow or disallow individual claims and thereby support or block an active role of national courts in reviewing of the exercise of public power by the State against standards of international law.[64] International courts, like the International Court of Justice in *LaGrand*,[65] can interpret and construe treaty obligations in a manner that supports such a role. Of course, national law may restrict standing where this is granted by international law, or it may provide for standing where international law does not do so. But from the perspective of international law, the proper starting point for any inquiry into the entitlement of a person to rely on international law for a particular claim is the content of the treaty.[66]

Fourthly, States may provide in a treaty that the treaty will be provisionally applied before its entry into force. At the domestic level,

---

62 Constitutional Court Case, Inter-American Court of Human Rights Series C No 55 (1999) para 36.

63 Authors who have used the concept of standing in this way in respect to international law in domestic courts include L Brilmayer, 'International Law in American Courts: A Modest Proposal' (1991) 100 Yale L J 2277, 2302; ME O'Connell, 'Enforcement and the Success of International Environmental Law' (1995) 3 Global L Studies J 47, 61; JJ Paust, *International Law as Law of the United States* (Carolina Academic Press, 1996) 239.

64 Buergenthal, 'Self-Executing and Non-Self-Executing Treaties …' (n 54) 319; M Sørensen, 'Die Verplichttungen Eines Staates im Bereich Seiner Nationalen Rechtsordnuung auf Grund eines Staatsvertrages' in *Mensenrechte im Staatsrecht und im Völkerrecht* (Verlag CF Müller, 1967) 15, 26.

65 *LaGrand Case (Germany v United States of America)*, Merits, ICJ Rep 2001, 466, 494.

66 S Riesenfeld, 'The Doctrine of Self-Executing Treaties and *US v Postal*: Win at Any Price?' (1980) 74 AJIL 895, 899–900.

such provisions circumvent the normal procedures and the usual allocation of powers regarding the implementation of treaty provisions, shifting powers from the legislative to the executive and possibly also to the judicial branch.

IV. THE NATIONAL LEVEL

This section will examine four techniques that States have employed, and may employ, in their national law in order to moderate the domestic effects of treaties: applicability (IV.1), supremacy (IV.2), direct effect (IV.3), and consistent interpretation (IV.4). The survey is by no means complete. Techniques that are not considered here include non-justiciability, which may limit the effect of treaties in domestic courts (as these will have to defer to the executive[67]) and the political questions doctrine, which may preclude the courts from examining whether the executive has acted in accordance with international law.[68]

1. Applicability

A first technique to moderate the effect of treaties at the domestic level is to grant, or deny, automatic legal effect of treaties once they are binding on the State as a matter of public international law.

There are two main approaches evident in the practice of States in making international law applicable domestically, with many varieties in between. At one end of the spectrum, a significant number of States have adopted a rule (often constitutional, whether written or unwritten) of domestic law that makes all or particular treaties part of domestic law automatically, that is without there being a need for implementing legislation. This is for instance the situation in Benin,[69] Cape Verde,[70] (in principle) China,[71] Cote d'Ivoire,[72] the Czech Republic,[73] the Dominican

---

[67] Eg, *Campaign for Nuclear Disarmament v The Prime Minister of the United Kingdom* [2002] EWHC 2777 (Admin) [47]; ILDC 662 (UK 2002). See for Ireland, High Court, *Edward Horgan v An Taoiseach* (2003 No 3739P); (2003) 2 IR 468; [2003] IEHC 64; 32 ILR 407, 440; ILDC 486 (IE 2003) paras 114–15.

[68] T M Franck, *Political Questions Judicial Answers* (Princeton UP, 1992).

[69] Article 147 Constitution of the Republic of Benin (1990).

[70] Article 11 Constitution of the Republic of Cape Verde (1980).

[71] S Guo, 'Implementation of Human Rights Treaties by Chinese Courts: Problems and Prospects' (2009) 8 Chinese J Intl L 161, 165.

[72] Article 87 Constitution of the Republic of Cote d'Ivoire (2000).

[73] Article 10 Constitution of the Czech Republic (1992).

Republic,[74] Egypt,[75] Ethiopia,[76] France,[77] Greece,[78] Japan,[79] the Netherlands,[80] Portugal,[81] Senegal,[82] the Russian Federation,[83] Switzerland,[84] Turkey[85] and the United States.[86]

A choice in favour of automatic incorporation of treaties may reflect the aim to secure effective performance of treaties. It may also reflect a will to control executive power. Indeed, this choice has commonly been made in post-revolutionary constitutional developments.[87] A decision to open constitutions towards treaties so as to allow for control of the previously unassailable government was made in the Constitution of the Weimar Republic of 1919, the German Constitution of 1949, the 1946 Constitution of Japan,[88] the 1974 Greek Constitution, the Spanish Constitution of 1978 and Eastern European constitutions after 1989.[89]

---

[74] Article 3 Constitution of the Dominican Republic (1994).

[75] Article 151 Constitution of the Arab Republic of Egypt (1971).

[76] Article 9(4) Constitution of Federal Democratic Republic of Ethiopia (1994).

[77] Article 55 Constitution of the French Republic (1958).

[78] Article 28(1) Constitution of the Hellenic Republic (1974/2008).

[79] Y Iwasawa, 'The Relationship between International and National Law: Japanese Experiences' (1993) 64 BYIL 343, 345.

[80] A Nollkaemper, 'The Netherlands' in D Sloss et al (eds), *The Role of Domestic Courts in Treaty Enforcement: A Comparative Study* (CUP, 2009) 326.

[81] Eg, Article 8(2) Constitution of Portugal (1976); see, eg, Portugal, Supreme Administrative Court, *A and B v Portuguese State*, Case no 0308/07; ILDC 1441 (PT 2007).

[82] Article 91 Constitution of the Republic of Senegal (2001).

[83] Article 15(4) Constitution of the Russian Federation (1993); VI Kuznetsov and BR Tuzmukhamedow (eds), *International Law: A Russian Introduction* (Eleven, 2009) 188.

[84] Switzerland, Federal Supreme Court, *A and B v Government of the Canton of Zurich*, BGE 126 I 242; ILDC 350 (CH 2000) para 2b.

[85] Article 90(5) Constitution of the Republic of Turkey (1982); see also Turkey, Court of Cassation, *Ray Sigorta AS v Nunner Lojistik Ticaret Limited Sti*, E 2007/2970, K 2008/4599; ILDC 1034 (TR 2008).

[86] Article VI Constitution of the United States of America (1787).

[87] E Stein, 'International Law in Internal Law: Towards Internationalization of Central-Eastern Constitutions' (1994) 88 AJIL 427, 428; A Cassese, 'Modern Constitutions and International Law' (1985) 192 Recueil des Cours 331, 351.

[88] Iwasawa, '... International and National Law: Japanese Experiences' (n 79) 375.

[89] VS Vereschetin, 'New Constitutions and the Old Problem of the Relationship between International Law and National Law' (1996) 7 EJIL 29.

The main alternative approach to making international law part of the applicable domestic law is to transform international obligations into domestic law. This is for instance the situation in Australia,[90] Botswana,[91] India,[92] Israel,[93] Italy,[94] Kenya,[95] Malawi,[96] Nigeria,[97] Norway,[98] Uganda,[99] the United Kingdom[100] and Zambia.[101] In these States, a treaty will not be part of national law until the legislature has acted to transform the provisions of the treaty into domestic law. For instance, it was only the Finnish legislation that had incorporated the International Covenant on Civil and Political Rights (ICCPR) into domestic law, and not the ICCPR as such, that has made the ICCPR applicable in Finnish courts.[102]

Both avenues can lead to domestic effect of treaties. Nonetheless, some institutions have expressed a clear preference for the former method. The

---

[90] Australia, High Court, *Dietrich v the Queen* [1992] HCA 57; (1992) 177 CLR 292 (13 November 1992) 24.

[91] Botswana, Court of Appeal, *Good v Attorney-General*, Civil Appeal No 028; ILDC 8 (BW 2005) [33].

[92] India, Supreme Court, *Daya Singh Lahoria v India*, AIR 2001 SC 1716; ILDC 170 (IN 2001) [A1].

[93] Israel, Supreme Court sitting as a Court of Appeals, *Anonymous (Lebanese citizens) v Minister of Defence*, FCrA 7048/97; ILDC 12 (IL 2000) [20].

[94] Italy, Constitutional Court, *EP v Municipality of Avellino*, Case No 349/2007; (2008) 91 *Rivista di Diritto Internazionale* 230; ILDC 301 (IT 2007) [6.1].

[95] Kenya, High Court, *Okunda v Republic* (3 November 1969), [1970] East Africa Law Reports 453; (1970) 51 ILR 414.

[96] Article 211 of the Constitution of the Republic of Malawi (1994) (providing that '[a]ny international agreement ratified by an Act of Parliament shall form part of the law of the Republic if so provided for in the Act of Parliament ratifying the agreement'.).

[97] Article 12 Constitution of Nigeria (1999).

[98] See, eg, Norway, Supreme Court, *A v The Norwegian Immigration Appeals Board*, HR-2008-681-A, *Norwegian Supreme Court Gazette* (Rt, Retstidende) 2008, 513; ILDC 1326 (NO 2008) [35]–[36].

[99] Uganda, Constitutional Court, *Uganda Law Society and Jackson Karugaba v Attorney General*, Constitutional Petitions Nos 2 and 8 of 2002; ILDC 1284 (UG 2009) [A4].

[100] *Re McFarland* [2004] UKHL 17; ILDC 102 (UK 2004).

[101] Zambia, Supreme Court, *Re Order 53 of the Rules of the Supreme Court and Re Application for Leave for Judicial Review by Roy Clarke, Attorney General v Roy Clarke*, Appeal No 96A/2004; ILDC 1340 (ZM 2008).

[102] See, eg, Finland, Supreme Administrative Court, *Geological Survey of Finland v Ministry of Trade and Industry,* 31 March 1999/692 KHO:1999:14; ILDC 930 (FI 1999).

ECtHR,[103] the Human Rights Committee (HRC)[104] and the UN Committee on Economic, Social and Cultural Rights[105] have suggested that incorporation of the treaty as such in domestic law is the preferred way of implementation of international obligations.

It may be said that there is ground for reconsideration of the traditional neutrality of international law on the question of domestic validity. Such neutrality was understandable in the situation where treaties were primarily concerned with interstate affairs. Once treaties have, to a larger extent, an internal focus, other States party to a treaty acquire an interest in the degree in which an obligation is made effective domestically.[106] However, there is not much practice that supports a development in that direction. In any case, the benefits of automatic incorporation have to be seen in the context of its drawbacks. It may open the door to treaty obligations that are wanting in terms of democracy and rule of law quality.[107] This holds particularly for treaties that are exempted from parliamentary approval, and for decisions of international organizations that may raise constitutional questions about the permissibility of delegating law-making functions to an international body.[108] All these provisions moreover raise legitimacy concerns.[109]

In any case, the explanatory power of the distinction between the monist and dualist models for explaining the domestic effect of treaties is

---

103 *Ireland v United Kingdom* App no 5310/71 (1978) 25 EHRR 239.

104 Human Rights Committee, General Comment 31, Nature of the General Legal Obligation on States Parties to the Covenant, UN Doc CCPR/C/21/Rev.1/Add.13 (2004) para 31.

105 *See* UN Committee on Economic Social and Cultural Rights, 'General Comment 9' (1998) UN Doc E/C.12/1998/24 [8].

106 Sørensen, 'Die Verplichttungen …' (n 64) 32; Stein, 'International Law in Internal Law …' (n 87) 450; S Stirling-Zanda, 'Obtaining Judicial Enforcement of Individual Conventional Rights' (2004) 42 *Archiv des Völkerrechts* (2004) 184, 209.

107 JO MacGinnis and I Somin, 'Should International Law Be Part of Our Law?'(2007) 59 Stanford L Rev 1175; S Clarkson and S Wood, 'Canada's External Constitution and Its Democratic Deficit' in OE Fitzgerald (ed), *The Globalized Rule of Law: Relationships between International and Domestic Law* (Irwin Law, 2006) 97.

108 *Natural Resources Defense Council v Environmental Protection Agency*, ILDC 525 (US 2006) [A2], commentary by D Shelton.

109 D Bodansky, 'The Legitimacy of International Governance: A Coming Challenge for International Environmental Law?' (1999) 93 AJIL 596; R Wolfrum and V Röben (eds), *Legitimacy in International Law* (Springer, 2009); D Georgiev, 'Politics or Rule of Law: Deconstruction and Legitimacy in International Law' (1993) 4 EJIL 1.

relatively limited. On the one hand, in States where treaties are automatically incorporated, multiple barriers may exist that prevent organs from actually applying them. On the other hand, it is not uncommon for courts in dualist States to rely on treaties not incorporated in national law. In Kenya, even though the system appears formally dualist,[110] the High Court held that international law was applicable so long as it was not in conflict with existing domestic law.[111] In such cases, the formal constitutional position only reflects part of the actual competence of organs to give effect to international law. It is to be added that this practice sits somewhat uneasily with the principles of democratic legitimacy and separation of powers.

2. Supremacy

The supremacy of international law prioritizes international law over national law.[112] In the event of a conflict between a treaty and domestic law, international law will have to prevail in the international legal order. The principle is at the heart of the law of treaties.[113]

In principle, the claim to supremacy of international law has no necessary legal consequences domestically.[114] State practice shows no general acceptance of the supremacy of international law in the national legal order. What is wrong in the international law sphere may be right in the national sphere, and what is unlawful in the national legal order may be perfectly legal in international law.[115]

Nonetheless, the principle of supremacy is key to the effect of treaties in national law. Where the principle is fully recognized, it allows courts to set aside a law adopted by the political branches, in particular the legislature, and thereby to ensure conformity of the policy and law of the State with its treaty obligations. There is substantial State practice that

---

110 *Okunda v Republic* (n 95).

111 *Kamunzyu v Kamunzyu*, Succession Cause 303 of 1998, [2005] eKLR; ILDC 1342 (KE 2005).

112 See for a comprehensive treatment of this aspect of the principle of supremacy: D Carreau, *Droit International* (Pedone, 2004) 43; G Fitzmaurice, 'The General Principles of International Law Considered from the Standpoint of the Rule of Law' (1957) 92 Recueil des Cours 68. See also C Santulli, *Le Statut International de L'Ordre Juridique Étatique* (Pedone, 2001) 427.

113 Articles 27 and 46 of the Vienna Convention on the Law of Treaties.

114 M Virally, 'The Sources of International Law' in M Sørensen (ed), *Manual of Public International Law* (St Martin's Press, 1978) 116, 170.

115 The International Court of Justice held in *Elettronica Sicula SpA (ELSI) (USA v Italy)*, Judgment, ICJ Rep 1989 15, para 73.

places treaties at the level of constitutional law, and thus accepts domestic supremacy of all or some (notably human rights) treaties.[116] This locks such treaty law in the constitution and provides a barrier against (easy) deviation through legislation.[117] This, for instance, is the case in Cape Verde,[118] the Czech Republic,[119] Greece,[120] Japan,[121] the Netherlands,[122] Bulgaria[123] and Portugal.[124] Some States have even done so in express recognition of the international principle of supremacy; examples can be found in cases from Argentina,[125] Belgium,[126] Chile,[127] Latvia[128] and Peru.[129]

Such a 'domestication of supremacy of international law' can significantly strengthen the power of the principle of supremacy to foster the efficacy and the effectiveness of international law.

However, these practices are relatively exceptional. On the whole, States have reserved the power under domestic law to limit the performance of treaty obligations where these may conflict with domestic law. Many States determine that in the case of a conflict between a treaty and domestic law, the latest expression of the will of parliament determines

---

116 Cassese, 'Modern Constitutions …' (n 87) 402.

117 T Ginsburg, 'Locking in Democracy: Constitutions, Commitment and International Law' (2006) 38 NYU J Intl L and Politics 707.

118 Article 11(4) Constitution of the Republic of Cape Verde (1980).

119 Article 10 Constitution of the Czech Republic (1992).

120 Article 28(1) Constitution of the Hellenic Republic (1974/2008).

121 Iwasawa, '… International and National Law: Japanese Experiences' (n 80) 372.

122 Article 94 Constitution of the Kingdom of the Netherlands (1983).

123 Bulgaria, Supreme Administrative Court, *Al-Nashif v National Police Directorate at the Ministry of the Interior*, Administrative Case No 11004/2002; ILDC 608 (BG 2003) [H11].

124 *A and B v Portuguese State* (n 81).

125 T Buergenthal, 'International Tribunals and Courts: The Internationalization of Domestic Adjudication' in U Beyerlin and others (eds), *Recht Zwischen Umbruch und Bewahrung. Festschrift für Rudolf Bernhardt* (Springer-Verlag, 1995) 687, 698.

126 Belgium, Court of Cassation, *ING België v B I*, Case No C.05.0154.N; ILDC 1025 (BE 2007); Belgium, Court of Cassation, *Minister for Economic Affairs v Franco-Suisse 'Le Ski'* [1972] CMLR 330.

127 Chile, Supreme Court, *Perú v Chile*, Rol No 2242-06; ILDC 1443 (CL 2007).

128 Latvia, Constitutional Court, *Linija v Latvia,* Case No 2004-01-06; ILDC 189 (LV 2004).

129 Peru, Constitutional Court, *Martin Rivas v Constitutional and Social Chamber of the Supreme Court*, 679-2005-PA/TC; ILDC 960 (PE 2007) [49].

which rule is supreme – whether or not that rule is contained in a treaty.[130] Most States have declared their constitutions to be supreme. Such States do not accept the supremacy of treaties as a formal principle, but make the effect of international law contingent on substantive conformity with fundamental values enshrined in national law.[131] In this respect it is relevant that many States restrict the precedence of international law in the domestic legal order to international human rights treaties.[132]

3. Direct Effect

Direct effect is a technique that can be used to facilitate or to block domestic effect of a treaty. On the one hand, it allows a court or other organ to apply a treaty obligation irrespective of any intervening legislative step. An organ can then give effect to an international obligation even when organs of other political branches have failed to give it effect.[133] This compliance-inducing potential can be caught in the notion of direct effect as a 'sword'.

On the other hand, direct effect can function as a shield. The mere fact that a rule of international law has been made part of national law is not sufficient for it to be applied on the same footing as domestic law.[134] This shield can fix the separation of powers, by protecting other branches of government from review by national courts on the basis of international law. For instance, although Article VI of the US constitution says that treaties are the supreme law of the land, the self-executing treaties doctrine imposes restrictions on judicial enforcement.[135]

---

[130] A Peters, 'The Globalization of State Constitutions' in J Nijman and A Nollkaemper (eds), *New Perspectives on the Divide between International and National Law* (OUP, 2007) 251, 260. See also the overview in Carreau, *Droit International* (n 112) 58–68.

[131] T Cottier and D Wüger, 'Auswirkungen der Globalisierung aus das Verfasungsrecht: Eine Diskussionsgrundlage' (1997) 16 *Kolloquium der Schweizerischen Akademie der Geistes- und Sozialwissenschaften* 241, 263.

[132] Peters, 'The Globalization of State Constitutions' (n 130) 260 and 269.

[133] V Skouris, ´Effet Utile versus Direct Effect: The Case-Law of the Court of Justice on the Direct Effect of Directives´ (2006) 17 European Business L Rev 241, at 242.

[134] That also holds for use of the concept in EU law: see, eg, J Gerkrath, 'Chapter 6 – Direct Effect in Germany and France: A Constitutional Comparison' in JM Prinssen and AAM Schrauwen (eds), *Direct Effect: Rethinking a Classic EC Legal Doctrine* (Europa Law Publishing, 2002) 129.

[135] *Foster v Neilson,* US Supreme Court, 2 Pet 253, 314 (1829).

International law is neutral on the question of direct effect.[136] It respects the right of States to determine for themselves whether or not they allow their courts to give direct effect to a treaty obligation. This liberty also means that we have to reject what Iwasawa called the 'given-theory': the idea that international law would determine whether or not a particular rule of international law has direct effect.[137]

Whether or not treaties can have direct effect thus is a choice of domestic (constitutional) legislators and the courts. Direct effect appears possible in a considerable number of States, including Argentina,[138] Bulgaria,[139] the Czech Republic,[140] the Dominican Republic,[141] Egypt,[142] France,[143] Japan,[144] Latvia,[145] the Netherlands[146] and Switzerland.[147]

---

[136] *Request for Interpretation of the Judgment of 31 March 2004 in the Case concerning Avena and Other Mexican Nationals (Mexico v United States of America)* ICJ Rep 2009 3 para 44.

[137] Y Iwasawa, 'The Doctrine of Self-Executing Treaties in the United States: A Critical Analysis' (1986) 26 Virginia J Intl L 627, 650.

[138] Section 31 of the Constitution of Argentina (1853). See for an example, *Simón (Julio Héctor) v Office of the Public Prosecutor*, Appeal Judgment, S. 1767. XXXVIII, ILDC 579 (AR 2005), Fallos 328:2056, 14 June 2005, Sup Ct (Argentina).

[139] Bulgaria, Supreme Court of Cassation, *Council of Ministers v TSD and ors,* Judgment No 1177, Civil Case No 241/2007 (2007); ILDC 972 (BG 2007).

[140] Article 10 Constitution of the Czech Republic (1992); see, eg, for an application, *Minister of Justice v Šenk,* Supreme Court of the Czech Republic, 8 Tz 38/2000; ILDC 1444 (CZ 2000).

[141] Article 3 Constitution of the Dominican Republic (1994). See, eg, *Gallardo Montilla v Gallardo Concepción,* Supreme Court of Justice, ILDC 1490 (DO 1997).

[142] Article 151 Constitution of the Arab Republic of Egypt (1971). See, eg, *Public Prosecution of Egypt v Salah Aldian Mustafa Ismail,* Supreme Court of State Security of Egypt, No 4190/86 Ozbekia (121 Koli Shamal) (1987); ILDC 1483 (EG 1987).

[143] France, Court of Cassation, *X v Y,* Cassation Appeal, Information Bulletin of the Court of Cassation No 626 of 1 October 2005, No. 1810 (2005); ILDC 770 (FR 2005).

[144] Y Iwasawa, *International Law, Human Rights, and Japanese Law: The Impact of International Law on Japanese Law* (Clarendon, 1998) 13, 25, 33.

[145] Latvia, Constitutional Court, *Re Latvian Education Law,* Constitutional Review, Case No. 2004-18-0106 (2005); ILDC 190 (LV 2005).

[146] Netherlands, Council of State, *Reinier van Arkel Foundation and ors v Minister for Transport, Public Works and Water Management,* 200401178/1 (2004); ILDC 129 (NL 2004).

[147] Switzerland, Federal Supreme Court, *A and B v Government of the Canton of Zurich,* Appeal Judgment, Case No 2P.273/1999 (2000); ILDC 350 (CH 2000).

In the practice of these States, there seems to be a close connection between direct effect and the allocation of individual rights by treaties. For instance, the Federal Supreme Court of Switzerland held that a provision of a treaty is only self-executing if it regulates the legal position of an individual, even though the question of whether that is the case is then made dependent on the substantive completeness of the norm.[148]

4. Consistent Interpretation

The term consistent interpretation refers to the interpretation of domestic law in conformity with international obligations. Through consistent interpretation, courts can achieve a result that is in conformity with international law and thus secure the performance of treaty obligations.[149]

The practice of courts that engage in consistent interpretation is widespread. It includes both civil law[150] and common law systems.[151] It also includes States that allow for automatic incorporation and those that require transformation. The former category includes States like Austria,[152] Ethiopia,[153] Japan,[154] Latvia,[155] the Netherlands,[156] Poland[157] and the United States;[158] in the latter category are States like Australia,[159]

---

148 *A and B v Government of the Canton of Zurich* (n 84) para 2b. Similarly Belgium, see *Art Research & Contact Naamloze Vennootschap v BS* (n 55) para 29.

149 Cassese, 'Modern Constitutions …' (n 87) 398.

150 Eg, *Switzerland v A and B*, Federal Supreme Court of Switzerland, BGE 128 IV 117; ILDC 347 (CH 2002) [6d].

151 Eg, *Minister for Immigration and Ethnic Affairs v Teoh* (n 18); HCA 20, 128 ALR 353 (1995); ILDC 779 (AU 1995).

152 Balthasar, '"Pacta sunt servanda." Zur innerstaatlichen Relevanz von durch Staatsvertrages eingegangenen Verpflichtungen Osterreichs', 50 ZOR (1996) 161, 169.

153 Article 13(4) Constitution of the Federal Democratic Republic of Ethiopia (1995).

154 Y Iwasawa, 'The Domestic Impact of International Human Rights Standards: The Japanese Experience' in P Alston and J Crawford (eds), *The Future of UN Human Rights Treaty Monitoring* (CUP, 2000) 245, 259.

155 *Re Latvian Education Law* (n 145) 5.

156 *TSM Compagnie d'Assurance Transports v Geisseler Transport AG*, Supreme Court of the Netherlands, NJ 1992/107, (1990).

157 *Stanisław K v Zakład Techniczno-Budowlany P Spółka Zoo*, Supreme Court of Poland, II PK 100/05; ILDC 388 (PL 2005) 10.

158 *Murray v The Charming Betsy*, 2 *Cranch 64*, US Supreme Court, 6 US 64 (1804) 118.

159 *Minister for Immigration and Ethnic Affairs v Teoh* (n 18) 202, 27.

Canada,[160] Iceland,[161] Israel,[162] Uganda,[163] South Africa,[164] Zambia[165] and the United Kingdom.[166]

It may be possible to infer from this practice a general principle of interpretation such that, within the limits of their domestic powers, national courts should interpret domestic law in conformity with the international obligations of the State.[167] However, there are major differences in the concept as it applies in different States and the normative guidance of such a principle would in any case be limited.

In domestic practice we can distinguish three broad categories in which the principle of consistent interpretation is applied. First, consistent interpretation is commonly applied when a provision of national law is ambiguous. For instance, when the Canadian Supreme Court was concerned with finding a definition of terrorism that provided a sufficiently well understood basis for adjudication, it found that the definition provided in Article 2(1)(b) of the International Convention for the Suppression of the Financing of Terrorism of 1999 embodied the essence of what is meant by 'terrorism'.[168]

---

160 *United States (Minister of Justice) v Burns and Rafay,* Supreme Court of Canada, 1 SCR 283, 2001 SCC 7; (2001) 195 DLR (4th) 1; ILDC 187 (CA 2001).

161 *State Social Security Institute v Organization of the Disabled in Iceland,* Supreme Court of Iceland, Case No. 125/2000, H 2000 4480 (2000); ILDC 68 (IS 2000).

162 *Kurtz and Letushinsky v Kirschen,* Supreme Court of Israel sitting as a Court of Civil Appeal, 21 Piskei Din (II) 20; (1967) 47 ILR 212, 214–15; *Kav La'oved Association v Israel,* Supreme Court of Israel sitting as the High Court of Justice, HCJ 4542/02; ILDC 382 (IL 2006) 37.

163 *Onynango-Obbo and Mwenda v Attorney-General,* Supreme Court of Uganda, Case No 2 (2002); ILDC 166 (UG 2004).

164 *Mazibuko v City of Johannesburg,* High Court of South Africa, ZAGPHC 128 (2008); ILDC 973 (ZA 2008) 31.

165 *Re Order 53 of the Rules of the Supreme Court and Re Application for Leave for Judicial Review by Roy Clarke, Attorney General v Roy Clarke* (n 101).

166 *R v Secretary of State for the Home Department, ex parte Brind, House of Lords,* 1 AC 696 (1991).

167 This was suggested by the ECtHR in *Jorgic v Germany* ECHR (2007) 70.

168 *Suresh v Canada (Minister of Citizenship and Immigration) and Attorney-General of Canada* [2002] 1 SCR 3; 37 Admin LR (3d) 159; ILDC 186 (CA 2002) [93]–[98]. See also Kenya, High Court, *RM and Cradle v Attorney General*, Civil Case 1351; ILDC 699 (KE 2006) [73].

Second, courts may engage in consistent interpretation whenever the wording of national law allows for it.[169] If a term has one meaning in domestic law and another in international law, the latter should prevail, to the extent that national law allows room for that interpretation.[170]

Third, courts may give effect to treaty obligations in reviewing the exercise of discretion by the executive in the light of such obligations. Treaty provisions may come in as an element in the grounds for review, in particular in the principles of reasonableness and legitimate expectations.[171]

The relevance of consistent interpretation is particularly clear in so-called dualist States, where delays may occur between the entry into force of treaties and domestic implementation, and courts may, through a process of interpretation, ensure domestic compliance with a treaty even if the political branches are not (yet) ready for it.[172]

In monist States, the practice of consistent interpretation is particularly relevant since it is not contingent on the question of whether a rule of international law can be given direct effect, and thus may allow a court to circumvent the shield that the concept of direct effect may set up. While courts generally restrict direct effect to a narrow category of rules that satisfies the criterion of completeness, consistent interpretation is not dependent on any a priori qualities of a rule of international law.[173]

In both these situations, consistent interpretation can circumvent limitations flowing from the separation of powers. When a court can achieve through consistent interpretation a result which it could also have brought about by granting a treaty provision direct effect (and which, however, it might wish to avoid because of separation of power concerns) consistent interpretation may help subtly shift powers to the courts. Indeed, the principle of separation of powers itself operates to limit the

---

[169] JF Coyle, 'Incorporative Statutes and the Borrowed Treaty Rule' (2010) 50 Virginia J Intl L 655.

[170] Australia, High Court, *Povey v Qantas Airways Ltd and British Airways Plc* [2005] HCA 33; (2005) 216 ALR 427; (2005) 79 ALJR 1215; ILDC 506 (AU 2005) [128] (Separate Opinion of Kirby J).

[171] M Allars, 'International Law and Administrative Discretion' in B Opeskin and D Rothwell (eds), *International Law and Australian Federalism* (Melbourne UP, 1997) 232, 256.

[172] *State v Metropolitan Police Commissioner*, Supreme Court of Bangladesh, 60 DLR (2008) 660; ILDC 1410 (BD 2008), 28; see also *Ershad v Bangladesh*, Supreme Court of Bangladesh, 21 BLD (AD) (2001) 69; ILDC 476 (BD 2000) 3 (Bimolendu Bikash Roy Chowdhury).

[173] Ibid; *Ziers v Gedeputeerde Staten Gelderland*, Council of State of the Netherlands, Case No AB 1995/24 (1993).

power of courts to engage in consistent interpretation. For instance, this limit has led courts to construe their interpretative use of international law in reviewing the exercise of discretion by other branches in strictly procedural terms.[174]

V. OUTLOOK: AN AGENDA FOR RESEARCH

To some extent the topic of domestic effects of treaties is static – not much has changed in the basic principles of international law reflecting its neutrality on domestic effects. On the other hand, if we consider the content of treaties, the (sometimes contested) role of international institutions, and in particular the evolving practice at national level, the topic appears to be in considerable flux. In relation to these dynamic dimensions, several topics can be identified that could – and perhaps should – guide further research.

A first area that has hardly been researched is how States, by including particular properties in treaties, seek to control, enhance or limit the domestic effects of treaties. What properties are relevant in this sense? What patterns, if any, can we see over time, relating to the increasing degree in which treaties substantively connect to national law?

A second, related question is whether any changes that we may identify in practice would call for a reconsideration of the largely neutral principles in general international law and the law of treaties specifically.

Turning to the domestic level, one area for research relates to the empirical question of to what extent States have opened their national legal orders to the effect of treaties, or rather have sought to limit such effect. What factors underlie such developments? Do we see a variation in subject matter of treaties and between regions? How do separation of power considerations, that themselves are in a state of flux, influence the reception of treaties?

A follow-up set of questions relates to the normative issues underlying and raised by this practice. Does the practice of treaty making, when viewed from the perspective of modern understandings of the legitimacy

---

[174] *Minister for Immigration and Ethnic Affairs v Teoh* (n 18) para 28 (Mason CJ and Deane J); Australia, High Court, *Re Minister for Immigration and Multicultural and Indigenous Affairs* (2003) 214 CLR 1; [2003] HCA 6; (2003) 195 ALR 502; (2003) 77 ALJR 699; ILDC 203 (AU 2003) [99]; Ireland, Supreme Court, *Kavanagh (Joseph) v Governor of Mountjoy Prison* ILDC 488 (IE 2002) para 38.

of international law-making, justify open national legal orders allowing for full effect of treaties, or does it rather call for increasing filters?

The increasing focus of treaties on matters of domestic law calls for and necessitates a reconsideration of the rather classic field of the law of treaties from the perspective of the evolving interface between the international and the national level.

PART II

DIMENSIONS

6. The temporal dimension: Non-retroactivity and its discontents

Markus Kotzur[*]

I. INTRODUCTION: NON-RETROACTIVITY AND THE DYNAMICS OF 'LIVING LAW'

The principle of non-retroactivity – a law would be retroactive if it 'alters the status of legal acts that were performed before it came into existence'[1] – is well established both in national and public international law.[2] Within a domestic legal system geared towards respect of the rule of law, non-retroactivity primarily qualifies as a remedy to avoid the abuse of legislative power in the adoption of a law (eg, the retroactive infringement of individual rights and freedoms by the lawmaker) or the abuse of executive power in the application of this law (eg, the retroactive infringement of individual rights and freedoms by the executive/administrative branch of government).[3] Being aware of this principle-oriented rule of law perspective, public international law – in particular treaty law (Article 28 of the Vienna Convention on the Law of Treaties 1969 (VCLT)) – has to consider the issue from another, but not completely different, angle. It must take into account that many of the

* The author would like to thank his scientific research assistant, Pauline Mattern, very much for her most helpful assistance in researching for this chapter, conceptualizing its structure and proof-reading the drafts.

1 JSR Munzer, 'Retroactive Law' (1977) 6 The Journal of Legal Studies 373, 373.

2 JT Woodhouse, 'The Principle of Retroactivity in International Law' (1955) 41 Transactions/The Grotius Society 69; A Chua and R Hardcastle, 'Retroactive Application of Treaties Revisited: Bosnia-Herzegovina v Yugoslavia' (1997) 44 Netherlands Intl L Rev 414, 414; ME Villiger, *Commentary on the 1969 Vienna Convention on the Law of Treaties: Article 28 – Non-Retroactivity of Treaties* (Martinus Nijhoff, 2009) 381 para 1; MN Shaw, *International Law* (6th edn, CUP, 2008) 926; A von Arnauld, *Völkerrecht* (C.F. Müller, 2012) 74.

3 Specifically see, GE Do Nascimento e Silva, 'Le Facteur Temps et les Traités' (1977) 154 Recueil des Cours de l'Académie de Droit International 272.

most fundamental changes in the international legal order are treaty-driven and thus result from conventional norms. In other words: treaties, entered into by equally sovereign States (Article 2(1) of the Charter of the United Nations 1945 (UNC)),[4] are the most effective means of enabling public international law to meet the needs and expectations of the globalized world in the 21st century. Treaties, to some extent radically, change public international law *pro futuro* because the parties to the treaties have consented to *henceforth* accept and adjust to these changes. A general retroactive application of the treaties would go beyond that consent and, at least indirectly, carry the risk of imposing retroactive obligations on the individual.[5] With regard to the latter point, the rule of law and the State consent-based dimensions of non-retroactivity go hand in hand. Article 28 VCLT, in addressing the temporal scope of a treaty, therefore reflects both: the traditional consent-orientation of public international law as well as its more recently discussed attachment to a rule of law-based scheme of global governance.[6]

Non-retroactivity, however, is a rather static concept and as such has its limits. All legal codifications should be seen, at least to some extent, as 'living instruments', the purpose of which is to adjust the achievements that have to be preserved from the past to the ever-changing present-day circumstances and beyond that to the more or less predictable needs of

---

4 B Fassbender, 'Article 2' in B Simma et al (eds), *The Charter of the United Nations*: *Volume I* (3rd edn, OUP, 2012) 133 para 64 *et seq.*

5 Again, reference has to be made to Do Nascimento e Silva, 'Le Facteur Temps …' (n 3) 272:

> *En droit international il faut examiner le problème sous un autre angle. D'abord, il faut tenir compte que les modifications dans l'ordre juridique international résultent de normes conventionnelles, c'est-à-dire des traités, qui constituent le principal moyen d'adaption du droit international à la réalité moderne. Ce phénomène peut être vérifié par quelques modifications radicales dans l'ordre juridique international, qui ont été le résultat de quelques conventions multilatérales. A ce sujet, il faut observer que, comme le principe de l'autonomie de la volonté est presque absolu et donne aux Etats un pouvoir presque discrétionnaire, les Etats doivent éviter l'adoption de règles rétroactives qui puissent être préjudicielles à leurs nationaux ou aux étrangers, qui sont, au fond, les destinataires de toutes les règles de droit international.*

6 This is reflected in particular in discussions of the 'transferability of domestic legacy to contexts beyond the State', see T Kleinlein, 'Between Myths and Norms: Constructivist Constitutionalism and the Potential of Constitutional Principles in International Law' (2012) 81 Nordic J Intl L 79 *et seq.*

the future. Public international law is – as law, as culture, and as human life are in general – 'deeply imbedded in time';[7] in the course of time law aims on the one side to *preserve* and on the other side to *modify* the ordering structures any polity is based upon; it is both a social mechanism of *continuity* and of *change*; it is both an instrument of *stability* and of *flexibility*.[8] As the Institut de Droit International (IDI) stated in its resolution on 'The Intertemporal Problem in Public International Law' (adopted 1975 in Wiesbaden): international law must, at the same time, 'promote the development of the international legal system whilst preserving the principle of legal stability which is an essential part of any juridical system'.[9] The more important universal legal standards become, the more important it becomes to have an appropriate balance between these dichotomies. This dialectical structure is expressly reflected by the Canadian Supreme Court's 'living tree doctrine' – a doctrine which can be transferred to public international law regulatory regimes: 'The "frozen concepts" reasoning runs contrary to one of the most fundamental principles of Canadian constitutional interpretation: that our Constitution is a living tree which, by way of progressive interpretation, accommodates and addresses the realities of modern life.'[10] Progressive interpretation, however, can have retroactive (side-)effects; and possible tensions between contemporaneous and present-day understandings of the language utilized need to be balanced when interpreting treaties or other agreements. Facts or acts can occur more than once, they can be repeated, and situations might continue to exist – they '*live on*', not

---

[7] JG Rodas, 'The Doctrine of Non-Retroactivity of International Treaties' (1973) 68 Revista da Faculdade de Direito de São Paulo 341, 341.

[8] P Häberle, 'Zeit und Verfassungskultur' in P Häberle, *Rechtsvergleichung im Kraftfeld des Verfassungsstaates* (Duncker & Humblot 1992) 627; W Berg, 'Die Zeit im öffentlichen Recht – Das öffentliche Recht in der Zeit' (2008) 56 Jahrbuch des öffentlichen Rechts 23, 23–24; S Kirste, 'Die Zeit der Verfassung' (2008) 56 Jahrbuch des öffentlichen Rechts 35, 35; M Kotzur, 'Zeitlichkeit und Ungleichzeitigkeiten im Völkerrecht' in U Hösch (ed), *Liber Amicorum W Berg* (Richard Boorberg Verlag, 2011) 199, 199–200.

[9] IDI Resolution, 'The Intertemporal Problem in Public International Law' (1975) 56 AnnIDI 536; Do Nascimento e Silva, 'Le Facteur Temps …' (n 3) 272; see also Rodas, 'The Doctrine of Non-Retroactivity …' (n 7) 341, 344.

[10] *Reference re Same-Sex Marriage* (Supreme Court of Canada) [2004] 3 SCR 698, 2004 SCC 79 para 22; WJ Waluchow, *A Common Law Theory of Judicial Review: The Living Tree* (CUP, 2007).

allowing for a strict bar against retroactive application.[11] Newly established *jus cogens* might open a specific backdoor for retroactive effects and so, too, might the distinction between the non-retroactivity of a treaty's substantive provisions, on the one hand, and its judicial enforcement (retroactive jurisdiction), on the other.[12] The fabric or texture of public international law is one of dynamics and continuity both of which can also be seen as the essence of a *'living' rule of law*.

II. NON-RETROACTIVITY IN PUBLIC INTERNATIONAL LAW – CONTEXTUALIZING PRINCIPLES

1. The Baseline Principle: An International Rule of Law

Even though international affairs are mostly conducted in the political rather than the strictly legal sphere, public international law has throughout the 20th and the beginning of the 21st centuries introduced many advanced international institutions. With this process of institutionalization comes a tremendous amount of new international regulations (such as peace and security law, human rights law, international environmental law, international economic law, etc).[13] This, so to speak, 'legalization of international relations'[14] implicitly reflects an 'international rule of

---

[11] A Buyse, 'A Lifeline in Time: Non-Retroactivity and Continuing Violations under the ECHR' (2006) 75 Nordic J Intl L 63, 65 with explicit reference to P Reuter, *Introduction to the Law of Treaties* (Kegan Paul International, 1995) 100.

[12] Buyse, 'A Lifeline in Time …' (n 11) 63, 65; A Aust, *Modern Treaty Law and Practice* (2nd edn, CUP, 2000) 142.

[13] S Chesterman, 'Rule of Law' (2012) MPEPIL, www.mpepil.com, accessed 11 February 2013, para 46; A Segura-Serrano, 'The Transformation of International Law' (2009) Jean Monnet Working Paper 12/09, 8, http://centers.law.nyu.edu/jeanmonnet/papers/09/091201.html, accessed 2 July 2012.

[14] KW Abbott, RO Keohane, A Moravcsik, A-M Slaughter and D Snidal, 'The Concept of Legalization' (2000) 54 Intl Organization 401; D Bindschedler-Robert, 'De la Rétroactivité en Droit International Public' in Faculté de Droit de l'Université de Genève, Institut Universitaire de Hautes Études Internationales, Genève (eds), *Recueil d'études de droit international – En Hommage à Paul Guggenheim* (Imprimerie de La Tribune de Genève, 1968) 185: '*C'est un truisme de constater que le droit international, comme tout ordre juridique, constitue un ordre normatif*'.

law'[15] in the making. The more *public* powers – *public* in a functional sense – are exercised by transnational actors, the more urgent becomes an adequate scheme to *legitimize*, *limit*, and *control* the empowerment of the actors, on the one hand, and the exercise of the relevant powers, on the other. At least to some extent, the actors have to be bound to 'rule of law' mechanisms. This does not mean to simply contend the existence of an international rule of law or to disregard the structural discrepancies between the national and the international realm. On the contrary, a simple analogy would be an obvious – *semantic* and *conceptual* – shortcoming. From a functional point of view, however, universal needs for not more but also not less than a rule of law-*orientation* become quite obvious. Among these needs, a particularly high significance can be allocated to the publicity of the law and to legal certainty.[16]

Here, an apparent nexus between an international rule of law and the principle of non-retroactivity can be made out. The underlying justification for non-retroactivity is legal certainty as well as foreseeability.[17]

---

[15] J Carter, 'The Rule of Law and the State of Human Rights' (1991) 4 Harvard Human Rights J 1 *et seq*; A Watts, 'The International Rule of Law' (1993) 36 German YB Intl L 15 *et seq*; D Thürer, 'Internationales "Rule of Law" – Innerstaatliche Demokratie' (1995) 5 Schweizerische Zeitschrift für Internationales und Europäisches Recht 455 *et seq*; I Brownlie, *The Rule of Law in International Affairs: International Law at the Fiftieth Anniversary of the United Nations* (Martinus Nijhoff, 1998); G Hafner, 'The Rule of Law and International Organizations' in K Dicke et al (eds), *Liber Amicorum J Delbrück* (Duncker & Humblot, 2005) 307 *et seq*; M Wittinger, 'Das Rechtsstaatsprinzip – vom Nationalen Verfassungsprinzip zum Rechtsprinzip der Europäischen und der Internationalen Gemeinschaft?' (2009) 57 Jahrbuch des öffentlichen Rechts 427 *et seq*; S Chesterman, 'An International Rule of Law?' (2008) 56 American J Comparative L 331–61; NYU Law School, Public Law Research Paper No 08-11, http://ssrn.com/abstract=1081738, accessed 14 July 2012; Chesterman, 'Rule of Law' (n 13).

[16] M Kotzur, 'Der Rechtsstaat im Völkerrecht' in M Breuer, A Epiney, A Haratsch, S Schmahl and N Weiß (eds), *Der Staat im Recht: Festschrift für Eckart Klein zum 70. Geburtstag* (Duncker & Humblot, 2013) 797, 809. Legal certainty is a principle of EU law, too, see Case 70/83 *Gerda Kloppenburg v Finanzamt Leer* [1984] ECR 1075.

[17] Buyse, 'A Lifeline in Time …' (n 11) 63, 64. As to legal certainty, see Villiger, *Article 28 – Non-Retroactivity of Treaties* (n 2) 386: 'There remains one conceptual difficulty relating to non-retroactivity, not raised in the *travaux préparatoires*, namely the conflict which arises with the principle of legal certainty: before the treaty's entry into force, the situation was governed (and enforceable) by other then prevailing legal rules which, with the "retroactive" advent of the treaty, may suddenly become obsolete.'

Non-retroactivity ensures that the application of legal regulations is not extended to facts or situations that have taken place before the regulations entered into force and when accordingly the impact of the regulations could not have been predicted. Non-retroactivity moreover avoids, or at least limits, uncertainties about the temporal application (*ratione temporis*) of a rule.[18] It is worthwhile to refer to Article 102 UNC in this context. Treaties, the content or even the existence of which are unknown to the public, create legal uncertainty and thus destabilize international relations. One of the most prominent examples of an attempt to eliminate this risk of uncertainty is given by the first of US President Woodrow Wilson's famous Fourteen Points. In the aftermath of World War I, he demanded, among others, '[o]pen covenants of peace, openly arrived at, after which there shall be no private international understanding of any kind but diplomacy shall proceed always frankly and in the public view'.[19] The so-called principle of 'legal publicity' and non-retroactivity of the law therefore share a common aim, in ensuring certainty and predictability of legal rules and obligations. The two categories of legal certainty and predictability are of the utmost importance when it comes to international criminal law. Penal provisions may not – according to the principle *nullum crimen, nulla poena sine lege stricta, (scripta), praevia* – have any retroactive effect to the detriment of the accused.[20] This was intensively discussed in the context of the Nuremberg and Tokyo tribunals[21] and finds continuous reflection in recent debates on international criminal law measures.[22] The European Court of Justice (ECJ)

---

[18] Buyse, 'A Lifeline in Time … ' (n 11) 63, 65 with reference to E Wyler, 'Quelques Réflexions sur la Réalisation dans le Temps du Fait Internationalement Illicite' (1991) 95 Revue Générale de Droit International Public 881, 896.

[19] Quoted according to E Martens, 'Article 102' in B Simma et al (eds), *The Charter of the United Nations: Volume II* (3rd edn, OUP, 2012) 2089 para 1.

[20] W-D Krause-Ablass, *Intertemporales Völkerrecht: Der zeitliche Anwendungsbereich von Völkerrechtsnormen* (Metzner, 1970) 43 *et seq*; G Werle, *Principles of International Criminal Law* (2nd edn, TMC Asser Press, 2009) 36–9; M C Bassiouni, *Introduction to International Criminal Law* (2nd revised edn, Martinus Nijhoff, 2013) 246–53; finally for European Union Law, see S Heikkilä, 'Prohibition of the Retroactive Application of Legislative Measures in the European Community Law' (1998) 9 The Finnish YB of Intl L 483 *et seq.*

[21] Already a classic, H Kelsen, 'Will the Judgment in the Nuremberg Trial Constitute a Precedent in International Law?' (1947) 1 The Intl L Q 153 *et seq.*

[22] B Van Schaack, 'Crimen Sine Lege: Judicial Lawmaking at the Intersection of Law and Morals' (2008) 97 Georgetown L J 119; A Cassese, *International Criminal Law* (OUP, 2003) 147–53. As to recent case law on the European plane, reference can be made to *M v Germany* ECHR 2009–VI 169;

also strictly refuses retroactivity in penal law. In *Kirk*, the Court held that 'such retroactivity may not, in any event, have the effect of validating *ex post facto* national measures of a penal nature which impose penalties for an act which, in fact, was not punishable at the time at which it was committed'.[23]

2. The Rule of Intertemporal Law

Next to the rule of law, non-retroactivity has to be contextualized with the rule (or principle) of intertemporal law.[24] Importantly, the two must not be confused: non-retroactivity itself – explicitly enshrined in Article 28 VCLT – forms only a part of the rule of intertemporal law (which, in general, aims at resolving a temporal conflict of laws).[25] Whenever the law changes, in particular by the entry into force of a new treaty, it becomes necessary to determine the field of application of the past rules and the new law.[26] This determination or 'delimitation' is, in the words of João G Rodas, 'the task of the intertemporal law'.[27] It has a primary focus not on the *temporal validity* but on the *temporal applicability* of a norm. Intertemporal problems are not limited to public international law. They arise in all fields of law and on all levels of political integration: civil law, criminal law, public law (constitutional law, administrative law), be it within the nation State, within regional entities such as the European Union,[28] or within the international community.[29] As far as public international law is concerned, the intertemporal approach was affirmed in the famous *Island of Palmas* arbitration (1928) by Swiss

Jendrowiak v Germany App no 30060/04 (ECtHR, 14 April 2011) (retrospectively imposed preventive detention).

[23] Case 63/83 *Regina v Kent Kirk* [1984] ECR 2689, 2718; for further details see Heikkilä, 'Prohibition of the Retroactive Application …' (n 20) 482, 487.

[24] M Kotzur, 'Intertemporal Law' (2008) MPEPIL, www.mpepil.com, accessed 11 February 2013, paras 1–3.

[25] K Odendahl, 'Article 28' in O Dörr and K Schmalenbach (eds), *Vienna Convention on the Law of Treaties: A Commentary* (Springer, 2012) 477 para 2; TO Elias, 'The Doctrine of Intertemporal Law' (1980) 74 AJIL 285 *et seq.*

[26] Rodas, 'The Doctrine of Non-Retroactivity …' (n 7) 341, 342.

[27] Ibid.

[28] For example, Case 113/81 *Otto Reichelt GmbH v Hauptzollamt Berlin-Süd* [1982] ECR 1957.

[29] As to the notion of an international community in general, AL Paulus, *Die Internationale Gemeinschaft im Völkerrecht* (Beck, 2001); M Payandeh, *Internationales Gemeinschaftsrecht: Zur Herausbildung gemeinschaftsrechtlicher Strukturen im Völkerrecht der Globalisierung* (Springer, 2010).

arbitrator Max Huber. He emphasized that 'a juridical fact must be appreciated in the light of the law contemporary with it, and not of the law in force at the time when the dispute in regard to it arises or falls to be settled'.[30] Huber, however, goes on distinguishing between the creation of rights and the existence of rights: 'The same principle which subjects the acts creative of a right to the law in force at the time the right arises, demands that the existence of the right, in other words its continued manifestation, shall follow the conditions required by the evolution of law'.[31]

This oft-quoted distinction between the creation and the existence of rights is the most decisive point in Huber's approach. The first element, that rights should be analysed in the light of the legal system contemporaneous with their creation, has been widely accepted. The second element, which refers to the necessity to pay attention to change and evolution in the existence of these rights as well, has been criticized as threatening legal titles and hence causing instability. However, the two key elements of the *Island of Palmas* arbitration should not be conceived as primarily antithetic but complementary principles. The stability due to the creation of rights and the necessary flexibility due to evolution of the law relating to the existence of these rights supplement each other.[32] An advanced restatement of the intertemporal doctrine has been given by the IDI. In 1975, led by Rapporteur M Sørensen, the IDI adopted a resolution regarding 'The Intertemporal Problem in Public International Law' ('IDI Resolution 1975').[33] The general principle is outlined in Article 1 of the resolution: 'Unless otherwise indicated, the temporal sphere of application of any norm of public international law shall be determined in

---

[30] *Island of Palmas Case (Netherlands v USA)* (1928) 2 RIAA 829, 845. See also Bindschedler-Robert, '… Rétroactivité en Droit … ' (n 14) 188–9:

> *C'est donc le moment où s'est produit le fait dont le juge doit déterminer la règle applicable, lorsque de règles différentes sur le même objet se sont succédé dans le temps. Ainsi, c'est la règle contemporaine à l'acte dont on affirme le caractère illicite qui devra être appliquée pour apprécier ce caractère. Ce droit n'est pas nécessairement le droit en vigueur au moment de la naissance du conflit, celui-ci pouvant être né postérieurement sinon à l'acte prétendument illicite, du moins aux faits qui conditionnent le caractère de cet acte.*

[31] *Island of Palmas Case* (n 30) 845.

[32] For the subsequent development and the case law of the ICJ, see Kotzur, 'Intertemporal Law' (n 24) para 7.

[33] IDI Resolution, 'The Intertemporal Problem in Public International Law' (n 9) 536.

accordance with the general principle of law by which any fact, action or situation must be assessed in the light of the rules that are contemporaneous with it'.[34]

III. NON-RETROACTIVITY IN PUBLIC INTERNATIONAL LAW: ITS LEGAL CHARACTER AND ITS SCOPE OF APPLICATION

Whether non-retroactivity (of treaties) is limited to Article 28 VCLT, or qualifies as a rule of international customary law, or even amounts to a general principle of law is not quite clear and is therefore disputed.[35] The constant State practice (in most cases States do not provide for retroactivity of the treaties they enter into), the approval by conventional practice, by international organizations, as well as by international courts and tribunals, clearly indicates the existence of a rule of customary law.[36] Additionally, as already stated above, non-retroactivity is a fundamental principle in most domestic legal orders as well as in international law. It is therefore also liable to be considered as a 'general principle of law recognized by civilized nations' in the sense of Article 38(1)(c) of the Statute of the International Court of Justice 1945 (ICJ Statute).[37] Even

---

[34] Ibid.

[35] Odendahl, 'Article 28' (n 25) 479 para 5. Some even deny the necessity or very existence of such a principle, see the illustrating references made by Rodas, 'The Doctrine of Non-Retroactivity …' (n 7) 343:

> 'Charles Rousseau and Baade recognize the necessity of the principle of non-retroactivity, though they admit that this principle has certain limits. However other internationalists doubt such necessity. Some Italian jurists – as Cavaglieri for instance – deny the possibility of a transitory law in International Law and consequently reject the existence of a principle of non-retroactivity.'

By contrast, in *Questions Relating to the Obligation to Prosecute or Extradite (Belgium v Senegal)* (Judgment) [2012] ICJ Rep 422, 457 the International Court of Justice held that Article 28 VCLT 'reflects customary law on the matter (para 100).

[36] Villiger, *Article 28 – Non-Retroactivity of Treaties* (n 2) 386 with further references; Odendahl, 'Article 28' (n 25) 478 para 5 (with reference to *Victrawl Pty Ltd v AOTC Ltd et al* 117 ALR 347, No 37 Federal Court Australia (1993); Rodas, 'The Doctrine of Non-Retroactivity …' (n 7) 343; HW Briggs, 'Reflections on Non-Retroactivity of Treaties' (1968) 21 Revista Española de Derecho Internacional 320, 320.

[37] Odendahl, 'Article 28' (n 25) 478; Bindschedler-Robert, '… Rétroactivité en Droit …' (n 14) 185; see furthermore the cases *De Becker v Belgium* (1958–1959) 2 Yearbook of the ECHR 214, 231 and WTO Panel Report on *United States – Countervailing Duties on Non-Rubber Footwear from Brazil,*

beyond that, the very nature of the law as a reliable and predictable normative order is repugnant to any general or uncircumscribed acceptance of retroactivity.[38] All in all, non-retroactivity reflects both a rule of customary international law and a general principle of law.[39] The same holds true for the principle of intertemporal law in general. It is well settled in international customary law that the legal significance of any subjective right or objective rule is governed by the legal standards valid at the time of its enactment. This notion is sometimes described as a theory, sometimes as a principle or doctrine, and, supported by a comparison of domestic legal systems, it amounts to a general principle of law (Article 38(1)(c) ICJ Statute).[40] Intertemporal law gained more importance with the increasing universalization of international legal standards. There is a clear nexus between universality, on the one hand, and an appropriate balance between legal stability and legal flexibility, on the other.[41] Given the so characterized principle-oriented nature of non-retroactivity, not only treaty-based norms but also international customary law norms do not have a general retroactive effect. As far as the latter are concerned, one has to add the argument that State practice and the relevant *opinio juris* only work *pro futuro*. It seems to be a

---

SCM/94, BISD 42S/208, para 4.10 (reference to these cases is made by Odendahl, 'Article 28' (n 25) 478 para 5 and 482 paras 16, 17). For a different view, see Woodhouse, 'The Principle of Retroactivity …' (n 2) 69.

[38] This is made very clear by Bindschedler-Robert, '… Rétroactivité en Droit …' (n 14) 185:

> *Si l'on peut donc dire que le droit international, comme tout ordre juridique, répugne à la rétroactivité des normes et qu'il est dominé par le principe de non-rétroactivité, ce n'est pas seulement par référence à un principe général de droit reconnu par les nations civilisées, mais pour une raison plus profonde qui réside en son caractère d'ordre normatif. Cette constatation ne signifie pas nécessairement que la rétroactivité soit toujours exclue, mais bien qu'il existe une présomption de non-rétroactivité, de sorte que la norme sera supposée être non-rétroactive à moins d'une intention contraire explicite du législateur.*

[39] F Dopagne, 'Article 28' in O Corten and P Klein (eds), *Les Conventions de Vienne sur le Droit des Traités: Commentaire Article par Article* (Bruylant, 2006) 1166–8; Odendahl, 'Article 28' (n 25) 479 para 5.

[40] For reference to state practice and case law, see Kotzur, 'Intertemporal Law' (n 24) para 5.

[41] Ibid para 4.

contradiction in terms to assume the retroactive nature of new State practice.[42]

The principle of non-retroactivity is not a norm of *jus cogens*.[43] This follows from Article 28 VCLT, which clearly allows that a different intention might appear from the treaty or be otherwise established. The contracting parties are free to agree on retroactive effects as long as the principle *pacta tertiis nec nocent nec prosunt* is respected.[44] It might nevertheless be the case that substantive *jus cogens* norms – such as the *nulla poena sine lege* principle – prohibit any retroactive effect and in so far also limit the freedom of the contracting parties in concluding an international treaty.[45] As already emphasized, the rule of law-oriented principle of non-retroactivity is valid for material provisions. Procedural rules, however, can have retroactive effect.[46]

The principle of non-retroactivity furthermore applies to behaviour that lies in the past and thus the potential negative consequences of which were not foreseeable at the time it took place. Norms that intend to regulate future behaviour might nevertheless go back to situations or pre-conditions of this behaviour which lie in the past.[47] The scope of application of the non-retroactivity principle has to be evaluated, in the final analysis, from a *functional* point of view taking into account the consequences of retroactive application. Double taxation agreements, for example, might impose possible liability for past lawful acts on a party.[48] Bindschedler-Robert uses the famous *Nottebohm Case*[49] to show that when the ICJ applies a new rule – in that case in the field of diplomatic

---

42 Bindschedler-Robert, '… Rétroactivité en Droit …' (n 14) 186 with reference to classical writings of Alfred Verdross.

43 H Kelsen, *Principles of International Law* (Rinehart, 1952) 95; Buyse, 'A Lifeline in Time …' (n 11) 63, 65.

44 Bindschedler-Robert, '… Rétroactivité en Droit …' (n 14) 186.

45 Ibid.

46 Heikkilä, 'Prohibition of the Retroactive Application …' (n 20) 492, using ECJ case law examples such as Joined Cases 212 to 217/80 *Amministrazione delle Finanze dello Stato v Salumi* [1981] ECR 2735, 2754, 2755, where Advocate-General Rozes stated: 'according to a principle generally accepted in the law of the Member States, procedural laws apply immediately to all actions pending at the time of their entry into force …'.

47 Bindschedler-Robert, '… Rétroactivité en Droit …' (n 14) 199.

48 Briggs, 'Reflections on Non-Retroactivity …' (n 36) 321–2.

49 *Nottebohm Case (Liechtenstein v Guatemala)* (Second Phase, Judgment) [1955] ICJ Rep 4.

protection – retroactively the Court not only changes the legal relationship between the parties but also the structures of international law and thus affects legal certainty in general.[50]

Furthermore, a distinction has to be made between 'true retroactivity' (*rétroactivité véritable*) and 'material retroactivity' (*rétroactivité matérielle*).[51] The former 'means the application of a legislative measure to a situation which is fully completed or the effects of which have ceased to exist before the entry into force of that measure'.[52] The latter 'refers to the application of a legislative measure to the future effects of a situation which has arisen under the former law'.[53] The ECJ, for instance, strictly applies 'material retroactivity' – since legitimate expectations, acquired rights, or the respect for the continuity of an already existing legal regime are to be protected – but is more reluctant to accept and enforce 'true retroactivity'.[54] Where only rights or benefits are conferred, a deviation from the principle of non-retroactivity becomes possible since neither human rights nor the rule of law are endangered.[55] The same is true for interpretative provisions[56] and interpretative judgments. The preliminary rulings procedure before the ECJ provides an illustration: the Court can declare legal acts invalid from the date of their adoption, that is, *ex tunc*.[57]

---

[50] Bindschedler-Robert, '... Rétroactivité en Droit ...' (n 14) 200.

[51] Heikkilä, 'Prohibition of the Retroactive Application ...' (n 20) 486.

[52] Ibid.

[53] Heikkilä, 'Prohibition of the Retroactive Application ...' (n 20) 486.

[54] Ibid with manifold references to the relevant case law, see, eg, *Salumi* (n 46) 2751–2 (interest of the legislator that a measure shall have retroactive effect); Case 98/78 *A. Racke v Hauptzollamt Mainz* [1979] ECR 69, 86 (public interest); Case 350/88 *Declare and Others v Commission* [1990] ECR 395 (legitimate expectations must be respected); Case 88/76 *Exportation des Sucres v Commission* [1977] ECR 709,726.

[55] Heikkilä, 'Prohibition of the Retroactive Application ...' (n 20) 489–91.

[56] Ibid 491, referring to Case 234/83 *Gesamthochschule Duisburg v Hauptzollamt München-Mitte* [1985] ECR 327, 341; Case 183/73 *Osram GmbH v Oberfinanzdirektion Frankfurt/Main* [1974] ECR 477, 485; Case 158/78 *P. Biegi v Hauptzollamt Bochum* [1979] ECR 1103, 1119.

[57] Heikkilä, 'Prohibition of the Retroactive Application ...' (n 20). The annulment of a legal act of the European Union with effects *ex nunc* pays respect to the principle of non-retroactivity if otherwise an unacceptable (financial) burden would be placed either on the individual or on a Member State. In such cases the Court explicitly strengthens legal certainty – which has to be guaranteed even in illegal situations, see Case 43/75 *Defrenne v Sabena* [1976] ECR 455. See also P Ludewig, *Die zeitliche Beschränkung der Wirkung von Urteilen des EuGH im Vorabentscheidungsverfahren* (Duncker & Humblot, 2012).

IV. NON-RETROACTIVITY AND INTERNATIONAL CUSTOMARY LAW

There is minimal scientific – theoretical as well as empirical – research regarding the temporal scope of international customary law. This might be, among other reasons, due to the fact that the 'entry into force' of customary law cannot be exactly determined.[58] The *longa consuetudo* that has to be supported by *opinio juris*[59] qualifies as a process of continuous development, and cannot be limited to a certain moment in time. When deciding about the very existence of international customary law, a court implicitly also decides on its application *ratione temporis* and might rely on a somewhat 'hidden' retroactivity when deciding that a certain case is governed by customary law already existing at the time when the decisive event took place. The relevant problems have already been discussed in the context of intertemporal law.[60] Some eminent scholars even hold that, in a strict sense, retroactivity of customary international law norms was impossible since customary standards only exist when the aforementioned legal practice is supported by explicit legal conviction and a 'retroactive' conviction would be logically impossible.[61] Villiger expressly states that 'customary law is only active, not retroactive'.[62] Nevertheless, it may not be excluded that international courts and tribunals retroactively apply a – beyond any doubt – new norm of customary law without directly addressing the question of retroactivity.[63] To avoid the practical as well as dogmatic discontents of the non-retroactivity principle requires first of all awareness of changes in international customary law and their relevance regarding a contemporaneous 'reading' of the legal landscape.

---

[58] Krause-Ablass, *Intertemporales Völkerrecht* (n 20) 35.

[59] I Brownlie, *Principles of Public International Law* (7th edn, OUP, 2008) 6–12; Shaw, *International Law* (n 2) 72–6.

[60] See text to n 42; in general, Kotzur, 'Intertemporal Law' (n 24).

[61] Bindschedler-Robert, '… Rétroactivité en Droit …' (n 14) 186, referring to the work of, eg, Alfred Verdross.

[62] Villiger, *Article 28 – Non-Retroactivity of Treaties* (n 2) 385.

[63] See the examples given by Rodas, 'The Doctrine of Non-Retroactivity …' (n 7) 347:

> 'In the Veloz-Mariana Case that opposed France and Spain in 1823 and in the Anglo-Brazilian Arbitration of 1904, to solve the problems of frontiers of British-Guyana, the arbiters applied retroactively a new customary rule. They attributed retroactive effect without posing the question of retroactivity.'

V. NON-RETROACTIVITY OF TREATIES – ARTICLE 28 VCLT

1. The Historical Development and the Negotiation Process

Article 28 VCLT – forming a part of the intertemporal law described earlier – regulates the temporal application (application *ratione temporis*) of a treaty.[64] The norm is based upon the general presumption of non-retroactivity holding that – 'unless a different intention appears from the treaty or is otherwise established' – the treaty's provisions 'do not bind a party in relation to any act or fact which took place or any situation which ceased to exist before the date of the entry into force of the treaty with respect to that party'.[65] The Vienna Convention on the Law of Treaties itself has non-retrospective (or -retroactive) effect and 'applies only to treaties which are concluded by States after the entry into force of present Convention with regard to such States' (Article 4 VCLT).[66] What Article 28 VCLT comprises is the non-retroactivity of treaties as a *dispositive* rule;[67] what Article 28 VCLT does not comprise is a general rule of non-retroactivity of the law as, for example, provided

---

[64] The personal scope (application *ratione personae*) and the material scope (application *ratione materiae*) are dealt with in such different provisions as Articles 6–18, 34–38, 41 VCLT and Articles 13–19, 31–33, 39–40 VCLT. The territorial scope (application *ratione loci*) is addressed by Article 29 VCLT, see Odendahl, 'Article 28' (n 25) 477 para 1. In general, E Orihuela Calatayud, *Los Tratados Internacionales y su Aplicación en el Tiempo* (Dykinson, 2004).

[65] See J Brunnée and SJ Toope, *Legitimacy and Legality in International Law: An International Account* (CUP, 2010) 49.

[66] Aust, *Modern Treaty Law* (n 12) 8; K Schmalenbach, 'Article 4' in O Dörr and K Schmalenbach (eds), *Vienna Convention on the Law of Treaties: A Commentary* (Springer, 2012) 81 para 1; A Haratsch and S Schmahl, 'Die Anwendung Ratione Temporis der Wiener Konvention über das Recht der Verträge' (2003) 58 Zeitschrift für Öffentliches Recht 105 *et seq*.

[67] Schmalenbach, 'Article 4' (n 66) para 13; as made clear by the famous *Ambatielos Case*, this dispositive rule displays international customary law that existed long before the entry into force of the Vienna Convention. The Court argued as follows:

> [T]o accept this theory would mean giving retroactive effect to Article 29 of the Treaty of 1926, whereas Article 32 of this Treaty states that the Treaty, which must mean all the provisions of the Treaty, shall come into force immediately upon ratification. Such a conclusion might have been rebutted if there had been any special clause or any special object necessitating retro-active interpretation. There is no such clause or object in the present case. It is therefore impossible to hold that any of its provisions must be deemed to have

by many national constitutions. The latter provisions might help to shed light on the overall rule of law-oriented importance of the non-retroactivity principle; they need, however, to be strictly distinguished from the more limited scope of Article 28 VCLT.[68]

As made clear by the historical background and the negotiations of Article 28 VCLT, the norm re-emphasizes and codifies a pre-existing rule of public international law.[69] In a detailed study Albert Bleckmann outlines two different approaches that determined the negotiation process.[70]

What distinguishes the two approaches is the difference between the entry into force of a treaty, on the one hand, and its temporal application and effects, on the other.[71] The first approach is evident in Sir Gerald Fitzmaurice's 1956 draft Article 41(6) which focuses on the entry into force of a treaty.[72] Sir Humphrey Waldock and the Drafting Committee followed that concept in their draft only modifying the wording in what now – according to Waldock's paper – should become draft Article 21(1)(c): 'Unless the treaty itself shall expressly provide for the retrospective operation of all or any of its clauses, the rights and obligations laid down in the treaty shall come into operation for each party only from the date of the entry into force of the treaty with respect to that particular party'.[73] The Drafting Committee changed Waldock's proposal slightly into draft Article 20(4) of its 1962 draft: 'The rights and obligations

---

been in force earlier. (*Ambatielos Case (Greece v United Kingdom)* (Preliminary Objection, Judgment) [1952] ICJ Rep 28, 40)

See also Krause-Ablass, *Intertemporales Völkerrecht* (n 20) 137.

[68] A Bleckmann, 'Die Nichtrückwirkung völkerrechtlicher Verträge, Kommentar zu Art 28 der Wiener Vertragsrechtskonvention' (1973) 33 Zeitschrift für Ausländisches Öffentliches Recht und Völkerrecht 38, 53–4.

[69] See again *Ambatielos Case* (n 67) 40; Odendahl, 'Article 28' (n 25) 478 para 5.

[70] Bleckmann, 'Die Nichtrückwirkung …' (n 68) 38 *et seq*.

[71] Krause-Ablass, *Intertemporales Völkerrecht* (n 20) 16 *et seq*.

[72] Article 41(6): 'Entry into force can never be retroactive, either generally or for any particular state, in the absence of express provision to the contrary' (Yearbook of the ILC (1956) vol 2, 104, 116). The intention of this approach was – as highlighted by Odendahl, 'Article 28' (n 25) 479 para 6 – to reject the overcome American retroactivity doctrine according to which a treaty did not enter into force on the date of its ratification (or acceptance, approval, accession) but retroactively on the date when it was signed. See also Do Nascimento e Silva, 'Le Facteur Temps …' (n 3) 277–8 and Rodas, 'The Doctrine of Non-Retroactivity …' (n 7) 353–60.

[73] Yearbook of the ILC (1962) vol 2, 27, 71.

contained in a treaty become effective for each party as from the date when the treaty enters into force with respect to that party, unless the treaty expressly provides otherwise'.[74] In the 1965 draft, the provision was transformed, without any change as to its content and wording, into draft Article 23(4).[75] Shortly afterwards, however, the idea was dropped.[76]

Instead, the second approach – focusing on the application and the effects of a treaty – was pursued further. In the third Waldock draft (1964) two different provisions dealing with the problem of intertemporal law can already be found. Draft Article 56, titled 'The inter-temporal law', holds in paragraph 1 that a 'treaty is to be interpreted in the light of the law in force at the time when the treaty is drawn up'. Paragraph 2 follows saying: 'Subject to paragraph 1, the application of a treaty shall be governed by the rules of international law in force at the time when the treaty is applied'. Draft Article 57 then explicitly refers to the 'Application of treaty provisions *ratione temporis*': '(1) Unless a treaty expressly or impliedly provides otherwise, its provisions apply to each party only with respect to facts or matters arising or subsisting while the treaty is in force with respect to that party'.[77] In 1966, draft Article 56 was dropped and the former draft Article 57 reformulated as new draft Article 56 under a new heading ('Application of a treaty in point of time') and with a different wording: '(1) The provisions of a treaty do not apply to a party in relation to any fact or act which took place or any situation which ceased to exist before the date of entry into force of the treaty with respect to that party, unless the contrary appears from the treaty. (2) Subject to article 53, the provisions of a treaty do not apply to a party in relation to any fact or act which takes place or any situation which exists after the treaty has ceased to be in force with respect to that party, unless the treaty otherwise provides'.[78]

In the Final Draft, draft Article 56(1) was changed into draft Article 24 (with a slightly different wording) and draft Article 56(2) was deleted. The newly shaped draft Article 24 ('Non-retroactivity of treaties') read as follows: 'Unless a different intention appears from the treaty or is

---

[74] Yearbook of the ILC (1962) vol 1, 258.
[75] Yearbook of the ILC (1965) vol 1, 99.
[76] Ibid, 273, 285.
[77] Paragraph 2 goes on:

> 'On the termination or suspension of the operation of a treaty, its provisions remain applicable for the purpose of determining the rights and obligations of the parties with respect to facts or matters which arose or subsisted whilst it was in force'

Yearbook of the ILC (1964) vol 2, 5, 8 *et seq.*

[78] Yearbook of the ILC (1966) vol 1, Part II, 38.

otherwise established, its provisions do not bind a party in relation to an act or fact which took place or any situation which ceased to exist before the date of the entry into force of the treaty with respect to that party'.[79] The final version of today's Article 28 VCLT corresponds to draft Article 24 – the only difference is that 'an act' was replaced by 'any act'; it was unanimously adopted by the Vienna Conference with one abstention.[80]

2. Article 28 VCLT in Systematic Context: Articles 4, 18, 24, 25, 34 VCLT

Article 28 VCLT is not the only intertemporal provision contained in the Convention's framework.[81] Article 4 – reiterating the principle of non-retroactivity in regard to the Convention's own application – has already been mentioned.[82] The interim obligation of Article 18 VCLT imposes the duty on a State not to frustrate the object and purpose of a treaty prior to its entry into force.[83] Notwithstanding this temporal aspect, the norm, being an exception to Article 28 VCLT, does not qualify as a retroactive provision but as a rule of good faith.[84] The temporal dimension is also present in Article 24(4) VCLT. The norm requires all provisions on the entry into force of a treaty and 'all matters arising necessarily before the entry into force' of that treaty to be applied from the adoption of that treaty.[85] In other words, Article 24(4) contains an unstated assumption of

---

79 Ibid, 169; Yearbook of the ILC (1966) vol 2, 180, 211.

80 For reference, see Bleckmann, 'Die Nichtrückwirkung …' (n 68) 38–40; Odendahl, 'Article 28' (n 25) 479 para 7; furthermore, Rodas, 'The Doctrine of Non-Retroactivity … ' (n 7) 350–2; for details as to the *travaux préparatoires* of the Vienna Conference, see Do Nascimento e Silva, 'Le Facteur Temps …' (n 3) 273–7.

81 In detail, see Do Nascimento e Silva, 'Le Facteur Temps …' (n 3) 272–3.

82 For the *travaux préparatoires* of Article 4 VCLT, ibid 286–91; Villiger, *Article 28 – Non-Retroactivity of Treaties* (n 2) 385–6; Odendahl, 'Article 28' (n 25) 478 paras 3–4.

83 See, eg, J Klabbers, 'How to Defeat a Treaty's Object and Purpose Pending Entry into Force: Toward Manifest Intent' (2001) 34 Vanderbilt J of Transnational L 283 *et seq*; O Dörr, 'Article 18' in O Dörr and K Schmalenbach (eds), *Vienna Convention on the Law of Treaties: A Commentary* (Springer, 2012) 219 with further references.

84 Odendahl, 'Article 28' (n 25) 478 paras 3–4; Do Nascimento e Silva, 'Le Facteur Temps …' (n 3) 286 with further references.

85 H Krieger, 'Article 24' in O Dörr and K Schmalenbach (eds), *Vienna Convention on the Law of Treaties: A Commentary* (Springer, 2012) 402–3 para 28.

the parties to a treaty that '*ses provisions formelles deviendront opératives (entreront en vigueur) dès l'adoption du texte pour que ces dispositions deviennent effectives*'.[86]

Article 25 VCLT, concerning a treaty's provisional application, relates to its 'pending entry into force',[87] whereas Article 28 VCLT presupposes a treaty's 'definitive' entry into force. Nevertheless, as Villiger states, a 'certain overlapping' may be seen: 'if State parties declare certain provisions retroactive according to Article 28 before a treaty's entry into force, there is in effect little difference with the treaty's provisional application according to Article 25'.[88] At the very moment of its provisional application, or at the latest when it enters into force, a treaty becomes binding, which is to say applicable to the parties.[89] Finally, Article 34 VCLT – the *pacta tertiis* rule – has an implicit intertemporal moment, too: consent *pro futuro*.[90] The implications of the *pacta tertiis* rule for retroactivity are obvious: a non-party to a treaty cannot retroactively be bound by any obligations stemming from that very treaty. However, the party is completely free to join the treaty for the future and then to accept the treaty obligations it lays down. Accession to treaties establishing international organizations, as for instance the accession to the EU, provides a striking example.[91]

3. The Content and Characteristics of Article 28 VCLT

a) The legal nature of Article 28 VCLT

Article 28 VCLT, providing for the non-applicability of a new treaty (based on progressive – and thus prospective – consent for the future) without deciding on the law that has to be applied instead, constitutes a unilateral, negative, and retroactive conflict rule.[92] The norm is, at least formally, unilateral since it only requires the non-applicability of certain

---

86 Do Nascimento e Silva, 'Le Facteur Temps ...' (n 3) 286 with reference to IM Sinclair, *The Vienna Convention on the Law of Treaties* (Manchester UP, 1984) 55.

87 Krieger, 'Article 24' (n 85) 416 para 20.

88 Villiger, *Article 28 – Non-Retroactivity of Treaties* (n 2) 385.

89 Odendahl, 'Article 28' (n 25) 487 para 26.

90 Villiger, *Article 28 – Non-Retroactivity of Treaties* (n 2) 385. Article 34 provides that 'a treaty does not create either obligations or rights for a third State without its consent'. For details, see Proelss (in this volume).

91 R Geiger, 'Article 49 TEU' in R Geiger, D-E Khan and M Kotzur (eds), *EUV/AEUV: Kommentar* (Beck, 2010) 166.

92 Bleckmann, 'Die Nichtrückwirkung ...' (n 68) 40–1; Odendahl, 'Article 28' (n 25) 477 para 2.

aspects of the new law. Logically, the old or pre-existing law has to be applied under these circumstances, and consequently Article 28 contains a bilateral conflict rule in a material sense. The unilateral form is due to the Convention's limitation on treaties. The applicable 'old law' does not necessarily have to be treaty law; it can stem from other sources of public international law.[93] The norm is negative since it determines in which cases a new treaty cannot be applied.[94] The norm furthermore is a retroactive conflict rule since it is oriented towards the past.[95] From a functional point of view, the rule of non-retroactivity works as a status quo guaranty, in particular seeking to prevent any subsequent creation of substantive liability.[96]

b) The parties' intention and the treaty's binding force

Article 28 VCLT refers to a treaty's entry into force as governed by Article 24 VCLT.[97] The unambiguous wording of the VCLT ('unless a different intention') leaves no doubt that the parties are free to give some provisions or the whole treaty retroactive effect. They are the 'masters of their own treaty', but nevertheless there is a clear presumption of non-retroactivity; retroactivity remains the exception.[98] The parties' 'different intention' can either 'appear from the treaty' directly[99] or be

---

[93] For a further detailed analysis, see Bleckmann, 'Die Nichtrückwirkung …' (n 68) 40–1.

[94] Odendahl, 'Article 28' (n 25) 478 para 2.

[95] Ibid.

[96] Briggs, 'Reflections on Non-Retroactivity …' (n 36) 322:

> What the rule of non-retroactivity properly seeks to prevent is the subsequent creation of a substantive liability which did not exist at the time a particular act took place. Where, on the contrary, potential liability under applicable legal principles arose contemporaneously with the commission of an act or series of acts, care should be taken in drafting the non-retroactivity clause not to bar consideration of past facts or to exclude the possible applicability of the treaty by stating ambiguously that the provisions of a treaty do not 'bind' a party in relation to past acts.

[97] In general, Krieger, 'Article 24' (n 85); Villiger, *Article 28 – Non-Retroactivity of Treaties* (n 2) 382–3.

[98] Villiger, *Article 28 – Non-Retroactivity of Treaties* (n 2) 384.

[99] Odendahl, 'Article 28' (n 25) 480, refers to Article 7 para 2 of the 1978 Vienna Convention on Succession of States in Respect of Treaties as a good example. Villiger, *Article 28 – Non-Retroactivity of Treaties* (n 2) 381, mentions Article 17 of the Peace Treaty of Lausanne of 1923 'which provided that Turkey's renunciation of certain rights concerning Egypt and Sudan applied as from 1914'.

otherwise established. The second option also allows the taking into account of the 'very nature and purpose of a treaty'[100] or other proof of the parties' consent, even though an explicit formulation in the treaty, as required by the first option, is missing.[101] Typically, treaties establish retroactive effect if they either have an interpretative nature or explicitly intend to govern a past situation.[102] The literature very often refers to the *Chamizal Tract* case[103] as an example of 'a treaty aimed at interpreting a prior treaty'.[104] Equally frequent reference is made to the famous *Mavrommatis Palestine Concessions* case.[105] In its decisions the Permanent Court of International Justice stressed, when addressing Protocol XII to the Treaty of Lausanne (1923), that this protocol 'was drawn up in order to fix the conditions governing the recognition and treatment by the contracting Parties of certain concessions granted by the Ottoman authorities before the conclusion of the protocol. Therefore, even if the protocol did not contain an explicit clause it nevertheless had to be retroactively applied since the protocol would otherwise be ineffective'.[106] Relying on the *effet utile* principle, the Court felt free to apply the protocol's guarantees to infringements of rights which took place before the protocol had come into force.[107]

---

[100] With further examples, Chua and Hardcastle, 'Retroactive Application of Treaties Revisited ...' (n 2) 417.

[101] Ibid paras 8, 9 with reference to the older literature (eg, V Haak, '"Unless the Treaty Otherwise Provides" and Similar Clauses in the International Law Commission's 1966 Draft Articles on the Law of Treaties' (1967) 27 Zeitschrift für Ausländisches Öffentliches Recht und Völkerrecht 540 *et seq*).

[102] For further details, Bleckmann, 'Die Nichtrückwirkung ...' (n 68) 52; Rodas, 'The Doctrine of Non-Retroactivity ...' (n 7) 345:

> 'The reasons which seem to have led the States to stipulate the retroactivity are chiefly the interpretative or complementary character of the convention or the necessity of regulating a situation arisen before the treaty.'

[103] International Boundary Commission, *International Title to the Chamizal Tract (United States v Mexico)* (1911) 5 AJIL 785 *et seq*.

[104] Odendahl, 'Article 28' (n 25) 481.

[105] *The Mavrommatis Palestine Concessions* PCIJ Rep Series A No 2, 7; R Uerpmann-Wittzack, 'Mavrommatis Concessions Case' (2006) MPEPIL, www.mpepil.com, accessed 11 February 2013.

[106] *Mavrommatis* (n 105) 34; reference to that quote is, eg, made by Odendahl, 'Article 28' (n 25) 481.

[107] Uerpmann-Wittzack, 'Mavrommatis Concessions Case' (n 105) para 8. Today, the *effet utile* principle finds an explicit guarantee in Article 31(1) VCLT, see Bleckmann, 'Die Nichtrückwirkung ...' (n 68) 51–2; Villiger, *Article 28 – Non-Retroactivity of Treaties* (n 2) 384.

When Article 28 VCLT states that new treaty law does not 'bind' a party, this wording does not limit the Article's effect to *legal obligations* only. Such a narrow focus – setting aside pre-existing rights – would betray both the consent- and the rule of law-oriented *comprehensive* nature of the non-retroactivity clause.[108] Making the dualism between rights and obligations the decisive criterion would furthermore leave out treaties with an objective nature – such as founding treaties of international organizations or status agreements – the structure of which do not necessarily display the typical contractual '*synallagma*' of rights and corresponding duties (or vice versa).[109] Therefore the verb 'bind' has to be read as 'having legal consequences' or being 'applicable with respect to a party'; this understanding last but not least clarifies, as supported by the Convention's background and drafting process, that any retroactive effect of a treaty refers to its application and not to its entry into force.[110]

c) A question of timing – the past incidents (acts, facts, situations) Article 28 VCLT refers to

aa) The general scheme The past incidents Article 28 VCLT refers to are acts, facts, and situations, and at any rate only such of those that fall within the treaty's personal, material, as well as territorial scope of application, and that qualify as prerequisites of the treaty's provisions.[111] What distinguishes the three types of incidents is, in particular, the question of continuity.[112] Acts and facts share the character of a brief incident with a precisely determinable beginning and end. Acts describe forms of behaviour – action but also omission or toleration – being attributable to an 'actor'; acts may be factual in nature, and they may further have legal effects; given the Vienna Convention's overall regulatory framework the actors need to be subjects of law (not necessarily of international law: next to states and international organizations, natural or legal persons under domestic law are covered, too).[113] A fact can be either the result of a previous act (facts created purposefully or accidentally by man – Kerstin Odendahl, *exempli causa*, refers to 'emissions,

---

[108] Bleckmann, 'Die Nichtrückwirkung …' (n 68) 42–3; Odendahl, 'Article 28' (n 25) 478 paras 12, 13.

[109] Bleckmann, 'Die Nichtrückwirkung …' (n 68) 42–3.

[110] Odendahl, 'Article 28' (n 25) 482 paras 13, 14.

[111] Odendahl, 'Article 28' (n 25) 483 para 18.

[112] Buyse, 'A Lifeline in Time …' (n 11) 71–3.

[113] Odendahl, 'Article 28' (n 25) 482 para 15; Bleckmann, 'Die Nichtrückwirkung …' (n 68) 44.

damage, prescription, acquisition') or happen independently from any human action (a natural disaster, the passage of time, etc); facts can also have a legal (*Rechtstatsachen*) or an exclusively factual character.[114] As far as situations are concerned, things get more complicated. A situation covers and comprises both acts and facts; the difference, however, is the continuity or duration. A situation lasts for a longer period of time, is somewhat more 'ongoing', is per se dynamic (not static), and, as a consequence thereof, has often no clearly determinable beginning or end.[115] A sharp distinction between acts/facts on the one hand and situations on the other cannot be drawn; this, however, is not very problematic since Article 28 VCLT emphasizes that any relevant 'incident' has to be a *past* incident which has come to an end prior to the treaty's entry into force ('any act or fact which took place'; 'any situation which ceased to exist').[116]

This 'prior' soon turns out to be the problematic point since incidents are dynamic in nature, and acts may cause effects long after they have been completed; facts may continue in time and, most importantly, situations may continue in time, too.[117] Most tellingly, Odendahl describes these dynamics of continuity as 'a large number of successive acts/facts/situations that together constitute a new, comprehensive incident'.[118] The influential Waldock Report had already stressed this aspect:

> In these cases the treaty does not, strictly speaking, apply to a fact, act or situation falling partly within and partly outside the period during which it is in force; it applies only to the fact, act or situation which occurs or exists after the treaty is in force. This may have the result that prior facts, acts or situations are brought under consideration for the purpose of the application of the treaty; but it is only because of their causal connection with the subsequent facts, acts or situations to which alone in law the treaty applies.[119]

In constellations like these, parts of the acts/facts/situations might have already ended, 'while the overall incident is still going on'.[120] If the

---

[114] Odendahl, 'Article 28' (n 25) 482 para 16; Bleckmann, 'Die Nichtrückwirkung ...' (n 68) 44.

[115] Odendahl, 'Article 28' (n 25) 483 para 17.

[116] Bleckmann, 'Die Nichtrückwirkung ...' (n 68) 44.

[117] See also Bindschedler-Robert, '... Rétroactivité en Droit ...' (n 14) 188–9.

[118] Odendahl, 'Article 28' (n 25) 483 para 20.

[119] H Waldock, *Sixth Report on the Law of Treaties*, Yearbook of the ILC (1966) vol 2, 51, 63 para 3.

[120] Odendahl, 'Article 28' (n 25) 483 para 20.

treaty is not limited to one single incident that has already come to an end, then Article 28 VCLT does not apply, since the overall incident may still be ongoing.[121]

Just to determine when an act, fact, or situation has come to an end does not suffice to determine fully the scope of Article 28 VCLT.[122] One has furthermore to clearly distinguish between past incidents (the so-called *facta praeterita*), the ongoing incidents (the so-called *facta pendentia*) and finally future incidents (the so-called *facta futura*).[123] As to *facta praeterita* the new treaty law is clearly not applicable; they are, following the intertemporal rule, governed by the old law. Conversely, as to *facta futura* the new treaty law is obviously applicable – they are governed by progressive – and thus prospective – consent *pro futuro*. Of a more problematic nature are, as always, the in-betweens, the *facta pendentia*. Whether these are governed by the old or by the new law depends on whether public international law favors a 'principle providing for the immediate effect of a new rule' or, on the contrary, a principle

---

121 Ibid; Villiger, *Article 28 – Non-Retroactivity of Treaties* (n 2) 383:

> Even acts or facts the effects of which extended over a longer period of time, ie, any continuing situation, do not fall under the treaty, if they ceased to exist before the date of the entry into force of the treaty. More important, however, is the implication here *e contrario*: if the situation, commencing in the past, continues to exist *after* the treaty's entry into force, it is "caught" by the treaty.

The International Law Commissison also took a clear position regarding that point, see Yearbook of the ILC (1966) vol 2, 212:

> If, however, an act or fact or situation which took place or arose prior to the entry into force of a treaty continues to occur or exist after the treaty has come into force, it will be caught by the provisions of the treaty. The non-retroactivity principle cannot be infringed by applying a treaty to matters that occur or exist when the treaty is in force, even if they first began at an earlier date. Thus, while the European Commission of Human Rights has not considered itself competent to inquire into the propriety of legislative, administrative *or* judicial acts completed and made final before the entry into force of the European Convention, it has assumed jurisdiction where there were fresh proceedings or recurring applications of those acts after the Convention was in force.

122 For the following, Odendahl, 'Article 28' (n 25) 484 para 21.

123 These categories can already be found in the classical treatise by P Roubier, *Les Conflits de Lois dans le Temps (Théorie Dite de la Non-Rétroactivité de la Loi)* (Sirey, 1929) 547 *et seq.*

supporting the survival of the old rule.[124] The International Law Commission (ILC) disregarded the latter principle and, instead, was very affirmative as to the existence of the former one: if

> an act or fact or situation which took place or arose prior to the entry into force of a treaty continues to occur or exist after the treaty has come into force, it will be caught by the provisions of the treaty. The non-retroactivity principle cannot be infringed by applying a treaty to matters that occur or exist when the treaty is in force, even if they first began at an earlier date.[125]

bb) Special aspects and problems

(1) *Human rights treaties*: The last aspect is of crucial importance in the context of human rights treaties, when – comparable to a 'continuing situation' – the human rights violation which started before the treaty's entry into force continues afterwards.[126] One could speak of a 'concept of continuing human rights violations' trying to reconcile the rule of law-based necessity to effectively protect human rights, on the one hand, and the equally rule of law-based principle of non-retroactivity, on the other.[127] Article 14(2) and (3) of the ILC Articles on Responsibilty of States for Internationally Wrongful Acts (2001) (ILC Articles on State Responsibility) reflect the problem, too. Human rights treaties are not generally exempt from the non-retroactivity principle. Only that part of a human right's infringement that takes place within a human rights treaty's temporal scope of application qualifies as a

---

[124] Odendahl, 'Article 28' (n 25) 484 para 21; see also Bleckmann, 'Die Nichtrückwirkung …' (n 68) 46.

[125] The Final Draft, Yearbook of the ILC (1966) vol 2, 212 para 3; see for further reference, Odendahl, 'Article 28' (n 25) 485 para 22, and Bleckmann, 'Die Nichtrückwirkung …' (n 68) 46–8.

[126] Buyse, 'A Lifeline in Time …' (n 11) 73–8; reference to the position of the European Commission and the European Court of Human Rights is made at 82–7. In manifold situations of 'continuing' violations, the Court has affirmed its jurisdiction, see *Blečić v Croatia* (GC) ECHR 2006–III 51, 74 para 73 *et seq*; *Posti and Rahko v Finland* ECHR 2002–VII 301, 314 para 39; *Kalashnikov v Russia* ECHR 2002–VI 93, 121 para 111. On the development of the jurisprudence of the European Court of Human Rights also, E Bjorge, 'Right for the Wrong Reasons: *Šilih v Slovenia* and Jurisdiction *Ratione Temporis* in the European Court of Human Rights' in (2013) 83 British YB of Intl L 115.

[127] LG Loucaides, 'The Concept of "Continuing" Violations of Human Rights' in P Mahoney, *Protecting Human Rights: The European Perspective. Studies in Memory of R Ryssdal* (Carl Heymanns Verlag, 2000) 803–15.

relevant violation. However, as Buyse clearly states, 'the prior acts, facts or situations can … , in the instances at hand, be taken into account for the determination of a violation. In other words, the time-limit is not a jurisdictional blindfold which prevents gazing into the past'.[128] To avoid such blindfolds, the European Court of Human Rights (ECtHR) as well as earlier on the European Human Rights Commission try to distinguish between continuing situations (clearly without the scope of the non-retroactivity principle) and instantaneous acts or facts with continuing effects (see also Article 14(2) of the ILC Articles on State Responsibility).[129] In general, the Court asks whether or not a 'necessary continuity' is established.[130] In various jurisdictions, the intertemporal rule has been modified in order to protect human dignity-based human rights.[131]

(2) '*Composite acts*': A parallel problem arises in the context of the so-called composite acts as laid down in Article 15 of the ILC Articles on State Responsibility. Article 15 addresses the scenario where not a single act per se infringes an international law obligation but several acts, when taken together, amount to a breach of international law. Following the non-retroactivity principle *stricto sensu*, only those acts which occur after the respective treaty's entry into force may be taken into account. Earlier facts (acts, situations), however, may not be disregarded if they 'establish

---

[128] Buyse, 'A Lifeline in Time …' (n 11) 75; Villiger, *Article 28 – Non-Retroactivity of Treaties* (n 2) 383 gives an example with regard to the (procedural) right to a fair trial:

> For instance, if a human rights treaty provides for international jurisdiction in respect of alleged unfairness of a trial, any complaint will be incompatible ratione temporis with the provisions of the treaty if the conviction and sentence following the trial became final before the treaty's entry into force. … If, on the other hand, at least the decision of the final judicial instance is given after the treaty's entry into force, the complaint may be entertained in respect of that part, as well as the outcome, of the proceedings.

[129] From the ECtHR's jurisprudence, see notably *Loizidou v Turkey* (GC) (Preliminary Objections) (1995) Series A no 310 para 99 *et seq*; and further Odendahl, 'Article 28' (n 25) 484; Draft Articles on Responsibility of States for Internationally Wrongful Acts with Commentaries, Yearbook of the ILC (2001) vol 2, Part II, 61.

[130] See Buyse, 'A Lifeline in Time …' (n 11) 87.

[131] For (case law) reference, see Kotzur, 'Intertemporal Law' (n 24) para 13.

a factual basis for the later breaches' or 'provide evidence of intent'.[132]

(3) *Acquired rights*: Acquired rights[133] are likely to create legitimate expectations and thus a retroactive infringement thereof has to be dealt with the greatest scrutiny. In general, as many domestic constitutions also provide, the legislator is banned from violating (limiting, abolishing, etc) these rights *pro futuro*.[134] The very concept of acquired rights presupposes that all conditions necessary for their genesis – as laid down by law – and all further transactions on which they depend have been performed.[135] An infringement of these rights as legal facts *praeterita* qualifies as 'retroactive in the true meaning of the word'.[136] Acquired rights are governed by the old law even after the enactment of the new law.[137]

d) Exceptions as recognized by Article 28 VCLT

This sub-section provides a summary of the already discussed 'exceptions' to the principle of non-retroactivity – exceptions not necessarily in a technical sense. Doubtlessly, a treaty can have retroactive effect when this is explicitly provided for or implied by the treaty's purpose and intention (see above).[138] Moreover, if a particular treaty provision is nothing but codified pre-existing customary international law (in particular a so-called declaratory clause) it can be applied retroactively since no legitimate expectations of whatever kind will be betrayed.[139] If an act,

---

[132] J Crawford, *The International Law Commission's Articles on State Responsibility* (CUP, 2002) 144; Odendahl, 'Article 28' (n 25) 484 para 20.

[133] P Tavernier, *Recherches sur l'Application dans le Temps des Actes et des Règles en Droit International Public (Problèmes de Droit Intertemporel ou de Droit Transitoire)* (Paris, 1970) 234 *et seq.*

[134] Bindschedler-Robert, '… Rétroactivité en Droit …' (n 14) 190.

[135] Heikkilä, 'Prohibition of the Retroactive Application …' (n 20) 496–8.

[136] Ibid.

[137] Bleckmann, 'Die Nichtrückwirkung …' (n 68) 48. This is going so far, that, as Heikkilä, 'Prohibition of the Retroactive Application …' (n 20) 496–7, states, the 'individual rights remain in force even if the act creating that right would be abolished. If the Court annuls a regulation, it has the power to restrict the *erga omnes* and the retroactive effects of the judgment in order to protect acquired rights.'

[138] For further details, Rodas, 'The Doctrine of Non-Retroactivity …' (n 7) 349–50.

[139] *Armed Activities on the Territory of the Congo (New Application: 2002) (Democratic Republic of the Congo v Rwanda)* (Jurisdiction and Admissability, Judgment) [2006] ICJ Rep 6, 52 para 125:

fact, or situation continues to exist, the new law can be applied since these continuing situations lay beyond the scope of non-retroactivity.[140]

Regarding important decisions of international courts and tribunals, attention has to be paid to the ICJ decision in the *Bosnia and Herzegovina Genocide* case.[141] In addition to the aforementioned and well-established exceptions the Court hints at a complementary one: obligations *erga omnes* anyway going beyond a treaty's (not only temporal) scope.[142] However, it is not exactly clear whether it was the fact that the Convention on the Prevention and Punishment of the Crime of Genocide (1948) (Genocide Convention) might be seen as reflective of international customary law or whether it was the Court's reliance on *erga omnes* obligations or even on the *jus cogens* nature of the relevant provisions that sustains retroactive application. A general retroactive application of new norms determining standards of the *ordre public*,[143] however, cannot be found in public international law.[144] In case of *jus cogens* the situation is very different (a fact supported by Article 53 VCLT).[145] *Jus cogens* norms, whether understood to be based on consent or not, are binding on every subject of public international law; *jus cogens* transcends the traditional consent principle.[146] What qualifies as *jus cogens* has an impact not only *ex nunc*, but *ex tunc*. Consequently, newly established norms of *jus cogens* clearly limit a contemporaneous

---

The Conventions on Genocide and Racial Discrimination were concluded before the latter date. Thus in the present case the rules contained in the Vienna Convention are not applicable, save in so far as they are declaratory of customary international law.

[140] Buyse, 'A Lifeline in Time …' (n 11) 70.

[141] *Application of the Convention on the Prevention and Punishment of the Crime of Genocide (Bosnia and Herzegovina v Serbia and Montenegro)* (Preliminary Objections, Judgment) [1996] ICJ Rep 595.

[142] Chua and Hardcastle, 'Retroactive Application of Treaties Revisited …' (n 2) 415; see furthermore, Rodas, 'The Doctrine of Non-Retroactivity …' (n 7) 344.

[143] M Gebauer, 'Ordre Public (Public Policy)' (2007) MPEPIL, www.mpepil.com, accessed 8 February 2013.

[144] Bleckmann, 'Die Nichtrückwirkung …' (n 68) 52.

[145] In general, K Schmalenbach, 'Article 53' in O Dörr and K Schmalenbach (eds), *Vienna Convention on the Law of Treaties: A Commentary* (Springer, 2012) 897 *et seq.*

[146] See generally, JA Frowein, 'Ius Cogens' (2009) MPEPIL, www.mpepil.com, accessed 4 October 2013.

understanding and also puts into question the principle of non-retroactivity.[147] This was pointed out in the joint declaration of Judges Shi and Koroma of 26 February 2007 regarding the aforementioned case on the *Application of the Convention on the Prevention and Punishment of the Crime of Genocide (Bosnia and Herzegovina v Serbia and Montenegro).*[148] The two judges emphasized that 'in some respects the interpretation of a treaty's provision cannot be divorced from developments in the law subsequent to its adoption'.[149] *Jus cogens* has to be seen as the most significant of these 'respects'. Consequently, the declaration continues: 'even though a treaty when concluded did not conflict any rule of *jus cogens*, it will become void if there subsequently emerges a new rule of *jus cogens* with which it is in conflict'.[150] Where *jus cogens* is at stake, the stability of a legal title is doubtless outweighed by the present-day concept of law and justice.

As previously mentioned, special attention has also to be paid to human rights treaties and their distinctive nature.[151] If human rights are inherent and thus pre-existing rights, if the contracting parties express their belief in the human being's 'inherent dignity', a supposedly 'retroactive' application of a human rights treaty might turn out to be nothing but a reference to natural law.[152] At least the wording found in the preambles of various human rights treaties and declarations suggest such an understanding. Thus, for example, the preamble of the 1948 Universal Declaration of Human Rights, which states: 'Whereas recognition of the inherent dignity and of the equal and inalienable rights of all members of the human family is the foundation of freedom, justice and peace in the world'.[153] Both the International Covenant on Civil and

---

[147] Kotzur, 'Intertemporal Law' (n 24) paras 11–12.

[148] See n 141.

[149] *Application of the Convention on the Prevention and Punishment of the Crime of Genocide (Bosnia and Herzegovina v Serbia and Montenegro)* (Joint Declaration of Judges Shi and Koroma) [2007] ICJ Rep 279, 280 para 2.

[150] Ibid.

[151] Buyse, 'A Lifeline in Time …' (n 11) 66.

[152] See Kotzur, 'Der Rechtsstaat im Völkerrecht' (n 16) 807–8.

[153] The declaration, based upon a UN General Assembly resolution, is not a binding treaty but soft law, that to some extent amounts to customary international law, see M Olivier, 'The Relevance of "Soft Law" as a Source of International Human Rights' (2002) 35 Comparative and Intl L J of Southern Africa 289, 301 *et seq*; RB Lillich, 'Growing Importance of Customary International Human Rights Law' (1995–1996) 25 Georgia J Intl and Comparative L 1 *et seq*.

Political Rights (1966) and the International Covenant on Economic, Social and Cultural Rights (1966) state in their opening phrases:

> The States Parties to the present Covenant, considering that, in accordance with the principles proclaimed in the Charter of the United Nations, recognition of the inherent dignity and of the equal and inalienable rights of all members of the human family is the foundation of freedom, justice and peace … recognizing that these rights derive from the inherent dignity of the human person …[154]

The States parties to the European Convention for the Protection of Human Rights and Fundamental Freedoms (1950) reaffirm in the Convention's preamble 'their profound belief in those fundamental freedoms which are the foundation of justice and peace in the world'.[155]

These emphatic text examples may not, however, obscure the fact that many of the mentioned treaties' operative clauses resemble a progressive development in public international law which by no means can be traced back to pre-existing foundations. In its *Loizidou* case[156] the ECtHR outlined what could be described as a 'duality of character of human rights treaties in general'.[157] Even though a human rights treaty's object and purpose might be the protection of some long acknowledged pre-existing rights, the non-retroactivity principle remains the general rule, whereas the specific purpose- or natural law-oriented dimension has to be substantiated on a case-by-case basis.[158]

Specific consideration has also to be given to jurisdictional clauses where a treaty's application to the so-called *facta pendentia* is at issue. It is up to the parties to regulate in some detail over which facts and incidents the relevant court shall have jurisdiction.[159] If this is not done, an international court or tribunal doubtlessly has jurisdiction over all

---

[154] International Covenant on Civil and Political Rights (entered into force 23 March 1976) 999 UNTS 171 (ICCPR) www.ohchr.org/EN/ProfessionalInterest/Pages/CCPR.aspx, accessed 14 May 2014; International Covenant on Economic, Social and Cultural Rights (entered into force 3 January 1976) 993 UNTS 3 (ICESCR) www.ohchr.org/EN/ProfessionalInterest/Pages/CESCR.aspx, accessed 14 May 2014.

[155] European Convention for the Protection of Human Rights and Fundamental Freedoms, www.echr.coe.int/Documents/Covention_ENG.pdf, accessed 14 May 2014.

[156] *Loizidou v Turkey* (n 129) para 99 *et seq.*

[157] Buyse, 'A Lifeline in Time …' (n 11) 67.

[158] See ibid, 67–70.

[159] For examples, see Krause-Ablass, *Intertemporales Völkerrecht* (n 20) 136 and Chua and Hardcastle, 'Retroactive Application of Treaties Revisited …' (n 2)

disputes that existed at the date when the treaty in question entered into force.[160] To ensure that the parties' intention is not for the Court to have jurisdiction over matters occurring prior to the treaty's entry into force, the parties should 'specifically provide that the Court's jurisdiction *ratione temporis* is limited'.[161] This is all the more important since in its

---

419, both addressing the Permanent Court of International Justice's case *Phosphates in Morocco (Italy v France)* (Preliminary Objections) PCIJ Rep Series A/B No 74, 10, 23.

[160] Odendahl, 'Article 28' (n 25) 485–6 para 24; analysing the ECtHR's jurisdiction, Buyse, 'A Lifeline in Time …' (n 11) 81, states:

> Concluding on the point of jurisdiction we have seen that when states indicated clear temporal limitations, the limitations were respected by the supervisory organs. On the other hand, when parties to the ECHR left the time frame open, both the Commission and the Court have taken the opportunity to extend their jurisdiction backwards to the moment of entry into force of the Convention. In those instances they thereby gave the declarations of states retroactive effect. When possible the jurisdiction *ratione temporis* was therefore at least not made smaller than the temporal scope of the ECHR, but as large.

In *The Mavrommatis Palestine Concessions*, the PCIJ held:

> The Court is of opinion that, in cases of doubt, jurisdiction based on an international agreement embraces all disputes referred to it after its establishment … The reservation made in many arbitration treaties regarding disputes arising out of events previous to the conclusion of the treaty seems to prove the necessity for an explicit limitation of jurisdiction and, consequently, the correctness of the rule of interpretation enunciated above. (PCIJ Rep Series A No 2, 7, 35).

[161] Chua and Hardcastle, 'Retroactive Application of Treaties Revisited …' (n 2) 418–19. See also the abovementioned decision on the application of the Genocide Convention:

> Yugoslavia, basing its contention on the principle of the non-retroactivity of legal acts, has indeed asserted … that, even though the Court might have jurisdiction on the basis of the Convention, it could only deal with events subsequent to the different dates on which the Convention might have become applicable as between the Parties. In this regard, the Court will confine itself to the observation that the Genocide Convention, and in particular Article IX, does not contain any clause the object or effect of which is to limit in such manner the scope of its jurisdiction *ratione temporis*, and nor did the Parties themselves make any reservation to that end, either to the Convention or on the occasion of the signature of the Dayton-Paris Agreement. The Court thus finds that it has jurisdiction in this case to give effect to the Genocide Convention with regard to the relevant facts which have occurred since the beginning of the conflict which took place in Bosnia-Herzegovina. (*Application of the Convention on the Prevention and Punishment of the Crime of*

preliminary objections in the *Bosnia and Herzegovina Genocide* case,[162] the ICJ held jurisdictional clauses to be applicable to *facta pendentia* by inverting the burden of proof. Following that approach, an international court has jurisdiction – if the parties to the treaty do not expressly otherwise provide – over all cases brought before it, even if the incidents occurred before the entry into force of the respective treaty.[163] The rules of procedure, however, are not considered to fall under the prohibition of retroactivity since they do not affect the content of the substantive law applicable to the dispute.[164]

VI. OUTLOOK AND CONCLUSION

To some extent, the principle of non-retroactivity – in its contents as well as in its discontents – displays the oft-discussed fragmentation of public international law.[165] Non-retroactivity is not an overall coherent principle, as already hinted at by Hans Kelsen: 'There is no rule of general international law prohibiting the establishment – especially by treaties – of norms with retroactive force'.[166] Non-retroactivity requires different scrutiny in different fields of public international law. As far as treaty law is concerned, Article 28 VCLT provides, as shown above, for a rather precise regulatory scheme. Unilateral juridical acts are a different

---

Genocide (Bosnia and Herzegovina v Serbia and Montenegro) (Preliminary Objections, Judgment) [1996] ICJ Rep 595, 617 para 34)

162 *Bosnia and Herzegovina Genocide* case (n 161).

163 Odendahl, 'Article 28' (n 25) 486 para 25; for further discussion, see Chua and Hardcastle, 'Retroactive Application of Treaties Revisited ...' (n 2) 418, and in detail, also S Maljean-Dubois, 'L'Affaire Relative à l'Application de la Convention pour la Prévention et la Répression du Crime de Génocide (Bosnie-Herzégovine c. Yugoslawie) Arrêt du 11 Juillet 1996, Exceptions Préliminaires' (1996) Annuaire Français de Droit International 357, 372.

164 Bindschedler-Robert, '... Rétroactivité en Droit ...' (n 14) 192 *et seq*; Heikkilä, 'Prohibition of the Retroactive Application ...' (n 20) 492 with refence to the case law of the ECJ.

165 Report of the Study Group of the ILC, *Fragmentation of International Law: Difficulties Arising from the Diversification and Expansion of International Law* (finalized by M Koskenniemi, A/CN.4/L.682, 13 April 2006); P-M Dupuy, 'A Doctrinal Debate in the Globalisation Era: On the "Fragmentation" of International Law' (2007) 1 European J L Studies, www.ejls.eu/1/4UK.pdf, accessed 11 February 2013; C Thiele, 'Fragmentierung des Völkerrechts als Herausforderung für die Staatengemeinschaft' (2008) 46 Archiv des Völkerrechts 1.

166 Kelsen, *Principles of International Law* (n 43) 95.

story.[167] In international criminal law the principle *nullum crimen, nulla poena sine lege* has to be strictly applied; they qualify as *jus cogens*, whereas Article 28 VCLT clearly shows that there is no general *jus cogens* standard hindering the parties from providing for the retroactive application of a treaty (or some of its provisions).[168] However, this freedom of the parties will find its limits if a retroactive infringement of human rights is at stake. Human rights standards, supplemented by an international rule of law, limit the freedom of consent of the contracting parties. This is all the more true since the Vienna Convention itself – namely in its preamble – refers to 'universal respect for, and observance of, human rights'. Consequently, 'it can be held that the non-retroactivity principle should not interfere with the individual's enjoyment of his or her human rights or at least be interpreted as favourably as possible in that respect'.[169] On the other side, human rights guarantees – in so far as resembling inherent 'natural' rights – might be applied retroactively. One aspect, however, has to be made very clear: the distinction between strict non-retroactivity and the conscious retroactive application of a treaty (or public international law in general) may not depend on the wishful outcome. As with all law, public international law deserves better than wishful thinking. Keeping that in mind, future research might notably focus on the following aspects:

- Future research could usefully address the interrelation between non-retroactivity as a principle protected by national constitutions and non-retroactivity as a principle of public international law.
- While it is agreed that non-retroactivity qualifies as a rule of international customary law, there seems to be a need for empirical studies analysing State practice in greater detail; these could provide a firmer empirical basis for claims as to the scope of the customary rule and exceptions to it.
- Non-retroactivity is, moreover, a fundamental principle in most domestic legal orders. Additional research needs to be carried out on the question of how new constitutional systems, for instance those evolved in 1989/1990 after the collapse of the Soviet Union, introduce the principle of non-retroactivity after the regime change.
- Furthermore, the principle of non-retroactivity has to be evaluated in relation to *jus cogens*. Newly developed *jus cogens* by its very

---

167 Bindschedler-Robert, '... Rétroactivité en Droit ...' (n 14) 187–8.
168 Bindschedler-Robert, '... Rétroactivité en Droit ...' (n 14) 186.
169 Buyse, 'A Lifeline in Time ...' (n 11) 67.

nature is liable to put into question the principle of non-retroactivity. It remains to be analysed to what extent this finding is reflected in State practice, especially in cases where core human rights issues, for instance the prohibitions against slavery and torture, are at stake.

– Finally, attention should be paid to the application of the non-retroactivity principle not only by the ICJ and the International Criminal Court but also by regional human rights courts, particularly taking into consideration human rights treaties and their special nature.

More generally, given the legal and constitutional pluralism characteristic of the 21st century, public international law has to take account of regional and domestic legal regimes, which can inform the interpretation and application of general standards such as non-retroactivity. Most importantly, however, that interpretation and application is to draw on the overarching principle of legalism – that is, the rule of law in international affairs.[170] An international legal order based on the rule of law will find convincing answers as to the non-retroactivity principle – and to many more legal issues concerning all humankind.

---

[170] S Chesterman, 'Rule of Law' (2007) MPEPIL, www.mpepil.com, accessed 4 October 2013.

7. The spatial dimension: Treaties and territory

Marko Milanovic[*]

I. INTRODUCTION

This chapter will explore the spatial dimension of treaties – their operation in, and with regard to, territory. Because Statehood continues to be the primary ordering principle in the global arena, because States conclude treaties to regulate their own behaviour, as well as (less often) the behaviour of certain non-State actors, and because States themselves are defined in territorial terms, as entities effectively governing territory and laying claim to it, examining the territorial scope of application of treaties is an obvious line of inquiry. Yet that inquiry either quickly exhausts itself or runs into conceptual hurdles that are difficult to overcome. As we will see, from the broad generalization that States, as the primary treaty makers and subjects thereof, are defined by the sovereign title they hold over territory comes very little by way of general rules regarding the territorial application of treaties.

Indeed, one could almost say that no such rules exist. The 1969 Vienna Convention on the Law of Treaties (VCLT) gives us one paltry provision in its Article 29, widely accepted as customary precisely because it says so little: '[u]nless a different intention appears from the treaty or is otherwise established, a treaty is binding upon each party in respect of its entire territory.' While this chapter will deal with Article 29 in detail, it is not meant to be a commentary thereof – such works already exist and there is no need to duplicate them.[1] Rather, like the other contributions in

* I would like to thank Shehzad Charania, Jacob Cogan, Monica Hakimi, Nico Krisch, Maximo Langer, Barbara Miltner, Anthea Roberts, Michael Waibel, Chanaka Wickremasinghe and Michael Wood for their very helpful comments.

[1] See especially, S Karagiannis, 'Article 29,' in O Corten and P Klein (eds), *Les Conventions de Vienne sur le Droit des Traités. Commentaire Article par Article* (Bruylant, 2006) 1189; K Odendahl, 'Article 29,' in O Dörr and K Schmalenbach (eds), *Vienna Convention on the Law of Treaties: A Commentary* (Springer, 2012) 489; M Villiger, *Commentary on the 1969 Vienna Convention on the Law of Treaties* (Nijhoff, 2009) 387.

this handbook, this chapter is meant as a 'think piece,' trying to think afresh and from a conceptual perspective about the spatial dimension of treaties, or the relationship between treaties and territory.

In that regard, despite Article 29's lofty heading ('territorial scope of treaties') implying that it is somehow an exhaustive rule on the matter, we will see that it in fact constitutes a very small piece of a complex puzzle. Instead of being an overarching rule, Article 29 VCLT actually deals with a very specific problem – treaty-making by federal States or States with overseas territories – and creates a presumption in favour of the applicability of the treaty to the whole territory of the State, that is, to all areas of the Earth's landmass over which it has title, unless a contrary intention is established.[2] That is the only thing it does, and it does not do it particularly well. Consider, for instance, how the formulation 'unless a different intention appears from the treaty or is otherwise established' leaves entirely unclear what exactly this 'intention' is, how and when it may be expressed and by whom. While there is a wealth of treaty practice relevant to the application of this provision, from the inclusion of explicit colonial or federal clauses into treaties to unilateral declarations by States defining the specific treaty's scope of application, such practice is confined to a very small number of States, with the vast bulk remaining silent, and is itself far from uniform. The political importance of former colonial powers has of course waned with colonialism itself, but as a purely legal matter, serious conceptual issues remain. For example, are States' unilateral declarations setting out to which of their territories a particular treaty applies to be regarded as reservations, or as a *sui generis* method of expressing a 'contrary intention' within the meaning of Article 29 VCLT?[3]

II. TERRITORIAL APPLICATION OF TREATIES

A major problem in discussing the territorial application of treaties is that the very notion of 'territorial application' can bear several different meanings, and that these different meanings are often confused or used

---

[2] See generally, S Karagiannis, 'The Territorial Application of Treaties,' in D Hollis (ed), *The Oxford Guide to Treaties* (OUP, 2012) 305; A Aust, *Modern Treaty Law and Practice* (2nd edn, CUP, 2007) 200 *et seq*, and the sources cited therein. See also, I Hendry and S Dickson, *British Overseas Territory Law* (Hart, 2011) 253–7; and I Sinclair, *The Vienna Convention on the Law of Treaties* (2nd edn, Manchester UP, 1984) 87–92.

[3] See *infra* section IV.

interchangeably. First, we can speak of territorial application of a treaty in the sense of the spatial extent of a State's obligations under the treaty, that is, in the process of (a) ascertaining what obligations a State has and (b) where these obligations are to be performed. Second, the words 'territorial application' can be used to denote the locus of a State's obligations, but this time confined strictly to *nothing but* the territory over which the State has sovereignty. Third, the words 'territorial application' or the 'territorial scope of application' can be used in the sense of ascertaining what *parts of the State's organic structure*, that is, its territorial sub-divisions, are subject to the obligations arising from the treaty. Whether the first and the third sense of territorial application can completely be distinguished from one another is a difficult question which I will address below.

First, however, let us deal with the idea of territorial application of a treaty as the locus of the State's obligations. In that sense, a treaty's territorial application is purely a function of its subject-matter. The variety of treaty subject-matters being endless, the rules, principles and policy considerations that underpin territorial application will thus vary from treaty to treaty.

To see the dependence of territorial application on the treaty's subject-matter at work we need only look at the example of human rights treaties.[4] They impose obligations solely on the States parties, not on third States or private individuals.[5] Moreover, they create obligations not only between the States parties themselves, but also between States and individuals – indeed, that is their whole purpose. The *application* of a human rights treaty to a particular individual thus implies that the State owes that individual some legal obligation under the treaty. *Territorial* or *spatial* application is hence a question of whether such obligations extend to a particular individual in a given location. Does the United Kingdom have human rights obligations under the 1950 European Convention on Human Rights (ECHR) to the inhabitants of London? Did the UK have obligations under the ECHR to the people of British-occupied Basra? Did

---

[4] This discussion draws heavily from M Milanovic, *Extraterritorial Application of Human Rights Treaties: Law, Principles, and Policy* (OUP, 2011) 7 *et seq*. This chapter inevitably builds on my prior work on the territorial application of treaties, and thus I hope that readers will forgive any excessive self-citation.

[5] By and large, a notable exception is the 1981 African Charter on Human and Peoples' Rights, which in its Articles 27–9 purports to impose duties on individuals, without, however, specifying the consequences of any breach of such duties.

the United States have human rights obligations under the 1966 International Covenant on Civil and Political Rights (ICCPR) to Osama bin Laden when its agents killed him in a covert operation in Pakistan?

Here we can distinguish between a treaty's territorial application in the first sense, as an inquiry into the extent of State obligations with regard to the location of a particular subject or object of regulation, and territorial application in the second sense, as the treaty's applicability within the State's own territory, over which it possesses sovereign title. *Extraterritorial* application would thus relate to spaces or areas over which the State does *not* have title. This is indeed how the terms are most frequently used in the human rights context; the very words 'extraterritorial application of human rights treaties' imply that there is something important about sovereignty or title over territory when it comes to the extent of States' obligations under these treaties, that is, that there is a legally meaningful distinction between the territorial and the extraterritorial application of, say, the ECHR or the ICCPR. But that may well be an unwarranted assumption, its intuitive appeal misplaced. I have thus argued that title over territory should have absolutely no bearing on the question of whether a particular inhabitant of that territory is owed human rights obligations.[6]

With this distinction in mind, my point is simply this: the territorial scope of application (in the first sense) of human rights treaties depends on the particular framework of these treaties and their text, concepts such as State 'jurisdiction' that we find in various clauses in these treaties (eg, Article 1 ECHR and Article 2(1) ICCPR), and various legal and policy factors that we may or may not deem to be relevant in their particular context. Whatever answers we come up with when it comes to particular scenarios of their application (eg, with regard to the killing of Bin Laden), these do not depend on some general rules of the law of treaties *ratione loci* – there are no such rules. We may, for example, think that de facto control over territory by a State, regardless of title over that territory, should mean that the State has human rights obligations to the territory's inhabitants,[7] but we arrived at that conclusion through an interpretative exercise involving the human rights treaties' text and object and purpose, not through the application of Article 29 VCLT.

It is also necessary to dispel the misconception that in the law of treaties generally, and in Article 29 VCLT specifically, there is some sort

---

6 See further, Milanovic, *Extraterritorial Application* (n 4) 58 *et seq.*

7 Cf *Loizidou v Turkey*, App No 15318/89, Judgment (Preliminary Objections), 23 February 1995.

of presumption against the extraterritorial effect of treaties. Again, no such presumption exists. The International Law Commission (ILC) commentaries to Article 25 of the Draft Articles on the Law of Treaties, which became Article 29 VCLT with a slightly different formulation, clarify that this provision has nothing to say on the matter:

> In [the ILC's] view, the law regarding the extra-territorial application of treaties could not be stated simply in terms of the intention of the parties or of a presumption as to their intention; and it considered that to attempt to deal with all the delicate problems of extra-territorial competence in the present article would be inappropriate and inadvisable.[8]

Presumptions against extraterritorial effect are creatures of domestic law, used by domestic courts to circumscribe the applicability of municipal legislation. They are avoidance techniques, used to conform domestic statutes to the international legal rules on the scope of the prescriptive jurisdiction of States and thus avoid conflicts between internal and international law, at least absent a clearly expressed wish of the domestic legislature to the contrary.[9] While the international rules on prescriptive jurisdiction serve to delimit the overlapping municipal legal orders of States on the basis of criteria such as territoriality or active or passive personality, domestic courts implement these rules through presumptions against extraterritorial effect and the like, thereby preventing their State from infringing on the sovereignty of another.

From the law of treaties' standpoint, the extraterritorial applicability of treaties is not per se troublesome or sovereignty-infringing. The *pacta tertiis* rule generally suffices to protect the sovereignty of third States, coupled with substantive rules like the prohibition of intervention. Depending on its subject-matter, a treaty with extraterritorial effect may indeed somehow violate the sovereignty of other States, but that is *not* generally the case. For instance, saying that when occupying southern Iraq the United Kingdom had human rights obligations under the ECHR to that territory's population – that is, that the ECHR applied extraterritorially – in no way whatsoever impinges on the sovereignty of Iraq, as the State of Iraq itself was in no way obliged to respect the ECHR, to

---

[8] ILC,'Draft Articles on the Law of Treaties with Commentaries,' Yearbook of the ILC (1966) vol 2 187, 214.

[9] See, eg, in the context of American law, W Dodge, 'Understanding the Presumption against Extraterritoriality,' (1998) 16 Berkley JIL 85; J Knox, 'The Unpredictable Presumption against Extraterritoriality,' (2011) 40 *Southwestern Law Review* 635.

which it was not a party, while the UK was bound only with respect to the acts of its own organs and agents.[10]

That there is no presumption against extraterritoriality does not mean that there is a presumption *in favour* of extraterritoriality. Again, as the ILC put it, the law cannot be stated simply in terms of such presumptions. Whether a particular treaty is capable of territorial application generally, and if so whether it can have extraterritorial effect, is a question of the interpretation of that particular treaty and of what its States parties actually wanted to achieve.

What can we then say generally about the territorial applicability of treaties in the first sense of ascertaining the place in which a State's obligations are to be performed? Again, the subject-matter of a particular treaty is the key consideration. In the words of the ILC:

> Certain types of treaty, by reason of their subject-matter, are hardly susceptible of territorial application in the ordinary sense. Most treaties, however, have application to territory and a question may arise as to what is their precise scope territorially.[11]

Bearing the centrality of treaty subject-matter in mind, we can broadly classify treaties in three different categories. First, we have treaties in which territory is the direct object of regulation – think of treaties involving the disposition of or cession of territory, or border agreements and the like. The second, and largest, category includes treaties that are in principle susceptible of territorial application. How and why territory exactly factors in of course depends on each particular treaty. For instance, it may or may not have dedicated clauses on territorial application. Both the treaty's territorial applicability and its precise scope of application may be plain with regard to some treaties and ambiguous and contested with others. Third, and lastly, we have treaties which are not susceptible to territorial application at all – the treaty's subject-matter would essentially be completely indifferent to territory.

---

[10] See further, Milanovic, *Extraterritorial Application* (n 4) 61 *et seq*. Note that in the UK/Iraq example the UK might find itself in the position of having assumed two contradictory obligations, ie, that its obligation to respect human rights under the ECHR might run against its obligation to respect the sovereignty of Iraq, but that does not mean that the ECHR's extraterritorial application is itself violating Iraqi sovereignty. Cf *Al-Saadoon and Mufdhi v United Kingdom* (dec), App No 61498/08, 30 June 2009; *Al-Saadoon and Mufdhi v United Kingdom*, App No 61498/08, Judgment, 2 March 2010.

[11] ILC, 'Draft Articles on the Law of Treaties with Commentaries,' Yearbook of the ILC (1966) vol 2 187, 213.

More precisely, these categories can and do overlap. Different provisions in a given treaty may not apply to territory in the same way, and indeed might not be susceptible of territorial application at all. It is thus through interpreting each provision in the treaty (while bearing in mind the treaty as a whole) that we can tell *whether* and *how* it can apply to territory and it is only then that we can ask *where* it applies.

For example, if we look at the 1998 Rome Statute of the International Criminal Court (ICC), we will see that most of its provisions, for instance those dealing with the organization of the Court and procedure before it, are not susceptible of territorial application in any truly meaningful sense. Others, however, are not only susceptible of territorial application but directly refer to territory, as for instance Article 4(2): 'The Court may exercise its functions and powers, as provided in this Statute, on the territory of any State Party and, by special agreement, on the territory of any other State.' The most politically sensitive provisions of the Statute – those dealing with the jurisdiction of the Court – definitely raise questions of territorial application, with Article 12(2) providing that the Court may exercise its jurisdiction if the crime in question was committed by a national of a State party or on a State party's territory. The interpretation of these provisions is seemingly straightforward – the extent of the Court's authority, and the extent of State obligations, is tied to States possessing title over territory, and that is that. But what, say, are we to do in situations where a crime is committed in a disputed territory, over which a State claims title that it might not actually have in law? Deeper issues still arise if the Rome Statute is seen not only as delineating the subject-matter and territorial jurisdiction of the Court, but also as creating substantive norms of criminal law that directly bind individuals.[12]

If, to consider another example, we take a look at the 1984 Convention Against Torture (CAT), we will see that many of its provisions tie the extent of State obligations to territories under their *jurisdiction*; for example, Article 2(1) CAT provides that '[e]ach State Party shall take effective legislative, administrative, judicial or other measures to prevent acts of torture in any territory under its jurisdiction.' Again, most human rights treaties contain similar jurisdiction clauses, but with significant differences between them – for instance, while under Article 1 ECHR the State obligation to secure human rights extends to *individuals* within its jurisdiction, under the CAT it is the *territory* that must be under the

---

[12] On which see M Milanovic, 'Is the Rome Statute Binding on Individuals? (And Why We Should Care),' (2011) 9 JICJ 25.

State's jurisdiction for the specific obligations to arise. The central question then becomes how to interpret this concept of jurisdiction, which may or may not take into account the State's *title* over a particular territory. In other words, while the treaty's provisions clearly are susceptible of territorial application, sovereignty over territory might be (and indeed is) perfectly irrelevant – properly interpreted, these provisions only require de facto control.[13]

Similarly, looking at the 1948 Convention on the Prevention and Punishment of the Crime of Genocide, we can see that a variety of its provisions are capable of application to territory. Notably, in Article I of the Convention the contracting parties 'undertake to prevent and to punish' the crime of genocide, without defining either what the obligations to prevent genocide actually involve or how they extend spatially. Both the obligations to prevent genocide and to punish it are by their nature capable of application to territory, for example, with respect to the place where the genocide or an ancillary act was committed. In that regard, Article VI provides inter alia that persons charged with genocide 'shall be tried by a competent tribunal of the State in the territory of which the act was committed.' It thus does not require – but neither does it prohibit – States to prosecute acts of genocide occurring outside their borders.[14] Yet in the *Bosnian Genocide* case the International Court of Justice (ICJ) interpreted Article I very broadly, in effect making it territorially unlimited – any State party has the due diligence obligation to do all it reasonably can to prevent any genocide in the world, no matter where it might happen.[15] Assuming that the Court's interpretation of Article I was correct, we can thus observe two different provisions in the same treaty which are both capable of application to territory yet whose territorial scope of application differs.

To take a final example, we can look at the 1949 Geneva Conventions, which contain dozens of obligations regarding the treatment of various kinds of persons during armed conflict. By their subject-matter, the performance of these obligations can, like hostile acts, only take place in

---

[13] See further, Milanovic, *Extraterritorial Application* (n 4) 58 *et seq.*

[14] A particularly thorny question is whether States would have the obligation to prosecute in territories which they occupy, as, eg, with Nazi Germany and Poland during World War II. See further, M Milanovic, 'Territorial Application of the Convention and State Succession,' in P Gaeta (ed), *The UN Genocide Convention: A Commentary* (OUP, 2009) 473.

[15] *Application of the Convention on the Prevention and Punishment of the Crime of Genocide (Bosnia and Herzegovina v Serbia and Montenegro)*, Judgment, 26 February 2007, paras 162–7, 183, 430.

some defined space. Most, if not all, of the Geneva Conventions' provisions are thus capable of territorial application. Common Article 1 of the Conventions provides that '[t]he High Contracting Parties undertake to respect and to ensure respect for the present Convention in all circumstances,' while Common Article 2 sets out their primary object of regulation, international armed conflict, defined as conflict between two States. Hostilities in international armed conflicts by their very nature occur outside the territory of at least one of the belligerent parties. By design, therefore, in times of international armed conflict the Geneva Conventions apply wherever persons protected by the Conventions are brought within the power of the enemy, whether the fighting occurred on the territory of one of the belligerents, on the territory of a third State, on the high seas, or on Antarctica.

The situation is more complex when it comes to Common Article 3, covering 'conflict[s] not of an international character occurring in the territory of one of the High Contracting Parties.' Such non-international armed conflicts were for a long time regarded as being completely synonymous with purely internal armed conflicts between a State and an organized armed group or between two such groups. Even then issues arose as to whether the humanitarian guarantees in Common Article 3 applied throughout the affected State or only in areas in which the fighting took place. Today, however, the issue of cross-border conflicts between States and non-State actors is of enormous relevance and is highly controversial.[16]

We can see from these examples how territorial applicability can depend not only on the subject-matter of each particular treaty, but can also vary from provision to provision in the same treaty, depending on how these provisions are to be interpreted. Article 29 VCLT comes into the picture, only once this interpretative process is well underway, if at all.

This observation brings us to the third possible sense of 'territorial application' in terms of whether treaty obligations extend to the acts of a State's territorial sub-units, and this is where Article 29 comes to the fore. Some authors argue that a distinction must be made between territories in which a treaty is applied and those territories in respect of which a treaty is binding,[17] or territorial application from the material

---

[16] See further, M Milanovic and V Hadzi-Vidanovic, 'A Taxonomy of Armed Conflict,' in N White and C Henderson (eds), *Research Handbook on International Conflict and Security Law* (Elgar, 2013), accessed 1 May 2014, at http://papers.ssrn.com/sol3/papers.cfm?abstract_id=1988915.

[17] Odendahl, 'Article 29' (n 1) 495.

application of treaty provisions that happen to relate to territory.[18] Both Odendahl and Karagiannis cite favourably the following statement by the ILC's then Special Rapporteur on the law of treaties, Sir Humphrey Waldock:

> [S]ometimes the provisions of a treaty expressly relate to a particular territory or area, e.g. the Antarctic Treaty; and in that event the territory or area in question is undoubtedly the object to which the treaty applies. But this is not what the territorial application of a treaty really signifies, nor in such a case is the application of the treaty confined to the particular territory or area. The 'territorial application' of a treaty signifies the territories which the parties have purported to bind by the treaty and which, therefore, are the territories affected by the rights and obligations set up by the treaty. Thus, although the enjoyment of the rights and the performance of the obligations contained in a treaty may be localized in a particular territory or area, as in the case of Antarctica, it is the territories with respect to which each party contracted in entering into the treaty which determine its territorial scope.[19]

These various distinctions are meaningful, but only to a limited extent. Yes, in principle, we can distinguish between territories (or various spaces) as the direct objects of treaty regulation (as, eg, with regard to treaties of cession or boundary delimitation) and the issue of the territorial application of various treaty provisions. However, it is misleading at best to say that the latter is a question of which territories *the parties have purported to bind* by the treaty. Territories cannot be legally bound by themselves, no more than any other inanimate object. It is the *State* as an actor or a subject of the law that is bound, even if the State itself is defined in territorial terms.

As a subject, the State is in the eyes of international law always seen as an aggregate.[20] The reality is of course different. States are vastly complicated entities, and that complexity can extend to how they organize themselves, territorially or otherwise. Article 29 VCLT thus attempts to address this complexity by setting a default rule as to how treaties should apply with respect to composite States with overseas territories or with decentralized territorial units. When, for instance, the 1959 Antarctic Treaty in its Article V prohibits 'nuclear explosions in Antarctica and the disposal there of radioactive waste material,' with

---

[18] Karagiannis, 'Territorial Application …' (n 2) 317.

[19] Yearbook of the ILC, (1964) vol 2, 12.

[20] See in particular, Article 4 of the ILC Articles on State Responsibility (ASR) and commentary thereto, setting out the principal rule of attribution of conduct based on organ status.

Article VI defining the relevant area as everything south of 60 degrees South latitude, the territorial scope of application in the first sense, as the area in which treaty obligations are to be performed, is as clear as it can be. It is to my mind confusing to say, as Waldock does, that with regard to the United Kingdom, the territorial scope of the treaty actually refers to its own sovereign territory, which is as such bound by the treaty. Rather, one could ask instead whether the UK as a State, a single subject of international law, is bound to perform these obligations with respect to the acts of all of the public authorities that international law normally regards as being part of that State. Would, in other words, the UK be in violation of the Antarctic Treaty if the authorities of the Falklands, rather than the central authorities of the UK, dumped radioactive waste in Antarctica? This is then less a question of territorial application, and more one of the treaty penetrating, or not, the fiction of a State as an aggregate – whether, in other words, the State had *bound itself* when concluding the treaty with respect to the conduct of all of its organs or agents, including its territorially organized sub-units, or whether it has in effect limited the scope of its obligations.

III. VARYING TERRITORIAL APPLICATION THROUGH DEDICATED TREATY CLAUSES

While we can conceptually distinguish between the territorial application of a treaty in the sense of a space or area in which a treaty obligation is to be performed and the treaty's binding effect in respect of the territorial sub-units of a State, this distinction is far from clear cut in practice.[21] To see how this is so we need to look at some examples, but let us first examine the different types of dedicated clauses that States include in treaties in order to set out their territorial scope of application. There are two broad types of these – colonial clauses and federal clauses – but the two categories are not set in stone. Both types have overlapping policy rationales, since their purpose is to limit a State party's obligations under the treaty. At least originally, the reason for doing so with regard to colonies was frequently a blatant policy of double standards – a colonial power did not want to be subject to the same obligations in its metropolitan territory and in its far-flung overseas dominions.[22] Today,

---

21 See also Villiger, *Commentary* (n 1) 391.

22 For a magisterial overview of the impact of still-extant colonialism, especially the British one, on the drafting of the ECHR and the ICCPR, see B Simpson, *Human Rights and the End of Empire* (OUP, 2001).

however, that politically incorrect rationale no longer holds. The process of decolonization has dismantled the former colonial empires, with their remaining overseas possessions usually being rather small and politically and economically unimportant, while at the same time having a large degree of autonomous self-government.

The rationale of colonial clauses – or of unilateral declarations on territorial application in the absence of such clauses, which we will examine shortly – thus resembles that of federal clauses: the central government does not wish to assume obligations which it cannot effectively or easily implement in its decentralized territorial sub-units due to domestic constitutional considerations. Or, to put it differently, because these obligations have to be complied with by the sub-units themselves, the central government will generally not undertake them without the sub-units' consent to that effect and wants flexibility at the treaty level, either through a dedicated clause or through unilateral declarations. Rather than promoting double standards, therefore, the rationale for such clauses would be respect for democratic self-governance and specific local circumstances.

This, of course, is not necessarily how the *other* States parties would see the matter. If a treaty is normally a grand bargain consisting of a number of reciprocal commitments between the States parties, limiting one State's obligations merely because of how it chose to organize itself can obviously affect the interests of the other States parties. This always made federal clauses hard to negotiate and include in treaties. Colonial clauses, on the other hand, were historically more widespread, but as decolonization progressed and colonialism itself became politically more and more unacceptable, so did colonial clauses, which were seen by many to somehow validate colonialism as such.[23]

Dedicated territorial application clauses are thus both rare and likely to affect only a relatively small number of States. This is not to say that they are not capable of creating a number of serious interpretative problems. To make this discussion somewhat less abstract, let us look at some examples. Article 19(7)(b) of the 1919 Constitution of the International Labour Organization (ILO) is often cited as the prototype federal clause, since it limits in various ways a federal State party's obligations 'in respect of [ILO] Conventions and Recommendations which the federal government regards as appropriate under its constitutional system, in whole or in part, for action by the constituent States, provinces, or

---

23 See, eg, Aust, *Modern Treaty Law* (n 2) 202–3; Karagiannis, 'Territorial Application …' (n 2) 310.

cantons rather than for federal action.' Similarly, Article 41(b) of the 1951 Refugees Convention provides that:

> With respect to those articles of this Convention that come within the legislative jurisdiction of constituent States, provinces or cantons which are not, under the constitutional system of the federation, bound to take legislative action, the Federal Government shall bring such articles with a favourable recommendation to the notice of the appropriate authorities of states, provinces or cantons at the earliest possible moment.

Note how federal clauses such as these are about the territorial application of a treaty only indirectly. Indeed, a treaty with such a clause would still apply in the federal State *throughout its territory* when it comes to matters that come within the jurisdiction of the federal government *as a matter of domestic law*. A federal clause, in other words, limits the federal State's international legal obligations by subjecting them to its own domestic law – something that both international law and other (potential) States parties would generally disfavour. The *physical location* of the regulated object (eg, whether a potential refugee lands in the United States in Alabama or in Washington, DC) matters only to the extent that domestic law makes it relevant (eg, whether under domestic law the processing of asylum seekers falls within the competence of the federal government or of the federal units).

Colonial clauses are different in that they do explicitly refer to territory. They can be framed in several different ways.[24] The first, and if you will the most colonial, is that of setting a presumption that the treaty will apply only to the State party's metropolitan territory while allowing it to *extend* the treaty's application to some or all of the (euphemistically termed) territories for whose international relations it is responsible – in effect, these clauses simply reverse Article 29 VCLT.[25] Secondly, we can have clauses that take Article 29 as the starting point but allow a State party to *exclude* certain territories from the treaty's reach.[26] Thirdly, we

---

[24] See Karagiannis, 'Territorial Application …' (n 2) 309–13; Odendahl, 'Article 29' (n 1) 492–3.

[25] See, eg, Article XII of the Genocide Convention: 'Any Contracting Party may at any time, by notification addressed to the Secretary-General of the United Nations, extend the application of the present Convention to all or any of the territories for the conduct of whose foreign relations that Contracting Party is responsible.' See also Article 40 of the Refugee Convention and Article 40 of the 1991 Energy Charter Treaty.

[26] See, eg, Article 70 of the 1965 Convention on the Settlement of Investment Disputes between States and the Nationals of Other States (ICSID Convention):

have clauses that specifically set out the territories to which the treaty will apply by name.[27] Finally, we have the more politically correct clauses that allow a State party to (neutrally) *define* the territories to which the treaty will apply. In all these cases, the territorial extension, exclusion or definition is done by the State party through unilateral declarations or notifications to the treaty depositary made either at the time of signature, ratification or accession or thereafter.[28]

While the application of these colonial clauses is normally straightforward, in some cases they can lead to serious interpretative problems. Consider, for example, the relationship between the State obligation to prevent genocide in Article I of the Genocide Convention and the colonial clause in Article XII thereof. As interpreted by the ICJ, Article I requires States parties to exercise due diligence and do all that they reasonably can to prevent genocide wherever it might occur. The implicit State obligation not to commit genocide is similarly territorially unlimited.[29] On the other hand, Article XII allows a contracting State 'to extend the application of the present Convention to all or any of the territories for the conduct of whose foreign relations that Contracting Party is responsible,' thereby reversing the Article 29 VCLT's presumption and implying that the Convention does not apply to overseas territories absent such an extension. On the face of it, there is a conflict between these two provisions. Let us assume that the United Kingdom did not extend the application of the Convention to Bermuda (which in actual fact it did). Does this mean that the UK would have an obligation not to commit genocide as well as prevent it wherever it might occur

---

'This Convention shall apply to all territories for whose international relations a Contracting State is responsible, except those which are excluded by such State by written notice to the depositary of this Convention either at the time of ratification, acceptance or approval or subsequently.'

[27] This is notably the case with European Union/European Community treaties – see generally Karagiannis, 'Territorial Application …' (n 2) 312–13; J Ziller, 'The European Union and the Territorial Scope of European Territories, (2007) 38 Victoria U of Wellington L Rev 51.

[28] This is the case with most recent Council of Europe treaties, which normally employ the model final clauses adopted by the Committee of Ministers of the Council of Europe at its 315th meeting, in February 1980, accessed 2 May 2014, at http://conventions.coe.int/Treaty/EN/Treaties/HTML/ClausesFinales.htm. Article d(1) thereof provides that 'Any State may at the time of signature or when depositing its instrument of ratification, acceptance, approval or accession, specify the territory or territories to which (this Agreement) (this Convention) shall apply.'

[29] See n 15.

except in Bermuda? Bearing in mind the object and purpose of the Convention, this is not a result that seems particularly sensible.

It seems that we can approach this apparent conflict in four different ways. First, we could say that the conflict exists only due to the ICJ's mistaken overly expansive interpretation of the obligations to prevent and not to commit genocide. If these obligations were to be limited to the State party's own metropolitan territory then the regime of the colonial clause would make sense – the UK would not have the obligation to prevent genocide in Bermuda, but neither would it have the obligation to prevent it in Bosnia or Rwanda, for example. Clearly, while this option removes the conflict, it also runs against important moral and policy considerations that led to the expansive interpretation of Article I in the first place.[30]

Second, we could embrace the conflict and say that the colonial clause does indeed allow for the States parties to carve out parts of their own territory to which their obligations would not apply. States may precisely have wanted the possibility of employing double standards. Yet the sheer moral arbitrariness of this position (ie, that the UK would have the obligation to prevent genocide in Bosnia but not in Bermuda) makes it singularly unappetizing.[31]

Third, we could try to avoid the conflict by splitting the Convention by reference to the territorial scope of the particular obligations that it imposes on its States parties. I have thus argued that the colonial clause and the declarations made under it should have no effect whatsoever on those obligations in the Convention which are territorially unlimited, that is, the obligations to prevent and not to commit genocide. However, the colonial clause would apply to those obligations which are subject to a territorial limitation, here mainly the obligation to punish genocide.[32] Hence, while the UK would have the obligation to prevent genocide both in Bosnia and in Bermuda, it would only have the obligation to prosecute suspected *génocidaires* when the genocide was committed on its own metropolitan territory or on the territory of one of its colonies to which it extended the Convention.

This is an interpretation that at the time to me seemed reasonable, and still does, but I had neglected the possibility of a fourth option. Recall Waldock's insistence that a distinction must be made between the

---

[30] See in that regard, Milanovic, 'Territorial Application …' (n 14).

[31] Of course, it does so in the context of this particular treaty – different policy considerations with regard to a different treaty may call for a different outcome.

[32] Ibid.

territory or area in which a treaty obligation is to be performed and the territory that is bound by the treaty or to which the treaty extends.[33] I have explained above why that distinction is terminologically imprecise and conceptually unclear, at least if we think of it in territorial terms – what really matters is whether we see the State as a single entity, an aggregate in the eyes of international law, or whether we exclude from it some of its subordinate political entities. In other words, the State's obligations would just like with a federal clause be *substantively* rather than territorially limited, here by reference to the actor which has to comply with the obligation.

To put this in more concrete terms, we could say that despite not extending the Convention to Bermuda the *central authorities* of the United Kingdom would still have the obligation not to commit genocide in Bermuda, just as with my third option above. However, the UK's obligations would not cover the acts of the autonomous authorities in Bermuda itself, even though their acts would normally, as a matter of the law of State responsibility, be attributable to the UK.[34] In short, the UK would be in violation of the Convention if it sent its navy, air force and army to commit genocide in Bermuda, but it would not be in violation of the Convention if the authorities of Bermuda itself were to go on a genocidal spree. While the Convention could thus be violated in the *territory* of Bermuda, this would depend on the identity of the potential violator as a political sub-unit of a State party.

This fourth option lacks the simplicity of the third, but it perhaps better describes the complex reality of States with autonomous sub-units and intricate internal constitutional arrangements. Now, which of these four options (if any) was intended by the Convention's States parties when the treaty was drafted is anyone's guess. As is so often the case, the Convention's *travaux* are more confusing than they are illuminating.

---

[33] See n 19 and accompanying text.

[34] The acts of the authorities of an autonomous territory would be equally attributable to the UK as, for instance, the acts of Scottish or Welsh devolved authorities – in the eyes of international law, these are all organs of the UK under Article 4 ILC ASR, and they would be attributable to the UK even if they were ultra vires so long as they were committed in their official capacity (Article 7 ASR). One would need an outright rebellion to dissolve this organic link. Thus, for instance, an intense salvo of missiles fired by the authorities of Bermuda against the United States could constitute an armed attack against the US by the *United Kingdom*, even if the action in question was contrary to the instructions of the central authorities.

Consider, for example, the views of the Swedish representative in the General Assembly's Sixth Committee, who is reported as saying that:

> [a] State which committed an act of genocide on the territory of another State after having signed the convention, would undoubtedly be guilty of a violation of the convention. Should a colonial Power commit or tolerate an act of genocide in one of its colonies, the situation would be similar. If, on the other hand, there were independent authorities capable of exercising decisive influence in the colony concerned, it was difficult to see how the colonial Power could be held responsible. He therefore wondered whether it was really necessary to introduce a clause on that point.[35]

What are we to make of this statement? On the one hand, it clearly supports the proposition that the Convention prohibits States from committing genocide on the territory of other States, as well as within their dependent territories. On the other, it implies that a colonial power could not be held responsible for committing or failing to prevent genocide in one of its territories, if that territory possessed independent authorities. It is completely unclear whether this would have been so because the Convention would not extend to such a territory, or (erroneously) because the act complained of could not be attributed to the State concerned. The other delegates made no statements either for or against the one of the Swedish delegate. The UK's concern, on the other hand, was with its domestic constitutional position that it does not legislate normally for its overseas territories without their prior consent.[36]

In short, none of the four options presented above can be easily excluded; the legal position is essentially under-determinate, and which option one favours depends on the weighing of the relevant moral and policy considerations. As I have explained above, to my mind options three and four are the most sensible, but the uncertainty remains, and is likely to remain – the odds of a case involving both the Genocide Convention and its colonial clause being litigated before the ICJ seem to be vanishingly small.

We can witness the same basic conflict between general principles regarding a treaty's territorial application and the specific provisions of its colonial clause in the ECHR, and here the issues are not merely part of a fairly abstract intellectual puzzle. It is now firmly established in the case law of the European Court of Human Rights that the ECHR will apply extraterritorially in situations in which a State party exercises effective overall control of an area or territory outside its national

[35] UN Doc A/C.6/SR.107, 474.
[36] Ibid, 476.

boundaries – this is the spatial model of the jurisdictional clause in Article 1 ECHR, as set out in *Loizidou*.[37] More controversial is the Convention's extraterritorial application under the *personal* model of jurisdiction as State authority and control over an individual victim of a human rights violation. The Court has endorsed this model in *Al-Skeini* even if its exact parameters remain unclear.[38] That notwithstanding, even if we look at the extraterritorial application of the ECHR solely through the prism of the spatial model, we can see a clear contradiction between this interpretation of Article 1 and the colonial clause in Article 56 (formerly Article 63) of the Convention, under which '[a]ny State may at the time of its ratification or at any time thereafter declare by notification addressed to the Secretary General of the Council of Europe that the present Convention shall … extend to all or any of the territories for whose international relations it is responsible.' Under Article 56(3) the 'Convention shall be applied in such territories with due regard, however, to local requirements.' Similar colonial clauses can be found in the additional protocols to the Convention.

Thus, on one hand, as per *Loizidou*, Turkey must comply with the Convention in Turkish-occupied northern Cyprus, an area under its de facto control, on the other hand the United Kingdom can pick and choose whether to apply the Convention to its overseas territories, over which it not only has de facto control but also de jure sovereignty. And as with the Genocide Convention, we have the same four options for dealing with this apparent conflict.[39]

First, the only way of avoiding the conflict entirely would be to say that all of the case law on the ECHR's extraterritorial application is wrongly decided, and that the proper position is that the treaty admits of no extraterritorial application whatsoever. And again as with the Genocide Convention this option is not appealing precisely because it runs against those considerations of policy and morality that motivated the development of the case law on extraterritorial application in the first place. Second, we could embrace the contradiction by saying that yes, the colonial clause does allow for carving out the colonies from the ECHR's protective reach but no, that this will not have an impact on the general principles regarding the ECHR's extraterritorial application. This now

---

[37] *Loizidou* (n 7).

[38] *Al-Skeini and others v United Kingdom* [GC], App No 55721/07, 7 July 2011.

[39] See also L Moor and AWB Simpson, 'Ghosts of Colonialism in the European Convention on Human Rights,' (2006) 76 BYBIL 121.

seems to be the position adopted by the European Court when it stated in *Al-Skeini* that:

> The 'effective control' principle of jurisdiction set out above does not replace the system of declarations under Article 56 of the Convention (formerly Article 63) which the States decided, when drafting the Convention, to apply to territories overseas for whose international relations they were responsible. Article 56 §1 provides a mechanism whereby any State may decide to extend the application of the Convention, 'with due regard … to local requirements,' to all or any of the territories for whose international relations it is responsible. The existence of this mechanism, which was included in the Convention for historical reasons, cannot be interpreted in present conditions as limiting the scope of the term 'jurisdiction' in Article 1. The situations covered by the 'effective control' principle are clearly separate and distinct from circumstances where a Contracting State has not, through a declaration under Article 56, extended the Convention or any of its Protocols to an overseas territory for whose international relations it is responsible (see *Loizidou* (preliminary objections), cited above, §§ 86–89 and *Quark Fishing Ltd v. the United Kingdom* (dec.), no. 15305/06, ECHR 2006- …).[40]

Note that the one thing that the Court does make clear in this paragraph is that the contradiction between its interpretation of Article 1 and the colonial clause in Article 56 will not lead to narrowing down its reading of Article 1. Why? Because the colonial clause was the product of 'historical reasons' which we have outgrown in our 'present conditions' – an argument that looks suspiciously like an invocation of the 'living instrument' doctrine without doing so by name, and despite the fact that in *Bankovic* the Court thought the living instrument approach to be inapposite to the question of extraterritorial application.[41] Note also how the Court's statement that colonies to which the Convention has not been extended are 'clearly separate and distinct' from foreign territories under the State's effective control is completely unreasoned, since (at least presumptively) a State's colonies *are* under its effective control, and since there is no reason why the Convention could not apply to such colonies if a *third* State occupies them and subjects them to its effective control.

In short, while the Court in *Al-Skeini* killed off the colonial clause as an argument against the spatial model of jurisdiction as it applies to foreign territories under a State's control, it remains unclear how Articles

---

[40] *Al-Skeini* (n 38) para 140.

[41] *Bankovic and Others v Belgium and Others* [GC] (dec), App No 52207/99, 12 December 2001, paras 64–6.

1 and 56 are to be squared with regard to the colonies themselves.[42] The Court may have endorsed the second option, that is, that of exclusion – even if a particular colony would normally be considered a territory within the effective control of the colonial State, and therefore within its jurisdiction, the absence of an Article 56 declaration would carve out an exception from the spatial model of Article 1, effectively allowing colonial States to create Convention-free zones. The approving references to *Loizidou* and *Quark* may bear out such an interpretation.

Yet the Court did not do so explicitly, and in any event, regardless of what it might think at least two other options seem to be possible. As with the Genocide Convention, the third option would require us to distinguish between those State obligations that are dependent on sovereignty or jurisdiction over territory, and those that are not. I have thus argued that the negative obligation to respect human rights should be completely territorially unlimited, as would those procedural or prophylactic positive obligations that are tied to a potential violation of the negative obligation to respect, while on the other hand the overarching positive obligation to secure or ensure human rights would only apply to those territories over which the State has effective control, that is, jurisdiction.[43] The colonial clause could then only affect this overarching positive obligation, but the negative obligation to respect would apply equally to the State's acts within its metropolitan territory, within its colonies and anywhere else in the world.

The fourth option would focus on the distinction between the central authorities of the colonial State and the autonomous authorities of an overseas territory, limiting the scope of the State's obligations to the acts of the former on the basis of the distribution of competences between the two as a matter of domestic law. Thus, in the absence of a declaration extending the Convention to the colony, the colonial State would not be in violation of the Convention if the authorities of the colony tortured an individual in the colony's territory or failed to take all reasonable measures to prevent private or third party mistreatment. However, if the *central authorities* of the colonial State brought the individual to the colony and tortured him there, the State would indeed be in violation of the Convention – it would not be able to exploit the colony as a legal black hole.

---

[42] For more analysis on the interplay between Articles 1 and 56 in light of *Al-Skeini*, see B Miltner, 'Revisiting Extraterritoriality after *Al-Skeini*: The ECHR and its Lessons,' (2012) 33 Michigan JIL 693.

[43] See Milanovic, *Extraterritorial Application* (n 4) 209 *et seq.*

To see how this fourth option would work we can look at the example of the British Indian Ocean Territory (BIOT), a UK overseas possession comprised of several atolls of the Chagos Archipelago.[44] The largest island of the archipelago is Diego Garcia, site of a joint UK and US military base which is of vast strategic importance for US operations in the Indian Ocean and beyond. Until 1965, BIOT was part of the then British possession of Mauritius, to which the ECHR was extended by UK declaration on the basis of the colonial clause. In order to make way for the construction of the military facility on Diego Garcia, the UK split off BIOT from Mauritius, which became independent in 1968. Mauritius is today protesting the splitting off of BIOT, claiming that it was contrary to the principle of self-determination and arguing that it remains its rightful sovereign.[45] The UK proceeded to depopulate the islands, transferring some 1,000-2,000 of their inhabitants to Mauritius and the Seychelles, under the pretence that they were merely temporarily resident in the Chagos Archipelago. The UK government later acknowledged that the deportation was unfortunate and provided a limited amount of compensation. From 1998 onwards a number of Chagos Islanders living in the UK challenged the ban on their return to the islands, with mixed success. The history of the litigation is complicated and will not be repeated here; the last word so far is the 2008 judgment of the House of Lords which, by 3 votes to 2, upheld the 2004 Orders in Council re-instating the (previously quashed) ban on the islanders' return.

---

[44] For general background, see J Lunn, 'The Chagos Islanders,' House of Commons Library Standard Note SN04463, 20 April 2012, accessed 2 May 2014, at www.parliament.uk/briefing-papers/SN04463.

[45] See, eg, the statement of the official Mauritian position in the Comments by the Government of Mauritius to the concluding observations of the Human Rights Committee on the United Kingdom of Great Britain and Northern Ireland and Overseas Territories, CCPR/CO/73/UK – CCPR/CO/73/UKOT/Add.1, 28 May 2002. The dispute has been exacerbated by the UK government's decision to establish a marine protected area in the waters around the archipelago, to the exclusion of the territorial sea of Diego Garcia, with leaked cables indicating that one motive for this was to make human resettlement, ie, the return of the Chagos Islanders, more difficult. Mauritius, on the other hand, initiated arbitral proceedings against the UK under Article 287 and Annex VII of the 1982 UN Convention on the Law of the Sea, which are pending. See further, Lunn, 'The Chagos Islanders' (n 44) 13 *et seq*.

Most of the litigation centred on issues of UK public law and the scope of the relevant principles of judicial review.[46] What interests us here, however, is the conformity of the deportation and the subsequent ban on resettlement with the ECHR. The deportation itself was outside the scope of the UK judicial review proceedings, and deadlines for raising that claim have long lapsed. As for the ban on resettlement, the ECHR, applicable within the UK domestic legal system by virtue of the Human Rights Act 1998, was not the object of significant argument between the parties and ultimately merited only a couple of paragraphs in the House of Lords judgment. In the words of Lord Hoffmann:

> I do not think that the Human Rights Act 1998 has any application to BIOT. In 1953 the United Kingdom made a declaration under article 56 of the European Convention on Human Rights extending the application of the Convention to Mauritius as one of the 'territories for whose international relations it is responsible.' That declaration lapsed when Mauritius became independent. No such declaration has ever been made in respect of BIOT. It is true that the territory of BIOT was, until the creation of the colony in 1965, part of Mauritius. But a declaration, as appears from the words 'for whose international relations it is responsible' applies to a political entity and not to the land which is from time to time comprised in its territory. BIOT has since 1965 been a new political entity to which the Convention has never been extended. … If the Convention has no application in BIOT, then the actions of the Crown in BIOT cannot infringe the provisions of the Human Rights Act 1998.[47]

The *Bancoult* case is currently pending before the European Court, and here of course the issue of the ECHR's application to BIOT becomes central. Note how the House of Lords' judgment rests solely on BIOT's separation from Mauritius and its transformation into a new colony or political entity, which would require a new extension declaration. This is where the judgment could be open to attack – bearing in mind the object and purpose of the Convention, the exceptional nature of the colonial clause which departs from the general regime of Article 1, the lack of any explicit mention in Article 56 of the State having the authority to withdraw a declaration once it has been extended to a territory, and the potential for abuse inherent in allowing colonial States to carve up colonies and thus create vacuums unprotected by the Convention, the

---

[46] See further, M Elliott and A Perreau-Saussine, 'Pyrrhic Public Law: *Bancoult* and the Sources, Status and Content of Common Law Limitations on Prerogative Power,' (2009) PL 697.

[47] *R (Bancoult) v Secretary of State for Foreign and Commonwealth Affairs* [2008] UKHL 61, [2008] 3 WLR 955, paras 64–5 (per Lord Hoffmann).

Court may well conclude that the Mauritius extension declaration continued to apply to BIOT. But then again, it may not.[48] What interests me here is whether the islanders would have an ECHR claim *even if* the Mauritius declaration is considered to have lapsed with respect to BIOT.

The answer to this question would clearly be a no under the exclusive option two and a yes under the inclusive option three, since the negative obligation to respect human rights would be territorially unlimited.[49] Under option four, however, the question to be asked would be whether the alleged human rights violation – the deportation itself or the later Order in Council prohibiting the islanders from returning – was an act of the central authorities of the United Kingdom, in which case the Convention would apply regardless of any extension declaration, or an act of the autonomous authorities of BIOT as a political entity, in which case the UK's obligations would either be severely limited or non-existent altogether. Indeed, for the purposes of UK litigation under domestic public law principles under *Quark*, it is a key issue whether the disputed executive act was that of the Crown in right of the UK or that of the Crown in right of the colony.[50] Whatever its validity as a matter of domestic law, from an international legal standpoint it would be fictional at best to say that BIOT somehow possesses authorities functionally independent from the UK central government. Since there is no colonial self-governance to be protected in a territory deliberately depopulated by the central government, the basic rationale behind the colonial clause is lacking. It would seem, therefore, that even under the fourth option the Convention would apply to the 2004 Orders in Council prohibiting the Chagossians from returning – whether they would be able to make out a substantive case may be a different matter.

Incidentally, Diego Garcia provides a setting for yet another example of the Convention's extraterritorial application. There have been a number of credible reports that the CIA used the Diego Garcia facility for the purpose of detaining so-called high-value Al-Qaeda detainees, including

---

48 Cf Aust, *Modern Treaty Law* (n 2) 205.

49 This of course assumes that on the facts there would be an arguable claim that a substantive provision of the Convention was violated.

50 *R (Quark Fishing Ltd) v Secretary of State for Foreign and Commonwealth Affairs* [2006] 1 AC 529. A further issue, which yet remains unresolved in UK courts, is whether the Human Rights Act as a UK domestic statute can apply to issues arising from territories to which the Convention has been extended under Article 56. See also *R (Barclay & Ors) v Secretary of State for Justice & Ors* [2009] UKSC 9, paras 100–12, 117, 119.

Khalid Sheikh Mohammed, the mastermind of 9/11, and the UK government admitted to instances of the base being used for rendition.[51] One issue is whether the United States owed extraterritorial obligations under the human rights treaties to which it is party, that is, the ICCPR and the CAT, to these detainees or those detained in other CIA 'black sites.'[52] Another issue, however, is whether the *United Kingdom* had obligations towards these detainees, and not just under the ICCPR and the CAT but also under the ECHR, and similar considerations as with the Chagossians themselves would apply here as well – but I will let the matter rest for now.

IV. VARYING TERRITORIAL APPLICATION THROUGH UNILATERAL DECLARATIONS OR RESERVATIONS

We have seen above how after the Second World War colonial clauses have increasingly attracted (not necessarily justified) criticism as somehow validating colonialism itself. As such resistance has grown it became correspondingly harder to include them in multilateral treaties, except for treaties in the Council of Europe where the issue was politically not seen in the same terms. If a treaty lacks an explicit clause dealing with territorial application, the question arises how it would apply to a colonial State's overseas territories.

A few States with remaining overseas territories, chief among them the UK, but prominently also Australia, Denmark, New Zealand and the Netherlands, thus developed a new practice, whereby they would declare at the time of signature or ratification of a treaty whether it would apply to the metropolitan territory alone or to (specified) overseas territories as well. For example, when it ratified the Rome Statute of the ICC Denmark declared that '[u]ntil further notice, the Statute shall not apply to the Faroe Islands and Greenland.' Subsequently, on 17 November 2004 and

---

[51] See, eg, secret detentions and illegal transfers of detainees involving Council of Europe member States: second report by Special Rapporteur Dick Marty, 7 June 2007, accessed 2 May 2014, at www.sacc.org.uk/sacc/docs/coe-rendition-second-marty-report.pdf, para 70; 'British Island "Used by US for Rendition,"' *The Guardian*, 2 March 2008, accessed 2 May 2014, at www.guardian.co.uk/world/2008/mar/02/ciarendition.unitednations.

[52] See further, Milanovic, *Extraterritorial Application* (n 4) 122–4, 129–33, 153–4.

20 November 2006, respectively, Denmark notified the United Nations (UN) Secretary-General as the treaty depositary that:

> With reference to the Rome Statute of the International Criminal Court, done at Rome on 17 July 1998, [the Government of Denmark informs the Secretary-General] that by Royal [Decrees of 20 August 2004 entering into force on 1 October 2004, and 1 September 2006 entering into force on 1 October 2006, respectively] the above Convention will also be applicable in [Greenland and the Faroe Islands]. Denmark therefore withdraws its declaration made upon ratification of the said Convention to the effect that the Convention should not apply to the Faroe Islands and Greenland.[53]

The UK practice is not as unambiguous, since it frequently ratifies a treaty as applying to the 'United Kingdom of Great Britain and Northern Ireland,' which is of course how the State is known internationally, but is in fact code for the metropolitan territory only. For domestic constitutional purposes, the Crown dependencies of Jersey, Guernsey and the Isle of Man and the numerous British overseas territories are not part of the UK proper.[54] Then, however, the UK would declare or notify to the depositary that the treaty *would be extended* to some or all of its overseas territories.

The conformity of this practice with the VCLT is open to debate and can be challenged on several grounds. First, it raises serious issues of interpretation of Article 29 VCLT's general rule that '[u]nless a different intention appears from the treaty or is otherwise established, a treaty is binding upon each party in respect of its entire territory,' as we will now see. Second, it effectively negates the utility of colonial clauses – if States can unilaterally vary the territorial applicability of treaties through declarations, what was the point of negotiating colonial clauses in the

---

[53] Similarly, the Netherlands ratified the Statute '[f]or the Kingdom in Europe, the Netherlands Antilles and Aruba,' while New Zealand declared that:

> consistent with the constitutional status of Tokelau and taking into account its commitment to the development of self-government through an act of self-determination under the Charter of the United Nations, this ratification shall not extend to Tokelau unless and until a Declaration to this effect is lodged by the Government of New Zealand with the Depositary on the basis of appropriate consultation with that territory.

See the relevant UN Treaty Collection (UNTC) entries, accessed 2 May 2014, at http://treaties.un.org/pages/ShowMTDSGDetails.aspx?src=UNTSONLINE&tabid=1&mtdsg_no=XVIII-10&chapter=18&lang=en.

[54] See Aust, *Modern Treaty Law* (n 2) 206–8.

first place? Indeed, in its commentary to the Draft Articles on the Law of Treaties, the ILC stated that:

> One Government proposed that a second paragraph should be added to the article providing specifically that a State, which is composed of distinct autonomous parts, should have the right to declare to which of the constituent parts of the State a treaty is to apply. Under this proposal the declaration was not to be considered a reservation but a limitation of the consent to certain parts only of the State. The Commission was of the opinion that such a provision, however formulated, might raise as many problems as it would solve. It further considered that the words 'unless a different intention appears from the treaty or is otherwise established' in the text now proposed give the necessary flexibility to the rule to cover all legitimate requirements in regard to the application of treaties to territory.[55]

Third, the UK practice in particular looks suspiciously like setting Article 29 on its head by having treaties presumptively apply to the metropolitan territory only, with their application to overseas territories requiring an explicit extension.[56]

That said, this practice has attracted little or no protest from other States, while as the principal depositary of multilateral treaties the UN Secretary-General has by and large endorsed it. Thus, the Secretary-General's *Summary of Practice* states that as the depositary he:

> has felt that he was not to pass judgement on the admissibility of such declarations and he has duly circulated them … This position would not appear inconsistent with the provisions of article 29 of the Vienna Convention on the Law of Treaties since it may be considered that the constant practice of certain States (which still comprise 'non-metropolitan' Territories) in respect of territorial application and the general absence of objections to such practices have 'established a different intention' within the meaning of article 29.[57]

This raises a first-order question that needs to be answered: are declarations on territorial application by their legal nature reservations or, rather, *sui generis* means of expressing a 'different intention' under Article 29 VCLT? If they are the former, the legal regime that would apply to them would be both clearer and less permissive than the current

---

[55] ILC, 'Draft Articles on the Law of Treaties' (n 8) 213.

[56] Cf Aust, *Modern Treaty Law* (n 2) 206 on the effective reversal of the presumption.

[57] Summary of Practice of the Secretary-General as the Depositary of Multilateral Treaties, UN Doc ST/LEG/7/Rev. 1 (1999), para 285.

state of the practice seems to be. In that regard, while the Secretary-General does not consider territorial declarations as impermissible, and while they are not classified in the same rubric as reservations in the UN Treaty Collection, the *Summary of Practice* does frequently refer to them as reservations or 'reservations,' as the case may be.[58] More clearly, in his work as the ILC's Special Rapporteur on reservations, Alain Pellet considered such declarations to be reservations since, in his view, they fulfilled the definitional elements of a reservation under Article 2(1)(d), namely they 'purport to exclude or to modify the legal effect of certain provisions of the treaty in their application to [the reserving] State.' According to Pellet, '[s]uch statements are genuine reservations because they purport the partial exclusion or modification of the treaty's application, which constitutes the very essence of a reservation.'[59]

While Pellet's position was endorsed by France, it was opposed by most other States with overseas territories, most notably by the UK, New Zealand and the Netherlands.[60] In the UK government's view, Pellet's position was flawed for three basic reasons. First, while reservations purport to exclude or modify the legal effect of *certain* provisions of a treaty, territorial declarations purport to exclude or extend the application

---

[58] Ibid, paras 273 ('may a State, when becoming a party to a treaty that is silent as to territorial application include in its instrument a territorial reservation, ie, a reservation to the effect that the treaty or some of its provisions shall not apply to certain Territories'); 275 ('When one State made a declaration concerning the non-application to certain of its non-metropolitan Territories of the Convention on the Privileges and Immunities of the Specialized Agencies, the Secretary-General advised States parties to the Convention and the specialized agencies that the instrument had been transmitted for deposit accompanied by a territorial reservation.'); 277 ('When neither the nature of the treaty nor other special circumstances (eg, the fact that the treaty is the constitutive act of an international organization) mandate the non-acceptance of the instrument containing a declaration as to the limited application or non-application of a treaty to Territories, the Secretary-General has been guided by the general principles of resolution 598 (VI), which he has deemed to apply, *mutatis mutandis*, to "reservations" as to the applicability to Territories. Accordingly, he has accepted instruments containing reservations as to the limited application or non-application to Territories, leaving it to the other parties to draw the legal consequences of such declaration that they may see fit.').

[59] See Report of the International Law Commission on the Work of its Fiftieth Session, 20 April – 12 June and 27 July – 14 August 1998, UN Doc A/53/10, 104–5.

[60] See, eg, Reservations to Treaties: Comments and Observations Received from Governments – Addendum, UN Doc A/CN.4/639/Add.1, 29 March 2011, 8 (France, New Zealand) and 9–10 (UK).

of the *entire* treaty to a particular territory. Second, such declarations are a form of expressing a 'different intention' under Article 29 VCLT. Third, these declarations are generally not objected to by other States, except when they have competing claims to sovereignty over the territory to which the particular treaty is extended.[61]

While there is force in these arguments, none of them are unassailable.[62] The first relies on a rather formal and seemingly arbitrary distinction between the modification of the legal effects of the entire treaty or some provisions of that treaty. As a general matter, this distinction is untenable. There is abundant practice of general or across-the-board reservations, whose permissibility of course may vary.[63] If that is so, there is no reason of principle why this distinction would suddenly become valid when it comes to the treaty's application *ratione loci* rather than *ratione materiae.* Second, unilateral territorial declarations may well be means of expressing a different intention under Article 29, but why would that necessarily entail that they are not reservations? Why cannot they be both? Finally, the lack of any objection by other States and the depositary is easily explained. By and large, the applicability of a particular treaty to overseas territories is today of zero political relevance; it is more a curiosity than anything else. Who cares, after all, whether this or that convention applies to the Pitcairn Islands, population 67?[64] Even the ministries of foreign affairs of well-to-do, developed States have better things to do, let alone those of the vast majority of resource-strapped governments. States routinely fail to object to statements that are reservations beyond any doubt, even when there are plenty of good

---

[61] For instance, Argentina routinely objects to UK declarations extending a given treaty to the Falklands/Malvinas, as it did, eg, with regard to the ICCPR and the Rome Statute of the ICC.

[62] But see Aust, *Modern Treaty Law* (n 2) 205–6.

[63] See guideline 1.1(2) of the ILC Guide to Practice on Reservations to Treaties, Report of the ILC on the Work of its 63rd Session, General Assembly, Official Records, 66th Session, Supplement no. 10, Addendum 1, UN Doc A/66/10/Add.1, providing that the VCLT definition should be interpreted 'as including reservations which purport to exclude or to modify the legal effect of certain provisions of a treaty, or *of the treaty as a whole with respect to certain specific aspects*' (emphasis added). See also paras 16–22 of the commentary.

[64] Who cares, that is, until a case like that of the displaced Chagos Islanders or that of rendition at Diego Garcia comes along. Note also that a number of overseas territories are acting as tax havens and thus attract incorporation of foreign companies; the permissibility of investment arbitration including such companies may very well depend on the territorial scope of UK bilateral investment treaties, and financially this is certainly not a minor issue.

reasons to do so. As for the practice of the UN Secretary-General as the principal depositary of multilateral treaties, not only are his views on the matter not entirely clear, as we have seen above, but bearing in mind that States have long resisted the depositary having a more active role in assessing the lawfulness of treaty actions, that is, moving beyond the strictly administrative role of a 'letter box depositary,' the legal relevance of his ambiguous non-objection is questionable at best.[65]

Be that as it may, due to the opposition it encountered, as well as disagreements in the Commission itself, the ILC abandoned Pellet's initial position in its final Guide to Practice. Guideline 1.1.3, which initially provided that '[a] unilateral statement by which a State purports to exclude the application of a treaty or some of its provisions to a territory to which that treaty would be applicable in the absence of such a statement constitutes a reservation,' was redrafted to say that:

> [a] unilateral statement by which a State purports to exclude the application of some provisions of a treaty, or of the treaty as a whole *with respect to certain specific aspects*, to a territory to which they would be applicable in the absence of such a statement constitutes a reservation.[66]

When, in other words, a State excludes the application of the *entire treaty* as such (ie not with regard to 'certain specific aspects') to a particular territory this would *not* constitute a reservation. The commentary now explicitly states that:

> While at first glance it might seem that a declaration by which a State purports to exclude the application of the treaty *as a whole* to all or part of its territory could also be considered as purporting to exclude or modify the application of the legal effect of the treaty, such declarations are not necessarily reservations within the meaning of guideline 1.1 but rather the expression of a 'different intention' in the sense of article 29 of the Vienna Conventions. The State is not excluding the legal effect of the treaty in respect of a particular territory but is identifying 'its territory,' in the sense of article 29, where the treaty is applied. The legal effect of the provisions of the treaty remains intact within its territorial scope.[67]

And that:

---

[65] On both points, see M Wood, 'Institutional Aspects of the Guide to Practice on Reservations,' (2013) 24 EJIL 1099.

[66] ILC, Report on the 63rd Session, UN Doc A/66/10/Add.1, 2 and 48. Emphasis added.

[67] Ibid, 50.

> On reflection, it would hardly seem possible to consider such declarations purporting to exclude the application of a treaty as a whole to a particular territory as actual reservations. In fact, it was noted that such an assimilation would deprive a State representing a Non-Self-Governing Territory at the international level from becoming a party to a treaty prohibiting reservations for as long as the Territory was unable, for one reason or another, to undertake the same commitments.
>
> It was for this reason that the Commission decided not to include in guideline 1.1.3 cases of declarations that purport to exclude the application of a treaty as a whole to a particular territory. In principle, these are not reservations in the sense of the Vienna Convention.[68]

Note how the Commission's almost total withdrawal from Pellet's initial position validates that of the UK and others, but does so purely on instrumentalist grounds. Even though now to the Commission they 'hardly seem possible,' good arguments can certainly be made in favour of Pellet's original view. It is at best an exaggeration to say that there is a categorical difference between, say, the UK stating that it reserves the right not to apply Article 11 ICCPR in Jersey (undoubtedly a reservation according to the ILC) and it saying that it does not want to apply the ICCPR to Jersey altogether (not a reservation). Nor is there something magical about the distinction between metropolitan and non-metropolitan territories. The promotion of self-governance policy argument can apply with equal force, if not more force, to federal units or other forms of territorial decentralization. Is it *really* categorically different for the UK to say that a treaty would not apply to Jersey or Guernsey from it saying that the treaty would not apply to Scotland, Wales or even London? In other words, if it can unilaterally do the former why could it not do the latter, and under the same legal conditions? Incidentally, everyone would agree that if the United States declared that a particular treaty did not apply to Alabama or if Canada declared it did not apply to Alberta these statements would constitute federal reservations.[69]

The ILC's decision to validate the (itself far from uniform) practice of unilateral territorial declarations by a few States was not based on some clear-cut principle, but was a pragmatic and political one. It would simply be far too messy to question long-established treaty relations, especially in cases where State made territorial declarations while the treaty in question explicitly prohibited reservations, bearing in mind that this practice has been tolerated by the vast silent majority mostly because it is politically too unimportant. Accepting that decision for what it is and

---

68 Ibid, 51.

69 See also Aust, *Modern Treaty Law* (n 2) 212–13.

consequently that territorial declarations are generally not to be thought of as reservations,[70] a number of uncertainties still remain.

While the application of the reservations regime might have been too strict, and thus unappealing, it would at least have brought some clarity. Hence, even if we considered territorial declarations to be *sui generis* means of expressing a different intention within the meaning of Article 29 VCLT, we could still ask whose intention this must be. Is this the intention solely of the declaring State, or that of the States parties collectively? Does, in other words, the variance of territorial application constitute a unilateral right of each contracting State, or does it depend on an explicit or tacit agreement by other States parties, who can have a say on the matter? Can their silence be interpreted as consent, and if so when and how? What if States *did* object to a territorial declaration, for whatever reason? What would be the legal effects of such an objection on treaty relations? Should declaring States make their intention reasonably explicit so that other States may be able to react adequately? Can territorial declarations once made be varied only in the direction of extending a treaty to a territory from which it was previously excluded, or can a territory that was once included be subsequently excluded from the treaty's territorial scope?[71]

None of these questions has a clear answer. We could perhaps reason through some of them by analogy to the reservations regime, but this would obviously again raise the question why we do not apply the reservations regime in the first place. Let us consider as an example of this complexity the UK's ratification of the Rome Statute of the ICC. When it ratified the Rome Statute in 2001, the UK made no declaration on territorial application – unlike those of Denmark, the Netherlands and New Zealand,[72] its instrument of ratification mentioned no limitation

---

[70] In that regard, note that even if the reservations hypothesis was valid, one could question whether a declaration of territorial *extension* as opposed to *exclusion* could be considered a reservation.

[71] For example, the UK argues that it:

> has been the long-standing practice of the United Kingdom (since at least 1967), in relation to multilateral treaties which are silent on territorial application, to specify in the instrument of ratification (or accession) the territories in respect of which the treaty is being ratified (or acceded to). Territories may be included (or excluded) at a later stage by means of a separate notification made by the United Kingdom to the depositary power. (UN Doc A/CN.4/639/Add.1, 10)

[72] See n 52 and accompanying text.

whatsoever.[73] The UN Treaty Collection entry on the status of ratifications of the Statute similarly made no mention of any territorial limitation; as far as the depositary was concerned, on whose practice the UK so relies, the UK's ratification of the Statute was no different in territorial terms than that of any other State.

Then, on 11 March 2010 the UK informed the Secretary-General that it wished that its ratification of the Rome Statute of the ICC 'be extended to the following territories for whose international relations the United Kingdom is responsible: Anguilla, Bermuda, British Virgin Islands, Cayman Islands, Falkland Islands, Montserrat, Pitcairn, Henderson, Ducie and Oeno Islands, St Helena, Ascension and Tristan da Cunha, Sovereign Base Areas of Akrotiri and Dhekelia, Turks and Caicos Islands.' The declaration added that the United Kingdom 'considers the extension of the aforesaid Statute … to take effect from the date of deposit of this notification …' The only State to object to the UK's declaration was Argentina on the basis that it referred to the Falkland Islands, which Argentina considers to be its own territory.[74] For its part, Article 120 of the Rome Statute stipulates that '[n]o reservations may be made to this Statute.'

The first problem we encounter in analysing this example is whether the UK's instrument of ratification contains an (implicit) territorial exclusion, whereby the UK ratified the Statute only with respect to its metropolitan territory. Unlike the comparable instruments from other States, the UK's instrument is simply not clear enough; no signal was given to prompt a third State to even consider making some kind of objection. A reasonable reader may well have thought that the UK made

---

[73] The instrument of ratification is dated 28 September 2001, was signed and sealed by the Foreign Secretary and reads as follows:

> Whereas the Rome Statute of the International Criminal Court, adopted in Rome on 17 July 1998, was signed on behalf of the United Kingdom of Great Britain and Northern Ireland on 30 November 1998;
>
> Now therefore the Government of the United Kingdom of Great Britain and Northern Ireland, having considered the Rome Statute aforesaid, hereby confirm and ratify the same and undertake faithfully to perform and carry out all the stipulations therein contained.

The instrument itself is not available through the UNTC but is on file with the author – I am very grateful to Chanaka Wickremasinghe, Legal Counsellor at the FCO, for providing me with a copy.

[74] See the UN Treaty Collection website, accessed 2 May 2014, at http://treaties.un.org/Pages/ViewDetails.aspx?src=TREATY&mtdsg_no=XVIII-10&chapter=18&lang=en.

no attempt to rebut the Article 29 VCLT presumption, as did the Secretary-General in his depositary capacity. If the instrument of ratification contained no exclusion, then the 2010 declaration would likely be devoid of any legal effect, unless one accepts the view that States can simply switch particular territories on and off at will for the purpose of a treaty's application. And what are we to make of the objection by Argentina? Does it have any effect whatsoever? Would that or should that even depend on who lawfully possesses title over the Falklands?

This discussion is of course fairly academic. In most cases no dispute will arise and nobody will care as to how a treaty exactly applies to a minor overseas possession. Here, however, we have the territorial jurisdiction of the ICC depending on what we make of the UK's instrument of ratification, its 2010 territorial declaration and the objection by Argentina, with regard to a territory over which the two States have already fought one war. The likelihood of this becoming a live issue may be small, but it is not nil.

V. TERRITORIAL CHANGES AND SUCCESSION

Finally, I will very briefly deal with the effect of territorial change on treaties. Consider first the scenario in which territory T first belonged to State A and was then ceded to State B. To the extent that a treaty's application in the sense of the space in which an obligation is to be performed actually depends on sovereignty over territory, treaties will generally follow the moving frontiers rule. So will territorial application in the sense of treaties' binding effect on the State's territorial sub-units.[75] Since it is the State as a single legal person that is and remains bound by treaties, not territories as such, A's treaties will generally cease applying, while B's will now extend to the ceded territory. This, again, will depend on the subject-matter of a given treaty and on any special arrangements that the two States might come to.[76]

The moving frontiers principle can be simply stated, but its application in a given case may give rise to certain complexities. Even more complex are those scenarios involving the creation of new States and the law of State succession. I will here refer the reader to the chapter in this

---

[75] See generally, Odendahl, 'Article 29' (n 1) 498 *et seq* and the references cited therein.

[76] Such as, for instance, the arrangements between China and the UK on the application of treaties to Hong Kong – see Aust, *Modern Treaty Law* (n 2) 213–14.

handbook dealing with this topic in detail,[77] except to briefly remark on how absolutely crucial it is to distinguish between succession to a treaty as such from succession to any State responsibility already arising from the breach of that treaty.

Consider in this regard the issue of State succession to the Genocide Convention and State responsibility for genocide in the former Socialist Federal Republic of Yugoslavia (SFRY), specifically the July 1995 Srebrenica massacre. Succession to the Genocide Convention is a particular mode for a successor State of the SFRY to become a party to that treaty. Some argue that the succession to the Genocide Convention or other treaties of a humanitarian character is automatic, and happens *ipso facto* upon the new State's emergence on the international plane and regardless of its wishes. Others (perhaps most) contend that the same rules on succession apply across the board and that new States have a choice as to whether to succeed to their predecessors' treaties or not. This is succession to the treaty itself, whether automatic or completely voluntary. But what happens once a *breach of the treaty* had already occurred and the predecessor State became responsible for an internationally wrongful act is an entirely different matter. Thus, in July 1995 the rump Federal Republic of Yugoslavia (FRY), consisting of the federal units Serbia and Montenegro, committed such an act, by failing to prevent the Srebrenica genocide. Montenegro became independent in 2006, while Serbia remained a continuator of the former FRY. The question, thus, is whether Montenegro as a successor State of the FRY now bears any part of the FRY's responsibility for a wrong already committed. The answer to that question is far from clear, except to say that the clean slate rule that generally applies to the succession to treaties should not automatically apply to a case of succession to responsibility.[78] In deciding the *Bosnian Genocide* case in 2007, after Montenegro's independence, the ICJ managed to avoid this issue by holding that regardless of whether Montenegro succeeded to the whole or part of the FRY's responsibility it did not succeed to the ongoing litigation before the Court, that is, it did not provide its consent to have proceedings brought before it.[79] On the other hand, the European Court of Human Rights did hear cases in which the alleged violation of the ECHR occurred when Serbia and Montenegro were part of the joint State but the

---

77 See the contribution of Andreas Zimmermann to this volume.

78 The leading study on the issue remains P Dumberry, *State Succession to International Responsibility* (Nijhoff, 2007). On the particular example of genocide in Bosnia, see also Milanovic, 'Territorial Application …' (n 14).

79 *Bosnian Genocide* (n 15) paras 76–8.

judgment was delivered after Montenegro's independence.[80] In doing so, it applied a functional approach whereby it allocated responsibility to that (new) State which organically continued the part of the old joint State whose conduct was the object of the case. Thus, if it were Montenegrin courts that were alleged to have breached the applicant's right to a fair trial before Montenegro's independence, it would be the State of Montenegro and not Serbia that would be responsible for that act post-independence. Whether that pragmatic approach, which fits the circumstances of those concrete cases before the Court, is transposable to other contexts is a difficult matter that is best left open.

VI. PROSPECTS FOR FURTHER RESEARCH

I hope that this chapter has shown how there is ample room for further research with regard to the territorial or spatial application of treaties. Indeed, the point of the chapter was more to raise issues than to resolve them. It was certainly not to claim that solutions appropriate in the human rights context and related matters can appropriately be transplanted to other settings, such as trade or investment. Rather, the examples I have drawn upon were used merely to explain the different conceptual issues we can encounter in discussing the territorial application of treaties more generally. We have seen how the very concept of the territorial application of treaties is capable of having several different meanings and is burdened by terminological confusion. First, when it comes to territorial application as examining the space in which a particular treaty's obligations are to be performed, the prospects for further research are endless, since the variety of treaty subject-matters is equally endless, and territorial application in this sense is purely a function thereof. Thus, while some of us can write about the territorial application of human rights treaties, others can write about status of forces agreements and environmental, labour or investment treaties.[81] This scholarship will to an extent necessarily be area-specific, and is subject to few, if any, overarching principles or generalizations.

---

[80] See *Bijelic v Montenegro and Serbia*, App No 11890/05 (ECHR, 28 April 2009).

[81] For a brief overview of various kinds of territorial application clauses in BITs, see UNCTAD, 'Bilateral Investment Treaties 1995–2006: Trends in Investment Rulemaking,' 18 April 2007, accessed 2 May 2014, at http://aimp.apec.org/Documents/2007/IEG/IEG-GOS1/07_ieg-gos_wksp1_005.pdf, 17–19.

Second, when it comes to territorial application as an enquiry into whether a State is bound by a treaty obligation with regard to the acts of one of its territorial sub-units, not only is this enquiry complicated by the perhaps inherently incomplete separation of this set of issues from those dealing with the locus of State's obligations, but here we have to contend with the often mind-boggling complexity of colonial and federal clauses, unilateral declarations and reservations. Add to this mix, inter-State disputes about sovereignty over particular pieces of territory, as for example with the Falklands/Malvinas,[82] and the opportunities for further research grow as the determinacy of the law diminishes.

---

[82] See, eg, M Waibel, 'Oil Exploration around the Falklands (Malvinas),' EJIL: Talk!, 13 August 2012, accessed 2 May 2014, at www.ejiltalk.org/oil-exploration-around-the-falklands-malvinas/ (discussing the territorial applicability of US and Argentine BITs to the disputed islands).

8. The personal dimension: Challenges to the *pacta tertiis* rule

Alexander Proelss

I. INTRODUCTION

The maxim *pacta tertiis nec nocent nec prosunt* (agreements neither harm nor benefit third parties) concerns the legal effects produced by treaties in relation to States that are not party to them. From the perspective of a ('third') State that has not expressed its consent to be bound by its terms,[1] a treaty constitutes *res inter alios acta*. As such, the *pacta tertiis* rule, which as the Permanent Court of International Justice (PCIJ) stated in 1923 stems from the operation of the principle of sovereign equality of States,[2] may be described as a negative formulation of the principle of *pacta sunt servanda*.

[1] Note that the *pacta tertiis* rule is not applicable to other sources of international law. In particular, there is no need to measure the legality (not: validity) of binding decisions of international organizations against the requirements of this rule, as the power to adopt such decisions directly follows from the statute of the organizations concerned, ie, from treaties concluded between States; cf Christian Tomuschat, 'International Organizations as Third Parties under the Law of International Treaties', in Enzo Cannizzaro (ed), *The Law of Treaties beyond the Vienna Convention*, (OUP, 2011) 206, at 217. Even in the case of the UN, the potential third-party effect of the resolutions of the Security Council does not result from the resolutions themselves, but from the powers transferred to it by the 1945 Charter of the United Nations (UN Charter), or by the validity of the relevant Charter provisions under customary international law respectively (Stefan Talmon, 'Article 2(6) UN Charter', in Bruno Simma, Daniel-Erasmus Khan, Georg Nolte and Andreas Paulus (eds), *The Charter of the United Nations: A Commentary* (OUP, 2012) paras 46–75). Concerning customary international law, the central importance of the element of consent is safeguarded by the concept of persistent objection (cf Olufemi Elias, 'Persistent Objector', in Rüdiger Wolfrum (ed), *Max Planck Encyclopedia of Public International Law*, Vol VIII (OUP, 2012) 280, para 2).

[2] *Status of Eastern Carelia* (Advisory Opinion) [1923] PCIJ Ser B No 5, 27; cf also International Law Commission, 'Report of the International Law Commission on the Work of its Eighteenth Session' (1966) UN Doc. A/6309/Rev.l, 226.

Historically, the *pacta tertiis* rule has its roots in the Roman law of contract.[3] Notwithstanding several attempts by the Great Powers (Austria-Hungary, France, Great Britain, Prussia and Russia) to create 'objective law' (in other words, law binding on third States) on several occasions following the Congress of Vienna in 1815, the *pacta tertiis* rule has never been called into question generally.[4] During the work of the International Law Commission (ILC) on the law of treaties, the effects of treaties on 'third' States[5] were comprehensively dealt with by Special Rapporteurs Fitzmaurice[6] and Waldock.[7] Settled jurisprudence on the matter prompted Special Rapporteur Fitzmaurice to state that the principles *pacta tertiis nec nocent nec prosunt* and *res inter alios acta* 'are so fundamental, self-evident and well-known, that they do not really require the citation of much authority in their support'.[8] Ultimately, the *pacta tertiis* rule was adopted as Art. 34 of the 1969 Vienna Convention on the Law of Treaties (VCLT). A similar rule was included in the 1986 Vienna

---

[3] Ronald Francis Roxburgh, *International Conventions and Third States* (Longmans, Green & Company, 1917) 6.

[4] *Certain German Interests in Polish Upper Silesia* (Merits) [1926] PCIJ Ser A No 7, 29; *The Factory at Chorzów (Claim for Indemnity)* (Merits) [1928] PCIJ Ser A No 17, 45; *Case Relating to the Territorial Jurisdiction of the International Commission of the River Oder* [1929] PCIJ Ser A No 23, 20; *Customs Régime between Germany and Austria* (Advisory Opinion) [1931] PCIJ Ser A/B No 41, 48; *Case of the Free Zones of Upper Savoy and the District of Gex (France v Switzerland)* (Judgment) [1932] PCIJ Ser A/B No 46, 141; PCA, 1928: 842; *Anglo-Iranian Oil Co Case* (Preliminary Objection) [1952] ICJ Rep 93, 109.

[5] The notion 'third State' is defined in Art. 2(1)(h) VCLT as a 'State not a party to the treaty'. This provision is logically linked to Art. 2(1)(g) stating that '"Party" means a State which has consented to be bound by the treaty and for which the treaty is in force'. A third State in terms of the VCLT is thus not only a State which is wholly a stranger to the treaty but also a State which participated in the drafting of the treaty but has not yet signed it. In his fifth report, Special Rapporteur Fitzmaurice pointed to the fact that the term 'third State' is 'strictly appropriate only for the case of a bilateral treaty', but referred to the common usage of this term within the contract laws of many States (International Law Commission, 'Fifth Report by Sir Gerald Fitzmaurice, Special Rapporteur' (1960) UN Doc. A/CN.4/130, 83).

[6] International Law Commission, 'Fifth Report by Sir Gerald Fitzmaurice, Special Rapporteur' (1960) UN Doc. A/CN.4/130, 69–107.

[7] International Law Commission, 'Third Report on the Law of Treaties, by Sir Humphrey Waldock, Special Rapporteur' (1964) UN Doc. A/CN.4/167 and Add.1-3, 5–65.

[8] International Law Commission, 'Fifth Report by Sir Gerald Fitzmaurice, Special Rapporteur' (1960) UN Doc. A/CN.4/130, 83.

Convention on the Law of Treaties between States and International Organizations or between International Organizations (VCLTSIO). At least in inter-State relations, the *pacta tertiis* rule is generally held to reflect customary international law.[9]

However, despite consensus regarding its normative value in general, the exact scope of the *pacta tertiis* rule has remained the subject of considerable controversy. This controversy stems from three main sets of challenges to the operation of the rule.

First of all, owing to the fact that the *pacta tertiis* rule very much flows from the broader concept of State sovereignty, the allegedly waning importance of State sovereignty has inevitably brought criticism of the *pacta tertiis* rule. As such, a number of commentators have argued that the operation of the *pacta tertiis* rule must necessarily decrease in line with the marginalization of the concept of State sovereignty.[10] There are a number of areas in which the declining significance of State sovereignty can arguably be evidenced, including the operation of *erga omnes* obligations.[11] As one highly recognized authority states:

> The rule that treaties cannot validly impose obligations upon dissenting third states follows clearly from the sovereignty of states and from the resulting fact that there is no international legislative process by which rules of law are imposed upon a dissenting minority of states. However, as international society becomes a more integrated community, a departure from the accepted principle becomes unavoidable, in particular in the sphere of preservations of international peace and security.[12]

To give just one example, in the field of international environmental law a small number of States have been able to rely on their sovereign status

---

[9] See only International Law Commission, 'Third Report on the Law of Treaties, by Sir Humphrey Waldock, Special Rapporteur' (1964) UN Doc. A/CN.4/167 and Add.1-3, 18; Case C-386/08, *Brita GmbH v Hauptzollamt Hamburg-Hafen* [2010] ECR I-01289, paras 42–4; Arnold Duncan McNair, *The Law of Treaties* (2nd ed, Clarendon Press, 1961) 309; Budislav Vukas, 'Treaties, Third-Party Effect', *Max Planck Encyclopedia of Public International Law*, Vol X (OUP, 2012) para 3.

[10] See only Georg Dahm, Jost Delbrück and Rüdiger Wolfrum, *Völkerrecht*, Vol I/3 (De Gruyter, 2002) 626.

[11] Georg Dahm, Jost Delbrück and Rüdiger Wolfrum, *Völkerrecht*, Vol I/3 (De Gruyter, 2002) 625; Bruno Simma, 'From Bilateralism to Community Interest in International Law' (1994) 250 *Recueil des Cours* 217, 331.

[12] Robert Jennings and Arthur Watts, *Oppenheim's International Law*, Vol I (9th ed, OUP, 1992) 1264.

to prevent the adoption of a sustainable climate change policy – much to the frustration of many other States, international organizations and non-governmental organizations.

Secondly, the fact that customary international law and the VCLT recognize that there are a number of situations to which the *pacta tertiis* rule does not apply has generated considerable debate regarding the scope of a number of exceptions to this rule. To elaborate, Arts 35–38 VCLT set out the circumstances under which a treaty may lawfully provide for obligations or rights of third States. Accordingly, it can be said that the *pacta tertiis* rule codified in Art. 34 VCLT is best understood as creating a *presumption* against creating effects for third States.[13] Whether or not the *pacta tertiis* rule is subject to further exceptions is an unclear and controversial issue that divided the ILC at the time of drafting the VCLT[14] and continues to split opinion today. In the words of two commentators, 'the classic exposition does not provide the full story today'.[15]

Finally, further challenges to the *pacta tertiis* rule arise as a result of uncertainties and controversies surrounding the application of that rule in specific situations. In this respect, the question of what constitutes an obligation or a right under Art. 34 VCLT is rarely discussed at all.[16] Further, it should be noted that the wording of Art. 34 VCLT does not cover the creation of rights and obligations for a third party that is not a State, such as an international organization for instance. Art. 34 VCLT-SIO addresses the situation with regard to treaties concerning one or more States and international organizations. With regard to all other treaties, however, whether or not the *pacta tertiis* principle applies appears to be a matter of customary international law. At the same time, it will be shown below that the *pacta tertiis* rule has been frequently

---

[13] Ian McTaggart Sinclair, *The Vienna Convention on the Law of Treaties* (Manchester University Press, 1984) 101.

[14] International Law Commission, 'Report of the International Law Commission on the Work of its Eighteenth Session' (1966) UN Doc. A/6309/Rev.l, 226.

[15] Alan Boyle and Christine Chinkin, *The Making of International Law* (OUP, 2007) 239.

[16] But see Christine Chinkin, *Third Parties in International Law* (OUP, 1993) 18–22; Philippe Cahier, 'Le problème des effets des traités à l'égard des États tiers' (1974) 143 *Recueil des Cours* 589, 597–605; Ronald Francis Roxburgh, *International Conventions and Third States* (Longmans, Green & Company, 1917) 31–3; Alexander Proelss, 'Commentary on Art. 34', in Oliver Dörr and Kirsten Schmalenbach (eds), *Vienna Convention on the Law of Treaties: A Commentary* (Springer, 2012), paras 13–28.

relied upon by States in situations which on closer examination have not given rise to issues of third-party effects.

The present chapter aims to provide a brief assessment of these three challenges that may ultimately call the *pacta tertiis* rule into question. It will start with an examination of the elements and scope of this rule before turning to potential exceptions that go beyond those codified in Arts 35–38 VCLT. While it is impossible here to comprehensively analyse the relevant State and treaty practice, individual examples will be used in order to substantiate the general conclusions drawn in this chapter. First and foremost, the examples chosen affect the fields of international criminal law, the United Nations (UN) Charter and the international law of the sea. This selection of areas of public international law is not surprising: by its very nature (and as evidenced, inter alia, by Art. 2(6)), the UN Charter aims at establishing a universal legal order, as does, taking into account the international character as well as the humanity-based nature of the crimes concerned, international criminal law. With regard to the international law of the sea, particular relevance for the *pacta tertiis* rule derives from the century-old doctrine of freedom of the seas, which, as far as fisheries, shipping and the protection of the marine environment are concerned, has brought about problems as to how the conduct of 'free riders', that is, States that have decided to not become members of the relevant (freedom-restricting) treaties, can be regulated. The chapter concludes that ultimately none of the challenges analysed present any meaningful threat to the *pacta tertiis* rule in the long run.

II. SCOPE OF APPLICATION OF THE *PACTA TERTIIS* RULE

1. Treaties Not Covered by the *pacta tertiis* Rule

The *pacta tertiis* rule can only constitute an obstacle vis-à-vis the third-party effect of an international agreement to the extent that an agreement creates either obligations or rights for one or more third State(s).

The first group of challenges may be illustrated best by reference to the argument made by the United States (US) according to which the exercise of jurisdiction by the International Criminal Court (ICC) on the basis of Art. 12(2)(a) of the 1998 Rome Statute of the International

Criminal Court (Rome Statute) would violate the *pacta tertiis* principle.[17] This provision refers to situations where the territorial State, in other words the State where the alleged offences were committed, has accepted the jurisdiction of the Court. In such cases, the ICC may exercise its jurisdiction even if the State of nationality of the accused is not a party to the Rome Statute, provided that either a situation exists in which one or more of such crimes appears to have been committed is referred to the prosecutor by a State party in accordance with Art. 14 of the Rome Statute, or the prosecutor has initiated an investigation in respect of such a crime in accordance with Art. 15 of the Rome Statute.[18] The possibility of US military personal operating overseas being subjected to the jurisdiction of the ICC remains a concern for the US despite the fact it has thus far refrained from becoming a party to the Rome Statute.

However, it is submitted that such concerns are without basis since the right of a State to exercise criminal jurisdiction over crimes committed on its territory is a well-established principle in public international law.[19] Nationality and territoriality are each an independent and sufficient basis for jurisdiction.[20] Indeed, '[t]here is no rule of international law prohibiting the territorial State from voluntarily delegating to the ICC its sovereign ability to prosecute'.[21] Against this background, the alleged 'third-party effect' of Art. 12(2)(a) of the Rome Statute is not one in law, but is a natural practical consequence of the foundation of the ICC. It may in fact best be described, in terms used by Special Rapporteur Fitzmaurice in 1960, as a treaty producing 'effects incidentally unfavourable to a third State'.[22] Such 'incidental effects', however, are compatible

---

[17] Cf Ruth Wedgwood, 'The International Criminal Court: An American Perspective' (1999) 10 *European Journal of International Law* 93, 99–102.

[18] Cf Rome Statute of the International Criminal Court (17 July 1998) 2187 UNTS 90, Art. 13(a) and (c).

[19] Ian Brownlie, *Principles of Public International Law* (7th ed, OUP, 2008) 301–3.

[20] Gerhard Hafner, Jonathan Huston, Anne Rübesame and Kristen Boon, 'A Response to the American View as Presented by Ruth Wedgwood' (1999) 10 *European Journal of International Law* 108, 117. Note that the same ought to be regarded as true in respect of the third 'original' category of jurisdiction of States, ie, flag State jurisdiction; see Art. 12(2)(a) of the Rome Statute of the International Criminal Court (17 July 1998) 2187 UNTS 90.

[21] Sharon A Williams and William A Schabas, 'Commentary on Art. 12', in Otto Triffterer (ed), *Commentary on the Rome Statute of the International Criminal Court* (Hart, 2008) para 15.

[22] International Law Commission, 'Fifth Report by Sir Gerald Fitzmaurice, Special Rapporteur' (1960) UN Doc. A/CN.4/130, 81; see also Alexander

with the *pacta tertiis* rule. One might add that the impact of the Rome Statute is further mitigated by the principle of complementarity[23] safeguarding the position of third States.[24]

It is occasionally debated whether references to other international agreements included in a treaty that result in the parties to that treaty being indirectly bound to the terms of the other agreements are compatible with the *pacta tertiis* rule. An example of such a situation is Art. 210(6) of the 1982 United Nations Convention on the Law of the Sea (UNCLOS) according to which '[n]ational laws, regulations and measures [relevant to the prevention, reduction and control of pollution of the marine environment by dumping] shall be no less effective in preventing, reducing and controlling such pollution than the global rules and standards.' It is generally accepted that the term 'global rules and standards' refers to the rules contained in the 1972 Convention on the Prevention of Marine Pollution by Dumping of Wastes and Other Matter (London Convention). Thus, by acceding to the UNCLOS, a State is obliged ('shall') to comply with the minimum standards of the 1972 Convention, irrespective of whether it has become a party to that treaty or not.

It should be noted, however, that States are of course, in accordance with their sovereignty, free to decide whether or not to become a party to the UNCLOS. Arguably, as a result, the decision of whether or not to become a party to the UNCLOS necessarily includes the decision to accept the obligations contained in the London Convention. If viewed from this perspective Art. 210(6) UNCLOS cannot be regarded as affecting the *pacta tertiis* principle.[25]

Proelss, 'Commentary on Art. 34', in Oliver Dörr and Kirsten Schmalenbach (eds), *Vienna Convention on the Law of Treaties: A Commentary* (Springer, 2012) para 15.

[23] According to this principle codified in the preamble, Art. 1 and Art. 17(1) of the Rome Statute, a case before the ICC is only admissible where a State is unwilling or unable genuinely to carry out the investigation or prosecution, or where a case has been investigated by the State which has jurisdiction over it, but that State has decided afterwards not to prosecute the person concerned due to its unwillingness or inability genuinely to prosecute.

[24] Gerhard Hafner, Jonathan Huston, Anne Rübesame and Kristen Boon, 'A Response to the American View as Presented by Ruth Wedgwood' (1999) 10 *European Journal of International Law* 108, 118.

[25] For the same reason, a fictional decision by the parties to the 1992 United Nations Framework Convention on Climate Change (UNFCCC) emphasizing that all measures adopted under the regime of that Convention ought to comply with the rules and principles contained in the UNCLOS would not violate Art. 34

The issue becomes more complicated, however, if one asks the question whether the minimum standards in terms of Art. 210(6) UNCLOS also comprise those that have been introduced into the London Convention after the entry into force of the UNCLOS, or after accession of the State concerned to the UNCLOS. It does not seem to be indefensible to read Art. 210(6) UNCLOS in a manner according to which that provision would have to be seen as containing a dynamic reference that would also include future amendments to, or a major revision of, the London Convention regime.[26] Whether or not such a broad reading deserves approval is a matter of treaty interpretation. In this respect, it should be noted that the International Maritime Organization (IMO), while having repeatedly emphasized that the 'global rules and standards' in terms of Art. 210(6) UNCLOS would have to be understood as a reference to the London Convention,[27] has refrained to this day from stating that Art. 210(6) UNCLOS would also include future developments, or even a substantial revision of relevant parts of the London Convention, as has happened with the adoption of the 1996 London Protocol to the 1972 Convention on the Prevention of Marine Pollution by Dumping of Wastes and Other Matter. Also in light of the general recognition of the *pacta tertiis* rule it arguably seems difficult to assume that States acceding to the UNCLOS were or are willing to automatically subject themselves to developments within a different treaty regime which they might not be able to anticipate at the time of accession. In any event, the fact that Art. 210(6) UNCLOS speaks of '*global* rules and standards' suggests that the rules and standards concerned have to be widely accepted and may thus not be referred to as minimum standards within the UNCLOS regime as long as the amendments to or revisions of the London Convention have not entered into force and additionally have been approved by the majority of States.

VCLT as it would only be applicable between the parties to the UNFCCC, see Harro Van Asselt, Francesco Sindico and Michael A Mehling, 'Global Climate Change and Fragmentation of International Law' (2008) 30 *Law & Policy* 423, 432.

[26] See Don Rothwell and Tim Stephens, *The International Law of the Sea* (Hart, 2010) 374.

[27] See only International Maritime Organization, 'Implications of the United Nations Convention on the Law of the Sea for the International Maritime Organization' (19 January 2012) IMO Doc. LEG/MISC.7, 67.

2. 'Obligations' and 'Rights' under the *pacta tertiis* Rule

The second group of challenges referring to the scope of application of the *pacta tertiis* rule concerns the interpretation of its constitutive elements. As stated above, it is somewhat surprising that the elements of 'obligations' and 'rights' have found only little attention by the relevant authorities, given that the impact of a treaty on a third State may take various forms and manifest itself in different grades of intensity. This author has submitted elsewhere that indirect obligations can, depending on the degree of intensity of the negative impact of the treaty concerned on a third State, qualify as obligations in terms of the *pacta tertiis* rule, and that a right *stricto sensu*, in contrast to a mere legal interest, involves the existence of a *ius standi*.[28] With regard to the distinction between a 'right' and a 'legal interest', Rosenne has suggested that 'the word "right" [was] to mean a right that was legally enforceable by whatever means were available in international law or international relations.'[29] Recent authorities have supported this conclusion by stating that '[t]he acid test of a genuine right, as distinct from a mere interest, is that the third State – on which the treaty right is conferred – has a *ius standi* to insist directly on its implementation'.[30] It is submitted that the International Court of Justice (ICJ) accepted the link between a material right and a *ius standi* in its decision in the *Barcelona Traction* case.[31]

As far as obligations are concerned, Art. 2(6) UN Charter according to which '[t]he Organization shall ensure that states which are not Members of the United Nations act in accordance with these Principles so far as may be necessary for the maintenance of international peace and security', may, in light of its mandatory wording ('shall ensure'), serve as an example of a provision that imposes indirect legal obligations on third States. From a third State's perspective, it does not make any difference

28 Alexander Proelss, 'Commentary on Art. 34', in Oliver Dörr and Kirsten Schmalenbach (eds), *Vienna Convention on the Law of Treaties: A Commentary* (Springer, 2012) paras 13–28.

29 [1964-I] *Yearbook of the International Law Commission*, 84.

30 Yoram Dinstein, 'The Interaction between Customary International Law and Treaties' (2006) 322 *Recueil des Cours* 243, 334 (original emphasis); see also Malgosia Fitzmaurice, 'Third Parties and the Law of Treaties' (2002) 6 *Max Planck Yearbook of United Nations Law* 37, 104 *et seq.*

31 *Case Concerning the Barcelona Traction, Light and Power Co Ltd (Belgium v Spain)* (Second Phase) [1970] ICJ Rep 3, para 44: '[c]reditors do not have any right to claim compensation from a person who, by wronging their debtor, causes them loss. In such cases, no doubt, the *interests* of the aggrieved are affected, but not their *rights*' (emphasis added).

whether a legal rule directly obliges it to comply with the regulations of a treaty, or whether the parties to the treaty are under an obligation to apply and/or enforce its standards vis-à-vis the third State. As stated by Jennings and Watts:

> [t]he obligation, it will be noted, is not a direct one. However, inasmuch as a legal rule is conceived as a precept of conduct enforced by external sanction, the difference is one of form rather than of substance.[32]

State practice seems to support the conclusion drawn here according to which Art. 2(6) UN Charter imposes indirect legal obligations on third States. For example, in the proceedings before the ICJ that led to the advisory opinion on the unilateral declaration of independence in respect of Kosovo, Norway submitted a Royal Decree of 28 May 2008 which stated that '[a]ccording to Article 2(6) of the UN Charter, even a state that is not a member of the UN has the obligation to act in accordance with the principles of the Charter so far as may be necessary for the maintenance of international peace and security, and it must comply with Security Council resolutions, including resolution 1244'.[33] Corresponding statements were made in the debates leading to the imposition of sanctions against Southern Rhodesia in 1966.[34] The UN Security Council has, with occasional exceptions, essentially given up the distinction between 'Member States' on the one hand and 'all States' or 'States not Members to the United Nations' on the other made in the early years of its resolution practice,[35] but has not clarified whether it regards Art. 2(6) UN Charter as the legal basis of the alleged third-party effect. That said, no indication exists that the majority of relevant ('third') subjects of international law has agreed to implement preventive or enforcement measures adopted by the Security Council only on a voluntary basis, or on the basis of general international law respectively.[36] If this line of

---

[32] Robert Jennings and Arthur Watts, *Oppenheim's International Law*, Vol I (OUP, 1992) 1264, note 4.

[33] Annex 2 to the Written Statement of the Kingdom of Norway, 16 April 2009, accessed 28 August 2013 at www.icj-cij.org/docket/files/141/15650.pdf.

[34] See the references collected by Stefan Talmon, 'Article 2(6) UN Charter', in Bruno Simma, Daniel-Erasmus Khan, Georg Nolte and Andreas Paulus (eds), *The Charter of the United Nations: A Commentary* (OUP, 2012) para 65.

[35] Ibid, paras 46–50.

[36] See ibid, paras 55–65.

argument is followed, then Art. 2(6) UN Charter is indeed in need of justification in light of the *pacta tertiis* rule.[37]

The opposite view according to which there is no contradiction between Art. 34 VCLT and Art. 2(6) UN Charter as the latter provision ought to be interpreted in a restrictive manner, that is, as a mere statement of attitude that does not contain any indirect legal obligation,[38] appears to be somewhat of a circular argument. It rests on the assumption that Art. 2(6) UN Charter cannot create any actual obligation for the third State simply due to the fact that it would otherwise violate the *pacta tertiis* rule. Such a reading would render Art. 2(6) UN Charter essentially superfluous – a conclusion that does not seem to sufficiently take into account the wording and drafting history of the provision and would furthermore cast into doubt the entire discussion on its effects.

It is thus submitted that there are two alternative ways to reconcile Art. 2(6) UN Charter with international law in general and the *pacta tertiis* rule in particular: Art. 2(6) UN Charter can be 'justified' either by recourse to the general interest of the international community as embodied in the UN Charter,[39] or by reference to the status of the principles contained in Art. 2 UN Charter as customary international law.[40] This does not necessarily imply that the third-party effect flows from general international law rather than Art. 2(6) UN Charter. While it is true that where a rule of treaty law has developed into a rule of

---

[37] But contrast Budislav Vukas, 'Treaties, Third-Party Effect', in Rüdiger Wolfrum (ed), *Max Planck Encyclopedia of Public International Law*, Vol X (OUP, 2012) para 16.

[38] See Stefan Talmon, 'Article 2(6) UN Charter', in Bruno Simma, Daniel-Erasmus Khan, Georg Nolte and Andreas Paulus (eds), *The Charter of the United Nations: A Commentary* (OUP, 2012) para 28 *et seq* with further references.

[39] Robert Jennings and Arthur Watts, *Oppenheim's International Law*, Vol I (OUP, 1992) 1264; Hans Kelsen, *The Law of the United Nations* (Praeger, 1950) 110; Alan Boyle and Christine Chinkin, *The Making of International Law* (OUP, 2007) 240; see also Stefan Talmon, 'Article 2(6) UN Charter', in Bruno Simma, Daniel-Erasmus Khan, Georg Nolte and Andreas Paulus (eds), *The Charter of the United Nations: A Commentary* (OUP, 2012) paras 39–75, who argues that the provisions of the UN Charter establishing a universal system of collective security have acquired the status of rules of customary international law and are as such binding on all States and non-State actors.

[40] Malcolm N Shaw, *International Law* (Cambridge University Press, 2008) 929; Ian Brownlie, *Principles of Public International Law* (OUP, 2008) 628; Mark E Villiger, *Commentary on the 1969 Vienna Convention on the Law of Treaties* (Martinus Nijhoff, 2009) Art. 34 para 9.

customary international law, it is usually the rule of customary international law rather than the treaty rule which binds the third State,[41] the situation may arguably be assessed differently in the case of the singular legal regime established by the UN Charter to which, as far as the scope of legal personality of the UN is concerned, the ICJ referred in its advisory opinion on *Reparation for Injuries Suffered in the Service of the United Nations*.[42] Jennings and Watts convincingly stated that the UN Charter itself (and not general international law) has to be regarded as 'having set a limit, determined by the general interest of the international community, to the rule that a treaty cannot impose obligations upon States which are not parties to it'.[43] In all that, it should be noted that the debate on the legal nature of Art. 2(6) UN Charter has lost much of its relevance due to the quasi-universal character of the UN.

A potential objection to the view advocated here, according to which indirect legal effects deriving from a treaty provision can – and as a matter of law generally will – contravene the *pacta tertiis* rule, may be based on the fact that third States are free to comply with the treaty or not and thus enjoy an 'autonomous scope of manoeuvre'. The latter notion has been used, inter alia, by Special Rapporteur Fitzmaurice to substantiate what he understood as incidental effects of a treaty that would not be covered by the provision that eventually became Art. 34 VCLT.[44] However, it should be noted that Fitzmaurice exclusively referred to treaties of guarantee and mutual assistance, that is, treaties that cover situations in which a third State resorts to the use of force and, thus, acts contrary to general international law. With regard to such situations, Ago stated in the course of the deliberations of the ILC that:

> [T]he Commission had henceforth established the principle of inequality as between the aggressor State and the others, and … in contemporary international law, an aggressor State was no longer to be regarded as being on an equal footing with other States.[45]

---

41 See Alexander Proelss, 'Commentary on Art. 34', in Oliver Dörr and Kirsten Schmalenbach (eds), *Vienna Convention on the Law of Treaties: A Commentary* (Springer, 2012) para 4.

42 *Reparation for Injuries Suffered in the Service of the United Nations* (Advisory Opinion) [1949] ICJ Rep 174, 185.

43 Robert Jennings and Arthur Watts, *Oppenheim's International Law*, Vol I (OUP, 1992) 1264.

44 International Law Commission, 'Fifth Report by Sir Gerald Fitzmaurice, Special Rapporteur' (1960) UN Doc. A/CN.4/130, 100–101.

45 [1966-I/2] *Yearbook of the International Law Commission*, 67.

It would seem to be absurd to allow an aggressor State to challenge the application of a treaty of guarantee and mutual assistance to its own conduct by recourse to the principles of sovereignty and independence on which the *pacta tertiis* rule is founded. Indeed, as stated by Fitzmaurice, the effect of such a treaty on the third State depends exclusively on whether the State concerned, in exercising its autonomous scope of manoeuvre, decides to act in conformity with general international law or not. It is submitted that such a situation ought to be distinguished from that of 'regular' indirect legal obligations, which is why it cannot be relied upon in order to challenge the position advocated here according to which indirect obligations are included in the scope of the *pacta tertiis* principle.

Based on the aforementioned, it is arguably difficult to reject the conclusion that the 1949 North Atlantic Treaty (NATO Treaty) as specified by the new strategic concept of 1999 is perfectly in line with the rule contained in Art. 34 VCLT. Under this concept, security interests of the alliance are not only affected by armed attacks on the territory of the States parties, but also cover acts of terrorism, organized crime and gross violations of human rights.[46] Since any reaction by NATO, or its member States respectively, to such acts taken in accordance with the expanded mandate of the existing framework of collective self-defence (assuming that their operation can be justified under general international law) only come into play if and to the extent to which they are provoked by a third State's illegal conduct, which, due to its grave character, corresponds in substance to resorting to the use of force, the situation may well be compared to that of the operation of traditional alliance clauses (to which, as stated above, the *pacta tertiis* principle is not applicable).[47] This line of argument could offer an alternative reasoning[48]

---

[46] See the Alliance's Strategic Concept of 1999, NATO Press Release NAC-S(99)65.

[47] Alexander Proelss, 'Commentary on Art. 34', in Oliver Dörr and Kirsten Schmalenbach (eds), *Vienna Convention on the Law of Treaties: A Commentary* (Springer, 2012) para 19.

[48] Traditionally, the exercise of jurisdiction by the ICTY with regard to citizens of third States is justified by reference to the validity of the principle of universality under customary international law or the UN Charter's 'quasi-constitutional' character. See, eg, *Prosecutor v Milan Milutinović and others*, ICTY-IT-99-37-AR72.2, para 34 *et seq*; Andreas Zimmermann, 'Violations of Fundamental Norms of International Law and the Exercise of Universal Jurisdiction in Criminal Matters', in Christian Tomuschat and Jean-Marc Thouvenin (eds), *The Fundamental Rules of the International Legal Order* (Martinus Nijhoff, 2006) 335, 343.

for accepting that the International Criminal Tribunal for the former Yugoslavia (ICTY) created by the UN Security Council on the basis of Chapter VII UN Charter was entitled to lawfully exercise its jurisdiction vis-à-vis citizens of the Federal Republic of Yugoslavia even though that State was, at the relevant point of time,[49] not a member of the United Nations.[50] Taking into account that the jurisdiction *ratione materiae* of the ICTY covers gross violations of international law such as genocide and crimes against humanity, the conclusion could be drawn that it is legally impossible for the accused to rely on the *pacta tertiis* rule in order to challenge the jurisdiction of the Tribunal, provided that that rule is at all applicable in favour of non-State actors such as individuals.

3. Obligations and Rights of Non-State Actors

The third group of challenges concerning the application of the *pacta tertiis* rule is related to the fact that the wording of Art. 34 VCLT only addresses obligations or rights of third 'States'. Therefore, the question arises as to whether the *pacta tertiis* rule under customary international law also covers treaties that establish obligations or rights of third parties other than States, namely international organizations, non-governmental organizations and individuals. In a recent case, the (then) European Court of Justice (ECJ, now Court of Justice of the European Union (CJEU)) relied on the *pacta tertiis* principle as a rule of customary international law in order to dismiss the argument that an obligation had been placed on the Palestinian Authority as a result of the EU–Israel Association Agreement.[51] The ECJ/CJEU did not clarify, however, whether it regarded the *pacta tertiis* rule as operating only due to the parallel

---

[49] The ICTY's Trial Chamber III stated in *Prosecutor v Milan Milutinović and others*, ICTY-IT-99-37-PT (6 May 2003) para 62:

> The constitutional character of the Charter, its near universal membership, the critical importance to the international community of the goal of the maintenance of international peace and security, are all factors that combine to render the Chapter VII resolution establishing the Tribunal applicable to any country that was a part of the former SFRY, irrespective of its United Nations membership at the time of the adoption of that resolution, or at the time of the commission of the offences.

[50] See only *Legality of the Use of Force (Serbia and Montenegro v Belgium)* (Judgment) [2004] ICJ Rep 279, 310 *et seq.*

[51] Case C-386/08, *Brita GmbH v Hauptzollamt Hamburg-Hafen* [2010] ECR I-01289, paras 44, 52.

existence of the 1997 Interim Euro-Mediterranean Association Agreement for Trade and Cooperation concluded between the EU and the PLO or due to the fact that it considered the Palestinian Authority as a State-like entity or an entity exercising effective jurisdiction vis-à-vis the specific subject matter of the case, or whether it acted on the assumption that this rule is generally applicable with regard to third non-State actors. The opinion of the Advocate General was similarly silent on this issue.[52]

Most authorities agree that the *pacta tertiis* rule under customary international law covers treaties concluded between States that confer rights or obligations on international organizations.[53] However, there is little State practice that supports this position. On the contrary, the UN Security Council has repeatedly addressed third international organizations, that is, organizations other than UN bodies or agencies, in binding resolutions.[54] While one may counter the argument that this practice implies that the *pacta tertiis* rule is not applicable to rights and obligations conferred on third organizations with reference to the singular legal regime established by the UN Charter, practice shows that treaties concluded between States that are members of an international organization frequently impose direct or indirect obligations on that organization.[55] Arguably, the 2011 Treaty Establishing the European Stability Mechanism (ESM Treaty) is a recent example which illustrates this point. This treaty is an agreement with regard to which the EU, being the organization affected by its terms, cannot, on the basis of a substantive approach, be considered a 'third' party *stricto sensu*. It is thus submitted

---

[52] However, in Case C-499/04 *Hans Werhof v Freeway Traffic Systems GmbH & Co KG* [2006] ECR I-2399, para 52, Advocate General Colomer stated that '[i]f future collective agreements were to have a permanent effect on an employer who had not participated in their negotiation, the consequences would be similar to those of contracts imposing obligations on third parties, in breach of the general principle *pacta tertiis nec nocent*'. This could be read as an implicit recognition of the applicability of the *pacta tertiis* rule vis-à-vis non-State actors.

[53] Note that the question relevant here is not, at least not exclusively, one referring to Art. 34 VCLTSIO. This provision addresses third-party effects of treaties concluded between States and international organizations, or between international organizations respectively, whereas the present situation deals with third-party effects of treaties concluded between States.

[54] See, eg, UN Res 687 of 3 April 1991, para 25; UN Res 748 of 31 March 1992, para 7; UN Res 917 of 6 May 1994, para 12; UN Res 1333 of 19 December 2000, para 17.

[55] Cf Christian Tomuschat, 'International Organizations as Third Parties under the Law of International Treaties', in Enzo Cannizzaro (ed), *The Law of Treaties beyond the Vienna Convention* (OUP, 2011) 212–16.

that the relationship between the member States and the international organization of which they are a member differs from that between States and an international organization of which they are not, and consequently cannot be adequately understood by reference to the *pacta tertiis* rule. The fact that international organizations are neither sovereign nor equal further militates against an undifferentiated application of that rule to these actors.[56] At the same time, it ought to be emphasized that treaties concluded by an international organization may well, according to its statute,[57] unfold legal effects on its member States, but this situation is not one affecting the validity of the *pacta tertiis* rule due to the consent by the member States embodied in the conclusion of, or accession to, the statute.

It is also noteworthy that the ICTY, faced with the need to request the cooperation of non-State actors such as NATO and the NATO-led Stabilization Force in Bosnia and Herzegovina (SFOR) under Art. 29 of the Statute of the ICTY,[58] held that:

> Article 29 applies to all States, whether acting individually or collectively. In principle, there is no reason why Article 29 should not apply to collective enterprises undertaken by States, in the framework of international organizations and, in particular, their competent organs such as SFOR in the present case. A purposive construction of Article 29 suggests that it is as applicable to such collective enterprises as it is to States.[59]

---

[56] Ibid, at 210–11.

[57] See, eg, Art. 216(2) of the Treaty on the Functioning of the European Union, according to which '[a]greements concluded by the Union are binding upon the institutions of the Union and on its Member States'.

[58] The Statute of the ICTY is contained in the annex to a report of the UN Secretary-General (UN Doc. S/25704 [1993] and S/25704/Add.1 [1993]) and was adopted on 25 May 1993 by Resolution 827 of the UN Security Council (see UN Doc. S/RES/827 [1993] of 25 May 1993). Art. 29 of the Statute reads:

> (1) States shall cooperate with the International Tribunal in the investigation and prosecution of persons accused of committing serious violations of international humanitarian law. (2) States shall comply without undue delay with any request for assistance or an order issued by a Trial Chamber, including, but not limited to: (a) the identification and location of persons; (b) the taking of testimony and the production of evidence; (c) the service of documents; (d) the arrest or detention of persons; (e) the surrender or the transfer of the accused to the International Tribunal.

[59] *The Prosecutor v Blagoje Simic, Milan Simic, Miroslav Tadic, Stevan Todorovic and Simo Zaric* (Decision) ICTY-IT-95-9-PT (18 October 2000) para 46.

Thus, although Art. 29 ICTY Statute (which is, again, indirectly based on an international treaty, namely the UN Charter) is, according to its wording, only applicable to States, the ICTY considered the organizations concerned to be bound to comply with requests under that provision.[60] The implications of this line of argument with regard to the *pacta tertiis* rule are not fully clear, however. On the one hand, it appears that the ICTY did not consider the *pacta tertiis* rule to be applicable to international organizations. This might seem particularly obvious in light of the fact that the ICTY stated in the *Blaškić* case that:

> [a]s for States which are not Members of the United Nations, in accordance with the general principle embodied in Article 35 of the Vienna Convention on the Law of Treaties, they may undertake to comply with the obligation laid down in Article 29 by expressly accepting the obligation in writing.[61]

Had the Tribunal found that the *pacta tertiis* rule was equally applicable to non-State actors it could have relied on the reasoning in this decision in its subsequent jurisprudence. That said, it is perhaps significant that the ICTY did not expressly refer to the inapplicability of that rule to international organizations but rather decided to lift the 'organizational veil' of the entities concerned. In this respect, it should be noted that it remains controversial whether NATO (or an operation such as SFOR conducted under its leadership) possesses independent legal personality or whether it is only to be regarded as a collective enterprise of States without independent legal personality.[62] If the latter is correct, then the jurisprudence of the ICTY does not appear to present any challenge to the *pacta tertiis* rule. Assuming *arguendo* that NATO is an international organization *stricto sensu*, that is, an organization with international legal personality, the reasoning of the ICTY not only ignored that separate

---

[60] The ICTY came to the same conclusion in *The Prosecutor v Milan Milutinovic, Nikola Sainovic, Dragoljub Ojdanic, Nebojsa Pavkovic, Vladimir Lazarevic and Sreten Lukic* (Decision) ICTY-IT-05-87-PT (17 November 2005) paras 36–7. The Appeals Chamber upheld this jurisprudence in *The Prosecutor v Milan Milutinovic, Nikola Sainovic, Dragoljub Ojdanic, Nebojsa Pavkovic, Vladimir Lazarevic and Sreten Lukic* (Decision) ICTY-IT-05-87-AR108bis.1 (15 May 2006) para 8.

[61] *Lašva Valley, Prosecutor (on the Application of Croatia) v Tihomir Blaškić* (Judgment) ICTY-IT-95-14-AR108bis (29 October 1997) para 26.

[62] Guido Acquaviva, 'Non-State Actors from the Perspective of International Criminal Tribunals', in Jean d'Aspremont (ed), *Participants in the International Legal System: Multiple Perspectives on Non-State Actors in International Law* (Routledge, 2011) 194–5.

legal personality[63] but through resorting to the 'collective enterprise of States' formula also avoided having to justify why the *pacta tertiis* rule did not apply.

Seen in this light, the course of action taken by the Tribunal seems to be based more on strategic considerations in order to find a practical solution to its cooperation problems than on a clear expression of the law governing the scope of the *pacta tertiis* rule. Indeed, insisting on the validity of this rule in situations such as the one relevant here could also lead to a conflict of values with the law on State responsibility, as the member States would theoretically be enabled to avoid their obligations by 'outsourcing' them to an organization which could again refuse to accept these obligations in accordance with Art. 35 VCLT, or corresponding customary international law respectively. It has thus been submitted that since NATO and other agencies that are involved in conflict or post-conflict areas in accordance with a UN mandate directly participate in the restoration of peace and security within the framework of Chapter VII UN Charter, they should be considered to be bound to comply with requests of the ICTY under Art. 29 ICTY Statute in the same way as their member States.[64] With regard to non-governmental organizations and individuals, it has been argued that they too could be bound to a treaty concluded by States should they choose to be.[65] This argument has been used, inter alia, to justify the compatibility of common Art. 3 of the Geneva Conventions[66] and the Additional Protocol II to the Geneva Conventions[67] with the *pacta tertiis* rule. In fact, both common Art. 3 and Protocol II are based on the assumption that, while not treaty parties, rebel groups and other non-State forces are generally bound to the standards contained in these documents. It has been alleged that since the applicability of international humanitarian law will usually be in the interest of non-State actors, they could be presumed to have

---

63 Ibid, 193–4.

64 Ibid, 196–7.

65 Antonio Cassese, 'The Status of Rebels under the 1977 Geneva Protocol on Non-International Armed Conflict', (1981) 30 *International and Comparative Law Quarterly* 416, 428.

66 1949 Geneva Convention for the Amelioration of the Condition of the Wounded and Sick in Armed Forces in the Field; 1949 Geneva Convention for the Amelioration of the Condition of Wounded, Sick and Shipwrecked Members of Armed Forces at Sea; 1949 Geneva Convention relative to the Treatment of Prisoners of War; 1949 Geneva Convention relative to the Protection of Civilian Persons in Time of War.

67 1977 Protocol II relating to the Protection of Victims of Non-International Armed Conflicts.

implicitly consented to the rights and obligations of the treaties.[68] The potential objection that consent would have to be expressed in writing with regard to such obligations may be challenged by recourse to the argument that the written form requirement contained in Art. 35 VCLT has not yet developed into a rule of customary international law.[69] Nevertheless, it is submitted that there is a good case that the aforementioned situation should be assessed differently since a general presumption of implicit consent of the non-State actor concerned will in many situations not be in accordance with the facts.

If a different position is taken, common Art. 3 of the Geneva Conventions as well as the provisions of the second Protocol to the Geneva Conventions ought to be interpreted as directly creating obligations for non-State actors irrespective of the fact they are not contracting parties. The application of obligations contained within an agreement to individuals or non-State actors without their prior consent is by no means precluded under international law. For example, the ICJ held in the *LaGrand* and *Avena* cases that Art. 36(1) of the 1963 Vienna Convention on Consular Relations creates individual rights which, by virtue of Art. 1 of the Optional Protocol, may be invoked by the national State of the detained person.[70] While these decisions, similar to the findings of the ECJ/CJEU regarding the basic freedoms codified in the 2007 Treaty on the Functioning of the European Union,[71] did not deal with the imposition of obligations on individuals, it seems doubtful whether the requirements for the allocation of rights under Art. 36 VCLT were fulfilled in the cases concerned. In particular, even though the second phrase of Art. 36(1) VCLT clarifies that the element of 'assent' does not depend on the fulfilment of any kind of formal requirement but is rather

---

[68] Michael Bothe, 'Friedenssicherung und Kriegsrecht', in Wolfgang Graf Vitzthum (ed), *Völkerrecht* (De Gruyter, 2013) 657–8.

[69] Caroline Laly-Chevalier, 'Commentary on Art. 35 VCLT', in Olivier Corten and Pierre Klein (eds), *Vienna Convention on the Law of Treaties: A Commentary*, Vol I (OUP, 2011) para 20; Alexander Proelss, 'Commentary on Art. 35', in Oliver Dörr and Kirsten Schmalenbach (eds), *Vienna Convention on the Law of Treaties: A Commentary* (Springer, 2012) para 19.

[70] *LaGrand (Germany v USA)* (Judgment) [2001] ICJ Rep 466, para 77; *Avena and other Mexican Nationals (Mexico v USA)* (Judgment) [2004] ICJ Rep, para 40.

[71] Case 26/62, *NV Algemene Transport- en Expeditie Onderneming van Gend & Loos v Netherlands Inland Revenue Administration* [1963] ECR 1, 24–5.

generally presumed,[72] it would not seem to be compatible with the object and purpose of Art. 36(1) of the Vienna Convention on Consular Relations if the existence (not: application) of the right contained therein would depend on the free will of the individual concerned.

In relation to obligations, it has been persuasively argued that the Rome Statute should be considered as imposing direct obligations on individuals.[73] Indeed, if one takes into account that the *pacta tertiis* rule is based on the principles of sovereignty and independence of States, attempts to automatically widen the scope of that rule so as to include individuals and other non-State actors (with the sole exception of inter-State entities such as classical international organizations) do not seem to be convincing.[74] Taking such a position does not provide a persuasive reason for why a State is, based upon its prescriptive jurisdiction arising out of its sovereignty, entitled to enact laws applicable within its territory or even abroad that directly criminalize certain conduct but should be prevented by law from doing so by way of an international treaty. Denying the possibility of direct applicability of international norms would fundamentally call into question the status of individuals as subjects of international law. To so challenge the status of the individual in international law, it is submitted, is not justifiable in light of the developments that have taken place in the fields of human rights and international criminal law since the creation of the United Nations in 1945. The question is thus not whether or not public international law can have direct effect on individuals but rather in what situations such an effect may be determined. In other words, this is in

---

72 Cf Alexander Proelss, 'Commentary on Art. 36', in Oliver Dörr and Kirsten Schmalenbach (eds), *Vienna Convention on the Law of Treaties: A Commentary* (Springer, 2012) para 26.

73 Marko Milanović, 'Is the Rome Statute Binding on Individuals? (And Why We Should Care)' (2011) 9 *Journal of International Criminal Justice* 25, 25–52). The basis of the argument is essentially twofold, namely (1) that some provisions of the ICC Statute, in particular Arts 22 and 24, are difficult to read as exclusively setting out the scope of the Court's subject matter jurisdiction and not addressing the responsibility of individuals directly, and (2) that the Statute goes beyond customary law without having created new customary law. Assuming that the Rome Statute is exclusively of jurisdictional nature, the latter reasoning would involve serious problems concerning the *nullum crimen sine lege* principle.

74 Marko Milanović, 'Is the Rome Statute Binding on Individuals? (And Why We Should Care)' (2011) 9 *Journal of International Criminal Justice* 25, 39; Christine Chinkin, *Third Parties in International Law* (OUP, 1993) 121.

fact a matter of treaty interpretation.[75] As the PCIJ held in its advisory opinion concerning *Jurisdiction of the Courts of Danzig*:

> the very object of an international agreement, according to the intention of the contracting Parties, may be the adoption by the Parties of some definite rules creating individual rights and obligations and enforceable by the national courts. … The intention of the Parties, which is to be ascertained from the contents of the Agreement, taking into consideration the manner in which the Agreement has been applied, is decisive.[76]

This statement is particularly remarkable due to the fact that it was made in a time when the status of individuals as subjects of international law had not yet been widely accepted. With the increasing relevance of non-State actors in modern times the question discussed here will arguably become more and more important.[77] In contrast, if the direct applicability of international treaties is rejected, an alternative approach to explain how treaties concluded between States (or between States and international organizations, or between international organizations) may well create rights and obligations for other non-State actors would rely on customary law exceptions to the *pacta tertiis* rule on the fields concerned.[78] While ultimately, both lines of argument lead to the inapplicability of the *pacta tertiis* rule, the second option faces the challenge that it will usually be difficult to determine the necessary elements of State practice and *opinio juris* before the conclusion of the treaty whose third-party effect is under consideration.

---

[75] Marko Milanović, 'Is the Rome Statute Binding on Individuals? (And Why We Should Care)' (2011) 9 *Journal of International Criminal Justice* 25, 45.

[76] *Jurisdiction of the Courts of Danzig* (Advisory Opinion) [1928] PCIJ, Ser B No 15, 17–18.

[77] For example, while the Federal Constitutional Court of Germany was correct in stating that Art. 3 of the 1907 Convention (IV) respecting the Laws and Customs of War on Land cannot be interpreted as containing an individual right for compensation (see Federal Constitutional Court of Germany, Order of 15 February 2006 – 2 BvR 1476/03, *Neue Juristische Wochenschrift* 59, 2543), the situation could well have to be assessed differently if that provision was included in a treaty concluded in modern times.

[78] Liesbeth Zegveld, *Accountability of Armed Opposition Groups in International Law* (Cambridge University Press, 2002) 10–12; see also Alexander Proelss, 'Commentary on Art. 34', in Oliver Dörr and Kirsten Schmalenbach (eds), *Vienna Convention on the Law of Treaties: A Commentary* (Springer, 2012) para 12.

III. POTENTIAL EXCEPTIONS TO THE *PACTA TERTIIS* RULE

1. Development of New Customary International Law

Numerous authorities have relied on alleged exceptions to the *pacta tertiis* rule. Prima facie, it seems that reference could be made in this respect to the development of rules of customary law. Indeed, Art. 38 VCLT is based on the assumption that Arts 34–37 VCLT do not have any impact on the accepted principle that a rule of treaty law may, depending on the circumstances, develop into a rule of customary law. In such cases, however, it is generally the rule of customary international law rather than the treaty rule which binds the third State.[79] As such, since the process described by Art. 38 VCLT does not actually concern the legal effects of a treaty on third States the development of rules of customary law on the basis of treaty rules cannot be characterized as an exception to the *pacta tertiis* rule.[80] The declaratory nature of Art. 38 VCLT also becomes manifest in the fact that while the provision only addresses the situation in which a treaty rule generates a new rule of customary international law that did not exist at the time when the treaty entered into force,[81] it does not at all exclude the general validity of treaties evidencing corresponding norms of customary law ('declaratory treaties').

[79] International Law Commission, 'Fifth Report by Sir Gerald Fitzmaurice, Special Rapporteur' (1960) UN Doc. A/CN.4/130, 96; Ronald Francis Roxburgh, *International Conventions and Third States* (Longmans, Green & Company, 1917) 73–4. It is submitted that the mere fact that a State decides not to accede to an international agreement does not automatically imply that it ought to be considered as a persistent objector concerning the development of a corresponding rule of customary international law (but see *Asylum Case (Colombia v Peru)* (Judgment) [1950] ICJ Rep 266, 277–8). A State complies with the requirements of the concept of persistent objection only if it has permanently and expressly objected to the application of the rule concerned; cf *Fisheries Case (United Kingdom v Norway)* (Judgment) [1951] ICJ Rep 116, 131.

[80] Budislav Vukas, 'Treaties, Third-Party Effect', in Rüdiger Wolfrum (ed), *Max Planck Encyclopedia of Public International Law*, Vol X (OUP, 2012) para 14, 16; Alexander Proelss, 'Commentary on Art. 34', in Oliver Dörr and Kirsten Schmalenbach (eds), *Vienna Convention on the Law of Treaties: A Commentary* (Springer, 2012) paras 4–5.

[81] Christos L Rozakis, 'Treaties and Third States: A Study in the Reinforcement of the Consensual Standards in International Law' (1975) 35 *Zeitschrift für ausländisches öffentliches Recht und Völkerrecht* 1, 12; Alexander Proelss,

2. *Pacta tertiis* and Objective Regimes

The search for treaties that do create legal effects vis-à-vis third States has occupied legal doctrine for decades. As pointed out by Simma, the debate has concentrated on so-called 'status-creating', 'dispositive' or 'constitutive' treaties, or treaties providing for 'objective régimes'.[82] These categories, which can arguably not be differentiated from each other in a clear-cut manner, can be traced back to a famous statement made by McNair in his separate opinion on the ICJ's advisory opinion in the *South West Africa Case*:

> From time to time it happens that a group of great Powers, or a large number of States both great and small, assume a power to create by a multipartite treaty some new international régime or status, which soon acquires a degree of acceptance and durability extending beyond the limits of the actual contracting parties, and giving it an objective existence. This power is used when some public interest is involved, and its exercise often occurs in the course of the peace settlement at the end of a great war.[83]

The ILC dealt with this issue on several occasions but, following intense debate, ultimately opted to reject the draft article suggested by Special Rapporteur Waldock.[84] In its 1966 report on the law of treaties to the UN General Assembly, it stated that:

> [s]ince to lay down a rule recognizing the possibility of the creation of objective regimes directly by treaty might be unlikely to meet with general acceptance, the Commission decided to leave this question aside in drafting the present articles on the law of treaties.[85]

The concept of objective regimes may well be qualified as the overall concept of the aforementioned treaty categories. Notwithstanding a

---

'Commentary on Art. 34', in Oliver Dörr and Kirsten Schmalenbach (eds), *Vienna Convention on the Law of Treaties: A Commentary* (Springer, 2012) para 12.

[82] Bruno Simma, 'From Bilateralism to Community Interest in International Law' (1994) 250 *Recueil des Cours* 217, 358.

[83] *International Status of South West Africa* (Advisory Opinion) [1950] ICJ Rep 128, 153.

[84] Cf Alexander Proelss, 'Commentary on Art. 34', in Oliver Dörr and Kirsten Schmalenbach (eds), *Vienna Convention on the Law of Treaties: A Commentary* (Springer, 2012) paras 35–8.

[85] International Law Commission, 'Report of the International Law Commission on the Work of its Eighteenth Session' (1966) UN Doc. A/6309/Rev.l, 231.

considerable degree of ambiguity as to its individual elements, it is based on the assumption that certain treaties are, either by their very nature or by the semi-legislative authority of their States parties, valid *erga omnes*.[86] Potential examples include treaties establishing international waterways, treaties establishing a boundary between two or more States, treaties whose subject is the demilitarization of a certain area, treaties establishing a special regime of common usage of marine or land territory, and peace treaties.[87]

However, whether the concept of objective regimes is valid under public international law remains disputed in international legal scholarship. The issue cannot be dealt with here in detail. The intention of the contracting States to act in the 'general interest' that is required according to legal doctrine for a treaty to be valid *erga omnes* in terms of an objective regime[88] is a concept open to abuse. Furthermore, if the dispositive character of the treaty concerned is cumulatively made dependent on the fact that all or the large majority of States have become parties to it,[89] or that existence of the competence of the contracting parties to settle the respective matter with *erga omnes* is presumed vis-à-vis all third States which have not objected to the assertion made by the contracting parties to act in the general interest,[90] the question arises whether there is really anything special about objective regimes as opposed to the *inter partes* validity of ordinary treaties. As has been discussed more fully elsewhere, a closer inspection of relevant State and treaty practice reveals that the concept of objective regimes has not received general recognition on the international plane, the sole exception being the UN Charter.[91] Rather, on closer examination third-party effects

---

[86] See, eg, Ian McTaggart Sinclair, *The Vienna Convention on the Law of Treaties* (Manchester University Press, 1984) 104; Georg Dahm, Jost Delbrück and Rüdiger Wolfrum, *Völkerrecht*, Vol I/3 (De Gruyter, 2002) 619–32; S P Subedi, 'The Doctrine of Objective Regimes in International Law and the Competence of the United Nations to Impose Territorial or Peace Settlements on States' (1994) 37 *German Yearbook of International Law* 162, 167; Francesco Salerno, 'Treaties Establishing Objective Regimes', in Enzo Cannizzaro (ed), *The Law of Treaties beyond the Vienna Convention* (OUP, 2011) 240–3.

[87] International Law Commission, 'Third Report on the Law of Treaties, by Sir Humphrey Waldock, Special Rapporteur' (1964) UN Doc. A/CN.4/167 and Add.1-3, 28–32.

[88] Georg Dahm, *Völkerrecht*, Vol I (Kohlhammer, 1958) 23.

[89] Ibid.

[90] Eckart Klein, *Statusverträge im Völkerrecht* (Springer, 1980) 209–13.

[91] Alexander Proelss, 'Commentary on Art. 34', in Oliver Dörr and Kirsten Schmalenbach (eds), *Vienna Convention on the Law of Treaties: A Commentary*

of treaties either derive from acceptance of a right or obligation in terms of Arts 35 and 36 VCLT, or result from the development of a treaty rule into a rule of customary law. *Cahier* was thus right to conclude that 'la notion de traité établissant des situations objectives est surtout une création de la doctrine'.[92] This may be demonstrated by reference to the following examples.

A category of treaties frequently referred to as dispositive or 'real' treaties characterized by their third-party effect are treaties establishing boundaries between two or more neighbouring States. Indeed, such treaties are valid *erga omnes* and ought to be respected by third States. However, the legal basis for this can arguably not be found in the concept of objective regimes but rather in the fact that only the States concluding the agreement have the competence to regulate the subject matter.[93] If the contracting parties have undisputed and exclusive territorial competence concerning the subject of the treaty the matter has nothing to do with potential exceptions to the *pacta tertiis* rule.[94] The situation should be assessed differently, though, in cases where the conclusion of a boundary

---

(Springer, 2012) paras 41–59; see also Philippe Cahier, 'Le problème des effets des traités à l'égard des États tiers' (1974) 143 *Recueil des Cours* 589, 677; Eric David, 'Commentary on Art. 34 VCLT', in Olivier Corten and Pierre Klein (eds), *Vienna Convention on the Law of Treaties: A Commentary*, Vol I (OUP, 2011) paras 10–11.

92 Philippe Cahier, 'Le problème des effets des traités à l'égard des États tiers' (1974) 143 *Recueil des Cours* 589, 677; see also Theodor Schweisfurth, 'International Treaties and Third States', (1985) 45 *Zeitschrift für ausländisches öffentliches Recht und Völkerrecht* 653, 665.

93 International Law Commission, 'Fifth Report by Sir Gerald Fitzmaurice, Special Rapporteur' (1960) UN Doc. A/CN.4/130, 99; Eric David, 'Commentary on Art. 34 VCLT', in Olivier Corten and Pierre Klein (eds), *Vienna Convention on the Law of Treaties: A Commentary*, Vol I (OUP, 2011) para 10; Philippe Cahier, 'Le problème des effets des traités à l'égard des États tiers' (1974) 143 *Recueil des Cours* 589, 670.

94 Arts 11 and 12 of the 1978 Vienna Convention on Succession of States in Respect of Treaties do not militate against the position taken here. While these provisions demonstrate that a State is precluded from relying on the *pacta tertiis* principle in the context of State succession (Malgosia Fitzmaurice, 'Third Parties and the Law of Treaties' (2002) 6 *Max Planck Yearbook of United Nations Law* 37, 77–82), a statement made by the ILC reveals that acceptance of the concept of objective regimes embodied in the Convention was limited to the field of State succession, and that according to State practice a successor State cannot be considered as a third State *stricto sensu* (International Law Commission, 'Report of the International Law Commission on the Work of its Twenty-Sixth Session' [1974] UN Doc. A/9610/Rev.1, 204).

agreement affects the territorial jurisdiction of a third State, the territorial scope of areas beyond the limits of national jurisdiction such as the high seas or the deep seabed ('Area') respectively (lack of exclusive territorial competence), or where the territorial competence of the contracting parties is disputed (lack of undisputed territorial competence). With regards to the first alternative, the ICJ indicated in the *Case Concerning the Frontier Dispute* that a delimitation agreement only has legal and binding effect as between the parties to it if the agreement concerns the territory of a third State not a party to the agreement.[95]

A more recent example of a treaty that has been considered as potentially producing third-party effects is the 1995 United Nations Agreement for the Implementation of the Provisions of the United Nations Convention on the Law of the Sea of 10 December 1982 relating to the Conservation and Management of Straddling Fish Stocks and Highly Migratory Fish Stocks (UNFSA). Some of its provisions, in particular Arts 8(4), 17, 21 and 23, are indeed intended to be binding on third States.[96] These articles aim at tackling the problem of 'free riders' by restricting access to fisheries resources to States which are either members of the competent regional fisheries management organizations (RFMOs) or which agree to apply the management measures established by them (Art. 8(4)), by subjecting States not being members of RFMOs or participating in subregional or regional fisheries management arrangements to further obligations (Art. 17), and by introducing stricter enforcement standards (Arts 21, 23). On closer inspection, however, the agreement cannot be held to modify the *pacta tertiis* rule.[97] Notwithstanding its character as an independent treaty, the UNFSA aims to implement and substantiate the pertinent provisions contained in the UNCLOS. According to Art. 4 UNFSA, '[n]othing in this Agreement shall prejudice the rights, jurisdiction and duties of States under the

---

95 *Case Concerning the Frontier Dispute (Burkina Faso v Mali)* (Judgment) [1986] ICJ Rep 554, para 46.

96 Peter G G Davies and Catherine Redgwell, 'The International Legal Regulation of Straddling Fish Stocks' (1996) 67 *British Year Book of International Law* 199, 265–6.

97 Erik Franckx, '*Pacta tertiis* and the Agreement for the Implementations of the Straddling and Highly Migratory Fish Stocks Provisions of the United Nations Convention on the Law of the Sea' (2000) 8 *Tulane Journal of International and Comparative Law* 49, 62–71; Joost Pauwelyn, 'Conflicts of Norms in Public International Law' (PhD thesis, Université de Neuchâtel 2001) 60; contra Francesco Salerno, 'Treaties Establishing Objective Regimes', in Enzo Cannizzaro (ed), *The Law of Treaties beyond the Vienna Convention* (OUP, 2011) 228.

Convention. This Agreement shall be interpreted and applied in the context of and in a manner consistent with the Convention'. In light of this special status, it is thus submitted that the UNFSA must generally be interpreted in a restrictive manner, or in other words in a manner compatible with the *pacta tertiis* rule.[98] Consequently, the rights and obligations contained in the agreement are only applicable to non-parties if and to the extent that it can be argued that relevant provisions have become part of customary law. As far as the enforcement jurisdiction of port States is concerned, this could be achieved by reference to the element 'in accordance with international law' contained in Art. 23(1) UNFSA. Assuming *arguendo* that this element cannot be applied to the detailed enforcement measures contained in Art. 23(2) and (3) UNFSA,[99] the only option seems to be to reduce the scope of these provisions on teleological grounds.

Finally, in relation to treaties that provide for a right of passage through international waterways, Art. I(1) of the 1888 Constantinople Convention may serve as an example. This provision states that '[t]he Suez Maritime Canal shall always be free and open, in time of war as in time of peace, to every vessel of commerce or of war, without distinction of flag'. When Egypt nationalized the Suez Canal in 1958, it issued a declaration in which it expressly accepted its obligations concerning freedom of passage 'for all nations within the limits of and in accordance with the provisions of the Constantinople Convention of 1888'. Against this background, the right of third States to freedom of passage through the Suez Canal has arguably less to do with the functional argument that 'international waterways and similar transit routes must be maintained open for the smooth operation of international commerce and security'[100] than either with the process described in Art. 36 VCLT in conjunction with the terms of the Constantinople Convention, or with the development of customary international law.[101]

---

[98] Alexander Proelss, 'Commentary on Art. 34', in Oliver Dörr and Kirsten Schmalenbach (eds), *Vienna Convention on the Law of Treaties: A Commentary* (Springer, 2012) para 58.

[99] Alexander Proelss, *Meeresschutz im Völker- und Europarecht* (Duncker & Humblot, 2004) 174 *et seq.*

[100] Alan Boyle and Christine Chinkin, *The Making of International Law* (OUP, 2007) 240.

[101] Alexander Proelss, 'Commentary on Art. 34', in Oliver Dörr and Kirsten Schmalenbach (eds), *Vienna Convention on the Law of Treaties: A Commentary* (Springer, 2012) para 47.

3. *Pacta tertiis* and the Concepts of *jus cogens* and *erga omnes* Obligations

The last group of potential challenges to the *pacta tertiis* rule arises from developments concerning special categories of international norms, namely the concepts of *jus cogens* and obligations *erga omnes*. As will be shown, on closer examination both concepts arise out of international custom, which is why they cannot be qualified as exceptions to, or an evolution of, the *pacta tertiis* rule. The issue is thus one concerning the sources of international law in general rather than treaty law in particular. Notwithstanding this, it is noteworthy that they are oftentimes assessed in connection with the *pacta tertiis* rule. Prima facie, the specific nature of the norms concerned seems to indicate that they may be relied upon in order to substantiate the legal relevance of the concept of objective regimes and that, as such, they potentially call into question the general validity of the *pacta tertiis* rule.[102] In this respect, one source has argued that norms of *jus cogens* can be drawn from conventions or treaties whose objects and purposes render them more important, and that in such situations 'States not party to them will also be bound by their terms'.[103] It is therefore justifiable to elaborate in more detail on the relationship between the *pacta tertiis* rule and the aforementioned concepts.

The legal foundation and mutual relationship of the concepts of *jus cogens* and *erga omnes* obligations cannot be addressed here in detail. It suffices to refer to the fact that both concepts are characterized by the interest of the international community in the protection of certain fundamental values and that seek to facilitate their effective implementation. In this respect, Art. 53 VCLT defines a *jus cogens* norm, or a peremptory norm of general international law, as 'a norm accepted and recognized by the international community of States as a whole as a norm from which no derogation is permitted and which can be modified only by a subsequent norm of general international law having the same

---

102 For an in-depth discussion of the relationship between the concepts relevant here, see Maurizio Ragazzi, *The Concept of International Obligations* Erga Omnes (OUP, 1997) 18–42; see also Alan Boyle and Christine Chinkin, *The Making of International Law* (OUP, 2007) 239 *et seq*.

103 Rafael Nieto-Navia, 'International Peremptory Norms (*Jus Cogens*) and International Humanitarian Law', in Lal Chand Vohrah, Fausto Pocar, Yvonne Featherstone, Olivier Fourmy, Christine Graham, John Hocking and Nicholas Robson (eds), *Man's Inhumanity to Man: Essays on International Law in Honour of Antonio Cassese* (Kluwer, 2003) 613.

character'. With regards to *erga omnes* obligations, the ICJ famously held in the *Barcelona Traction* case that these obligations are 'obligations of a State towards the international community as a whole', and that '[i]n view of the importance of the rights involved, all States can be held to have a legal interest in their protection'.[104] Examples include the prohibition against committing acts of aggression and genocide, the basic human rights including protection from slavery and racial discrimination,[105] the principle of self-determination of peoples,[106] and the basic obligations under international humanitarian law.[107]

As in the case of objective regimes, accepting that a certain group of States would, by way of conclusion of a treaty, be able to determine what norms ought to be considered as being of peremptory nature, or valid *erga omnes* respectively, involves serious problems of legitimacy. In this respect, the normative basis on which the contracting parties could rely for (1) identifying objects and purposes that are more important than others, and (2) binding other States by way of conclusion of a treaty to which they have not become a party, is far from clear. The fact that certain treaty provisions are framed in absolute terms or prohibit the conclusion of special agreements which would adversely affect the object and purpose of the treaty concerned does not justify the assumption that that treaty entails third-party effects. To argue such would be to put the contracting parties in the position of essentially determining the scope and validity of international legal rules. As Oxman has rightly stated, 'profound conviction of public benefit is, in itself [not] sufficient to generate law binding on those who disagree',[108] and the same is true with regard to the alleged need to fill the normative gaps that result from the structural deficiencies of the international law-making process.[109]

---

[104] *Barcelona Traction, Light and Power Company, Limited (Belgium v Spain)* (Judgment) [1970] ICJ Rep 3, para 33.

[105] Ibid, para 34; *Legality of the Threat or Use of Nuclear Weapons* (Advisory Opinion) [1996] ICJ Rep 226, para 31.

[106] *East Timor (Portugal v Australia)* (Judgment) [1995] ICJ Rep 90, para 29; *Legal Consequences of the Construction of a Wall in the Occupied Palestinian Territory* (Advisory Opinion) [2004] ICJ Rep 136, para 155.

[107] *Legal Consequences of the Construction of a Wall in the Occupied Palestinian Territory* (Advisory Opinion) [2004] ICJ Rep 136, para 157.

[108] Bernhard Oxman, 'Comment', in Jost Delbrück (ed), *New Trends in International Lawmaking: International 'Legislation' in the Public Interest* (Duncker & Humblot, 1997) 111.

[109] But see Francesco Salerno, 'Treaties Establishing Objective Regimes', in Enzo Cannizzaro (ed), *The Law of Treaties beyond the Vienna Convention* (OUP, 2011) 240–1.

Concerning obligations *erga omnes*, the ICJ stated in its judgment in the *Barcelona Traction* case that '[s]ome of the corresponding rights of protection have entered into the body of general international law …; others are conferred by international instruments of a universal or quasi-universal character',[110] and it is true that the second alternative of that phrase ('international instruments of a universal or quasi-universal character') seems to suggest that a treaty rule may indeed become valid *erga omnes*. That said, it has convincingly been demonstrated that the statement concerned is 'best interpreted as an indication that obligations *erga omnes* are often *also* protected by international treaties'.[111] Indeed, in its advisory opinion on the *Legality of the Threat or Use of Nuclear Weapons*, the ICJ observed that a great majority of rules of humanitarian law were binding on 'all States whether or not they have ratified the conventions that contain them, because they constitute intransgressible principles of international customary law'.[112] By exclusively relying on that statement, the ICJ determined in its advisory opinion on *Legal Consequences of the Construction of a Wall in the Occupied Palestinian Territory* that 'these rules incorporate obligations which are essentially of an *erga omnes* character'.[113] Finally, with regard to peremptory norms of international law, the ICJ held in a recent judgment that 'the prohibition of torture is part of customary international law and it has become a peremptory norm (*jus cogens*)'.[114] In light of the aforementioned, it seems justifiable to conclude that *erga omnes* obligations and peremptory norms of international law (*jus cogens*) arise out of international custom.[115] While international treaty practice may undoubtedly contribute to

---

[110] *Barcelona Traction, Light and Power Company, Limited (Belgium v Spain)* (Judgment) [1970] ICJ Rep 3, para 34.

[111] Christian Tams, *Enforcing Obligations* erga omnes *in International Law* (Cambridge University Press, 2005) 123.

[112] *Legality of the Threat or Use of Nuclear Weapons* (Advisory Opinion) [1996] ICJ Rep 226, para 79.

[113] *Legal Consequences of the Construction of a Wall in the Occupied Palestinian Territory* (Advisory Opinion) [2004] ICJ Rep 136, para 157.

[114] *Questions relating to the Obligation to Prosecute or Extradite (Belgium v Senegal)* (Judgment) 2012, [2012] ICJ Rep 422, para 99.

[115] Christian Tams, *Enforcing Obligations* erga omnes *in International Law* (Cambridge University Press, 2005) 120–8; Jerzy Sztucki, Jus Cogens *and the Vienna Convention on the Law of Treaties: A Critical Appraisal* (Springer, 1974) 74. See also W Michael Reisman, *The Quest for World Order and Human Dignity in the Twenty-First Century: Constitutive Process and Individual Commitment* (Brill, 2013) 132, who qualifies *jus cogens*, as far as the human rights discurse is concerned, as 'a type of super-custom'.

the formation of a new rule of customary international law, it cannot by itself serve as an independent basis from which *jus cogens* and *erga omnes* obligations could directly be drawn. If this reasoning is correct, the concepts of *jus cogens* and *erga omnes* obligations cannot be referred to as a doctrinal basis for potential third-party effects of treaties.

The recent judgment of the ICJ in the *Case Concerning Questions relating to the Obligation to Prosecute or Extradite* does not contradict the view advocated here. While the Court expressly referred to a common interest in compliance with the obligations contained in the 1984 Convention against Torture and Other Cruel, Inhuman or Degrading Treatment or Punishment (CAT) by the State in whose territory an alleged offender is present, it limited the *erga omnes* effect attributed to that common interest (which, again, implied a *jus standi* of any State party to bring a claim against the alleged offender State) to the States parties to the Convention.[116] Such 'obligations *erga omnes partes*' do not at all affect the nature and scope of the *pacta tertiis* rule.

IV. OPEN QUESTIONS: A RESEARCH AGENDA

In light of the ambiguities surrounding the individual elements and scope of the *pacta tertiis* rule, as well as current challenges presented by the constant development of international law such as the rise of non-State actors, the conclusions drawn in this chapter are preliminary in nature. While taking into account that this rule is based on the independence and sovereignty of States, the research agenda on the personal dimension of the law of treaties is intrinsically linked to future developments related to the concept of Statehood. Further, the impact that potentially influential concepts such as 'functional sovereignty' will have on the scope of the law of treaties *ratione personae* remain to be assessed in future. Against this backdrop, the following topics constitute no more than an initial approach to the establishment of a research agenda:

- The legal basis and evolutionary history of the *pacta tertiis* rule are comparatively well researched. In contrast, the elements of this rule are still characterized by a considerable degree of uncertainty. This affects the notion of obligations as well as that of rights. State practice remains to be comprehensively examined with regards to the relevance of indirect obligations and their relationship to mere

[116] *Questions relating to the Obligation to Prosecute or Extradite (Belgium v Senegal)* (Judgment) 2012, [2012] ICJ Rep 422, paras 68–9.

incidentally unfavourable effects of treaties. Finally, the potential application of the *pacta tertiis* rule to the resolution of conflict of norms has arguably not been sufficiently clarified.

- In relation to the personal scope of the *pacta tertiis* rule, the question of whether and to what extent non-State actors can rely on this rule should be given particular attention. In this respect, whether or not non-State actors can be subjected to common standards or whether there is a need to differentiate between international organizations on the one hand and other non-State actors on the other falls to be assessed. The relationship between international organizations and 'their' member States deserves further examination particularly in the context of the law of treaties as State practice does not seem to be consistent in this respect.[117] Regarding individuals, the decisive issue is whether the status of individuals as subjects of international law produces particular effects that affect the scope of the *pacta tertiis* principle.
- Finally, research should focus on the continued development of the concepts of *jus cogens* and *erga omnes* obligations in relation to the *pacta tertiis* rule. In this respect, one of the central questions seems to be whether the statement made by the ICJ in its recent decision in *Belgium v Senegal*[118] on the relevance of 'obligations *erga omnes partes*' will ultimately turn out to be applicable also vis-à-vis third States, namely States that have not acceded to the treaty concerned. How would it be possible to justify a departure from the *pacta tertiis* rule by recourse to certain values that are held to be in the interest of mankind as a whole? And how could one overcome the legitimacy issues involved in this question?

Time will tell whether practice and legal scholarship will appropriately address the challenges to the *pacta tertiis* rule identified in this chapter.

---

[117] Christian Tomuschat, 'International Organizations as Third Parties under the Law of International Treaties', in Enzo Cannizzaro (ed), *The Law of Treaties beyond the Vienna Convention* (OUP, 2011) 220–21.

[118] *Questions relating to the Obligation to Prosecute or Extradite (Belgium v Senegal)* (Judgment) 2012, [2012] ICJ Rep 422.

PART III

TENSIONS

9. Formalism versus flexibility in the law of treaties

Jean d'Aspremont

I. INTRODUCTION

The common narrative about treaties is rather one-dimensional. Both treaties and their legal regime are meant to be formal. First, treaties themselves, albeit possibly made through non-formal processes, are usually construed as formal instruments aimed at regulating a given aspect of international life. Second, and more fundamentally, the making, identification, validation, application, interpretation, modification and termination of treaties are regulated by a set of formal constraints meant to formally organize various aspects of their existence and functioning. In that sense, treaty law is traditionally perceived as a toolbox providing instruments for the formal translation of the exercise of public authority at the international level.[1] Treaty law thus contrasts with customary law, which in some ways could be seen as the realm of *laissez-faire*.

This contribution aims to show that the law of treaties can be read very differently, and that the dominance of formalism in treaty law is much more nuanced and qualified than the general perception sketched out in the preceding paragraph suggests. It will be argued that from its making to its termination, a treaty see-saws between formalism and flexibility, and that the body of rules designed by international lawyers to regulate the life of treaties mirrors this constant oscillation: the law of treaties, as codified in the two Vienna Conventions (the 1969 Vienna Convention on the Law of Treaties and the 1986 Vienna Convention on the Law of Treaties between States and International Organizations or between International Organizations), displays both formal rationality and flexibility. This chapter aims to shed some light on the various, and disparate, features of this fundamental tension.

[1] ILC, *Study on Treaties and Times: Effect on Treaties of Subsequent Agreement and Practice* (Preliminary Study by G Nolte, A/63/10,) Annex A, para 5.

It is more specifically submitted here that the oscillation between formal rationality and flexibility comes to a head at three different levels: at the moment of the creation of the treaty, at the moment of its validation and identification as a treaty properly so-called and, finally, at the moment of its application, that is when the provisions of a treaty are confronted with the facts and accordingly need to be interpreted. At each of these stages, the tension between formal structures and flexibility is solved according to a different equilibrium. The different balances struck are themselves unstable and in a constant state of flux, for they are treaty-dependent and have not been definitively concretized by the rules of the Vienna Conventions. It is true that the constant oscillation between formalism and flexibility also infuses the rules on suspension and termination. However, as suspension and termination form the subject of a separate contribution, the 'unmaking' of treaties will be addressed only briefly.

The three dimensions of the life of a treaty studied here – creation, identification/validation and application/interpretation – while interwoven, need to be distinguished so as to understand how the balance between formalism and flexibility in treaty law is struck.[2] This is why, after some preliminary remarks on the terminology (II), this chapter separately addresses the tension between formalism and flexibility in the making of treaties (III), their identification/validation (IV) and their application/interpretation (V).

II. FORMALISM AND FLEXIBILITY AS POWER-DELEGATING STRUCTURES

The following paragraphs aim to spell out what is meant by formalism – that is, formal structures of thought – and flexibility in the design of

---

[2] The distinction between law-identification and content-determination is at the heart of my earlier study *Formalism and the Sources of International Law* (OUP, 2011). In the same vein, see A Orakhelashvili, *The Interpretation of Acts and Rules in Public International Law* (OUP, 2008) 285–6; J Beckett, 'Behind Relative Normativity: Rules and Process as Prerequisites of Law' (2001) 12 EJIL 627–50; J Beckett, 'Countering Uncertainty and Ending Up/Down Arguments: Prolegomena to a Response to NAIL' (2005) 16 EJIL 213–17; O Corten, *Méthodologie du Droit International Public* (Editions de l'Université de Bruxelles, 2009) 213. See contra P Reuter, 'Traités et Transactions. Réflexions sur l'Identification de Certains Engagements Conventionnels', in *International Law at the Time of its Codification: Essays in Honour of Roberto Ago* (Giuffrè, 1987) 399 *et seq*.

some of the secondary rules pertaining to international treaties. For the purpose of the arguments made here, *formalism* means the erection of formal structures within which the creation, identification/validation and application/interpretation of a treaty must be carried out. Formalism entails that these three operations will function against the backdrop of a set of predefined standards, thereby limiting the leeway of the makers, addressees, interpreters or observers of a treaty. These standards may be mostly procedural (at the making stage), cognitive (at the identification stage) or hermeneutic (at the application stage). In themselves, these standards do not dictate a particular result for any of these three operations, as such a result cannot be predicted by the law of treaties. Yet, the formal standards therein set formal limits as to what these operations can generate. In that sense, formalism in treaty law does not provide predictability as to what kind of regulation is contained within a treaty. It does not dictate how a treaty must be made, identified and validated or applied and interpreted. Instead, formalism provides a surface of predictability for the users and consumers of treaty law as to what *cannot* be achieved by these three operations. Thus, the predictability provided by formalism as it is understood here is negative. These constraints, formally imposed on the creation, identification/validation and application/interpretation of treaty, are all informed by the presupposition that such formal standards provide a firmer basis for coherence in treaty-making. In their absence, treaty law, as a tool for international regulation and governance, may be seen as lacking any distinct value as a regulatory instrument over other sources of rules.

On the other hand, *flexibility*, as it is understood here, is based on the delegation of power to the maker, the addressee, the observer or the interpreter of the treaty. It presupposes that each of these actors will have the ability to competently address questions of making, identification/validation or application/interpretation that may arise in the life of a treaty. Flexibility is thus premised on the idea that such answers are not knowable *in abstracto* and cannot be anticipated by the law of treaties. Further, even if they could be known and predicted, it is not appropriate that they are. Flexibility thus shies away from attempting to predict what will happen during the creation, identification/validation or application/interpretation stages. It transfers the burden of predicting any outcomes to the makers, addressees, interpreters or observers of the treaty. It is thus a form of regulation characterized by *laissez-faire* and, as a result, allows for the constant adjustment of an agreement to ensure its survival in a constantly changing environment.

The use of the term *flexibility* in this chapter should be distinguished from *semantic flexibility* within the text of the treaty itself. Indeed, the words and phrasing contained within a treaty text can be vague in varying degrees. The reasons for this vagueness can be reduced to several categories. It can be ordinary – that is, inherent in the indeterminacy of language, transparent – that is, intentionally indeterminate, as this is the limit of the consensus that was reached during negotiations or to award a greater leeway for interpretation to the authority applying the treaty – or, as legal philosophers have termed it, 'extravagant'.[3] Any one of these categories of vagueness, when present in the text of a treaty, brings about semantic flexibility, especially at the level of application/interpretation. This type of flexibility is of only indirect concern in this chapter. Certainly, semantic flexibility raises questions of indeterminacy, and these will be touched upon in section IV. However, the focus here is on the tension between formalism and flexibility in techniques designed by the law of treaties to address semantic flexibility, and not on semantic flexibility itself.

The choice of more or less formalism or flexibility in treaty-making is sometimes made consciously and at other times it is not. In some instances it is the result of a political choice for more formal constraints or, conversely, for more *laissez-faire*. This choice is never one-dimensional or absolute. The rigidity associated with the law of treaties can be qualified by flexible mechanisms, while the uncertainty inherent in flexibility (particularly with regard to the delegation of power) is allayed by the inclusion of formal structures. At the same time, it is important to note that the balance between formalism and flexibility is itself the result of internal systemic dynamics and evolves with the practice of those authorities in charge of the interpretation and application of treaties. Indeed, flexibility can be self-generated, and the balance between formalism and flexibility may not always stem from a conscious decision. This is why the oscillations between formalism and flexibility found in the making, identification/validation and application/interpretation of treaties are inherently variable. The following paragraphs will confirm this.

---

[3] On the various types of vagueness, see generally A Marmor, 'Varieties of Vagueness in the Law' (2013) USC Legal Studies Research Paper No 12-8, accessed at http://ssrn.com/abstract=2039076.

III. FORMALISM AND FLEXIBILITY IN THE MAKING (AND UNMAKING) OF TREATIES

In international law, the process by which rules are made can be formalized.[4] This is usually manifested by resort to compulsory formal procedures. If such procedures are not respected, the norm in question will be deprived of legal effect. In the design of the law of treaties, it could have potentially been decided that international treaty-making abide by a strictly formal procedure. In this framework, the existence and validity of the treaty would be determined, inter alia, by reference to whether this formalized procedure had been respected by the contracting parties. The drafters of the Vienna Conventions decided not to follow this particular course. First, oral agreements have been left outside the scope of the Vienna Conventions, are governed by customary international law and are not subject to any specific procedural requirements. Second, even for written agreements, treaty-making has not been made subject to any formal procedure. The expression of individual consent and the meeting of all individual consents can generate a valid treaty falling within the scope of the Vienna Conventions, irrespective of the process of their expression. Indeed, for written treaties there is also great flexibility as to how a text can be authenticated, as the parties themselves determine the authentication process.[5] Likewise, an expression of consent can be done through one of the various modes suggested by the Vienna Conventions or 'any other means if so agreed'.[6] The regime of the Vienna Conventions in respect of the making of treaties is inherently flexible. It does not require that the method of expressing consent be subject to strict formal procedures but rather provides some signposts or suggestions as to how this may be carried out. It is interesting to note that in early debates within the International Law Commission, the necessity of codifying the conclusion and adoption process was not deemed to be necessary.[7]

There is certainly a degree of healthy pragmatism behind this *laissez-faire* approach, and the flexibility of the Vienna Conventions. Indeed, it would have been detrimental to the success of the Conventions if too formal a procedure for treaty-making had been imposed, as it could

---

[4] J Salmon (ed), *Dictionnaire de Droit International Public* (Bruylant, 2001) 516.

[5] Article 10 of the 1969 and 1986 Vienna Conventions.

[6] Article 11 of the 1969 and 1986 Vienna Conventions.

[7] Yearbook of the ILC (1950) vol I, 67–99.

potentially discourage subjects of international law from translating their agreements into treaties falling within the ambit of the Conventions. In that sense, the flexibility regarding treaty-making found in the law of treaties can be seen to promote the appeal of treaty law as a method for concluding international agreements in general.

Albeit primarily flexible, the regulation of international treaty-making under the Vienna Conventions contains some aspects which have been subject to formal standardization. It is necessary to mention here some important qualifications, as these endeavours to formalize certain dimensions of treaty-making remain modest and continue to allow for the possibility of more flexible options agreed by the parties to prevail.

1. The definition of the powers of the delegates in charge of adopting or authenticating a treaty has been formalized.[8] The infringement of such formal standards can deprive an act relating to the conclusion of a treaty of legal effect, when performed by a person who cannot be considered to represent the State in question.[9] Such an infringement can even lead to the invalidity of a treaty in the case of a manifest violation of a rule of internal law of 'fundamental importance' regarding the competence to conclude treaties.[10] Such formalization is, however, qualified. First, it is stipulated that 'if it appears from the practice of the States concerned or from other circumstances that their intention was to consider that person as representing the State for such purposes and to dispense with full powers' this person is deemed to represent the State in question for the purpose of expressing consent to be bound by a treaty.[11] Second, this formalization is significantly tempered by a system of presumptions with regards to positions held which are automatically deemed to represent the State in question for the purpose of adopting, authenticating or expressing consent to be bound by a treaty.[12] Third, the verification of such powers is, in practice, very flexible.[13] There even are international organizations where mutual confidence between delegates is said to suffice for conferences or

8 Article 7(1) of the 1969 and 1986 Vienna Conventions.

9 Article 8 of the 1969 and 1986 Vienna Conventions.

10 Article 46 of the 1969 and 1986 Vienna Conventions.

11 Article 7(1)(b) of the 1969 and 1986 Vienna Conventions.

12 See Article 7(2) of the 1969 and 1986 Vienna Conventions.

13 Report of the Special Rapporteur Fitzmaurice, Doc A/CN.4/101, Yearbook of the ILC (1956) vol II, 123; G Scelle, *Précis de Droit des gens* (Sirey, 1932) 462.

treaties negotiated under their auspices.[14] In this respect it is noteworthy that at the Vienna Conference of 1968–69, the powers of the delegates were only verified at the very end.[15]

2. The modes of adoption, authentication and consent are the object of some attempts at formalization. For instance, the Vienna Conventions suggest that a two-thirds majority of those present and voting should be the mode of adoption of a treaty.[16] Signature is also considered to be the traditional mode of authentication.[17] Likewise, it is accepted that signature, exchange of instruments constituting a treaty, ratification, acceptance, approval or accession can all be means of expressing consent to be bound by the treaty.[18] However, these formalized suggestions by the Vienna Conventions as to the modes of adoption, authentication and consent are only indicative, and the parties can agree on any other mode. The specific modes agreed upon by the parties will always prevail over those laid out in the Conventions.
3. The *laissez-faire* approach of the Vienna Conventions regarding international treaty-making is often qualified in practice by domestic rules or the internal procedures of international organizations. At the domestic level, and although the constitutional rules of most States increasingly allow simplified forms of agreement,[19] the treaty-making rules of some States dictate strict formalities. Such formal procedural requirements can impinge upon the negotiation phase and require pre-negotiation arrangements. This is the case, for instance, with domestic procedural requirements in some federal

---

[14] See the examples cited by P Kovacs, 'Article 7', in O Corten and P Klein (eds), *Les Conventions de Vienne sur le Droit des Traités. Commentaire Article par Article* (Bruylant, 2006) 210–11.

[15] Ibid, 211.

[16] Article 9 of the 1969 and 1986 Vienna Conventions.

[17] Article 10 of the 1969 and 1986 Vienna Conventions.

[18] Article 11 of the 1969 and 1986 Vienna Conventions.

[19] See generally GS Krutz, *Treaty Politics and the Rise of Executive Agreements: International Commitments in a System of Shared Powers* (University of Michigan Press, 2009); A Gras, 'Les "executive agreements" aux E´tats-Unis' (1972) 76 Revue générale de droit international public 973–1045; AP Knoll, 'International Executive Agreements: Their Constitutionality, Scope and Effect' (1969) 2 Case Western Reserve J Intl L 94–119; EM Byrd, *Treaties and Executive Agreements in the United States: Their Separate Roles and Limitations* (Nijhoff, 1960); A Aust, *Modern Treaty Law and Practice* (CUP, 2000) 160–61.

States.[20] Most of the time, however, such requirements are only relevant in the post-negotiation phase and pertain to the ratification, incorporation or implementation of treaties. Be that as it may, these domestic procedural requirements do not, as such, curb the flexibility of treaty-making at the international level.

4. The law of some international organizations sometimes lays down procedural requirements prior to the negotiation. This is the case in relation to some of the mixed agreements between the European Union and Member States with third parties.[21] This is where neither the Community nor the Member States have exclusive competence in a particular area. Representation of Member States must be ensured and formal coordination mechanisms are put in place.
5. Some treaties are adopted through the decision-making procedures, and by virtue of instruments, of international organizations. In this case, the treaty-making process is – partly – subject to the formal procedure of the organization concerned.[22]

---

[20] See, eg, the Belgian constitutional rules on the negotiation of treaties pertaining to matters falling within the competences of the federated entities. In particular, see the Cooperation Agreement of 8 March 1994 between the Federal State, the Communities and the Regions on the procedure to be followed for the conclusion of mixed treaties, *Moniteur belge*, 17 December 1996. For the English version of this agreement, see A Alen and R Ergec, *Federal Belgium After the Fourth State Reform of 1993* (Ministry of Foreign Affairs, External Trade and Development Cooperation, 1994) 57. On this matter, see generally J Wouters and L De Smet, 'The Legal Position of Federal States and their Federated Entities in International Relations: The Case of Belgium' (2001) Institute for International Law, KU Leuven, Working Paper No 7, June 2001, accessed at www.law.kuleuven.be/iir/nl/onderzoek/wp/WP07e.pdf.

[21] See D McGoldrick, *International Relations Law of the European Union* (Longman, 1997) 78–9:

> an agreement can be regarded as mixed if the European Community and one or more of the Member States are parties to it. … An agreement can also be regarded as mixed if the European Community and the Member States share competence in relation to it, even if only Member States can be parties. Finally, an agreement can be in a mixed form because of requirements relating to its financing or relating to its provisions on voting … if competence in the subject matter of a Treaty lies partly with the European Community and partly with the Member States, then the agreement is described as a mixed one.

[22] See GA Res 42/263 (28 July 1994) pertaining to Agreement Relating to the Implementation of Part XI of the United Nations Convention on the Law of the Sea of 10 December 1982.

6. Although as a matter of principle the organization of treaty-making under the Vienna Conventions regime rests on a high degree of flexibility, there is one aspect which is the object of much stricter formalization: the formulation of reservations. Indeed, the Vienna Conventions prescribe limits as to the content,[23] the moment of formulation,[24] the form of communication to other parties,[25] the necessity of the confirmation of reservations made upon signature,[26] and, particularly in the case of reservations to constitutive elements of international organizations, the procedure of acceptance of reservations.[27] Paradoxically, however, the enforcement mechanisms of these formal limitations remain flexible. There is no formalized annulment procedure for invalid reservations and enforcement depends upon the objections of other parties. These objections in themselves have no specific legal effect and bring about substantially the same effects as the acceptance of the reservation in question.[28] Thus, even in the case of reservations, flexibility remains the dominant paradigm.
7. Parties to international treaties are under an obligation to register the treaty with the Secretary General of the United Nations.[29] Although such a procedural requirement does not bear upon the validity of treaties, it has the effect of significantly formalizing the process of treaty-making. Its importance is undermined by the non-registration of 'agreements in simplified form' and the lack of firm sanction for non-performance (other than non-invocability before UN organs).
8. Finally, the most important qualification to the flexible approach of the law of treaties in relation to treaty-making lies in the common resort to formal intergovernmental conferences[30] or the use of

---

[23] Article 19 of the 1969 and 1986 Vienna Conventions.

[24] Article 19 of the 1969 and 1986 Vienna Conventions.

[25] Article 23 of the 1969 and 1986 Vienna Conventions.

[26] Article 23(2) of the 1969 and 1986 Vienna Conventions.

[27] Article 20 of the 1969 and 1986 Vienna Conventions.

[28] Cf para 1 and para 3 of Article 21 of the 1969 and 1986 Vienna Conventions. On this point, see J Verhoeven, *Droit International Public* (Larcier, 2000) 410.

[29] Article 80 of the 1969 Vienna Convention and Article 81 of the 1986 Vienna Convention. See also Article 102 of the UN Charter.

[30] See generally Aust, *Modern Treaty Law* (n 20) 66–70.

> international organizations as a forum for the conclusion of treaties.[31] In both cases, treaty-making processes are subject to strict formal procedural requirements. The importance of this qualification to the overall flexibility of treaty-making under the general regime ought not to be exaggerated, particularly in the light of the flourishing practice of 'agreements in simplified form', especially for bilateral agreements.[32] 'Agreements in simplified form' are treaties proper, although they originate in ad hoc and often non-formal procedures which depart from the traditional, solemn treaty-making procedures and are usually not subject to registration with the Secretariat of the United Nations.[33] It is precisely this non-formal character in their creation, especially at the domestic level, that entices States to conclude such agreements.[34]

In the light of the foregoing, it appears reasonable to assert that treaty-making, albeit occasionally subject to formal standards, remains largely flexible. The dimensions of treaty-making that have been subject

---

31 See GA Res 42/263 (n 22).

32 C Lipson, 'Why Are Some International Agreements Informal?' (1991) 45 *International Organization* 495; M Fitzmaurice, 'The Identification and Character of Treaties and Treaty Obligations Between States in International Law' (2003) 73 British YB Intl L 141, 142; GM Danilenko, *Law-Making in the International Community* (Martinus Nijhoff Publishers, 1993) 55. Such a finding was already made by M Lachs, 'Some Reflections on Substance and Form of International Law', in Wolfgang Friedmann, Louis Henkin and Oliver Lissitzyn (eds), *Transnational Law in a Changing Society: Essays in Honor of P Jessup* (Columbia UP, 1972) 99.

33 On agreements in simplified form, see C Chayet, 'Les accords en forme simplifiée' (1957) 3 AFDI 205–26; FS Hamzeh, 'Treaties in Simplified Form: Modern Perspective' (1968/69) 43 BYIL 179–89; J Salmon, 'Les accords non formalisés ou "solo consensu"' (1999) 45 AFDI 1, 22; P Gautier, 'Les accords informels et la Convention de Vienne sur le droit des traités entre Etats, Mélanges Jean Salmon: Droit du pouvoir, pouvoir du droit (Bruylant, 2007) 425–54; see also P Gautier, *Essai sur la définition des traités entre Etats* (Bruylant, 1993) 149–309. For an earlier recognition of agreement in simplified form, see the 1935 codification of the law of treaties by the Harvard Research (1935) 29 AJIL Sup 697–8 (although it excluded simple exchange of notes from its definition of treaty).

34 A Aust, 'The Theory and Practice of Informal International Instruments' (1986) 35 ICLQ 787, 811; J Klabbers, *The Concept of Treaty in International Law* (Kluwer, 1996) 29; Fitzmaurice, 'The Identification and Character of Treaties …' (n 32) 142.

to formal standardization are limited and largely leave open the possibility for the parties to agree on more flexible options. Thus, as far as the making of treaties is concerned, the parties enjoy considerable leeway as to how they organize their negotiations, express their consent or make reservations.

Although the present chapter is not concerned with modification or termination, it is interesting to note that the flexibility paradigm which dominates the making of treaties also produces effects in the *modification* and *termination processes*. In the case of modification of treaties, for instance, it is widely acknowledged that subsequent practice can alter the effects of treaties.[35] By the same token, it is accepted that a treaty which establishes a boundary can be modified by a non-formal act.[36] In the case of termination, non-formal action can sometimes be deemed to terminate a treaty even in the presence of a formal termination procedure.[37] Further, behaviour at odds with treaty prescriptions can in some instances lead to termination, even in the presence of a formal termination procedure.[38] As modification and termination form the subject of other chapters of this work, they will not be further expanded on here. It suffices to show that the flexibility that informs the regulation of treaty-making can also dominate the unmaking of treaties.

IV. FORMALISM AND FLEXIBILITY IN THE IDENTIFICATION OF TREATIES

The identification of a treaty is the operation whereby an international agreement is identified as a treaty proper and thus as belonging to the international legal order. It is as a result of this identification that an agreement becomes subject to the secondary rules of the international legal order pertaining to the law of treaties. It is also by virtue of such identification that the treaty produces primary rules within that legal

---

35 ILC, *Study on Treaties and Times* (n 1).

36 *Sovereignty over Pedra Branca/Pulau Batu Puteh, Middle Rocks, and South Ledge (Malaysia/Singapore)*, Judgment ICJ Rep 2008 (23 May) para 120.

37 *Aerial Incident of 10 August 1999 (Pakistan v India)*, Jurisdiction Judgment ICJ Rep 2000 (21 June) 25, para 28.

38 Article 60 of the 1969 and 1986 Vienna Conventions. See also the termination of the mandate of South Africa over Southern Africa, *Legal Consequences for States of the Continued Presence of South Africa in Namibia (South West Africa) notwithstanding Security Council Resolution 276 (1970)*, Advisory Opinion ICJ Rep 1971 (21 June) paras 42–105.

order. Identification of a rule as a legal rule simultaneously entails a process of validation. Because validity is the specific form of existence of rules,[39] identifying a treaty amounts to validating it. Identification and validation are thus intertwined operations, and they rest on the same equilibrium between formalism and validity. The following paragraphs will thus engage simultaneously with questions of identification and validation.

If a treaty is invalid, it ceases to belong to the international legal order and its membership of this legal order is retroactively terminated. Some of the reasons for *retroactive* termination are a direct reflection of the main treaty-identification parameter, that is, *intent*. If there was no intent to create a treaty, the agreement concerned cannot belong, or ever have belonged, to the international legal order.[40] Not all the grounds of invalidity are related to intention and consent.[41] This section only focuses on the balance struck between formalism and flexibility in the processes of identification and validation and does not deal with the invalidity of treaties in any broader sense.

As a preliminary remark, it should be stated that the fact that the regime of treaty-making is primarily informed by flexibility does not automatically entail that the identification of treaties is equally flexible. Indeed, an agreement can originate in a very non-formal process and still be identified as a treaty using formal criteria. Conversely, an agreement that has been elaborated by virtue of a very formal procedure may be subject to a non-formal identification process, that is, it can be ascertained by virtue of non-formal indicators. In that sense, formalism and flexibility at the law-making level are intrinsically separate from formalism and flexibility at the identification level.

It is truistic to say that the parties to a treaty make a norm and elevate it into a conventional legal rule to achieve a given purpose. According to mainstream treaty theory, a norm that has been agreed on and enshrined in a treaty is classically called the *negotium*. If the parties decide to translate their agreement into a written instrument, the written instrument enshrining the norm is called the *instrumentum*. The *instrumentum* is the

---

39 This is a point compellingly made by Kelsen. On the extent of this conceptual revolution, see N Bobbio, 'Kelsen et les Sources du Droit' , in *Essais de Théorie du Droit* (M Guéret tr, Bruylant/LGDJ, 1998) 235.

40 See Articles 46–52 of the 1969 and 1986 Vienna Conventions on the Law of Treaties.

41 Article 53 of the 1969 and 1986 Vienna Conventions on the Law of Treaties.

formal 'container' of the obligation.[42] According to this position, authors of a treaty have complete control over both the *negotium* and the *instrumentum*. They determine both the content and the formal container.[43] In terms of treaty identification, it is essential to point out that both the content and container can potentially indicate whether the norm in question is an international legal rule. It goes without saying that such a possibility does not exist for oral treaties; whose identification is intended to be entirely flexible and non-formal. The following paragraphs accordingly solely address written treaties, as the existence of an *instrumentum* makes it possible for formalism to play a role in the identification process.

Theoretically speaking, a written agreement's membership of the international legal order could be determined by either a predefined content (*negotium*) or a predefined type of container (*instrumentum*). This means that identification could be made either flexibly or formally. If it were made dependent on the substance on the norm, the identification process would leave it to the fluctuating substantive content of the agreement to elevate it to the status of an international agreement. On the

42 Such a distinction was already made by Kelsen, 'Theorie du Droit International Public' (1953-III) 84 Collected Courses 1, 136. This distinction was also made by the Special Rapporteur Brierly of the ILC on the Law of Treaties, Yearbook of the ILC (1950) vol II, A/CN.4/32 para 30. See also the report of Fitzmaurice, Yearbook of the ILC (n 13), Article 14 and commentary No 24; the dissenting opinion of Judge Basdevant, *Ambatelios*, ICJ Rep (1 July 1952) 169; the 1935 codification of the Harvard Research (n 33) 690. Some authors have preferred the words *actum* and *actus* to draw such a distinction between the content of the act and the instrument where it is enshrined: see J Dehaussy, cited by J-P Jacqué, *Elements Pour une Théorie de l'Acte Juridique en Droit International Public* (LDGJ, 1972) 52. Jacqué, however, draws a distinction between, on one hand, the *negotium–instrumentum* dichotomy, which are two constitutive elements of the legal act, and the act–norm dichotomy on the other hand. See Jacqué, *Elements Pour une Théorie* 47–56.

43 In the same vein, K Raustiala, 'Form and Substance in International Agreements' (2005) 99 AJIL 581; H Hillgenberg, 'A Fresh Look at Soft Law' (1999) 10 EJIL 499, 504–5. For criticism of the correlative idea that States can freely decide whether to activate international law, see Klabbers, *The Concept of Treaty* (n 34) and J Klabbers, 'Not Re-Visiting the Concept of Treaty' in A Orakhelashvili and S Williams (eds), *40 Years of the Vienna Convention on the Law of Treaties* (BIICL, 2010) 29–39. On the choice between law and non-law, see J Klabbers, 'The Commodification of International Law' (2006) Select Proceedings of the European Society of International Law (vol 1, Hart, 2008) 341–58. See also the account of the cost and benefits of non-law by Lipson, 'Why Are Some International Agreements Informal?' (n 32).

other hand, if it is the written instrument that determines an agreement's membership of the international legal order, the identification process could be considered as being primarily formalistic.

According to mainstream theory, the decisive criterion in the identification of treaties is never found in the *negotium* but only in the *instrumentum*. In particular, the formulation of clear obligations is not considered a *constitutive element* of any legal act.[44] The *instrumentum* has usually been preferred to the *negotium* as the basis for the identification of written treaties.[45] As a result, the *negotium* has been left without any treaty-ascertainment effect, and treaties whose content is totally non-normative, that is, treaties that do not contain any firm obligations, can still qualify – and be identified – as international treaties.[46] This

[44] For a classical example, see Rousseau, *Principes Généraux du Droit International Public* (vol 1, Pedone, 1944) 156–7; J Basdevant, 'Règles Générales du Droit de la Paix', (1936) 58 *Recueil des Cours de l'Académie de Droit International* 471–692, 208. It is true that, in the international legal scholarship, some authors have attempted to elevate the content of a norm into a formal criterion to ascertain international legal rules, the most famous of them being Hersch Lauterpacht. See Separate Opinion of Judge Lauterpacht, *Certain Norwegian Loans*, ICJ Rep 1957 (6 July) 48; also his dissenting opinion to the *Interhandel* case, ICJ Rep 1959 (21 March) 116. This also permeates his work as Special Rapporteur on the Law of Treaties of the International Law Commission. See generally ILC Report, (1953, A/2456 (A/8/9)) chp V(II)(i), para 164 *et seq* and ILC Report (1954, A/2693 (A/9/9)) chp I(III), para 8. See also 1935 codification of the law of treaties by the Harvard Research (n 33). Gautier, *Essai sur la Définition* (n 33) 63–74. Interestingly, some of these scholars have subsequently relented from this view. Compare Jacqué, *Elements Pour une Théorie* (n 42) 69–70 and J-P Jacqué, 'Acte et Norme en Droit International' (1991-II) 227 Recueil des Cours 357, 383.

[45] For a classical affirmation of that position, see P Reuter, *Introduction au Droit des Traités* (3rd ed, Presses Universitaires de France, 1995) 30 *et seq*. For criticism of that conceptual construction according to which States, through the choice of *instrumentum*, can freely decide to activate international law or not, see Klabbers, The Concept of Treaty (n 34); more recently, see Klabbers, 'Not Re-Visiting the Concept of Treaty' (n 43).

[46] Numerous treaties nowadays enshrine such a soft *negotium*. One of the most obvious examples is provided by the 1995 Framework Convention on the Protection of National Minorities of the Council of Europe which deliberately falls short of defining the concept of minorities, leaving it to the parties to determine whether there are national minorities on their territory. On the legal problems generated by this convention, see generally J d'Aspremont, 'Les Réserves aux Traités. Observations à la Lumière de la Convention-cadre du Conseil de l'Europe Pour la Protection des Minorités Nationales', in *Les Minorités, Recueil des Travaux de l'Association Henri Capitant* (vol LII,2002) 487–514. Another example of an instrument with a soft *negotium* is provided by

instrumentum-based identification of international treaties has also been espoused in case law.[47]

The foregoing demonstrates the dominant role played by formalism in treaty-identification. It is argued here, however, that this is as far as the role of formalism extends in the identification of a treaty. Indeed, even though the model of formal law-identification, based on the *instrumentum*, lays down an adequate framework for the identification of written treaties, this identification remains ultimately dependent on the intention of the authors of these agreements. As a result, as is explained below, formalism in the treaty-identification process yields to flexibility.

It is well established that the identification yardstick provided by the 1969 Vienna Convention on the Law of Treaties ('governed by international law')

---

those agreements which are not self-sufficient in the sense that they require complementary instruments in order that their scope can be fully defined. This is commonly the case of framework conventions which abound in the field of environmental law or nuclear non-proliferation. These types of soft *negotium* usually are accompanied by provisions that require the parties to adopt complementary instruments (*pacta de contrahendo* or *de negociando*) that will flesh out the obligations contained in the original instrument. See the illustrations provided by A Kiss, 'Les Traités-cadres: une Technique Juridique Caractéristique du Droit International de l'Environnement', (1993) 39 Annuaire Français de Droit International 792. See also R-J Dupuy, 'Declaratory Law and Programmatory Law: From Revolutionary Custom to "Soft Law"', in R Akkerman et al (eds), *Declarations of Principles: A Quest for Universal Peace* (Sijthoff, 1977) 247, 254; See also the *International Status of South-West Africa*, Advisory Opinion ICJ Rep 1950 (11 July) 128, especially 140.

[47] For instance, in the *North Sea Continental Shelf* case, the Court deemed that the principle of equidistance enshrined in Article 6 of the 1958 Convention on the Continental Shelf was not normative but did not challenge its legal character (ICJ Rep 1969, para 72). Likewise, in the case pertaining to the *Military and Paramilitary Activities in Nicaragua, (Nicaragua v United States of America)*, the Court, despite contending that Article 3(d) of the Charter of the Organization of American States does not provide for any sort of obligation to the parties, it did not reject its legal character (ICJ Rep 1986, paras 259–61). The same is true with respect to its judgment on the preliminary objections in the *Oil Platforms* case. In that case, although it considered that Article I of the 1955 Treaty of Amity, Economic Relations and Consular Rights between Iran and the United States, according to which 'there shall be firm and enduring peace and sincere friendship', did not contain any obligation, the Court did not disqualify it as an international legal rule (ICJ Rep 1996, paras 28 and 31). For an analysis of this aspect of the case, see J d'Aspremont, 'Les Dispositions Non-Normatives des Actes Juridiques Conventionnels' (2003) 36 *Revue Belge de Droit International* 496, 518; See also A Boyle and C Chinkin, *The Making of International Law* (OUP, 2007) 221.

is of little use, as it only refers to the consequence of an agreement being identified as a treaty rather than the process of its identification.[48] Although the Vienna Convention is silent as to the decisive criterion in treaty-identification, it is the view of the International Law Commission that the legal nature of an act hinges upon the intent of the parties. Indeed, apart from Fitzmaurice who argued that an explicit criterion should be included,[49] the International Law Commission and its Special Rapporteurs deemed it to be self-evident and found it unnecessary to specify in their definition of a treaty.[50] This opinion is shared by most international legal scholars.[51] Thus, although treaty-ascertainment remains formal on its surface, the legal nature of such an instrument is itself determined on the basis of a non-formal criterion: *intent*.[52] This means that in the treaty-identification process, the inherent formalism of the function of a formal written instrument is subsequently replaced by the non-formal criterion of intent, thereby aligning the process much more with the notion of flexibility.

Nothing can be seen to be more flexible than an intent-based treaty-identification criterion.[53] Such a criterion ultimately grounds the identification of international treaties on an often indiscernible psychological element, and makes treaty-identification a deeply speculative operation aimed at reconstructing the author(s)' intent.[54]

---

[48] Fitzmaurice had explicitly made a distinction between the law-ascertainment criterion and the consequence of an agreement being ascertained as a treaty. See ILC Report (1956, A/3159 (F) (A/11/9)), chp III(I), para 34 *et seq.*

[49] Ibid.

[50] ILC Report (1966, A/6309/Rev.1 (F) (A/21/9)), part I(E) paras11–12, and part II, chp II, paras 9–38.

[51] Among others, see A Aust, *Modern Treaty Law and Practice* (2nd edn, CUP, 2007) 20; Oppenheim's International Law (Vol I, 9th edn, Jennings & Watts eds, 1992) 1202. Klabbers, *The Concept of Treaty* (n 34) 68; Fitzmaurice, 'The Identification and Character of Treaties …' (n 34) 145 and 165–6; Orakhelashvili, *The Interpretation of Acts* (n 2) 59. See also the general remarks of I Seidl-Hohenveldern, 'Hierarchy of Treaties', in J Klabbers and R Lefeber (eds), *Essays on the Law of Treaties: A Collection of Essays in Honour of Bert Vierdag* (Martinus Nijhoff, 1998) 7. See Jacqué, *Elements Pour une Théorie* (n 42) 121; See C Chinkin, 'A Mirage in the Sand? Distinguishing Binding and Non-Binding Relations Between States' (1997) 10 Leiden J Intl L, 223–47.

[52] See, eg, Orakhelashvili, *The Interpretation of Acts* (n 2) 59–60.

[53] In the same vein, see Klabbers, *The Concept of Treaty* (n 34) 11 *et seq.* See also the remarks of Danilenko, *Law-Making* (n 32) 57 (who pleads for the necessity of a formal act of acceptance).

[54] The *Czech Republic v European Media Ventures SA* [2007] EWHC 2851 (QB) (Comm), para 17: 'The search for a common intention is likely to be … elusive … because the contracting parties may never have had a common intention'.

It is noteworthy that, confronted with the impossibility of establishing intention on the basis of formal criteria, international scholars and judges have repeated their attachment to a formal evidentiary process to ascertain such an intention.[55] This has particularly been the tendency of the International Court of Justice, which has striven to devise a formal methodology for the ascertainment of the intention of the parties.[56] This methodology, as well as lacking consistency, has failed to alleviate the problems inherent in the establishment of intent. This is why international lawyers continue to struggle establishing intent as a basis for distinguishing treaties from other non-legal agreements.[57] The difficulty of systematizing intent likely explains why the Court appears to have moved away from the idea of a strict methodology in more recent cases, as can be seen in its decisions in *Land and Maritime Boundary between Cameroon and Nigeria*[58] and *Pulp Mills on the River Uruguay*.[59]

Against this backdrop, suggestions have been made to abandon intent as a criterion in the identification of treaties.[60] The author of this chapter

---

[55] See, eg, K Widdows, 'On the Form and Distinctive Nature of International Agreements' (1976–1977) 7 Australian YB Intl L 114. On this point, see the remarks of Fitzmaurice, 'The Identification and Character of Treaties …' (n 34) 145.

[56] As regards the identification of international treaties, see *Aegean Sea Continental Shelf (Greece v Turkey)*, Judgment ICJ Rep 1978 (19 December) paras 95–107: emphasis is put on the actual terms and circumstances. Compare *Maritime Delimitation and Territorial Questions between Qatar and Bahrain (Qatar v Bahrain)*, Judgment ICJ Rep 1994 (1 July). Regarding the identification of unilateral promise, see *Nuclear Tests (Australia v France)*, ICJ Rep 1974 (20 December) para 43; *Military and Paramilitary Activities in and against Nicaragua* (n 47) Merits. See *Frontier Dispute (Burkina-Faso/Mali)* ICJ Rep 1986. See the remarks of J Klabbers, '*Qatar v Bahrain*: The Concept of "Treaty" in International Law' (1995) 33 ARV 361–76.

[57] See generally Klabbers, *The Concept of Treaty* (n 34) especially 245–50.

[58] See the laconic consideration of the Court regarding the nature of the Maroua Declaration adopted by Cameroon and Nigeria in *Land and Maritime Boundary between Cameroon and Nigeria (Cameroon v Nigeria: Equatorial Guinea intervening)*, ICJ Rep 2002 (10 October) para 263:

> The Court considers that the Maroua Declaration constitutes an international agreement concluded between States in written form and tracing a boundary; it is thus governed by international law and constitutes a treaty in the sense of the Vienna Convention on the Law of Treaties (see Article 2, para l), to which Nigeria has been a party since 1969 and Cameroon since 1991, and which in any case reflects customary international law in this respect.

[59] *Pulp Mills on the River Uruguay (Argentina v Uruguay)*, Judgment ICJ Rep 2010 (20 April) para 138.

[60] Klabbers, *The Concept of Treaty* (n 34) especially 245–50.

has himself attempted to devise a new framework to construe the sources of international law in a dynamic fashion, grounded in the practices of law-applying authorities, which would overcome the difficulties inherent in the flexibility associated with intention as the decisive criterion in the identification of a treaty.[61] Such propositions, however, have yet to be endorsed and substantiated by international legal scholarship or law-applying authorities. Until that occurs, it seems that identification of treaties will continue to be informed by flexibility, despite the formal trappings provided by the general theory of treaty-identification.

V. FORMALISM AND FLEXIBILITY IN THE APPLICATION AND INTERPRETATION OF TREATIES

Stating that there cannot be any application of treaties without interpretation is extremely mundane.[62] Indeed, it is uncontested that those authorities empowered to apply international treaties must inevitably interpret them. Treaty-application is primarily about confronting a conventional rule with facts.[63] As a result, applying the treaty to the specific facts of each case requires an operation of interpretation which constructs a specific meaning for a particular rule for the specific situation to which it is applied. This is also why treaty-application and interpretation are not operations on which judges have a monopoly. Both legal scholars and addressees of treaties themselves are similarly engaged in the application and interpretation of treaties.

In terms of the argument put forward in this chapter, it is important to highlight that treaty-interpretation is ubiquitous and accompanies any attempt to apply a legal rule contained within a treaty to a factual situation. Interpretation, and the determination of a treaty's content in order to establish a standard of behaviour for a particular situation, simultaneously empowers the interpreter who is placed in a unique position. This can be explained as follows.

---

[61] d'Aspremont, *Formalism and the Sources* (n 2).

[62] For a classical affirmation of that idea, see Scelle, *Précis de Droit des gens* (n 13) Vol II, 488. See also G Schwarzenberger, 'Myths and Realities in Treaty Interpretation' (1968) 9 Virginia J Intl L 1 8.

[63] For an earlier affirmation, see J Bentham, *Rationale of Judicial Evidence: Specially Applied to English Practice: From the Manuscripts of Jeremy Bentham* (Hunt and Clarke, 1827).

Stating that the indeterminacy of ordinary language has contaminated the language of treaties is utterly unremarkable. Indeterminacy commonly stems from the openness of the ordinary language through which rules in treaties are expressed. Likewise, treaty rules, being the product of human thought,[64] are beset by ambiguities. These ambiguities may have been desired because they were the only manner in which the (absence of) consensus reached during negotiations could be translated into a written agreement. They could also manifest a deliberate delegation of powers of interpretation to the law-applying authority.[65] Whatever the foundations of the indeterminacy in the content of treaties, it is important to highlight here that, as a result of such indeterminacy, treaty-application and interpretation are necessarily accompanied by a wide discretionary power for the authority in charge of carrying out these functions.

While both the flexibility and wide discretion of law-applying authorities are necessary to preserve the meaningfulness of treaties when applied to factual situations,[66] it is not surprising that this discretionary power is subject to checks and formal constraints. In general, the drafters of treaties have attempted to restrict the powers of judges and other law-applying authorities as much as possible. The restriction of the discretionary powers of law-applying authorities has been seen as indispensable to the preservation of their legitimacy.

Attempts to constrain the powers of law-applying authorities have traditionally amounted to attempts to formalize and standardize their legal reasoning. More specifically, attempts to formalize the rationality of law-application and to constrain law-applying authorities' powers has usually meant the elaboration of rules of interpretation that guide content-determination by these authorities. It is this attempt that has given rise to the rules of interpretation found in Articles 31–33 of the Vienna Conventions,[67] which have now come to be viewed as reflecting

---

[64] In the same vein, R Ago, 'Positive Law and International Law' (1957) 51 AJIL 691, 727–8.

[65] This is what A Marmor has called 'transparent vagueness'. See Marmor, 'Varieties of Vagueness in the Law' (n 3). On the vagueness of treaties and the powers of international judges, see generally M Forteau, 'Les Sources du Droit International Face au Formalisme Juridique' (2011) 30 Observateurs des Nations Unies 61–71. On the distinction between ambiguity (words' connotation) and vagueness (words' denotation), see the work of Michael Thaler as reported by J Kammerhofer, *Uncertainty in International Law: A Kelsenian Perspective* (Routledge, 2010) 118.

[66] ILC, *Study on Treaties and Times* (n 1) Annex A, 365.

[67] It is interesting to note that, although it has proved less successful, a similar endeavour has also been undertaken for unilateral acts and promises. See

customary international law and are frequently resorted to by courts and tribunals in practice.[68] This is not to say that there were no standards of interpretation before the Vienna Conventions. Informed by earlier scholarly work,[69] the formal standards of interpretation prescribed by the Vienna Conventions came to replace the sovereignty-protective principles of interpretation devised by international courts in the first half of the 20th century[70] by a toolbox of formal principles.[71]

Needless to say, the elaboration of formal standards of interpretation was not an easy enterprise. Such an achievement – which was deemed a

---

the Fourth Report on Unilateral Acts of States, (A/CN.4/519) paras 101–54 and Fifth Report on Unilateral Acts of States, (A/CN.4/525) add 1, paras 120–35. See the comments of J d'Aspremont, 'Les Travaux de la Commission du Droit International sur les Actes Unilatéraux des Etats' (2005) 109 Revue Générale de Droit International Public 163–89. See the contribution of V Rodríguez Cedeño, and MI Torres Cazorla, 'Unilateral Acts of States', in *Max Planck Encyclopedia of International Law* (OUP, 2008). See also C Goodman, '*Acta Sunt Servanda?* A Regime for Regulating the Unilateral Acts of States at International Law (2006) 25 Australian YB Intl L 43 or Orakhelashvili, *The Interpretation of Acts* (n 3) 465–86. Interestingly, the International Court of Justice asserted that the interpretation of unilateral acts is not necessarily governed by the same principles as international treaties. See *Accordance with International Law of the Unilateral Declaration of Independence in Respect of Kosovo*, Advisory Opinion ICJ Rep 2010 (22 July) para 94.

[68] See, eg, *Case Concerning the Arbitral Award of 31 July 1989 (Guinea-Bissau v Senegal)*, Judgment ICJ Rep 1991, 69–70, para 48; *Land, Island and Maritime Frontier Dispute (El Salvador/Honduras: Nicaragua intervening)*, Judgment ICJ Rep 1992, 582–3, paras 373, 380 and 586; *Territorial Dispute (Libyan Arab Jamahiriya/Chad)*, Judgment ICJ Rep 1994, 21–2, para 41; *Maritime Delimitation and Territorial Questions between Qatar and Bahrain (Qatar v Bahrain)*, Jurisdiction and Admissibility Judgment ICJ Rep 1995, 18, para 33.

[69] See the Annuaire de l'Institut de Droit International (1956) 46, 364–5. See also, accessed at www.idi-iil.org/; AD McNair, *The Law of Treaties* (Clarendon Press, 1961) 466; L Siorat, *Le Problème des Lacunes en Droit International. Contribution à l'Étude des Sources du Droit et de la Fonction Judiciaire* (LGDJ, 1958) 134 *et seq*; Rousseau, *Principes Généraux du Droit* (n 44) 676 *et seq*; P Verzijl, *Georges Pinson* case (1927-8) AD No 292, cited by C McLachlan, 'The Principle of Systemic Integration and Article 31(3)(c) of the Vienna Convention' (2005) 54 ICLQ 279, 279. On the work of the International Law Commission, see MS McDougal, 'The International Law Commission's Draft Articles upon Interpretation: Textuality Redivivus' (1967) 61 AJIL 992–1000.

[70] *Interpretation of Article 3, Paragraph 2, of the Treaty of Lausanne*, Advisory Opinion, PCIJ 1925 Series B, No 12, 7 at 25.

[71] On the rebuttal of that idea, see L Crema, 'Disappearance and New Sightings of Restrictive Interpretation(s)' (2010) 21 EJIL 681–700.

miracle[72] – was particularly painstaking work due to the difficulty in striking the subtle balance between the necessity to preserve flexibility in treaty-application and interpretation, on the one hand, and the necessity of constraining the powers of law-applying authorities (by formal standardization of their legal reasoning), on the other.[73] The final balance struck by Articles 31–33 of the Vienna Conventions is thus the result of the tension and interaction between the opposing logics of flexibility and formalism.

The existence of formal rules of interpretation makes the application and interpretation of treaties, at least on the surface, a formal operation. Indeed, the existence of such principles shrouds these operations with a veil of formalism. These rules purport to provide a formal methodology for the interpretation of international legal rules.[74] They are grounded in the idea that there is an inherent objective intelligibility and rationality in the logic of treaty-application.[75] They convey what one could describe as a 'Montesquian myth of textualism',[76] sometimes supplemented by internationalist and purpositivist techniques, equating the interpretation of treaties with textual mining – that is, extracting an idea or rule from the text which exists objectively. In contrast to treaty-making and treaty-identification, formalism, at least on the surface, seems to dominate treaty-application and treaty-interpretation.

This is, however, as far as formalism has penetrated treaty-application and interpretation. Indeed, the interpretation and application of treaties shows far more flexibility in practice. First, the elaboration of formal rules of treaty-interpretation and application has not definitively struck a balance between flexibility and formalism. In fact, the balance between the two appears to be in a constant flux in international practice. This

---

72 P Reuter, *Introduction au Droit des Traités* (Armand Colin, 1972) 103. See Pellet and Dailler, *Droit International Public* (No 170, 6th ed, 1999) 262.

73 JM Sorel, 'Article 31', in Klein and Corten (eds), *Les Conventions de Vienne* (n 14) 1291.

74 See generally S Sur, *L'Interprétation en Droit International Public*, (LGDJ, 1974). See also, Sorel, 'Article 31' (n 73) 1289–338; Orakhelashvili, *The Interpretation of Acts* (n 2) 301–92; Kammerhofer, *Uncertainty in International Law* (n 65) 92 *et seq*.

75 On the quest for immanent rationality, see EJ Weinrib, 'Legal Formalism: On the Immanent Rationality of Law' (May 1988) 97(6) The Yale L J 949–1016; SV Scott, 'International Law as Ideology: Theorizing the Relationship Between International Law and International Politics' (1994) 5 EJIL 313–25, especially 322.

76 This is an expression I have used elsewhere. See J d'Aspremont, 'Wording in International Law' (2012) 25 Leiden J Intl L.

oscillation between normative creativity and formalization of content-determination can be observed in the decisions of courts and tribunals. In that sense, the tension between formalism and flexibility in the interpretation and application of treaties continues to be very dynamic. It is illustrative to mention two examples demonstrating the unstable character of the balance struck by the Vienna Conventions.

The controversies surrounding the use of subsequent practice and other relevant rules of international law as recognized by Article 31(3) of the Vienna Conventions provide an example of this uneasy balance between formalism and flexibility. Although formally anchoring interpretation in the existing normative environment of the rule or existing practice,[77] Article 31(3) has clearly reinforced the flexibility in treaty-application and interpretation. The extent of that flexibility has not been objectively determined in practice and demonstrates decided variation. The ambition of the International Law Commission to provide guidelines related to this issue shows an acknowledgment that the use of this provision has been incoherent and unpredictable in practice and that further formalization is necessary.[78]

A further example of the fluctuating balance between formalism and flexibility in the standards of interpretation found in the Vienna Conventions is provided by the development of conflicting and opposing techniques of interpretation under the same formal umbrella. These two interpretation techniques are namely: the (re)interpretation of a treaty on the basis of its *evolutive character*, and the (re)interpretation of a treaty on the basis of the *subsequent practice* of the parties; and they are both regularly found in the practice of international courts and tribunals. The former is based on an extrapolation of the intention of the parties.[79] The

---

[77] Specifically on Article 31(3)(c), see P Merkouris, 'Debating the Ouroboros of International Law: The Drafting History of Article 31(3)(c)' (2007) 9 Intl Comm L Rev 1; McLachlan, 'The Principle of Systemic Integration …' (n 69); see also J d'Aspremont, 'The Systemic Integration of International Law by Domestic Courts: Domestic Judges as Architects of the Consistency of the International Legal Order' in A Nollkaemper and OK Fauchald (eds), *The Practice of International and National Courts and the (De-)Fragmentation of International Law* (Hart, 2012) 141–66.

[78] ILC, *Study on Treaties and Times* (n 1) Annex A, 365.

[79] On evolutive interpretation, see M Fitzmaurice, 'Dynamic (Evolutive) Interpretation of Treaties, Part I' (2008) Hague YB Intl L 101, 153. A famous example of interpretative interpretation of a treaty is that endorsed by the European Court of Human Rights (see, eg, *Tyrer v the United Kingdom* (Judgment) App no 26 (ECHR 25 April 1978) para 31; *Marckx v Belgium* (Judgment) App no 31 (ECHR 13 June 1979) para 41; *Airey v Ireland*

latter is grounded in a determination of subsequent and current practice of the parties, in line with Articles 31(1) and 31(3)(b).[80] It is not necessary here to carry out a detailed assessment of the natures, benefits and limitations of these two techniques;[81] for the argument put forward in this chapter it suffices to highlight that the availability of both techniques under the Vienna Conventions shows how unstable the equilibrium between formalism and flexibility in the application and interpretation of treaties continues to be.

This constant flux between formalism and flexibility falls short of shedding some light on the true extent of the limits of the formalization of the interpretation and application of treaties attempted by the regime of the Vienna Conventions. Indeed, there is a much more fundamental reason why the formalization of treaty content-determination has remained in limbo despite the elaboration of Articles 31–33 of the Vienna Conventions. A century of rule-scepticism and legal realism,[82] as well as two decades of deconstructivism and critical legal studies,[83] have compellingly demonstrated the illusive character of formalism in law-interpretation and shed some light on the 'abuse of

---

(Judgment) App no 32 (ECHR 9 October 1979) para 26; *Loizidou v Turkey* (Preliminary Objections) App no 310 (ECHR 23 March 1995) para 7).

[80] The use of subsequent practice in treaty-interpretation is widely recognized as an interpretation technique (see, eg, Report of the Study Group of the ILC, *Fragmentation of International Law: Difficulties Arising from the Diversification and Expansion of International Law*, (finalized by M Koskenniemi, A/CN.4/L.682, 13 April 2006) and justifies that the ILC, as indicated above, deemed it necessary to embark on the study of subsequent practice (see ILC, *Study on Treaties and Times* (n 1).

[81] On the motives that can potentially inform the choice for one of these two techniques, see J Arato, 'Subsequent Practice and Evolutive Interpretation: Techniques of Treaty Interpretation over Time and Their Diverse Consequences' (2010) 9 The Law and Practice of Intl Courts and Tribunals 443–94.

[82] On the realist criticisms of formalism as a theory of legal reasoning in adjudication, see generally AJ Sebok, 'Misunderstanding Positivism' (1994–1995) 93 Michigan L Rev 2054, 2071.

[83] See, eg, D Kennedy, 'The Disciplines of International Law and Policy' (1999) 12 Leiden JIL 84; D Kennedy, 'When Renewal Repeats: Thinking Against the Box' (1999–2000) 32 NYU JILP 335; M Koskenniemi, *The Gentle Civilizer of Nations: The Rise and Fall of International Law 1870–1960* (CUP, 2002) 502; M Koskenniemi, *From Apology to Utopia: The Structure of International Legal Argument* (CUP, 2005) 306; N Purvis, 'Critical Legal Studies in Public International Law' (1991) 32 Harvard JIL 81; T Skouteris, 'Fin de Nail: New Approaches to International Law and its Impact on Contemporary International Legal Scholarship' (1997) 10 Leiden JIL 415; T Skouteris, *The Notion*

logic',[84] the 'abuse of deduction'[85] and the 'mechanical jurisprudence'[86] inherent in such a formal determination of the content of legal rules. The practice of law-application – including treaty-application – shows how flexibility has remained unchallenged despite the attempts to formally standardize both the application and interpretation of law.[87] Through these scholarly movements, the idea that the application of treaties is made behind a veil of ignorance has been severely undermined.[88]

Interestingly, despite the demystification of formalism in the interpretation and application of treaties, observers and actors have continued to perpetuate the 'Montesquian myth of textualism' in the judicial application of law and continued to demote their function to textual mining. Everyone in the epistemic community of international law politely repeats that courts simply unearth the semantics that objectively exist in texts. At the same time, however, very few members of the community of international legal scholars still believe in such a parable. Despite the abovementioned compelling critiques of the myth of formal treaty-application in legal scholarship, the perpetuation of this Montesquian myth in international law is far from accidental and can be explained as follows. The Montesquian myth of textualism has been deemed indispensable to preserve the legitimacy of judicial decision-making

---

of Progress in International Law Discourse (LEI Universiteit Leiden, 2008) chapter 3; for a similar interpretation of formalism from the vantage point of critical legal studies, see I Scobbie, 'Towards the Elimination of International Law: Some Radical Scepticism about Sceptical Radicalism' (1990) 61 BYBIL 339, 345.

84 Sebok, 'Misunderstanding Positivism' (n 82) 2093.

85 D Kennedy, *The Rise and Fall of Classical Legal Thought*, (re-edited in 2006, Beard Books) xviii.

86 This is the famous expression of Roscoe Pound, 'Mechanical Jurisprudence' (1908) 8 Columbia L Rev 605.

87 See JHH Weiler, 'The Interpretation of Treaties: A Re-Examination Preface' (2010) 21(3) EJIL 507; this was already expressed by Lauterpacht before the adoption of the Vienna Convention on the Law of Treaties, 'Restrictive Interpretation and the Principle of Effectiveness in the Interpretation of Treaties' (1949) 26 British YB Intl L 48, 53.

88 This is the reason why I am convinced that international legal positivism is not about providing means to establish authoritative interpretation. The complex theories of interpretation that have been established to provide rationality (and hence authority) to argumentative reasoning are, in my view, alien to the knowledge of international law. They are, more simply, theories of argumentation. See J d'Aspremont, 'Herbert Hart in Post-Modern International Legal Scholarship' in J d'Aspremont and J Kammerhofer (eds), *International Legal Positivism in a Post-modern World* (CUP, 2013) (forthcoming).

processes. Without this myth, the exercise of governance by courts and tribunals would be made far more transparent, which would not be without severe repercussions on their authority and on the entire adjudicative process. Once the exercise of power by law-application authorities is uncovered and made transparent, other modes of legitimation in judicial decision-making will be needed to sustain the authority of courts and tribunals.[89] This is likely why theories of interpretation continue to flourish in international legal scholarship.[90]

The foregoing has attempted to demonstrate that, to a far greater extent than in the making or identification of treaties, it is the application and interpretation of treaties that serves to magnify the dynamic tensions between formalism and flexibility. The constant oscillation between the necessity for legitimization through the formal constraint of the powers of law-applying authorities, and the necessity of preserving flexibility to allow treaties to remain normatively meaningful, makes the equilibrium between formalism and flexibility here the most dynamic of the three examined in this study.

VI. CONCLUDING REMARKS

The statement that international law is the continuation of the struggle of politics by more civilized means[91] is nowadays an uncontroversial assertion. It is generally accepted that international law brings about a displacement, rather than a neutralization, of the political confrontations in the international arena. Such a displacement of politics is carried out by virtue of a wide variety of different means.

Treaty law certainly constitutes one attempt to displace politics. Indeed, treaty law seeks to stabilize agreements reached among the main international actors by virtue of a formal standardization of (some aspects

---

[89] For such an endeavour, see I Venzke, *How Interpretation Makes International Law: On Semantic Authority, Legal Change and Normative Twists* (OUP, 2012); see also I Venzke, 'The Role of International Courts as Interpreters and Developers of the Law: Working Out the Jurisgenerative Practice of Interpretation' (2012) 34 Loyola of Los Angeles Intl and Comparative L Rev, accessed at http://papers.ssrn.com/sol3/papers.cfm?abstract_id=1868423.

[90] In recent years, no fewer than six monographs have been written on interpretation. For a critical review of these works, see M Waibel, 'Demystifying the Art of Interpretation' (2011) 22 EJIL 571, 571–88.

[91] This has been one of the lessons learnt from the last decades of international critical thinking. See, eg, M Koskenniemi, 'What is International Law For?' in M Evans, *International Law* (2nd ed, OUP, 2006) 57, 77.

of) the making, identification, application and interpretation thereof. As indicated above, it does not dictate how treaties must be made, identified and validated or applied and interpreted, but provides a formal surface of predictability for the users and consumers of treaty law as to what cannot be achieved with these three operations. In that sense, like any formalization of politics,[92] the type of formalism found in treaty law can be understood as an endeavour to control the making, identification, application and interpretation of norms through abstract categories. Treaty law should be seen as nothing more than a formal norm-management instrument.

It is important to realize that, albeit resting on an effort to formalize – to varying extents – the making, identification, application and interpretation of treaties, treaty law, like any other attempts to displace politics, does not seek to stifle it completely. On the contrary, politics survives on the formal surface in flexibility-friendly spaces, permitting the constant adjustment of the agreement and ensuring its survival in a constantly changing environment. In other words, in treaty law, politics are internalized in spaces which have been specifically designated for that purpose. In such pockets of flexibility provided by the Vienna Conventions, the law of treaties operates to delegate power to the maker, addressee, observer or interpreter of the treaty. This is well illustrated by the three dimensions of treaty law addressed in this chapter.

It is true that the creation of (or systemic self-generation of) pockets of flexibility found in the law of treaties can also be seen in other areas of international law, for example, international adjudication[93] or the rules

---

[92] D Kennedy, 'A New Stream of International Legal Scholarship' (1988–1989) 7 Wisconsin Intl Law J 1, 30.

[93] For instance, it is interesting to note that the International Court of Justice, following the Permanent Court of International Justice, in interpreting the conditions of its jurisdiction and its ability to seize itself of the cases submitted to it, has demonstrated a strong endeavour to preserve as much flexibility as possible. See, eg, *Application of the Convention on the Prevention and Punishment of the Crime of Genocide (Bosnia and Herzegovina v Serbia and Montenegro)*, Judgment on the Preliminary Objections ICJ Rep 1996 (11 July) para 26; *Temple of Preah Vihear (Cambodia v Thailand)*, Preliminary Objections ICJ Rep 1961 (26 May) 31; *Northern Cameroons (Cameroon v United Kingdom)*, ICJ Rep 1963, 28; *Military and Paramilitary Activities in and against Nicaragua (Nicaragua v United States of America*), ICJ Rep 1984, 428–9, para 83;. More recently, see the joint declaration of Judges Al-Khasawneh, Simma, Bennouna, Cançado Trindade and Yusuf appended to the case concerning *Ahmadou Sadio Diallo (Republic of Guinea v Democratic Republic of the Congo)*, ICJ Rep 2010 (30 November), accessed at www.icj-cij.org/docket/index.php?p1=3&p2=3&k=

of international responsibility.[94] This means that, when it comes to preserving flexibility, the law of treaties behaves in a similar manner to other secondary rules of international law. The previous sections have demonstrated that, with regard to the law of treaties, the articulation between the formal surface for the 'domestication' of politics and the pockets of flexibility is particularly variable in practice. Indeed, as this study has attempted to demonstrate, the equilibrium between formalism and flexibility in treaty-making, treaty-identification and treaty-application varies considerably. For each of these dimensions of the life of a treaty, formalism and flexibility strike different balances and fluctuate according to disparate dynamics. Furthermore, the balance between flexibility and formalism found in each of these dimensions of the law of treaties is also unstable and subject to constant variation.

In conclusion, it is argued that the complexity of the equilibrium between formalism and flexibility is symptomatic of the nature of the law of treaties. It is a manifestation of the very special nature of this branch of international law. In that sense, the complex, unstable and dynamic articulation between formalism and flexibility found in the law of treaties is anything but surprising. Indeed, it is the view of this author that the law of treaties boils down to an agglomeration of secondary rules which are of very different natures. Put simply, treaty law is primarily a composite set encompassing rules of change[95] and, to a very limited extent, rules of adjudication.[96] This set of rules is remarkably heterogeneous, and far more so than other sets of secondary rules found in

---

7a&case=103&code=gc&p3=4. For the case law of the PCIJ on this question, see *The Mavrommatis Palestine Concessions (Greece v Britain)*, Judgment PCIJ 1924 (30 August) Series A, No 2, 34; *Certain German Interests in Polish Upper Silesia*, PCIJ Series A, No 6, 14.

[94] On the flexibility left in the rules on international responsibility by virtue of the undefined concept of causality, see, 'The Articles on the Responsibility of International Organizations: Magnifying the Fissures in the Law of International Responsibility' (2012) Intl Organizations L Rev (forthcoming).

[95] On the difficulty in distinguishing the rules of recognition and the rules of changes, see J Waldron, 'Who Needs Rules of Recognition?' (2009) New York University School of Law, Public Law and Legal Theory Research Paper Series, Working Paper No 09-21, April 2009, accessed at http://ssrn.com/abstract=1358477.

[96] It is true that rules of recognition are strikingly absent from the Vienna Conventions and the pedigree by virtue of which treaties are identified is not directly determined by the Vienna Conventions and has been left to practice and scholarship (see section IV).

international law.[97] It is in this context that the intricate, multi-layered nature of the articulation between formalism and flexibility in the law of treaties should be seen as an expression of the deeply complex and composite structure of this area of international law.

Where does the foregoing leave us in terms of research agenda? This chapter has shown that the dichotomy of flexibility versus formalism sheds a new light on the systemic dynamics at work within the law of treaties. It simultaneously reveals another layer of complexity which is too often ignored in the mainstream legal scholarship. The few observations formulated here at the level of the making, identification and application of treaties have been inevitably cursory. They would benefit from additional exploration of the (various facets of the) inextricable tension between flexibility and formalism.

Although the tension between flexibility and formalism at play in treaty law unfolds, as has been highlighted here, in a way that is very specific to the law of treaties, it should not be seen as an isolated phenomenon in international law. Albeit in different ways, other areas of international law are riven by such a tension. Any further research into the tension between flexibility and formalism in treaty law should thus also take into account the more structural character of this dichotomy. In that sense, it seems that research on this question should necessarily be anchored into a broader research agenda on the foundational and similarly inextricable tension(s) between formalism and deformalization which permeate(s) (the theory of) international law as a whole.

---

[97] It is true that the rules on international responsibility could be said to be equally heterogeneous as is illustrated by the inclusion of primary norms as well as rules on attribution which bears effect beyond the system of responsibility or rules of self-help.

10. Integrity versus flexibility in the application of treaties

Katherine Del Mar

I. INTRODUCTION

This chapter examines the inherent tension that exists between treaty integrity and flexibility in the application of treaties. It focuses on flexibility devices which can be triggered unilaterally and which are available when entering multilateral treaties, namely reservations and other unilateral statements made upon ratification of a treaty, such as interpretative declarations.[1] Consequently, amendment and modification procedures are not examined. A reservation is the flexibility device *par excellence* by which the integrity of a treaty is softened.[2] This is because reservations are exceptions to a party's consent to be bound by the provisions of a treaty where their intended effect is to condition consent on the terms of the reservation.[3] Reservations constitute an attempt to reconcile two conflicting but fundamental requirements in treaty making: preserving the integrity of a treaty and encouraging universality of participation.[4] The drawback of reservations is the possibility for them to undermine the integrity of a treaty regime.[5] A principal concern with

[1] Reservations cannot be made to bilateral treaties; see International Law Commission, 'Guide to Practice on Reservations to Treaties', adopted by the United Nations General Assembly, Sixty-Third Session (2011), UN doc A/66/10, 19–51, reproduced in Yearbook of the ILC (2011) vol II, Part 2 (hereinafter ILC Guide to Practice), Guideline 1.6.1. On the United States practice in this regard, see A Aust, *Modern Treaty Law and Practice* (CUP, 2000) 106–7.

[2] Reservations have been described as 'the most significant' flexibility device: B Simma, 'Consent: Strains in the Treaty System' in RStJ MacDonald and DM Johnston (eds), *The Structure and Process of International Law* (Martinus Nijhoff Publishers, 1983) 485, 491.

[3] P Reuter, *Introduction au Droit des Traités* (2nd edn, Presses Universitaires de France, 1985) 71.

[4] *Reservations to the Convention on the Prevention and Punishment of the Crime of Genocide*, Advisory Opinion, ICJ Rep 1951 (28 May) 15, 24.

[5] International Law Commission, 'Guide to Practice on Reservations to Treaties with Commentaries Thereto', adopted by the UN General Assembly,

regard to reservations, therefore, is how far this flexibility device can go without harming the integrity of a treaty.[6]

The 'integrity of a treaty' is a notion traditionally understood to mean that 'no reservation [is] valid unless it [is] accepted by all contracting parties without exception, as would have been the case if it had been stated during the negotiations.'[7] In its advisory opinion on *Reservations to the Convention on Genocide*, the International Court of Justice ('the Court') departed from the unanimity rule by following the practice of the Pan American Union, the precursor to the Organization of American States.[8] The Court thus established a flexible system for reservations, whereby the consent of all contracting parties to a reservation is not required. This flexible system was adopted by the International Law Commission ('ILC'), in its draft Articles on the Law of Treaties, which became Articles 19 and 20 of the 1969 Vienna Convention on the Law of Treaties,[9] and the equivalent Articles in the 1986 Vienna Convention on the Law of Treaties.[10]

Many thorny issues arise in consideration of the balance struck between the integrity of the treaty and the reservations system, which remains a highly contentious area of scholarship and practice.[11] To some extent, this is a result of lacunae and ambiguities in the 1969 and 1986 Vienna Conventions on the Law of Treaties. The natural starting point for any discussion on reservations today are the relevant provisions of the 1969 and 1986 Vienna Conventions read together with the colossal *Guide on Practice to Reservations to Treaties*, completed under the auspices of the ILC, the final version of which was adopted in 2011 ('the ILC Guide'). The ILC Guide is a non-binding 'code of recommended

---

Sixty-Third Session (2011), Supplement No. 10, UN doc A/66/10/Add.1 (hereinafter Commentary to the ILC Guide), Guideline 2.5.3, 208, para (4).

6 S Spiliopoulou Åkermark and O Mårsäter, 'Treaties and the Limits of Flexibility', (2005) 74 Nordic J Intl L 509, 509.

7 *Reservations to the Convention on Genocide* (n 4) 21.

8 Ibid, 22. See JM Ruda, 'Reservations to Treaties', (1975) 146 *Recueil des Cours de l'Académie de Droit International* 95, 115–33.

9 Vienna Convention on the Law of Treaties, 23 May 1969, entered into force on 27 January 1980, 1155 UNTS 331 ('1969 Vienna Convention').

10 Vienna Convention on the Law of Treaties between States and International Organizations or between International Organizations, 21 March 1986, (1986) 25 ILM 543, not yet in force ('1986 Vienna Convention').

11 Aust, *Treaty Law* (n 1) 125.

practices,'[12] which consists of a consolidation of the *lex lata* and a progressive development of the law on reservations to treaties.[13]

Three difficulties that arise with regard to reservations to treaties are the focus of this chapter. The first is determining the existence of a reservation. Only the flexibility device of reservations, as opposed to other kinds of unilateral statements made upon ratification of a treaty, may condition consent to be bound by a treaty, and affect the existence or scope of treaty relations between the reserving entity and other contracting parties. The way in which the ILC Guide has sought to provide guidance in this respect is examined. Secondly, the status of the author of an invalid reservation is addressed. This remains one of the most contentious matters concerning reservations, and one on which the ILC has adopted a controversial stance by attempting to strike a new balance between preserving the integrity of the treaty and respecting the conditioned consent of reserving entities. Thirdly, auto-interpretation of the compatibility of reservations with the object and purpose of a treaty will be considered with a view to considering the role of third parties in this determination, particularly with respect to human rights treaties. As will be seen, much the same issues have bedevilled this area of treaty law for over sixty years. With this in mind, the future direction of research is finally considered in light of the most recent attempt by the ILC to formulate guidance for practitioners.

II. DETERMINING THE EXISTENCE OF A RESERVATION: DISTINGUISHING BETWEEN INTERPRETATIVE DECLARATIONS AND RESERVATIONS TO TREATIES

Determining the existence of a reservation is important to understanding the treaty obligations that the author of a reservation and other contracting parties bear in their bilateral relations with one another. This is because a reservation is an attempt 'to modify the legal effect of certain provisions of the treaty in their application to that [reserving] State.'[14] In this respect, reservations must be distinguished from other flexibility

---

[12] Commentary to the ILC Guide (n 5) Commentary to Guideline 2.5.3, 207, para (2).

[13] A concise overview of the ILC Guide to Practice (n 1) is provided in D McRae, 'The Work of the International Law Commission, 2007–2011: Progress and Prospects', (2012) 106 AJIL 322, 325–9.

[14] 1969 and 1986 Vienna Conventions, Article 2, para 1(d).

devices in the form of unilateral statements made upon ratification of a treaty that are not regulated by the Vienna Conventions, but which are commonplace in practice: interpretative declarations and other unilateral declarations. The ILC Guide makes a positive contribution to the law on reservations in this respect by dealing expressly with interpretative declarations in a number of its Guidelines, as well as statements of non-recognition,[15] and statements concerning the modalities of implementation of a treaty at the internal level.[16]

The ILC Guide distinguishes between reservations and interpretative declarations on the basis of the attempt by the former to modify the legal effects of certain provisions of the treaty,[17] in keeping with the definition of a reservation provided in the Vienna Conventions under Article 2(1)(d). By contrast, an interpretative declaration is defined in the ILC Guide as 'a unilateral statement, however phrased or named, made by a State or an international organization, whereby that State or that organization purports to specify or clarify the meaning or scope of a treaty or of certain of its provisions.'[18] The decision to label a unilateral statement as a reservation, or an interpretative declaration, is of course a matter left to the author of the unilateral statement. This raises the problem of 'disguised reservations,'[19] namely statements labelled as unilateral declarations but which behave like reservations insofar as they purport to modify the legal effect of certain provisions of the treaty in their application to the author of the statement. The Vienna Conventions settled the matter by holding that a reservation is a unilateral statement 'however phrased or named,' which purports to modify the legal effects of certain provisions of the treaty.[20] Like a book, a reservation should not be judged by its cover.[21]

Whilst repeating the *lex lata* and acknowledging that the substance of the unilateral statement is determinative as to whether it constitutes a

---

15 ILC Guide to Practice (n 1) Guideline 1.5.1.

16 Ibid, Guideline 1.5.2.

17 Ibid, Guideline 1.3.

18 Ibid, Guideline 1.2.

19 Aust, *Treaty Law* (n 1) 104–5.

20 1969 and 1980 Vienna Conventions, Article 2(d).

21 This point is discussed in DW Bowett, 'Reservations to Non-Restricted Multilateral Treaties', (1976–1977) 48 BYBIL 67, 68. See also *Delimitation of the Continental Shelf between the United Kingdom of Great Britain and Northern Ireland, and the French Republic*, Decision of 30 June 1977, UNRIAA, Vol XVIII, paras 54–55; *Temeltasch v Switzerland*, (Decision) App no 9116/80 (European Commission of Human Rights 5 May 1982) paras 69–82; *Belilos v Switzerland* (Judgment) App no 10328/83 (ECHR 29 April 1988) paras 48–49.

reservation or interpretative declaration, rather than its nomenclature, the Commentary to the ILC Guide also suggests that the name of a unilateral statement made upon ratification is 'an element of appraisal which must be taken into consideration and which can be viewed as being of particular (although not necessarily vital) significance.'[22] Guideline 1.3.2 of the ILC Guide *thus* provides that '[t]he phrasing or name of a unilateral statement provides *an indication* of the purported legal effect.'[23] This would appear to create a rebuttable presumption according to which the substance of the unilateral statement corresponds with the name it has been given.[24] Thus, although Guideline 1.3.2 makes clear that the particular label attached to the unilateral statement cannot be conclusive, it nevertheless considers the name accorded to the statement should play some role in determining the nature of the substance of the statement.

This rebuttable presumption is carried across in the ILC Guide to treaties which prohibit reservations to all, or specific, treaty provisions.[25] It is proposed that a rebuttable presumption should apply according to which a unilateral statement formulated in respect of a treaty which prohibits reservations per se, or with regard to certain treaty provisions to which the statement pertains, is not a reservation. This approach is justified in the Commentary to the ILC Guide as an application of the

---

22 Commentary to the ILC Guide (n 5) Commentary to Guideline 1.3.2, 82, para (8).

23 ILC Guide to Practice (n 1) Guideline 1.3.2 (emphasis added).

24 Although Guideline 1.3.2 does not expressly establish a rebuttable presumption, the Commentary to Guideline 1.3.2 explains that the 'indication' provided by the name given to a unilateral statement in effect operates as a rebuttable presumption. See Commentary to the ILC Guide (n 5) Commentary to Guideline 1.3.2, 82, paras (10) and (11).

25 ILC Guide to Practice (n 1) Guideline 1.3.3, which provides:

> When a treaty prohibits reservations to all or certain of its provisions, a unilateral statement formulated in respect of those provisions by a State or an international organization *shall be presumed not to constitute a reservation*. Such a statement nevertheless constitutes a reservation if it purports to exclude or modify the legal effect of certain provisions of the treaty, or of the treaty as a whole with respect to certain specific aspects, in their application to its author. (emphasis added)

A recent survey of over 300 multilateral treaties concluded since 1951 found that 46% contained some form of no-reservations clause: J Galbraith, 'Treaty Options: Towards a Behavioral Understanding of Treaty Design', (2013) 53(2) Virginia J Intl L 309, 316–17.

general principle that bad faith is not to be presumed;[26] a general principle which was formulated in the context of inter-State adjudication for the purpose of adjudging the merits of a claim of international responsibility.[27] In this vein, the general principle that bad faith is not to be presumed was reformulated more narrowly by the Rapporteur in the *Spanish Zone of Morocco Claims* as the principle according to which '*la responsabilité internationale de l'Etat ne se présume pas* ('the international responsibility of a State is not presumed').'[28]

The difficulty with applying the general principle that bad faith is not to be presumed to the task of distinguishing between interpretative declarations and reservations is that this is a task undertaken by contracting parties individually, for the purpose of protecting their own interests, and not by an objective third party for the purpose of adjudging a claim of international responsibility. Good faith should moderate the arbitrariness of this task undertaken by individual States and international organizations,[29] but in exercising good faith themselves, it does not follow that these same States and international organizations need presume good faith on the part of the author of the statement. Indeed, rather than taking the author of a unilateral statement at its word that the statement titled 'interpretative declaration,' 'declaration,' 'understanding' or a similarly neutral term does not purport to modify the legal effect of treaty provisions, a certain vigilance needs to be exercised by (prospective) contracting parties in identifying so-called reservations-in-fact.[30] Indeed the very reason why a unilateral statement may be called an 'interpretative declaration' by its author may be because the treaty prohibits the making of reservations, and to label the statement a

---

26 Commentary to the ILC Guide (n 5) Commentary to Guideline 1.3.3, 83, para (2).

27 The general principle that bad faith is not to be presumed was formulated by the tribunal in the *Lake Lanoux* arbitration: *Affaire du Lac Lanoux (France c Spain)*, Award of 16 November 1957, UNRIAA, Vol XII, 281, 305.

28 *Affaires des biens britanniques au Maroc espagnol (Espagne c Royaume-Uni), Réclamation XXVIII: Tanger, Chevaux – Haj Mohamed Harrej*, Award of 1 May 1925, UNRIAA, Vol II, 699, para 4.

29 C Fernández de Casadevante Romani, *Sovereignty and Interpretation of International Norms*, (Springer, 2007) 14.

30 ET Swaine, 'Treaty Reservations' in DB Hollis (ed), *The Oxford Guide to Treaties* (OUP, 2012) 277, 293. See also Commentary to the ILC Guide (n 5) Commentary to Guideline 4.5.3, 280, para (1).

reservation 'in such circumstances almost certainly would be regarded as invalid.'[31]

Practice demonstrates the vigilance exercised by contracting parties in analysing statements based on an analysis of their content, rather than their nomenclature, and reacting negatively to such statements if they are considered to amount to reservations-in-fact.[32] Although a reservation-in-fact could not be relied upon by its author to alter any obligations under the treaty where such reservations are prohibited, it has been suggested that such prohibited reservations nevertheless 'run the risk of subtly altering obligations.'[33] For example, the United Nations Convention on the Law of the Sea ('UNCLOS') prohibits reservations under its Article 309.[34] Article 310 provides that a State upon signing or ratifying UNCLOS may make a declaration or statement 'provided that such declarations or statements do not purport to exclude or to modify the legal effects of the provisions of this Convention in their application to that State.'[35] Upon ratification, the Philippines made a 'statement,' which provided inter alia that the 'concept of archipelagic waters is similar to the concept of internal waters under the Constitution of the Philippines …' This 'statement' was understandably objected to by a number of contracting parties.[36]

By contrast to the Philippines example, other statements made upon ratification of a treaty may be interpreted by contracting parties as

---

[31] I Cameron, 'Treaties, Declarations of Interpretation' in R Wolfrum (ed), *Max Planck Encyclopaedia of International Law* (OUP, accessed at http://opil.ouplaw.com/home/EPIL) (article last updated 2010) para 9.

[32] Negative reactions to reservations-in-fact are not objections, strictly speaking; as such they cannot oppose the entry into force of the treaty. Rather, a negative reaction may be viewed 'as a safeguard measure, a protest against establishing an interpretation of the treaty that it might consider opposable, which it does not find appropriate, and about which it must speak out': Report of the ILC, Sixty-First Session (2009), UN doc A/64/10, 262, para 11. See also A McNair, *The Law of Treaties* (Clarendon Press, 1961) 430–31.

[33] Swaine, 'Treaty Reservations' (n 30) 293. See also Commentary to the ILC Guide (n 5) Commentary to Guideline 4.5.3, 280, para (1).

[34] United Nations Convention on the Law of the Sea, 10 December 1982, entered into force on 14 November 1994, 1833 UNTS 396, Article 309.

[35] Ibid, Article 310.

[36] States which objected to the Philippines' statement included Australia (3 August 1988), Belarus (24 June 1985), the Russian Federation (25 February 1985), and Ukraine (8 July 1985). Declarations and objections relating to UNCLOS are reproduced on the website of the Treaty Section of the Office of Legal Affairs of the United Nations, accessed 11 June 2014 at http://treaties.un.org/Pages/ViewDetailsIII.aspx?&src=TREATY&mtdsg_no=XXI~6&chapter=21&Temp =mtdsg3&lang=en.

corresponding in substance to the neutral name they have been given by their authors. Practice demonstrates that contracting parties more often than not do not react at all – either positively or negatively – to such statements. For example, Romania made a declaration upon signature of UNCLOS, confirmed upon ratification, according to which it inter alia states that 'according to the requirement of equity – as it results from articles 74 and 83 of [UNCLOS] – the uninhabited islands without economic life can in no way affect the delimitation of the maritime spaces belonging to the mainland coasts of the coastal States.'[37] No contracting State interpreted this statement as amounting to a reservation-in-fact, or reacted negatively to it.[38]

By virtue of the vigilance that contracting parties must exercise in evaluating whether the substance of a unilateral statement made upon ratification corresponds with the name it has been given by its author, it is difficult to see the value added by the rebuttable presumption proposed in Guideline 1.3.3. There are many reasons why a reservation-in-fact may be referred to in more neutral terms by its author, including that the treaty in question may prohibit reservations per se or the specific reservation its author wishes to make. Arguably there is greater necessity

---

[37] Declaration by Romania made upon signature of UNCLOS on 10 December 1981, confirmed upon ratification on 17 December 1996, para 3 (see treaty website, n 36).

[38] In the *Maritime Delimitation in the Black Sea* case, Romania contended that Ukraine had accepted the applicability of Article 121(3) UNCLOS in the delimitation of the continental shelf and exclusive economic zones, as interpreted by Romania when signing and ratifying it: *Maritime Delimitation in the Black Sea (Romania v Ukraine)*, Judgment, ICJ Rep 2009 (3 February) 76, para 35; ibid, Romania's Memorial, 91–4, paras 8.20–8.30; ibid, CR 2008/18, 18–19, paras 39–41 (Aurescu) (translation by the Registry of the Court); and ibid, CR 2008/20, 53–4, paras 73–9 (Lowe). Consequently, Romania argued that Ukraine had accepted that the only role Serpent Island may play in the maritime delimitation between the two States is that determined by Article 121(3) UNCLOS: ibid, CR 2008/18, 2 September 2008, 20, para 45 (Aurescu) (translation by the Registry of the Court). Ukraine, in turn, simply pointed out the difference between a declaration and a reservation, noting that a declaration does not call for any response from the other contracting parties. Thus, it argued that its silence could not be implied as reacting positively to Romania's interpretation: ibid, CR 2008/29, 12 September 2008, 20, para 63 (Malintoppi). For its part, the Court considered that 'Romania's declaration… has no bearing on the Court's interpretation [of UNCLOS]': ibid, Judgment, 78, para 42. It thus appears that the Court confirmed that silence in response to an interpretative declaration does not automatically imply acquiescence: RK Gardiner, *Treaty Interpretation* (OUP, 2010) iv.

with regard to such treaties to pay no heed to the nomenclature of unilateral statements made upon ratification, much less to apply a presumption in favour of the name they have been accorded.

The ILC Guide also provides guidance concerning the matters to which reservations can pertain. Such matters include the territorial application of the treaty, addressed under Guidelines 1.1.3 and 1.1.4. Significantly, Guideline 1.1.3 purports to cure a problem that arises in practice when a State makes a unilateral statement that it is extending the scope of the treaty to cover specified parts of its territory, thereby suggesting that unless such a unilateral statement is made, the treaty applies only to part of a State's territory. For example, the United Kingdom has a practice of declaring upon ratification of a multilateral treaty to which, if any, overseas territories the treaty will extend.[39] Such a practice jars with Article 29 of the Vienna Conventions, which applies a rebuttable presumption that a treaty is binding on a State with respect to its *entire* territory.[40]

Guideline 1.1.3 is carefully worded. It does not propose that a unilateral statement made upon ratification which purports to exclude the application of the treaty *as a whole* to a particular territory constitutes a reservation. Such a formulation would preclude a State representing a non-self-governing territory at the international level from becoming party to a treaty which prohibits reservations for such time as the Territory in question is unable to commit to the same treaty obligations.[41] Instead of constituting a reservation, the ILC Guide proposes that a statement which purports to exclude the treaty *as a whole* from specific territory should be considered as an expression of a 'different intention' under Article 29 of the Vienna Conventions,[42] thereby rebutting the presumption set out under this provision that the treaty is binding on a State with respect to its entire territory. In line with Article 29 of the 1969 Vienna Convention, Guideline 1.1.3 thus proposes to treat unilateral

---

[39] See United Kingdom Foreign & Commonwealth Office, 'Guidelines on Extension of Treaties to Overseas Territories', 19 March 2013, accessed 14 June 2014 at www.gov.uk/government/publications/guidelines-on-extension-of-treaties-to-overseas-territories, para 5.

[40] Article 29 of the 1969 and 1986 Vienna Conventions provides that '[u]nless a different intention appears from the treaty or is otherwise established, a treaty is binding upon each party in respect of its entire territory.' For more on the territorial scope of treaties, see Marko Milanovic's contribution to the present volume.

[41] Commentary to the ILC Guide (n 5) Commentary to Guideline 1.1.3, 51, para (9).

[42] Ibid, 50, para (5).

statements made upon ratification which purport to exclude '*some provisions* of a treaty or of the treaty as a whole *with respect to certain specific aspects*' from a territory to which they would be applicable in the absence of such a unilateral statement as a reservation.[43]

III. STATUS OF THE AUTHOR OF AN INVALID RESERVATION

The reservations system is binary in the potential legal effects of a reservation depending on whether the reservation is considered valid or invalid. Valid reservations are those which do not fall foul of any of the three limbs of Article 19 of the Vienna Conventions, that is, the reservation is prohibited either by a clause prohibiting reservations per se, or by a clause providing that only specific reservations may be made, which do not include the reservation in question,[44] or the reservation is incompatible with the object and purpose of the treaty.[45] A valid reservation can be expressly accepted, or it will be deemed to have been accepted by a contracting party if this party remains silent for a period of more than twelve months after being notified of the reservation.[46] Only once it is accepted by at least one contracting party will an act expressing a reserving entity's consent to be bound by the treaty be effective.[47] Express or implied acceptance of a valid reservation will create bilateral treaty relations between the reserving and accepting parties.[48]

If, however, a contracting party objects to a valid reservation then – depending upon the intention expressed by the objecting party – the reserving entity and the objecting party may, or may not, enter into treaty relations. Article 20, paragraph 4(b), reworded with a slightly different emphasis in Guideline 4.3.5,[49] provides that an objection to a reservation

[43] ILC Guide to Practice (n 1) Guideline 1.1.3 (emphasis added).

[44] 1969 and 1986 Vienna Conventions, Article 19(a) and (b).

[45] Ibid, Article 19(c).

[46] Ibid, Article 20, para 5. The customary nature of this rule is doubtful.

[47] Ibid, Article 20(c). Conversely, an act expressing a reserving entity's consent to be bound will produce no effect as long as there has been no (express or implied) acceptance: A Pellet and D Müller, 'Reservations to Treaties: An Objection to a Reservation Is Definitely Not an Acceptance' in E Cannizzaro (ed), *The Law of Treaties Beyond the Vienna Convention* (OUP, 2011) 37, 42.

[48] 1969 and 1986 Vienna Conventions, Article 20(a).

[49] Unlike Article 20, para 4(b), of the 1969 and 1986 Vienna Conventions, Guideline 4.3.5 words the preclusion of the entry into force of the treaty in positive terms as follows:

does not preclude the entry into force of the treaty between the reserving entity and the objecting party, 'unless a contrary intention is definitely expressed' by the objecting entity. An objection therefore can have 'maximum effect,' whereby an objecting contracting party can definitely express its intention not to enter into treaty relations with the reserving entity.[50]

By contrast to valid reservations, multilateral treaties rarely stipulate the consequences flowing from an invalid reservation, and State practice is inconsistent in this regard. The length of the commentary to some provisions in the ILC Guide provides a first indication of the contentious nature of some areas of practice regarding reservations to treaties. This is certainly the case with the status of the author of an invalid reservation, 'one of the most serious lacunae' in the Vienna Conventions on the Law of Treaties,[51] and addressed under Guideline 4.5.3. The focus in this section is the status of the author of a reservation which may be considered invalid by reason of its incompatibility with the object and purpose of the treaty under Article 19(c) of the Vienna Conventions.

In theory, there exist three possibilities governing the legal relations between an entity which has formulated a reservation, which is objected to by a contracting party on the basis that it is incompatible with the treaty's object and purpose and therefore invalid:

(i) There are *no treaty relations* between the reserving entity and the objecting entity;
(ii) The *treaty is in force only in part* between the reserving entity and the objecting entity, because those treaty provisions to which the reservation is attached are severable from the regime of treaty provisions which otherwise apply in their bilateral relations;

An objection by a contracting State or a contracting organization to a valid reservation *precludes the entry into force of the treaty* as between the objecting State or organization and the reserving State or organization, *if the objecting State or organization has definitely expressed an intention to that effect* in accordance with guideline 2.6.7. (emphasis added)

50 Examples are provided in the Commentary to the ILC Guide (n 5) Commentary to Guideline 2.6.7, 259, para (2).

51 Pellet and Müller, 'Reservations to Treaties …' (n 47) 54. Article 19(c) of the 1969 and 1986 Vienna Conventions simply provides that 'A State [or an international organization] may, when signing, ratifying, accepting, approving or acceding to a treaty, formulate a reservation unless … the reservation is incompatible with the object and purpose of the treaty.'

(iii) The *treaty in full* – including those provisions to which the reservation attaches – *is in force* between the reserving entity and the objecting entity, as the effect of the objection is to render the reservation severable from the reserving entity's consent to be bound.[52]

As explained above, the first possibility is an option with respect to a valid reservation, and it is contingent on the objecting contracting party definitely expressing its intention not to enter into treaty relations with the reserving entity. In relation to invalid reservations, however, the approach taken by the ILC was to reject the first option of precluding treaty relations as a result of the formulation of an invalid reservation. There is scant practice in support of the first possibility,[53] even though precluding treaty relations may be an appealing outcome to impose on the reserving entity by contracting parties which view the reservation in question as offending the very core of the treaty, and thus making a mockery out of the reserving entity's adhesion to the treaty instrument. However, to preclude treaty relations between the reserving entity and the objecting contracting party would oppose both the will expressed by the reserving entity to be bound by the treaty, and the freedom of the objecting party to choose whether or not the treaty should enter into force between it and the reserving entity.[54]

The ILC Guide characterizes its methodology as striking a middle path between two opposing schools of thought, referred to in the doctrine as

---

[52] These three possibilities are worded slightly differently by C Redgwell, 'Universality or Integrity? Some Reflections on Reservations to General Multilateral Treaties', (1993) 64 BYBIL 245, 274. A different formulation of the three possibilities, also presented in a different order, is provided by R Goodman, 'Human Rights Treaties, Invalid Reservations, and State Consent', (2002) 96 AJIL 531, 531.

[53] See Commentary to the ILC Guide (n 5) Commentary to Guideline 2.6.6, 257, para 8. In the Sixth Committee, the view was expressed that 'once a reservation was determined to be invalid, following objections by several contracting parties, the reserving State should not be considered bound by the treaty with the exception of human rights, humanitarian law treaties and treaties relating to the law of armed conflict': UN General Assembly, Topical Summary of the Discussion Held in the Sixth Committee of the General Assembly during its Sixty-Second Session, 2008, UN doc A/CN.4/588, 12, para 57.

[54] See views expressed by delegations in the Sixth Committee: UN General Assembly, Topical Summary of the Discussion Held in the Sixth Committee of the General Assembly during its Sixty-Second Session, 2008, UN doc A/CN.4/588, 13, para 59.

the 'permissibility' and 'opposability' schools of thought.[55] These two schools of thought represent two different positions on where the balance should be struck between preserving the integrity of the treaty and allowing the flexibility device of reservations to soften it. According to the permissibility school, invalid reservations are void *ab initio*.[56] For advocates of the permissibility school, the integrity of the treaty is not sufficiently protected by objections to reservations.[57] Rather, an objective threshold of impermissibility of a reservation is set out under each limb of Article 19 of the Vienna Conventions. Advocates of the permissibility school thus consider the object and purpose test under Article 19(c) of the Vienna Conventions to apply independently of objections.[58] By contrast, the opposability school considers reservations only to be opposable by other States.[59] At the heart of this approach is awareness of the enforceability of reservations, as each (prospective) contracting partner has to decide for itself whether a reservation is compatible with the treaty's object and purpose.

The compromise reached in the ILC Guide between these disparate positions is influenced by the remedy recommended by treaty bodies and scholars with regard to human rights treaties, including the so-called Nordic approach to reservations.[60] It comes in the form of a rebuttable

---

55 An overview of these two schools of thought is provided by JK Koh, 'Reservations to Multilateral Treaties: How International Legal Doctrine Reflects World Vision', (1982) 23 Harvard Intl L J 71, 97–9. See also ET Swaine, 'Reserving', (2006) 31 Yale J Intl L 307, 314–16.

56 Bowett, 'Reservations …' (n 21) 83.

57 Swaine, 'Treaty Reservations' (n 30) 285.

58 A Pellet and D Müller, 'Reservations to Human Rights Treaties: Not an Absolute Evil …' in U Fastenrath, R Geiger, D-E Khan, A Paulus, S von Schorlemer, and C Vedder (eds), *From Bilateralism to Community Interest: Essays in Honour of Bruno Simma* (OUP, 2011) 526. In this vein, some delegations in the Sixth Committee expressed the view that:

> all States becoming parties to a treaty should commit themselves to its object and purpose. Central provisions could not be nullified through reservations. Such reservations should be considered null and void, as indicated clearly in article 19 of the Vienna Convention on the Law of Treaties. Objections were not necessary to establish that fact.

See UN General Assembly, Topical Summary of the Discussion Held in the Sixth Committee of the General Assembly during its Sixty-Second Session, 2008, UN doc A/CN.4/588, 7, para 15.

59 Ruda, 'Reservations to Treaties' (n 8) 190.

60 See J Klabbers, 'Accepting the Unacceptable? A New Nordic Approach to Reservations to Multilateral Treaties', (2000) 69 Nordic J Intl L 179.

presumption that leans heavily in the direction of the permissibility school of thought:[61] '[u]nless the author of the invalid reservation had expressed a contrary intention or such an intention is otherwise established, it is considered a contracting State or a contracting organization without the benefit of the reservation.'[62] The ILC has thus sanded down the hard edges of the third option outlined above, and proposes that the treaty in full – including those provisions to which the reservation attaches – will be in force between the reserving entity and the objecting contracting party, *unless* the reserving entity has expressed a contrary intention. Pursuant to the ILC's guidance, the effect of the objection is to render the reservation severable from the reserving entity's consent to be bound, in the absence of an intention on the part of the reserving entity not to become a party to the treaty without the protection of the terms of its reservation.

This is not a happy compromise. Although a certain amount of deference is given to the author of the reservation by relying heavily on the intention expressed by the reserving State or international organization as to whether it intends to be bound by the treaty without the benefit of its reservation,[63] in the absence of a discernable intention in this respect, the author of such a reservation is deemed to be a contracting party 'without the benefit of the reservation.' This opens up the possibility for a State or international organization to consent to be bound by a treaty on the condition that the treaty provisions apply only in accordance with the terms set out in its reservation, and subsequently for this State or international organization to be deemed to be bound by the treaty in its entirety on the basis that its reservation was invalid, and its intention not to be bound by the treaty without the benefit of its reservation was not discernable. This result would seem to conflict with the well-settled rule that a legal subject only bears those treaty obligations it consents to be bound by.[64] As the Court stated in its advisory

---

[61] Commentary to the ILC Guide (n 5) Commentary to Guideline 4.5.3, 525, para (1).

[62] ILC Guide to Practice (n 1) Guideline 4.5.3, para 2.

[63] Ibid, Guideline 4.5.3, para 1, provides: 'The status of the author of an invalid reservation in relation to a treaty depends on the intention to be bound by the treaty without the benefit of the reservation or whether it considers that it is not bound by the treaty.'

[64] *Case of the SS Wimbledon*, Judgment, PCIJ, 1923 Series A, No 1, 25 ('the right of entering into international engagements is an attribute of State sovereignty'); *Exchange of Greek and Turkish Populations*, Advisory Opinion, PCIJ, 1925 Series B, No 10, 21; *International Status of South-West Africa*, Advisory

opinion on *Reservations to the Convention on Genocide*, '[i]t is well established that in its treaty relations a State cannot be bound without its consent, and that consequently no reservation can be effective against any State without its agreement thereto.'[65]

An additional hurdle in Guideline 4.5.3 is determining the intention of the reserving State, namely 'deciding whether the invalid reservation constituted an essential condition of the state's consent to be bound.'[66] The difficulty of this hurdle is augmented by the uncertainty introduced in paragraph 3 of Guideline 4.5.3, by which 'the author of the invalid reservation may express *at any time* its intention not to be bound by the treaty without the benefit of the reservation.'[67] A time limit is introduced by the ILC only if the reservation is first considered invalid by a treaty-monitoring body. In that case, the reserving entity has twelve months from the date at which the treaty-monitoring body made its assessment to express its intention that it is not bound by the treaty without the benefit of its reservation.[68]

In defence of the approach taken by the ILC, it may be argued that States and international organizations have a right to make reservations only if they are consistent with the terms of the treaty.[69] Specifically with regard to the object and purpose of the treaty, by expressing its consent to be bound by the treaty, a reserving entity is expressing its consent to be bound by the very core of the treaty and it must be taken as having foreseen the possibility that its reservation (presumably made in good faith) would be found incompatible with the treaty's object and purpose.[70] If the State or international organization does not then have recourse to the withdrawal mechanisms at its disposal, it should be treated as intending to be bound by the treaty in its entirety. The

---

Opinion, ICJ Rep 1950 (11 July) 128, 139 ('An "agreement" implies consent of the parties concerned … The parties must be free to accept or reject the terms of a contemplated agreement. No party can impose its terms on the other party').

65 *Reservations to the Convention on Genocide* (n 4) 21.

66 Goodman, 'Human Rights Treaties …' (n 52) 532.

67 ILC Guide to Practice (n 1) Guideline 4.5.3, para 3 (emphasis added).

68 Ibid, Guideline 4.5.3, para 4.

69 With regard to the object and purpose of the treaty, the Court stated that '[t]he object and purpose of the Convention thus limit both the freedom of making reservations and that of objecting to them': *Reservations to the Convention on Genocide* (n 4) 24.

70 B Simma and GI Hernández, 'Legal Consequences of an Impermissible Reservation to a Human Rights Treaty: Where Do We Stand?' in E Cannizzaro (ed), *The Law of Treaties Beyond the Vienna Convention* (OUP, 2011) 60, 82.

difficulty with this argument is that although – in line with the permissibility school of thought – the compatibility of a reservation with the object and purpose of a treaty is an objective threshold test for determining the validity of a reservation, the decision-maker is each individual contracting party, rather than an objective third party or an abstract 'adjudicator.' It may be difficult to ascertain the object and purpose of a treaty and subsequently to determine whether the reservation is compatible with it. The entity which determines the compatibility of reservations is discussed in the next section. Rather than settling the matter, the compromise in Guideline 4.5.3 continues the debate.

IV. THE ENTITY WHICH DETERMINES THE COMPATIBILITY OF RESERVATIONS

Following the approach of the permissibility school of thought, the nullity of an invalid reservation does not depend on the objection or the acceptance by a contracting State or organization.[71] In practice, however, the reservation system links the formulation of a reservation to the acquiescence or the objections formulated thereto made by contracting parties for the determination of the compatibility of the reservation with the object and purpose of the treaty in question. This is because '[d]enying a reservation legal effect does not, unfortunately, determine the residual treaty relations between the reserving [entity] and the (other) ... parties.'[72] The Commentary to the ILC Guide notes in this respect that:

> Guideline 4.5.1 [nullity of an invalid reservation] does not resolve all issues concerning the effects of the nullity of an invalid reservation. While it is established that such a reservation cannot produce legal effects, it is essential to answer the question of whether its author becomes a contracting party without the benefit of its reservation, or whether the nullity of its reservation also affects its consent to be bound by the treaty.[73]

In identifying entities competent to determine the compatibility of a reservation, international law proceeds from a decentralized approach, which it then seeks to mitigate through presumptions and cautious

---

[71] ILC Guide on Practice (n 1) Guidelines 4.5.1, and 4.5.2, para 1.

[72] Swaine, 'Treaty Reservations' (n 30), 293. See also Commentary to the ILC Guide (n 5) Commentary to Guideline 4.5.3, 525, para (1).

[73] Ibid, Commentary to Guideline 4.5.1, 525, para (1).

attempts to vest particular institutions with competence to make authoritative assessments.

1. A Decentralized System for Assessing Reservations

Pursuant to the ICJ's advisory opinion, the compatibility of a particular reservation was to be assessed by each of the other State parties 'individually and from its own standpoint.'[74] This clearly corroborated the lack of certainty concerning the legal effects of invalid reservations and the related question of the status of the author of an invalid reservation (discussed in the preceding section). Based on this, Article 19(c) of the Vienna Conventions establish a system of auto- (or self-) interpretation that places emphasis on the reactions of contracting parties to reservations,[75] with the exception of the obligation under Article 20, paragraph 3, of the 1986 Vienna Convention according to which reservations to constituent treaties require the relevant international organization's approval.[76] Interpretation is a powerful tool.[77] Contracting parties individually interpret reservations made to the treaty so as to determine the validity and scope of such reservations, to accept or make objections thereto, and ultimately to determine whether they have entered into bilateral treaty relations with the reserving entity, and if so, with regard to which treaty rules.

Auto-interpretation is commonplace in both international and domestic legal practice. It simply refers to a legal subject's power to interpret its own legal obligations for its own purposes.[78] However, whereas a dispute that arises as a result of conflicting interpretations of contractual obligations made by different legal subjects at the domestic level may be

---

[74] *Reservations to the Convention on Genocide* (n 4) 24.

[75] Ibid, 26.

[76] 1986 Vienna Convention, Article 20, para 3. See ILC Guide to Practice (n 1) Guideline 2.8.8.

[77] See J Klabbers, 'On Rationalism in Politics: Interpretation of Treaties and the World Trade Organization', (2005) 74 Nordic J Intl L 405, 407.

[78] Auto-interpretation is defined by Bin Cheng as 'the right under international law of parties to a dispute each to maintain its own interpretation of the law (and of the facts) without being subject to any legal duty to accept any third-party settlement of the dispute': B Cheng, 'Custom: The Future of General State Practice in a Divided World' in RStJ MacDonald and DM Johnston (eds), *The Structure and Process of International Law* (Martinus Nijhoff Publishers, 1983) 513, 522. See also L Gross, 'States as Organs of International Law, and the Problem of Auto-Interpretation' in GA Lipsky (ed), *Law and Politics in the World Community* (California UP, 1953) 59, 76–7.

judicially determined and definitively settled, auto-interpretation at the international level often constitutes both the start and end point of the matter, as the issue may never be judicially determined or otherwise settled despite the existence of such possibilities. This in turn creates uncertainty in legal relations. With regard to the interpretation of a reservation to a treaty, uncertainty arises in relation to the scope of a State or international organization's consent to be bound by certain provisions, and thus whether certain treaty obligations apply between parties to a treaty and the validity of the reservation, and thus whether the reservation is severable from the instrument of ratification, or whether the treaty provisions to which the reservation attaches are severable from the treaty rules otherwise applicable in bilateral relations between the reserving and objecting parties.

2. Mitigating Uncertainty through Presumptions?

The system of auto-interpretation for determining the compatibility of reservations with the object and purpose of a treaty is a matter that has garnered special attention with regard to human rights treaties. This is because reservations to human rights treaties are particularly popular and numerous,[79] and because by virtue of the nature of the obligations that these kinds of treaties contain, they resist the logic underpinning the reservations system set out under the Vienna Conventions, which is premised on the reciprocal exchange of obligations, and with regard to reservations, auto-interpretation of their compatibility. By contrast, human rights treaties 'are inspired in superior common values and are applied in conformity with the notion of *collective guarantee*.'[80] Auto-interpretation in relation to the compatibility of reservations with the object and purpose of the treaty implies three decisions: determining the object and purpose of a treaty; determining the compatibility of the reservation with the treaty's object and purpose; and, if a reservation is

---

[79] Simma and Hernández, 'Legal Consequences …' (n 70) 61.

[80] AA Cançado Trindade, *The Access of Individuals to International Justice* (OUP, 2011) 90 (emphasis in the original). See also the separate opinions of Judge Cançado Trindade in the Inter-American Court of Human Rights cases of *Blake v Guatemala*, Reparations, Judgment of 22 January 1999 (Ser. C) No. 48 (1999), and *Caesar v Trinidad and Tobago*, Judgment of 11 March 2005 (Ser. C) No. 123 (2005).

considered incompatible, deciding whether to react by objecting to the reservation in question.[81]

The 'object and purpose' test was formulated by the Court,[82] which referred to the right of each contracting party to appraise the validity of the reservation, and is exercisable individually and from its own standpoint.[83] It is the object and purpose of the treaty that the Court thought would mitigate possible divergent views among contracting parties because '[i]t must clearly be assumed that the contracting States are desirous of preserving intact at least what is essential to the object of the Convention.'[84] Rather than mitigating divergent views, dissenting members of the Court thought administration of the object and purpose test would mean that 'there will be no finality or certainty as to the status of the reserving State as long as the admissibility of any reservation that has been objected to is left to the subjective determination by individual States.'[85] The task that each contracting party must undertake is itself complex because the object and purpose of a treaty is an 'unaffiliated and metaphysical concept,'[86] which is difficult to administer in practice because 'Article 19 [of the Vienna Conventions] sheds no light on how a treaty's object and purpose is to be discerned and in fact borders on the self-referential.'[87]

As a result of the nature of the obligations contained in human rights treaties, there may be an inclination to view all the substantive provisions of such treaties to reflect their object and purpose. Dinah Shelton argues

---

[81] ILC Guide to Practice (n 1) Guideline 4.5.2, para 2, recommends that 'a State or an international organization which considers that a reservation is invalid should formulate a reasoned objection as soon as possible.'

[82] *Reservations to the Convention on Genocide* (n 4) 24.

[83] Ibid, 26.

[84] Ibid, 27.

[85] Ibid, Dissenting Opinion of Judges Guerrero, Sir Arnold McNair, Read and Hsu Mo, 44.

[86] Koh, 'Reservations to Multilateral Treaties ...' (n 55) 98.

[87] Simma and Hernández, 'Legal Consequences ...' (n 70) 64. As William Schabas has noted, to follow the interpretative approach set out in the Vienna Conventions could lead to the absurd requirement of having recourse to the treaty's object and purpose in order to establish its object and purpose; see WA Schabas, 'Reservations to Human Rights Treaties: Time for Innovation and Reform', (1994) 32 Canadian Ybk Intl L 39, 48. See also J Klabbers, 'Treaties, Object and Purpose' in Rüdiger Wolfrum (ed.), *Max Planck Encyclopaedia of International Law* (OUP, accessible at http://opil.ouplaw.com/home/EPIL) (article last updated 2013) para 11. The approach taken by the ILC Guide to Practice is to propose that the treaty as a whole be taken into account in order to determine its object and purpose (n 1) Guideline 3.1.5.1.

in this respect that because many human rights treaties codify minimum standards of treatment, 'it would seem inherently incompatible to allow reservations by which guarantees would fall below agreed-upon levels.'[88] The distinction between substantive and procedural obligations in a treaty was drawn in the case concerning *Armed Activities on the Territory of the Congo*, where Rwanda's reservation to Article IX of the Convention on the Prevention and Punishment of the Crime of Genocide, 78 UNTS 277, 9 December 1948, entered into force on 12 January 1951, was argued by the Democratic Republic of the Congo to be incompatible with the object and purpose of the Convention because it would exclude Rwanda from any mechanism for the monitoring and prosecution of genocide.[89] Rwanda argued that its reservation was not incompatible as it related only to a procedural provision of the Convention.[90] The Court favoured the Rwandan argument, noting that the reservation 'does not affect substantive obligations relating to acts of genocide themselves under the Convention,' and consequently, it held in the double negative that it could not conclude that the reservation was incompatible with the object and purpose of the Convention.[91] The ILC attempted to incorporate this approach into its guidance, by providing the general rule under Guideline 3.1.5.7 that '[a] reservation to a treaty provision concerning dispute settlement or the monitoring of the implementation of the treaty is not, in itself, incompatible with the object and purpose of the treaty.'[92]

Other commentators consider that reservations to non-derogable rights in human rights treaties would be incompatible with the object and purpose of a human rights treaty.[93] Judge Cançado Trindade thus writes that 'such reservations would be, in my understanding, without any *caveat*, incompatible with the object and purpose of those treaties.'[94]

---

[88] D Shelton, 'State Practice on Reservations to Human Rights Treaties', (1983) 1 Canadian Human Rights Ybk 205, 209.

[89] *Armed Activities on the Territory of the Congo (New Application: 2002) (Democratic Republic of the Congo v Rwanda)*, Jurisdiction and Admissibility, Judgment, ICJ Rep 2006 (3 February) 30, para 57.

[90] Ibid, 30, para 61.

[91] Ibid, 32, para 67.

[92] ILC Guide to Practice (n 1) Guideline 3.1.5.7.

[93] Human Rights Committee, General Comment No 24, CCPR/C/21/Rev.1/Add.6, 11 November 1994, para 10: 'While there is no automatic correlation between reservations to non-derogable provisions, and reservations which offend against the object and purpose of the Covenant, a State has a heavy onus to justify such a reservation.'

[94] Cançado Trindade, *Access of Individuals to International Justice* (n 80) 90.

The ILC follows this approach in broad brushstrokes, but includes a caveat that reservations to provisions concerning rights from which no derogation is permissible under any circumstances will not contravene the prohibition set out in Guideline 3.1.5.4 if 'the reservation in question is compatible with the essential rights and obligations arising out of that treaty.'[95] This singling out of non-derogable obligations for the protection afforded under the object and purpose test has 'a certain surface attractiveness,'[96] but is problematic given the fact that reservations to some derogable obligations could also be considered incompatible with the object and purpose of a treaty.[97]

It is also the task of a contracting party to consider the compatibility of the reservation in question with the object and purpose of the treaty. This is a task that will not necessarily follow consecutively from a determination of the object and purpose of the treaty. Indeed, the two tasks are likely to be closely entwined, with the terms of the reservation under consideration testing the parameters of the treaty's object and purpose. Whether undertaken separately or jointly, both tasks risk placing political and other interests of the objecting State above the protection of the integrity of the treaty, particularly in the case of human rights treaties. The Human Rights Committee noted in this respect that '[i]t is an inappropriate task [for the determination of the compatibility of a reservation with the object and purpose of the treaty] for States parties in relation to human rights treaties.'[98] Bruno Simma considers the assessment to be one which will be carried out in a 'typically bilateralist and subjective way.'[99]

There is an assumption that when making a determination about a treaty's object and purpose, and whether a reservation is incompatible with the object and purpose, contracting parties 'are desirous of preserving intact at least what is essential to the object of the [treaty].'[100] Even assuming good faith on the part of contracting parties in adhering to this

---

95 ILC Guide to Practice (n 1) Guideline 3.1.5.4.

96 R Higgins, 'United Nations: Still a Force for Peace', (1989) 52 MLR 1, reprinted in R Higgins, *Themes and Theories: Selected Essays, Speeches, and Writings in International Law* (OUP, 2009) 509, 522.

97 Ibid.

98 Human Rights Committee, General Comment No 24 (n 93) para 18.

99 B Simma, 'Reservations to Human Rights Treaties: Some Recent Developments' in A Rest, G Hafner, G Loibl, K Zemanek and L Sucharipa-Behrmann (eds), *Liber Amicorum Professor Seidl-Hohenveldern in Honour of his 80th Birthday* (Kluwer Law International, 1998) 659, 662–3.

100 *Reservations to the Convention on Genocide* (n 4) 27.

'rule of conduct'[101] there nevertheless arises in connection with reservations to human rights treaties the particular difficulty of the reaction – or, more commonly, the lack of reaction – by other contracting parties to a reservation that on its face appears incompatible with the treaty's object and purpose. A contracting party may remain silent and not object to a reservation for any number of 'weighty political reasons,'[102] or some other reason, unconnected to its determination of the compatibility of the reservation with the object and purpose of the treaty. Rosalyn Higgins has gone further and suggested that 'one might say there is a collusion to allow penetrating and disturbing reservations to go unchallenged.'[103] With this in mind, silence with regard to a reservation should be regarded as just that. It should not be inferred that by remaining silent, a contracting party views a reservation as being compatible with the treaty's object and purpose.[104]

3. Towards Authoritative Pronouncements?

The issues raised by auto-interpretation with respect to reservations in turn raise the question whether an objective third party would be competent to determine the object and purpose of a treaty, and the compatibility of reservations with it. The competence of an international court to adjudge such matters, in line with the principle of the free choice of means for the peaceful settlement of a dispute,[105] is uncontroversial. As the Court itself acknowledged in the *Reservations to the Convention on Genocide* case, contracting parties may 'decide to adopt a position on the jurisdictional plane in respect of [a] divergence [of views regarding the compatibility of a reservation with the treaty's object and purpose] and to settle the dispute which thus arises either by special agreement or by the procedure laid down in [the treaty in question].'[106]

---

[101] Ibid, 24.

[102] Aust, *Treaty Law* (n 1) 119.

[103] Higgins, 'United Nations …' (n 96) 519.

[104] Cançado Trindade, *Access of Individuals to International Justice* (n 80) 90.

[105] UNGA Res 2625 (XXV), 'Declaration on Principles of International Law Concerning Friendly Relations and Cooperation among States in Accordance with the Charter of the United Nations', UN doc A/RES/2625(XXV), para 5 of the 'Principle that States shall settle their international disputes by peaceful means in such a manner that international peace and security and justice are not endangered'. See also *East Timor (Portugal v Australia)*, Judgment, ICJ Rep 1995 (30 June) 101, para 26.

[106] *Reservations to the Convention on Genocide* (n 4) 27.

Of greater debate is the role of treaty-monitoring bodies in deciding such matters. Guideline 3.2.1 recognizes the competence of a treaty-monitoring body to assess the permissibility of reservations pursuant to discharging the functions entrusted to it. In slightly convoluted terms, the Guideline then specifies that '[t]he assessment made by such a body in the exercise of this competence has no greater legal effect than that of the act which contains it.'[107] In other words, 'the legal force of their findings in that regard cannot exceed that which is generally recognized for the instruments that they are competent to adopt.'[108] The ILC is cautious not to suggest that the assessment of a treaty-monitoring body is binding as the legal force of any such assessment will depend on the particular treaty in question. It merely recommends that a State or international organization which formulates a reservation is required to 'give consideration' to an assessment of the permissibility of its reservation carried out by a relevant treaty-monitoring body.[109]

The approach taken by the ILC of deferring to the relevant treaty in question, and not pushing development in this area further, may be disappointing to those who consider that reservations to human rights treaties should be subject to 'a system of objective determination of the compatibility or otherwise of [the] reservations with the object and purpose of human rights treaties' made by treaty bodies rather than contracting parties.[110] The means for achieving assessments by treaty bodies with the necessary legal force could include the inclusion of 'an express provision in future human rights treaties' or 'the adoption of protocols to the existing instruments.'[111] However, the ILC refrained from recommending that States and international organizations include specific clauses conferring competence on a treaty-monitoring body to assess the permissibility of reservations and specifying the legal effects of such assessment, 'even though that would undoubtedly be desirable when feasible.'[112]

Others will be troubled that the ILC Guide has recognized the capacity of some treaty bodies to engage in such a practice, and for 'promoting

---

[107] ILC Guide to Practice (n 1) Guideline 3.2.1, para 2.

[108] Commentary to the ILC Guide (n 5) Commentary to Guideline 3.2.1, 400, para (4).

[109] ILC Guide to Practice (n 1) Guideline 3.2.3.

[110] Cançado Trindade, *Access of Individuals to International Justice* (n 80) 96.

[111] Ibid.

[112] Commentary to the ILC Guide (n 5) Commentary to Guideline 3.2.2, 401, para (3).

this kind of authority.'[113] Opposition to treaty bodies playing such a role are based on a concern that their participation would augment the number of entities assessing objections to reservations, thereby 'increas[ing] the likelihood that potentially problematic objections will be caught, but also increas[ing] the likelihood of conflicting pronouncements.'[114] This was a problem foreseen by the ILC, but one which it was thought would be the lesser of two evils: 'it is probably better to have too much assessment than no assessment at all.'[115] There is also some uncertainty inbuilt in the timing of such assessments by human rights bodies. Whereas contracting parties must formulate objections to reservations within twelve months,[116] the same is not the case for treaty-monitoring bodies. There have thus been proposals for a similar time limit to apply to assessments made by treaty-monitoring bodies. However, such bodies do not have the same control as the contracting parties over the timing of their assessment or pronouncements concerning the permissibility of reservations.

The difficulties that arise with respect to human rights treaties have led to claims of a fragmented system,[117] and calls for human rights treaties to be formally subject to a different reservations regime than the regime in place under the 1969 and 1986 Vienna Conventions.[118] This proposal presupposes the ability to clearly identify treaties falling within such a category. The problems with safeguarding the values set out in 'human rights treaties' through an application of the Vienna Conventions' system of reservations could equally be argued to arise with regard to treaties pertaining to international humanitarian law and environmental law, which are also 'normative treaties' insofar as they display an '*imperméabilité à la réciprocité*' ('impermeability to reciprocity').[119] In this

---

[113] Swaine, 'Treaty Reservations' (n 30) 300.

[114] Ibid.

[115] Commentary to the ILC Guide (n 5) Commentary to Guideline 3.2, 398, para (12).

[116] 1969 and 1986 Vienna Conventions, Article 20, para 5. The time limit applies from the date of receipt of notification of the reservation (or the date of the expression of the objecting contracting party of its consent to be bound).

[117] Cançado Trindade, *Access of Individuals to International Justice* (n 80) 97.

[118] E Riedel, 'International Covenant on Economic, Social and Cultural Rights (1966)' in Rüdiger Wolfrum (ed.), *Max Planck Encyclopaedia of International Law* (OUP, available online at http://opil.ouplaw.com/home/EPIL) (article last updated, 2007) para 24.

[119] F Coulée, 'A Propos d'une Controverse Autour d'une Codification en Cours: les Réactions aux Réserves Incompatibles avec l'Objet et le But des Traités de Protection des Droits de l'Homme' [Concerning a controversy about

respect, it has been argued that human rights treaties are not a special case. Rather, they face the same difficulties under the reservations regime as any other treaty that attempts to reconcile different religious and social systems,[120] and that the reservations regime under the Vienna Conventions is flexible enough to provide appropriate solutions for all kinds of treaties, including human rights treaties.[121] The approach taken by the ILC not to propose a separate reservations regime for a particular kind of treaty is in keeping with its provision of guidance in conformity with the reservations regime under the Vienna Conventions.

V. OPEN QUESTIONS: A RESEARCH AGENDA

The knotty issues that arise out of the lacunae and ambiguities in the 1969 and 1986 Vienna Conventions with regard to reservations to treaties continue to subsist despite the most recent effort by the ILC to provide practical guidance to States and international organizations. These issues include matters addressed in this chapter, namely mechanisms for protecting the integrity of human rights treaties from reservations that are incompatible with the treaty's object and purpose, identifying the object and purpose of a treaty, and the uncertainty that continues to prevail regarding the status of the author of an invalid reservation. In many respects, the research agenda in this area of treaty law corresponds to these persisting uncertainties and remains unchanged since the ILC first started its work, despite its most recent contribution.

The continuing lack of consensus on key issues concerning reservations to treaties, despite lengthy, vigorous debate, raises a more fundamental question for the future direction of research posed many years ago by Catherine Redgwell: should such matters be resolved at all?[122] Should we even strive to reach consensus? The current ambiguities that dog this area of treaty law could paradoxically provide the necessary flexibility to encourage greater levels of treaty participation. By contrast, settled rules

---

an ongoing codification: Reactions to reservations incompatible with the object and purpose of Treaties for the Protection of Human Rights] in P Amselek (ed.), *Liberté, Justice, Tolérance. Mélanges Offerts à Gérard Cohen-Jonathan* [Liberty, Justice, Tolerance. Collection in honour of Gerard Cohen-Jonathan] (Bruylant, 2004) 500, 502. See also Redgwell, 'Universality or Integrity? …' (n 52) 280.

120 Aust, *Treaty Law* (n 1) 122.

121 Pellet and Müller, 'Reservations to Human Rights Treaties …' (n 58) 523.

122 Redgwell, 'Universality or Integrity? …' (n 52) 279.

on some of the stickier issues relating to reservations could have a deterrent effect on treaty participation. States and international organizations may be more reluctant to participate in a treaty if they are unable to agree to be bound by certain provisions, in the knowledge that a reservation may not adequately protect their interests. Alternatively, if the current ambiguities about reservations were clarified, ambiguity may be sought elsewhere by watering down treaty provisions during treaty negotiations, and thereby dispensing with the need to formulate reservations at all.

It is preferable to encourage treaty participation conditioned by reservations, rather than diluting the original treaty obligations, because reservations may over time become redundant. In the case of a State, a reservation may become redundant as a result of its internal law changing so as to no longer conflict with a particular treaty provision to which the reservation pertains, which could follow a regime change from an undemocratic State to a democratic State.[123] In such cases, contracting parties are encouraged to withdraw their reservations.[124] The net result of this activity is that over time there will be high levels of treaty participation and increasingly fewer reservations to undiluted treaty obligations. Ambiguity about the effect of a reservation or the status of a contracting party which has formulated a reservation can thus buy time for the reservation to become redundant, and for it subsequently to be withdrawn.

The choice by the Special Rapporteur Alain Pellet to produce a non-binding instrument in the form of the ILC Guide undoubtedly had a strong bearing on the substance of the Guidelines contained therein, as it was open to the Special Rapporteur to take – sometimes quite controversial – positions on highly contentious matters that a different form of instrument would not have allowed. However, this was a savvy choice of instrument because as a guide, it not only poses no threat to the

---

[123] An additional point is that it may be in a State's overriding interests to become a party to certain treaties, such as a human rights treaty. An undemocratic State's interests should not be privileged at the time of ratification with regard to a reservation it has formulated over the interests of a successor democratic State at a later point in time, when the reservation comes into question and perhaps could be withdrawn. See Goodman, 'Human Rights Treaties …' (n 52) 554.

[124] ILC Guide to Practice (n 1) Guideline 2.5.3 entitled 'Periodic review of the usefulness of reservations.' Undertaking a periodic review of reservations to consider withdrawing those which no longer serve their purpose is an approach advocated by treaty-monitoring bodies, particularly in the field of human rights; see Cançado Trindade, *Access of Individuals to International Justice* (n 80) 97.

reservations regime under the Vienna Conventions, but it also preserves the ambiguities prevalent in that system. It is submitted that the prevailing ambiguity about reservations could constitute an important flexibility device that serves to protect the integrity of treaties. This is an open question to research more carefully before continuing the ongoing debate about key issues concerning reservations.

11. *Pacta sunt servanda* versus flexibility in the suspension and termination of treaties

Sotirios-Ioannis Lekkas and Antonios Tzanakopoulos

I. INTRODUCTION

Pacta sunt servanda – the rule that treaties are binding on the parties and must be performed in good faith – is universally accepted as the 'basis of all treaty law'.[1] Still, fundamental as it may be, it is neither unqualified nor completely isolated from other considerations.[2] Treaties are the principal means that States and/or other subjects of international law use to formalize their mutual commitments. It would defeat the very purpose of their conclusion if they were not resistant to subsequent developments, or if the commitments undertaken therein could be easily retracted by

[1] GG Fitzmaurice, 'Second Report on the Law of Treaties' in Yearbook of the ILC ('YBILC') (1957) vol. II (A/CN.4/107) 16, 20 para 6. The rule is codified in Article 26, Vienna Convention on the Law of Treaties (adopted 23 May 1969, entered into force 27 January 1980) 1155 UNTS 331 ('VCLT'); see also Preamble, para 3 VCLT; also Article 26, 'Vienna Convention on the Law of Treaties between States and International Organizations or between International Organizations' (adopted 21 March 1986, not yet into force) UN Doc A/CONF.129/15. Although some of the issues we discuss might have implications for international organizations, we focus primarily on inter-State relationships. Cf commentary to Article 23(1), ILC, 'Draft Articles on the Law of Treaties with Commentaries' YBILC (1966) vol. II (A/CN.4/SER.A/1966/Add.1) 177 ('DALT'), 211.

[2] See initial phrasing of the provision in Article 5(1), GG Fitzmaurice, 'Report on the Law of Treaties' YBILC (1956) vol. II (A/CN.4/101) 104, 108. Article 26 provides that only treaties 'in force' are covered by the rule. Questions of invocation aside, validity is thus a qualification of, not an exception to, the rule (cf J Salmon, 'Article 26: Convention of 1969' in O Corten and P Klein, *The Vienna Conventions on the Law of Treaties: A Commentary* (OUP, 2011) 660, 666, 668–70; ME Villiger, *Commentary to the 1969 Vienna Convention on the Law of Treaties* (Martinus Nijhoff, 2009) 325).

one party.[3] On the other hand, if no room is left to accommodate change, a treaty may lose its foundation on the agreement of the parties, or its object and purpose may be frustrated over time, turning its provisions into a dead letter.[4] More pragmatically, the negotiating parties would more likely be reluctant to enter into an agreement that binds them unconditionally in perpetuity.[5]

The tension between stability and change underlies international law in its entirety and, particularly, the law of treaties.[6] It is exemplified in the *pacta sunt servanda* rule's juxtaposition to grounds for invoking unilaterally the suspension or termination of the *pactum*, as is, for example, the *clausula rebus sic stantibus*.[7] How can one such rule be admitted without fundamentally weakening the other? And how is a proper balance between stability and flexibility to be struck?

The need for flexibility pervades all stages of the life of a treaty, and there are ways to accommodate it without affecting the duty of performance.[8] At the stage of negotiation and conclusion, the parties may, for example, devise appropriate substantive provisions or exceptions, or submit interpretative declarations, or reservations, if permitted.[9] During the operation stage, subsequent developments may be accommodated

---

[3] M Lachs, 'The Developments and General Trends of International Law in our Time' (1980) 169 *Recueil des cours de l'académie de droit international* 9, 190.

[4] C Tomuschat, '*Pacta sunt servanda*' in A Fischer-Lescano, H-P Gasser, T Marauhn and N Ronzitti (eds), *Frieden in Freiheit – Peace in Liberty – Paix en liberté: Festschrift für Michael Bothe zum 70. Geburtstag* (Nomos, 2008) 1047, 1048.

[5] LR Helfer, 'Exiting Treaties' (2005) 91 *Virginia Law Review* 1579, 1599–1601.

[6] H Lauterpacht, *The Function of Law in the International Community* (first published 1933, reissue OUP, 2011) 266.

[7] For a discussion of this 'contradiction' from a particular angle, see M Koskenniemi, *From Apology to Utopia: The Structure of International Legal Argument* (first published 1989, reissue CUP, 2005) 342–5.

[8] For a concise and comprehensive illustration, see LR Helfer, 'Flexibility in International Agreements' in JF Dunoff and MA Pollack (eds), *Interdisciplinary Perspectives on International Law and International Relations: The State of the Art* (CUP, 2012) 175, 179.

[9] See the recent work of the ILC, 'Guide to Practice on Reservations to Treaties' in 'Report of the International Law Commission on the Work of its 63rd Session' (26 April–3 June 2011 and 4 July–12 August 2011) UN Doc A/66/10, 19 para 75.

through interpretation and modification or amendment.[10] These matters are not covered here, as they are dealt with by Jean d'Aspremont in his contribution to this *Research Handbook*.

By contrast, certain circumstances may call for non-compliance with obligations under the treaty. In such cases, the law of treaties provides, *in extremis*, for the formal dissolution of the *pactum* as such (termination of the treaty), or for the withdrawal of a certain party, or for the suspension of operation of the treaty. This takes place when all the parties so agree, or by operation of the law, or in accordance with the treaty's own terms.[11] Most importantly, a party may take action to unilaterally assert the termination of a treaty, to withdraw from it, or to suspend its operation. The International Law Commission ('ILC') Working Group on 'Treaties over Time' drew particular attention in its initial recommendations to the grounds of termination or suspension that clearly relate to the passage of time, such as the supervening impossibility of performance and the fundamental change of circumstances.[12] Other grounds, potentially beyond the VCLT, such as *desuetude* or obsolescence, were also highlighted.[13] Besides, a breach of a treaty obligation might be excused in the exceptional cases of *force majeure* or necessity under the law of responsibility.[14]

General international law, however, has always been reticent towards allowing unilateral action to abdicate treaty obligations,[15] and this is reflected in its codification in the VCLT. The parties to a treaty may agree to more flexible modalities in advance, and most treaties concluded nowadays indeed provide expressly for their duration, and/or for denunciation or withdrawal ('exit clauses').[16] Yet again, the tension seems to persist on that level only slightly altered: how to achieve consent, while

---

[10] G Nolte, 'Treaties over Time in Particular: Subsequent Agreement and Practice' in ILC, 'Report of the International Law Commission on the Work of its 60th Session' (5 May–7 June and 7 July–8 August 2008) UN Doc A/63/10, Annex A ('Treaties over Time Recommendations'), 366 paras 7–10; cf Articles 31–32 and 39–41 VCLT.

[11] Fitzmaurice, 'Second Report …' (n 1) 25.

[12] Treaties over Time Recommendations (n 10) 366 para 8.

[13] Ibid 366 paras 8 and 10.

[14] Pt I Ch. V, ILC, 'Draft Articles on State Responsibility for Internationally Wrongful Acts with Commentaries' in ILC, 'Report of the International Law Commission on its Fifty-Third Session' YBILC (2001) vol. II (A/56/10) 31 ('ARSIWA').

[15] A McNair, *The Law of Treaties* (OUP, 1961) 493; Fitzmaurice, 'Second Report …' (n 1) 22.

[16] A Aust, *Modern Treaty Law and Practice* (2nd edn, CUP, 2007) 277.

preventing opportunistic exit?[17] As a counterbalance, general international law (reflected in Articles 70 and 72 VCLT) only allows operation of termination or withdrawal for the future, without affecting acquired rights of the parties, while – more importantly – some treaties provide for their continuing operation even after termination or withdrawal takes effect in order to safeguard rights of third parties and private entities who were the beneficiaries of the now dissolved *pactum* ('survival clauses').[18] In principle then, the internalization of such concerns to the treaty itself, rather than tension between commitment and exit, could be more aptly described as an expression and reaffirmation of the *pacta sunt servanda* rule.[19]

This chapter starts with a rough sketch of the balance drawn in general international law between treaty stability and the need for change as reflected in the current law of treaties on suspension and termination, and its relationship with the law of responsibility. It then turns to the practical methods of internalization used to accommodate exit without compromising the expectations of the other parties and third party beneficiaries. In what follows, we discuss the grounds allowing for unilateral termination of, withdrawal from, or suspension of a treaty (section II). While the general international law of treaties allows for such 'flexibility' in termination or suspension, in reality it does so under such strict conditions as to confirm the fundamental principle that *pacta sunt* indeed *servanda,* and unilateral exit is heavily circumscribed. The law of State responsibility may be resorted to for help in this connection: while doctrinally clearly distinguishable (defence for the violation of the obligation as opposed to grounds for its extinction), circumstances precluding wrongfulness may be seen as having a function similar to that of suspension (section III). However, such defences are also difficult to invoke successfully, so as to confirm, in practice, the *pacta sunt servanda* rule. The apparent tension between *pacta sunt servanda* and the seemingly multifarious bases for terminating, withdrawing from, or suspending a treaty reveals itself then as only apparent. Section IV turns to the provisions of treaties providing their own rules for termination, withdrawal, or suspension, as indeed allowed under general international law. Here, whatever apparent tension completely disappears: the exit *is* (part of) the *pactum,* so that unilateral termination or withdrawal merely serves to reinforce the *pacta sunt servanda* rule. And not only that, but parties to

---

17 Helfer, 'Exiting …' (n 5) 1599–1601.

18 Eg, Aust, *Modern Treaty Law* (n 16) 286–8.

19 SE Nahlik, 'The Grounds of Invalidity and Termination of Treaties' (1971) 65 AJIL 736, 746.

treaties have devised methods to guarantee, in certain situations, the continued operation of provisions in the dissolved *pactum*. Section V concludes, setting out an agenda for future research on the subject.

II. *PACTA SUNT SERVANDA* AND UNILATERAL SUSPENSION AND TERMINATION UNDER GENERAL INTERNATIONAL LAW

The current general international law of treaties is premised upon a fundamental distinction between the formal and procedural aspects of a treaty, and the obligations embodied in that treaty.[20] The VCLT was never meant as a comprehensive code on an international 'law of obligations'.[21] Indeed, the only provision that deals expressly with performance as such is the *pacta sunt servanda* rule,[22] this 'cornerstone of international relations'[23] that seems all-encompassing. It is in the context of this 'staccato statement'[24] that the rules on grounds for unilateral termination and suspension were developed and subsequently cautiously codified as default rules providing for the formal end or the temporary disruption of the life of treaties subject to a complex and cumbersome procedure.[25]

When it is possible for one of the parties to the *pactum* to unilaterally disengage from it, the basic rule that *pacta sunt servanda* evidently comes under pressure. Indeed general international law is inimical to such unilateral action, and the VCLT itself codified this reluctance in establishing a presumption against unilateral disengagement in Article 56, when the treaty is silent as to its suspension or termination or to withdrawal from it.[26] The VCLT further allows, through the operation of

---

[20] Eg, ILC, 'Report of the International Law Commission Covering its Second Session' YBILC (1950) vol. II (A/1316) 364, 380 para 161; S Rosenne, 'Bilateralism and Community Interests in the Codified Law of Treaties' in W Friedmann, L Henkin and O Lissitzyn (eds), *Transnational Law in a Changing Society: Essays in Honor of Phillip C Jessup* (Columbia UP, 1972) 202, 210–11.

[21] S Rosenne, *Breach of Treaty* (Grotius, 1985) 4.

[22] J Crawford and S Olleson, 'The Exception of Non-Performance: Links between the Law of Treaties and the Law of State Responsibility' (2000) 21 AYBIL 55, 59.

[23] Villiger, *Commentary* (n 2) 363.

[24] Ibid 368.

[25] Articles 60–62, 65–68 VCLT; Fitzmaurice, 'Second Report …' (n 1) 19 para 2.

[26] See, eg, Villiger, *Commentary* (n 2) 700–701.

pacta sunt servanda, a number of methods that can bring about suspension or termination of treaties. This can be done, for example, through the conclusion of a new treaty between the same parties which is incompatible with the previous treaty (that is, through a new *pactum*), whether explicitly[27] or implicitly.[28] Most importantly the parties may allow for unilateral unconditional (or otherwise) termination or withdrawal in the treaty itself.[29] This latter issue is dealt with in section IV below. We focus here instead on the grounds which can be unilaterally invoked to terminate, withdraw from, or suspend a treaty, as these are the ones traditionally seen as being in tension with the *pacta sunt servanda* rule.

The grounds provided in the VCLT – reflecting 'in many respects' customary international law[30] – could be divided roughly into two categories. Article 60 VCLT is 'inward looking' in that only the will and conduct of the parties is implicated: no external events affect the treaty, but only party conduct. The rule aims at re-establishing the contractual

---

[27] Eg, the new international investment agreements ('IIAs') to be entered into between the EU, which now has exclusive competence on issues of investment after the Lisbon Treaty, and third States will include, according to the Commission, an explicit provision replacing all EU member States' IIAs with the relevant State with the new EU IIA: see the leaked Comprehensive Economic and Trade Agreement ('CETA') draft investment chapter at section 7 on final provisions, accessed 1 October 2013 at www.tradejustice.ca/wp-content/uploads/2013/10/Investment-chapter-annotated-consoldated-text-31-May-2013.doc.

According to an EU suggestion, a provision on relationship of the CETA investment chapter with other agreements would be worded in part as follows: 'This Agreement replaces the agreements between Member States of the European Union and Canada listed in Annex (Y). The provisions of such agreements shall cease to apply from the date of entry into force of this Agreement'. See also Regulation (EU) No 1219/2012 of the European Parliament and of the Council establishing transitional arrangements for bilateral investment treaties ('BITs') between Member States and third countries, OJ L 351/40 (12 Dec 2012) Article 3. This may create interesting problems, such as whether relevant survival clauses (on which see section IV below) in the EU member States' BITs with that State will operate and allow an investor to seek to rely on them, eg, because they offer better protection than the new EU IIA with the relevant State.

[28] See Articles 57–59 VCLT.

[29] See Article 42(2) VCLT.

[30] Eg, *Gabčíkovo-Nagymaros Project (Hungary/Slovakia)*, Judgment, ICJ Rep 1997, 7, 38 para 46; *Fisheries Jurisdiction (United Kingdom v Iceland)*, Jurisdiction, ICJ Rep 1973, 18 para 36; *Fisheries Jurisdiction (Germany v Iceland)*, Jurisdiction, ICJ Rep 1973, 63 para 36.

symmetry that has been upset due to a material breach by a party.[31] Conversely, Articles 61, on supervening impossibility of performance, and 62 VCLT, on fundamental change of circumstances, address situations where the source of frustration is independent from the actions of the parties and external to the treaty in question.[32] The latter two grounds are of particular interest to this inquiry.

The provision of Article 61, despite its somewhat deceiving title, provides for a specific case of supervening impossibility of performance resulting from the 'disappearance or destruction of an object indispensable for the execution of the treaty'.[33] These grounds of termination or suspension, however, may not be invoked if the impossibility is the result of a breach by the party invoking the relevant grounds of any obligation under the treaty or any other international obligation owed to any other party to the treaty.[34] The provision raises several questions of interpretation, indicatively, whether it encompasses only the disappearance of a physical object or also that of a legal situation or regime,[35] and whether the resulting impossibility must be absolute.[36] Yet, in the two cases where Article 61 was invoked none of these questions was resolved. In

---

[31] LA Sicilianos, 'The Relationship between Reprisals and Denunciation or Suspension of a Treaty' (1993) 4 EJIL 341, 345; Villiger, *Commentary* (n 2) 738; B Simma and CJ Tams, 'Reacting against Treaty Breaches' in DB Hollis (ed), *The Oxford Guide to Treaties* (OUP, 2012) 576, 582. See further the contribution by CJ Tams in this *Research Handbook.*

[32] Classification based on H Waldock, 'Second Report on Law of Treaties' YBILC (1963) vol. II (A/CN.4/156 and Add.1-3) 36, 78; see also Q D Nguyen, P Dailler and A Pellet, *Droit International Public* (8th edn, LGDJ, 2009) 339, 344; S Rosenne, *Developments in the Law of Treaties 1945–1986* (CUP, 1989) 337.

[33] P Bodeau Livinec and J Morgan-Foster, 'Article 61: Convention of 1969' in Corten and Klein, *The Vienna Conventions* (n 2) 1382, 1383.

[34] Article 61(2) VCLT. The qualification added by Waldock (Fifth Report YBICL (1966) vol. II (A/CN.4/183 and Add. 1-4) 1, 39) was rejected in the initial ILC draft, but was restated later during the Vienna Conference 1968-1969: see Villiger, *Commentary* (n 2) 755.

[35] The ILC appears to have accepted some scenarios of legal impossibility (Commentary to Article 61 para 3, 'Draft Articles on the Law of Treaties between States and International Organizations or between International Organizations with Commentaries' YBILC (1982) vol. II(2) (A/37/10) 17). The ICJ did not pronounce on the matter *Gabčíkovo-Nagymaros* (n 30) 63–4 para 103.

[36] See Bodeau Livinec and Morgan-Foster, 'Article 61 …' (n 33) 1395–6; T Giegerich, 'Article 61' in O Dörr and K Schmalenbach (eds), *Vienna Convention on the Law of Treaties: A Commentary* (Springer, 2012) 1051, 1057; for a concise summary of the ILC's discussions on the issue, see M Fitzmaurice,

LAFICO/Burundi, the contested issue was whether the severance of diplomatic relations and the expulsion of several Libyan managers of the company owned jointly by the two States parties could amount to impossibility to perform the agreement establishing the joint venture.[37] On the other hand, in *Gabčíkovo-Nagymaros*, Hungary argued that the essential object of the agreement – in the event, a joint economic investment consistent with environmental protection – had permanently disappeared.[38] The impossibility was found in both cases to have resulted from a breach on the part of the State invoking the relevant grounds of termination.[39]

Turning to the second grounds, Article 62 originates from the proverbial opposite (or implied condition[40]) of *pacta sunt servanda* – *rebus sic stantibus* – and recognizes the need for dissolution of treaties in case of fundamental change of circumstances rendering them inapplicable.[41] The provision is worded in negative terms in order to stress its exceptional character.[42] It requires cumulatively a change that is fundamental; unforeseen by the parties; the circumstances that have changed to have constituted an essential basis of the consent of the parties to be bound by the treaty; and the effect of the change to be such as to radically transform the obligations still to be performed.[43] Additionally, these grounds of termination may not be invoked with respect to treaties establishing a boundary or if the change is the result of a breach by the

'Exceptional Circumstances and Treaty Commitments' in Hollis, *The Oxford Guide* (n 31) 605, 607–10.

37 *LAFICO/Republic of Burundi* [1991] 96 ILR 279, 317–18 para 54.

38 *Gabčíkovo-Nagymaros* (n 30) 63–4 para 103. It should be highlighted that the Court also took note of the fact that the treaty established procedures for negotiation and readjustment.

39 Ibid; *LAFICO/Burundi* (n 37) para 54; see also Fitzmaurice, 'Exceptional Circumstances … ' (n 36) 610–12; C Binder, 'Stability and Change in Times of Fragmentation: The Limits of *Pacta Sunt Servanda* Revisited' (2012) 25 LJIL 909, 914.

40 According to which all agreements are made under the implied condition that the circumstances will remain as they are: *conventio omnis intellegitur clausula rebus sic stantibus*.

41 Waldock, 'Second Report …' (n 32) 80; see, eg, L Oppenheim, *International Law: A Treatise* (Longman, 1920–21) 698: 'this exceptional condition is as necessary for International Law and international intercourse as the rule *pacta sunt servanda*'.

42 *Gabčíkovo-Nagymaros* (n 30) 64–5 para 104.

43 Ibid; Article 62(1) VCLT; DALT Commentary to Article 59 (n 1) para 9.

invoking party of any obligation under that treaty or any other international obligation owed to any other party to the treaty.[44]

The sparse case law on Article 62 or on the customary rule that it 'in many respects' reflects has been well recorded and need not be examined thoroughly here.[45] The ICJ found in *Icelandic Fisheries* and *Gabčíkovo-Nagymaros* that the requirements of the provision were not met.[46] Notably, in that latter case the ICJ dismissed Hungary's claim that the economic and political changes brought about by the dissolution of the USSR had a sufficiently close link to the object and purpose of the joint investment project agreement. Additionally, the later shifts in environmental protection and law 'were not entirely unforeseen', and could have been accommodated through relevant mechanisms within the treaty.[47] A rather unique instance of judicial acceptance of a fundamental change of circumstances as allowing unilateral termination was that before the European Court of Justice in the *Racke* case.[48]

Under the VCLT, the substantive grounds for unilaterally asserting suspension or termination of a treaty are complemented by a cumbersome procedural regime.[49] Article 65(1) VCLT makes the invocation of grounds of termination or suspension contingent upon notification. Subsequent provisions set a minimum 3-month period during which any party may protest the claim.[50] In case the parties achieve no agreed solution the VCLT provides for dispute resolution chosen by the parties, and, in case of disagreement, for mandatory conciliation in accordance with its Annex 1.[51]

The cumbersome procedure established by the VCLT is clearly aimed at curbing unilateral exit from treaty obligations: the grounds can be unilaterally invoked but can produce no automatic effect. Following the VCLT procedure will effectively lead either to agreement between the parties for termination or suspension of the treaty (even if achieved through diplomatic methods of dispute settlements), or to the resolution

---

44 Article 62(2) VCLT.

45 Eg, Binder, 'Stability and Change ...' (n 39) 912–14; Fitzmaurice, 'Exceptional Circumstances ...' (n 36) 615–20.

46 *UK Fisheries Jurisdiction* (n 30) 20 para 40; *German Fisheries Jurisdiction* (n 30) 64 para 40.

47 *Gabčíkovo-Nagymaros* (n 30) 64–5 para 104.

48 Case 162/96, *Racke GmbH & Co v Hauptzollamt Mainz* [1998] ECR I-3655 paras 55–8.

49 Articles 65–68 VCLT.

50 Article 65(2) VCLT.

51 Articles 65(3), 66 VCLT.

of the dispute by an independent third party, again as a result of the agreement of the parties to that effect. In reality, the procedure completely safeguards the *pacta sunt servanda* rule by requiring agreement (read: a new *pactum* of sorts) in order to effectuate suspension or termination.

In practice the dispute resolution provisions have found little application.[52] In *Gabčíkovo-Nagymaros*, the ICJ stated that '[b]oth Parties agree that Articles 65 to 67 of the Vienna Convention on the Law of Treaties, if not codifying customary law, at least generally reflect customary international law'.[53] Although it is sometimes cited as proof for the customary status of the provisions,[54] it reads more like an acknowledgment of an agreement between the parties as to applicable international law. Indeed, in *Armed Activities on the Territory of the Congo* the ICJ considered that the rules of Article 66 were 'not declaratory of customary international law'.[55] It went on to clarify that '[n]or have the Parties otherwise agreed to apply Article 66 between themselves', as Hungary and Slovakia obviously had done in *Gabčíkovo-Nagymaros*.[56] Finally, the European Court of Justice found in *Racke* that the procedural requirements laid down in Article 65 of the VCLT 'do not form part of customary international law'.[57]

If the procedural regime does not reflect customary law, as argued above, two cogent questions arise: the first is whether there can be further grounds for unilateral termination or suspension beyond the VCLT and thus not subject to its procedural regime. The second is whether the – in most respects – customary norms of Articles 60 to 64, and especially the rules on supervening impossibility of performance and the *clausula rebus sic stantibus* (could) have the same content in customary law as under the VCLT, in view of the lack of a strict procedural regime under customary law. It is to these questions we now turn, taking the second one first.

It could be claimed that the availability of grounds for unilaterally asserting the suspension or termination of a treaty – something which

---

52 Simma and Tams, 'Reacting against Treaty Breaches' (n 31) 593; Aust, *Modern Treaty Law* (n 16) 300; H Krieger, 'Article 65' in Dörr and Schmalenbach, *Vienna Convention* (n 36) 1131, 1134.

53 *Gabčíkovo-Nagymaros* (n 30) 66 para 108.

54 Aust, *Modern Treaty Law* (n 16) 300; Villiger, *Commentary* (n 2) 814.

55 *Armed Activities on the Territory of the Congo (New Application: 2002) (Democratic Republic of the Congo v Rwanda)*, Jurisdiction and Admissibility, ICJ Rep 2006, 6, 52 para 125.

56 Ibid.

57 *Racke* (n 48) para 59.

States have generally been wary to accept as part of the general international law of treaties – were allowed in the VCLT precisely due to the counterbalancing effect of the procedure for invocation of such grounds.[58] In other words, the purpose of the procedural provisions is to curb pretextual recourse to grounds of suspension or termination and to ensure that the suspension or termination sought will only be achieved in the final analysis through agreement or dispute settlement.[59] Lacking such a procedural regime in general international law, would the content of the unilateral grounds be the same?

In fact it can be claimed that the general international law of treaties provides for by and large the same strictly conditioned content of unilateral grounds for termination. And it can be further claimed that it only allows these to be unilaterally invoked but not to produce automatically upon invocation the effects of suspension or termination. Even if the procedural regime is not part of custom, the requirement that whatever effect of the unilateral grounds is agreed upon between the parties – even if the outcome of diplomatic methods of dispute settlement, or brought about through the decision of a court or tribunal to which the case has been submitted – can be argued to reflect customary international law.

But, to come to the question on the availability of unilateral grounds beyond the VCLT, the latter does not contain a general savings clause, unlike, for example, Article 56 ARSIWA. Article 42(2) VCLT purports to regulate the issue of termination and suspension exhaustively.[60] Thus, at least as a matter of treaty law one would expect that Part V of the VCLT would preclude the invocation of other grounds.[61] The question relates mainly to treaties beyond the scope of the VCLT, and focuses on the legal status of Article 42(2) VCLT. The reference to all provisions relating to termination, in combination with the contested status of Articles 65–68,

---

[58] DALT Commentary to Article 62 (n 1) para 1. Cf I Sinclair, *The Vienna Convention on the Law of Treaties* (2nd edn, Manchester UP, 1984) 162–3.

[59] DALT Commentary to Article 62 (n 1) para 1.

[60] It reads: 'The termination of a treaty, its denunciation or the withdrawal of a party, may take place only as a result of the application of the provisions of the treaty or of the present Convention. The same rule applies to suspension of the operation of a treaty.' Conversely, Article 56 ARSIWA reads: 'The applicable rules of international law continue to govern questions concerning the responsibility of a State for an internationally wrongful act to the extent that they are not regulated by these articles.'

[61] *Gabčíkovo-Nagymaros* (n 30) 38 para 47: 'Thus the Vienna Convention of 1969 on the Law of Treaties confines itself to defining – in a limitative manner – the conditions in which a treaty may lawfully be denounced or suspended.'

seems to militate against the provision's customary status.[62] The counter-argument would be that the corresponding customary rule relates only to the substantive grounds, and not to procedure.[63] In *Gabčíkovo-Nagymaros* the ICJ held that in the absence of a contrary agreement by the parties the treaty in question 'could be terminated only on the limited grounds enumerated in the Vienna Convention', despite the VCLT being inapplicable as treaty law.[64] By stark contrast, the Court's stance was remarkably non-committal in the recent *Interim Accord* case as to the legal status of the *exceptio non adimpleti contractus*, and its relationship to the law of treaties and responsibility. In the event, the Court held that it did not have to pronounce on whether the *exceptio* formed part of contemporary international law since Greece had failed to substantiate the conditions it had itself asserted.[65] It should be noted that the VCLT was directly applicable in the case.[66] The way to read the two pronouncements consistently would be that in the latter case the Court's reservation referred to general international law; *not* to VCLT law. In other words, it could mean that the *exceptio* is an uncodified secondary rule belonging to the realm of responsibility,[67] or 'at best a specific feature of certain mutual or synallagmatic obligations'.[68] The Court's reservation might even be *ex abundanti cautela* since it could be argued that part of the *exceptio*, at least the part that could justify suspension or termination, is now subsumed under the 'material breach' grounds codified in the VCLT.

---

[62] M Kohen, 'Article 42: Convention of 1969' in Corten and Klein, *The Vienna Conventions* (n 2) 1016, 1017–18; K Odendahl, 'Article 42' in Dörr and Schmalenbach, *Vienna Convention* (n 36) 733, 737; Villiger, *Commentary* (n 2) 549; C Binder, *Die Grenzen der Vertragstreue im Völkerrecht* (Springer, 2013) 273–4.

[63] Along the lines of *Military and Paramilitary Activities in and against Nicaragua (Nicaragua v US)*, Merits, ICJ Rep 1986, 14, 105 para 200.

[64] *Gabčíkovo-Nagymaros* (n 30) 62–3 para 100.

[65] *Application of the Interim Accord of 13 September 1995 (The Former Yugoslav Republic of Macedonia v Greece)*, Judgment, ICJ Rep 2011, 644, 690–91 para 161. This stance is criticized by Judge Simma in his elaborate separate opinion (ICJ Rep 2011, 695, 703–4 para 20).

[66] *Interim Accord*, Judgment, ibid, 673 para 91.

[67] On the basis of Article 56 ARSIWA; J Crawford, *State Responsibility: The General Part* (CUP, 2013) 680; see, eg, Article 8 of Part II, W Riphagen, 'Fifth Report on State Responsibility' YBILC (1984) vol. II (A/CN.4/380 and Corr.1) 1, 3.

[68] ARSIWA Commentary to Pt I Ch V (n 14) para 9.

Other notable examples of such alleged grounds, besides the *exceptio*, would be *desuetude* or obsolescence. As there is no authoritative expression of the relevant doctrines, definitions can be only tentative. *Desuetude* is defined as 'the rejection of a rule through subsequent non-enforcement or non-compliance.'[69] In a sense, it is the opposite of *consuetude*, meaning negative practice coupled with corresponding *opinio juris*.[70] Obsolescence (or *caducité*), on the other hand, is a more elusive notion (if it is not seen to overlap with *desuetude*). Kohen defines it as 'the impossibility of applying the treaty due to the disappearance of a legal situation which constituted one of its essential conditions.'[71] Wouters and Verhoeven define it as 'the termination of a treaty or treaty obligation because of events other than lapse of time which make execution of the treaty unjust, detrimental, inopportune, or without sense, and therefore terminates or modifies the treaty.'[72] Under such a doctrine the termination of the treaty or parts thereof would be presumably automatic. Any State action would be just declaratory.[73]

As a preliminary point, both doctrines have been considered by the ILC but were not included in its draft articles on the law of treaties. The Commission decided that although *desuetude* or obsolescence might be the factual basis of termination, the legal basis is found in the consent of the parties.[74] Equally telling has been the relevant subsequent practice cited in support of the doctrine. Kohen notes, for instance, the 'enemy

---

69 J Wouters and S Verhoeven, 'Desuetudo' in R Wolfrum (ed), *The Max Planck Encyclopedia of Public International Law* (vol. III, OUP, 2012) 60.

70 MG Kohen, 'Desuetude and Obsolescence of Treaties' in E Cannizzaro (ed), *The Law of Treaties beyond the Vienna Convention* (OUP, 2011) 352.

71 Ibid 358.

72 Wouters and Verhoeven, 'Desuetudo' (n 69); Binder, *Die Grenzen ...* (n 62) 272.

73 Binder, *Die Grenzen ...* (n 62) 274.

74 DALT (n 1) Commentary on Article 39, 237 para 5; see also *Nuclear Tests (Australia v France)*, Joint Dissenting Opinion of Judges Onyeama, Dillard, Jiménez de Aréchaga and Sir Humphrey Waldock, ICJ Rep 1973, 337 para 53; cited anew with approval in the Report of the ILC Working Group: G Nolte, 'Jurisprudence of the International Court of Justice and Arbitral Tribunals of Ad Hoc Jurisdiction Relating to Subsequent Agreements and Subsequent Practice: Introductory Report for the ILC Study Group on Treaties over Time' reprinted in G Nolte (ed), *Treaties and Subsequent Practice* (OUP, 2013) 169, 207–8. But see for criticism, F Capotorti, 'L'extinction et la suspension des traités' (1971) 134 *Recueil des cours* de l'Academie de droit international de La Haye 417, 517–19, who sees *desuetude* as a potential outcome of supervening custom. The latter should not be seen, according to Capotorti, as some sort of tacit agreement, as it would have to be if one were to accept that *desuetude* is termination by implicit consent of the parties.

states' reference in Articles 53, 106 and 107 of the Charter of the United Nations. Although the reference eventually lost all practical effect, the practice of the UN General Assembly has been revealing. While in the preamble of its Resolution 50/52 the Assembly pronounced that 'the clauses have become obsolete', in the operative part it merely 'expresse[d] its intentions to initiate the procedure set out in article 108 ... to amend the Charter'.[75] In other words, the majority of States recognized that there is no automaticity in such a declaration.[76] Another commonly cited example would be the 1990 declaration of obsolescence of several provisions of the Austrian State Treaty of 1955 by Austria.[77] As Austria made clear in its observations to the ILC Working Group on 'Treaties over Time' such a declaration was made only after consultations with the other parties, and was subsequently accepted by them.[78] Nolte, reporting for the ILC Working Group, submitted accordingly that the occasion constituted an instance of tacit agreement to partially terminate the treaty pursuant to Article 54(b) VCLT, upholding the rule of Article 42(2) VCLT.[79] However, such agreement, albeit not necessarily explicit, needs to be proven and cannot be presumed.[80]

The need for consent and the lack of automaticity even in presumptive grounds for termination beyond the VCLT confirms the general position here that the tension between *pacta sunt servanda* and grounds for termination or suspension that can be unilaterally invoked by parties to a treaty is more apparent than real: in the end, the effects on the treaty are the outcome of a process aimed at achieving consent, or the outcome of a dispute settlement process which itself needs to be consented to. Even if it is not so, the tension remains at best apparent: grounds for termination can be unilaterally invoked, but in practice are hardly ever invoked successfully. But these are not the only grounds that parties to a treaty may invoke in order to (at least temporarily) disengage themselves from the obligations under the *pactum*. Defences in the law of State

---

75 UNGA Res 50/52 (15 December 1995) para 3; see also UNGA Res 60/1 (16 September 2005) para 177 deciding the deletion of the term.

76 Binder, *Die Grenzen* ... (n 62) 301–2 concedes the point but argues that it was unnecessarily formalistic.

77 Kohen, 'Desuetude...' (n 70) 358–9; Binder, *Die Grenzen* ... (n 62) 274–89.

78 G Nolte, 'Subsequent Agreements and Practice of States Outside of Judicial or Quasi-Judicial Proceedings: Third Report for the ILC Study Group on Treaties over Time' in Nolte, *Treaties* (n 74) 305, 358.

79 Ibid 357, 359.

80 Ibid 359.

responsibility, though doctrinally distinguishable from grounds of suspension or termination of a treaty, can have effects identical to suspension, and may thus create similar tension with the *pacta sunt servanda* rule. It is to these defences that we now turn.

III. CIRCUMSTANCES PRECLUDING WRONGFULNESS IN THE LAW OF RESPONSIBILITY: SUSPENSION THROUGH THE BACK DOOR?

As Special Rapporteur on State Responsibility Willem Riphagen remarked, the 'principle *pacta sunt servanda* form[s] the link between the law of treaties and the law of responsibility'.[81] Although at some point the ILC considered the inclusion of general defences for non-performance as part of the law of treaties,[82] these were left to be dealt with within the context of State responsibility.[83] The relationship between these two regimes had been contested in the past, largely due to its limiting effect on the *pacta sunt servanda* rule.[84] This is because the same factual setting may give rise to both grounds of termination or suspension of a treaty, and to circumstances precluding the wrongfulness of a treaty breach. The ICJ, however, made clear that the two fields of law remain distinct and operate at different levels,[85] as indeed they do.

First, they are different in scope. As the ICJ made clear in *Gabčíkovo-Nagymaros*:

---

[81] W Riphagen, 'Third Report on State Responsibility' YBILC (1982) vol. II (A/CN.4/354 Corr. 1 and Add. 1, 2) 22, 30 para 50.

[82] See Articles 9–18 in GG Fitzmaurice, 'Fourth Report on Law of Treaties' YBILC (1959) vol. II (A/CN.4/120) 37, 43–6.

[83] Article 73 VCLT; ILC, 'Report of the International Law Commission Covering its Sixteenth Session' YBILC (1964) vol. II (A/CN.4/173) 175–6 para 18.

[84] Eg, DW Bowett, 'Treaties and State Responsibility' in *Le droit international au service de la paix, de la justice et du développement – Mélanges Michel Virally* (Pedone, 1991) 137–45; S Marks, 'Treaties, State Responsibility, and Remedies' (1990) 3 CLJ 387; or more recently, Fitzmaurice, 'Exceptional Circumstances …' (n 36) 631.

[85] V Gowland-Debbas, 'The Role of the International Court of Justice in the Development of the Contemporary Law of Treaties' in CJ Tams and J Sloan (eds), *The Development of International Law by the International Court of Justice* (OUP, 2013) 25, 50.

> A determination of whether a convention is or is not in force, and whether it has or has not been properly suspended or denounced, is to be made pursuant to the law of treaties. On the other hand, an evaluation of the extent to which the suspension or denunciation of a convention, seen as incompatible with the law of treaties, involves the responsibility of the State which proceeded to it, is to be made under the law of state responsibility.[86]

In other words, circumstances precluding wrongfulness are defences *par excellence*, that is, they apply only after all the constituent requirements of the obligation have been found to exist, and there has been a breach of that obligation.[87] Moreover, they apply to international obligations regardless of their origin or character, save for *jus cogens* rules.[88]

Second, they have different effects than grounds for termination or suspension. Circumstances precluding wrongfulness merely justify or excuse a breach of an international obligation for the time being, that is, as long as they exist.[89] As soon as they cease to do so, the duty to comply revives.[90] Conversely, the successful invocation of grounds for termination or suspension displaces the underlying treaty obligation permanently or temporarily.[91] It should be noted, however, that the VCLT remains silent on the important practical issue of how the operation of the treaty will be resumed in case of suspension, which is by and large the same effect that circumstances precluding wrongfulness achieve. Particularly, it is unclear whether resumption of operation of the treaty would take place automatically, once the grounds of suspension cease to exist, or unilaterally by notification of the party that invoked them in order to suspend the treaty (by analogy from Article 68 VCLT), or with the consent of all the parties.[92]

---

86 *Gabčíkovo-Nagymaros* (n 30) 38 para 47; see also *Rainbow Warrior (New Zealand/France)* [1990] 20 RIAA 215, 251 para 75.

87 ARSIWA Commentary on Pt I Ch. V (n 14) para 7; *Gabčíkovo-Nagymaros* (n 30) 39 para 48.

88 Articles 12 and 26 ARSIWA.

89 Article 27(a) ARSIWA.

90 ARSIWA Commentary on Pt I Ch. V (n 14) para 2; *Gabčíkovo-Nagymaros* (n 30) 63 para 101.

91 Articles 70 and 72 VCLT.

92 P Couvreur and C Espaliù Berdud, 'Article 72: Convention of 1969' in Corten and Klein, *The Vienna Conventions* (n 2) 1631, draw a connection between Article 72 and *Gabčíkovo-Nagymaros* (n 30) 63 para 102; Crawford and Olleson, 'The Exception of Non-Performance …' (n 22) 59.

Third, circumstances precluding wrongfulness operate more or less automatically,[93] while grounds of termination or suspension do not,[94] as discussed above. This is so not only under the cumbersome procedure provided for in the VCLT, but even in custom: there may not be any specific procedure to follow upon the invocation of grounds of termination, but invocation alone is not enough to bring about automatic termination even under customary law. The effect of the grounds invoked will depend on the reaction of other parties to the treaty, and in the final instances on the agreement of all parties or on the outcome of a dispute settlement method.

Doctrinal differences aside, circumstances precluding wrongfulness could for reasons of convenience be largely classified in two categories.[95] Self-defence and countermeasures are contingent upon a wrongful act by a State, normally the one injured by another, prior, wrongful act, that is sought to be justified by recourse to these circumstances precluding wrongfulness.[96] Conversely, *force majeure* and necessity relate to external circumstances that compel – to a certain extent – the State to breach an international obligation.[97] It is the latter two we are going to focus on.

Force majeure, as envisaged in Article 23(1) ARSIWA, requires the existence of an irresistible force or an unforeseen event, beyond the control of the State, causing material impossibility to perform the obligation.[98] In addition, the defence is inapplicable if the situation of *force majeure* is due, either alone or in combination with other factors, to conduct of the invoking State, or if the invoking State has assumed the risk of that situation occurring.[99] The defence of *force majeure* is not at all new and has been invoked in many contexts in the past.[100] Yet, the

---

[93] On countermeasures: cf *Gabčíkovo-Nagymaros* (n 30) 56 para 84; Article 52 ARSIWA; Simma and Tams, 'Reacting against Treaty Breaches' (n 31) 576, 602–3.

[94] ARSIWA Commentary on Pt I Ch. V (n 14) para 4; Crawford, 'Second Report on State Responsibility: Addendum' (30 April 1999) UN Doc A/CN.4/498/Add.2 para 225.

[95] S Heathcote, 'Necessity' in J Crawford, A Pellet and S Olleson (eds), *The Law of International Responsibility* (OUP, 2010) 491, 496.

[96] Articles 21 and 22 ARSIWA. On the doctrinal challenges of consent, see Crawford, 'Second Report …' (n 94) paras 233–41.

[97] Articles 23 and 25 ARSIWA; Crawford, *State Responsibility* (n 67) 295.

[98] ARSIWA Commentary on Article 23 (n 14) para 2; FI Paddeu, 'The Genealogy of *Force Majeure* in International Law' (2012) 82 BYBIL 381, 463.

[99] Article 23(2) ARSIWA.

[100] See, eg, R Ago, 'Eighth Report on State Responsibility: Add. 1-4' YBILC (1979) vol. II(1) (A/CN.4/318/Add. 1-4) 3, 47–66.

judicial practice pertaining to the ILC Article is sparse and its legal status is still to a certain extent debatable.[101]

Force majeure is exceptional and its threshold of application is significantly high.[102] It is clear that the source of material impossibility can be a natural event or human intervention.[103] The Commission clarified that by irresistible force is meant 'a constraint which the State was unable to avoid or oppose by its own means'.[104] As to the 'unforeseeablity' condition, the ILC suggests that 'the event must have been neither foreseen nor of an easily foreseeable kind'.[105] In *LAFICO/Burundi*, the facts of the case were relatively straightforward. The arbitral tribunal in that case easily concluded that the unilateral acts of severance of diplomatic relationships and expulsion of certain nationals could not qualify as an unforeseen event or an irresistible force.[106] The Iran-US Claims Tribunal has found on different occasions that 'social and economic forces beyond the power of the State to control through the exercise of due diligence' would qualify as *force majeure*.[107] Another case cited in this context is the *Aucoven* award of an arbitral tribunal under the auspices of the International Centre for Settlement of Investment Disputes ('ICSID').[108] In that, the Tribunal found that intense civil unrest and threatened violence was not 'unforeseeable' for the purposes of justifying non-compliance with an obligation to raise toll rates pursuant to a relevant concession agreement.[109] It should be noted, however, that the plea of *force majeure* in that case was primarily based on the relevant concession agreement and domestic law.[110]

As to the condition that the situation of *force majeure* must make performance 'materially impossible', controversies still persist. It is clear

---

[101] Paddeu, 'The Genealogy …' (n 98) 484–7, 490–93.

[102] S Szurek, 'Force Majeure' in Crawford, Pellet and Olleson, *The Law …* (n 95) 475, 477.

[103] ARSIWA Commentary on Article 23 (n 14) para 3.

[104] Ibid para 2.

[105] Ibid.

[106] *LAFICO/Republic of Burundi* (n 37) 318.

[107] See Crawford, *State Responsibility* (n 67) 297; e.g., *Gould Marketing, Inc. v Iran et al.* (1983) 3 Iran-USCTR 147, 153; *General Dynamics Telephone Sys. Ctr. v The Islamic Republic of Iran* (1985) 9 Iran-USCTR 153, 160; *Anaconda-Iran Inc. v Iran et al.* (1986) 13 Iran-USCTR 199, 213.

[108] *Autopista Concecionada de Venezuela (Aucoven) SA v Bolivarian Republic of Venezuela*, ICSID Case No ARB/00/5, Award, 23 September 2003; Binder, 'Stability and Change …' (n 39) 919–20.

[109] *Aucoven*, ibid, paras 117–19.

[110] Ibid para 107; Paddeu, 'The Genealogy …' (n 98) 486.

that material impossibility means, at least, more than material difficulty.[111] The arbitral tribunal in *Rainbow Warrior* found that 'the test of [the] applicability of [draft Article 31][112] is of absolute and material impossibility, and … [that] a circumstance rendering performance more difficult or burdensome does not constitute a case of *force majeure*.'[113] On the other hand, the ILC, drawing from *Gabčíkovo-Nagymaros*, clarified that the threshold of applicability of Article 23 'though considerable, is lower than is required by Article 61 on termination or suspension of treaties'.[114] Along similar lines, Crawford opined against the conflation of material impossibility and absolute impossibility, *Rainbow Warrior* notwithstanding, material impossibility falling by logical implication short of absolute.[115] Such a view is reflected also in the *Aucoven* award.[116] This conundrum is only but an indication of the profound effects of the tension between stability and flexibility in the context of circumstances precluding wrongfulness.

In the same vein, the content and the effects of the necessity defence have been a matter of intense controversy given the defence's propensity for

---

[111] Crawford, *State Responsibility* (n 67) 299; ILC, 'Report of the International Law Commission on the work of its thirty-first session' YBILC (1979) vol. II (A/34/10) 87, 133 para 40: 'the adverb "materially" preceding the word "impossible" is intended to show that … it would not suffice for the "irresistible force" or the "unforeseen external event" to have made it *very difficult* for the State to act in conformity with the obligation' (emphasis in original).

[112] See ILC, Report 1979, ibid, 122.

[113] *Rainbow Warrior* (n 86) 77; Ago, 'Eighth Report …' (n 100) 51 para 110; *idem*, 'Eighth Report on State Responsibility: Add. 5-7' YBILC (1980) vol. II (A/CN.4/318/Add.5-7) 13, 19 *et seq.* paras 12–26 and para 31; cf also, *Sempra Energy International v Argentine Republic*, ICSID No ARB/02/16, Award, 28 September 2007, para 246.

[114] *Gabčíkovo-Nagymaros* (n 30) 63 para 102; ARSIWA Commentary on Article 23 (n 14) para 4.

[115] Crawford, *State Responsibility* (n 67) 299.

[116] *Aucoven* (n 108) paras 122–4: having found that the applicable standard was the same as the one in international law, the tribunal went on to say:

> Venezuela admits that the civil protest was not irresistible in the sense that it could not have been mastered by the use of force. This being so, the question then becomes: by all reasonable judgment how much force can a State be legally required to deploy to perform its contract obligations? The answer to this question implies a delicate assessment that calls in part for political judgment. … Suffice it to state that this Tribunal is rather inclined to find that … the impossibility requirement appears met.

abuse.[117] Although the ICJ has acknowledged necessity's legal status as a defence under customary international law, it has done so with caution, stressing its exceptional character.[118] As enshrined in Article 25 ARSIWA, the conduct in breach of an international obligation needs to be 'the only means for the state to safeguard an essential interest against a grave and imminent peril'. Conversely, the conduct in question must not 'seriously impair an essential interest' of the injured State or of the international community as a whole. Also, the plea of necessity is precluded if the international obligation in question excludes the possibility of invoking it or 'the state has contributed to the situation of necessity'. The 'non-contribution' requirement, notably, is stricter than the corresponding provisions on *force majeure* and distress, where the situations need be 'due' to the conduct of the State for the defences to be inapplicable.[119]

Recent practice relating to the defence of necessity as elaborated by the ILC shows that international courts and tribunals have not been receptive to relevant pleas.[120] Two aspects of the circumstance of necessity – in combination or separately – have more often than not proven fatal for the successful invocation of the plea in a judicial setting. The first such obstacle is the 'only means' requirement that has been decisive in the only relevant cases before the ICJ and the International Tribunal for the Law of the Sea ('ITLOS'), as well as in several cases before arbitral tribunals.[121] Likewise, the requirement set out in Article 25(2)(b) ARSIWA that 'the state has not contributed to the situation of necessity' appears equally restrictive. As an ICSID Annulment Committee has critically remarked, 'a liberal interpretation … [could

---

117 ARSIWA Commentary on Article 25 (n 14) para 2; Heathcote, 'Necessity' (n 95) 492.

118 *Gabčíkovo-Nagymaros* (n 30) 40 para 51; *Legal Consequences of the Construction of a Wall in the Occupied Palestinian Territories*, Advisory Opinion, ICJ Rep 2004, 194–5 para 140; but see *Rainbow Warrior* (n 86) 254 para 78.

119 Crawford, *State Responsibility* (n 67) 313.

120 Binder, 'Stability and Change …' (n 39) 918–19.

121 T Christakis, '"Nécessité n'a pas de loi"? La nécessité en droit international' in Société française pour le droit international (ed), *La nécessité en droit international – Colloque de Grenoble* (Pedone, 2007) 11; *LAFICO/Burundi* (n 37) 318–19 para 55; *Gabčíkovo-Nagymaros* (n 30) 40 para 51; *Wall* (n 118) 194–5 para 140; *M/V "Saiga" (No 2) (Saint Vincent and the Grenadines v Guinea)*, ITLOS Rep 1999, 10 para 135; also, eg, *Enron Corporation Ponderosa Assets v Argentine Republic*, ICSID Case No Arb/01/3, Award, 22 May 2007, paras 308–9; *Suez, Sociedad General de Aguas de Barcelona SA, and Vivendi Universal SA v Argentine Republic*, ICSID Case No 03/19, Award, 30 July 2010, para 260, although one should be cautious about the precedential value of these awards due to the particularities of the bilateral investment treaties in question.

encompass] any causal link between the conduct of the state and the situation of necessity'.[122] In *Gabčíkovo-Nagymaros,* the ICJ held that even if all the other requirements of necessity were met, Hungary could still not have relied on it 'as it had helped, by act or omission, to bring it about'.[123] The ILC suggests that the contribution must be 'sufficiently substantial and not merely incidental or peripheral'.[124] Nonetheless, there are but few examples in recent judicial practice to highlight the meaning of the requirement.[125]

Circumstances precluding wrongfulness under the general international law of State responsibility may achieve the same effect as that of suspension under the general international law of treaties, introducing tension between the stability guaranteed by *pacta sunt servanda* and the flexibility inherent in unilateral (even if only temporary) disengagement from the *pactum.* However, they are as difficult to invoke successfully as the unilateral grounds of termination or suspension under the law of treaties, if not more. An analysis of general international law then reveals the tension between *pacta sunt servanda* and the grounds for suspension and termination of treaties as apparent, rather than real – in reality *pacta sunt servanda* appears as a rule that seems extremely difficult to dislodge, even temporarily. The only sure means of escaping a *pactum* is by means of a new *pactum* of sorts; any other exit route seems particularly difficult to follow.

But the rules discussed so far are only general, default rules. States remain free to condition the *pacta sunt servanda* rule by providing for unconditional (or loosely conditioned) rights of unilateral suspension or termination of treaties. How does this flexibility square with *pacta sunt servanda*? It is to this question that the final substantive section of this chapter now turns.

IV. FLEXIBILITY OF EXIT CLAUSES IN TREATIES

The rules of the VCLT on grounds of termination and suspension are default rules. As the VCLT itself provides explicitly at the outset of Part V, States are free to devise by agreement their own provisions for

---

[122] See, eg, *Enron Creditors Recovery Corp. Ponderosa Assets LP v Argentine Republic*, ICSID Case No Arb/01/3, Decision on the Application for Annulment by the Argentine Republic, 30 July 2010, para 387.

[123] *Gabčíkovo-Nagymaros* (n 30) 46 para 58.

[124] ARSIWA Commentary to Article 25 (n 14) para 20.

[125] Christakis, 'Nécessité …' (n 121) 30; eg, *LG&E Energy Corp. et al. v Argentine Republic*, ICSID Case No ARB/02/1, Decision on Liability, 3 October 2006, paras 245–61.

termination or suspension of a treaty, and they may freely dispose of any substantive or procedural limitations on the right to terminate or withdraw from a treaty.[126] Mindful of the rather demanding conditions for the invocation of grounds of unilateral suspension or termination under the general international law of treaties, States have reacted by including special clauses providing for termination or withdrawal in international agreements, making these rather common.[127] These 'exit clauses' pervade all areas of treaty practice, and they vary in form.[128]

By stark contrast to the relevant grounds in general international law, treaty provisions on termination are mostly skeletal, focusing on form and procedure rather than substance. For instance, some treaties are only concluded for a fixed duration providing expressly for their termination, with or without provision for extension.[129] Many international investment agreements ('IIAs'), for example, are of limited duration (mostly 10–20 years).[130] Less frequently, a treaty might provide for its suspension.[131] More importantly, most treaties provide expressly for conditions of unilateral termination or withdrawal.[132] Such conditions are more often than not only procedural, ranging from notice effective immediately[133] and set notice periods,[134] to fixed intervals[135] and minimum periods of application.[136]

---

[126] Articles 42(2) and 54 VCLT; on the use of terms, see Aust, *Modern Treaty Law* (n 16) 277.

[127] Helfer, 'Flexibility …' (n 8) 182.

[128] Aust, *Modern Treaty Law* (n 16) 278.

[129] DB Hollis, 'The End of Treaty Relations' in *idem*, *The Oxford Guide* (n 31) 758, 765–9.

[130] UNCTAD, *Bilateral Investment Treaties 1995–2006: Trends in Investment Rulemaking* (United Nations, 2007) 20–21.

[131] UN Legal Department, *Final Clauses of Multilateral Treaties: Handbook* (United Nations, 2003) 107–8.

[132] For a comprehensive classification, see Helfer, 'Exiting …' (n 5) 1597.

[133] Eg, Article XV(1), Articles of Agreement of the International Monetary Fund (adopted 22 July 1944, entered into force 27 December 1945) 2 UNTS 39.

[134] Eg, Article 30, UN Convention against Illicit Traffic in Narcotics and Psychotropic Substances (adopted 20 December 1988, entered into force 11 November 1990) 1582 UNTS 95.

[135] Eg, Article 9, ILO Convention No 111, Discrimination (Employment and Occupation) Convention (adopted 25 June 1958, entered into 15 June 1960), accessed 1 October 2013 at www.ilo.org/dyn/normlex/en/f?p=NORMLEXPUB:1:0.

[136] Eg, Article 47(1), Energy Charter Treaty (adopted 17 December 1994, entered into force 16 April 1998) 2080 UNTS 95 ('ECT'); most BITs fall into that category, UNCTAD, *Bilateral Investment* (n 130) 20–21.

Termination or withdrawal clauses very rarely require any substantive justification by the denouncing or withdrawing party.[137] Arms-control and non-proliferation treaties are almost unique in that regard.[138] The relevant clause is almost identical in a series of non-proliferation treaties ('extraordinary events' clause):

> Each Party shall, in exercising its national sovereignty, have the right to withdraw from the Treaty if it decides that extraordinary events, related to the subject matter of this Treaty, have jeopardized the supreme interests of its country. It shall give notice of such withdrawal to all other Parties to the Treaty and to the United Nations Security Council three months in advance. Such notice shall include a statement of the extraordinary events it regards as having jeopardized its supreme interests.[139]

The phrasing of the provision might be deceiving. There is some truth in the observation that the clause might seem very close to the *rebus sic stantibus* rule. Some authors have gone as far as suggesting that certain instances of denunciation were based on Article 62 VCLT, the extraordinary events clause notwithstanding.[140] One might concede that the provision does not theoretically preclude the application of the rule

---

[137] Helfer, 'Exiting …' (n 5) 1598.

[138] DH Joyner and M Roscini, 'Withdrawal from Non-Proliferation Treaties' in DH Joyner and M Roscini, *Non-Proliferation Law as a Special Regime: A Contribution to Fragmentation Theory in International Law* (CUP, 2012) 151.

[139] Article 20(2), Convention on the Prohibition of the Use, Stockpiling, Production and Transfer of Anti-Personnel Mines and on their Destruction (Ottawa Convention) (adopted 18 September 1997, entered into force 1 March 1999) 2056 UNTS 211; Article X, Treaty on the Non-Proliferation of Nuclear Weapons (adopted 12 June 1968, entered into force 5 March 1970) 729 UNTS 161. See also Article IV, Treaty Banning Nuclear Weapon Tests in the Atmosphere, in Outer Space and Under Water (adopted 5 August 1963, entered into force 10 October 1963) 480 UNTS 43; Article XIII, Convention on the Prohibition of the Development, Production and Stockpiling of Bacteriological (Biological) and Toxin Weapons and on their Destruction (Biological Weapons Convention) (adopted 10 April 1972, 26 March 1975) 1015 UNTS 163; Article XVI, Convention on the Prohibition of the Development, Production, Stockpiling and Use of Chemical Weapons and on their Destruction (Chemical Weapons Convention) (adopted 3 September 1992, entered into force 29 April 1997) 1974 UNTS 45.

[140] M Fitzmaurice and TO Elias, 'The Doctrine of Fundamental Change of Circumstances' in M Fitzmaurice and TO Elias, *Contemporary Issues in the Law of Treaties* (Eleven Publishing, 2005) 185–98; R Müllerson, 'The ABM Treaty: Changed Circumstances, Extraordinary Events, Supreme Interests and International Law' (2001) 50 ICLQ 509, 524–31, more tentatively.

reflected in Article 62 VCLT in so far as it does not contradict it.[141] However, in practical terms, it seems rather dubious that any such denunciation can be construed as falling within the VCLT grounds, the key phrase of the clause being 'if [the party] decides'. The self-judging character of the clause alongside the conspicuous absence of third party dispute settlement provisions in arms-control agreements would make invocation of fundamental change of circumstances superfluous.[142]

It has been suggested that the latitude provided by the extraordinary events clause fails to provide a balance between *pacta sunt servanda* and flexibility in withdrawal or termination,[143] leaning very heavily towards allowing unfettered exit. Although we see the merits of this point, legally speaking, *pacta sunt servanda* is neatly, if not rigidly, upheld. Such unfettered exit clauses are, after all, part of the *pactum* that must be performed subject to the obligation of good faith.[144] As such, there is no tension between such flexible exit clauses and *pacta sunt servanda*: exiting the *pactum* as allowed by the *pactum* merely serves to reinforce the rule.

And yet, below this formal surface some tension is evident. A self-judging exit clause is tantamount to a 'get out of jail free' card; tantamount to assuming an obligation 'except if you don't' – or at least it could be so portrayed. This necessarily indicates some pressure on the *pacta sunt servanda* rule. Similar understandings of such self-judging release clauses have been expressed notably with respect to reservations to treaties and 'reservations' in (or better: limitations of the scope of) unilateral declarations submitting to the jurisdiction of the International Court of Justice under Article 36(2) of its Statute.[145] The difference,

---

[141] Joyner and Roscini, 'Withdrawal ...' (n 138) 159.

[142] As Müllerson, 'The ABM Treaty ...' (n 140) 503, admits.

[143] A Vermeer-Künzli, 'The Merits of Reasonable Flexibility: The Contribution of the Law of Treaties to Peace' in G Nolte (ed), *Peace through International Law* (Springer, 2009) 67, 85–8.

[144] See Nahlik, 'The Grounds ...' (n 19) 746; on the limits of discretion under self-judging clauses, see, eg, *Certain Questions of Mutual Assistance in Criminal Matters (Djibouti v France)*, ICJ Rep 2008, 177, 229 paras 145 *et seq.*

[145] Statute of the International Court of Justice (adopted 26 June 1945, entered into force 24 October 1945) 33 UNTS No 993; A Pellet, 'Article 36' in A Zimmermann, K Oellers-Frahm, C Tomuschat and CJ Tams (eds), *The Statute of the International Court of Justice: A Commentary* (2nd edn, OUP, 2012) 633, 688–9; S Rosenne, *The Law and Practice of the International Court, 1920–2005* (vol. II, Martinus Nijhoff, 2006) 748–51; JG Merrills, 'The Optional Clause Revisited' (1993) 64 BYBIL 197, 237–9. See also Lauterpacht's separate opinion in *Norwegian Loans (France v Norway)*, ICJ Rep 1957, 9, 48:

however, is that in these latter cases there is no general consent at the outset with regard to the disengagement from the *pactum*. In the case of special exit clauses in treaties, the consent of all parties is indeed provided at the outset. Even if so, the underlying tension comes to bear when third party beneficiaries of the treaty are affected. We turn now to this issue.

According to Article 70 VCLT, which reflects customary international law,[146] termination or withdrawal releases all the parties or the withdrawing party from any obligation further to perform the treaty. Moreover, 'it does not affect rights, duties and legal situations of the parties created through the execution of the treaty' (Article 70(1)(b)). As a preliminary point, it was clear from the outset that Article 70(1)(b) VCLT relates only to '[a] right, obligation or legal situation of the states parties to the treaties created through the execution, and is not in any way concerned with the question of "vested interests of individuals"'.[147] States, however, may freely extend benefits to non-parties, especially private entities, on the basis of a treaty, and indeed devise appropriate clauses to accommodate benefits established before the exit takes effect, along the lines of Article 70 VCLT.[148] Still, the latter provision deals with rights, obligations, and legal situations established while the treaty was in force, and

---

> the Acceptance embodying the "automatic reservation" is invalid as lacking in an essential condition of validity of a legal instrument. This is so for the reason that *it leaves to the party making the Declaration the right to determine … the very existence of its obligation* … An instrument in which a party is entitled to determine the existence of its obligation is not a valid and enforceable legal instrument of which a court of law can take cognizance. It is not a legal instrument. It is a declaration of a political principle and purpose. (emphasis added)

[146] See, eg, Villiger, *Commentary* (n 2) 875; A Nollkaemper, 'Some Observations on the Consequences of the Termination of Treaties and the Reach of Article 70 of the Vienna Convention on the Law of Treaties' in IF Dekker and H Meijers (eds), *On the Foundations and Sources of International Law* (TMC Asser, 2003) 187; H Ascensio, 'Article 70: Convention of 1969' in Corten and Klein, *The Vienna Conventions* (n 2) 1585, 1590–91.

[147] DALT Commentary to Article 66 (n 1) para 3.

[148] *Jurisdiction of the Courts of Danzig*, Advisory Opinion, 1928, PCIJ Ser B No 15, 17–18; for third states, see Articles 34–38 VCLT. For private entities, see, eg, Article 78(2) American Convention on Human Rights (adopted 22 November 1969, entered into force 18 July 1978) 1144 UNTS 123; Article 58(2) Convention on the Protection of Human Rights and Fundamental Freedoms (adopted 4 November 1950, entered into force 3 September 1953) 213 UNTS 222; Article 72, Convention on the Settlement of Investment Disputes Between States and

does not look into the future. It merely seeks to establish the rule of non-retroactivity, that is, to clarify that termination or withdrawal only operate *ex nunc*.[149] By contrast, the invalidity of a treaty operates *ex tunc*, and the safeguarding of 'acquired rights' of parties is much more limited.[150] The parties may by agreement, however, extend the operation of the treaty (or rather, of some of its provisions) even after the termination or withdrawal takes effect. This is done by the adoption of relevant 'survival clauses'.

Survival clauses are not as common as denunciation or withdrawal clauses. They are most common in IIAs.[151] For example, the Energy Charter Treaty provides that:

> [t]he provisions of this Treaty shall continue to apply to Investments made in the Area of a Contracting Party by Investors of other Contracting Parties or in the Area of other Contracting Parties by Investors of that Contracting Party as of the date when that Contracting Party's withdrawal from the Treaty takes effect for a period of 20 years from such date.[152]

But IIAs are not the only area of treaty law where one can find survival clauses. The Geneva Conventions of 1949 provide that notwithstanding the parties' 'liberty to denounce the Convention[s]' and the fact that denunciation 'shall take effect one year after the notification thereof has been made', 'a denunciation of which notification has been made at a time when the denouncing Power is involved in a conflict shall not take effect until peace has been concluded, and until after operations connected with release and repatriation of the persons protected by the

---

Nationals of Other States (adopted 18 March 1965, entered into force 14 October 1966) 575 UNTS 159.

149 See also Article 71 VCLT, relating to the operation of Article 64 VCLT according to which '[i]f a new peremptory norm of general international law emerges, any existing treaty which is in conflict with that norm becomes void and *terminates*' (emphasis added). This is an instance of termination through invalidation and is meant to operate, like all other instances of termination, only *ex nunc*, subject to the special provisions of Article 71(2), which largely mirror those of Article 70.

150 See Article 69 VCLT, which safeguards only 'acts performed in good faith before the invalidity was invoked', which 'are not rendered unlawful by reason only of the invalidity of the treaty'.

151 J Harrison, 'The Life and Death of BITs: Legal Issues Concerning Survival Clauses and the Termination of Investment Treaties' (2012) 13 *Journal of World Investment & Trade* 928, 931.

152 Article 47(3) ECT (n 136).

present Convention have been terminated'.[153] While technically this is a special provision regarding the notice period for automatic withdrawal, its effect is rather one similar to that of survival clauses. Such clauses function as a remedy to the automaticity of termination or withdrawal under generous exit provisions, by providing that certain effects of the treaty will continue despite the treaty's extinction or a party's withdrawal from it.

The purpose of such survival clauses is clear: they aim not to allow the apparent flexibility in exiting a treaty (but which is really merely a manifestation of the *pacta sunt servanda* rule) to unduly impact on third party beneficiaries. This may be seen as creating a counterbalance to easy exit, turning 'flexibility' in suspension or termination of treaties on its head. The flexibility of the regime of exit in such circumstances is that termination or withdrawal covers only some, rather than all, the legal effects flowing from the provisions of the now extinct (or no longer applicable) treaty. In fact, termination or withdrawal is flexible because for a longer or shorter time it covers only part of the affected treaty.

V. EVALUATION AND AN AGENDA FOR RESEARCH

If *pacta sunt servanda*, then easy exit from the *pactum* through its suspension or termination puts pressure on the rule and creates tension between formal commitments and flexible means of disengaging from them. The analysis of means and methods for suspension or termination of treaties, however, reveals that whatever tension may be presumed is apparent, rather than real.

For one, the grounds that can be unilaterally invoked in order to bring about suspension or termination, even if not subject to the demanding procedural regime of the VCLT, are still subject to the consent of all parties in order to produce the desired effect. In any event, the conditions

---

[153] Common Article 63(3), Geneva Convention for the Amelioration of the Condition of the Wounded and Sick in Armed Forces in the Field (adopted 12 August 1949, entered into force 21 October 1950) 75 UNTS 35; Article 62(3) Geneva Convention for the Amelioration of the Condition of Wounded, Sick and Shipwrecked Members of Armed Forces at Sea Field (adopted 12 August 1949, entered into force 21 October 1950) 75 UNTS 81; Article 142(3) Geneva Convention relative to the Treatment of Prisoners of War (adopted 12 August 1949, entered into force 21 October 1950) 75 UNTS 135; Article 158(3) Geneva Convention relative to the Protection of Civilian Persons in Time of War (adopted 12 August 1949, entered into force 21 October 1950) 75 UNTS 287; see also, eg, Article 20(3) Ottawa Convention (n 139).

for the invocation of such grounds are so strict as to guarantee that successful invocation will be exceptional indeed. The latter is also true with respect to defences under the law of international responsibility, which may achieve an effect tantamount to suspension. *Pacta sunt servanda* thus appears to be able to accommodate whatever 'tension' by relying on the need for consent with respect to unilateral assertions (thereby engendering a new *pactum* of sorts), which are anyway only exceptionally successful.

More importantly, the general international law of treaties (as reflected in large part in the VCLT) seems willing to 'pay the price' for the strict and narrow general exit rules by relying on other forms of treaty adaptation when rigid adherence to *pacta sunt servanda* would produce inequitable or undesirable results. These include flexibility in the interpretation of treaties, which allows taking into consideration subsequent events whether in the form of practice or of agreement, and – in the final analysis – even the possibility of 'living with breaches'. Evolutive or dynamic interpretation allows parties to 'play around' with *pacta sunt servanda*, redefining and adjusting the '*pacta*' part. Furthermore, a breach of treaty need not necessarily be pursued. Even if it is, the international responsibility which it will engage will not necessarily be enforced. Rather, the breach may bring the parties together in an attempt to find a practicable solution, which may take the form of a new *pactum* or some informal agreement or arrangement.

Finally, the general international law of treaties seems willing to 'pay the price' for strict and narrow grounds for unilateral termination by allowing parties to devise their own exit clauses. Here, however, no pressure is put on the *pacta sunt servanda* rule, at least formally: the exit clause is indeed part of the *pactum*. In any event, the flexibility that the law of treaties – viz., the *pacta sunt servanda* rule – allows here permits the parties to a treaty to counterbalance easy exit with survival clauses to protect third party beneficiaries.

Future research on the tension between stability and flexibility of treaty commitments could focus on a careful examination of the mechanics of invocation of grounds seeking termination or suspension of treaties under general international law. Even when they are resisted, very rarely will such invocations (as is the case with most disputes) end up before formal dispute settlement mechanisms (and when they do, they are bound to be well documented and studied). In most cases they will not, and it will be interesting to see how such invocations may in fact engender practicable solutions through cooperation of the parties, as is presumed above. In this connection, it would be interesting to see what arguments within the framework of *pacta sunt servanda* are made in order to accommodate change, and to what extent these actually assist in avoiding the termination or suspension of the *pactum*, achieving rather its readjustment or modification. In that, the formal commitment is maintained through the flexibility inherent in the general international law of treaties in areas other than unilateral termination or suspension.

Overall, as we have seen, a robust re-examination of the general rules on suspension and termination of treaties seems rather unlikely. Interesting legal issues, however, are unavoidably arising in the interstices and remain unexplored. Given the variety of exit and survival clauses in specific regimes, two types of interactions are likely to occur. First, the interpretation and application of treaty-specific rules on suspension and termination will be informed by the relevant general rules. Whether the special rules are to be applied or interpreted consistently with the general regime, or, conversely, call for a departure from it will depend on the specific provisions at play. Second, further issues might arise in the interaction of special rules on suspension and termination *inter se* as in the cases of interrelated treaties.[154] In other words, the tension between stability and flexibility of treaty obligations in times of complexity and fragmentation is expected to raise issues of compatibility between specific regimes *inter se*, and between such regimes and general international law.[155]

---

[154] An example has been the controversy relating to the suspension or termination of the ICSID Convention and its effects on dispute settlement provisions under IIAs: see, eg., OM Garibaldi, 'On the Denunciation of the ICSID Convention, Consent to ICSID Jurisdiction, and the Limits of the Contract Analogy' in C Binder, U Kriebaum, A Reinisch and S Wittich (eds), *International Investment Law for the 21st Century: Essays in Honour of Christian Schreuer* (OUP, 2009) 251; A Tzanakopoulos, 'Denunciation of the ICSID Convention under the General International Law of Treaties' in R Hofmann and CJ Tams (eds), *International Investment Law and General International Law: From Clinical Isolation to Systemic Integration?* (Nomos, 2011) 75.

[155] See also Binder, *Die Grenze* (n 62) 934.

12. Uniformity versus specialization (1): The quest for a uniform law of inter-State treaties

Malgosia Fitzmaurice and Panos Merkouris

I. INTRODUCTION

The recent proliferation of international courts and tribunals,[1] accompanied by the expansion of areas regulated by international law with ever increasing density, has led to an equally increasing fear of fragmentation both at an institutional and at a normative level.

The present chapter examines whether the 1969 Vienna Convention on the Law of Treaties (VCLT) rules or their customary law equivalents provide the actors in the international arena with a uniform set of rules, or whether practice has demonstrated that they are only a 'springboard' allowing the States flexibility to adopt more tailor-made solutions. In order to avoid any overlaps with other contributions in the present handbook, the analysis will focus on three main areas of the law of treaties: i) the provisions relating to the creation of conventional obligations, that is, what is a treaty, ii) the issues relating to consent to be bound, and iii) the provisions relating to amendment of treaties. These areas refer, on the one hand, to the emergence of a binding treaty and, on the other, to its continued, albeit somewhat transformed, existence. In this manner a complete overview of the genesis and life of a treaty can be

[1] See C Brown, 'The Proliferation of International Courts and Tribunals: Finding Your Way through the Maze' (2002) 3 Melbourne J Intl Law 453; T Buergenthal, 'Proliferation of International Courts and Tribunals: Is it Good or Is it Bad?' (2001) 14 Leiden J Intl L 267; H Thirlway, 'The Proliferation of International Judicial Organs: Institutional and Substantive Issues: The International Court of Justice and Other International Courts' in NM Blokker and HG Schermers (eds), *Proliferation of International Organizations: Legal Issues* (Kluwer Law International, 2001) 251–78.

given[2] and certain conclusions can be reached as to the existence or not of a characteristic of uniformity of the relevant provisions amongst inter-State treaties.

II. UNIFORMITY VERSUS SPECIALIZATION: AN OVERVIEW

Before embarking on the analysis of the relevant provisions, we need to clarify what is meant by the bipole 'uniformity versus specialization' used in the title of the present chapter. These terms refer to the idea of fragmentation that has been in the forefront of international legal academic discourse since the beginning of the 21st century. This is reflected by the fact that the Sixth Committee of the United Nations (UN) delegated to the International Law Commission (ILC) the discussion on the issue of fragmentation and how it could be addressed. The ILC, in its turn, established a Study Group to examine the intricacies and possible consequences of fragmentation.[3] The Study Group eventually submitted a report finalized by Martti Koskenniemi.[4] It is interesting to note that in the title of the finalized report of the Study Group the term 'fragmentation' has been dropped in *lieu* of 'diversification', despite that on numerous occasions in the report the ILC uses the term fragmentation. This was done because it was considered that fragmentation had negative connotations, whereas diversification was somewhat more positive in the sense that it did not create a sentiment of foreboding and fear for the future of public international law.

The Report of the ILC Study Group tackled a variety of issues,[5] and it included an analysis of the notion of 'self-contained regimes'. As the ILC Study Group noted '[t]he fragmentation of the international social world has attained legal significance especially as it has been accompanied by the

---

[2] The provisions relating to the effects of breach and to the termination of the treaty (eg, bases of suspension or termination of a treaty) are not addressed here, as they are covered by a separate chapter: see Tams (in this volume).

[3] UN GAOR, 57th Session, Supplement No 10 (A/57/10), chp IX.A, paras 492–4 and 511.

[4] Report of the Study Group of the ILC, *Fragmentation of International Law: Difficulties Arising from the Diversification and Expansion of International Law* (finalized by M Koskenniemi, A/CN.4/L.682, 13 April 2006) (hereinafter ILC Study Group).

[5] Such as fragmentation as a phenomenon, conflict of norms, Article 103 of the 1945 UN Charter, *jus cogens* norms, and Article 31(3)(c) VCLT and the principle of systemic integration.

emergence of specialized and (relatively) autonomous rules or rule-complexes, legal institutions and spheres of legal practice'.[6] This was a direct reference to the so-called self-contained regimes.[7] One can find this notion mentioned in the ILC Commentary to Article 55 (*lex specialis*) of the Articles on Responsibility of States for Internationally Wrongful Acts. In this Commentary the ILC makes a distinction between 'weaker forms of *lex specialis*, such as specific treaty provisions on a single point' and 'strong forms of *lex specialis*, including what are often referred to as self-contained regimes'.[8] This dichotomy was based on two examples taken from international jurisprudence: the *SS 'Wimbledon'* case[9] of the

---

[6] ILC Study Group, (n 4) para 8, referring also to A Fisher-Lescano and G Teubner, 'Regime-Collisions: The Vain Search for Legal Unity in the Fragmentation of Global Law' (2004) 25 Michigan J Intl L 999. Also LANM Barnhoorn and KC Wellens (eds), *Diversity in Secondary Rules and the Unity of International Law* (Martinus Nijhoff, 1995).

[7] On self-contained regimes, see B Simma, 'Self-Contained Regimes' (1985) 16 Netherlands YB Intl L 112; Barnhoorn and Wellens (eds), *Diversity in Secondary Rules*, (n 6); V Lowe, 'The Politics of Law-Making: Are the Method and Character of Norm Creation Changing?' in M Byers (ed), *The Role of Law in International Politics: Essays in International Relations and International Law* (OUP, 2000) 207 *et seq*; M Koskenniemi and P Leino, 'Fragmentation of International Law? Postmodern Anxieties' (2002) 15 Leiden J Intl L 553; Fisher-Lescano and Teubner, 'Regime Collisions ...', (n 6); B Simma and D Pulkowski, 'Of Planets and the Universe: Self-Contained Regimes in International Law' (2006) 17 EJIL 485; E Klein, 'Self-Contained Regime' in R Wolfrum (ed), MPEPIL (2010) www.mpepil.com, accessed 1 July 2012; B Simma and D Pulkowski, '*Leges Speciales* and Self-Contained Regimes' in J Crawford, A Pellet and S Olleson (eds), *The Law of International Responsibility* (OUP, 2010) 139.

[8] ILC, Draft Articles on State Responsibility, Commentary on Article 55, in UN GAOR, Fifty-Sixth Session, Supplement No 10 (A/56/10), (2001) 358–9.

[9] *Case of the SS 'Wimbledon'*, Judgment, PCIJ 1923 Series A, No 1, 23–4:

> [T]he Treaty [of Versailles] has taken care not to assimilate [the Kiel Canal] to the other internal navigable waterways of the German Empire. A special section has been created at the end of the Part XII ... and in this special section rules exclusively designed for the Kiel Canal have been inserted; these rules differ on more than one point from those to which other internal navigable waterways of the Empire are subjected ... *The provisions relating to the Kiel Canal in the Treaty of Versailles are therefore self-contained* ... The idea which underlies [those rules] is not to be sought by drawing an analogy from [provisions on other waterways] but rather by arguing *a contrario*, a method of argument which excludes them. (emphasis added).

Permanent Court of International Justice (PCIJ) and the *Hostages* case[10] of the International Court of Justice (ICJ).

The ILC Study Group in its analysis identifies three types of different[11] self-contained regimes.

i) In a narrow sense, the term self-contained regime denotes 'a special set of secondary rules under the law of State responsibility that claims primacy to the general rules concerning consequences of a violation';[12]
ii) In a broader sense, self-contained regimes can 'refer to interrelated wholes of primary and secondary rules, sometimes also referred to as "systems" or "subsystems" of rules that cover some particular problem differently from the way it would be covered under general law';[13] and
iii) self-contained regimes as a branch of international law that is characterized by its own principles and institutions (eg 'human rights', 'environmental law', 'humanitarian law').[14]

---

10 *Case Concerning the United States Diplomatic and Consular Staff in Tehran (United States of America v Iran)*, Judgment, ICJ Rep 1980 (24 May) 40, para 86:

> The rules of diplomatic law, in short, *constitute a self-contained regime* which, on the one hand, lays down the receiving State's obligations regarding the facilities, privileges and immunities to be accorded to diplomatic missions and, on the other, foresees their possible abuse by members of the mission and specifies the means at the disposal of the receiving State to counter any such abuse. (emphasis added)

11 But these different regimes are not always clearly distinguishable and are sometimes overlapping.

12 ILC Study Group, (n 4) para 128; Simma also refers to those regimes as 'embracing, in principle, a full (exhaustive and definite) set of secondary rules' and 'which is intended to exclude more or less totally the application of the general consequences of wrongful acts, in particular the application of the countermeasures normally at the disposal of an injured party'; Simma, 'Self-Contained Regimes', (n 7) 117.

13 ILC Study Group, (n 4) para 128.

14 Ibid, para 129; One can see this division of public international law into branches reflected in a 1971 Report to the Commission by the United Nations Secretariat, where 17 different 'topics' or 'branches' of international law were identified; ILC, Survey of International Law (Working Paper Prepared by the Secretary-General) Yearbook of the ILC (1971) vol II, Part 1, 1–99; See also Barnhoorn and Wellens (eds), *Diversity in Secondary Rules*, (n 6); P Malanczuk, 'Space Law as a Branch of International Law' in Barnhoorn and Wellens (eds),

In the end the ILC Study Group reaffirmed the conclusion to which the World Trade Organization (WTO) Appellate Body (AB) had arrived at in its first case, the *US – Reformulated Gasoline* case, that is, that 'the General Agreement [GATT] is not to be read in *clinical isolation* from public international law';[15] a conclusion that finds support in a number of international decisions, not only within the WTO framework[16] but in other regimes as well.[17] This led to the following statement:

Diversity in Secondary Rules, (n 6) 144–6; Such a division has not been without criticism, see I Brownlie, *Principles of Public International Law* (6th edn, OUP, 2003) 529–30; A Pellet, 'Droit de l'hommisme et droit international' Gilberto Amado Memorial Lecture, 18 July 2000 (United Nations, 2000); T Kuokkanen, *International Law and the Environment: Variations on a Theme* (Kluwer Law International, 2002).

[15] (Emphasis added); *United States – Standards for Reformulated and Conventional Gasoline*, 29 April 1996, WT/DS2/AB/R, 17.

[16] Eg, *Korea – Measures Affecting Government Procurement*, 1 May 2000, WT/DS163/R, para 7.96, where the Panel stated: 'Customary international law applies generally to the economic relations between the WTO Members. Such international law applies to the extent that the WTO treaty agreements do not "contract out" from it.' In support of this impossibility of a *stricto sensu* self-containedness of the WTO regime, see PC Mavroidis and D Palmenter, 'The WTO Legal System: Sources of Law' (1998) 92 AJIL 398–9; JP Trachtman, 'The Domain of WTO Dispute Resolution' (1999) 40 Harvard Intl L J 333–77; J Pauwelyn, *Conflict of Norms in Public International Law: How WTO Law Relates to Other Rules of International* Law (CUP, 2003); G Marceau, 'Conflict of Norms and Conflict of Jurisdictions: The Relationship between the WTO Agreement and MEAs and Other Treaties' (2001) 32 JWT 757–79; A Lindroos and M Mehling, 'Dispelling the Chimera of "Self-Contained Regimes": International Law and the WTO' (2006) 16 EJIL 860–66.

[17] *Velásquez Rodríquez* Case, Judgment of 29 July 1988, OC-4/88, *Inter-American Yearbook on Human Rights* (1988) 990, para 184; *Al-Adsani v United Kingdom* (Judgment of 21 November 2001) 34 EHRR 11, paras 55–6; *Fogarty v United Kingdom* (Judgment of 21 November 2001) 34 EHRR 12, paras 36–7; *McElhinney v Ireland* (Judgment of 21 November 2001) 34 EHRR 13, paras 36–7; *Arbitration Regarding the Iron Rhine ('Ijzeren Rijn') Railway (Belgium v the Netherlands)*, Award of 24 May 2005, para 58, www.pca-cpa.org/upload/files/BE-NL%20Award%20corrected%20200905.pdf, accessed 1 July 2012; *Mamatkulov and Askarov v Turkey* (Judgment of 4 February 2005) 41 EHRR 494, para 111; *Georges Pinson Case (France v United Mexican States)*, Award of 13 April 1928, RIAA 5 (1952): 327 at 422, para 50(4); *Esphahanian v Bank Tejarat,* Award of 29 March 1983, Iran-USCTR 2 (1983/I): 157 at 161; *Case No. A/18*, Award of 6 April 1984, Iran-USCTR 5 (1984/I): 251 at 260. In most of these cases it has to be noted that various norms of public international law came into consideration for the purposes of interpretation of the relevant treaty provision or term, through the medium of Article 31(3)(c) of the VCLT.

> *Inappropriateness of the term 'self-contained'*. None of the Special Rapporteurs and none of the cases discussed by them implies the idea of special systems or regimes *that would be fully isolated from general international law. To this extent, the notion of a 'self-contained regime' is simply misleading*. Although the degree to which a regime or responsibility, a set of rules on a problem or a branch of international law needs to be supplemented by general law varies, there is no support for the view that anywhere general law would be fully excluded ... *such exclusion may not be even conceptually possible*. Hence, it is suggested that *the term 'self-contained regime' be replaced by 'special regime'*.[18]

Based on these considerations and for the purposes of the present chapter the aim will be to examine whether the relevant provisions of the VCLT form a uniform basis of creation and maintenance of international conventional obligations or whether 'special regimes' have adopted a series of *ad hoc* solutions that diverge considerably from those provided for in the VCLT.

III. TENSIONS CONCERNING THE IDENTIFICATION AND CHARACTER OF TREATIES AND TREATY OBLIGATIONS BETWEEN STATES

The succinct definition of a treaty in the 1969 VCLT may be subject to different interpretations and different understandings by States and various courts and tribunals.

Therefore the question that may be asked at the outset is whether there is one widely accepted definition of a treaty and whether State practice and the jurisprudence of international courts and tribunals have a common understanding and similar record of application of the VCLT definition. Is there in the jurisprudence of international courts any evidence of a uniform approach as to what constitutes a treaty, and, more importantly, of what type of instrument can be said to generate international rights and obligations for States?

The tensions relating to defining both treaties and treaty obligations contained in instruments which are treaties (or purporting to be treaties) are partly derived from the deceptively simple definition of a treaty contained in Article 2(1) of the 1969 VCLT, which defines the treaty as 'an international agreement concluded between States in written form

---

[18] ILC Study Group, (n 4) para 152 §5 (emphasis added); see also para 193.

and governed by international law, whether embodied in a single instrument or in two or more related instruments and whatever its particular designation'. The question of what constitutes a treaty and the binding nature of obligations deriving from it remains one of the most vexing issues in the law of treaties. In 1962 Judge Jessup expressed an opinion which still holds, that '[t]he notion that there is a clear and ordinary meaning of the word "treaty" is a mirage'.[19] Apart from the difficulties arising from the identification of the binding character or not of certain legal instruments, the development of international law in particular areas, such as environmental law, resulted in an increase of 'soft law' instruments, which are not legally binding, but which may appear to have the form of a treaty. Another problem is the distinction between treaties and unilateral statements of States, which under certain circumstances may create obligations for States. There is also a grey area of certain decisions of organs established by Multilateral Environmental Agreements (MEAs) which may in fact create new treaty obligations (this also creates problems of consent to be bound by a treaty, discussed below).

Essentially, as will be explained further, the question of what constitutes a treaty in the practice of international courts and tribunals is based on the analysis of whether an instrument creates international legal obligations. The decision in most cases is arbitrary, and frequently what appears to be a similar set of legal and factual issues results in different opinions of the courts. Such divergences create tensions and lack of certainty in inter-State relations. What is beyond doubt is that international obligations can be established on the basis of a treaty.[20]

---

[19] Separate Opinion, Judge Jessup in *South West Africa (Ethiopia v South Africa; Liberia v South Africa)*, Preliminary Objections, Judgment, ICJ Rep 1962 (21 December) 402. See also, GJH van Hoof, *Rethinking the Sources of International Law* (Kluwer Law and Taxation Publishers, 1983) 117.

[20] The International Law Commission stated that:

> international obligations may be established by customary rule of international law, by a treaty or by general principles applicable within international legal order. States may assume legal obligations by a unilateral act. An international obligation may arise from provisions stipulated in a treaty (a decision of an international organ of an international organisation competent on the matter, a judgment given between two States by the International Court of Justice or another tribunal, etc) … Moreover these various grounds of obligations interact with each other … Treaties, especially multilateral treaties, can contribute to the formation of general international law, customary law may assist interpretation of treaties; an obligation contained in a treaty may be applicable to a States by a reason of its unilateral act, and so on. (The

The creation of legal obligations by means of a treaty was the core of the drafts presented by the ILC Rapporteurs during the codification of the law of treaties. Fitzmaurice, in particular, referred in his Reports to the creation of a legal obligation or, in other words, to the intention of establishing a relationship governed by international law.[21]

Since the key characteristic of a treaty is the creation of international obligations, the name of a treaty is without importance and the nomenclature cannot provide any guidance as to the legal character of an instrument.[22] The ICJ stated very clearly that '[t]erminology is not a determinant factor as to the character of an international agreement or undertaking'.[23] Such lack of guidance makes tensions between States even more pronounced, as in the case of a dispute; they have to rely on an inconsistent jurisprudence of international courts and tribunals.

The first element of a treaty that can be a cause of uncertainty in inter-State relations is its form. There are several cases which were devoted to analysing the form of an instrument from the point of view of its treaty character.[24]

In the *Aegean Sea Continental Shelf* case a critical issue was the legal nature of the Joint Communiqué of the Greek and Turkish Prime Ministers, that is, whether that instrument constituted an agreement to submit the dispute over the delimitation of the continental shelf in the Aegean Sea to the ICJ. In this case the Court rejected the argument of Greece that the Joint Communiqué was a treaty on the basis that the legal

---

Report of the ILC, on its Fifty-Third Session (23 April–1 June and 2 July–10 August 2001), Chapter IV, 'State Responsibility' at 126, GAOR, Fifty-Fifth Session, Supplement 10 (UN Doc. A/56/10).

21 Sir G Fitzmaurice, First Report on the Law of Treaties, Yearbook of the ILC (1956) vol II, A/CN4/101, 90.

22 The ILC used many names for a treaty without according to them any special meaning. The ILC said that there are treaties, conventions, protocols, declarations, charters, pacts, statutes, etc. Yearbook of the ILC (1966) vol II, 188.

23 *South West Africa*, (n 19) 331.

24 *Aegean Sea Continental Shelf (Greece v Turkey)*, Jurisdiction, ICJ Rep 1978 (19 December) 4, at 39, para 95; *Maritime Delimitation and Territorial Questions between Qatar and Bahrain (Qatar v Bahrain),* Jurisdiction and Admissibility, ICJ Rep 1994 (1 July) 112; *Dispute Concerning Delimitation of the Maritime Boundary between Bangladesh and Myanmar in the Bay of Bengal*, Judgment of 14 March 2012, ITLOS Reports 2012, www.itlos.org/index.php?id=108&L=0, accessed 1 July 2012; *Case Concerning the Land and Maritime Boundary between Cameroon and Nigeria (Cameroon v Nigeria: Equatorial Guinea, Intervening)*, Judgment, ICJ Rep 2002 (10 October); *Legal Status of Eastern Greenland (Denmark v Norway)*, PCIJ 1933 Series A/B, No 53.

character of an instrument must be defined by reference to the actual terms of an act or transaction, and the particular circumstances in which it was drawn up. The Court, however, emphasized that a treaty can have a multitude of forms.[25] In two similar cases, *Qatar/Bahrain* case and *Bangladesh/Myanmar* the main point in dispute was the legal nature of Agreed Minutes. In *Qatar/Bahrain* minutes were alleged by Qatar to constitute an international agreement submitting the dispute to the Court. Bahrain was adamant that they were purely just a record of meetings. The ICJ stated as follows:

> Accordingly, and contrary to the contentions of Bahrain, the Minutes are not a simple record of a meeting, similar to those drawn up within the framework of the Tripartite Committee; they do not merely give an account of discussions and summarize points of agreement and disagreement. They enumerate the commitments to which the Parties have consented. They thus create rights and obligations in international law for the Parties. They constitute an international agreement.[26]

In the *Bangladesh/Myanmar* case, the International Tribunal for the Law of the Sea (ITLOS) reached the opposite conclusion having examined two sets of Agreed Minutes. As mentioned above, the ICJ was firmly of the view that the Agreed Minutes in question created rights and obligations for States, and thus constituted an international agreement. The ITLOS, on the other hand, having analysed two fairly detailed and precise sets of Agreed Minutes (of 1974 and 2008, respectively) was of the view they were nothing more but just the record of two meetings. Of course, if one goes through the analysis of both the ICJ and ITLOS on this aspect, one would be hard pressed to find any clear indication of conflict between these two judgments. Both of them use the same rules and tests to identify if these sets of documents constituted an international agreement and thus produced legal effects. Both the ICJ and ITLOS referred to the 'actual terms and to the particular circumstances in which [the Agreed Minutes had been] drawn up'.[27] The ICJ found that the terms used in paragraphs 1 and 2 of the Agreed Minutes, which included a 'reaffirmation of obligations previously entered into'.[28] and address the circumstances 'under which the dispute may subsequently be submitted to the Court'.[29] It is for this reason that the ICJ concluded that

25 *Aegean Sea*, (n 24) para 96.
26 *Qatar/Bahrain*, (n 24) para 25 of the Judgment.
27 This test was established in the *Aegean Sea*, (n 24) para 96.
28 *Qatar/Bahrain*, (n 24) para 25.
29 Ibid, para 24.

the intention of the parties was to enter into a binding agreement. ITLOS, on the other hand came to a different conclusion. According to its judgment the terms of the Minutes clearly demonstrated that the 1974 Agreed Minutes were not an international agreement. According to the reasoning of ITLOS '[t]his is supported by the language of these Minutes, in particular, in light of the condition expressly contained therein that the delimitation of the territorial sea boundary was to be part of a comprehensive maritime boundary treaty'.[30] However, the decisive element seems to have been the fact that '[f]rom the beginning of the discussions Myanmar made it clear that it did not intend to enter into a separate agreement on the delimitation of territorial sea and that it wanted a comprehensive agreement covering the territorial sea, the exclusive economic zone and the continental shelf'.[31]

The fact that for a very similar set of documents, both named 'Agreed Minutes', two international judicial bodies came to a different legal classification is not surprising. This stems from the fact that 'international agreements may take a number of forms and be given a diversity of names'.[32] This flexibility of the law of treaties is both a source of strength and of weakness. It allows its adaptation to the multifariousness of international relations and cooperation, but it may also be a cause for uncertainty as to what are the international obligations that each State has actually undertaken. As evinced by the two judgments just analysed, in order to identify the legal nature of these Agreed Minutes one had to refer to the terms of the documents in question and the circumstances surrounding their conclusion. Such a practice is by no means an easy and straightforward one, which can result in cases where documents that have been given the same title, that is, Agreed Minutes, may be qualified as having such opposite legal effects, one creating international obligations and the other not.

Another fundamental difference in the findings of both courts is one relating to the intention of the parties. In *Qatar/Bahrain* case the ICJ was adamant that the intentions of States as to the nature of an instrument is of no interest to the Court, which based its decision entirely on the objective text of the document before it. The ITLOS, however, took a different stand on this matter. It said as follows:

> From the beginning of the discussions Myanmar made it clear that it did not intend to enter into a separate agreement on the delimitation of territorial sea

---

30 *Bangladesh/Myanmar*, (n 24) para 92.
31 Ibid, para 93.
32 *Qatar/Bahrain*, (n 24) para 23.

> and that it wanted a comprehensive agreement covering the territorial sea, the exclusive economic zone and the continental shelf.[33]

The ITLOS also stressed that the fact that both parties did not submit Agreed Minutes to their respective constitutional procedures regarding treaties is one of the indications that the Agreed Minutes were not considered to be legally binding.[34] The deceptively simple difference between these two cases would be in assuming that in the *Qatar/Bahrain* case the Minutes contained the set of obligations, while in the *Bangladesh/Myanmar* case, they did not. We should remember, however, that the judgment in the first of these cases was very strongly contested by Bahrain, which always maintained that the Minutes were not treated by it as a treaty.[35] Therefore, the decisions of international judicial bodies on this matter are not devoid of highly specialized nuances that may be a cause of uncertainty and in some cases tension.

Another point of possible tensions between States can be the procedural issue regarding who is entitled to bind a State by signing, ratifying, and so on, a treaty. Classical international law codifies this issue in Articles 7 and 8 of the 1969 VCLT. However, recent developments in international law prompted the ICJ to state in the *Democratic Republic of Congo/Rwanda*[36] case the following:

> The Court notes, however, that with increasing frequency in modern international relations other persons representing a State in specific fields may be authorized by that State to bind it by their statements in respect of matters falling within their purview. This may be true, for example, of holders of technical ministerial portfolios exercising powers in their field of competence in the area of foreign relations, and even of certain officials.[37]

These developments in international law were not noted by the ITLOS, which adhered to the traditional rule and stated as follows:

> the head of the Burmese delegation, Commodore Hlaing, a naval officer, could not be considered as representing Myanmar for the purpose of expressing consent to be bound by a treaty as he was not one of those holders

---

33 *Bangladesh/Myanmar*, (n 24) para 93.

34 Ibid, para 97.

35 See also on the contested nature of these Minutes, *Qatar/Bahrain*, (n 24), Separate Opinion of Judge Valticos and Dissenting Opinion of Judge Oda.

36 *Armed Activities on the Territory of the Congo (New Application: 2002) (Democratic Republic of the Congo v Rwanda)*, Jurisdiction and Admissibility, Judgment, ICJ Rep 2006 (3 Febuary) 6.

37 Ibid, para 47.

> of high-ranking office in the State referred to in article 7, paragraph 2, of the Vienna Convention. Furthermore, the circumstances described in article 7, paragraph 1, of the Vienna Convention do not apply in the present case since Commodore Hlaing did not have full powers issued by the Government of Myanmar and there were no circumstances to suggest that it was the intention of Myanmar and Bangladesh to dispense with full powers.[38]

The possibility of confusion concerning obligations deriving from a treaty is not a recent phenomenon. The best example illustrating the limitations of any definition in the face of multifaceted sources of international obligations is the *Eastern Greenland* case before the PCIJ. This case is treated as an example of a unilateral act (*in casu* the declaration by Norwegian Foreign Minister Ihlen regarding sovereignty over Greenland) binding on a State. In 1919, the Danish Minister accredited in Norway, said in a conversation with Ihlen that Denmark would not object to any claim to Spitzbergen which Norway may submit at the Peace Conference, if Norway would not oppose the claim of Denmark at the same conference to the whole of Greenland. In another conversation, the same year, Ihlen stated: 'that the plans of the Royal [Danish] Government in regard to the sovereignty of Denmark over the whole of Greenland would not encounter difficulties on the part of Norway'.[39] These words were recorded by Ihlen in the form of minutes and submitted to his Government. One of the questions before the Court was the question of the legal nature of the 'Ihlen Declaration'.

It appears, however, from the exchange of views between Ihlen and the Danish Minister that the Ihlen Declaration was in fact an interdependent act, rather than a pure unilateral declaration in the sense of the *Nuclear Tests* cases.[40] The Court said as follows:

> It is clear from the relevant Danish documents which preceded the Danish Minister démarche at Christiania on July 14th, 1919, that the Danish attitude in the Spitzbergen question and the Norwegian attitude in the Greenland question were regarded in Denmark as interdependent, and this interdependence appears to be reflected also in M. Ihlen's minute of the interview. Even if this interdependence – which, in view of the affirmative reply of the Norwegian Government, in whose name the Minister of Foreign Affairs was speaking, would have created a bilateral engagement – is not held to have been established, it can hardly be denied that what Denmark was asking of Norway ('not to make difficulties in the settlement of [the Greenland]

38 *Bangladesh/Myanmar*, (n 24) para 83.

39 *Status of Eastern Greenland*, (n 24) 73.

40 *Nuclear Tests (New Zealand v France)*, Judgment, ICJ Rep 1974 (20 December) 457.

question') was equivalent to what she was indicating her readiness to concede in the Spitzbergen question (to refrain from opposing 'the wishes of Norway in regard to the settlement of this question'). What Denmark desired to obtain from Norway was that the latter should do nothing to obstruct the Danish plans in regard to Greenland. The declaration which the Minster for Foreign Affairs gave on July 22nd, 1919, on behalf of the Norwegian Government, was definitely affirmative: 'I told the Danish Minister to-day that the Norwegian Government would not make any difficulty in the settlement of this question.'[41]

This type of obligation undertaken by a State, in the view of the present authors, cannot be classified as arising from a unilateral statement, as the element *do ut des*, that is reciprocal recognition of mutual obligations, is clearly present. It is for determent of States that the Court refrained from an analysis of this interdependent obligation and instead derived the binding obligation on Norway from the statement made by Ihlen in his position as a Foreign Minster.

The above analysis indicates that there is no uniformity in approaches as to what constitutes a treaty, and therefore this creates tensions in inter-State relations concerning the character and scope of international obligations. The fragmented case law of international courts and tribunals offers nothing to ameliorate this situation. On the contrary, it aggravates it even further by an absolute lack of uniformity and a great degree of specialization in approaches to an almost identical set of factual and legal issues, the best example of which are the *Qatar/Bahrain* and *Bangladesh/Myanmar* cases.

The *Eastern Greenland* case also exemplifies that the variety of legal interrelationships between States preclude perhaps in certain areas the possibility of a uniform approach. At any rate, the question of obligations deriving from the treaty regime is definitely one of specialization rather than uniformity.

IV. CONSENT TO BE BOUND BY A TREATY

There is yet another area of the international law of treaties which is not uniform but due to developments in international law is highly specialized and a possible source of tensions. That area is the expression of consent to be bound by a treaty. In general, the law relating to the methods of expression of consent to be bound by a treaty is codified in Articles 11–17 of the VCLT. The role of the procedures of expressing

---

41 *Status of Eastern Greenland*, (n 24) 70–71.

consent to be bound is to establish a mechanism through which a treaty becomes binding on States. Article 11 of the VCLT lists classical means of consent to be bound by a treaty.[42] The lack of uniformity is particularly visible in allowing consent to be bound to be expressed by 'other means so agreed', as provided for in Article 11 VCLT.

The most legally interesting phenomenon in recent years in relation to consent to be bound is the growing legislative power of the Conferences or Meetings of the Parties (COPs or MOPs) established by certain Multilateral Environmental Agreements.[43] This phenomenon was aptly called by Churchill and Ulfstein 'autonomous institutional arrangements', which they believe 'mark a distinct and different approach to institutional collaboration between states, being more informal and flexible, and often innovative in relation to norm creation and compliance'. According to the same authors:

> A special feature of many MEAs is that they establish an institutional framework of what we have called autonomous institutional arrangements, in the form of COPs, subsidiary bodies, and secretariats, to develop and control their parties' environmental commitments, rather than setting up formal IGOs of the traditional kind ... In spite of their formal denomination, we nevertheless conclude that these self-governing, treaty-based AIAs [autonomous institutional arrangements] of MEAs may be considered to be IGOs, albeit of a less formal, more ad hoc nature than traditional IGOs.[44]

These organs of MEAs are equipped to adopt decisions which under certain treaty regimes can make binding modifications to the obligations of the parties to the treaty, not provided for and unforeseen by the original treaty. Therefore, consent to be bound to a treaty ceases to be expressed in any uniform manner and acquires a high degree of specialization. The necessity to create 'strong' regimes with possibly binding, rule-making power has warranted novel solutions. This may involve the development of new practices which were not previously covered by the

---

[42] Article 11 of the VCLT reads as follows: '[T]he consent of a State to be bound by a treaty may be expressed by signature, exchange of instruments constituting a treaty, ratification, acceptance, approval or accession, or by other means if so agreed'.

[43] Such as, eg, the 1985 Vienna Convention for the Protection of the Ozone Layer and the 1987 Montreal Protocol on the Substances that Deplete the Ozone Layer (the 'Montreal Protocol'); the 1992 United Framework Convention on Climate Change; and the 1997 Kyoto Protocol.

[44] R Churchill and G Ulfstein, 'Autonomous Institutional Arrangements in Multilateral Environmental Agreements: A Little-Noticed Phenomenon in International Law' (2000) 94 AJIL 623, 625.

law of treaties and which lead to further specialization in the area of consent to be bound. An example of this are the decisions taken by COPs and MOPs in various environmental treaties.[45]

There is a great degree of ambivalence between States in relation to such novel ways of consent to be bound. The special ways in which such new forms may be established is through consent of States to modify the terms of the treaty themselves by making amendments or adjustments and through fleshing out or extending treaty provisions through the use of 'enabling provisions'.

The question of the lack of uniformity arises in relation to the powers of COPs/MOPs when traditional (uniform) means of consent to be bound by a treaty are abandoned and modifications to the MEAs are brought about directly by the COP/MOP without a further act of validation by the parties, or where, also without such further act, other decisions of treaty bodies are intended to give rise to directly binding obligations on the parties. A principal example of a MEA which does precisely this is the Montreal Protocol. It provides for an 'adjustment procedure' in Article 2(9). This procedure concerns the modification of the scope of the parties' duties under the Protocol, such as the tightening of control measures by bringing forward the phasing out of certain substances. Decisions adopting an adjustment are as a rule adopted by consensus. However, in case of failure of all efforts to reach consensus, such decisions may be adopted by a two-thirds majority vote of all parties present and voting and representing a majority of both developed and developing countries. The decision has to be communicated to the parties and then enters into force for all parties, including those which opposed the adoption, six months from the date of circulation of the communication.

The little known example of specialization in the expression of consent to be bound regarding modification of treaty obligations by the majority of States parties to a treaty arises in relation to the International Maritime Organization (IMO) and is known as 'tacit acceptance procedure'. This procedure will be analysed in more detail *infra* in section V, but for present purposes it is sufficient to say that the IMO has very extensive regulatory powers in relation to shipping and marine environmental protection. In order to discharge its powers, the IMO elaborates drafts and manages agreements, makes recommendations and drafts non-binding codes. These soft law instruments are frequently incorporated

---

[45] P Davies, 'Non-Compliance: A Pivotal or Secondary Function of CoP Governance?' (2013) 15/1 *International Community Law Review* 77.

into conventions through their amendment procedure. This procedure of amendment also binds the minority. For example, in 1999, the voluntary 1993 Code for Safe Carriage of Packaged Irradiated Nuclear Fuel, Plutonium and High-Level Radioactive Waste on Board Ships (the INF Code) was adopted at the 71st Session of the Maritime Safety Committee (MSC) on the basis of Resolution 88(71). At the same session, Chapter VII (Carriage of Dangerous Goods) of the 1974 International Convention on the Safety of Life at Sea (SOLAS) was amended to incorporate this code.[46] This procedure merits attention, as it departs from the uniform pattern of expression of consent to be bound in international law. Amendments may be approved by majority vote in the MSC and are adopted if objections are raised only by a minority of less than 50 per cent of gross tonnage of the worlds' merchant fleet. It is thus possible than an amendment based on the decision of a majority in the MSC, and approved by only a majority of SOLAS contracting parties, may also be binding on the minority of the parties which objected to it. It is significant that such a method of adoption of an amendment might result in the imposition of a considerable burden on States. In this particular case, as of 1 January 2001 all ships, regardless of size, engaged in the carriage of packaged irradiated nuclear fuel, plutonium, and high-level radioactive wastes were required to hold a valid International Certificate of Fitness, which certified that a ship was constructed according to certain standards regarding such matters as strength, stability, fire protection, cargo securement, and so on.

A second method of modification of States' obligations under a treaty is derived from 'enabling clauses' in conventions or protocols which charge COPs/MOPs with the elaboration of rules in certain areas covered by a treaty without expressly providing for actual amendment of the treaty (even though they may in fact result in modification of States parties' obligations). The essential characteristic of such enabling clauses and the decisions made under them is that they do not provide for a detailed decision-making procedure to be followed by the COPs/MOPs and do not, in particular, make any express provision for decisions made

---

[46] Article VIII(b) reads as follows:

> Amendments shall be deemed to have been accepted on a particular date, unless more than one third of the Contracting Governments of SOLAS, or Contracting Governments the combined merchant fleets of which constitute not less than 50 percent of the gross tonnage of the world's merchant fleet, have notified their objections to the amendment.

under them to be binding (whether by consensus or by majority).[47] Despite this, matters decided by COPs/MOPs on the basis of enabling clauses are often claimed to be binding on the parties; or at least, they ought to be. But such claims are by no means undisputed.[48]

There are several examples of such enabling clauses. The Montreal Protocol reads in Article 8: 'The Parties, at their first meeting, shall consider and approve procedures and institutional mechanisms for determining non-compliance with provisions of this Protocol and for the treatment of Parties found to be in non-compliance.' The most extensive use of enabling clauses can be found in the Kyoto Protocol. In fact they are central to its structure. A series of key provisions regarding the climate change regime, elements which were also highly controversial, were left to be decided at the meeting of COP/MOP under enabling clauses. The most striking provisions are found in Articles 6, 12, and 17, which authorize the COP/MOP to elaborate guidelines and set up machinery to regulate the 'flexibility mechanisms', and in Articles 18 and 24, which charge the COP/MOP with elaborating a non-compliance procedure.[49] This procedure under the Kyoto Protocol is especially far-reaching, as it may be used to suspend the right of participation of a State party to the flexibility mechanisms. Therefore, this mechanism may be considered as a further specialization of a special method of consent to be bound by a treaty.

---

[47] Article 2(9) of the Montreal Protocol is an exception to this as it not only provides explicitly that these decisions are binding but also outlines the decision-making process.

[48] Churchill and Ulfstein, 'Autonomous Institutional Arrangements …', (n 44); generally on the debate surrounding the binding or not nature of COP/MOP decisions, see T Goehring, 'Treaty-Making and Treaty Evolution' in D Bodansky, J Brunnée and E Hey (eds), *The Oxford Handbook of International Environmental Law* (OUP, 2008) 467, 491 *et seq*; J Brunnée, 'COPing with Consent: Law-Making under Multilateral Environmental Agreements' (2002) 15 Leiden J Intl L 1; G Handl, 'International "Lawmaking" by Conferences of the Parties and Other Politically Mandated Bodies: Comment' in R Wolfrum and V Röben (eds), *Development of International Law in Treaty Making* (Springer, 2005) 127.

[49] Although the case of the Kyoto Protocol, as will be demonstrated in section V, is somewhat different than that of the Montreal Protocol, as Article 18 charges the COP with the duty to elaborate a non-compliance procedure, nonetheless for its decision to entail any binding consequences it specifically requires the amendment procedure of Article 20 to be followed.

The puzzling nature of new 'specialized' ways of consent to be bound has been the subject of many theoretical analyses. The theories which were put forward can be broadly grouped in three main categories:

i) Theories which accord binding force to the COP/MOP decisions as deriving from the intention of the parties, that is, as deriving, in the broadest sense, from consent to the treaty they are based on;
ii) Theories which assume that the decisions do not have formally binding legal effect but nevertheless attempt to find some intermediate ('soft' or '*de facto*') status; and
iii) Theories which also assume that the decisions do not have formally binding character on the basis of the intention of the parties but seek to substitute an alternative basis, outside the realm of the law of treaties, for its binding character.

The first of these theories (the intention of the parties) is based on two alternative explanations. One is based on the language of enabling clauses in the Kyoto Protocol, which use the word 'shall' (COP 'shall define the relevant principles, modalities and rules and guidelines'). This indicates the intention of the parties to give decisions of COPs/MOPs binding force.[50] An alternative approach focuses rather on COP/MOP decisions as the expression of the parties' intention that the decision be binding. In effect, this theory treats COPs/MOPs decisions taken by consensus as agreements in a simplified form, which are binding on parties.[51] In such cases it is the wording of the decision that is crucial. The creation of a non-compliance procedure under the 1989 Basel Convention on Transboundary Movement of Hazardous Wastes, which was adopted by a decision of the COP at its one motion and by consensus, and without being based on an enabling clause in the text of the Basel Convention, may be seen as an example where this theory comes to bear.

The theories of soft or *de facto* effect are based on the premise that even if decisions of COPs/MOPs do not have a fully binding effect on the parties' rights and obligations, the failure to comply with them may have consequences as regards compliance, and this may be described as '*de*

---

[50] J Brunnée, '"Reweaving" the Fabric of International Law? Patterns of Consent in Environmental Framework Agreements' in R Wolfrum and V Röben (eds), *Developments in International Law-Making* (Springer, 2005) 12.

[51] Churchill and Ulfstein, 'Autonomous Institutional Arrangements …', (n 44) 640.

facto law-making'.[52] The term may be criticized on the same basis as soft law: it may imply an attempt to blur what should be a clear distinction between what is legally binding and what is not. Nevertheless it is an accurate description of a real-world situation which has implications for international relations, for the effectiveness and functioning of treaty regimes, and for the formation of legally binding rules.

Finally, it has been suggested that international institutional law may be applicable to COPs/MOPs. The consequence of such an approach would be the applicability of the concept of 'implied powers', which would in turn provide another basis for holding the decisions of COPs/MOPs to be legally binding.[53]

V. AMENDMENT PROCEDURES

1. *Travaux Préparatoires* of the VCLT

The final area to be examined with respect to the possible tensions that may arise between uniformity and specialization in treaty law is that of amendment of treaties. A first issue that needs to be addressed is a definitional one. The terms 'amendment', 'revision' and 'modification' are sometimes used interchangeably.[54] Eventually, the ILC made use only of the terms amendment, and modification, with the former denoting an alteration of the provisions of the treaty, which produced effects on all of the parties, whereas modification addressed the issue of *inter se* agreements.[55]

The relevant provisions of the VCLT are Articles 39–41, and these offer from the very start an interesting insight as to whether they promote a uniform solution or a variety of solutions as to how a treaty, throughout its life cycle, may be amended or modified. Article 39, which functions as an introductory provision, clearly stipulates that the VCLT provisions on amendment and modification apply 'except insofar as the treaty may otherwise provide'. It is logical to infer from this that the VCLT rules on

---

52 Brunnée, '"Reweaving" ...', (n 50) 111.

53 Churchill and Ulfstein, 'Autonomous Institutional Arrangements ...', (n 44) 633–4.

54 United Nations, *Handbook of Final Clauses* (ST/LEG/6), 130 and 150.

55 Ie, agreements between only some of the parties to the treaty in question, and which produced effects only between those parties; Yearbook of the ILC (1966) vol II, 232, para 3.

amendment and modification were meant to be of a 'residual character'.[56] Of course one can argue that several provisions of the VCLT are of a residual character, however, in this context the term was even more relevant since it was used to denote the lack of uniformity in State practice as to amendment/modification provisions and the non-existence of a relevant customary international rule. This is confirmed by the *travaux préparatoires* of the VCLT. This admission made deducing – let alone agreeing on any – customary rules on amendment an impossible task.[57] For this reason, ILC discussions focused simply on trying to 'include a formulation of the basic rules concerning the process of amendment',[58] and the keyword throughout the discussions was that the relevant provisions would be of a residual character.[59]

Articles 40 and 41 reflect the clear separation that the ILC wanted to make between the processes of amendment and modification. In particular, Article 40(3) VCLT was the result of an intense debate as to whether parties should be given a right to become parties only to the amended treaty or whether this right should extend to the negotiating procedures, that is, whether States that had signed and ratified a treaty had a right only to become a party to the treaty as amended but not necessarily a right to participate in the negotiations, or whether that right included also a right of participation in the negotiations that lead to the amended version of the treaty. The latter solution (right to participate in the amendment negotiations and right to be party to the amended treaty) was the one found to be more in line with the spirit of the provisions of the VCLT.[60] Similarly, as regards Article 40(5) the ILC considered that the provision:

> should be based on two principles: *(a)* the right of the State, on becoming a party to the treaty, to decide whether to become a party to the treaty alone, to the treaty plus the amending agreement or to the amended treaty alone; *(b)* in the absence of any indication by the State, it is desirable to adopt a solution which will bring the maximum number of States into mutual relations under the treaty. Paragraph 5 therefore provides that, failing an expression of a different intention, a State which becomes a party after the amending agreement has come into force is to be considered as: *(a)* a party to the treaty

---

[56] Ibid, 233, para 7.

[57] Ibid, 232, para 2.

[58] Ibid.

[59] Ie, that they would apply only if the parties to the treaty had not inserted in its text any specific provisions on amendment and modification; see also ibid, 233, para 7.

[60] Ibid, 233–4, para 10.

> as amended, and *(b)* a party also to the unamended treaty in its relations with any party to the treaty which is not bound by the amending agreement.[61]

Finally, Article 41 regulates the procedure for *inter se* agreements. The importance of this provision is highlighted by the fact that consecutive Special Rapporteurs on the Law of Treaties were in agreement as to the fact that *inter se* agreements were the most often used and practical method for revising multilateral treaties.[62] This notwithstanding, the vast majority of multilateral treaties does not contain provisions either permitting or prohibiting *inter se* agreements.[63]

The ILC, although following the approach already enunciated in Article 39, that is, that of the 'residual nature' of the provisions, nonetheless felt it essential to impose two absolute limitations on the freedom of States to negotiate *inter se* agreements.

> [They should not] (i) … affect the enjoyment by the other parties of their rights under the treaty or the performance of their obligations; [and] (ii) [they should not] relate to a provision, derogation from which is incompatible with the effective execution of the object and purpose of the treaty as a whole.[64]

Based on the typology of international obligations suggested by Sir Gerald Fitzmaurice, it seems that with respect to treaties creating reciprocal obligations (ie, bilateral or bilateralizable obligations) it would be easier to make a case that an *inter se* agreement is in conformity with the limitations set by Article 41 than it would be in the case of treaties creating non-reciprocal obligations (ie, interdependent or integral obligations).

---

61 Ibid, 234, para 13.

62 See H Lauterpacht, Second Report, Yearbook of the ILC (1954) vol II, 136; Sir G Fitzmaurice, Third Report on the Law of Treaties, Yearbook of the ILC (1958) vol II, A/CN.4/115, 43, para 89; Sir H Waldock, Third Report on the Law of Treaties, Yearbook of the ILC (1964) vol II, 49.

63 ILC Study Group, (n 4) para 315; a notable exception is Article 3111 of the 1982 United Nations Convention on the Law of the Sea (UNCLOS).

64 Article 41 of the VCLT; these two limitations seem to be based on the typology of international obligations suggested by Sir Gerald Fitzmaurice, ie, a) reciprocal (which are further divided into bilateral and bilateralizable obligations) and b) non reciprocal (which, in turn, can be further divided to interdependent and integral obligations); in more detail, see Sir G Fitzmaurice, Second Report on the Law of Treaties, Yearbook of the ILC (1957) vol II, A/CN.4/107, 16, 54; Fitzmaurice, Third Report on the Law of Treaties, (n 62) 20, 27, Article 18, para 2; ibid, 41–5, paras 77–94; Waldock, Third Report on the Law of Treaties, (n 62) 39, para 17.

2. Uniformity versus Specialization of Amendment Procedures: Contemporary Critical Examples

In the previous section the analysis of the text and *travaux préparatoires* of Articles 39–41 of the VCLT demonstrated their residual character. What remains to be shown is whether this freedom, recognized to States, of regulating as they see fit the amendment procedures of the international treaties they enter into has been utilized, leading to unique amendment solutions. The following examples have been selected as the most demonstrative of these issues: i) the 'tacit acceptance procedure' common but not restricted to the IMO conventions; ii) disconnection clauses; iii) restrictions to the 'right of amendment' imposed by participation in international organizations such as the EU; and iv) the non-compliance procedure of the Kyoto Protocol.

a) The tacit acceptance procedure

One of the major problems of the 'unanimity rule' in amendment procedures is the fact that the greater the participation of States in a particular treaty the more difficult and time-consuming it is for an amendment to pass. This drawback becomes more pronounced in the case of treaties that are of a technical character and need to be updated regularly. The IMO conventions are examples of such technical treaties, and one of the most well known of these is the International Convention for the Safety of Life at Sea (SOLAS),[65] which adopts a tacit acceptance procedure.[66] Earlier versions of the SOLAS Convention followed the unanimity rule[67] or the 'percentage rule' with respect to updating.[68]

---

[65] The 1974 International Convention for the Safety of Life at Sea (SOLAS), 14 ILM 959.

[66] Tacit acceptance procedures can be found in other IMO conventions as well, such as the 1972 Convention on the International Regulations for Preventing Collisions at Sea, 1050 UNTS 16; the 1973 International Convention for the Prevention of Pollution from Ships as amended by the Protocol of 1978 (MARPOL 73/78), 17 ILM 546; the 1972 International Convention for Safe Containers, 29 UST 3707.

[67] SOLAS 1914, Article 74 (referring to 'common consent'), www.imo.org/KnowledgeCentre/ReferencesAndArchives/HistoryofSOLAS/Documents/SOLAS%201914.pdf, accessed 1 July 2012; SOLAS 1929, Article 61, www.austlii.edu.au/au/other/dfat/treaties/1936/9.html, accessed 1 July 2012.

[68] Ie, amendments entering into force when accepted by a certain percentage of the parties; SOLAS 1948, Article IX, www.austlii.edu.au/au/other/dfat/treaties/1960/1.html, accessed 1 July 2012; SOLAS 1960, Article IX, www.austlii.edu.au/au/other/dfat/treaties/1968/7.html, accessed 1 July 2012.

However, these procedures were far from successful, and in 1968 the IMO established a Working Group to identify areas for improvement of its functioning. The amendment procedure was one of the main points of consideration,[69] and the outcome of the work of the Working Group eventually led to the tacit acceptance procedure of Article VIII of the 1974 SOLAS Convention.[70]

According to this procedure, once a proposal for an amendment has been adopted by the International Maritime Safety Committee (IMSC),[71] it automatically enters into force once the required amount of time has lapsed. No additional action is required either by the organization or by the States parties.[72] Action is required only if the States want to block the passing of the relevant amendment. In such a case they have the option of objecting explicitly. But even that objection may not be sufficient in and of itself. In order to bar the entry into force of the amendment the States parties objecting must represent 'more than one third of Contracting Governments, or Contracting Governments the combined merchant fleets of which constitute not less than fifty per cent of the gross tonnage of the World's merchant fleet'.[73]

Only in that case of explicit objection does the amendment fail to enter into force. This procedure has been reserved for amendments to the chapters of the Annex, with the exception of Chapter I. The reason for this is that the relevant chapters are of a technical nature and need to be constantly updated in order to keep up with technological advances. The sheer number of amendments to the SOLAS Convention is the soundest proof of the efficacy of this procedure.[74] This fact is further highlighted if one considers that, prior to the incorporation of the tacit acceptance procedure in the workings of the SOLAS Convention, none of the amendments proposed to the 1960 version of the SOLAS Convention had entered into force.[75]

---

69 IMO, 'Conventions: Introduction – Adopting a Convention, Entry into force, Accession, Amendment, Enforcement, Tacit Acceptance Procedure' www.imo.org/About/Conventions/Pages/Home.aspx, accessed 1 July 2012.

70 A detailed history of the evolution of the tacit acceptance procedure in the IMO can be found at ibid.

71 In accordance with the procedure of Article VIII(b)(i)–(v).

72 1974 SOLAS Convention, Article VIII(b)(vi)(2) and (vii)(2).

73 1974 SOLAS Convention, Article VIII(b)(vi)(2).

74 The amendments adopted by the IMSC are listed in IMSC Resolutions, which can be found at www5.imo.org/SharePoint/mainframe.asp?doc_id=3710&topic_id=435, accessed 1 July 2012.

75 IMO, 'Conventions: Introduction …' (n 69).

b) Disconnection clauses

Another issue that has arisen with respect to amendment and modification of treaties is the recent increase in the use of 'disconnection clauses' in multilateral agreements to which the European Union (EU) is a party. The aim of such clauses is to ensure that the EU rules will continue to apply amongst the member States of the EU, while at the same time leaving unaffected the relationships and corresponding rights and obligations between EU members and non-EU members that are all parties to the treaty, in which the disconnection clause has been inserted.

A typical form that such a disconnection clause may have is:

> Notwithstanding the rules of the present Convention, those Parties which are members of the European Economic Community shall apply in their mutual relations the common rules in force in that Community.[76]

In its Report the ILC Study Group identified a number of conventions that had such a disconnection clause.[77] These clauses can be general,[78] partial,[79] or qualified.[80] What is interesting is that the ILC Study Group analyses them in the section devoted to Special Clauses, the greatest part

---

[76] Article 27 of the 1988 Convention on Mutual Administrative Assistance in Tax Matters, cited in ILC Study Group, (n 4) para 289.

[77] Eg, Council of Europe Convention on Laundering, Search, Seizure and Confiscation of the Proceeds from Crime and the Financing of Terrorism, 16 May 2005 Warsaw, Article 52(4); Council of Europe Convention on Action against Trafficking of Human Beings, 16 May 2005 Warsaw, Article 40(3); Council of Europe Convention on the Prevention on Terrorism, 16 May 2005 Warsaw, Article 26(3); Council of Europe Convention on Contracts Concerning Children, 15 May 2003 Strasbourg, Article 20(3); Agreement on Illicit Traffic by Sea, implementing Article 17 of the United Nations Convention against Illicit Traffic in Narcotic Drugs and Psychotropic Substances, 31 January 1995 Strasbourg, Article 30(3); Convention on Civil Liability for Damage Resulting from Activities Dangerous to the Environment, 21 June 1993 Lugano, Article 25(2); Protocol on Civil Liability and Compensation for Damage Caused by the Transboundary Effects of Industrial Accidents on Transboundary Waters, 21 May 2003 Kiev, Article 20(2).

[78] Covering the whole treaty.

[79] Article 20(2) of the Protocol on Civil Liability and Compensation for Damage Caused by the Transboundary Effects of Industrial Accidents on Transboundary Waters.

[80] Article 26(3) of the Council of Europe Convention on the Prevention of Terrorism; for more details on the various typologies and controversies over disconnection clauses, see CP Economides and AG Kolliopoulos, 'La clause de déconnexion en faveur du droit communautaire: une pratique critiquable' (2006) 110(2) RGDIP 273–302; E Neframi, 'La répartition intra-communautaire des

of which is devoted to Conflict Clauses. In fact it goes on to explicitly state that '[disconnection clauses] are thus *best analyzed as conflict clauses* added to treaties with the view to regulating potential conflicts between Community law and the treaty'.[81] However, such a categorization may be open to debate. As mentioned *supra* the object and purpose of such clauses is to ensure that EU rules will continue to apply amongst EU member States. The crux of this point is that EU rules are not to be understood merely as frozen in time, but as evolving over time. If this were not the case, then a kaleidoscope of possibly conflicting obligations would emerge. On the one hand, and under the convention incorporating a disconnection clause, EU member States would be bound by a set of norms as they stood at the time of the entry into force of the relevant convention and, on the other hand, they would also be bound by the amended or new EU rules, as they may have evolved over time. Such a situation would lead to an *absurdum* and clearly the aforementioned interpretation cannot be upheld. However, this brings us another question. If the disconnection clauses are aimed at allowing the EU member States that are parties to a particular convention to be bound *inter se* by a different set of rules, which may change over time, how is this different than the *inter se* agreements provided for in Article 41 of the VCLT?

The ILC Study Group faced with the same question and, somewhat bizarrely, immediately after categorizing disconnection clauses as conflict clauses acknowledges that 'this is scarcely different from regular *inter se amendments* that also apply between some parties only and that may be subject to future modification'.[82] The use of the term '*inter se amendment*' seems somewhat awkwardly placed. The flow of the Study Group's argument and its context seem to indicate that what was meant was '*inter se* agreement' or '*inter se* modification', that is, the process envisaged in Article 41 of the VCLT. This is reinforced by the fact that in the following paragraphs the Study Group takes its analysis in the realm of 'modification'.

The only thing that then remains to be examined is whether disconnection clauses can indeed be considered as *inter se* agreements under Article 41 of the VCLT. Firstly, the very inclusion of the disconnection clause in the body of a treaty satisfies the requirement of Article 41(1)(a), that is, that: '(*a*) the possibility of such a modification is provided for by

compétences et les états sous le prisme de la clause de déconnexion' (2008) 61 *Revue Hellénique de Droit International* 477–97; ILC Study Group, (n 4) paras 289–94.

[81] ILC Study Group, (n 4) para 292 (emphasis added).

[82] Ibid (emphasis added).

the treaty'. Secondly, the requirement of notification of the modification to other parties, under Article 41(2), is not applicable since the modification of the treaty is provided for in the disconnection clause. Finally, an open-ended disconnection clause will have the same limits as an *inter se* agreement, that is, it will have to respect the object and purpose of the treaty.[83]

The above analysis, thus, demonstrates that disconnection clauses are more appropriately categorized as *inter se* agreements under Article 41 VCLT rather than conflict clauses, but also that modern treaty practice leads to the emergence of new forms of treaty clauses that raise important theoretical and practical issues as to their correct characterization and the apposite requirements and consequences.

c) Curtailing the right of a state to propose amendments

As has been pointed out above, the rules enshrined in Articles 39–42 of the VCLT are of a residual nature. This gives States great discretion to set up amendment procedures that can either enhance or reduce their amendment rights. Examples of the latter are evident in the jurisprudence of the European Court of Justice (ECJ).

Before we proceed with an examination of the relevant cases, some background information is necessary. Article 351 of the 2007 Consolidated version of the Treaty on the Functioning of the European Union (CTFEU) provides that:

> The rights and obligations arising from agreements concluded before 1 January 1958 or, for acceding States, before the date of their accession, between one or more Member States on the one hand, and one or more third countries on the other, shall not be affected by the provisions of the Treaties.
>
> To the extent that such agreements are not compatible with the Treaties, the Member State or States concerned shall take all appropriate steps to eliminate the incompatibilities established. Member States shall, where necessary, assist each other to this end and shall, where appropriate, adopt a common attitude.
>
> In applying the agreements referred to in the first paragraph, Member States shall take into account the fact that the advantages accorded under the Treaties by each Member State form an integral part of the establishment of

---

[83] Chairman, 876th ILC Meeting of 22 June 1966, Yearbook of the ILC (1966) vol I, Part 2, 219; this is reflected in the final text of Article 41(b)(ii); similar considerations of respect of the object and purpose of the treaty permeated the ILC discussions on reservations; Report of the Special Rapporteur A Pellet, Tenth Report on Reservations to Treaties, Doc. A/CN.4/558/Add.1, (2005) 3–4; see also ILC Study Group, (n 4) para 293. Some disconnection clauses are even worded so as to be 'without prejudice to the object and purpose of the present Convention'; ILC Study Group, (n 4) para 294.

> the Union and are thereby inseparably linked with the creation of common institutions, the conferring of powers upon them and the granting of the same advantages by all the other Member States.[84]

The *Burgoa* case established that Article 351 CTFEU 'is of general scope and it applies to any international agreement, irrespective of subject-matter, which is capable of affecting the application of the treaty'.[85] Furthermore, according to the jurisprudence of the ECJ, Article 351 refers to rights of third States and obligations of member States, *but not to rights of member States*. In more detail:

> the terms 'rights and obligations' in Article [351] refer, as regards the 'rights', to the rights of third countries and, as regards the 'obligations', to the obligations of Member States and that, by virtue of the principles of international law, by assuming a new obligation which is incompatible with rights held under a prior treaty a State *ipso facto* gives up the exercise of these rights to the extent necessary for the performance of its new obligations.[86]

Based on this interpretation of Article 351, a member State cannot invoke its *rights* stemming from a different convention to circumvent its obligations under the EU regime. Only obligations of the member State fall within the framework of Article 351.

In *Commission v Greece*, the issue in question was that the Greek Government had submitted a proposal to the MSC of the IMO regarding the 'development of check lists or of other tools to assist SOLAS Contracting Governments in the verification of compliance of ship and of port facilities with the verification of compliance with the requirements of SOLAS chapter XI-2 and of the ISPS Code [the International Ship and Port Facility Security Code]'.[87] The Commission argued that since the setting of a common policy in the area of transport is one of the

---

[84] Article 351 of the CTFEU (ex Article 307 of the 1992 Treaty Establishing the European Community (TEC)).

[85] Case C-812/79, *Attorney General v Juan C Burgoa*, Judgment of 14 October 1980, ECR (1980) 2787, 2802, para 6.

[86] Case 10/61, *Commission of the European Economic Community v Italy*, Judgment of 27 February 1962, ECR 1, para II B 3; see also J Klabbers, 'Re-Inventing the Law of Treaties: The Contribution of the EC Courts' (1999) XXX Netherlands YB Intl L 45, 63–5.

[87] IMO, 'Measures to Enhance Maritime Security' (MSC 80/5/11), 18 March 2005, Executive Summary, www.sjofartsverket.se/upload/4017/80-5-11.pdf, accessed 1 July 2012.

objectives of the Community,[88] and bearing in mind Articles 90, 91, and 100 of the CTFEU in combination with Regulation (EC) No 725/2004 of the European Parliament and of the Council of 31 March 2004 on enhancing ship and port facility security, the EU enjoyed exclusive competence to regulate and assume international obligations in that particular area.[89]

The Court re-affirmed the distinction between 'rights' and 'obligations' of Article 351.

> [Article 351] is designed to *apply only* if there is an incompatibility between, on the one hand, *an obligation arising under the international convention*, concluded by the Hellenic Republic before its accession to the Community and by which that State became an IMO member, and, on the other, *an obligation arising under Community law*.[90]

Greece was not obliged to submit that proposal. Consequently, the case at hand was one of exercise of a right rather than adherence to an obligation.[91]

Furthermore Greece 'set in motion … a procedure with the contested proposal, [and] took an initiative likely to affect the provisions of the Regulation, which is an infringement of the obligations under [EU law]'.[92] The fact that the proposal of Greece would not lead by necessity to the adoption of that particular amendment was not considered to have any bearing on the case.[93]

For these reasons the ECJ held that Greece, by exercising its rights under the SOLAS Convention to propose an amendment to the MSC for consideration, was in violation of EU law and that therefore it should have abstained from such an action.

---

[88] As affirmed in Case 22/70, *Commission v Council* [1971] ECR 263, para 20.

[89] C-45/07, *Commission v Greece*, Judgment of 12 February 2009, ECR, paras 14–19, http://curia.europa.eu/jurisp/cgi-bin/form.pl?lang=EN&Submit=Rechercher$docrequire=alldocs&numaff=C-45/07, accessed 1 July 2012.

[90] Ibid, para 35 (emphasis added); referring also to Case C-62/98, *Commission v Portugal* [2000] ECR I-5171, paras 46 and 47. Additionally the Court held that since the crux of Greece's submission was that its proposal to the MSC was not clashing with its obligations under EU law, Article 351 could not be applied, as it requires the existence of a conflict.

[91] *Commission v Greece*, (n 89).

[92] Ibid, para 23.

[93] Ibid, paras 23 and 29.

In a similar and more recent case the ECJ following almost the same legal reasoning as in *Commission v Greece*, came to an identical conclusion. In *Commission v Sweden* the facts of the case were the following: Sweden had submitted a proposal for an amendment to Annex A of the 2001 Stockholm Convention on Persistent Organic Pollutants (Stockholm Convention). This amendment proposal consisted of the inclusion of a substance, perfluoroctane sulfonate (PFOS) in Annex A. However, the Commission had already presented a proposal for a Decision,[94] asking for authorization to submit amendment proposals in the Annexes to the 1998 UNECE Convention on Access to Information, Public Participation in Decision-making and Access to Justice in Environmental Matters (Aarhus Convention) and the Stockholm Convention. In this case as well the ECJ found that Sweden's actions were not in conformity with its obligations under EU law.[95]

What these two cases, taken from the recent jurisprudence of the ECJ, demonstrate is that matters are becoming increasingly complex in the area of interactions between treaties and treaty regimes. The fact that a convention provides for the possibility of a State to propose amendments may no longer suffice for that State to exercise that right. It will have to be examined and balanced alongside its other international obligations stemming from international treaties and/or participation in international organizations.

d) The Non-Compliance Procedure (NCP) of the Kyoto Protocol

A final issue that should be discussed is the Non-Compliance Procedure of the Kyoto Protocol regime. An important element of contemporary multilateral environmental treaties is the establishment of such non-compliance procedures (NCPs). The Kyoto Protocol is no exception to this. According to Article 18:

> The Conference of the Parties serving as the meeting of the Parties to this Protocol shall, at its first session, approve appropriate and effective procedures and mechanisms to determine and to address cases of non-compliance with the provisions of this Protocol, including through the development of an indicative list of consequences, taking into account the cause, type, degree and frequency of non-compliance. *Any procedures and mechanisms under this*

---

[94] COM(2004) 537 final.

[95] Case C-246/07, *Commission v Sweden*, Judgment of 20 April 2010, ECR, paras 69–105, http://curia.europa.eu/jurisp/cgi-bin/form.pl?lang=EN&Submit=Rechercher$docrequire=alldocs&numaff=C-246/07, accessed 1 July 2012.

> *Article entailing binding consequences shall be adopted by means of an amendment to this Protocol.*[96]

The Kyoto Protocol NCP was adopted during the first Conference of the Parties serving as the meeting of the Parties to the Kyoto Protocol (CMP1) in Montreal, by means of Decision 27/CMP.1.[97] No amendment was ever passed in accordance with Article 18.[98] The question that naturally arises is how does the lack of an amendment affect the NCP? According to Article 18 '[a]ny procedures and mechanisms under this Article *entailing binding consequences* shall be adopted by means of an amendment to this Protocol' (emphasis added). One way to resolve the issue would be to consider that either the NCP does not entail binding consequences or that any decision taken by the two branches of the NCP (the Facilitative and the Executive Branch) will have no binding effect.[99]

However, that does not seem to be the case. First of all, the Executive Branch may, according to Section XV of Decision 27/CMP.1 entitled 'Consequences applied by the Enforcement Branch', render a decision to the effect of deducting from a party's assigned amount for the second

---

[96] Emphasis added.

[97] UNFCCC, 'Decision 27/CMP.1: Procedures and Mechanisms Relating to Compliance under the Kyoto Protocol', FCCC/KP/CMP/2005/8/Add.3, 30 March 2006, http://unfccc.int/resource/docs/2005/cmp1/eng/08a03.pdf#page=92, accessed 1 July 2012; the Rules of Procedure were adopted during CMP2, with Decision 4/CMP.2; UNFCCC, 'Decision 4/CMP.2: Compliance Committee', FCCC/KP/CMP/2006/10/Add.1, 2 March 2007, http://unfccc.int/resource/docs/2006/cmp2/eng/10a01.pdf#page=17, last accessed 1 July 2012.

[98] A proposal by Saudi Arabia to incorporate the compliance procedures into the Protocol through an amendment has since then remained on the agenda of the CMP; S Oberthür and R Lefeber, 'Holding Countries to Account: The Kyoto Protocol's Compliance System Revisited after Four Years of Experience' (2010) 1 Climate L 133, 151 and fn 94.

[99] This argument was raised by Canada in 2008 in front of a Canadian Court; 'Memorandum of Fact and Law of the Respondent of 13 February 2008' in *Friends of the Earth v The Minister of the Environment* (Federal Court, Court File No T-1683-07), para 7. On the debate on this issue, see, Oberthür and Lefeber, 'Holding Countries to Account …', (n 98) 151, referring to J Brunnée, 'The Kyoto Protocol: Testing Ground for Compliance Theories?' (2003) 63 ZaöRV 255; G Ulfstein and J Werksman, 'The Kyoto Compliance System: Towards Hard Enforcement' in OS Stokke, J Hovi, and G Ulfstein (eds), *Implementing the Climate Regime: International Compliance* (Earthscan, 2005)39, 57–8; A Halvorssen and J Hovi, 'The Nature, Origin and Impact of Legally Binding Consequences: The Case of the Climate Regime' (2005) 6 Intl Environmental Agreements 157.

commitment period,[100] demand the development of a compliance action plan and/or suspend the eligibility of the party in question to make use of the flexibility mechanisms of the Kyoto Protocol.[101] Furthermore, the Executive Branch has already given a number of judgments and the parties have submitted themselves to this process without casting doubts on the legally binding nature of this process.[102]

The various theories regarding the legally binding nature of the COP/MOP decisions have been analysed in detail *supra* in section IV and may offer some insight as to the current status of the Kyoto Protocol NCP. In addition to these, Oberthür and Lefeber seem to argue that what is of import is the *de facto* effectiveness of the NCP, and that the debate on its formally binding status is somewhat irrelevant.[103] However, there is one more possibility that needs to be taken into consideration and this bring us full circle to the original analysis of the discussions on Articles 39–41 of the VLCT and, in particular, draft article 38, which provided for modification through subsequent practice of States and which never found its way into the final text of the VCLT. Based on the fact that Decision 27/CMP.1 was adopted unanimously, that the Executive and Facilitative Branches have been functioning without objection being raised as to the legal validity of their decisions, that the Executive Branch has rendered a number of judgments suspending parties from their eligibility to use the Kyoto Protocol flexibility mechanisms, and that countries like Greece have submitted themselves willingly to the process in order to reverse their suspension, it is argued that there is sufficient practice demonstrative of the intention of the parties to consider the NCP as producing binding consequences. There are two ways then that this subsequent practice could be used to provide the NCP with the required status: either through interpretation or through modification.

---

[100] The Kyoto Protocol system envisaged a number of Commitment Periods. During the First Commitment Period, States parties to the Kyoto Protocol undertook to reduce their greenhouse gas emissions (GHG emissions) by an agreed percentage. These commitments were provided for in Annex B to the Kyoto Protocol. The First Commitment Period was to last from 2008 to 2012. At the end of 2012, according to the initial scheme, an amendment to the Kyoto Protocol would be agreed upon and enter into force; this would regulate the GHG emissions reduction for a Second Commitment Period, starting from 2013 (end date was to be agreed upon).

[101] It is this last sanction that the Enforcement Branch has opted for in most of its decisions.

[102] With the possible exception of Canada, which, however, raised that objection in a domestic court; see 'Memorandum of Fact and Law …', (n 99).

[103] Oberthür and Lefeber, 'Holding Countries to Account …', (n 98) 151–2.

Article 31(3)(b) VCLT is, for our purposes, inapplicable as the ordinary meaning of the text of Article 18 of the Kyoto Protocol is quite clear. An amendment to the Kyoto Protocol is required.

The only other option remaining is to consider that the practice of the States is of such *gravitas* that it amounts to subsequent practice leading to a modification of the treaty, similarly to what draft article 38 prescribed. Since that article never came into existence, the basis will have to be its customary law equivalent. In this manner, that is, through modification by subsequent practice, the NCP of the Kyoto Protocol is endowed, both *de facto* and *de lege*, with binding consequences. Regardless of how one attempts to legally categorize the NCP of the Kyoto Protocol, the fact remains that this is one more illustrative example of the residual character of the amendment and modification provisions of the VCLT,[104] and how diverse and unique the solutions adopted by States are, when they are called to address issues of the continued functioning of multilateral treaties.

VI. CONCLUSIONS

In discussing the possibility of a uniform law of inter-State treaties, the present chapter examined three particular aspects of the law of treaties: what is a treaty, consent to be bound, and amendment procedures.

With respect to what constitutes a treaty the analysis of the international jurisprudence led us to the conclusion that there is no uniformity in approaches as to what constitutes a treaty, as illustrated by the *Qatar/Bahrain* and *Bangladesh/Myanmar* cases. This lack of uniformity, in turn, may create or intensify tensions between States.

As far as consent to be bound by a treaty is concerned, this area has been thought to be one of the most uniform of the law of treaties, as the issues of signature, ratification, or accession have demonstrated a rather high degree of consistency in State practice. However, as was shown, new developments in international environmental law have led to challenging and specialized methods of consent to be bound. Notably, when consenting to be bound by MEAs, States may also indirectly express their consent to be bound by future obligations (unforeseen at the time of the initial consent), which would result from treaty organs. This is somewhat different from the secondary law of international organizations, in the sense that with some notable, but scarce, exceptions such

[104] This time in the context of environmental treaties.

as Article 2(9) of the Montreal Protocol, MEAs usually do not offer any indication as to whether the nature of their decision is binding or not.

This new development is particularly striking in cases of binding decisions, such as in the non-compliance procedure under the Kyoto Protocol, when the State in non-compliance may be deprived by a binding decision of all privileges deriving from participation in flexibility mechanisms. The legal nature (or legal grounds) of such new methods of consent is neither fully understood nor is there an agreement as to their legal character. It is, however, incontrovertible that this method will further develop, as the number of MEAs has been growing and they have become very sophisticated from the point of view of innovative legal techniques.

A similar conclusion was also reached with respect to amendment procedures. Even the VCLT itself recognized the residual nature of the relevant provisions. This option has been put to use and tested to its limits in a variety of manners in international State practice, notable examples being the tacit acceptance procedure, the disconnection clauses, the limitation of the right to propose amendments, and the Kyoto Protocol non-compliance procedure. Despite this lack of uniformity though, one must not immediately jump to the conclusion that these solutions are characteristic of particular special regimes. Specialization does exist, but it is not a *regime-specific specialization* but rather a specialization stemming from the particular needs, the object and purpose of the treaty in question. Consequently what we are dealing with is not a *regime-specific specialization* but rather a *telos-specific specialization.*

VII. OPEN QUESTIONS: A RESEARCH AGENDA

The above analysis has indicated a number of areas where further research might be useful. In summation:

- **The definition of a treaty:** As shown *supra*, 'international agreements may take a number of forms and be given a diversity of names'.[105] For this reason, further research is required in order to clarify the process and the elements that are to be taken into account (and the gravity of each element in that process) when identifying whether a particular set of documents is to be considered an international agreement.

105 *Qatar/Bahrain*, (n 24) para 23.

- **Consent to be bound:** This area of research ties with the previous point. However, it goes even further. The promulgation of international organizations, international regimes ('self-contained'/ 'special' or not), and multilateral treaties has opened up the international legal arena to a true kaleidoscope of manners in which consent to be bound can be given. An in-depth analysis (updated at regular intervals) of the evolution of the concept to be bound in modern practice would be extremely useful in offering clarity and stability in international relations and would be an indispensable tool for practitioners and academics alike.
- **Amendment/modification procedures:** During the discussions on the VCLT it was clear that no customary rule on amendment/ modification existed. However, indispensable to those discussions was the United Nations *Handbook of Final Clauses*.[106] The importance of research in the diverse solutions adopted by States with regards to these clauses was not lost on the United Nations. In 2003, the United Nations published a new handbook called *Final Clauses of Multilateral Treaties Handbook*.[107] Nonetheless, there are two problems with this handbook that make further research on amendment/modification provisions imperative. Firstly, it was published almost ten years ago and, as evinced in the present chapter, several developments have come to pass. Secondly, and this is understandable since the handbook tries to cover a lot of diverse topics, only 13 pages are devoted to amendment and modification provisions. A study devoted entirely to this area of the law of treaties would produce information useful for anyone whose interest and/or practice lies within the field of law of treaties.

[106] United Nations, *Handbook of Final Clauses*, (n 54).
[107] United Nations, *Final Clauses of Multilateral Treaties Handbook* (2003) http://treaties.un.org/doc/source/publications/FC/English.pdf, accessed 1 July 2012.

13. Uniformity versus specialization (2): A uniform regime of treaty interpretation?

*Michael Waibel**

I. INTRODUCTION

'There is no part of the law of treaties which the text writer approaches with more trepidation than the question of interpretation.'[1]

Fragmentation of international law can occur at two levels: at the level of *substantive rules* (applicable law) and at the level of *interpretive* method. Whereas the substantive aspect of fragmentation has spawned an enormous literature over the last decade,[2] interpretive fragmentation has received less attention.[3] The focus of this chapter is on this second dimension: does international law know a single, unified method, or equivalently, regime or approach to treaty interpretation?

The emphasis in this chapter is on what treaty arbitrators in fact do, rather than on what they say they do in interpreting treaties. The chapter

* Thanks to Helmut Aust, John Avery Jones, Eirik Bjorge, Richard Gardiner and Isabelle van Damme for comments and discussions and to Kerim Uster and Anastasia Zolotar for research assistance.

1 AD McNair, *The Law of Treaties* (OUP, 1962) 392.

2 Report of the Study Group of the ILC, *Fragmentation of International Law: Difficulties Arising from the Diversification and Expansion of International Law* (finalized by M Koskenniemi, A/CN.4/L.682, 13 April 2006) 14 (hereinafter *ILC Report on Fragmentation*); see also, M Fitzmaurice and P Merkouris, 'Uniformity versus Specialization (1): The Quest for a Uniform Law of Inter-State Treaties', in this *Handbook*.

3 JHH Weiler, 'The Interpretation of Treaties: A Re-Examination Preface' (2010) 21 EJIL 507; J Pauwelyn and M Elsig, 'The Politics of Treaty Interpretation' in JL Dunoff and MA Pollack (eds), *Interdisciplinary Perspectives on International Law and International Relations* (CUP, 2012) 421; A Roberts, 'Power and Persuasion in Investment Treaty Arbitration: The Dual Role of States' (2010) AJIL 179, 225 (the debate about how interpretive authority is shared between the treaty parties and investment tribunals raises the broader question of 'the applicability of the Vienna Convention interpretive rules in different areas of international law, questioning whether common principles of interpretation can and should exist').

shows that, at times, treaty interpreters pay mere lip service to the 1969 Vienna Convention on the Law of Treaties' (VCLT) principles on interpretation. They give preference to one element of the International Law Commission's (ILC) 'crucible'[4] over another, rather than bringing all the elements to bear on treaty interpretation in a single combined operation. Whether one sees interpretive uniformity, or interpretive divergence, depends on the position of the zoom of the lens. When zoomed out, the picture is one of interpretive uniformity. When zoomed in, one discovers a much greater degree of interpretive divergence in international law. There are at least three types of interpretive fragmentation. First, fragmentation of interpretive methods across subfields of international law – for example, international criminal tribunals may emphasize textual interpretation, whereas human rights tribunals adopt broad purposive, rights-expanding interpretations.[5] Second, treaty interpreters on a given court within a particular subfield, such as investment law, may disagree on the appropriate interpretive methodology.[6] Third, even though the VCLT's interpretive framework has been in place since the early 1970s, the methods of interpretation that a particular tribunal employs may change over time.

The issue of interpretive fragmentation raises two central questions.[7] First, do we observe varieties of treaty interpretation depending on the type of treaty, the subfield or the treaty interpreter? Second, are interpretive methods tailored to specific fields and particular types of treaties normatively desirable?[8] The claim that the VCLT provides an appropriate framework for the interpretation of bilateral investment treaties (BITs),

---

[4] Doc A/CONF.39/11, Add 2, Yearbook of the ILC (1966), vol II, para 8 ('All the various elements, as they were present in any given case, would be thrown into the crucible…'); RK Gardiner, *Treaty Interpretation* (OUP, 2008) 9–10.

[5] L Grover, 'A Call to Arms: Fundamental Dilemmas Confronting the Interpretation of Crimes in the Rome Statute of the International Criminal Court' (2010) 21 EJIL 543, 551.

[6] *Golder v United Kingdom*, Application no. 4451/70, 21 February 1975, Separate Opinion of Judge Sir Gerald Fitzmaurice, (1975) 1 EHRR 524, paras 23–47.

[7] JHH Weiler, 'Prolegomena to a Meso-Theory of Treaty Interpretation at the Turn of the Century', IILJ International Legal Theory Colloquium: Interpretation and Judgment in International Law (NYU Law School, 14 February 2008) 14 (distinguishing between the prescriptive and the factual question); Pauwelyn and Elsig, 'Politics of Treaty Interpretation' (n 3) 445.

[8] Report of the Special Rapporteur H Waldock, Doc A/CN.4/156, Yearbook of the ILC (1964) vol II, 55.

for example, a proposition I defended elsewhere[9] – differs from the descriptive claim that all investment tribunals in fact rely on the VCLT when interpreting BITs.

Articles 31–33 VCLT purport to set out a unified approach to interpretation. Yet this chapter contends that the VCLT constrains treaty interpreters only on the margins, and that varieties of treaty interpretation lurk behind the veneer of the VCLT's general interpretive framework. On closer inspection, interpretive practices in international law diverge, just like in national law.[10] In the words of Weiler, we observe the emergence of 'distinctive hermeneutic languages or idioms' across fields[11] – a corollary of the increasing specialization of international lawyers and the proliferation of specialized dispute resolution fora.

The emergence of specialized interpretive methodologies in international law mirrors the earlier development of statutory and contract varieties of interpretation in domestic law.[12] In Roman and medieval law, the principles for the construction of contracts and legislation were broadly similar.[13] Yet distinct interpretative methods developed as a result of the great private law codifications.[14] In modern times, national legal systems typically know two or more general interpretive approaches.[15] At the same time, interpretive methods across countries for statutes or

---

[9] M Waibel, 'International Investment Law and Treaty Interpretation' in R Hofmann and CJ Tams (eds), *International Investment Law and General International Law: From Clinical Isolation to Systemic Integration?* (Nomos, 2011) 29–52.

[10] See Sections II and III below.

[11] Weiler, 'The Interpretation of Treaties ...' (n 3) 507 (the WTO Appellate Body has a 'very distinct vocabulary and hermeneutics').

[12] EA Farnsworth, '"Meaning" in the Law of Contracts' (1967) 76 YLJ 939, 957 ('plain meaning' has found particularly fertile territory in modern contract law).

[13] S Vogenauer, 'Interpretation of Statutes, History of' in J Basedow, KJ Hopt, and R Zimmermann (eds), *The Max Planck Encyclopaedia of European Private Law* (OUP, 2012) 987.

[14] Ibid, 989 (referring to Articles 4–5 French Civil Code and §§6–9 of the Austrian Civil Code); M Bos, 'Theory and Practice of Treaty Interpretation' (1980) 27 Neth Intl l Rev 3, 137; On statutory interpretation in US law, F Schauer, *Thinking Like a Lawyer: A New Introduction to Legal Reasoning* (Harvard UP, 2009) chp 8; for English law, see R Cross, J Bell, and Sir G Engle, *Statutory Interpretation* (3rd edn, OUP, 1995); EA Kramer, *Juristische Methodenlehre* (2nd edn, Stämpfli, 2005).

[15] Bos, 'Theory and Practice ...' (n 14) 155 ('one branch of the law may differ more or less considerably from another with respect to the legal method to be applied to it').

contracts, for example, are surprisingly similar.[16] The general tendency is for interpretation in private law to emphasize strict textual construction, as compared to more teleological interpretation in public law.

In origin international law borrowed principles of interpretation from the approaches common to various European laws in the 17th and 18th centuries.[17] The current debate in international law over the 'correct' interpretative approach, and the development of a differentiated interpretive framework, mirrors a similar debate and the earlier development of varieties of interpretation in domestic legal systems.

'Contract imagery' in treaty interpretation has long been influential and held sway over virtually all treaties.[18] The statutory analogy to treaty construction developed only in the 20th century.[19] Its emergence in modern international law provided an important impetus for different varieties of treaty interpretation in international law. In dualist systems such as the UK, statutory construction has come to play an important role in treaty interpretation because English courts generally interpret the domestic implementing statute rather than the treaty itself.[20]

---

[16] S Vogenauer, *Die Auslegung von Gesetzen in England und auf dem Kontinent: eine Vergleichende Untersuchung der Rechtsprechung und ihrer Historischen Grundlagen* (Mohr Siebeck, 2001).

[17] Bos, 'Theory and Practice ...' (n 14) 15.

[18] DJ Bederman, 'Revivalist Canons and Treaty Interpretation' (1993–1994) 41 UCLA Law Rev 953, 1012.

[19] Ibid, 1019–27; A Nollkaemper, 'The Netherlands' in D Sloss (ed), *The Role of Domestic Courts in Treaty Enforcement: A Comparative Study* (CUP, 2009) 326–69 (Dutch courts assimilate treaty to statutory interpretation); L Garlicki, M Masternak-Kubiak, and K Wójtowicz, 'Poland' in ibid, 379, 389 (Polish courts use the same rules of interpretation for domestic law as for treaties).

[20] Sir IM Sinclair, 'The Principles of Treaty Interpretation and their Application by the English Courts' (1963) 12 ICLQ 508 (the method by which legislative effect is given to a treaty determines materially the manner in which the courts will interpret and apply the treaty); contra, MP Van Alstine, 'The Role of Domestic Courts in Treaty Enforcement: Summary and Conclusions' in D Sloss (ed), *The Role of Domestic Courts in Treaty Enforcement: A Comparative Study* (CUP, 2009) (the formal distinction into dualist and monist States does not divide States on the role of the VCLT).

II. THE VCLT'S INTERPRETIVE FRAMEWORK

This chapter adopts a broad view of interpretation.[21] Pauwelyn and Elsig highlight that international tribunals face five core interpretive choices: (i) the dominant hermeneutic – text, intent or objective; (ii) static or dynamic meaning; (iii) deference to treaty parties or filling gaps in (incomplete) treaties; (iv) weight to earlier rulings versus a case-by-case approach; and (v) inward-looking or outward-looking with regard to the systemic consequences.[22]

Treaty interpretation is not primarily about attributing a particular meaning to a treaty, but involves the 'attempt to persuade the relevant interpretative community that a particular interpretation ... is the most appropriate meaning to adopt'.[23] In this way, '[s]emantic content is negotiated in the legal practice of interpretation'.[24] Judicial dialogue is an important part of the interpretive exercise.[25]

Compared to Article 29 VCLT on the territorial scope of application,[26] Articles 31–33 VCLT on interpretation are more detailed.[27] The use of mandatory language ('A treaty *shall* be interpreted') in Article 31(1) suggests that more than a mere hortatory principle was intended. Yet, are there any *rules* for practising the art of interpretation?

---

[21] J Crawford and P Nevill, 'Relations between International Courts and Tribunals' in M Young (ed), *Regime Interaction in International Law: Facing Fragmentation* (CUP, 2012) 235–60, 236 ('interpretive techniques in the broad sense' include tools to address norm conflict and fragmentation).

[22] Pauwelyn and Elsig, 'Politics of Treaty Interpretation' (n 3) 460.

[23] J Tobin, *The Right to Health in International Law* (OUP, 2012) 77; MS McDougal, HD Laswell, and JC Miller, *The Interpretation of International Agreements and World Public Order: Principles of Content and Procedure* (Martinus Nijhoff, 1994) xvi (a continuing process of communication). For criticism, see G Fitzmaurice, '*Vae Victis* of Woe to the Negotiations!' (1971) 65 AJIL 954.

[24] I Venzke, *How Interpretation Makes International Law: On Semantic Change and Normative Twists* (OUP, 2012) 53.

[25] E Criddle, 'The Vienna Convention on the Law of Treaties in US Treaty Interpretation' (2005) 44 VJIL 431, 496, 497 ('a universal legal grammar that may facilitate more effective communication, cooperation and decisional uniformity among domestic courts and foreign and international tribunals').

[26] See M Milanovic, 'The Spatial Dimension: Treaties and Territory' in this *Handbook* (186) ('one paltry provision', 'one could almost say that no such rules exist').

[27] Report of the Special Rapporteur R Ago, Doc A/CN.4/SER.A/1964, Yearbook of the ILC (1964) vol I, 23 (emphasis added).

1. Functions of the VCLT's Interpretive Principles

More than 40 years after the VCLT codified principles of interpretation, their practical operation remains contested and in flux. Neither the adoption of the VCLT by many, though not all, States,[28] nor the widespread recognition that Articles 31–33 represent customary international law,[29] has closed the debate over the 'correct' approach to interpretation.

According to the ILC, the underlying principle of Article 31 VCLT is that 'the text must be presumed to be the authentic expression of the intentions of the parties; and that, in consequence, the starting point of interpretation is the elucidation of the meaning of the text, not an investigation *ab initio* into the intentions of the parties'.[30] Textualists won the battle over teleologists and subjectivists at the Vienna Conference in 1968 and 1969, when the ILC adopted 'qualified textuality' as a compromise.[31]

The VCLT's principles on treaty interpretation represent the lowest common denominator among competing schools of interpretation. Their generality ensures their adaptability.[32] The VCLT does not contain interpretative rules, but codified interpretive principles that do not provide step-by-step guidance.[33] They *enable* the interpreter to use a set of methodological tools. Within the VCLT's broad parameters, interpreters are able to tailor the VCLT's interpretive framework to their own needs and preferences. They can, by and large, disengage from the VCLT's interpretive principles if and when it suits them. Referring to the VCLT only pro forma can provide convenient cover for an interpretive methodology that in substance disengages from the VCLT.

---

[28] Examples of non-parties include France, India, Indonesia, South Africa and the United States.

[29] *Arbitral Award of 31 July 1989 (Guinea Bissau v Senegal)*, Judgment, ICJ Rep 1991, 53, para 48; Gardiner, *Treaty Interpretation* (n 4) 12.

[30] Yearbook of the ILC (1966) vol II, 220.

[31] FG Jacobs, 'Varieties of Approaches to Treaty Interpretation: With Special Reference to the Draft Convention on the Law of Treaties before the Vienna Diplomatic Conference' (1969) 18 ICLQ 318, 338; R Bernhardt, 'Interpretation and Implied (Tacit) Modification of Treaties: Comments on Articles 27, 28, 29, and 38 of the ILC's 1966 Draft Articles on the Law of Treaties' (1967) 27 ZaöRV 497; Gardiner, *Treaty Interpretation* (n 4) 8.

[32] Gardiner, *Treaty Interpretation* (n 4) 9.

[33] Ibid, 9 (not 'simple precepts that can be applied to produce a scientifically verifiable result'); Yearbook of the ILC (1966) vol II, 218.

The VCLT provides 'authoritative internationalist canons for treaty construction',[34] with the aim of overcoming parochial interpretive canons. The VCLT provides for minimum harmonization rather than *laissez-faire*. Even though interpreters lack complete freedom of choice, they enjoy considerable leeway in how they interpret treaties. For instance, to accord primacy to the object and purpose over the text is to depart from the VCLT's interpretive framework.[35] The VCLT's interpretive principles nudge treaty interpreters towards the 'correct' meaning by constraining the interpreters, albeit only on the margin.[36] They provide an 'intellectual checklist'.[37]

The VCLT's interpretive framework responds to the need for harmonized interpretive principles, even if at a high level of generality.[38] It provides a common language for treaty interpreters to think conceptually about interpretive questions. It equips international lawyers with a 'rudimentary legal grammar'[39] that unites them, even if they disagree in particular cases how these principles should be applied. This grammar is part of the glue that keeps international law together.[40] The VCLT's interpretive principles are an essential infrastructure',[41] part of what Paulus calls the 'commonly agreed standards that go beyond the self-interest of the parties and the particularities of the functional sub-system in which the judge operates'.[42] They have become part of the DNA of

---

34 Criddle, '... US Treaty Interpretation' (n 25) 499.

35 See Section III below.

36 Christoph Schreuer, 'Comments' in R Hofmann and CJ Tams (eds), *International Investment Law and General International Law: From Clinical Isolation to Systemic Integration?* (Nomos, 2011) 71–4, 71.

37 Rules and principles of interpretation constrain the interpreter in choosing from the range of possible interpretive outcomes and guard against undue expansion of the interpretive function, OM Fiss, 'Objectivity and Interpretation' (1982) 34 Stanford L Rev 739 ('bounded objectivity'); D Vagts, 'Treaty Interpretation and the New American Way of Law Reading' (1993) 4 EJIL 480; I van Damme, 'Treaty Interpretation by the WTO Appellate Body' (2010) 21 EJIL 605, 620 ('(limited) constraints'); G Shaffer and J Trachtman, 'Interpretation and Institutional Choice at the WTO' (2011) 52 Virginia J Intl L 103, 115.

38 *ILC Report on Fragmentation*, (n 2) 427 ('[i]t is in fact hard to think of any approach to interpretation that would be excluded from articles 31–32').

39 Criddle, '... US Treaty Interpretation' (n 25) 436; Fiss, 'Objectivity ...' (n 37) 745.

40 M Foltea, *International Organizations in WTO Dispute Settlement* (CUP, 2012) 88.

41 Gardiner, *Treaty Interpretation* (n 4) 6.

42 A Paulus, 'International Adjudication' in S Besson and J Tasioulas (eds), *The Philosophy of International Law* (OUP, 2009) 224.

international lawyers, so much so that nowadays we can identify international lawyers by reference to those who regularly apply the VCLT.

Scepticism on the desirability and feasibility of interpretive rules predates the VCLT.[43] Two of the special rapporteurs on treaties (Brierly and Lauterpacht) did not even discuss interpretation in their reports, one was 'positively opposed to the idea that interpretation could ever be captured in a rule'[44] (Fitzmaurice) and final Special Rapporteur Waldock gave only 'lukewarm' support to formulating interpretive rules.[45] Klabbers attributes this lack of interest or reluctance to their legal training that made them suspicious about rules-based interpretive methodologies.[46] Viewed from this perspective, the level of generality of the VCLT's interpretive framework is hardly surprising.

It is facile to criticize the generality of the VCLT's interpretive framework. Such criticism might have some validity if the aim of the Convention had been to formulate a 'comprehensive code of the canons of interpretation'.[47] Yet the drafters of the Vienna Convention lacked this ambition.[48] Their aim was much more modest. Rather than create a detailed interpretive code, the interpretive principles found in the VCLT are mostly principles of logic and good sense.[49] The '[o]bviousness of [the VCLT's interpretive] provisions endows it with automatic acceptance from its users'.[50]

Due to the diversity of treaty interpreters and great cultural and legal diversity in international law, there was value in the VCLT's minimum

---

43 JL Brierly, *The Law of Nations* (Clarendon, 1928) 168; Harvard Draft Convention on the Law of Treaties (1935) 29 AJIL 657, 944.

44 J Klabbers, 'Book Review' (2013) 24 EJIL 718, 718.

45 Ibid, 719.

46 J Klabbers, 'On Rationalism in Politics: Interpretation of Treaties and the World Trade Organization' (2005) 74 Nordic J Intl L 405, 418–19.

47 Sir IM Sinclair, *The Vienna Convention on the Law of Treaties* (2nd edn, Manchester UP, 1984) 117–18.

48 van Damme, 'Treaty Interpretation …' (n 37) 620 ('the VCLT did not "over-codify" principles of treaty interpretation').

49 D Anzilotti, *Lehrbuch des Völkerrechts* (vol I, de Gruyter, 1929) 82; I Brownlie, *Principles of Public International Law* (2nd edn, OUP, 1973) 624; McNair, *Law of Treaties* (n 1) 365; Bos, 'Theory and Practice …' (n 14) 38 (noting absence of reservations on Articles 31–33 in Vienna).

50 J-M Sorel and V Boré Eveno, 'Article 31' in O Corten and P Klein, *The Vienna Convention on the Law of Treaties: A Commentary* (OUP, 2011) vol 1, para 1; Bederman, 'Revivalist Canons …' (n 18) 964 (adherence to treaty text as 'intuitively obvious').

harmonization.[51] Different treaty interpreters may variously construe the same applicable law, follow different guiding objectives, and may be part of diverse interpretive communities.[52] The VCLT may help to 'bridge the "gulfs in language, culture and values that separate nations" by providing a set of definitive "conventions of description, argument, judgment and persuasion" to facilitate interjudicial dialogue'.[53]

The VCLT's interpretive principles are important for transparency, consistency, predictability and accountability.[54] Principles of interpretation also aim to depoliticize the interpretive process, and adjudication more generally, by acting as procedural rationality requirements for treaty interpreters.[55] International courts and tribunals can use the VCLT to build credibility and legitimacy for the exercise of their judicial function.[56] In the early days of the World Trade Organization (WTO), the Appellate Body (AB) invoked the VCLT partly for reasons of 'judicial marketing'.[57] Once its legitimacy was established, the AB ceased 'excessive methodological justification by reference to the VCLT'.[58]

2. Interpretive Space

Interpretation also includes the degree of deference,[59] or margin of appreciation,[60] that adjudicators grant to auto-interpretations of treaties

---

51 Criddle, '... US Treaty Interpretation' (n 25) 498.

52 See Section IV below.

53 Criddle, '... US Treaty Interpretation' (n 25) 498 (citing *Trans World Airlines v Franklin Mint*, 66 US 243, 262 (1984) (Stevens, J, dissenting) and SE Fish, *Doing What Comes Naturally: Change, Rhetoric, and the Practice of Theory in Literary and Legal Studies* (Duke UP, 1989) 115); I Johnstone, 'Treaty Interpretation: The Authority of Interpretive Communities' (1990–91) 12 Michigan J Intl L 371–2, 378.

54 U Linderfalk, 'Doing the Right Thing for the Right Reason: Why Dynamic or Static Approaches Should be Taken in the Interpretation of Treaties' (2008) 10 Intl Community L Rev 109, 110.

55 Klabbers, 'On Rationalism in Politics ...' (n 46) 411 (to pacify apprehensive WTO members).

56 van Damme, 'Treaty Interpretation ...' (n 37) 639.

57 I van Damme, *Treaty Interpretation by the WTO Appellate Body* (OUP, 2009) 54; Sorel and Boré Eveno, 'Article 31' (n 50) para 33 (references to the VCLT are quasi automatic); Shaffer and Trachtman, '... Institutional Choice ...' (n 37) 115 (the AB refers to VCLT in 65 percent of its decisions).

58 van Damme, *Treaty Interpretation by the WTO* (n 57) 292.

59 Pauwelyn and Elsig, 'Politics of Treaty Interpretation' (n 3) 447.

60 Y Shany, 'Toward a General Margin of Appreciation Doctrine in International Law?' (2005) 16 EJIL 907; S McInerney-Lankford, 'Fragmentation of

by governments, the applicability of norms beyond the scope of a given subfield, and the conceptual lenses employed by treaty interpreters.[61] Even though deference to the executive is not an interpretive technique as such, it implies that the role of third-party adjudicators in treaty interpretation is limited.[62] In France, the Ministry of Foreign Affairs used to provide preliminary rulings on interpretations of treaties to the French courts.[63] Deference is said to be 'the single best predictor of interpretive outcomes in American treaty cases'.[64]

States can, and often do, abstain from delegating the power to interpret treaties to adjudicators, opting instead for auto-interpretation, joint interpretation or authentic interpretation by the treaty parties, or by organs in the case of international organizations. Foreign ministries play a particularly important role in construing the obligations undertaken by States. These forms of interpretation differ from interpretation by third-party adjudicators such as international tribunals and national courts for which the VCLT was primarily designed.[65]

International Law Redux: The Case of Strasbourg' 32 OJLS 609–32, 613; G Letsas, 'Two Concepts of the Margin of Appreciation' (2006) 26 OJLS 705–32, 721 (referring to the structural margin of appreciation as the decision not to substantively scrutinize decisions by domestic authorities).

[61] A Roberts, 'Clash of Paradigms: Actors and Analogies Shaping the Investment Treaty System' (2013) 107 AJIL 45.

[62] Bederman, 'Revivalist Canons …' (n 18) (citing *United States v Alvarez-Machain*, 504 US 655 (1992) as an example of extreme deference where majority on the Supreme Court 'manipulated rules of contract construction to favour the government's interpretation of the treaty'); Criddle, '… US Treaty Interpretation' (n 25) 433; SM Sullivan, 'Rethinking Treaty Interpretation' (2008) 86 Texas LJ 777 (explaining factors behind shift from limited to near total deference); cf for English law, *IRS v Commerzbank AG*, 63 TC 218 (1990), Mummery J (no deference to treaty interpretation of the government).

[63] V Fikfak, 'International Law before English and Asian Courts: Finding the Judicial Role in the Separation of Powers' Asian JIL 1, 14; Van Alstine, 'The Role of Domestic Courts …' (n 20) 591 (Russian Supreme Court); J Dutheil de la Rochère, 'France' in FG Jacobs and S Roberts (eds), *The Effects of Treaties in Domestic Law* (Sweet & Maxwell, 1987).

[64] Bederman, 'Revivalist Canons …' (n 18); J Dugard, 'South Africa' in D Sloss (ed), *The Role of Domestic Courts in Treaty Enforcement: A Comparative Study* (CUP, 2009) 472 (more deference in respect of unincorporated treaties and those not affecting the rights of individuals in South African law).

[65] L Gross, 'States as Organs of International Law and the Problem of Autointerpretation' in GA Lipsky (ed), *Law and Politics in the World Community: Essays on Hans Kelsen's Pure Theory and Related Problems in International Law* (University of California Press, 1953) 76.

Qualified textuality leaves considerable discretion to interpreters, and thereby facilitates judicial activism.[66] The purpose of the VCLT's interpretive framework is not only to guide adjudicators but also to constrain discretion and curb judicial activism. As decisions of international tribunals are typically final, international judges and arbitrators enjoy more discretion than national judges. The VCLT constrains treaty interpretation only on the margin, and opens the door to diverse interpretative approaches.[67]

Interpretative space varies by treaty type.[68] The more open-ended the treaty provisions (principles or standards as opposed to detailed obligations), the greater the tribunal's interpretive space. Due to a high degree of incompleteness, the role of interpretation ex post is potentially greater. Teleological interpretation has played a greater role for interpreting certain treaties with limited specificity establishing international organizations (eg, the UN Charter, or the European Union treaties) compared to treaties with detailed rules (such as the General Agreement on Tariffs and Trade (GATT 1947)).

Treaty interpreters typically enjoy more interpretive space in interpreting human rights treaties and BITs than in interpreting other subfields of international law, given such treaties' open-textured formulation. In the *Engel* case concerning the notion of criminal charges in Article 6 of the European Convention of Human Rights (ECHR), the European Court of Human Rights (ECtHR) could choose among at least eight plausible interpretations.[69] In international investment law, the divided jurisprudence on issues such as the interpretation of the fair and equitable treatment standard or the scope of most-favoured nation clauses suggests the presence of ample interpretive space.

---

66 F Zarbiyev, 'Judicial Activism in International Law: A Conceptual Framework for Analysis' (2012) 3 JIDS 14, 16–17; Pauwelyn and Elsig, 'Politics of Treaty Interpretation' (n 3) 448 (considerable 'wiggle room').

67 Pauwelyn and Elsig, 'Politics of Treaty Interpretation' (n 3) 448, 450 ('there is general agreement that the application of these VCLT rules, in any particular case, leaves ample scope for maneuver and allows different tribunals to prioritize different interpretive methods or elements (eg., text, context, or purpose)'); Shaffer and Trachtman, '… Institutional Choice …' (n 37) 115 ('some circumscription' with the goal of limiting judicial discretion).

68 Pauwelyn and Elsig, 'Politics of Treaty Interpretation' (n 3) 459–68 (developing a demand-and-supply theory of variations in interpretive approaches).

69 *Engel and Others v the Netherlands* (1976) Series A no. 22; G Letsas, 'The Truth in Autonomous Concepts: How to Interpret the ECHR' (2004) EJIL, 292–3.

The degree of interpretive freedom also varies by tribunal and over time. Tribunals are likely to enjoy a higher degree of interpretive freedom with multilateral treaties compared to bilateral treaties, especially if the treaty parties are diverse and unable to agree among themselves. Pauwelyn suggests that the WTO Appellate Body may enjoy greater interpretive freedom (and could as a result become more 'activist') in the future, given the growing diffusion of power among the WTO membership.[70] Conversely, ad hoc tribunals are likely to have more limited interpretive space than permanent international tribunals such as the International Court of Justice (ICJ) or the International Criminal Court (ICC) with a long-term view whose function is not ephemeral and tied to settling a particular dispute.[71]

3. Formal Invocation versus Interpretation in Action

In modern treaty interpretation, it is *de rigueur* to invoke the VCLT.[72] International courts and tribunals routinely refer to the VCLT principles, more frequently than domestic courts or other treaty interpreters.[73] Such invocation of the VCLT provides a shield against easy criticism of the decision at the methodological level, and indirectly offers some protection against substantive criticism. Yet formal invocation of the VCLT and interpretive practices may diverge.[74]

---

70 J Pauwelyn, 'Treaty Interpretation or Activism? Comment on the AB Report on United States: ADs and CVDs on Certain Products from China' (2013) 12 World Trade Rev 235, 241; Pauwelyn and Elsig, 'Politics of Treaty Interpretation' (n 3) 421–44.

71 Pauwelyn and Elsig, 'Politics of Treaty Interpretation' (n 3) 462 (a tribunal's lifespan, the composition of its constituency, and institutional competition as supply-side factors).

72 D Simon, *L'Interpretation Judiciaire des Traités D'Organisations Internationals (Morphologie des Conventions et Function Jurisdictionelle)* (Pedone, 1981) 59 (Article 31 has become a reference that must be cited, even if it will then be twisted); Gardiner, *Treaty Interpretation* (n 4)) 15 ('virtually axiomatic').

73 Nollkaemper, 'The Netherlands' (n 19) 362 (express references to VCLT by Dutch courts extremely rare).

74 Bederman, 'Revivalist Canons …' (n 18) 956:

> a court's selection of an interpretive method for construing any legal instrument (whether a contract, statute, or treaty), is often driven by the substantive result desired. It is not enough to credit what a court says about how it construes a treaty; one must understand what the court then does in applying the method of interpretation to reach some legal conclusion.

The focus on treaty interpretation is also likely to be too narrow, if what we are concerned with is interpretive *outcomes*. The methods of treaty interpretation, at least on the surface, may be largely homogenous. Most international courts and tribunals, particularly recently created ones, or those with a specialized mandate, are superficially attached to the VCLT principles. Yet at the same time, they adopt the methods to their own use. One important function of invoking the VCLT is to legitimize the adjudicative function of international courts and tribunals.

According to Sorel and Boré Eveno, 'there is a type of incantatory reference to this "sacred text"; this situation, however, does not necessarily imply that the ensuing reasoning always conforms strictly to the reference which, it must be said, leaves many doors open'.[75] Klabbers explains that 'often enough the rules of interpretation are paid tribute to but ignored, distorted or manipulated in actual use, either by design or out of ignorance'.[76] In his view, even the ICJ 'takes considerable liberties with [Articles 31 and 32], as it sees fit'.[77]

Even though tribunals often invoke the VCLT interpretative principles, they do not always studiously apply them. International courts and tribunals sometimes declare their fidelity to Articles 31–33 VCLT, while in reality using them in differentiated ways, and on occasion even openly deviating from the VCLT's interpretative framework.[78] In some cases, interpreters rely on a single principle of the VCLT read in isolation from the others.[79] They give great weight to object and purpose, and may too

---

75 Sorel and Boré Eveno, 'Article 31' (n 50) para 33.

76 Klabbers, 'On Rationalism in Politics …' (n 46) 416.

77 Ibid, 426.

78 Weiler, 'The Interpretation of Treaties …' (n 3) 507 (many tribunals claim to follow the universal rules of the VCLT); Klabbers, 'On Rationalism in Politics …' (n 46) 427 (the VCLT covers 'interpretive liberties under a fig leaf of prescriptions'); H Lauterpacht, 'Restrictive Interpretation and the Principle of Effectiveness in the Interpretation of Treaties' (1949) BYBIL 48, 49 (treaty interpreters refer to interpretive canons 'more out of piety than conviction' and emphasizing that these references serve often little other purpose than 'the form in which the judge cloaks a result arrived at by other means'); Pauwelyn and Elsig, 'Politics of Treaty Interpretation' (n 3) 449 ('in some cases, a tribunal's interpretive method may be little more than ex post justification or façade'); Bederman, 'Revivalist Canons …' (n 18) 1022; GS Goodwin-Gill, 'The Search for the One, True Meaning …' in Guy S Goodwin-Gill and Hélène Lambert (eds), *The Limits of Transnational Law: Refugee Law, Policy Harmonization and Judicial Dialogue in the European Union* (CUP, 2010) 204, 206.

79 Gardiner, *Treaty Interpretation* (n 4) 7.

readily go beyond the text of the treaty in relying on *travaux préparatoires* or other extraneous material. There is a tendency to pick and choose among the various elements of the crucible. At times, references to the VCLT are used as little more than a fig leaf.

References to the VCLT as such do not tell us much about whether an international court or tribunal is in fact deviating from the VCLT's interpretative canon.[80] Similarly, at the level of systemic integration, a statement by a tribunal that, for example, international trade law is part of the larger universe of international law could be 'cheap talk', nothing more than rhetoric, with little effect on interpretation and application of the law, or it could reflect a genuine commitment to interpret trade law as part and parcel of general international law.

What interpreters say they do may not be what they do. If a tribunal says it is applying the VCLT, this does not mean that it is in fact applying the VCLT *tel quel*, without tweaking the interpretive principles for its own purposes. The tribunal may invoke the VCLT, and then go on to apply its own hidden interpretive methodology. Or it may invoke the VCLT principles on interpretation, but then consciously proceed to do something different. It is an open question how often international courts and tribunals refer only pro forma to the VCLT to shield themselves from criticism or to build legitimacy.

III. VARIETIES OF TREATY INTERPRETATION

The question of whether treaty interpretation in one subfield of international law differs from treaty interpretation in another is linked to the idea that different types of treaties are to be interpreted differently, that is, that particular elements of the VCLT's interpretative armoury are more appropriate for specific types of treaties.

There are various ways of categorizing treaties.[81] The most common grouping of treaties is into law-making and contract-type treaties (*traités-lois* and *traité-contrats*). Contract-type treaties are characterized by their

---

[80] Contra Eirik Bjorge, *Evolutionary Interpretation of Treaties* (OUP, 2014) 56.

[81] AD McNair, 'The Functions and Differing Legal Character of Treaties' (1930) 11 BYBIL 100, 118, reprinted in McNair, *Law of Treaties* (n 1) 739–54 (distinguishing between conveyancing treaties, contract-treaties, law-making treaties and constitutive instruments of international organizations); R Kolb, *Interprétation et création du droit international. Esquisse d'une herméneutique juridique moderne pour le droit international public* (Bruylant, 2006) 202–3

reciprocal character.[82] They comport obligations voluntarily undertaken, and resemble private law contracts in this respect.[83] Arguably, they can reasonably be interpreted by relying heavily on the intention of the parties – in a way analogous to contracts.

By contrast, *traités-lois*, especially multilateral ones, serve the collective interest of States, and may call for a different interpretive approach.[84] Prior to the VCLT, '[t]reaty interpretation was mostly a matter of ad hoc interpretation of bilateral treaties',[85] and it was therefore natural to regard treaties as close analogues of contracts and interpret them through a contractual lens. With the rise of the community interest in international law,[86] the 'exclusively private law approach to the interpretation of treaties [was increasingly regarded as] antiquated'.[87]

The difficulty of drawing a distinction between contractual and law-making treaties is that particular treaties do not fit en bloc into either category. A given treaty often incorporates both law-making and contractual elements. The same applies to other ways of categorizing treaties. The more promising dimension is to look at whether interpretive methods differ by type of provision within treaties.[88] For example, Letsas explains that the ECtHR's method of interpretation can vary depending on the Convention right in question.[89] In a similar vein, Pauwelyn and Elsig

(contrasting treaties protecting *singuli* (contractual treaties) from treaties protecting public goods).

[82] H Lauterpacht, *Private Law Sources and Analogies in International Law* (Longman, 1927) 70.

[83] *Reservations to the Genocide Convention*, ICJ Rep 1991, 21 ('the notion of the integrity of the Convention … is directly inspired by the notion of contract'); P Daillier, M Forteau, NQ Dinh and A Pellet, *Droit international public* (8th edn, LGDJ, 2009) 283 ('L'opération d'interprétation est particulièrement délicate en droit international … elle est compatible avec la théorie classique inspirée de la notion de contrat' (the process of interpretation is particularly sensitive in international law … it is compatible with classical theory inspired by the notion of contract)).

[84] Bos, 'Theory and Practice …' (n 14) 156.

[85] van Damme, 'Treaty Interpretation …' (n 37) 619.

[86] B Simma, 'From Bilateralism to Community Interest in International Law' (1994) RCADI, VI, 217–384.

[87] Bos, 'Theory and Practice …' (n 14) 157.

[88] G Scelle, *Précis de Droit de Gens* (Sirey, 1934) 334 (no treaty as a whole requires one specific method of interpretation); S Sur, *L'Interprétation en Droit International Public* (LGDJ, 1974) 262–4.

[89] G Letsas, 'Intentionalism and the Interpretation of the ECHR' in M Fitzmaurice, O Elias, and P Merkouris (eds), *Treaty Interpretation and the*

conclude that 'most courts have central tendencies and generally prefer certain types of interpretation over others'.[90]

In empirical terms, the question is whether the hermeneutics employed by a tribunal in subfield A differ from the hermeneutics in subfield B. Does the ICJ's interpretive methodology differ from the one of the WTO Appellate Body? Do investment tribunals use a different set of interpretive tools compared to human rights treaty courts? We can distinguish two stylized schools: the unity and the diversity schools.

1. The Unity School

According to the unity school, international law's interpretive method is unified and does not differ by subfield of international law.[91] The VCLT is treaty-blind. In each case, the VCLT's interpretive principles inform treaty interpretation in the same way. Treaty interpretation draws no distinction based on the type of treaty – bilateral or multilateral, law-making or contractual.[92] Whether the text to be interpreted is a human rights convention, a boundary treaty or an inter-State loan agreement, the same set of interpretative rules apply.

Crawford, with reference to the ILC, concludes that the techniques of treaty interpretation 'seem to have a general character, whether they arise in the International Court of Justice, in the dispute system of the WTO, in the European Court of Justice or elsewhere'.[93] In support, he refers to *LaGrand*, in which the ICJ concluded that the Vienna Convention on Consular Relations of 1963 gave rise to individual rights on the basis of the 'principle of ordinary interpretation'.[94]

Bjorge concludes that the 'method [of treaty interpretation] is not fragmented; the law of treaties, the method used by various types of international tribunal in treaty interpretation, is a single, unified method

---

Vienna Convention on the Law of Treaties: 30 Years On (Martinus Nijhoff, 2010) 510 (torture vs freedom of speech).

[90] Pauwelyn and Elsig, 'Politics of Treaty Interpretation' (n 3) 450.

[91] On the unity of interpretation in the social sciences and humanities, R Dworkin, *Justice for Hedgehogs* (Harvard UP, 2011) 123 ('[A]ll … types of interpretation share important features that make it appropriate to treat interpretation as one of the two great domain[s] of intellectual activity').

[92] J Crawford, *Brownlie's Principles of Public International Law* (8th edn, OUP, 2012) 31.

[93] J Crawford, *International Law as an Open System: Selected Essays* (Cameron May, 2002) 37.

[94] *LaGrand (Germany v United States of America)*, Judgment, ICJ Rep 2001, 466; Crawford, *Brownlie's Principles* (n 92) 28–9.

of law'. He affirms that 'there is in international law *one* method, and that, even where tribunals insist that they are applying a particular style of interpretation'.[95] Notwithstanding some variation in interpretive methods by treaty type, treaty interpretation retains its fidelity to the VCLT's interpretive framework.

According to van Damme, the VCLT 'objectivised' treaty interpretation. The VCLT's edifice is built on the assumption that the principles of interpretation would 'apply generally to all types of treaty text, independently of who interprets and for whom the text is intended'.[96] She maintains that the interpretation of WTO agreements follows the same interpretive principles as all other treaties.[97]

2. The Diversity School

According to the diversity school, interpretive practices are too varied to be able to speak of a single general approach.[98] Weiler explains that Articles 31–33 are 'descriptively … an "unreal" signpost of contemporary treaty interpretation'.[99] Klabbers highlights that the 'awkward circumstance that both parties can present widely diverging interpretations with the help of the same rule does not seem to be regarded as an embarrassment'.[100] Brölmann concludes that 'not all interpretive rules are the same for all treaties'.[101]

Similarly, Bernhardt affirms that the principles of treaty interpretation do not apply uniformly across the various areas of international law. To him, the thesis that interpretive methods are uniform is 'either misleading or else correct only on a highly abstract level'.[102] Roberts notes that 'perhaps we will see a tailoring of the VCLT interpretive approaches with

---

[95] Bjorge, *Evolutionary Interpretation* (n 80) 54.

[96] van Damme, 'Treaty Interpretation …' (n 37) 643.

[97] Ibid, 607.

[98] Klabbers, 'On Rationalism in Politics …' (n 46) 413; R Bernhardt, 'Thoughts on the Interpretation of Human Rights Treaties' in F Matscher and H Petzold (eds), *Protecting Human Rights: The European Dimension: Studies in Honour of Gérard J Wiarda* (Carl Heymann, 1988) 65, 70–71.

[99] Weiler, '… Meso-Theory …' (n 7) 14.

[100] Klabbers, 'On Rationalism in Politics …' (n 46) 414; Simon, *L'Interpretation* (n 72) 130–34.

[101] CM Brölmann, 'Specialized Rules of Treaty Interpretation: International Organizations' in D Hollis (ed), *The Oxford Guide to Treaties* (OUP, 2012) 507–24, 507 (with reference to McNair, *Law of Treaties* (n 1)).

[102] Bernhardt, 'Thoughts …' (n 98) 70–71; M Craven, 'Legal Differentiation and the Concept of the Human Rights Treaty in International Law' (2000) 11

respect to different types of treaties and before different disputes resolution fora' in the future.[103]

Calls for specialized rules of treaty interpretation have been loudest in respect of human rights law. Human rights treaties are said to be 'special' in the sense that their interpretation diverges from received interpretive practices in international law.[104] In this view, human rights treaties are quasi-constitutional in character and resemble domestic bills of rights, rather than traditional treaties.[105] Notwithstanding these special characteristics, some authors consider that interpretive practices of the ECtHR and the Inter-American Court of Human Rights (IACtHR) are either based on or can be squared with the VCLT.[106]

Consider the emergence of a special approach to interpreting tax treaties as a second example.[107] Lang affirms that 'any interpretive rules concerning especially tax treaties take precedence as *lex specialis* over

---

EJIL 489, 492, 494, 497 (referring to the 'characteristic diffidence' of international legal doctrine towards the peculiarities of human rights treaties and the inappropriateness of the contractual paradigm to human rights treaties); McNair, 'Functions …' (n 81) 106 (call for 'free[ing] ourselves from the traditional notion that the instrument known as the treaty is governed by a single set of rules, however inadequate, and set ourselves to study the greatly differing legal character of the several kinds of treaties and to frame rules appropriate to the character of each kind'.

[103] A Roberts, 'Subsequent Agreements and Practice: The Battle over Interpretive Power' in G Nolte (ed), *Treaties and Subsequent Practice* (OUP, 2013) 95, 102.

[104] M Scheinin, 'Human Rights Treaties and the Vienna Convention on the Law of Treaties: Conflicts of Harmony?' (2005) IACL Report 4 (explaining the discomfort among human rights lawyers with a dogmatic application of the VCLT, and the reasons for the call for modified application of the VCLT); G Letsas, 'Strasbourg's Interpretative Ethic: Lessons for the International Lawyer' (2010) 21 EJIL 509, 512, 538, 541; cf also, R Ergec and J Velu, *La Convention Européenne des Droits de L'Homme* (Bruylant, 1990) 51 ('les canons classiques des traités doivent s'infléchir au contact des méthodes plus adaptée à cet aspect spécifique de la Convention').

[105] JHH Weiler, 'The Transformation of Europe' (1991) 100 YLJ 2403, 2416; Weiler, 'The Interpretation of Treaties …' (n 3) 507; Craven, 'Legal Differentiation …' (n 102) 493.

[106] JG Merrills, *The Development of International Law by the European Court of Human Rights* (2nd edn, Manchester UP, 1993) 69; L Lixinski, 'Treaty Interpretation by the Inter-American Court of Human Rights: Expansionism at the Service of the Unity of International Law' (2010) 21 EJIL 585.

[107] American Law Institute, Federal Income Tax Project, Tentative Draft No 16, 15 April 1991 (recommending rules for the interpretation of tax treaties).

the principles set out in the Vienna Convention'.[108] Even if tax treaties do not differ from other treaties, some interpretive methods are used only in relation to tax treaties.[109]

IV. EFFECTIVENESS AND THE MAGIC OF OBJECT AND PURPOSE

Object and purpose fulfil a special role in the crucible. The reference to object and purpose in Article 31 VCLT renders the principles of treaty interpretation malleable depending on the subfield of international law and the type of treaty. Two, seemingly contradictory, answers can therefore be given to the question of whether international law knows varieties of treaty interpretation. Were it not for object and purpose, the practice of treaty interpretation across different substantive fields of international law might be similar. Put differently, one source of the diversity in the methods of treaty interpretation across fields is the varying object and purpose of treaties.

The treaty's object and purpose can deploy its powerful effect in conjunction with effectiveness. Effectiveness is a 'vehicle to emphasize certain values in the treaty'.[110] Interpreters may deploy effectiveness linked to a treaty's object and purpose in different ways, depending on the treaty's character and the substantive area of international law at issue. The ILC decided not to incorporate effective interpretation in Article 31 VCLT to avoid 'extensive' or 'liberal' interpretation. Effectiveness, though not expressly mentioned in the VCLT, is implicit in the reference to 'object and purpose'.[111]

The drafters of the VCLT did not intend the object and purpose to be an independent principle of interpretation read in isolation of the rest of

---

108 M Lang (ed), *Tax Treaty Interpretation* (Kluwer Law, 2001) 82.

109 E Reimer, 'Tax Treaty Interpretation in Germany' in Michael Lang (ed), *Tax Treaty Interpretation* (Kluwer Law/Linde, 2000) 122; K Vogel, 'Double Tax Treaties and their Interpretation' (1986) 4 Berkeley J Intl L 1, 15, 30–37, 33 (as the VCLT contains 'only relatively general rules', 'it cannot make allowance for the peculiarities of tax treaties').

110 van Damme, 'Treaty Interpretation …' (n 37) 638.

111 D Nguyen, P Daillier, and A Pellet, *Droit International Public* (7th edn, LGDJ, 2002) 264; D Rietiker, 'The Principle of "Effectiveness" in the Recent Jurisprudence of the ECtHR: Its Different Dimensions and its Consistency with Public International Law: No Need for the Concept of Treaty *Sui Generis*' (2010) 79 NJIL 249, 256; *Territorial Dispute (Libyan Arab Jamahiriya/Chad)*, Merits, ICJ Rep 1994, 6, paras 51–2.

Article 31 VCLT. In the design of the VCLT the object and purpose is only one element of the crucible. Restrictive or expansive presumptions in interpretation have become suspect, and increasingly give way to a neutral approach operating without such presumptions.[112]

1. Human Rights Law

Many human rights lawyers regard effectiveness as central to realizing the object and purpose of human rights instruments. The principle has been a prominent feature in human rights adjudication.[113] Likewise, human rights tribunals have been at the forefront of developing the principle of evolutionary interpretation.[114] Treaty interpreters have gradually mainstreamed the principle,[115] culminating in the ICJ's endorsement in *Costa Rica-Nicaragua*.[116] Evolutionary interpretation has also found fertile territory in WTO law.

Interpreters of human rights treaties have extended the principle of effectiveness beyond its traditional scope, arguably in departure from general international law.[117] In *Golder*, the ECtHR relied on effectiveness and concluded that Article 6(1) ECHR conferred a right of access to the courts.[118] In his separate opinion, Judge Fitzmaurice criticized this extensive interpretation of Article 6(1) for inventing a new obligation

---

[112] Crawford, *Brownlie's Principles* (n 92); Roberts, 'Power and Persuasion' (n 3) 199.

[113] *Airey v United Kingdom*, App no 6289/73 (ECHR, 9 October 1979) para 24 ('to guarantee not rights that are theoretical or illusory but rights that are practical and effective'); *Nada v Switzerland*, App no 10593-08 (ECHR, 12 September 2012) paras 182 and 19 ('interpreted and applied in a manner that renders its guarantees practical and effective').

[114] Bjorge, *Evolutionary Interpretation* (n 80).

[115] B Simma, 'Mainstreaming Human Rights: The Contribution of the International Court of Justice' (2012) 3 JIDS 1, 20; Bernhardt, 'Thoughts …' (n 98) 65.

[116] *Dispute Regarding Navigational and Related Rights (Costa Rica v Nicaragua)*, Judgment, ICJ Rep 2009, 213.

[117] DJ Harris, M O'Boyle, and C Warbrick, *Law of the European Convention on Human Rights* (2nd edn, OUP, 2009) 15; A Mowbray, 'The Creativity of the European Court of Human Rights' (2005) 5 HRLR 57–79, 60; M Paparinskis, *The International Minimum Standard and Fair and Equitable Treatment* (OUP, 2013) 150 (ECtHR was aware that it introduced a new variant of interpretation).

[118] *Golder v United Kingdom* (n 6) especially para 36; Mowbray, 'Creativity of the ECtHR' (n 117) 58.

incompatible with the ECHR's 'ordinary meaning'.[119] Such teleological interpretation has led to the criticism that the ECtHR and other human rights bodies only pay lip service to the VCLT principles on interpretation.[120]

The ECtHR refers to the VCLT only sparingly.[121] It oscillates between the isolationist paradigm in *Loizidou*[122] that emphasizes the autonomous character of the ECHR and the open paradigm in *Banković*, according to which 'the Convention must be interpreted in the light of the rules of interpretation set out in the Vienna Convention',[123] and 'any relevant rules of international law' under Article 31(3)(c).

2. International Organizations

Teleological interpretation has been central to interpreting the UN Charter, given the UN's unique object and purpose.[124] Special interpretive principles could apply to the UN Charter and other treaties establishing international organizations. For example, Kunig contends

---

[119] *Golder v United Kingdom* (n 6) Separate Opinion of Judge Sir Gerald Fitzmaurice; cf also his earlier separate opinion in *National Union of Belgian Police v Belgium*, App No 4464/70 [1975] Ser A, No 19, para 9 (plea to follow the ordinary approach to interpretation); M Fitzmaurice, 'Dynamic (Evolutive) Interpretation of Treaties and the European Court of Human Rights' in A Orakhelashvili and S Williams (eds), *40 Years of the Vienna Convention on Treaties* (BIICL, 2010) 92, 151; Sinclair, 'Principles …' (n 20) 130–33.

[120] M Fitzmaurice, 'The Tale of Two Judges: Sir Hersch Lauterpacht and Sir Gerald Fitzmaurice: Human Rights and the Interpretation of Treaties' (2009) 61 Rev Hellen Dr Intern 140 (neglecting the fundamental canons of interpretation); cf also, Baroness Hale, 'Common Law and Convention Law: The Limits to Interpretation' [2011] EHRLR 534, 543.

[121] M Forowicz, *The Reception of International Law in the European Court of Human Rights* (OUP, 2010) 6.

[122] *Loizidou v Turkey*, App No 15318/89, Judgment (ECHR, 23 March 1995) para 75 ('a constitutional instrument of European public order').

[123] *Banković and Others v Belgium and 16 Other Contracting States*, App No 52207/99, Judgment (ECHR, 12 December 2001) 333; cf also, *ILC Report on Fragmentation* (n 2) para 164 (the ECHR is not a self-contained regime, with reference to *Banković*).

[124] E Gordon, 'The World Court and the Interpretation of Constitutive Treaties: Some Observations on the Development of an International Constitutional Law' (1965) 59 AJIL 794–833 ('object and purpose' as the dominant criterion); cf also, N Fennelly, 'Legal Interpretation at the European Court of Justice' (1996) 20 Fordham Intl LJ 656–79; J Arato, 'Treaty Interpretation and Constitutional Transformation: Informal Change in International Organizations' (2013) 38 YJIL, forthcoming.

that the 'normative side of the UN charter' is interpreted differently from the contractual side.[125] When interpreting constitutional treaties of international organizations (IOs), the treaty's object and purpose assumes a greater role than in the interpretation of ordinary treaties.[126]

In the *Nuclear Weapons* advisory opinion, the ICJ stated that: 'from a formal standpoint, the constituent instruments of international organizations are multilateral treaties, to which the well-established rules of treaty interpretation apply'.[127] Yet after this formalistic statement on the unity of interpretive methods, the Court immediately highlighted that constituent instruments of international organizations have 'special characteristics':

> Such treaties can raise specific problems of interpretation, owing, inter alia, to their character which is conventional and at the same time institutional; the very nature of the organization created, the objectives which have been assigned to it by its founders, the imperatives associated with the effective performance of its functions, as well as its own practice, are all elements which may deserve special attention when the time comes to interpret these constituent treaties.[128]

In finding that the European Community had 'exclusive competence' to negotiate the European Road Transport Agreement (ERTA), the ECJ adopted a 'teleological, purposive rule drawn from the book of constitutional interpretation'.[129] The Advocate General had warned that a finding of exclusive competence would require a 'teleological interpretation of

---

[125] P Kunig, 'United Nations Charter, Interpretation of' in R Wolfrum (ed), *Max Planck Encyclopaedia of Public International Law* (OUP, 2010) paras 2–4.

[126] *Reparation for Injuries Suffered in the Service of the United Nations*, ICJ Rep 1949, 174 (the UN's capacity to bring the claim, 'not settled by the actual terms of the Charter', was 'implied in [the UN]'s constituent documents'); E Lauterpacht, 'The Development of the Law of International Organizations by the Decisions of International Tribunals' (1976) 152 RCADI 381, 420; D Akande, 'International Organizations' in MD Evans, *International Law* (3rd edn, OUP, 2010) 263; Brölmann, 'Specialized Rules ...' (n 101); J Klabbers, *An Introduction to International Institutional Law* (2nd edn, CUP, 2009) 87–90; CF Amerashinge, *Principles of the Institutional Law of International Organizations* (2nd edn, CUP, 2004) 24–65.

[127] *Legality of the Use by a State of Nuclear Weapons in Armed Conflict*, Advisory Opinion, ICJ Rep 1996, 66, para 19.

[128] Ibid, para 19.

[129] Case C–22/70 *Commission of the European Communities v Council of the European Communities* [1971] ECR 263 ('ERTA'); Weiler, 'Transformation ...' (n 105) 2416; R Post, 'Constructing the European Polity: ERTA and the *Open Skies* Judgments' in M Poiares Maduro and L Azoulai (eds), *The Past and Future*

the treaties' characteristic 'of a constitutional court', rather than the kind of restrictive interpretation ordinarily accorded to treaties between independent States.[130] According to Weiler, the Court sidestepped 'the presumptive rule of interpretation typical in international law, that treaties must be interpreted in a manner that minimizes encroachment on State sovereignty'.[131]

The line between giving effect to the object and purpose of a particular treaty, such as human rights, investment or tax treaties, and giving undue weight to object and purpose, thereby disregarding the text and not applying the VCLT's interpretive framework, is fine indeed.

V. DIVERSE TREATY INTERPRETERS AND INTERPRETIVE COMMUNITIES

This section shifts focus from the text itself to the actors involved in the interpretation.[132] Central to interpretive outcomes are treaty interpreters. As the ILC recognized, the application of the VCLT principles on interpretation 'is not automatic but depends on the conviction of the interpreter'.[133] As a result, '[a]nswers to legal questions become dependent on whom you ask'.[134] How treaty interpreters approach the task of interpretation may ultimately matter more than the formulation of VCLT principles.[135]

---

of EU Law: The Classics of EU Law Revisited on the 50th Anniversary of the Rome Treaty (Hart, 2010) 234, 239–43; Klabbers, *International Institutional Law* (n 126) 87–8; Sinclair, 'Principles …' (n 20) 508.

130 T Tridimas and P Eckhout, 'The External Competence of the Community and the Case-Law of the Court of Justice: Principle versus Pragmatism' (1994) 14 YB of European L 143, 149; 'ERTA' (n 129) Opinion of AG Dutheillet de Lamothe, 10 March 1971, 289–93 (awarding exclusive competence to the Community to negotiate the ERTA would involve engaging in 'discretionary construction of the law … a judicial interpretation far exceeding the bounds which the court has hitherto set regarding its power to interpret the Treaty', similar to a finding of implied powers by the US Supreme Court).

131 Weiler, 'Transformation …' (n 105) 2416.

132 Cf also, Venzke, *Semantic Change* (n 24) 54.

133 Yearbook of the ILC (1966) vol II, 218, para 4; R Jennings, 'General Course on Principles of Public International Law' (1967) 121 RCADI 323, 544; van Damme, 'Treaty Interpretation …' (n 37) 641 (AB jurisprudence cannot 'be reduced to a mere synthetic application of Articles 31 to 33 VCLT).

134 *ILC Report on Fragmentation* (n 2) 483.

135 Sur, *L'Interprétation* (n 88) 223–5.

Competition between tribunals is one source of growing interpretive diversity in international law. Jennings famously referred to the 'tendency of particular tribunals to regard themselves as different, as separate little empires which must as far as possible be augmented'.[136] Courts may seek to expand their own influence and prestige. One way of increasing prestige is to develop a new, or distinctive, interpretive approach.

1. The Actors in Treaty Interpretation

Can the plurality of different treaty interpreters and their diverse perspectives – international courts and tribunals, national courts, government legal advisors, international organizations and non-State actors – all be accommodated within the VCLT's single interpretative framework?[137] Or is the growing diversity of actors a source of interpretive fragmentation? Are particular actors more sophisticated treaty interpreters than others?

Traditionally, ministries of foreign affairs have been the primary actors in treaty interpretation, much more so than national courts or international tribunals.[138] As a result, a lot of treaty interpretation has been auto-interpretation, and as a matter of fact, does not necessarily follow VCLT principles. Foreign ministries and other national treaty interpreters can of course follow the VCLT's approach. Yet they are likely to have more room to disengage from the VCLT principles, or to only invoke the VCLT pro forma, than either national courts or international tribunals.

The VCLT was largely designed with international third-party adjudicators in mind. Whereas international courts and tribunals apply the VCLT as part of general international law, national courts may in practice have considerable freedom in choosing their interpretive methodology, or even be mandated to use domestic interpretive methodologies, even in

---

[136] R Jennings, 'The Proliferation of Adjudicatory Bodies: Dangers and Possible Answers' in Implications of the Proliferation of International Adjudicatory Bodies for Dispute Resolution (1995) 9 ASIL Bulletin: Educational Resources on International Law 2, 6; R Jennings, 'The Judiciary, International and National, and the Development of International Law' (1996) 45 ICLQ 1, 5–6.

[137] M Bos, 'Legal Archetypes and the Normative Concept of Law as Main Factors in the Defining and Development of International Law' (1976) 23 Netherlands Intl L Rev 72, 74 (distinguishing three 'archetypes' of law appliers, namely the lawmaker, the judge and the scholar). He builds on the interpretation *authentica, usualis et doctrinalis* developed by CJ Bartolus de Saxoferrato, *Commentaria*, vol II; Vogenauer, 'Interpretation of Statutes ...' (n 13) 989.

[138] R Schaffer, 'Current Trends in Treaty Interpretation and the South African Approach' Au YB Intl L 129, 148.

treaty cases.[139] Theoretically, the growing role of national courts could herald more consistent interpretation of treaties across multiple jurisdictions, or exactly the opposite.[140] An important factor for whether national courts are part of the problem or part of the solution is the interpretive methodology that they apply.

Who has the authority to interpret constitutive documents of IOs is also likely to influence interpretive outcomes. Different actors are empowered to interpret constitutive documents, depending on the IO. The ICJ lacks the power to authoritatively interpret the UN Charter.[141] The Court is limited to interpreting the Charter in specific cases. Similarly, even though the United Nations High Commission for Refugees (UNHCR) under Article 35 of the Refugee Convention of 1951 has a 'duty of supervising the application of the provisions of the Convention', it does not have the power to issue authentic interpretations of the Convention.[142]

Other international organizations, such as the International Monetary Fund (IMF), have the power to authoritatively interpret their constituent document. Yet the drafters of the IMF Articles were keen to ensure that control over the meaning of the IMF's constitutive treaty rested with financial experts representing States, rather than with a tribunal external to the organization.[143] Not surprisingly, the VCLT plays no significant role in the interpretation of the IMF Articles of Agreement by the IMF.[144] When national courts interpret the IMF Articles of Agreement, such as Section VIII(2)(b) on the recognition of exchange controls,[145] they typically do not refer to the VCLT.

Treaty interpreters refer to VLCT principles on interpretation with varying frequency. References to the VCLT are common in trade and

---

139 See the various country chapters in D Sloss, *The Role of Domestic Courts in Treaty Enforcement: A Comparative Study* (CUP, 2009).

140 Goodwin-Gill, 'The Search …' (n 78) 204–41; *King v Bristow Helicopters* [2002] 2 AC 628 (emphasizing the desirability of uniform interpretation).

141 Kunig, 'UN Charter …' (n 125) para 7.

142 Goodwin-Gill, 'The Search …' (n 78).

143 EP Hexner, 'Interpretation by Public International Organizations of their Basic Instruments' (1959) 53 AJIL 341–70, 344.

144 A search of the IMF's *Selected Decisions* yielded not a single reference to the VCLT.

145 BS Meyer, Recognition of Exchange Controls after the International Monetary Fund Agreement (1953) 62 YLS 867; eg *Wilson, Smithett & Cope Ltd v Terruzzi* [1976] QB 703, CA; *de Boer, Widow Moojen v von Reeichert*, Court of Appeal, Paris 1962, 89 J Droit Intl 718.

investment law,[146] yet rarer in tax law and virtually absent in international monetary law. Why does treaty interpretation take a different shape in trade and investment law on the one hand, and monetary and tax law on the other hand?

Part of the explanation lies in who the treaty interpreters are: in the case of trade and investment, a standing dispute settlement body; in the case of investment law, ad hoc arbitral tribunals; in international tax law, national courts and other administrative agencies, and in international monetary law, the IMF with the occasional assistance of national courts.

2. Specialization and Interpretive Communities

A second source of interpretive diversity is the increasingly narrow legal education and specialization of adjudicators.[147] Closely linked to narrower legal education than in the past is the rise of distinct and self-contained interpretive communities.

These communities speak a common language.[148] They share certain historical, political and social contexts that provide the background for treaty interpretation.[149] Interpretation may also be influenced by practices and shared understandings within a particular interpretive community. These can, consciously or unconsciously, affect interpretation.[150]

Educational background and experience is likely to shape treaty interpretation. The interpretive methodology could differ depending on the interpreter's speciality and legal education. Roberts argues that

---

[146] C Schreuer, 'Diversity and Harmonization of Treaty Interpretation in Investment Arbitration' in M Fitzmaurice, O Elias, and P Merkouris (eds), *Treaty Interpretation and the Vienna Convention on the Law of Treaties: 30 Years On* (Martinus Nijhoff, 2010) 129; RJ Weeramantry, *Treaty Interpretation in Investment Arbitration* (OUP, 2012); Waibel, '... Treaty Interpretation' (n 9).

[147] Letter from Felix Frankfurter, Professor, Harvard Law School, to Mr Rosenwald, 13 May 1927, quoted in HT Edwards, 'The Growing Disjunction between Legal Education and the Legal Profession' (1992) 91 Michigan L Rev 34, 34 ('In the last analysis, the law is what lawyers are. And the law and the lawyers are what the law schools make them'); T Mayer-Maly, 'Der Jurist: Enzyklopädist oder Spezialist' in D Merten (ed), *Probleme der Juristenausbildung* (Duncker & Humblot, 1980) 15–28; AT Kronman, *The Lost Lawyers: Failing Ideals of the Legal Profession* (Harvard UP, 1995).

[148] Fiss, 'Objectivity ... ' (n 37); Vagts, '... New American Way ...' (n 37) 480.

[149] Shaffer and Trachtman, '... Institutional Choice ...' (n 37) 131.

[150] Johnstone, '... Interpretive Communities' (n 53) 371–2; Shaffer and Trachtman, '... Institutional Choice ...' (n 37) 119.

investment arbitral tribunals adopt different interpretative paradigms depending on who the arbitrators are.[151] It is an open question to what extent the background of adjudicators affects how they interpret treaties.

Generalists are a dying breed among lawyers, including among international lawyers. The higher level of specialization among international lawyers today goes hand in hand with a narrowing of one's perspective, a 'tunnel vision' that is the natural by-product of specialization.[152] WTO panel members and judges on human rights tribunals may no longer share the same interpretive outlook. As part of two distinct interpretive communities, they may increasingly speak different languages.

Does the emergence of interpretive communities change the process of interpretation, and lead, almost inevitably, to more fragmentation in international law?[153] Interpretive communities could add significantly to centrifugal tendencies in international law. The degree to which interpretive communities cause interpretive fragmentation hinges on how closely knit a given interpretive community is.[154]

3. Interpretive Home Bias

Treaty interpreters, especially judges in national courts, may owe primary allegiance to their home jurisdiction and approach treaty interpretation with their national glasses on.[155] National courts may be particularly prone to interpreting treaties through a national lens, and as a result of

---

151 Roberts, 'Clash of Paradigms …' (n 61).

152 H Muir Watt, 'Private International Law as Global Governance: Beyond the Schism, from Closet to Planet' ('PILAGG') (OUP, forthcoming, 2014, 26–30.

153 SE Fish, *Is there a Text in this Class? The Authority of Interpretive Communities* (Harvard UP, 1980); Johnstone, '… Interpretive Communities' (n 53); I Johnstone, 'Security Council Deliberations: The Power of the Better Argument' (2003) 14 EJIL 437, 443–7; Vagts, '… New American Ways …' (n 37) 480; Waibel, '… Treaty Interpretation' (n 9) 31.

154 Pauwelyn and Elsig, 'Politics of Treaty Interpretation' (n 3) 467 (referring to the closely knit epistemic community in human rights law and the GATT, as compared to the more diffuse epistemic community in general international law).

155 *R v Secretary of State for the Home Department, ex parte Adan* [2001] All ER 593, 617 (Steyn LJ) (interpretation of international law untainted by national legal culture); E Benvenisti, 'Judicial Misgivings Regarding the Application of International Law: An Analysis of the Attitudes of National Courts' (1993) 4 EJIL 159, 161; A Roberts, 'Comparative International Law? The Role of National Courts in Creating and Enforcing International Law' (2011) 60 ICLQ 57, 75; Crawford and Nevill, 'Relations …' (n 21) 249.

their growing role could constitute a major source of interpretive fragmentation.

The average national judge, even in higher courts, is likely to be more familiar with their national law's canon for statutory or contractual interpretation, rather than the VCLT. National approaches are likely to influence how they approach treaty interpretation. For example, US judges have a 'predilection' for applying 'unwittingly the rules of statutory construction to treaties'.[156]

The failure by some treaty interpreters to apply the VCLT's interpretive framework may be out of ignorance, rather than by design. As Bederman explains, 'rules of treaty construction are truly judge-made law, and [national judges] remain largely ignorant of international glosses on the subject ... There appears to have been little appreciation of substantive canons of treaty interpretation – default rules which favour particular interpretive or policy outcomes'.[157] Justice Blackmun remarked that unlike earlier treaty interpreters, '[t]oday's jurists, furthermore, are relatively unfamiliar with interpreting instruments of international law'.[158]

At times, national courts apply domestic canons of contract or statutory construction, rather than VCLT principles (though those may overlap). According to Bederman, US courts 'frequently apply different substantive canons of construction to different kinds of treaties',[159] depending on whether the legislative or contractual aspect of a treaty predominates.[160] Despite the persistence of the domestic contract analogy, courts have showed some openness to interpreting treaties more liberally than private law contracts.[161]

---

[156] Bederman, 'Revivalist Canons ...' (n 18) 964.

[157] David J. Bederman, *Classical canons: rhetoric, classicism and treaty interpetation* (Ashgate, 2001), 244.

[158] H Blackmun, 'The Supreme Court and the Law of Nations: Owing a Decent Respect to the Opinions of Mankind' (1994) 104 Yale LJ 39, 8.

[159] Bederman, 'Revivalist Canons ...' (n 18) 956 ('little consistency in the US; difficult to discern even a core set of domestically derived principles that US courts faithfully employ in interpreting treaties'); Restatement (Third) on the Foreign Relations Law of the United States, §432 (1987), 197–8 (interpretive power largely delegated to the executive branch due to its special expertise in foreign affairs).

[160] *Société Nationale Industrielle Aérospatiale v United States*, 482 US 522, 533 (1987) ('[i]n interpreting an international treaty, we are mindful that it is 'in the nature of a contract between nations [to which] [g]eneral rules of construction apply'); Bederman, 'Revivalist Canons ...' (n 18) 963; Criddle, '... US Treaty Interpretation' (n 25) 451.

[161] *Choctaw Nation of Indians v United States*, 318 US 423 (1943).

Criddle argues that the US Supreme Court erroneously relies on two domestic analogies: first, it generally interprets treaties pursuant to the contractual paradigm, and it analogizes deference to the treaty interpretations of the executive branch to the *Chevron* doctrine in US administrative law.[162] The danger in the contract analogy is that it leads to the adoption of parochial canons of treaty interpretation that depart from the VCLT.[163] It can lead to domestic law bias.[164]

4. Interpretive Fragmentation in International Tax Law

International tax law, though arguably on the fringes of international law, offers a good illustration of interpretive fragmentation. Avi-Yonah argues that a coherent international tax regime exists, and that it forms a significant part of international law.[165] Yet his book refers to the VCLT not once. This is reminiscent of the limited role played by the VCLT in GATT dispute settlement in the 1970s and 1980s. Whether tax treaty interpretation conforms to the VCLT's interpretive framework is unclear.

A major reason for departure from the VCLT's interpretive framework in international tax law is that national courts and administrative agencies are the central actors in this area, given the absence of commonly used dispute settlement methods at the international level. Tax disputes reach the international plane typically only incidentally, as part of a larger dispute involving other elements. For example, investment tribunals have

---

[162] *Chevron v Natural Resources Defense Council*, 467 US 837 (1984) (courts should ordinarily defer to reasonable interpretations of agencies); E Criddle, 'Chevron Deference and Treaty Interpretation' (2003) 112 YLJ 1927; CA Bradley, 'Chevron Deference and Foreign Affairs' (2000) 86 Virginia J Intl L 649; D Sloss, 'United States' in D Sloss (ed), *The Role of Domestic Courts in Treaty Enforcement: A Comparative Study* (CUP, 2009) 524, 553 (deference as the nationalist counterpoint); Bederman, 'Revivalist Canons …' (n 18) 972; Criddle, '… US Treaty Interpretation' (n 25) 459 (treaty interpretations by government agencies entitled to 'great weight').

[163] Criddle, '… US Treaty Interpretation' (n 25) 472 (the private law analogy 'set US treaty practice adrift from its international moorings').

[164] McDougal et al, *World Public Order* (n 23) 259 ('National judges appear to have voted for the position championed by their country about 80 percent of the time').

[165] RS Avi-Yonah, *International Tax as International Law: An Analysis of the International Tax Regime* (CUP, 2007). Other books on tax treaties do, however, refer to the VCLT.

on occasion considered the interaction between tax and investment treaties.[166]

How often then do national courts refer to the VCLT when interpreting tax treaties? English courts and agencies often employ strict construction, inspired by the statutory interpretation of tax statutes. Their 'judicial habits in statutory interpretation die hard'.[167] If one discounts differences between tax treaties and domestic tax legislation, the 'English courts have tended to adopt similar approaches to interpreting double taxation agreements as they have for other [domestic] legislation'.[168] Notwithstanding, at least since the judgment in *IRS v Commerzbank* in 1990, English courts have commonly referred to the VCLT in tax cases.[169] Yet the approach to interpreting tax treaties is inconsistent even within the English Court of Appeal.[170]

Over the last two decades, the English courts have come round to the view that the strictly literal approach that they use for domestic revenue statutes is inappropriate for international tax treaties. They have become more open to teleological arguments.[171] According to this newer trend in

---

[166] Eg, *EnCana v Ecuador*, Award (UNCITRAL), 3 February 2006.

[167] Schaffer, 'South African Approach' (n 138) 129 (South African courts adopt a statutory approach to treaty interpretation).

[168] P Baker, *Double Taxation Conventions and International Tax Law* (2nd edn, Sweet & Maxwell, 1994) para C-09, 27); J Freedman, 'Interpreting Tax Statutes: Tax Avoidance and the Intention of Parliament' (2007) 123 LQR 53–90 (discussing the prevalence of strictly textual approaches in statutory tax interpretation).

[169] *IRC v Commerzbank AG* [1990] STC 285, *IRC v Banco do Brasil SA* [1990] STC 285.

[170] *Bayfine UK Products v HMRC* [2011] EWCA Civ 304, para. 17 (refers to the VCLT while adopting a very purposive approach) contrasts with *Anson v HMRC* [2013] EWCA Civ 63 (strong emphasis on the text without a reference to the VCLT) and the intermediate position in *HMRC v FCE Bank* [2012] EWCA Civ 1290.

[171] *IRC v Exxon* [1982] STC 356, 369; *Union Texas Petroleum v Critchley* [1988] STC 691; *IRS v Commerzbank AG* (n 169); *Ben Nevis v IRC* [2013] EWCA Civ 578 (international tax enforcement); I.R. 128/80 (1985) 145 BFHE 341, 9 October 1985; *Great West Life Assurance Co. v United States*, (1982) 678 F. 2.d 180; Baker, *Double Taxation Conventions* (n 168) para C-10, 28; cf also *The Queen and Inland Revenue Commissioners ex parte: Commerzbank AG*, Case C-330/91, [1993] ECR I-4017 (a tax case involving the freedom of establishment).

the tax treaty jurisprudence, tax treaties should be interpreted 'unconstrained by technical rules of English law, or by English legal precedent, but on broad principles of general acceptation'.[172]

There is also some evidence of interpretive fragmentation across countries, with a competitive race to the bottom in tax treaty interpretation. National courts in developing countries compete to interpret double taxation agreements in favour of taxpayers, to become or remain an attractive investment destination. Similarly, courts in developing countries sometimes strategically choose among competing constructions to enhance their country's competitive position.[173]

VI. SPECIAL INTERPRETIVE INSTRUCTIONS AND JOINT INTERPRETATIONS

Special interpretive principles, rules or instructions give guidance or directions to adjudicators, often specific to a particular treaty, on how they should exercise their interpretive authority. As the VCLT's interpretive framework is dispositive,[174] States entering into treaties could adopt such specialized directions in analogy to Article 31(4). Yet they rarely provide more specific instructions to adjudicators. The low incidence of such instructions reflects the fact that States typically see no need to set out special interpretive rules or principles, given the wide latitude already left by the VCLT principles.

The existence of specialized interpretive rules or principles, as in Article 3(2) Dispute Settlement Understanding (DSU), Article 22(2) Statute of the International Criminal Court (ICC Statute), or Article 29 of the Inter-American Convention on Human Rights (IACHR) can limit the

---

172 *James Buchanan & Co Ltd v Babco Forwarding & Shipping (UK) Limited* [1987] AC 141, 152.

173 E Baistrocchi, 'The Use and Interpretation of Tax Treaties in the Emerging World: Theory and Implications' (2008) British Tax Rev 352–91, 355 (citing *Union of India v Azadi Bachao Andolan* (2003) SC 56 ITR 563).

174 Yearbook of the ILC (1966) vol II, 218, para 4; Paparinskis, *Minimum Standard* (n 117) 144; *United States-Anti-Dumping Measures on Certain Hot-Rolled Steel Products from Japan,* WT/DS184/AB/R, AB Report, 23 August 2001, DSR 2001:X 4697, note 40 ('The parties to a particular treaty might agree upon rules of interpretation for that treaty which differ from the rules of interpretation in Articles 31 and 32 of the *Vienna Convention*. But this is not the case here').

adjudicator's interpretive space.[175] Specialized interpretive rules or principles typically emerge when the treaty parties consider that adjudicators enjoy 'excessive' interpretive space, and could do with more guidance. Another mechanism is joint interpretation, which functions as a safety valve. States parties are able to react if the jurisprudence develops in unintended directions or if they consider jurisprudential trends to be undesirable ex post on policy grounds. Good example are NAFTA Articles 1131(2) and 2001(2)(c) that expressly enable NAFTA parties to issue joint interpretations that are binding on NAFTA tribunals.[176]

1. International Trade Law

The drafters of the WTO agreements could have adopted their own interpretative methodology, putting more emphasis on intent than the VCLT. Yet they limited themselves to instructing the Dispute Settlement Body (DSB) to interpret the WTO agreements 'in accordance with the customary rules of interpretation of public international law'. The drafters included Article 3(2) DSU for two primary reasons: first, to change the interpretive approach adopted by GATT panels with less emphasis on *travaux préparatoires*, and second, to interpret WTO law as part of the larger universe of international law.[177]

A good example of a more specific interpretive instruction in WTO law is Article 17(6) of the Anti-Dumping Agreement (A-D A). It calls on the interpreter to regard a measure to be in conformity with the A-D A provided one of several possible interpretations supports such conformity.

---

[175] Grover, 'Call to Arms ...' (n 5) 553 (Article 22.2 ICC Statute as a response to the 'perceived liberal interpretive reasoning' of the International Criminal Tribunal for the Former Yugoslavia (ICTY) and International Criminal Tribunal for Rwanda (ICTR); Lixinski, '... Expansionism at the Service of the Unity of International' (n 106) 587; D Akande, 'The Sources of International Criminal Law', in A Cassesse (ed), *The Oxford Companion to International Criminal Justice* (OUP, 2009) 44–5 ('the application of the principle *in dubio pro reo* should modify the application of the Vienna Convention methods of interpretation').

[176] North American Free Trade Agreement (Can.-Mex.-U.S.), 8, 11, 14, 17 December 2011, (1992) 32 ILM 289 and 605; 4 NAFTA Free Trade Commission, Notes of Interpretation of Certain Chapter 11 Provisions 31 July 2001 (fair and equitable treatment is equivalent to the international minimum standard); Roberts, 'Power and Persuasion ...' (n 3) 180–81.

[177] Pauwelyn and Elsig, 'Politics of Treaty Interpretation' (n 3) 461.

The aim of this provision is to ensure a larger degree of deference to national anti-dumping decisions than the VCLT would entail.[178]

Yet despite the explicit instruction, the AB has only paid mere lip service to this provision.[179] In *US-Hot-Rolled Steel*, the AB clarified that the VCLT principles of interpretation are to be applied first, followed by the special interpretive instruction for anti-dumping duties in a second step. The choice is between interpretations 'permissible under the rules of treaty interpretation in Articles 31 and 32'.[180]

In a declaration of principle, the AB added: 'the rules of treaty interpretation in Articles 31 and 32 of the Vienna Convention apply to *any* treaty, in *any* field of public international law, and not just to the WTO agreements. These rules of treaty interpretation impose certain common disciplines upon treaty interpreters, irrespective of the content of the treaty provision being examined and irrespective of the field of international law concerned'.[181]

The Doha Declaration on the Agreement on Trade Related Aspects of Intellectual Property Rights (TRIPS) and Public Health also contains specific interpretive instructions. It 'affirm[s] that the Agreement can and should be interpreted and implemented in a manner supportive of WTO members' right to protect public health and, in particular, to promote access to medicines for all'. WTO members collectively instructed all WTO organs to place greater emphasis on object and purpose than the VCLT allows and to interpret the TRIPS with additional flexibility: 'In applying the customary rules of interpretation of public international law, each provision of the TRIPS Agreement shall be read in the light of the object and purpose of the Agreement as expressed, in particular, in its objectives and principles.'[182]

Interpretive notes (called 'Ad notes' in WTO parlance) provide interpretive directions to the WTO panels and the AB. For example, the GATT contracting parties adopted an interpretive note to Article III (the 'Note Ad Article III') providing that if a domestic law applies to both an imported product and the 'like' domestic product, it should be analysed

---

178 van Damme, 'Treaty Interpretation ...' (n 37) 607.

179 van Damme, 'Treaty Interpretation ...' (n 37) 607 (citing the AB's refusal on the ground that it would be incompatible with its character as a judicial body).

180 *US-Hot-Rolled Steel* (n 174) para 60.

181 *US-Hot-Rolled Steel* (n 174), para 60 (emphases in original); affirmed in *US-Continued Existence and Application of Zeroing Methodology*, WT/DS350/AB/R, 19 February 2009, para 267.

182 WTO, Declaration on the TRIPS Agreement and Public Health, 20 November 2001, WT/MIN(01)/Dec/2, para 5(a).

under Article III rather than Article XI.[183] Ad notes differ from the principles of interpretation set out in the VCLT in the sense that they are tied to a particular substantive provision of the treaty. They are thus designed to guard against the risk that the DSB interprets a provision at odds with the intention of the treaty parties. The Appellate Body reads treaty provisions and Ad notes as 'one inseparable subject for interpretation'.[184]

2. International Tax Law

The Model Treaty of the Organization for Economic Cooperation and Development for the avoidance of double taxation and its associated Commentary are tools to foster common interpretations by national courts and administrative bodies in different States.[185] When interpreting tax treaties, national courts often refer to the OECD Convention as an 'aid to interpretation'.[186] The Commentary's influence on tax treaty interpretation and how it fits into the VCLT framework is one of the most controversial issues in the international tax literature.[187]

---

[183] Note Ad Article III GATT (stating that any law affecting the internal sale, offering for sale, purchase, transportation, distribution, or use of products 'which applies to an imported product and to the like domestic product and is collected or enforced in the case of the imported product at the time or point of importation' is to be treated as an internal regulation subject to Article III and (impliedly) not as an import restriction subject to Article XI). *Import, Distribution and Sale of Certain Alcoholic Drinks by Provincial Marketing Agencies*, GATT Dispute Panel Report, 18 February 1992, GATT B.I.S.D. (39th supp.) 27, para 5.28.

[184] van Damme, *Treaty Interpretation by the WTO* (n 57) 29. The same applies to interpretive footnotes, ibid, 76.

[185] Vogel, 'Double Tax Treaties ...' (n 109) 39–43.

[186] Baker, *Double Taxation Conventions* (n 168) C-10, 28, C-12, 28; OECD, Recommendation C(92) 122/FINAL of 23 July 1992.

[187] M Lang, P Pistone, J Schuch, and C Staringer, *The Impact of the OECD and UN Model Conventions on Bilateral Tax Treaties* (CUP, 2012) 4; M Lang and F Brugger, 'The Role of OECD Commentary in Tax Treaty Interpretation' (2008) 23 *Australian Tax Forum* 95; Article 31(2), Article 31(3) or Article 32 are possibilities, JA Jones et al, 'The Interpretation of Tax Treaties with Particular Reference to Article 3(2) of the OECD Model, *British Tax Review* (1984) 90 *et seq.* (the Commentary as a subsequent agreement under Art. 31(3) VCLT); N Blokker, 'Skating on Thin Ice? On the Law of International Organizations and the Legal Nature of the Commentaries on the OECD Model Tax Convention' in S Douma and F Engelen, *The Legal Status of the OECD Commentaries* (IBFD, 2008), 13–27; F Weiss, 'Interpretation of Tax Treaties in Accordance with the

Article 3(2) of the OECD Model Treaty contains an interpretive *lex specialis*, the so-called general *renvoi* clause[188] that provides:

> As regards the application of the Convention at any time by a Contracting State, any term not defined therein shall, unless the context otherwise requires, have the meaning which it has at that time under the law of that State for the purposes of the taxes to which the Convention applies, any meaning under the applicable tax laws of that State prevailing over a meaning given to the term under other laws of that State.

The aim of Article 3(2) is that the taxing State's domestic tax law definitions enjoy priority;[189] as a result, it is entirely possible that the treaty will be interpreted differently by the courts of different States parties.[190] Domestic tax law imposes tax, whereas tax treaties invariably relieve taxpayers from tax. Article 3(2) is favourable to taxpayers in that tax relief is given in respect of whatever is taxed as, for example, 'employment income' under domestic tax law. The double taxation treaty's relief is applied to all income that is defined as 'employment income' by the taxing State.

Such recourse to domestic law definitions is not foreseen in the VCLT. One particular difficulty that Article 3(2) has raised is whether the *renvoi* is to domestic law at the time the tax treaty was concluded or to domestic law at the time the treaty is applied. National courts used to differ on whether an evolutionary or static approach is correct.[191] Courts in virtually all countries now accept that the reference in Article 3(2) to domestic law is ambulatory (evolutionary) rather than static. From the perspective of the VCLT, another interesting feature of Article 3(2) is that its reference to 'context' is wider than that in Article 31 VCLT. It calls on tax treaty interpreters to use any material that sheds light on domestic law not applying (or the treaty definitions).

Commentaries on the OECD Model Tax Convention under the Vienna Convention on the Law of Treaties' ibid, 131–52.

[188] IFA, 'General Report on the Interpretation of Tax Treaties' (1960) 42 Cahier DFI 296.

[189] Reimer, '... Germany' (n 109) 123; Vogel, '... Double Tax Treaties' (n 109) 39–43, 68–75.

[190] Reimer, '... Germany' (n 109) 129.

[191] IFA, 'Interpretation of Tax Treaties' (1986) Bull. IBFD 75, at 81.

3. Treaties for the Benefit of Third Parties

By analogy to human rights law, Reisman argues that treaties for the benefit of third parties warrant 'special concern that interpretation by one or both of the States-parties not undermine the rights and expectations of the third-party beneficiaries'.[192] Recourse to *travaux préparatoires* when interpreting such treaties should be limited because human rights treaties and BITs are designed to influence the behaviour of private entities or individuals who often lack any or ready access to such documents.[193] Similarly, Roberts ventures that in disputes involving non-State actors, tribunals are likely to defer less to subsequent agreements between the State parties, compared to inter-State courts and tribunals.[194] This suggests a variety of interpretation based on the weight attached to subsequent agreements.

VII. OUTLOOK: AN AGENDA FOR RESEARCH

Whether different varieties of treaty interpretation exist in international law depends on the level of abstraction. Viewed from 10,000 feet, the method of treaty interpretation appears unified. However, viewed from close up, there are varieties of interpretation in international law, across and within regimes. Yet against the background of the VCLT's flexibility, codifying distinct interpretive methodologies for different fields of international law promises little benefit.

One way of reconciling the VCLT's unified interpretive framework with interpretive varieties is to characterize each and every divergence from the VCLT as an 'incorrect' application of the VCLT.[195] Sometimes, treaty interpretation is indeed off the rails. Yet as Section I showed, far from being an interpretive straightjacket, flexibility is a built-in feature of

---

[192] WM Reisman, Expert Opinion in *The Republic of Ecuador v United States of America*, 24 April 2012, para 26; contra, Paparinskis, *Minimum Standard* (n 117) 147 (dismissing the need for an interpretive *lex specialis* in investment arbitration).

[193] MH Arsanjani and WM Reisman, 'Interpreting Treaties for the Benefit of Third Parties: The "Salvors' Doctrine" and the Use of Legislative History in Investment Treaties' (2010) 104 AJIL 597, 603–4.

[194] Roberts, '... The Battle over Interpretive Power' (n 103) 102.

[195] C Harris and K Kakkaiyadi, 'Treaty Interpretation before the Supreme Court' CJICL (2013) 2, 113 (UK Supreme Court frequently misapplies VCLT).

the VCLT's interpretive armoury.[196] Treaty interpretations may be based on the VCLT, even though treaty interpreters attach different weights to the elements in Articles 31–33.

The VCLT represents the optimal level of interpretive fragmentation/convergence. The ILC did not aspire to a rigid interpretive toolbox, disregarding the different objects and purposes across its subfields. Subfields can serve as laboratories for testing new variants of established interpretive methods, or indeed for new methods entirely. Human rights law and the law of IOs have pioneered effectiveness – encouraging interpreters in other subfields to react to this initially isolated interpretive trend.

Treaties are by no means the only important written documents in international law: resolutions of IOs, memoranda of understanding and guidelines also require interpretation. The practice on whether the VCLT's interpretive framework applies to non-treaty instruments varies.[197] The ICJ in the *Kosovo* advisory opinion stated that the VCLT principles on interpretation 'may provide guidance' on the interpretation of UN Security Council Resolutions.[198] Similarly, the International Tribunal for the Law of the Sea (ITLOS) affirmed that the principles could be applied by analogy to binding non-treaty instruments.[199]

Future work could shed light on the empirical question of whether the VCLT's interpretive principles significantly affect outcomes. This is often simply assumed. We know very little about whether, and how, the VCLT affects outcomes. To what extent does the VCLT constrain treaty interpretation by actors other than international tribunals, such as national

---

196 *Alvarez-Machain* (n 62); another notorious example is the interpretation of 'torture' by the Office of Legal Counsel, see JL Goldsmith, *The Terror Presidency: Law and Judgment inside the Bush Administration* (WW Norton & Co, 2007); J Klabbers, 'Virtuous Interpretation' in M Fitzmaurice, O Elias, and P Merkouris (eds), *Treaty Interpretation and the Vienna Convention on the Law of Treaties: 30 Years On* (Martinus Nijhoff, 2010) 15–38, 33; Z Douglas, 'The MFN Clause in Investment Arbitration: Treaty Interpretation off the Rails' (2011) 2 Journal JIDS 97; B Schlütter, 'Aspects of Human Rights Interpretation by the UN Treaty Bodies' in H Keller and G Ulfstein (eds), *UN Human Rights Bodies: Law and Legitimacy* (CUP, 2012) 317.

197 A Orakhelashvili, *The Interpretation of Acts and Rules in Public International Law* (OUP, 2008) chps 12–14.

198 *Accordance with International Law of the Unilateral Declaration of Independence in Respect of Kosovo*, Advisory Opinion, ICJ Rep 2010, para 94.

199 ITLOS, Seabed Disputes Chamber, *Responsibilities and Obligations of States Sponsoring Persons and Entities with Respect to Activities in the Area*, Advisory Opinion, 1 February 2011.

courts and international organizations? Does the VCLT serve as a common frame of reference within which domestic courts carry out treaty interpretation, encouraging interpretive convergence? Alternatively, are national courts nowadays the primary source of interpretive divergence?

Would we see more interpretive divergence in a counterfactual world without the VCLT's interpretive glue? Was the process of treaty interpretation significantly different in, say, the 1930s compared to treaty interpretation today? Does the special interpretive instruction in Article 3(2) DSU affect treaty interpretation in the WTO? Would WTO panels and the AB not invoke, in any event, the customary principles of treaty interpretation?[200]

If the VCLT principles of interpretation were largely inconsequential for outcomes, why have they received so much attention in the academic literature over the last two decades? What insights does this debate hold for legal practitioners and judges who may be more acutely aware of the limitations of interpretive principles? Is the debate on interpretation in reality a proxy fight in order to advance particular normative visions of international law in its various subfields?

---

[200] van Damme, 'Treaty Interpretation …' (n 37) 608, citing *Case Concerning Kasikili/Sedudu Island, (Botswana/Namibia)*, ICJ Rep 1999, 1045, 1102, para 93.

PART IV

INTERACTIONS AND RUPTURES

14. Regime-collisions: Tensions between treaties (and how to solve them)

Jasper Finke

I. INTRODUCTION

Resolving conflicts between treaties was once a rather straightforward topic of public international law. In the last two decades, however, as treaties became regimes[1] and as conflicts or collisions turned into tensions, the topic has taken on a multidimensional character. The changes in terminology are therefore not merely an attempt to reclothe a well-studied topic.[2] Instead, each term (treaties or regimes, conflicts and collisions, or tensions) reflects a different perspective that addresses a

[1] The meaning of treaty is clearly defined in Article 2 (1)(a) Vienna Convention on the Law of Treaties, 23 May 1969, 1155 UNTS 331 (VCLT): 'treaty means an international agreement concluded between States in written form and governed by international law, whether embodied in a single instrument or in two or more related instruments and whatever its particular designation'. What constitutes a regime is, in contrast, not as easily defined because it is not a formal legal category. Based on the work of Krasner, regimes are understood as 'sets of implicit or explicit principles, norms, rules, and decision-making procedures around which actor's expectations converge in a given area of international relations'. S Krasner, 'Structural Causes and Regime Consequences: Regimes as Intervening Variables' in S Krasner (ed), *International Regimes* (Cornell UP, 1983) 1, 2.

[2] Early scholars such as Grotius and Vettel had already addressed the problem of conflicts between treaties in international law. In modern times the works of C Rousseau, 'De la Compatibilité des Normes Juridique Contradictoires dans l'Ordre International' (1932) 39 RGDIP 133, and W Jenks, 'The Conflict of Law-Making Treaties' (1953) 30 BYIL 655, have been especially influential. In the early 1990s, given the growing numbers of international treaties, courts, and tribunals, the topic was given once again a considerable amount of scholarly attention; see especially, W Czapliński and G Danilenko, 'Conflict of Norms in International Law' (1990) 21 NYIL 3; JB Mus, 'Conflicts between Treaties in International Law' (1998) XLV NILR 208; S-A Sadat-Akhavi, *Methods of Resolving Conflicts between Treaties* (Martinus Nijhoff, 2003); J Pauwelyn, *Conflict of Norms in Public International Law: How WTO Law Relates to Other Rules of International Law* (CUP, 2003); R Wolfrum and N Matz, *Conflicts in*

different set of problems. The main purpose of this chapter is to outline and categorize these problems as well as to sketch out possible solutions.

Usually, the starting point for every analysis of regime or treaty collision is to define and clarify the term collision or conflict. This chapter will depart from this traditional approach, not because it is incorrect but because it would imply that there is only one true meaning of conflict in this context. Indeed 'validity' can be found in all of the current definitions of regime – or treaty collision in the sense that they point to different problems and perspectives, and are as such the result of specific developments in public international law. These different problems and perspectives are captured by the terms compliance, coherence, and constitutionalism that will serve as the analytical framework of this chapter. In the remaining part of the introduction, I will explain how these terms structure the analysis of regime-collision, before focusing on the specific problems that each of them implies and possible ways to solve them.

The first and classical perspective on regime-collision is that of compliance, which focuses on specific obligations rather than treaties as a whole. No State should find itself in a 'quasi-tragic' situation in which it necessarily violates international law because norm A prescribes what norm B explicitly prohibits.[3] This approach – also called the narrow concept of conflicting treaties[4] – focuses on individual State behaviour within a system of bilateral treaty obligations. As long as a State can comply with its obligations, no conflict exists. With the changing conception of public international law as a legal system or order,[5] this individualized account of conflict, though still valid, proved to be inadequate to address broader concerns of coherence. Due to the fragmentation of public international law, the decentralized law-making processes, and treaty regimes that are limited to specific subject matters such as trade, the law of the sea, environmental law, and criminal law,

International Environmental Law (Springer, 2003); and E Vranes, 'The Definition of "Norm Conflict" in International Law and Legal Theory' (2006) 17 EJIL 395.

[3] 'A conflict arises when it is impossible to comply with both norms ...'; Sadat-Akhavi, *Resolving Conflicts* (n 2) 38.

[4] N Matz-Lück, 'Treaties, Conflicts between' in R Wolfrum (ed), MPEPIL, para 5, www.mpepil.com, accessed 16 October 2013.

[5] See E Benevisti, 'The Conception of International Law as a Legal System' (2008) 50 GYIL 393. That international law has developed into an order or system is also a precondition for assuming that something such as the international community exists and that we are currently witnessing the constitutionalization of that order or system.

scholars and practitioners were concerned that the unity of international law was at risk.[6] In this context conflicts are defined more broadly. Also referred to as programmatic conflicts, they are based on values and policies rather than on specific irreconcilable obligations.[7] Thus, conflicts emerge where treaty A prohibits certain behaviour even though treaty B either allows or even encourages such conduct. States that are parties to both treaties could, of course, comply with their obligations by adhering to the stricter prohibitions. Yet assuming that international law is, or at least should be, a coherent legal system, such situations should be avoided.

Broadening the scope to include matters of coherence brings one more aspect into the discussion: whereas the compliance perspective is only concerned with substantive treaty obligations, the notion of coherence introduces what one could call an institutional dimension. Maintaining a coherent international legal order, which consists to a large extent of treaty regimes, each limited to a specific subject matter, requires extensive coordination between these regimes. Such efforts not only include substantive coordination especially in the form of systemic interpretation[8] or the principle of mutual supportiveness,[9] but also coordination of the actions taken by a treaty's or regime's institutions, especially since inconsistencies often arise ex post during the implementation phase of a specific regime or due to uncoordinated policy shifts.

---

[6] See, inter alia, G Hafner, 'Risks Ensuing from Fragmentation of International Law', Official Records of the General Assembly, Fifty-Fifth Session, Supplement No 10 (A/55/10), Annex 321: '[T]he system of international law consists of erratic parts and elements which are differently structured so that one can hardly speak of a homogeneous nature of international law.' See also S Spelliscy, 'The Proliferation of International Tribunals: A Chink in the Armor' (2001) 40 Columbia J Transnational L 143; for a less skeptical perspective, see J Chaney, 'Is International Law Threatened by Multiple International Tribunals?' (1998) 271 Recueil des Cours de l'Académie de Droit Internationale 101.

[7] Matz-Lück, 'Treaties …' (n 4) para 6.

[8] See generally, C McLachlan, 'The Principle of Systemic Integration' (2005) 54 ICLQ 279; ILC, *Fragmentation of International Law: Difficulties Arising from the Diversification and Expansion of International Law: Report of the Study Group of the International Law Commission* (A/CN.4/L.682) 206–43; N Matz-Lück, 'Harmonization, Systemic Integration, and "Mutual Supportiveness" as Conflict-Solution Techniques: Different Modes of Interpretation as a Challenge to Negative Effects of Fragmentation?' (2006) 17 Finnish YB Intl L 39; for more details, see below II, 2, c) and b).

[9] R Paroni, 'Mutual Supportiveness as a Principal of Interpretation and Law-Making' (2010) EJIL 21, 649.

Even though taking coherence, instead of compliance, as the starting point for analyzing problems of regime – or treaty collision provides for a more comprehensive approach, this shift still takes place within the framework of international law as a legal order based on largely non-hierarchically structured, but overlapping, treaties. However, there is considerable weight behind the idea that international law is in a state or process of constitutionalization;[10] and despite the fact that no clear picture of the future constitutional order has yet emerged, aspects of this debate have found their way into the more confined realm of regime-collision – though these aspects are as diverse as the whole issue of constitutionalization itself. Those who support the idea of international law as a coherent legal order use the idea of constitutionalization as a means to introduce elements of hierarchy and priority of certain norms, especially those fundamental human rights that belong to the category of *jus cogens*.[11] A different strand in the literature, which relies heavily on sociological concepts of systems theory, is skeptical that international law could evolve into a single constitutional order. Instead it stresses the coexistence of different independent systems, which have been described as 'auto-constitutional regimes'.[12] Within the more traditional international law literature, this perspective is supported by research stressing the constitutionalization of specific treaty regimes, in particular that of the World Trade Organization (WTO) or the law of the sea.[13]

[10] See J Klabbers, 'Setting the Scene' in J Klabbers, A Peters, and G Ulfstein (eds), *The Constitutionalization of International Law* (OUP, 2010) 4 *et seq* with further references concerning the different strands in the literature.

[11] See the contributions in E de Wet and J Vidmar (eds), *Hierarchy in International Law* (OUP, 2012); D Shelton, 'Normative Hierarchy in International Law' (2006) 100 AJIL 291.

[12] See A Fischer-Lescarno and G Teubner, 'Regime-Collision: The Vain Search for Legal Unity in the Fragmentation of Global Law' (1999) 25 Michigan J Intl L 999, 1014–17. This perspective is closely connected to the idea of constitutional pluralism. In contrast to the concept of postnational constitutionalism that seeks to construe 'an overarching legal framework that determines the relationships of the different levels of law', pluralism emphasizes 'a model of order that relies less on unity and more on the heterarchical interaction of the various layers of law' as it assumes that the overarching framework that constitutes the core of the concept of postnational constitutionalism is 'neither practically possible nor normatively desirable'; see N Krisch, *Beyond Constitutionalism: The Pluralist Structure of Postnational Law* (OUP, 2010) 23.

[13] For the WTO, see DZ Cass, *The Constitutionalization of the World Trade Organization: Legitimacy, Democracy, and Community in the International Trading System* (OUP, 2005); E-U Petersmann, *Constitutional Functions and Constitutional Problems of International Economic Law* (University of Fribourg

This approach also offers a distinct perspective on how to solve problems that arise from a large number of constitutional orders. Assuming that these regimes are indeed independent and self-contained, scholars embrace a conflict of laws approach in order to determine which provisions of regime A might be applied within regime B – very similar to the situation where State A uses conflict of laws principles to determine the applicability of the laws of State B within its jurisdiction.[14] The underlying structure of this concept is closely linked to ideas of sovereignty as comprehensive autonomy, that is, that each order determines the extent to which it allows 'foreign' law to be applied. A similar approach assumes that all orders, national and international ones, are either vertically or horizontally interconnected in such a way that they form a single global legal order. Problems of overlap, inconsistencies, and competence are then solved with reference to the idea of federalism.[15]

In what follows, these three different perspectives will be discussed: compliance, coherence, and constitutionalization, and the methods that have been developed to address the underlying conflicts and tensions. In the last part and in lieu of a conclusion, the chapter outlines yet unanswered questions that could form the basis for a future research agenda.

II. COMPLIANCE

Analyzing conflicts between treaties with regard to the notion of compliance illustrates the primary underlying objective. In order to enable States to comply with all of their treaty obligations, conflicts between

---

Press, 1991) and his numerous related publications on the topic; for a description of the so-called constitutional model, see also J Langille, 'Neither Constitution nor Contract: Understanding the WTO by Examining the Legal Limits on Contracting Out through Regional Trade Agreements' (2011) 86 NYU L Rev 1482, 1491–4. Referring to LOSC as a constitution for the oceans dates back to Tommy Koh, the then Third President of the 1982 UN Conference on the Law of the Sea; see United Nations, *The Law of the Sea: United Nations Convention on the Law of the Sea* (New York, 1983) xxxiii–xxxvii.

[14] Fischer-Lescarno and Teubner, 'Regime Collision …' (n 12) 1000 *et seq.*

[15] I would like to thank Rike Krämer, who first drew my attention to the concept of federalism as a possible tool to solve inter-regime conflicts; a similar concept has also been developed by GB Dinwoodie and RC Dreyfuss, *A Neofederalist Vision of TRIPS: The Resilience of the International Intellectual Property Regime* (OUP, 2012).

treaties (that is, a situation in which a State must necessarily violate at least one of its obligations under a treaty in order to comply with an obligation under another treaty) must be avoided or, where they arise, resolved. Thus, there are two elements involved in dealing with conflicts between treaties: avoiding such situations and resolving them. Both aspects have been incorporated into the relevant provisions of the VCLT. Before turning to those, it is necessary to add a short note on conflicts and interpretation.

1. Conflicts and Interpretation

Usually, it is fairly straightforward to determine a conflict in the narrow sense: the legal consequences of two norms are mutually exclusive. Whereas provision A requires the extradition of X, provision B prohibits his or her extradition. States that knowingly conclude treaties – which contain mutually exclusive obligations, usually address the relationship between the two treaties or more specifically between the conflicting norms, especially by including so-called conflict clauses.[16] If, however, this is not the case, then the mere fact that States knowingly accept conflicting obligations is best understood as an implicit agreement to deviate from their earlier obligations (Article 59 VCLT). Yet, the language of treaty provisions is by and large vague and ambiguous. Thus, the existence of a conflict might not be apparent at the time when a treaty is concluded. Instead, it only crystalizes over time when the treaty provisions are interpreted either by the parties or a competent court or tribunal. In such cases, the existence of a conflict depends on the specific meaning of the relevant provisions, which highlights the close relationship of conflicts between treaties and interpretation. Nevertheless, should a conflict arise because treaty provisions are interpreted in such a way that they are mutually exclusive then the conflict must be resolved according to the provisions of the VCLT and arguably *lex specialis*.

---

[16] Borrowing from the ILC, conflict clauses are defined as provisions:

> intended to regulate the relation between the provisions of the treaty and those of another treaty or of any other treaty relating to the matters with which the treaty deals. Sometimes the clause concerns the relation of the treaty to a prior treaty, sometimes its relation to a future treaty and sometimes to any treaty past or future. (Report of the ILC on the Work of its 18th Session (4 May–19 July 1966), Yearbook of the ILC (1966) vol II, 214)

On the different types of conflict clauses, see ILC, *Report on Fragmentation* (n 8) paras 268–71; Sadat-Akhavi, *Resolving Conflicts* (n 2) 87–96; A Aust, *Modern Treaty Law and Practice* (2nd edn, CUP, 2007) 218–26.

Conflict avoidance through interpretation constitutes a different, yet related, topic. Just as conflicts can arise by giving a broad and ambiguous norm a specific meaning, interpretation can also be utilized to avoid conflicts. Even though a conflict-avoiding approach might be the most sensible one, there is no general obligation to do so. Still, in the absence of clear evidence to the contrary, it is safe to assume that States do not wish to enter into conflicting treaties (the so-called presumption against conflict).[17] Thus, it can be concluded that later treaties, even if they could be interpreted in such a way that they were to conflict with earlier obligations, are compatible with earlier ones.[18] Therefore, conflict through interpretation should only arise if there is either a discernable intention of the parties, or, that is, when those who interpret and apply an ambiguous and vague treaty provision do not realize that it conflicts with another treaty obligation.

2. VCLT

The most prominent provision dealing with the relationship of conflicting treaties or obligations is Article 30 VCLT (successive treaties relating to the same subject matter). Yet, other provisions such as Article 41 VCLT (so-called *inter se* agreements) and Article 59 VCLT (termination or suspension of the operation of a treaty implied by conclusion of a later treaty) are also relevant. In addition, Articles 53 and 64 VCLT address the more specific problem concerning the relationship between treaty provisions that conflict with peremptory norms of general international law, either when the treaty is concluded or at a later point in time when a new peremptory norm emerges after the treaty's conclusion.[19]

It is interesting to note that the VCLT uses the term 'conflict' only when describing the relationship between treaties and peremptory norms of general international law, but not with regard to what is generally considered to be the core of the problem, that is, how to deal with

---

[17] On the presumption against conflict, see Pauwelyn, *Conflict of Norms* (n 2) 240–44; ILC, *Report on Fragmentation* (n 8) paras 37–43.

[18] R Jennings and A Watts (eds), *Oppenheim's International Law* (9th edn, Longman 1992) 1275.

[19] See with further references, A Orakhelashvili, *Peremptory Norms in International Law* (OUP, 2006) 132–204; K Schmalenbach, 'Article 53 – Treaties Conflicting with a Peremptory Norm of General International Law' and 'Article 64 – Emergence of a New Peremptory Norm of General International Law ("Jus Cogens")' both in O Dörr and K Schmalenbach (eds), *Vienna Convention on the Law of Treaties* (Springer, 2012).

situations in which treaty obligations are mutually exclusive. Instead, Article 30 VCLT stipulates for its application that, firstly, treaties must be successive and, secondly, that they must relate to the same subject matter. If that is the case, and subject to the special provision of Article 103 UNC, it introduces a triad of solutions: first, a special case of conflict clauses; second, the principle of *lex posterior*; and third, a modification of this principle in case the parties to the later treaty do not include all the parties to the earlier one.

If the parties clarify the relationship between the current treaty and an earlier or later treaty in such a way that the current one is 'subject to' or 'not to be considered as incompatible with' either the earlier or later treaty, then the provisions of these treaties prevail in case of mutually exclusive obligations (Article 30(2) VCLT). If the treaty does not contain such or a similar clarification, Article 30(3) VCLT determines that the provisions of the earlier treaty apply only to the extent that they are compatible with the later treaty. Still, the paragraph adds two more important requirements for its application: the identity of parties between the treaties; and the requirement that the conclusion of the later treaty does not imply the termination or suspension of the earlier one according to Article 59 VCLT. If parties to the later treaty do not include all the parties to the earlier one, Article 30(4) VCLT provides the following solution: the *lex posterior* rule applies to all those who are parties to both treaties, whereas the relationship between States that are parties to both treaties and States that are parties to only one of the two treaties is governed by that treaty to which both States are parties.[20]

3. *Lex specialis*

The relationship between conflicting treaties, even in a narrow sense, is, however, more complex than this brief description of the relevant VCLT provisions indicates. One factor that complicates this account is the doctrine of *lex specialis derogat legi generali*, which has not been codified by the VCLT. Nevertheless, scholars and tribunals have referred to and applied it regularly over the course of a century in the context of conflicts between treaties.[21] Generally speaking, the principle of *lex specialis* provides that in case of conflict, the more specific provision should prevail

---

[20] On Article 30 VCLT generally, see A Orakhelashvili, 'Article 30 Convention of 1969' in O Corten and P Klein (eds), *The Vienna Conventions on the Law of Treaties: A Commentary* (vol I, OUP, 2011).

[21] For a comprehensive survey, see Pauwelyn, *Conflict of Norms* (n 2) 385 *et seq.*

over the more general one. Even though this approach seems to reflect an inner logic, it entails several problems. The first concerns the relationship to the *lex posterior* principle, which is still obscure. Part of this obscurity derives from the following fundamental question: what makes a provision special or specific, especially in cases in which norm A prescribes a certain behaviour that norm B prohibits? One could of course point to the fact that a 'special rule is more to the point … than a general one and it regulates the matter more effectively …'.[22] This, however, indicates that *lex specialis* is not an adequate tool for dealing with conflicts in the narrow sense because it seems hard to imagine why norm A, which prohibits a certain conduct, is either more to the point or regulates a matter more effectively than norm B, which requires such conduct. Thus, the *lex specialis* principle might be more suitable to address issues of coherence or fragmentation, especially with regard to treaties on the same subject matter or treaties that are part of the same regime, such as the WTO order.[23] It will therefore be discussed in more detail below.

III. COHERENCE

1. Three Different Perspectives

That the number of international treaties has sharply increased over the past 40 years is a trite statement in public international law; and as with most growth stories, it was first seen as a positive development. More international law seemed to signify the triumph of law over power, which had dominated international relations until the end of the Cold War. It was also taken as evidence that international law had evolved from its origins as a bundle of bilateral State obligations into a legal order or system. Yet, in the absence of a central law-making authority, this growth of international law has, in several ways, taken on an unstructured character.

---

[22] ILC, *Report on Fragmentation* (n 8) para 60.

[23] See, eg, the Appellate Body in *Guatemala – Cement* arguing that 'it is only where the provisions of the DSU and the special or additional rules and procedures of a covered agreement cannot be read as complementing each other that the special or additional provisions are to prevail'; *Guatemala – Anti-Dumping Investigation Regarding Portland Cement from Mexico*, Report of the Appellate Body (25 November 1998), WT/DS60/AB/R, para 65.

Instead of integrating new regimes into the United Nations (UN) structure, these regimes were established independently and without either substantive or institutional links. The most prominent example in this regard is the WTO. In addition, treaty making was divided into specific subject matters, in which States or groups of States had different interests. While the EU and the USA might have generally agreed on the further liberalization of international trade, they could not agree on a common position with regard to environmental protection beyond specific issues such as banning CFCs (chlorofluorocarbons). Thus, States formed expedient but shifting alliances to pursue different policy objectives, which in turn resulted in inconsistencies and contradictions. The controversies concerning the precautionary principle or food that contains GMOs (genetically modified organisms) are only the most well-known and politicized ones.

Yet, the phenomenon of fragmentation does not occur solely horizontally but also vertically or, in other words, regionally.[24] There exists, however, an important difference between these two forms of fragmentation. Whereas horizontal fragmentation is linked to matters of coherence across different subject matters, vertical fragmentation (or regionalism) is the result of parallel treaties addressing the same subject matter, but on different levels. In its extreme, it encompasses the competition or even rivalry between bilateral treaties on the one hand and a global treaty regime on the other hand, as evidenced by the increasing number of free trade agreements (FTAs) that are concluded not only between a number of States but on a truly bilateral level.[25] But bilateralism or regionalism is not limited to matters of economic relations. On the

---

[24] The issue of globalism versus regionalism is, of course, not a completely new development. Tendencies towards regionalism can always be observed after periods of universal law-making. Still, in the last two decades, the topic has found particular interest among scholars; see C Schreuer, 'Regionalism v Universalism' (1995) 6 EJIL 477; with regard to international economic law see, for example, the contributions in J Nakagwa (ed), *Multilateralism and Regionalism in Global Economic Governance: Finance, Trade, and Investment* (Routledge, 2011). In addition, the European Society of International Law has dedicated its 5th Biennial Conference on the topic of Regionalism and International Law; see www.uv.es/esil2012/, accessed 15 May 2014.

[25] The ongoing process of bilateralization in international economic relations is not necessarily one of regionalization as quite a few preferential trade agreements (PTA) are concluded trans-regionally. Still, the number of regional PTAs has increased as well; on regionalism and its impact on the future of

contrary, it can be observed in many other areas, for example, the protection of maritime resources as evidenced by the Southern Bluefin Tuna controversy in which the parties disagreed whether the 1982 United Nations Convention on the Law of the Sea (LOSC) or the regional treaty should govern the dispute, including the relevant dispute settlement procedures.[26] It may also be found within the area of human rights protection, in particular with regard to the question of extraterritorial application. Arguably the position of the European Court of Human Rights (ECtHR) with regard to the European Convention on Human Rights (ECHR) is more restrictive than that of the Human Rights Committee with regard to the International Covenant on Civil and Political Rights (ICCPR) even though the position of the ECtHR has developed over the last 12 years since its decision in *Banković*.[27] At the same time, the issue of regional fragmentation and lack of coherence already points to a broader and more fundamental question; that is, the question of whether or not coherence between regional and global treaties on the same subject matter is either necessary or even desirable. Based on a process-based perspective, differences in interpretation and adjudication may well be a source for development. In other words, competition between regimes may well lead to an overall advancement of legal protection.

The third aspect of coherence, at least in a broader sense, concerns the relationship of treaties that are part of the same regime. Again, the WTO represents one of the most prominent examples. Multiple issues can arise concerning the relationship of those multilateral trade agreements that are an integral part of the WTO legal order (so-called WTO Covered Agreements) as listed in Annex 1 to 3 of the 1994 Agreement Establishing the World Trade Organization (WTO Agreement). A treaty might include a justification for trade restrictions that is not included in another treaty, but both apply principally to the subject matter of a specific

economic integration, see C Brummer, 'Ties that Bind: Regionalism, Commercial Treaties, and the Future of Global Economic Integration' (2007) 60 Vanderbilt L Rev 1350.

26 See A Boyle, 'Southern Bluefin Tuna Case' in R Wolfrum (ed), MPEPIL, para 15, www.mpepil.com, accessed 16 October 2013.

27 *Banković et al v Belgium et al* App No 52207/99 (ECHR, 12 December 2001); for a description and evaluation of the Human Rights Committee's jurisprudence and how the jurisprudence of the ECtHR has evolved in the post-*Banković* case law, see *M Milanovic, Extraterritorial Application of Human Rights Treaties: Law, Principles, and Policy* (OUP, 2011) 175–87.

dispute. Similarly, justifications for trade restrictions might differ depending on which treaty is applicable. In these cases, it is not so much the coherence of the international legal order that might be at stake, but rather the coherence within a specific regime. Thus, these examples could also be described as matters of internal regime coherence.

2. Possible Solutions

What all the examples with respect to the notion of coherence have in common is that they embrace a more comprehensive understanding of conflict or collision than situations in which mere compliance is at stake. This, however, should not suggest that the underlying problems of these examples are necessarily identical. Possible solutions for conflicts between treaties that form part of one specialized regime such as the WTO must, for example, take the particularities of the regime itself into account, as well as the fact that the conflicting treaties belong to a more coherent system than that of international law in general. Suitable solutions might therefore differ from those that address conflicts between regimes belonging to different subject matters such as, for example, human rights obligations of States and their obligations to comply with Security Council resolutions under the 1945 Charter of the United Nations – a question that figured so prominently in the by now four *Kadi* decisions,[28] but which is also relevant in a number of cases concerning

[28] In the joined Cases C-402/05 P and C-415/05 P *Kadi and Al Barakaat International Foundation v Council and Commission* [2008] OJ 2008 C 285/2, the ECJ overturned the ruling of the Court of First Instance in the Case T 315/01 *Kadi* v *Council and Commission* [2005] ECR II 3649 and Case T 306/01 *Yusuf and Al Barakaat International Foundation* v *Council and Commission* [2005] ECR II 3533. After the Commission adopted Regulation (EC) No 1190/2008 amending for the 101st time Regulation 881/2002, OJ 2008 L322/25, thereby relisting Mr Kadi, the General Court in its decision Case T-85/09 *Kadi v Commission* [2010] ECR II 5177 annulled that regulation. The ECJ confirmed that decision in the latest judgment concerning Mr Kadi in the joined Cases C-584/10 P, C-593/10 P and C-595/10 P *Commission et al v Kadi* [2013], http://curia.europa.eu/juris/liste.jsf?num=C-584/10, accessed 19 October 2013; see generally, E de Wet, 'Human Rights Consideration and the Enforcement of Targeted Sanctions Europe' in B Fassbender (ed), *The Emergence of Core Standards of Judicial Protection in Securing Human Rights* (OUP, 2011) 141–71; J Kokott and C Sobotta, 'The Kadi Case: Constitutional Core Values and International Law – Finding a Balance' (2012) 23 EJIL 1015–24.

actions of European States under the authority of the UN Security Council.[29]

As indicated above, possible solutions could be hierarchical as well as coordinative or cooperative. The latter reflects the view that international law evolved into a legal order in which treaty regimes coexist on an equal footing, whereas hierarchical approaches are closely connected to the view that the international legal order is undergoing a process of constitutionalization. Solutions based on the constitutionalist's perspective are discussed further below, whereas the following illustration of possible problem-solving mechanisms will rely on coordinative and cooperative mechanisms. It should, however, be noted that just as a singular correct definition of conflict does not exist, neither is there a single way of solving them. One might disagree with regard to the effectiveness of coordinative solutions and propose more hierarchal mechanisms. Yet, international law, regardless of the extent to which it has been constitutionalized already, is still a system in the making. Thus, both perspectives should be treated as supplementary instead of incompatible.

a) *Lex specialis* and *lex posterior*

According to the Final Report of the ILC Study Group on Fragmentation, the well-established principles of *lex specialis* and *lex posterior* apply to broader categories of conflicts between treaties as well. What is more, they are also believed to be 'perfectly capable of resolving [such a] conflict or overlap'.[30] Even though this statement is certainly true for some conflicts caused by overlapping treaties, it seems challengeable with respect to others, especially if the overlap illustrates competing or even contradicting policy objectives. The following paragraph will thus elaborate on the effectiveness of these instruments in such cases.

---

[29] See, eg, *Behrami and Behrami v France* and *Saramati v France, Germany and Norway* App No 71412/01 and 78166/01 (ECHR, 5 May 2007) and *Berić and Others v Bosnia and Herzegovina* App No 36357/04 et al (ECHR, 16 October 2007). According to De Sena and Vitucci, these cases demonstrate 'clear tendency to guarantee the primacy of decisions of the United Nations Security Council … even at the expense of the legal order of the European Convention on Human Rights'; P De Sena and MC Vitucci, 'The European Courts and the Security Council: Between *Dédoublement Fontionnel* and Balancing of Values' (2009) 20 EJIL, 193, 193 *et seq*.

[30] ILC, *Report on Fragmentation* (n 8) para 410.

aa) Lex posterior The application of the *lex posterior* principle requires the existence of (a) successive treaties (b) relating to the same subject matter (Article 30(1) VCLT). Even though the term 'subject matter' is not defined, its general usage implies that the treaties in question must address the same substantive area such as environmental law, trade law, and the like.[31] Thus, the *lex posterior* doctrine cannot address problems that relate to conflicts of policy goals or values because these are usually pursued within treaties or regimes that belong to different subject matters. Even if certain environmental agreements either allow or encourage the use of trade restrictive measures, they do not address the same subject matter as the WTO regime. Trade restrictions are merely a means to achieve a certain end, in this case environmental protection, whereas the main objective of the WTO regime, depending on one's perspective, is either free trade or non-discriminatory trade relations.

Still, the fact that treaties do relate to the same subject matter does not automatically lead to the application of *lex posterior*. In particular, in cases of regime building, which are understood as processes of constitutionalization in a broad sense, its application runs contrary to the very idea of building such an order as this necessarily entails development over time. In such a case, the idea that a treaty of that regime shall not apply in case of conflict or collision because it was enacted earlier than the conflicting one is nonsensical. It is, however, not only the constitutional nature of regime building that rules out the *lex posterior* doctrine as a meaningful tool to solve the problem. Based on the language of Article 30 VCLT, the treaties must be successive, while in cases of regime building treaties are not successive but complementary. Therefore, the principle of *lex posterior* does not apply when determining the relationship of treaties that form part of a specific regime such as the WTO, or even in cases of regionalism in which certain treaties serve as a general framework. Especially with regard to the law of the sea, the underlying idea was that regional agreements would specify and implement the broad principles of LOSC. Relying on *lex posterior* in case of a conflict would undermine this regime-building function that such treaties have.

---

[31] This interpretation of 'same subject matter' is not uncontested; see Matz-Lück, 'Treaties ...' (n 4) para 13, for more details. Pauwelyn, for example, holds that the requirement merely indicates 'that there be a conflict or incompatibility'; Pauwelyn, *Conflict of Norms* (n 2) 365.

bb) Lex specialis A similar stance could be taken towards the application of *lex specialis*. Why should a regional agreement for the preservation of certain maritime resources be more specific if it collides with the underlying principles of LOSC? At the same time, scholarship has relied on *lex specialis* to determine the relationship between the WTO Covered Agreements,[32] although it is very much contested whether this principle is applicable in cases in which multilateral environmental agreements (MEAs) either allow, encourage, or even prescribe trade restrictions to accomplish an environmental goal. Is it the MEA or the relevant WTO Covered Agreement that is more specific? In order to be able to answer this question, two important aspects have to be considered. First, even though the conflicts that are addressed under the rubric of coherence have a common basis (they reflect concerns of fragmentation in a broad sense) they nevertheless still differ from each other to such an extent that a 'one-size-fits-all' solution simply does not exist. Second, the strict distinction between *lex specialis* as a derogation principle in case of conflict on the one hand, and interpretation as a means to avoid such conflicts on the other, is difficult to maintain.[33]

In order to explain why *lex specialis* is an appropriate tool to address or prevent conflicts in some but not in all cases, one must take into account its 'subjective nature', which is rooted in the contractual freedom of States. It would, therefore, be unwise to conceptualize *lex specialis* as a self-standing legal norm to resolve existing conflicts. Instead, like *lex posterior*, it is better understood as a practical method 'in search of the "current expression of state consent"'.[34] In other words: whether or not *lex specialis* is a meaningful approach depends on the specific circumstances in which treaties conflict. Especially in cases of framework conventions, treaties that establish the most fundamental principles for a specific subject matter or topic, the consent of States, expressed through their ratification of the relevant treaties, precludes them from then invoking *lex specialis* in cases of supposedly more specific rules that conflict with the fundamental principles set out in the framework convention or quasi-constitutional treaties. It might, of course, be difficult to determine whether or not a treaty actually fulfills these functions. If, however, widespread agreement exists in this regard, as in the case of

---

32 Pauwelyn, ibid, 399 *et seq*; see also the Appellate Body in *Guatemala – Cement* (n 23) para 65.

33 See also ILC, *Report on Fragmentation* (n 8) para 412: 'It follows that … *conflict resolution and interpretation cannot be distinguished* from each other' [emphasis added].

34 Pauwelyn, *Conflict of Norms* (n 2) 388.

LOSC, then the exclusion of *lex specialis* follows from the fact that States have agreed to this function by ratifying the relevant treaty.

Yet, not all regimes are built around a quasi-constitutional treaty. The WTO regime, for instance, derives its organizational structure from the WTO Agreement itself. Still, this treaty only forms part of the overall regime and does not exhaust its constitutional core, especially since it does not include any substantive provisions. Instead, the WTO consists of a number of treaties whose relationship – at least in the absence of a conflict clause – remains unclear in case of overlap. Whether or not *lex specialis* provides a meaningful solution in such a situation depends to a large extent on the WTO members' intention. This is, for example, reflected in the general approach that all relevant WTO Covered Agreements are applicable unless the intention of the members implies that some norms govern a certain dispute exclusively because the norms are more 'specific' and the application of the 'general' treaty or its provisions would render the 'specific' treaty meaningless. Thus, the WTO regime not only illustrates the close relationship between *lex specialis* and the intention of the parties but also reflects its double-sided nature as a derogation principle and an interpretive tool.

The type of conflict that has triggered most debate over the last 15 years is the 'WTO and …' dispute.[35] It has been argued, in particular by Pauwelyn, that *lex specialis* is indeed a reasonable approach that is applicable to this category of conflict.[36] Again, the answer to the question

---

[35] These debates started with the relationship of WTO and environmental law that was also 'institutionalized' with the establishment of the Committee on Trade and Environment (CTE); see generally, E Vranes, *Trade and the Environment: Fundamental Issues in International and WTO Law* (OUP, 2009) and G Marceau, 'Conflicts of Norms and Conflicts of Jurisdictions: The Relationship between the WTO Agreement and MEAs and other Treaties' (2001) 35 JWT 1081. With the growing importance of the WTO dispute settlement system, the debate expanded into related fields such as sustainable development, human rights, global health, and other issues; see, eg, GS Sampson, *The WTO and Sustainable Development* (UN University, 2005); G Marceau, 'WTO Dispute Settlement and Human Rights' (2002) 13 EJIL 753; HP Hestermeyer, *Human Rights and the WTO* (OUP, 2007); WHO and WTO Secretariat, *WTO Agreements and Public Health* (2002) www.wto.org/english/news_e/pres02_e/pr310_e.htm, accessed 16 October 2013; T Apps and A Green, *Reconciling Trade and Climate: How the WTO Can Help Address Climate Change* (Edward Elgar, 2011).

[36] According to Pauwelyn, the rules on trade restrictions included in the Cartagena Protocol on Biosafety are more specific than those included in the 1994 WTO Agreement on the Application of Sanitary and Phytosanitary Measures (SPS Agreement); see Pauwelyn, *Conflict of Norms* (n 2) 389.

whether or not *lex specialis* is applicable is less straightforward than such general propositions might suggest as, for example, that environmental treaties are always more specific and should thus prevail. One reason for that lies in the heterogeneous nature of environmental agreements with regards to trade restrictions. Some agreements ban trade in certain substances; of those, some – such as the Montreal Protocol – did so before the WTO was established (even though the 1947 General Agreement on Tariffs and Trade (GATT 1947) was already in force).[37] In that case the treaty was either considered to be compatible with GATT 1947 or it governed the issue of trade in the banned substance as the more specific regime. But even if we take the latter case, that is, the treaty governs the issue of trade more specifically, then the conclusion that *lex specialis* might apply here as well does not entail that it *always* should do so. That is so because banning or regulating trade in certain substances, such as GMOs, does not necessarily reflect the current expression of State consent. The USA, for example, is very outspoken against the Cartagena Protocol on Biosafety.[38] The Protocol thus merely illustrates consent among the States that are parties to the Protocol and can therefore not govern the economic relationship between a party to the Protocol and a non-party. Thus, *lex specialis* cannot be applied in cases when some parties (eg, the EU and its Member States) establish standards that regulate trade in certain substances outside the WTO regime, if these standards are incompatible with WTO obligations or at least require a radical re-interpretation of those agreements due to a lack of consent among States concerning these standards. Similarly, *lex specialis* does not control cases in which MEAs only allow trade restrictions as one of a range of possible options or even merely encourage restrictions rather than requiring them. Arguing that either one of the regimes – MEAs or the WTO regime – must be considered *lex specialis* is tantamount to saying that one of the two issues – free trade or environmental protection – is categorically more important than the other.

b) Systemic interpretation

Brownlie, as early as 1988, warned against the compartmentalization of public international law.[39] However, it was not until a further institutional development occurred, namely the rise of (quasi-)binding

---

[37] Montreal Protocol on Substances that Deplete the Ozone Layer, 16 September 1986, (1987) 26 ILM 1541.

[38] Cartagena Protocol on Biosafety to the Convention on Biological Diversity, 29 January 2000, (2000) 39 ILM 1027.

[39] I Brownlie, 'The Rights of Peoples in Modern International Law' in J Crawford (ed), *The Rights of Peoples* (Clarendon, 1988) 1, 15.

and (quasi-)obligatory dispute settlement procedures, that the ideal of a coherent legal order was substantially challenged. It was in particular the success of the WTO dispute settlement system that caused concern among non-trade lawyers and scholars about the inherent bias of the WTO legal order vis-à-vis matters such as human rights, environmental protection, global health, or the protection of cultural identities and its relationship with general public international law. Moreover, topics that are addressed within the WTO legal order are also dealt with in other fora. The issue of how to deal with thousands of treaties with either complete or partial substantive overlap is, however, not confined to matters of trade, even though this area is particularly relevant in a globalized economy. Based on the assumption that all specialized regimes are part of international law as a coherent legal system, a tremendous effort has been made over the last 10 years to solve those conflicts that are caused by fragmentation through interpretation and in particular through systemic interpretation.[40]

Article 31(3)(c) VCLT provides the basis for the systemic interpretation approach according to which 'any relevant rules of international law applicable in the relations between the parties' shall be taken into account. Until fragmentation became one of the 'hot topics' of international law, this provision had appeared to be fairly redundant. For this reason in international practice there appeared to be a general reluctance to refer to it.[41] This attitude changed dramatically by mid-2005 when systemic interpretation (or integration) took on a prominent position in the ILC's study on fragmentation and played a pivotal role in the ICJ's reasoning in the *Oil Platforms* case.[42] Indeed, it was precisely that case that revealed the dual issues inherent in the fragmentation debate.

The *Oil Platforms* case was not concerned with conflicts between two specific regimes. Instead, it addressed the relationship between a bilateral treaty and customary international law.[43] From this perspective, the primary aim of Article 31(3)(c) VCLT is to ensure coherence between a

---

[40] G Distefano and PC Mavroidis, 'Systemic Interpretation in International and WTO Law: The Glue of the International Legal Order' in O Guillod and C Müller (eds), *Pour un Droit Équitable, Engagé et Chaleureux* (Helbing Lichtenhahn, 2011) 743; McLachlan, '... Systemic Integration' (n 8) 279; J Kammerhofer, 'Systemic Interpretation, Legal Theory, and the International Law Commission' (2008) 19 Finnish YB Intl L 157.

[41] McLachlan, '... Systemic Integration' (n 8) 279 *et seq*.

[42] ILC, *Report on Fragmentation* (n 8) paras 410–80.

[43] *Oil Platforms (Islamic Republic of Iran v United States of America)*, Merits, ICJ Rep 2003 (6 November) 161, paras 40–41. For a list of decisions that

treaty and what is termed 'general international law'; as 'treaties are themselves creatures of international law',[44] they must 'be applied and interpreted against the background of the general principles of international law'.[45] Even though this approach is important for establishing and maintaining a coherent legal order, the more pressing problem today seems to be the harmonization or coordination of regimes that are confined to a specific subject matter. This does not render Article 31(3)(c) VCLT meaningless. Quite the contrary, the rule applies to 'any relevant rules of international law', which also include other treaty provisions as long as they are applicable in the relations between the parties.[46] These two requirements (applicability and relevance), however, provide ample space for disagreement.

In *EC Biotech*, for example, the Panel has interpreted 'applicable' to mean that a certain provision must not only be applicable between the parties to a dispute, but between all WTO members.[47] Such reasoning, however, would render the provision close to meaningless, at least in the case of treaties with widespread or even almost universal acceptance. Such narrow interpretation also stands in sharp contrast to the practice of the WTO Appellate Body in the *Shrimp* dispute in which it referred to a number of international instruments – binding and non-binding alike – to determine whether or not the US import restriction on certain shrimp products violated the *chapeau* of Article XX GATT.[48] Consequently, a

apply Article 31(3)(c) VCLT, see Kammerhofer, 'Systemic Interpretation …' (n 40) 159, fn 5.

[44] McLachlan, '… Systemic Integration' (n 8) 280.

[45] AD McNair, *Law of Treaties* (2nd edn, Clarendon, 1961) 466.

[46] Pauwelyn, *Conflict of Norms* (n 2) 254 *et seq*; Marceau, 'Conflicts of Norms …' (n 35) 1087.

[47] *European Communities – Measures Affecting the Approval and Marketing of Biotech Products*, Report of the Panel (29 September 2009), WT/DS291, 292, 293/R, para 7.68.

[48] The Panel in *EC – Biotech* introduced an interesting distinction: whereas Article 31(3)(c) VCLT requires a Panel to take into account any applicable law among the parties, there exist instances in which a Panel can take non-WTO law into account for its informative character, but it is not legally required to do so. In such a case it could also rely on other international law that does not bind all WTO parties or is even entirely non-binding; *EC – Biotech* (ibid) paras 7.90–7.96. Even though this would do justice to the language of Article 31(3)(c) VCLT, it raises two problems: firstly, the panel seems to suggest that non-WTO law is either more important or its impact on WTO law is somewhat greater in cases where the requirements of Article 31(3)(c) VCLT are met than in situations in which it is only taken into account because of its informative character. Yet, in both situations non-WTO law can only influence the process of interpretation

number of different interpretations of Article 31(3)(c) VCLT were proposed that aim at broadening its scope of application.

At least in cases in which a multilateral treaty can be bilateralized, that is, where it can be split into a set of bilateral treaty obligations, it is reasonable to understand 'applicable between the parties' to mean 'the parties to the dispute'.[49] Yet, the practicability of this approach is very uncertain. In particular, multilateral treaties that codify the most important rules and principles of a specific subject matter are often considered to fulfill quasi-constitutional functions. This would, of course, apply to the fundamental principles of free trade as codified in the GATT and GATS. However, at least in the case of the WTO, the structure of commitments and schedules that are negotiated on a bilateral level run counter to this description of constitutionalization.

Another approach would allow the application of other treaties as long as their provisions reflect customary international law. This approach would rather elegantly overcome the obstacles posed by the language of Article 31(3)(c) VCLT. Still, the effect would be that it did not have any effect different from that under the narrow interpretation mentioned above, which requires that the relevant treaty is applicable to all parties to the treaty under interpretation. Arguably the broadest construction, which is, however, at odds with the language of Article 31(3)(c) VCLT, 'does not require complete identity … , but … that the other rule relied upon can be said to be implicitly accepted or tolerated by all parties to the treaty'.[50] Thus, in case of the WTO all non-WTO treaties that could 'reasonably be said to express the common intentions or understanding of all [WTO] members' would be applicable.[51]

Despite the potential of Article 31(3)(c) VCLT for advancing the ideal of a coherent international legal order, it seems that it can fulfill this task best in cases in which a specific treaty or regime is interpreted with

---

within the frame set by its wording, its context, and the object and purpose. Secondly, it misreads the decision of the Appellate Body in *US–Shrimp*, in which the Appellate Body took into account non-binding international instruments as well as treaties that were not binding on all WTO members; see *US – Import Prohibition of Certain Shrimp or Shrimp Products*, Report of the Appellate Body (12 October 1998), WT/DS58/AB/R, para 158 and note 157.

49 D Palmeter and P Mavroidis, 'The WTO Legal System: Sources of Law' (1998) 92 AJIL 398, 411.

50 McLachlan, '… Systemic Integration' (n 8) 314 *et seq.*

51 Pauwelyn, *Conflict of Norms* (n 2) 261. See also Yassen, the then chairman of the ILC meeting, stating 'that to be taken into consideration in interpreting the treaty, those rules, although not "general", must be "common" to the parties of the treaty'; Yearbook of the ILC (1966) vol I/2, 197, para 52.

regard to general international law. Its feasibility is, however, limited in cases of 'true' regime-collisions, especially if these regimes express divergent policy objectives that might be highly contested, as is the case with the precautionary principle, for example.

c) Mutual supportiveness

Despite the emphasis placed by scholars and practitioners on Article 31(3)(c) VCLT as a vehicle to achieve coherence through systemic interpretation, this approach represents just one of several options. 'Reference to other rules of international law in the course of interpreting a treaty is an everyday, often unconscious part of the interpretation process'.[52] Interpretation understood as the task of giving meaning must, in order to maintain a base level of consistency, rely on some form of standards or benchmarks. The VCLT clarifies the relevant standard by making the ordinary meaning of the terms of the treaty, in their context, the starting point of all interpretive endeavours, seen in the light of the object and purpose of the treaty (Article 31(1) VCLT). Still, in situations in which broad and vague provisions must be interpreted and thereby specified before they can be applied to a concrete case, the ordinary meaning, or the object and purpose, do not provide sufficient direction. Such a provision can still be interpreted in different ways and interpreters – whether scholars, parties, or tribunals – often turn to other provisions in order to seek additional guidance.

It is in this context that the idea of mutual supportiveness becomes relevant. It made its first appearance in para 2(b) of the Agenda 21 – the voluntary action plan that was the product of the 1992 United Nations Conference on Environment and Development. 'The international economy should provide a supportive international climate for achieving environmental and development goals by … making trade and environment mutually supportive'.[53] It was endorsed by the WTO Committee on Trade and Environment as well,[54] and it found its way into the preamble of several MEAs as a surrogate for a conflict clause that until 1998 was the predominant method of clarifying the relationship between MEAs

---

52 McLachlan, '… Systemic Integration' (n 8) 280.

53 The text of Agenda 21 is available at http://sustainabledevelopment.un.org/content/documents/Agenda21.pdf, accessed 16 October 2013.

54 See, eg, the 1996 Report of the CTE to the Singapore Ministerial Conference; CTE, Report (1996) of the Committee on Trade and Environment (12 November 1996), WT/CTE/1, paras 167 and 171.

and other treaties.[55] This alternative to classic concepts of conflict resolution is significant in several ways. Mutual supportiveness clauses neither establish the priority of the relevant treaty nor do they subordinate the treaty to other agreements, especially to the WTO Covered Agreements. They are therefore characterized by a certain ambiguity: first, the parties recognize that trade and environment are mutually supportive; second, the clause states that nothing in the treaty shall be understood to change the rights and obligations of a party under any existing international agreements, particularly those relating to the trade aspect of the treaty's subject matter; and third, this does not establish any hierarchy between the treaties.[56]

One could, of course, doubt the effectiveness of such an ambiguous principle or in order to clarify its meaning neglect its third aspect, which would transform it into a subordination clause.[57] However, elimination of ambiguity is not the aim of mutual supportiveness. It cannot be: balancing trade and environmental policies across regimes, each with their own institutional particularities, is a complicated and continuous process. Thus, the main objective is to shift the trade and environment debate 'from a theory of conflictual relationships to one of co-existence, consistency, and complementarity'.[58] Even though mutual supportiveness represents a soft approach because it does not establish hard criteria that would decide hard cases one way or another, it is still a helpful tool for moving towards or establishing an international legal order that is not based on notions of hierarchy.

One could object to mutual supportiveness by arguing that it violates the principle that States cannot be bound to treaties without their consent.

---

[55] The first treaty that included a reference to the principal of mutual supportiveness instead of a conflict clause was the Convention on the Prior Informed Consent Procedure for Certain Hazardous Chemicals and Pesticides in International Trade, 10 September 1998, (1999) 38 ILM 1; see Paroni, 'Mutual Supportiveness ...' (n 9) 653.

[56] See, eg, the last three paragraphs of the preamble of the Cartagena Protocol on Biosafety to the Convention on Biological Diversity:

> *Recognizing* that trade and environment agreements should be mutually supportive with a view to achieving sustainable development, *Emphasizing* that this Protocol shall not be interpreted as implying a change in the rights and obligations of a Party under any existing international agreements, *Understanding* that the above recital is not intended to subordinate this Protocol to other international agreements.

[57] S Safrin, 'Treaties in Collision? The Biosafety Protocol and the World Trade Organization Agreement' (2002) 96 AJIL 606, 618 *et seq*.

[58] Paroni, 'Mutual Supportiveness ...' (n 9) 655.

Such a perspective does, however, mistake the factual consequences that such provisions might have for being legally bound in a formal sense. In other words: even the principle of mutual supportiveness will not bind a WTO member to a provision of an MEA to which it is not party, at least not in a legal sense. The MEA might inform a panel on how to construct the meaning of a provision of a WTO Covered Agreement, such as Article XX GATT, for example, which is within the WTO context the most important provision for justifying trade restrictions that serve an environmental purpose. And it is, of course, possible that Article XX GATT might have been interpreted differently if the MEA had not been concluded. Still, being legally bound is a formal category or concept. If a State does not comply with specific treaty obligations despite being legally bound, it can be held responsible for this non-compliance. The only obligations in the example given above are those of the WTO Covered Agreement and not the MEA. A panel or the Appellate Body who interpret a specific WTO provision will decide whether the member who introduced a trade restriction for environmental purposes has complied with its WTO obligations. Deciding that the measure is justified does not imply that the member against whom the trade restriction has been imposed is bound by the provisions of a MEA, even if these provisions were decisive in order to specify the meaning of Article XX GATT within the limits established by Article 31(1) VCLT: the ordinary meaning of the terms of the provision, in their context, and in light of its object and purpose.[59] The objection that considering non-regime law in order to interpret provisions that are part of the regime in question violates the *pacta tertiis nec nocent nec prosunt* rule should thus be understood as an attempt to influence the process of interpretation in one's favour. Influencing how to construe a broad provision is, however, categorically different from being formally bound without consent.

---

[59] That using other sources than the treaty itself to interpret its provisions might conflict with the *pacta tertiis non nec nocent nec prosunt* rule, especially if these sources are not binding on all parties to the treaty that is interpreted, can still be found in current scholarship; see Pauwelyn, *Conflict of Norms* (n 2) 257. Still, this approach neglects the differences of being legally bound and the process of interpretation. It is, of course, true that taking into account provisions that not all parties agreed to might neglect their intentions and interests; see Jennings and Watts, *Oppenheim's International Law*, vol I (n 18) 1268. Whether or not this might be the case is, however, a question of the specific circumstances, which illustrates that the problem is unrelated to the *pacta tertiis nec nocent nec prosunt* rule.

d) Institutional aspects and challenges

aa) General cooperation Regime coordination or inter-regime cooperation is not limited to systemic interpretations or the mutual supportiveness of substantive provisions. Failure to consider the institutional dimension has quite aptly been described as the 'blind spot' of this debate,[60] even though cooperation between international organizations is not a novelty. On the contrary – the whole concept of establishing a 'family' of organizations under the roof of the United Nations acknowledges the gap between specialized international organizations and problems that transcend their limited competence and jurisdiction. New regimes and international organizations have, however, been created outside this framework, which in turn requires new cooperation techniques. These techniques may be formal as well as informal. Important examples in the former category are the cooperation agreements between the WTO on the one hand and the International Monetary Fund (IMF) and World Bank on the other. These are part of an effort for greater coherence in economic policymaking.[61] Seen in broader historical context, these efforts to enhance cooperation could be qualified as a late attempt to implement the original Bretton Woods ideal: three separate institutions that are each responsible for a specific mandate and which are linked by close institutional ties.[62]

The continuing effort of these three organizations to coordinate their economic policies through close cooperation is, of course, an important step towards coherence. But at the same time, this only represents a very

---

[60] O Perez, 'Multiple Regimes, Issues Linkage, and International Cooperation: Exploring the Role of the WTO' (2005) 26 University of Pennsylvania J Intl Economic L 735.

[61] See M Aubon, 'Fulfilling the Marrakesh Mandate on Coherence: Ten Years of Cooperation between the WTO, IMF and World Bank', WTO Discussion Paper 13 (2007) www.wto.org/english/res_e/publications_e/disc_paper13_e.htm, accessed 16 October 2013.

[62] Originally, the 1947 Final Act of the United Nations Conference on Trade and Employment – today better known as the Havana Charter – would have established the International Trade Organization as a specialized UN organization. The basic rules for cooperation with the UN were laid down in Article 86 Havana Charter (the text of the Havanna-Charter is available at www.wto.org/english/docs_e/legal_e/prewto_legal_e.htm, accessed 16 May 2014). Article 87 addressed cooperation with other international institutions that have related responsibilities, in other words the World Bank and the IMF, including the possibility of joint committees, reciprocal representation at meetings and all other working relationships that were deemed necessary.

small part of the overall problem of coherence through cooperation and coordination, especially since the subject matters of the institutions involved – the WTO, the IMF, and the World Bank – are closely linked and interrelated. Yet, the difficulties in establishing institutional cooperation beyond this specific situation are illustrated by the still underdeveloped ties between the WTO and MEA secretariats. Even though WTO members agreed to negotiate the terms and conditions for regular information exchange between MEA secretariats and relevant WTO committees and for granting the former observer status in the latter,[63] these negotiations have not yet been concluded. The issue of observer status in particular is still contested, whereas the basic elements for regular information exchange, at least between the CTE and MEA secretariats, have been finalized.[64]

bb) Coherence and dispute settlement The task of establishing greater coherence in international dispute settlement faces two fundamental problems. The first, a rather WTO-specific one, is usually discussed as an aspect of systemic interpretation, even though all tribunals and courts whose subject matter is limited to a specific treaty regime might face it. The issue at stake is to what extent 'non-regime' law might be applied in these specific proceedings. If the assumption is correct that non-regime law cannot be taken into account in such cases, then institutional limitations would seriously hamper all efforts to strive for a more coherent international legal order.

The fundamental problem with regard to the 1994 Dispute Settlement Understanding (DSU) is that in contrast to other treaties establishing international courts or tribunals, it does not specify the applicable law, at least not explicitly. The Statute of the International Court of Justice (ICJ Statute), for example, clearly defines the applicable law in Article 38. Similarly, the LOSC distinguishes between the jurisdiction of International Tribunal for the Law of the Sea (ITLOS) or an arbitral tribunal established pursuant to the LOSC in Article 288 and the applicable law in Article 293, which includes the LOSC as well as any rule of international law that is compatible with it. In order to determine the applicable law in

---

[63] The mandate for these negotiations is found in para 31(ii) of the Doha Ministerial Declaration, 14 November 2001, www.wto.org/english/thewto_e/minist_e/min01_e/mindecl_e.htm, accessed 16 October 2013.

[64] CTE, Report by the Chairman to the Trade Negotiations Committee for the purpose of the TNC Stocktaking Exercise, TN/TE/19, Annex II, 9; and CTE, Report by the Chairman to the Trade Negotiations Committee, TN/TE/20, Annex I, 5; see also Perez, 'Multiple Regimes …' (n 60) 767 *et seq.*

WTO proceedings, scholars have turned to Article 3.2 DSU, which determines that WTO provisions shall be interpreted in accordance with the customary rules of interpretation.[65] As the rules for interpretation codified in Article 31 VCLT are believed to reflect customary international law, Article 31(3)(c) VCLT seems to be the plausible answer to the question under which circumstance non-WTO law might be applied. Yet, this conclusion rests on the assumption that because the DSU, in contrast to LOSC or the ICJ Statute, does not provide for any explicit rules with regard to the law applicable in WTO dispute settlement proceedings, it must be restricted to the WTO Covered Agreements. Thus, non-WTO law cannot be applied at all unless the WTO Covered Agreements provide a legal basis to do so. One of them, along this line of reasoning, is Article 31(3)(c) VCLT. Consequently, there is no difference between the law that can be enforced or the jurisdiction of a panel and the law that can be applied.[66] This conclusion is, however, not supported by either the DSU or the WTO regime in general.[67]

It is therefore not only customary international law that applies to the economic relationship of WTO members unless they have opted out of these rules by becoming WTO members.[68] Non-WTO treaty law may be applied as well to specify the meaning of the WTO provision as long as this application does not alter the rights and obligations of WTO members under the Covered Agreements.[69] That, however, is only the case if an interpretation exceeds the limits set by the sometimes vague and abstract language of the relevant WTO provision.

---

[65] Marceau, 'Conflicts of Norms …' (n 35) 1087 *et seq*; R Tarasofsky, 'Ensuring Compatibility between Multilateral Environmental Agreements and GATT/WTO' (1996) 7 YIEL 52, 67; Pauwelyn, 'The Role of Public International Law in the WTO: How far Can We Go?' (2001) 95 AJIL 535, 574 *et seq*; Palmeter and Mavroidis, 'The WTO Legal System …' (n 49) 410.

[66] G Marceau, 'A Call for Coherence in International Law: Praise for the Prohibition against "Clinical Isolation" in WTO Dispute Settlement' (1999) 33/5 JWT 87, 113.

[67] On the distinction between jurisdiction or enforceable law and applicable law, see Pauwelyn, *Conflict of Norms* (n 2) 457 *et seq*.

[68] See *Korea – Measures Affecting Government Procurement*, Report of the Panel (1 May 2000), WT/DS163/R, para 7.96: 'Customary international law applies generally to the economic relations between the WTO members. Such international law applies to the extent that the WTO treaty agreements do not "contract out" from it.'

[69] L Bartels, 'Applicable Law in WTO Dispute Settlement Proceedings' (2001) 35 JWT 499, 510 *et seq*.

A second aspect of coherence in the realm of international courts and tribunals concerns the allocation of disputes if multiple fora are available or the dispute settlement provisions of several treaties apply.[70] While *lis pendens* and *res judicata* may provide adequate solutions in cases in which identical disputes have been brought before different courts or tribunals,[71] they cannot address issues of partial overlap, as evidenced by the *MOX Plant* dispute.[72] Even though specialized courts, whose jurisdictions are restricted to the specific subject matter of the regime that has established them, may have recourse to non-regime law to specify the meaning of provisions that they are competent to interpret and enforce, they may not determine the rights and obligations of the parties under a non-regime treaty. If, however, these are relevant for a tribunal in order to determine its jurisdiction, then most rules of procedure do not provide any explicit mechanisms to deal with the situation. The decision of the Arbitral Tribunal, which was established pursuant to the LOSC, in the *MOX Plant* dispute, to suspend the proceedings until the ECJ had issued its judgment on whether or not the dispute was exclusively governed by EU law provides, of course, for a useful outcome.[73] Yet, the Tribunal had to rely on comity for its approach. This might suffice from a mere pragmatic perspective. But it seems preferable that courts should also be legally bound to engage in meaningful formal cooperation as this will contribute to avoid regime-collisions and resolve tensions.

---

70 See generally, Y Shany, *Competing Jurisdictions of International Courts and Tribunals* (OUP, 2004); J Finke, 'Competing Jurisdiction of International Courts and Tribunals in Light of the MOX Plant Dispute' (2006) 49 GYIL 307; V Lowe, 'Overlapping Jurisdiction of International Courts and Tribunals' (1999) 20 Australian YB Intl L 191; K Oellers-Frahm, 'Multiplication of International Courts and Tribunals: Problems and Possible Solutions' (2001) 5 MPEPIL 67.

71 V Lowe, '*Res judicata* and the Rule of Law in International Arbitration' (1996) 8 AJICL 38 with further reference to decisions of international courts and tribunals. With regard to *res judicata*, see also *Trail Smelter Case (United States v Canada)*, 15 April 1941, RIAA, vol III, 1905, 1951 *et seq*; the relevance of *lis pendens* has been analyzed by C McLachlan, *Lis pendens in International Litigation* (Martinus Nijhoff, 2009).

72 For a more detailed description of the different fora that were involved in this dispute, see Finke, 'Competing Jurisdiction …' (n 70) 319–25.

73 *The MOX Plant Case (Ireland v UK)*, Order No 3 – Suspension of Proceedings on Jurisdiction and Merits, and Request for Further Provisional Measures, 24 June 2003, www.pca-acp.org, accessed 16 October 2013; for the decision of the ECJ, see Case C-459/03 *Commission v Ireland* [2006] ECR I-4635.

IV. CONSTITUTIONALISM

The third lens through which regime-collision can be analyzed is that of constitutionalism, even though the term itself and its relevance in international law are very much debated.[74] Nevertheless, the evolving nature of international or global constitutionalism provides yet another perspective from which to reflect on the phenomenon of regime-collision.

1. Hierarchy and the Constitutionalization of the International Legal Order

The idea of a constitutionalized international legal order is closely linked to the notion of hierarchy. This hierarchy, it is hoped, could help to establish a coherent legal order that is based on shared values. The most obvious candidates for this set of norms are, of course, those that belong to the body of *jus cogens*, that is, those fundamental rules that reflect and protect the most fundamental values of the international community as a whole.[75] There is, of course, little doubt that *jus cogens* has introduced elements of hierarchy to international law that go beyond a constructed hierarchy based on subordination clauses as a means of conflict avoidance or solutions. It is, however, for several reasons doubtful whether *jus cogens* could be utilized to solve either tensions or conflicts between international regimes on a large scale.

The first reason for that lies in the relative obscurity of the concept of *jus cogens*, an obscurity that persists despite the fact that more than 40 years have passed since its (re-)introduction into international law by incorporation into the VCLT. Even though scholarship has developed a set of criteria that should help to determine whether or not a norm has acquired the status of *jus cogens*,[76] the process by which such a rule

---

[74] *The MOX Plant Case* (ibid) para 28.

[75] See Klabbers, 'Setting the Scene' (n 10) 16 *et seq* for the conflicting assumptions concerning 'the higher imperatives' of a global constitution: fundamental human rights on the one hand and the sovereign equality of States on the other.

[76] Article 53 VCLT defines a peremptory norm as one 'accepted and recognized by the international community of States as a whole as a norm from which no derogation is permitted'. One could argue that this description merely illustrates the effect of a peremptory norm, instead of defining it, as it does not provide any substantive criteria for determining a peremptory norm. Thus, additional indicators are needed. Informative is the approach taken by the International Criminal Tribunal for the former Yugoslava (ICTFY) which relied on the criteria 'most fundamental standards of the international community' and

comes into being is difficult to grasp. It seems that, as with States, recognition is an indispensable element even though it is not constitutive from a purely legal point of view.

In addition, the notion of *jus cogens* itself rests on an ambiguous concept, that is, the idea of the international community as a whole. Within scholarship, two major strands have emerged: a more formalist perspective versus a more substantive one. The latter perspective includes fundamental rules for the functioning of the international system, which is still being formed by States as the predominant actors.[77] These rules include but are not limited to: *pacta sunt servanda*, good faith, sovereign equality, and independence. The substantive perspective, in contrast, would place more emphasis on basic human rights such as the prohibition of torture, crimes against humanity, and war crimes. In that sense, peremptory norms are norms that 'serve as a public order embodying material constitutional provisions of international law'.[78] Thus, the struggle concerning the concept of *jus cogens* reflects, at least to some extent, conflicts between international regimes that illustrate not so much conflicting norms but conflicting policies and values that must be balanced in case of conflict. To date, though, no general concept of balancing (or proportionality) has emerged that, like its counterpart in national legal orders, could weigh the competing values and interests embodied in separate regimes.[79]

'the importance of the values [the norm] protects' in order to determine the *jus cogens* character of the prohibition of torture; see IT-95-17/I-T *Prosecutor v Furundija* [1998] para 153; for further reference see JA Frowein, '*Ius cogens*' in R Wolfrum (ed), MPEPIL, www.mpepil.com, accessed 16 October 2013.

[77] For a description of these two different perspectives and their proponents, see C Tams, *Enforcing Obligations* erga omnes *in International Law* (CUP, 2005) 141 *et seq.*

[78] A Orakhelashvili, 'State Immunity and International Public Order' (2002) 45 GYIL 226, 255.

[79] It has been argued that proportionality has emerged as a general principle of law within WTO law, especially since the decision of the Appellate Body in *Shrimp*; see generally, M Andenas and S Zleptnig, 'Proportionality: WTO Law in Comparative Perspective' (2007) 42 Texas Intl L J 370. For a more skeptical approach, see J Neumann and E Türck, 'Necessity Revisited: Proportionality in World Trade Organization Law after *Korea – Beef, EC – Asbestos* and *EC – Sardines*' (2003) 37/1 JWT 199, 233. Still, even those stressing the useful role of proportionality in WTO law do not apply this standard to inter-regime-collisions.

2. Global Legal Order and Auto-Constitutional Systems

Even though constitutionalization in international law is generally viewed as the constitutionalization of the international system itself, two other perspectives exist, which take into consideration the process of globalization and fragmentation. These two processes have questioned two assumptions that are crucial for the idea of a constitutionalized international legal order: first, the idea that such an order can be clearly distinguished from national legal orders, and second, that there *is* a single international legal order. Taken together, globalization and fragmentation will most likely create not one international and many national legal orders, but one global legal order that transcends the distinction of what is national and what is international. In addition, such a global legal order would not be based on a strict hierarchy of rules, but consist rather of largely independent and self-contained regimes. Thus regime-collision is not so much a problem of conflicting norms and obligations but instead illustrates the collision of 'distinct global social sectors'[80] that are each pursuing different special interests. As these types of conflicts are predominantly political, it is unsurprising that its supporters call for the 'politicization of legal norm collisions through power mechanisms, negotiations between relevant collective actors, public debate and collective decisions'.[81]

This perspective takes the ideal of legal pluralism to its global level, grounding it in the idea of a differentiated global society and a polycentric view on globalization that is quite distinct from the emphasis on a coherent international legal order. Based on such an understanding, this strand of the literature promotes principles for decentralized networking, which on an abstract level include (a) normative compatibility instead of hierarchical unity, (b) law-making through irritations, observations, and reflexivity, and (c) decentralized modes of coping with conflicts of laws.[82]

The insight that this perspective offers is especially valuable because it broadens the perspective on regime-collision and questions the feasibility of solutions that seek to uphold an ideal of unity and coherence of a system that is being challenged not only by vertical but also by horizontal fragmentation. Still, sociological and political concepts need translation into the language of law. One possible translation is the idea of federalism – not as a normative concept that is rooted in the division of

---

80 Fischer-Lescarno and Teubner, 'Regime-Collision …' (n 12) 1000.

81 Ibid, 1003; see also Krisch, *Beyond Constitutionalism* (n 12) 23.

82 Ibid, 1018.

power within a State, but as an organizational idea.[83] The essence of these concepts, also framed as neo-federalism, run counter to the idea of a coherent international legal order. They emphasize diversity over unity and experimentalism over harmonization.

V. CONCLUSION AND OUTLOOK: A RESEARCH AGENDA

The future research agenda is an ambitious one because it is situated at the fault lines of the international legal system, a system that is in part still characterized by bilateral treaty obligations, but that at the same time must meet the challenges of maintaining at least some degree of coherence, and that is also struggling with the transformation from the Westphalian system of sovereign States to some form of a global legal order. Even though this description might be considered trite, it also contains important insights for a possible research agenda: first, no easy answers exist; second, at least tensions between treaty regimes can have positive effects for legal development and should therefore not be regarded as being harmful to the international legal order; and third, conflicts between treaty regimes are not a static problem. Instead, in as much as the regimes change and develop over time, so does the problem of regime-collision.

Research on regime conflicts, collisions, or tensions must acknowledge that causes as well as solutions are multidimensional. They cannot be found in substantive or institutional law alone. In addition, all legal approaches should take into account the political dynamics of such conflicts. Thus, rather simple and straightforward solutions such as *lex specialis* are restricted to a limited set of cases, and cannot serve as a general approach. Instead, a thorough analysis of regime-collisions must start with the causes for conflict (and not with a definition of what constitutes a conflict). On the basis of such an analysis future research can develop a comprehensive set of mechanisms that is able to address these problems institutionally and solve them substantially. Both aspects and how they interact with each other as well as with the political dimensions of regime-collision should form the main focus of such research. In addition, lawyers should also take into account what has generally been neglected thus far, that is, the beneficial dimensions of

---

[83] See Dinwoodie and Dreyfuss, *Neofederalist Vision of TRIPS* (n 15) 14 *et seq* with regard to TRIPS.

tensions between treaty regimes. As evidenced by the *Kadi* cases, these tensions might provide the necessary impulse for the general advancement of legal protection.[84] Future research should therefore be able to reflect on and embrace the process-like nature of the problem of regime-collision, something that legal scholars and practitioners tend to underestimate, as they take a snapshot perspective on a specific problem or case.

---

[84] Security Council Resolution 1904 (2009) and Security Council Resolution 1989 (2011) established, respectively enhanced the Office of the Ombudsperson thereby incorporating 'some of the human rights requirements that had been sacrificed for the sake of international security'; P De Cesari, 'Recent Developments in the Fight against Terrorism: The Role of the European Courts' in N Boschiero, T Scovazzi and C Ragni (eds), *International Courts and the Development of International Law* (Asser Press, 2013) 655, 657. Arguably, the *Kadi* cases and thus the jurisprudence of the ECJ helped to create this mechanism; A Tzanakopoulos, '*Kadi* Showdown: Substantive Review of (UN) Sanctions by the ECJ', EJIL: Talk!, 19 July 2013, www.ejiltalk.org/kadi-showdown/, accessed 20 October 2013.

15. Responding to deliberately created treaty conflicts

Surabhi Ranganathan[*]

I. INTRODUCTION

What are treaty conflicts? Why do they arise? And, how should we – scholars, practitioners and students of international law – respond to them?

Jasper Finke's chapter[1] in this *Handbook* answers the first of these questions, and offers partial answers to the other two. With respect to the first question, he introduces three frameworks within which we might understand treaty conflicts. Importantly, he reminds us not to take a narrow view of such conflicts as being problematic purely when they take the form of incompatibility between treaty *obligations*. On the second question, Finke suggests that many treaty conflicts are the result of increasing numbers of international legal agreements. And, on the third question, he focuses on methods of *resolving* treaty conflicts, exploring the role that principles of *lex posterior*, *lex specialis* and coordination may play. At the end of the chapter, however, Finke also notes that the 'causes' of treaty conflicts are multidimensional and 'solutions' to them must address them *institutionally* and *substantially*, responding to their *political* dimensions.

The present chapter takes these concluding comments as its point of departure, to focus on some usually underexplored issues. The chapter first explains that treaty conflicts do not only arise due to the increasing numbers of international legal agreements; in many cases they are deliberately created. Section II furnishes several examples in support of the argument that States often deliberately use conflicting treaties as a strategy to challenge, or change, existing multilateral treaty-based regimes. It also explains that the strategy is effective not least because it

* I would like to thank James Crawford and Christian Tams for reading and commenting on earlier drafts of this chapter, and Athene Richford for her careful editing.

1 Chapter 14 in this volume.

exploits fundamental principles that govern treaty-making and application. The politics of treaty conflict is, in other words, rooted in the law of treaties.

Section III offers a fresh perspective on the frequently criticized 1969 Vienna Convention on the Law of Treaties (VCLT) provision on treaty conflict, Article 30. It views this provision as an attempt by its drafters to reconcile three things: that States often would, and did, create treaty conflicts deliberately; that it was not possible in the abstract to consider all conflicts as 'bad' and therefore urgently needing *resolution*; and, the sense that, nevertheless, international law must *regulate* treaty conflicts. It explains that this last idea was important not only to avoid the most pernicious results of treaty conflicts but also because, otherwise, treaty conflicts pose a serious challenge to thinking of international law as 'law'.

Section IV continues with the theme of how treaty conflicts may be addressed in a pragmatic way. It outlines three proposals that focus upon preserving the effective operation of multilateral treaties facing challenges such as from conflicting treaties. Notably all three proposals contemplate that specific institutions may modify the relevant multilateral treaties. Section IV focuses on how the authors of these proposals deal with questions of lack of State consent and institutional competence to make modifications.

A final section then sets out an agenda for future research.

II. DELIBERATELY CREATED TREATY CONFLICTS

Treaty conflicts are not always the contingent or inadvertent by-products of the increasing numbers of treaties; the international system is rife with instances in which States create new treaties to overcome old ones. Consider the following examples:

In 1990, the United States and the European Union withdrew from the Uruguay Round on the expansion of the 1947 General Agreement on Tariffs and Trade (GATT). They concluded, bilaterally, a modified trade agreement, which they 'invited' other States to join. This grew into the World Trade Organization, including the 1994 GATT.[2]

The United States and the European Community have pressured developing countries to sign bilateral 'TRIPs-plus' agreements that

---

[2] E Benvenisti and G Downs, 'The Empire's New Clothes: Political Economy and the Fragmentation of International Law' (2007) 60 Stanford L Rev 595, 616.

exceed the standards of intellectual property protection provided in the 1994 Agreement on Trade Related Aspects of Intellectual Property Rights, and inter alia, seriously limit access to affordable medicines.[3]

In the 1980s, the newly concluded 1982 United Nations Convention on the Law of the Sea provided for a regime for deep seabed mining based on the principle that seabed minerals were the common heritage of mankind. Immediately, eight States (the United States, the United Kingdom, France, Germany, the Netherlands, Belgium, Japan, Italy), some of them parties to the UN Convention, concluded an alternative regime that embraced the view that seabed mining was a freedom of the high seas. This regime was underpinned by two treaties, a 1982 treaty between four of the States and a 1984 treaty between all eight States.[4]

Some years previously, the movement for a New International Economic Order had seen, amongst other things, the adoption of the 1976 Bogotá Declaration by eight developing equatorial States (Brazil, Colombia, Congo, Ecuador, Indonesia, Kenya, Uganda, Zaire). The Declaration claimed sovereignty over the geostationary orbit, and asserted that the 1967 Outer Space Treaty:

> cannot be considered as a final answer to the problem of the exploration and use of outer space, even less when the international community is questioning all the terms of international law which were elaborated when the developing countries could not count on adequate scientific advice and were thus not able to observe and evaluate the omissions, contradictions and consequences of the proposals which were prepared with great ability by the industrialized powers for their own benefit.[5]

At the turn of the century, and up to 2005, the United States concluded numerous (more than 100) 'bilateral immunity agreements' with States party and not party to the 1998 Rome Statute for the International Criminal Court. Contrary to the Part IX provisions of that Statute, these bilateral agreements stipulated non-cooperation with the Court's requests

---

3 L Helfer, 'Regime Shifting: The TRIPs Agreement and the New Dynamics of Intellectual Property Lawmaking' (2004) 29 Yale J Intl L 1, 24.

4 See RR Churchill and AV Lowe, *Law of the Sea* (3rd edn, Manchester UP, 1999) Chp 12.

5 Conclusion 4, Declaration of the First Meeting of Equatorial Countries, Bogotá, Colombia, 3 December 1976. In his book, space law expert Ricky Lee treats the Bogotá Declaration as a treaty, using VCLT provisions to assess its implications: see R Lee, *Law and Regulation of Commercial Mining of Minerals in Outer Space* (Springer, 2012) 172.

for surrender of US nationals and, in some cases, nationals of the other signatory to a bilateral immunity agreement.[6]

In 2005, the United States and India announced plans to conclude a civil nuclear cooperation agreement, under which the United States would supply nuclear fuel and technology to India. India, unlike the United States, is not a party to the 1968 Nuclear Non-Proliferation Treaty (NPT), but like the United States, maintains a nuclear weapons programme. The NPT recognizes the United States as a nuclear weapons State (along with the United Kingdom, France, China and Russia) but does not endorse India's programme. Moreover, the NPT founded a nuclear trade regime which appears to exclude the sort of nuclear cooperation envisaged by the two States in 2005 and finalized in a 2007 bilateral agreement.[7]

The above examples attest to the deliberate creation of treaty conflicts in a range of fields and by a variety of States – though some names do crop up rather more often than others. Several features are common to these examples. First, we can see that in each, the effort by a few States to conclude bilateral or small group treaties that were inconsistent with the provisions of existing multilateral treaty regimes. In most cases, these States did so to challenge, and/or change such multilateral treaty regimes. The challenge is clear in case of the Bogotá Declaration vis-à-vis the Outer Space Treaty and the US-led bilateral immunity agreements vis-à-vis the Rome Statute. In the other instances, the intent to alter the existing multilateral regime, whether on trade, intellectual property rights protection, law of the sea or nuclear governance, can be easily inferred. Let us, for simplicity's sake, call this common feature the 'small treaty/large treaty dynamic'.

The second common feature is perhaps even more noteworthy. In many of the above cases, we see that the small treaty includes at least some States not party to the large treaty. India is not a party to the NPT, while the United States is; the United States is not party to the Rome Statute, while some of the co-signatories of its bilateral immunity agreements are and some are not; Brazil, Colombia and Ecuador were parties to the

[6] See J Crawford, P Sands, and R Wilde, 'Joint Opinion in the Matter of the Statute of the International Criminal Court and in the Matter of Bilateral Agreements Sought by the United States under Article 98(2) of the Rome Statute', (5 June 2003), accessed 19 May 2014 at www.amicc.org/docs/Art98-14une03FINAL.pdf.

[7] See S Ranganathan, 'Visions of International Law: Lessons from the 123 Agreement', Special Issue on India, the 123 Agreement, and Nuclear Energy: Issues of International Law, (2011) 51(2) Indian J Intl L 146.

Outer Space Treaty, the other five States endorsing the Bogotá Declaration were not; France and the Netherlands were party to the UN Convention on the Law of the Sea, the other States parties to the 1984 agreement were not; the United States and the European Union (EU) both exited the 1947 GATT before inviting other States party to that treaty to join the WTO. In other words, in most cases, the conflicting treaties have 'non-identical parties'. In literature, they are often notified as 'AB/AC conflicts', with the letters signifying common (A) and distinct (B and C) parties.

In short, we see in these examples the attempts by a few States to challenge or change existing multilateral treaty regimes by deliberately concluding conflicting bilateral or small group treaties that include some non-identical parties. Of course, then, the immediate question that arises is why such conflicts should provide an effective means to that end?

The answer lies in a combination of law and fact. As a matter of fact, coding desired aims into treaty form vests these aims with legal significance. There is a difference between stating that some end – an expanded trade agreement, for example – *should be* pursued, and asserting that several States have *already undertaken* to pursue it in their relations with each other. The latter may generate additional momentum for other States to adapt to the new legal development as well. A new treaty offers fresh focus for inter-State interactions: it may alter the negotiating context; a State may use it as leverage vis-à-vis another State; individual States may perceive it as a ground for justification of their actions, and a new factor to consider in policymaking. In short, a new, conflicting, treaty may catalyze new political dynamics and foster a shift from the existing legal status quo. Furthermore, a new treaty may challenge the legitimacy of an existing multilateral treaty for reasons other than showing it up as outdated. To take one theory of legitimacy, a rule is legitimate if it is determinate, coherent with other rules, adherent to a secondary framework which determines how rules are made and applied, and symbolically validated, as having been enacted in accordance with proper procedures.[8] The conclusion of a new, conflicting, treaty at least clouds the determinacy and coherence of the rules inscribed in the existing treaty, eroding its overall legitimacy. This is only exacerbated if the new treaty becomes the locus of State practice. Empirically then, concluding a new treaty is a plausible way to challenge or change an existing treaty.

Moreover, a new small treaty with non-identical parties may offer effective challenge to an existing large multilateral treaty for conceptual

8 T Franck, *The Power of Legitimacy among Nations* (OUP, 1990).

reasons emerging from the founding features of the law of treaties. To begin with, the law of treaties – as is currently reflected in the VCLT – does not distinguish between small and large or bilateral and multilateral treaties; it regards all types of treaties as equally normative. (As Section II shows, this was not always the case; earlier drafts of the VCLT attached greater normative significance to multilateral treaties.)

In addition, as Jan Klabbers notes,[9] the law of treaties emanates from fundamental principles that preclude any legal rule to suppress or invalidate a treaty even if it has been deliberately created to conflict with an existing one. These principles are: State's freedom to contract, *pacta sunt servanda*, *res inter alios acta*, and *pacta tertiis nec nocent nec prosunt*. The first two confirm that all States have the right to enter into treaties, and the treaties they conclude are legally binding upon them. However, this does not imply that by concluding one treaty, States sign away their competence to conclude other treaties even if they are conflicting ones. For here comes into play the third principle, *res inter alios acta*, that every treaty is effective as between the parties to it.

Now, it may be argued that where the parties to the two treaties are identical, the *res inter alios acta* principle together with the *pacta sunt servanda* principle should exclude the deliberate conclusion of conflicting agreements. But it does not: Article 30 VCLT clarifies that where treaties have identical parties, and the same subject matter, new treaties override existing ones to the extent of their incompatibility. In practice the parties, or perhaps a court or treaty body, may attempt first to reconcile the two treaties by way of interpretation; but would apply the later treaty in preference to former if the two cannot be reconciled (following the *lex posterior* principle). Indeed, Article 59 VCLT clarifies that the earlier treaty may be considered as terminated or suspended in such cases. Where the two treaties have different subject matter, then the parties, or a court or treaty body, might also consider which treaty is the more specific in relation to the issue in dispute (*lex specialis*).

The situation is more complicated where the treaties have non-identical parties, that is, are AB/AC conflicts. For here the *pacta tertiis* principle is also relevant. This principle states that no treaty can alter the rights and obligations of any State without its consent. By implication, it excludes attempts to reconcile treaties through the interpretation of one (say AB) by reference to the other (AC) where this would affect the rights or obligations of State B, unless B's consent is also obtained. For the same reason, neither AB nor AC may be invalidated, or subordinated to each

---

[9] J Klabbers, *Treaty Conflict and European Union* (CUP, 2009) 99–100.

other by application of *lex posterior* or *lex specialis*, without the consent of all parties. The Central American Court of Justice made this point in *Costa Rica v Nicaragua*, which it decided in 1916.[10] The Court found that Nicaragua's treaty with the United States was incompatible with its previous treaty with Costa Rica, but could not invalidate the Nicaragua/US treaty because the United States was not party to the dispute before it. More recently, as Klabbers notes, the Court of Justice of the European Union has found EU treaties to override other treaties entered into by EU member States (including those with non-members),[11] but such decisions cannot bind those non-member States; from their perspective, their treaties continue to govern their rights and obligations vis-à-vis EU members.

As Section III discusses, for these reasons, the VCLT drafters too found it very hard to achieve a treaty conflict rule that was both conceptually and practicably satisfactory. They finally agreed to the present Article 30 VCLT as the only plausible conflict rule.

III. A SUITABLE CONFLICT RULE

In drafting the VCLT, the International Law Commission (ILC) had to consider several issues. First, how to define 'conflict' – should they include only situations where two treaties provided mutually incompatible obligations between States; or also situations where a right or privilege granted in one treaty clashed with another right or privilege or obligation granted in another, or the object and purpose of one treaty was inconsistent with that of another? This was an important question, because it would determine – secondly – the remedies to be provided: if the ILC limited themselves to a strict definition of treaty conflict (where two treaties had mutually incompatible obligations) then they could address treaty conflicts on the plane of State responsibility alone. But, if they were also concerned about impairments of treaties per se, then they would have to suggest rules according to which one treaty could be given precedence over another. Third, in the latter case, what rules should they provide: should they consider a treaty to be invalidated by its conflict with an existing treaty; or should they consider it merely subordinated to the existing treaty; or, should they flip the rule altogether and consider the later treaty to take precedence over the earlier because more up-to-date (but would that not send the wrong message to States,

[10] (1917) 11 American J Intl L 181.

[11] Klabbers, *Treaty Conflict* (n 9) Chps 6, 9.

encouraging them to violate existing treaties with impunity)? Fourth, in any of these cases, what about States that were only party to one treaty, and not the other conflicting one – how might their rights be protected? How could conflict rules take into account the special difficulties presented by AB/AC conflicts (bringing the *pacta tertiis* principle into play)? Fifth, was it important to take into consideration the different types of treaties: for example, treaties that are merely *contractual* in character – conglomerates of reciprocal bilateral rights and obligations between States – such that it may be appropriate for States to qualify their contracts by entering into further treaties with each other? How could a rule provide for this, and at the same time distinguish the case of *legislative* treaties that established general rules or regimes and could not be contracted out of? Moreover, what if one legislative multilateral treaty was concluded in conflict with another or was in conflict with a previous contractual treaty. Should it be invalidated or subordinated merely because that other treaty was put in place first?

These were only some of the many complicated questions that the ILC had to address by way of a conflict rule. Moreover, they had to find a way to reconcile the competing interests of stability and change – that is, recognize on the one hand that States had the right to conclude new treaties – and indeed, this was an important means of development and change of international law – and on the other hand protect the integrity of existing treaties. The task was a difficult one, made all the more complicated by the Commission's recognition that many conflicts would be deliberately created and their determination to provide rules that would also address the additional challenges (discussed above) posed by AB/AC conflicts. This section discusses how the Commission dealt with this task.

1. Article 30 and its Discontents

When the ILC first met to discuss drafting the law of treaties in 1949, it probably did not foresee that the subject of treaty conflicts (and particularly, conflicts between treaties with non-identical parties) would be amongst the few that would exercise it even well into the 1960s. Certainly, it was not one of the topics that the first ILC Special Rapporteur, JL Brierly, chose to focus upon. However, from the time of the appointment of the second Special Rapporteur, Sir Hersch Lauterpacht in 1952, through the tenure of his successors Sir Gerald Fitzmaurice (1955–61) and Sir Humphrey Waldock (1961–66), the subject was considered at length. The Rapporteurs discussed it extensively in their reports. It was also debated multiple times during ILC sessions,[12] and later when the United Nations Conference on the Law of Treaties was convened in Vienna in March 1968 in order to adopt the VCLT.[13] The culmination of these efforts was, principally, Article 30 of the VCLT, which provides:

> Article 30 Application of successive treaties relating to the same subject-matter
>
> 1. Subject to Article 103 of the Charter of the United Nations, the rights and obligations of States parties … shall be determined in accordance with the following paragraphs.
> 2. When a treaty specifies that it is subject to, or that it is not to be considered as incompatible with, an earlier or later treaty, the provisions of that other treaty prevail.
> 3. When all the parties to the earlier treaty are parties also to the later treaty … the earlier treaty applies only to the extent that its provisions are compatible with those of the later treaty.
> 4. When the parties to the later treaty do not include all the parties to the earlier one:
>   (a) as between States parties to both treaties the same rule applies as in paragraph 3;
>   (b) as between a State party to both treaties and a State party to only one of the treaties, the treaty to which both States are parties governs their mutual rights and obligations.
> 5. Paragraph 4 is without prejudice to article 41, or to any question of the termination or suspension of the operation of a treaty under article 60 or to any question of responsibility which may arise for a State from the conclusion or application of a treaty, the provisions of which are incompatible with its obligations towards another State under another treaty.

Article 30, thus, opens by giving overriding priority to States' obligations under the UN Charter and to *non obstante* clauses that may be found in either of the conflicting treaties. It then provides that where the parties to one treaty are all parties to a later treaty of the same subject matter, the *lex posterior* principle should apply. Cases where parties to the later treaty are a subset of the parties to the earlier are more complicated: Article 30(4)(a) suggests that normally, in such cases too, between that

---

[12] Following Waldock's assumption of the role of Special Rapporteur, the ILC discussed the topic over three meetings in the fifteenth session (1963), three meetings at the sixteenth session (1964) and four meetings at the eighteenth session (1968) of the ILC.

[13] The Committee of the Whole discussed the topic in three meetings, it was then discussed in a plenary meeting, during which draft Article 30 was adopted.

subset of parties the *lex posterior* rule applies, unless the earlier treaty had forbidden its parties from entering into an inconsistent later treaty, or the later treaty would infringe on the rights of other parties to the earlier treaty, or derogate from a provision essential to accomplish that treaty's object and purpose.[14] Clause (4)(b), addressing conflicts between treaties with non-identical parties provides, in a nutshell, that each of the conflicting treaties is valid, and effective, between its parties. A State party to both (or all) conflicting treaties may find it necessary to determine how best to comply with its commitments to both; when this is not possible, it would 'simply have to choose which one to honour'.[15] The decision would not be without cost, for Article 30(5) refers to State responsibility in the event of a breach of obligation as a result of choosing one of the treaties over the other. In also referring to Article 60, clause (5) further notes the possibility of termination or suspension of one or both of the treaties, as a result of a material breach of the obligations owed under them.

This scheme may be criticized on two counts. First, it appears to take a reductive view of treaty conflict, concerning itself only with situations where a conflict results in a breach of treaty obligations. This ignores other consequences of treaty conflict – these include, as discussed, challenges to the legitimacy of multilateral treaty regimes. This may be the case even where there is no specific breach of obligation, but the treaties' objects and purposes are incompatible. To draw from the above mentioned examples, the US-led bilateral immunity agreements stipulating non-surrender of nationals to the International Criminal Court were on the surface justified as falling under an exception for such agreements provided in Article 98 of the Rome Statute itself. Most of the bilateral agreements specifically referred to this provision. However, there was a clear purpose behind their conclusion: they formed part of an aggressive US campaign to undermine the Court. And, they did so, by reflecting the US and the other signatories' lack of confidence in the Court's investigative and judicial processes. Similarly, the seabed mining regime concluded by the eight western States in divergence from the UN Convention on the Law of the Sea was superficially justified as 'interim', intended to operate only until the entry into force of the UN Convention. However, in fact, given the likelihood of much delay in the Convention's entry into force (it finally happened in 1994) – exacerbated not least by these States' own unwillingness to ratify it – the alternative regime was

---

[14] This follows from the reference to Article 41 in Article 30(5).

[15] Klabbers, *Treaty Conflict* (n 9) 88.

intended, within that time, to crystallize a different set of principles to govern seabed mining. In its 2006 Report on Fragmentation, the ILC recognized that '[a] treaty may sometimes frustrate the goals of another treaty without there being any strict incompatibility between their provisions'.[16] Moreover, two treaties 'may possess different background justifications, or emerge from different legislative policies or aim at divergent ends'.[17] All of these may have consequences for the effective functioning of the treaties. Article 30 ignores these aspects.

A second possible criticism, specifically of Article 30's scheme for conflicts involving treaties with non-identical parties, is that it provides no indication of how the treaties must be reconciled, or which of the two must take priority. It is thus unlike provisions relating to conflicts where the parties are identical or where the later treaty is concluded between parties to the earlier. Nor if, as is suggested above, a State must indeed choose between its commitments to the conflicting treaties, does it adopt any other principle that weights the choice in favour of either treaty. Perhaps the only provisions – in the whole of the VCLT – that offer guidance are Articles 30(1), 53 and 64: Article 30(1) draws on Article 103 of the UN Charter to confirm that Charter obligations take priority; Articles 53 and 64 specify that a treaty will be invalidated if it conflicts with a peremptory norm of international law. This still leaves us without guidance in most cases of treaty conflict. (Of course, had the ILC recommended the application of priority principles to such cases, we might have criticized it for ignoring the *pacta tertiis* principles.)

Many international law scholars have found Article 30 inadequate to address the challenges posed by treaty conflicts. Sir Ian Sinclair, who served as the United Kingdom's representative to the Vienna Conference, has observed that Article 30 is:

> in many respects, not entirely satisfactory. The rules laid down fail to take account of the many complications where there coexist two treaties relating to the same subject-matter, one negotiated at the regional level among States between whom there is a high level of confidence and another negotiated within the framework of a universal organisation.[18]

---

[16] Report of the Study Group of the ILC, *Fragmentation of International Law: Difficulties Arising from the Diversification and Expansion of International Law*, (finalized by M Koskeniemmi, A/CN.4/L.682, 13 April 2006) 19, para 24.

[17] Ibid.

[18] I Sinclair, *The Vienna Convention on the Law of Treaties* (Manchester UP, 1984) 98.

This is, in many respects, a specific instance of the larger category of small treaty/large treaty conflicts that Article 30 fails to address. Gregory Fox has described Sinclair's evaluation as a 'typical British understatement', considering, for his part, Article 30 'an entirely unsatisfactory response to treaty conflicts'.[19] In particular, the approach taken in Article 30(4)(b), 'seems simply out of place in a world of proliferating legislative treaties. It is a mechanistic rule that wholly ignores the substantive claims at issue in a clash between two comprehensive treaty regimes.'[20] Of course, similar complications may also arise where the clash is between one comprehensive treaty regime and another treaty; the VCLT does not differentiate large treaties, or treaties founding comprehensive regimes, from other treaties.

2. Explaining Article 30

Yet a fair judgment on Article 30 would have to take into account the considerations acting upon its drafters. I have explained above some of the questions that they faced. I have also offered a preview into some of the reasons why Article 30 follows the approach it does – other alternatives may not be compatible with the founding principles of the VCLT. However, it is worth reflecting on the stages through which Article 30 evolved into its present form, for previous drafts were quite different. Here, I briefly outline the proposals advanced by the various ILC Special Rapporteurs on the law of treaties. In parsing these, it is worth noting that each Rapporteur saw his task as that of resolving two dilemmas.

First, between 'stability' and 'change': each Rapporteur had to consider whether his proposal should protect the earlier treaty or accept the later one as a conduit for change in international law. The second dilemma was even more complicated, for it required the Rapporteurs to find a medium between considerations of 'integrity' and 'instrumentality' of the conflict rule. On the one hand, the rule had to express disapproval of strategies of deliberate erosion of existing agreements, particularly multilateral ones, and remind States of their good faith obligations to observe all treaty commitments. Moreover, it had to be consistent with the other founding principles of the law of treaties. On the other hand, the rule had to effectively promote whatever resolution between stability and change the Rapporteur had determined to be appropriate; and it had

---

[19] G Fox, 'International Organizations: Conflicts of International Law' (2001) 95 Proceedings of the Annual Meeting of ASIL 183, 185.

[20] Ibid, 186.

to *convey* that treaty conflicts could be regulated in a practical way through international law. A rule that overreached, that exceeded the development of international organizations at the time, could be ignored by States; a modest, enabling rule would be harder to reject. We see the two concerns reflected in these quotes, taken from Lauterpacht's and Waldock's commentaries on their proposed conflict rules:

> Treaties, woven into the structure of customary international law, are the substance of the growing and changing law of nations. International law cannot recognise and it must actively discourage a state of affairs in which the law-creating faculty of states is abused for violating existing law as laid down in valid agreements. Governments cannot be permitted to discredit international law and to render it unreal by filling it with mutually exclusive obligations and by reducing treaties to conflicting makeshifts of political expediency.[21]

And:

> The imperfect state of international organization and the manifold uses to which treaties are put seem to make it necessary for the Commission to be cautious in laying down rules which brand treaties as illegal and void[22] ... . [I]t seems safer for the Commission, in the present state of the development of international law to abide by a more flexible rule.[23]

These quotes succinctly outline both the challenge that treaty conflicts were considered to pose to the idea of international law as 'law' and the normative and practical considerations that bracketed the ILC members' efforts to formulate a suitable conflict rule. Even so, within these brackets, the Rapporteurs offered a range of responses, all the while claiming to only further the logic of their predecessors' drafts and relying on the same materials: nineteenth- and early twentieth-century scholarship and a few judicial decisions.[24]

---

[21] H Lauterpacht, First Report on the Law of Treaties, Yearbook of the ILC (1953) vol II, A/CN.4/63, 158.

[22] H Waldock, Second Report on the Law of Treaties, Yearbook of the ILC (1963) vol II, A/CN.4/156 and Add.1-3, 56, para 14.

[23] Ibid, 60, para 29.

[24] Permanent Court of International Justice: *Oscar Chinn*, PCIJ 1934 Series A/B, No 63, 65; *European Commission of the Danube*, PCIJ 1927 Series B, No 14, 6; *Mavrommatis Palestinian Concessions*, PCIJ 1924 Series A, No 2, 6; *Austro-German Customs Union*, PCIJ 1931 Series A/B, No 41, 37. Central American Court of Justice: *Costa Rica* v *Nicaragua*, (1917) 11 American J Intl L 181; *El Salvador* v *Nicaragua*, (1917) 11 American J Intl L 674 (1917).

In his two reports, written in 1953 and 1954, Lauterpacht adopted what may be broadly described as an 'invalidity approach', but which was accompanied by several qualifications. Indeed, the invalidity rule included in the 1953 report[25] was further narrowed in the 1954 report.[26] In sum, Lauterpacht suggested that a bilateral or multilateral treaty, or treaty provision, would be void if 'its performance involve[d] a breach of a treaty obligation previously undertaken by one or more of the contracting parties' *and* if the breach was such as to 'interfere seriously with the interests of the other parties to that treaty' or 'seriously impair an essential aspect of the original purpose of the treaty'.[27] That the breach would have to be a serious one was thus doubly emphasized.

Lauterpacht, moreover, provided a series of exceptions under which various types of multilateral treaties would not be void even if their performance involved breach of previously undertaken treaty obligations. These were: treaties of a general legislative character; treaties which could be deemed as concluded in the international interest; and treaties revising multilateral conventions, either in accordance with their provisions or by a substantial majority of the parties. These suggestions reflect an effort to reconcile considerations of stability and change; they give specific recognition to multilateral treaties as the fabric of international law; and they follow the *pacta sunt servanda* principle.

Lauterpacht also proposed that if the later treaty was invalidated, a State party only to that treaty would be entitled to damages if it was unaware of the existence of the earlier treaty. This provision reinforced the requirement of good faith in the conclusion of treaties, aiming to discourage States from participating in other States' attempts to challenge or change their existing treaty commitments. Perhaps, it was also an attempt to mitigate possible challenges from States party to the invalidated treaty on the ground that to declare that treaty void only because of its conflict with another to which they had no obligation was contrary to the *pacta tertiis* principle.

As to how a treaty would be pronounced to be void, Lauterpacht took the view that this would be judicially determined; he expected (and hoped!) that States would take treaty conflict disputes before a court if they failed to negotiate an appropriate settlement amongst themselves. He

---

[25] H Lauterpacht, *Article 16: Consistency with Prior Treaty Obligations*, First Report on the Law of Treaties (n 21) 156.

[26] H Lauterpacht, *Article 16: Consistency with Prior Treaty Obligations*, Second Report on the Law of Treaties, Yearbook of the ILC (1954) vol II, A/CN.4/87 and Corr.1, 133.

[27] Ibid.

considered, however, that in many cases, the conflict would be resolved by agreement of parties; or, if brought before a court, by interpretations that would reconcile the conflicting treaties or by according priority to one of the treaties vis-à-vis the other.

The pulls of the twin considerations of stability and change and integrity and instrumentality that we see in Lauterpacht's formulation are even more evident in Fitzmaurice's proposal.[28] Fitzmaurice, first of all, substituted a 'priority' approach for Lauterpacht's invalidity rule, providing that in cases of conflict the earlier treaty would take priority over the later. However, he retained the invalidity approach for some special cases. The later treaty would be invalidated where it was an *inter se* agreement amongst some parties to the earlier; and the earlier prohibited conclusion of inconsistent treaties or the later treaty required parties to take action 'in direct breach' of their obligations under the earlier. Invalidity would also result where the earlier treaty was of an *integral* or *interdependent* character and the later treaty conflicted with it in a material particular. He considered as integral those treaties under which every State's obligation was absolute and not dependent on a corresponding performance by any other State, such as a human rights treaty. Interdependent treaties, on the other hand, were those where one party's breach could justify the termination of the treaty as a whole, for example, disarmament treaties. Finally, he took the position that in all these cases of priority or invalidity States party only to the later treaty would be entitled to compensation unless aware of the conflict with the earlier.

Fitzmaurice recognized that in not invalidating one of the conflicting treaties, the priority rule would serve more as suggestion than constraint. For, in practice, States would choose either of the treaties to follow ('in the existing state of international organisation, it may not be possible to prevent a *power* of election from being in fact exercised'[29]). However, it was provided precisely in order to reconcile the ideas of integrity (frowning upon a later, deliberately concluded, conflicting treaty) and instrumentality (recognizing that such later treaty may be a conduit for change of international law). In Fitzmaurice's view the priority rule was also more in keeping with the *res inter alios acta* principle, which a general invalidity rule violated; though it was not any more compatible with the *pacta tertiis* principle. His carefully calibrated exceptions in favour of invalidity – when the conflict involved certain types of treaties

[28] G Fitzmaurice, *Article 18: Legality of the Object (Conflict with Previous Treaties – Normal Cases)*, Third Report on the Law of Treaties, Yearbook of the ILC (1958) vol II, A/CN.4/115 and Corr.1, 27.

[29] Ibid, 42, para 85.

and was of a material character or the result of action in direct breach – were an apparent effort to reconcile ideas of stability and change.

Waldock's proposal further refined Fitzmaurice's priority thesis. Revising his initial proposal which had retained some elements of the invalidity rule,[30] he suggested that as between a State party to both treaties and a State party only to the earlier treaty, the earlier treaty should prevail; while, as between States parties to both treaties, the later treaty should prevail. Moreover, as between a State party to both treaties and a State party only to the later treaty, the later should prevail, unless that State was aware that the earlier treaty was in force; if so, that State party only to the later treaty could not demand its specific enforcement or damages for its non-performance.[31] Thus Waldock eliminated invalidity for all cases of treaty conflict. The choice in favour of a priority rule was governed by the same considerations that are reflected in Fitzmaurice's proposal; and the decision to eliminate the invalidity rule entirely was explained by reference to its impracticability in the 'present stage of international organization'.[32]

The language of priority, that one treaty would 'prevail' over the other, subsisted well into the ILC Drafting Committee's discussions of the draft rule. So did the provision on the unenforceability of later treaties that were not concluded in good faith (that is, without knowledge of the conflict with an earlier treaty). Even though ILC members recognized the priority rule's limited practical significance for the reason that Fitzmaurice too had acknowledged, they continued to view it as essential to convey disapproval of deliberately created treaty conflicts. Many also called for the reinstatement of some sort of invalidity rule. Over the course of the discussion, however, Waldock's point about the present state of underdevelopment of international organization won out.[33] The language of priority was translated into the current Article 30(4). The provision on the unenforceability of treaties that had been concluded with

---

[30] H Waldock, *Article 14: Conflict with a Prior Treaty*, Second Report on the Law of Treaties (n 22) 53.

[31] H Waldock, *Article 65: Priority of Conflicting Treaty Provisions*, Third Report on the Law of Treaties, Yearbook of the ILC (1964) vol II, A/CN.4/167 and Add.1-3, 34.

[32] H Waldock, *Article 14: Conflict with a Prior Treaty*, Second Report on the Law of Treaties (n 22) 56, para 14 and 60, para 29; and H Waldock, *Article 65: Priority of Conflicting Treaty Provisions*, Third Report on the Law of Treaties (n 31) 44, para 34.

[33] Summary Record of the 703rd meeting of the ILC, A/CN.4/SR.703, 19 June 1963, para 5, 75.

knowledge of conflict was dropped as being contradictory to States' freedom to contract. The special treatment for multilateral treaties, present in both Lauterpacht and Fitzmaurice's formulations, was also excluded.

Under Waldock's stewardship then, Article 30 took on many of the features that later met with criticism. But in defending it, Waldock – who, of the three Rapporteurs, showed the keenest appreciation for the *instrumentality* of the chosen rule – made the important point that the rule squarely addressed:

> whether, as between two States, one of them could invoke the fact that it was already a party to a prior treaty with another State as a ground for non-performance of the later treaty. That in essence was the problem of the relativity of treaties, and it had real practical significance in the case of a conflict between treaty obligations.[34]

The rule set out in Article 30(4) and (5) indeed clarified the absolute validity of both treaties such that the breach of either one due to performance of the other would lead to State responsibility. This, of course, sets it apart from Lauterpacht and Fitzmaurice's formulations. But it also arguably makes Article 30 a practicable basis for resolving treaty conflicts. Its practicability stems from the fact that it enables other States, affected by the breach, to invoke State responsibility, and grounds efforts by other actors to pressure States to comply with their treaty commitments. Recently, Klabbers has suggested that Article 30 embodies a 'principle of political decision' that:

> allows states and in particular decision-makers (think of judges) to choose the treaty they deem the most worthy in the circumstances … What is more, it allows others to pressure the state or the tribunal concerned into making the right choice: human rights advocates, for example, may use the principle of political decision in advocating that in a conflict between a human rights convention and another treaty, the state concerned ought to give preference to the human rights treaty; environmentalists may invoke it to advocate the priority … of an environmental treaty … [I]t is precisely the indeterminacy of the principle of political decision that allows for flexible and responsive politics and makes it possible for society at large (civil society, if you will) to participate in international decision-making processes.[35]

Article 30 is perhaps thus best understood as an effort to comprehend and respond to (or avoid!) the challenges – to specific international treaties

---

[34] Summary Record of the 857th meeting of the ILC, A/CN.4/SR.857, 24 May 1966, para 59.

[35] Klabbers, *Treaty Conflict* (n 9) 90.

and to the normative force of international law – embodied in deliberately created treaty conflicts. Certainly, the rule does not, in itself, safeguard multilateral treaties against challenges posed by deliberately created conflicts. But, perhaps, its confirmation of the continued validity of such treaties provides the relevant incentives for States to engage towards finding solutions. Even so, in many cases of deliberately created treaty conflicts, we see that where States do propose solutions, these consist in limiting or reinterpreting the scope of the treaty that they were seeking to alter in the first place. For instance, in the treaty conflict relating to seabed mining discussed earlier, the eight western States claimed there was no conflict because their alternative treaty was compatible with the 'spirit' of the UN Convention, a claim which sought to discount the specific mining regime outlined in the UN Convention. Parties to the UN Convention claimed there was no conflict because the alternative treaty was illegal at the outset. In the case of the conflict between the Rome Statute and US-led bilateral immunity agreements, the bilateral agreements purported to limit the International Criminal Court's access to various categories of individuals by reinterpreting the Rome Statute's provisions to this effect; States party to the Statute and Court officials insisted that it was up to the Court to determine the appropriate scope of the bilateral agreements.

Of course, in some cases States may display a more constructive attitude even in contexts of deliberately created treaty conflicts. They may also approach a judicial institution or treaty body to mediate the conflict. Or, indeed, such institutions may get involved at their own instance, particularly in order to safeguard the effective operation of the regimes underpinned by the treaties in conflict. The next section will discuss some suggestions made to this effect.

IV. WHAT INSTITUTIONS CAN DO

A key feature of many deliberately created treaty conflicts is the challenge posed to the effective operation of regimes established by specific multilateral treaties. In such cases, international institutions of various types might play an important role in meeting this challenge and mitigating the impact upon the multilateral treaty. They may persuade States party to the multilateral treaty to comply with their treaty commitments or otherwise enforce compliance. They may, of course, also play the role of judging that the conflict leads to a material breach of the multilateral treaty, necessitating its termination and the application of State responsibility. These roles are usually in keeping with the specific legal mandates held by these institutions, and as such do not call for further comment in this chapter. This section will focus on a 'grey zone', that is, three proposals in which legal scholars suggest the institutions might *alter* a challenged multilateral treaty to secure its effective operation.

These suggestions fall into a grey zone because, ordinarily, institutions do not have the authority to alter multilateral treaties at their own behest. Treaties are products of State consent and it is up to member States to amend them (following procedures prescribed in the treaty, or if not, in part IV of the VCLT) or modify them by subsequent practice (as provided for in VCLT Article 31(3)(b)). Of course, some scholars have noted that institutional practices, including interpretative practices, might lead to the transformation of a treaty.[36] The proposals discussed here take note of such practices, but focus on their extreme aspect: when institutions go beyond simply interpreting treaties to actually varying treaty terms. It is important to consider the grounds on which their doing so might be justified.

1. The Doctrine of Approximate Application

The first relevant proposal emerges from Lauterpacht's separate opinion in the 1956 advisory opinion in the *Admissibility of Hearings of Petitioners* case.[37] The case was one of several South West Africa cases decided by the International Court of Justice (ICJ), in relation to South Africa's Mandate over present-day Namibia. The Mandate had been established under the League of Nations' Mandates System. In 1950, the ICJ decided that the UN General Assembly (UNGA) could succeed to the League Council's supervisory powers over the Mandate.[38] However, the 1950 opinion also provided that the UNGA must confine itself to the degree of supervision and procedures followed by the League Council. South Africa's rejection of this opinion and its refusal to cooperate with the UNGA-established supervisory Committee on South West Africa, led the Committee to embrace a series of creative measures to maintain effective supervision. The 1956 opinion responded to the UNGA's query on whether one such measure – to admit oral hearings by South West

---

[36] See M Waibel, 'Demystifying the Art of Interpretation' (2011) 22 EJIL 571.

[37] *Admissibility of Hearings of Petitioners by the Committee on South West Africa*, Advisory Opinion, ICJ Rep 1956, 23.

[38] *International Status of South-West Africa*, Advisory Opinion, ICJ Rep 1950, 128.

African petitioners – was compatible with the degree and procedures of supervision followed by the League Council. The League had never actually granted oral hearings.

In the Court's opinion, the Committee could grant oral hearings and would *not* overstep the degree and procedures followed by the League. In Lauterpacht's opinion too the Committee could grant oral hearings, but not for the reason expressed by the Court.[39] He considered that the decision to grant oral hearings would ordinarily overstep the degree and procedure of supervisions followed by the League; thus in granting oral hearings the Committee would be acting contrary to the supervision regime that had subsisted under the League and was applied to the UNGA under the ICJ's 1950 Opinion.

However, he took the view that the ICJ could lawfully alter this regime to permit oral hearings, because three conditions were satisfied. First, the ICJ was here dealing with an instrument not of the ordinary contractual type but one which established a 'regime of continuing validity',[40] that was not affected by changes in attitudes, status or the 'very survival of individual parties or persons affected'.[41] Second, the party upon whom the alteration would impose a greater burden had itself acted in a manner as to make it impossible to implement the regime in its original, literal, scope. Third, the alteration was only to the extent needed to preserve effective operation of the regime; it was thus not substantial but akin to 'removing a clog or filling a lacuna or adopting an alternative in order to prevent a standstill of the entire system on account of a failure in any particular link or part'.[42] It was Lauterpacht's view, in sum, that such an alteration amounted to no more than giving effective interpretation to a regime as a whole. In his own words:

> It is a sound principle of law that whenever a legal instrument of continuing validity cannot be applied literally owing to the conduct of one of the parties, it must, without allowing that party to take advantage of its own conduct, be applied in a way approximating most closely to its primary object. To do that is to interpret and give effect to the instrument – not to change it.[43]

In short, Lauterpacht justified alterations to legal instruments (including treaties) both on the basis of State consent (deemed as given because the

---

39 *Admissibility of Hearings of Petitioners,* Separate Opinion of Sir Hersch Lauterpacht, ICJ Rep 1956, 35.
40 Ibid, 45.
41 Ibid, 48.
42 Ibid, 48.
43 Ibid, 46.

instrument in question was established to be of continuing validity) and institutional competence (the court, acting judicially, was merely interpreting an instrument of continuing validity).

This doctrine of approximate application was taken up by Shabtai Rosenne in his classic work *Breach of Treaty*,[44] where indeed it was given a slightly expanded form:

> [W]hat we have termed the doctrine of 'approximate application' means that faced with a situation of established breach … the parties themselves in the first instance, renegotiate and apply the treaty in good faith and where they are not successful in doing this themselves, then acting through or with the assistance of a competent international organ, whether judicial or not are legally obliged to take steps to redraft the treaty or reformulate the subsystem so as to ensure its continued effective application.[45]

To Rosenne, thus, the doctrine implied the duty of States, and the competence of judicial *and* some other international *institutions*, to alter a treaty to preserve its effective operation.

However, the doctrine has received few airings thereafter. Slovakia invoked it in the *Gabčíkovo-Nagymaros Project* case,[46] but in a highly distorted way. In effect, it argued that the doctrine enabled Slovakia to unilaterally alter the terms of a bilateral treaty concluded with Hungary to construct some waterworks, which treaty Hungary had decided not to carry out. Hungary strongly rejected this argument. While the thrust of its objections focused on Slovakia's use of the doctrine, it also contended that the doctrine was not well established in international law, having been cited only in one separate opinion and one significant scholarly work. Slovakia's use of the doctrine, moreover, persuaded some judges of the dangers associated with too loose a reading of the doctrine. To Judge Bedjaoui, the doctrine afforded the opportunity to States to modify treaties unilaterally, at will, he considered that 'because of its dangers' the doctrine 'deserved wholehearted censure'.[47] However, the Court, while not accepting Slovakia's use of the doctrine, did not consider whether the doctrine was, or not, an established 'principle of international law or a general principle of law'.[48] It merely noted that 'if such

---

[44] (Grotius, 1985).

[45] Ibid, 100.

[46] *Gabčíkovo-Nagymaros Project (Hungary/Slovakia)*, Judgment, ICJ Rep 1997, 7.

[47] *Gabčíkovo-Nagymaros Project,* Separate Opinion of J Bedjaoui, ICJ Rep 1997, 120, 127, para 30.

[48] *Gabčíkovo-Nagymaros Project,* Judgment (n 46) para 76.

a principle existed, it could by definition only be employed within the limits of the treaty in question';[49] that is, more or less rehearsing Lauterpacht's position on the manner of alterations that could be supported by the doctrine.

The ICJ is unlikely to find that the doctrine is well established in international law whenever it next considers the problem of breach of a multilateral treaty regime. But, it is fair to say that within the limits so clearly spelt out by Lauterpacht, the doctrine does offer judicial institutions (and if we follow Rosenne, some other international organs) a basis to secure effective operation of multilateral treaties that may be challenged by a deliberately created treaty conflict. Moreover, it does not implicate the institutions' capacity to *resolve* the treaty conflict, shifting the focus to its competence to adjust one of the conflicting treaties. It thus avoids some of the issues relating to consistency with the fundamental principles of treaty law that constrain efforts to design conflict rules.

2. Treaties Bodies and the Managerial Approach

The second proposal is elaborated by Abram Chayes and Antonia Handler Chayes in *The New Sovereignty*.[50] In this book, which is one of the leading lights of a large body of compliance scholarship in the United States, the Chayeses explore the role of treaty bodies in fostering compliance with multilateral treaties. While they do not specifically comment on treaty conflict, their 'managerial approach' is applicable to the compliance problems created by (particularly deliberately created) treaty conflicts.

According to the Chayeses, treaty bodies may promote compliance by *persuading* States to comply with their obligations. They may do so by promoting the flow of information and States' interactions within a treaty regime, as well as through undertaking, where relevant, activities such as reporting, data collection, verification, monitoring, policy review, capacity building, dispute settlement and adaptation of the treaty. In addition, they may also promote compliance by *tailoring* treaty obligations to the circumstances of the member States. The Chayeses' core argument is that compliance is not an 'on-off phenomenon'; rather most regimes can allow an acceptable margin of 'what would be strictly speaking non-compliance'.[51] Thus, treaty bodies may calibrate an appropriate margin based on the treaty's objects, context, State behaviour, State capacity to

---

[49] Ibid.
[50] (Harvard UP, 1998).
[51] Ibid, 18–20.

comply, urgency of the circumstances leading to non-compliance, etc. They insist that such calibration must be through an interactive process reflecting 'the perspectives and interests of the participants', rather than 'some external, scientifically or market-validated standard'.[52]

A crucial element of both *persuasion* and *tailoring*, in context of the managerial approach, is that treaty bodies may alter some treaty terms in order to promote compliance with the treaty regime as a whole. While it must be noted that the Chayeses avoid a detailed discussion of the possibility of actual changes being introduced by treaty bodies, preferring to describe instead the practice of 'authoritative or semi-authoritative interpretation by a designated body of the organisation, often the secretariat or a legal committee',[53] the suggestion runs right through the book, and indeed is implied in the use of terms such as adaptation and tailoring. And express discussion or not, the Chayeses also provide the grounds on which treaty bodies may base the authority to introduce changes, and these will be extrapolated below. They are, partly, institutional competence and State consent.

Occasionally, the treaty (which is both the constitutive treaty of the treaty body and one of the conflicting treaties) may have provided the legal basis for the treaty body to take what action is required. But even where these powers are not expressly spelt out, they may be implied in the very setting up of the treaty body. As the Chayeses point out, a treaty body's '*raison d'etre* is the treaty. At least presumptively, it will be committed to treaty compliance'.[54] In other words, it would be natural for a treaty body to take steps towards supporting effective operation of the treaty. However, they also acknowledge the loose nature of this justification, noting that States have 'developed a deep skepticism about bureaucracies' that 'generate a degree of autonomy that impinges on the states' freedom of action'.[55] Thus powers to alter should not be easily implied. The Chayeses instead point to two other factors that guide the actions of treaty bodies. The first is adherence to (what we would now term) principles of global administrative law (GAL), that is, principles that ensure procedural regularity of the actions undertaken by the treaty bodies.

The second is that the treaty body makes (or, in the Chayeses' view should make) these decisions not in a vacuum but in the course of an interactive process. Essentially the body operates as site, moderator and

---

52 Ibid.
53 Ibid, 209.
54 Ibid, 274.
55 Ibid, 111.

participant to a dialogue between the erring State and other relevant actors, seeking from the former justification of its non-compliance and building consensus amongst the latter for the alterations needed. In this way, State consent is obtained afresh. Essential here is also that the treaty body serves to 'intensify the legal content of the discourse'.[56] Per the Chayeses, arguments of law permit a more reasoned, intersubjective basis for taking action. Other types of arguments have characteristic problems:

> Arguments invoking the other parties' interests and broadly utilitarian appeals face the familiar difficulties of divining subjective preferences and aggregating utilities … . Alternatively, justification of questioned conduct often relies on broadly accepted background principles rooted in practical experience and common sense: rough fairness, the status quo, precedent and custom … . In most situations however, there will be more than one plausible objective criterion, and none of them will be neutral.[57]

The Chayeses consider that legal argumentation is not only best suited to enable parties to comprehend and evaluate each others' positions, but it also produces its own constraints. In an earlier work, *The Cuban Missile Crisis,* based on his experience of the event while a Legal Adviser of the US Department of State, Abram Chayes had argued that, in practice, being forced to justify actions in terms of international law could influence States. Even under such fraught circumstances as persisted during the crisis, the US government did not take positions that would 'trivialize the whole effort at legal justification'.[58] In *The New Sovereignty* the Chayeses insist that it is hard for any party having debated seriously and at length via legal norms to dismiss them as unimportant; the managerial approach thus consolidates a general respect for international law. This further serves the end of promoting effective operation of international legal agreements.

Certainly, there is much that the Chayeses do not spell out for us, including the specifics of what makes for an appropriate legal discourse. But, the broad idea that, faced with a situation of challenge to a multilateral treaty regime by threats of non-compliance, treaty bodies can take steps, including altering its terms, to promote compliance is a creative one. Moreover, it makes the effort to marry its practical orientation with fidelity to legal principle, in providing that the role of treaty bodies is subject to the regulative influence of legal discourse (and the State consent that is generated through it) and to scrutiny of the

---

[56] Ibid, 125.
[57] Ibid, 120.
[58] A Chayes, *The Cuban Missile Crisis* (OUP, 1974) 65.

procedural regularity of their actions, based on administrative law-type principles.

3. Accommodation by Treaty Interaction

The third idea is that of 'treaty coordination' or 'regime interaction', which is best fleshed out by Rudiger Wolfrum and Nele Matz in *Conflicts in International Environmental Law*[59] and Margaret Young in *Trading Fish, Saving Fish.*[60] The ILC too referred to it as a possible approach particularly where two instruments fall within the same regime, in its report on the *Fragmentation of International Law.*[61]

The suggestion is, broadly, that faced with a treaty conflict, or regime conflict, various institutions should seek, and may be able, to transform the conflict into an opportunity for mutual learning between the conflicting treaties (or regimes), and may broker small adjustments to both, such that they accommodate each other even if their conflict is not fully resolved. It emerges from the presumption that there is usually a reason underlying treaty conflicts: a new conflicting treaty is a hint that the existing treaty did not adequately address a particular issue or represent a particular viewpoint. Of course, the new treaty too may be focused on specific issues only or represent specific views to the exclusion of others. The treaty conflict makes these exclusions and biases apparent. The authors of these suggestions do not fully clarify their count of relevant institutions, though their focus is on treaty bodies and intergovernmental organizations (IGOs) functionally related to the issue-areas that are concerned in the treaty conflict.

How do they justify their suggestions that in pursuit of mutual accommodation, institutions may essentially alter one or more of the conflicting treaties? I focus here mainly on Young's justification; these are quite similar to Wolfrum and Matz's, but more expressly stated.

In part, the justification is of institutional competence. Young relies not solely on expressly provided competence but also on implied powers of institutions, deriving from the functional necessity to take the various conflicting treaties into account.[62] She draws on the *Reparation* case,[63] in which the ICJ found that 'the rights and duties of an entity like the UN

---

59 (Springer, 2003).

60 (CUP, 2011).

61 ILC, *Fragmentation* (n 16) 140 *et seq.*

62 Young, *Trading Fish* (n 60) 272.

63 *Reparation for Injuries Suffered in the Service of the United Nations*, Advisory Opinion, ICJ Rep 1949, 174.

"must depend upon its purposes and functions as specified or implied in its constituent documents and developed in practice"'.[64] In the same way, '[i]n fisheries governance, it is functionally necessary for IGOs to take account of … interests [that] are variously economic, consumerist, ecological and ecocentric'.[65] Wolfrum and Matz also suggest this in a more veiled way: '[e]ven if cooperation with other institutions is not expressly mentioned in a treaty, it is likely that the authority to cooperate could be based upon a general competence to deal with issues necessary for better implementation of an agreement'.[66]

In support of this idea of implied functional competence, Young suggests, moreover, that we need to move away from a State consent-based paradigm. Indeed even where some degree of consent to interaction is indicated in a treaty, it will rarely encompass treaties to which some of the member States are not party, thus bringing up the usual problems of dealing with conflicts between treaties with non-identical parties. Rather than State consent, the capacities of IGOs to further treaty or regime interaction 'arise from the necessity of either enhanced representation or deliberation'.[67] Young points out that States may only reflect specific viewpoints in their treaties, leaving others entirely unrepresented; similarly their treaties may take some, but not all, issues into account. In such case IGOs have the capacity to engage with other views (whether of States, NGOs or other bodies) and other interests, bringing them into conversation with each other, and promoting 'diverse and pluralistic solutions'.[68]

A central plank of the argument in favour of the legitimacy of such an approach is that such interaction is, and must be, amenable to scrutiny of its process. For, Young recognizes that treaty interaction in the absence of State consent and based on a functional approach can 'lead to abuse … may signal a "technicalisation" of international affairs, where managerial procedures and decision-making by unseen experts begins to control global politics'.[69] This, however, may be addressed by review of the mechanisms used by the relevant institutions to promote regime interaction, both as to the sources of the norms being brought into interaction and as to the openness, participation and transparency of the process. Such review, she notes, may be carried out by States and, moreover, is

64 Young, *Trading Fish* (n 60) 272.
65 Ibid, 273.
66 Wolfrum and Matz, *Conflicts* (n 59) 167.
67 Young, *Trading Fish* (n 60) 276.
68 Ibid, 275.
69 Ibid, 276.

organically carried out in some situations by institutions – where more than one institution is involved – vis-à-vis each other.[70] Young references, in this regard, GAL scholarship on accountability, which focuses on procedural accountability of institutions that undertake rule- and decision-making and implementation such that their role takes on the character of administration,[71] and which 'locate[s] accountability structures in non-traditional sites of globalised lawmaking, including by market actors and international committees of IGOs'.[72] Indeed, GAL scholars take a fairly broad approach to institutional accountability, finding it may be facilitated by a host of mechanisms including legal, fiscal, supervisory, hierarchical, electoral, market-based, reputational, and peer-review based.[73]

The interaction approach is thus a creative response to treaty conflict, providing for a wide scope for institutional action. Its basis in law as it *is*, is less clear, particularly as regards the suggestion that it is time to move beyond a State consent-based paradigm. In many ways international law *has* moved beyond direct State consent as the basis for international law and towards recognizing the authority of autonomous institutional action. But it is doubtful that international law sanctions the subordination of clearly established rights and obligations under international legal agreements to the demands of 'functional necessity', even if this is in the service of greater representation and deliberation. Nevertheless, given that the theatre for evaluating institutions' moves to promote interaction is more likely to be diplomatic than judicial, the approach provides fairly distinctive criteria – procedural accountability in promoting representation and deliberation – for review and criticism. And while the one concept should not be lightly used as substitute for the other, it is fair to

---

[70] Ibid, 278–84.

[71] B Kingsbury, N Krisch, and R Stewart, 'The Emergence of Global Administrative Law' (2005) 68 L and Contemporary Problems 1.

[72] Young, *Trading Fish* (n 60) 281.

[73] To be fair, Richard Stewart describes the last three as 'responsiveness-promoting' rather than accountability mechanisms. See R Stewart, 'Accountability, Participation and the Problem of Disregard in Global Regulatory Governance' (7 February 2008) Institute for International Law and Justice International Legal Theory Colloquium, New York University School of Law, 15, accessed 19 May 2014 at http://iilj.org/courses/documents/2008Colloquium.Session4.Stewart.pdf. However, the broader view, embraced by Ruth Grant and Robert Keohane, is also widely cited in GAL scholarship. See R Grant and R Keohane, 'Accountability and Abuses of Power in World Politics' (2005) 99 American Political Science Rev 29.

say that the approach suggests that interaction may be legitimate, even if its legality is not yet fully grounded.

4. To Sum Up

The three proposals discussed above are all creative responses to the challenges that situations like treaty conflict pose to the effective implementation of multilateral treaties. Each envisages the alteration of at least one of the treaties in question and justifies this on a combination of institutional authority to effect changes and State consent (or the lack of need for it). Some of the proposals may come across as more grounded in law than the others but that feature has not, in fact, had any relationship at all to their practice. Indeed, 'administrative management' and 'interaction' claim to build upon what treaty bodies and other institutions actually do in practice. Approximate application has made rare appearances in judicial procedures and in legal scholarship, but is arguably equally prevalent in the practice of institutions, where the focus is on adapting treaty terms to foster the effective functioning of a treaty regime rather than compliance of specific States or improvement of one/both conflicting treaties. I will not go into a discussion of examples here, but will conclude with the short point that these approaches, as well as the VCLT conflict rules, in fact reflect the presence of a dynamic attitude that, in response to the politics of treaty conflicts, offers methods to channel such politics through forms and procedures of international law, and that grounds efforts to preserve the effective functioning of hard-won multilateral regimes challenged by treaty conflicts.

V. PROGRAMME FOR FURTHER RESEARCH

What directions should future research take? Here, instead of outlining specific research questions let me focus on a few themes and ideas.

First, as a general theme, it is important to fully embrace the politics of international law. This includes accepting that political factors do influence the creation and operation of both treaties and the law of treaties. It also means avoiding two extremes: of regarding the doctrine of international law (including of treaties) as wholly disconnected from politics, or as entirely subsumed by it. The politics of international law is no reason to disregard its normative role in international relations. Instead, the effort should be to illuminate the intimate, and mutually influential, connections between treaty law and politics, to provide a richer, more grounded picture of this role.

Second, the need to reconsider the paradigms within which we think about treaties and consequently challenges to, or conflicts between, treaties. As discussed above, the focus on breach and State responsibility is inadequate to respond to all the functions served by treaties or all the interests that may be implicated in their operation. It also ignores that some treaties do have a different character than others. This may be because of the content of their substantive obligations (recall Fitzmaurice's categories of integral and interdependent treaties). Or, they may be structurally different, for they establish administrative bodies to oversee their own effective implementation. It is perhaps time to revisit the importance of these distinctions for the law and politics of treaties.

Third, the need to explore more deeply into the bases for institutional authority in international law. This includes the need to engage with the discourses of constitutionalization, administrative governance, and pluralism, that have become popular narratives of international legal order, and that provide visions of institutional competence, as well as *other* procedural and/or substantive criteria (beyond competence) for evaluating the legitimacy of institutional action. How do these discourses relate to the State-based conception of international law? Do they offer a foundation on which we might rethink the core principles of treaty law? Or, are they at best weakly descriptive, and even only weakly normative, visions?

Fourth, the need to take seriously the argument that treaty conflicts are no more than a symptom of the fact that any treaty is, at best, an expression of what *some* States (or actors) consider appropriate or desirable at a given time. In other words, they may only serve particular interests, and do so by excluding others. Moreover, these interests may be subject to change with time. Thus, it is not constructive to approach treaty conflicts in terms of a condemnatory attitude or on the presumption that the conflicts must, somehow, be *resolved*. It *is* important, however, to attend to the underlying value- and interest-contestations that are revealed by treaty conflicts, to consider ways in which international law can provide frameworks within which these contestations can take place, and to critically evaluate those that it does provide.

16. Treaty breaches and responses

Christian J. Tams

I. INTRODUCTION

As a general rule, treaties are not concluded to be breached; but treaty breaches are quite common. They are bound to occur, as so much of international life is covered by international treaties (and hence there is so much treaty law to be breached), and as States, like other subjects of the law, are not perfect. None of this is particularly surprising or particularly problematic. No legal system can exclude non-compliance with accepted voluntary commitments (under treaties, under contracts, under pledges or promises, etc); and all legal systems anticipate non-compliance. It is in the way they deal with instances of non-compliance that legal systems differ.

This chapter assesses how one particular legal system – international law – addresses one particular form of non-compliance – treaty breaches. It proceeds on the basis of two fairly straightforward questions. The *first question* is addressed to the substance of international law: what does international law have to say on treaty breaches and responses? For reasons of convenience, this question will be broken into two sets of issues. What amounts to a treaty breach? And what are the consequences of treaty breaches, and how other States obtain redress? The *second question* concerns the *locus* of regulation: what branches of international law address treaty breaches and responses? In assessing this second question, and in line with the overall focus of the *Research Handbook*, the subsequent contribution looks to the general law of treaties, as codified in the 1969 Vienna Convention on the Law of Treaties (VCLT). However, as the general law of treaties has surprisingly little to say on treaty breaches, general rules of responsibility (as set out in the International Law Commission's (ILC) 2001 Articles on State Responsibility (ASR)[1]) and special provisions of particular treaties will also be looked at. The overall intention is to clarify in what way, and where, international law regulates an

[1] The Articles are reproduced, with commentaries, in Yearbook of the ILC (2001) vol II, Part 2, 31.

essential problem of international treaty relations that 'plays an important rôle in both international law and foreign office practice'.[2]

II. WHAT AMOUNTS TO A TREATY BREACH?

Before addressing reactions against breaches, legal systems need to clarify what amounts to a treaty breach. This question is rarely discussed in the abstract.[3] Typically, States disagree on whether a particular treaty provision has been violated: whether an invasion justified as self-defence breaches the UN Charter (UNC, Charter) provision against the use of force, whether the stop and search of a foreign attaché violates rules of diplomatic immunity, whether the seizure of a foreign ship violates the freedom of navigation, and so on. Yet these specific disputes presuppose a general understanding of the concept of 'treaty breach'; and of course international law recognizes the need for such a concept.[4] It deals with it rather *en passant*, though, and perhaps not in the most natural way. The subsequent sections briefly identify the main elements of the international legal regime.

1. The General Law of Treaties: Limited Guidance

The general law of treaties, as codified in the 1969 Vienna Convention, is the obvious starting point for the analysis. Given its status as the central text on treaty law, one might expect the Vienna Convention to regulate

---

[2] RB Bilder, 'Breach of Treaty and Response Thereto' (1967) 61 Proceedings ASIL 193, 193.

[3] In her exhaustive study, Caroline Laly-Chevalier pertinently notes: '*La violation du traité est "rebelle" à toute définition a priori. Terrain propice au jeu croisé des prétensions contradictoires, la violation du traité n'a d'ailleurs jamais fait l'object, en droit international, de tentative d'objectivation,*' C Laly-Chevalier, *La Violation du Traité* (Bruylant, 2005) 83. Christine Chinkin agrees: 'No comprehensive definition of breach to serve as a guide for decisionmakers has yet been formulated,' C Chinkin, 'Nonperformance of International Agreements' (1982) 17 Texas Intl L J 387, 388. For an abstract definition, but one including a now obsolete element of will, see G Schwarzenberger, *International Law as Applied by International Courts and Tribunals* (vol I, 3rd edn, Stevens & Sons, 1957) 575: 'a breach of treaty may be defined as unjustified non-compliance against the will of another party with a treaty in circumstances in which, in the light of the *jus aequum* rule, such an act or omission is attributable to a contracting party and voluntary'. Cf further below, II.3.

[4] In Bilder's words, 'the concept of obligation logically presupposes a concept of breach': Bilder, 'Breach of Treaty ...' (n 2) 194.

questions of treaty breaches and responses, and perhaps even do so in some detail. However, it does so only in passing: in the words of Shabtai Rosenne, 'the provisions of the Convention, taken in their entirety, only touch the fringe of the legal and political problems which breach of a treaty … will create'.[5] In fact, the term 'breach' appears in merely three provisions (Articles 60, 61, 62) and is only central to one of them (Article 60). As a result of a number of strategic decisions taken by the drafters (consciously taken, pragmatic, and as such neither right nor wrong) the general law of treaties sidesteps most legal issues raised by treaty breaches. The Vienna Convention notably provides very little guidance on what amounts to a breach of treaty. In its Article 60(3), it offers a (controversial) definition of 'material breaches',[6] but neither that provision, nor any other, says anything on breaches as such. Treaty breaches simply did not feature on the drafters' agenda as they set out to devise a general regime of treaty law. The drafters' approach has been rationalized as a result of their desire to focus on 'the treaty as an instrument' as opposed to 'the treaty as a source of obligation'.[7] However, that distinction is a fairly subtle one and not maintained strictly.[8] The more plausible explanation is that, irrespective of the drafters' general understanding of terms such as 'law of treaties' and 'law of obligations', they pragmatically decided that the (already cumbersome) drafting of a general law of treaties need not be burdened with questions of treaty breaches – and that these would be better addressed elsewhere.

2. Filling Gaps: Particular Treaties as Primary Rules

There are two main aspects to this silence. First, and unsurprisingly, the Convention as a 'treaty on treaties' does not attempt to spell out the *substantive* obligations imposed by particular treaties.[9] It left this task to each particular treaty – or to what a later codification project would refer to as the 'primary rules'. And of course, this was a meaningful approach

---

[5] S Rosenne, *Breach of Treaty* (Grotius, 1985) 44. For a similar observation, see B Simma, 'Reflections on Article 60 of the Vienna Convention on the Law of Treaties and its Background in General International Law' (1970) 20 ÖZÖR 5, 83.

[6] See below, III.1, for brief comment.

[7] Rosenne, *Breach of Treaty* (n 5) 3–8.

[8] Cf Rosenne, *Breach of Treaty* (n 5) 44 ('subtle, and at times … artificial').

[9] Only occasionally does the Vienna Convention impose its own (primary?) obligations, Article 18 being a notable example.

for a treaty laying down meta-rules of general application, which could never be expected to reflect the totality of existing treaty obligations at force at any given point.

It is worth noting, however, how little the Vienna Convention engages with the primary rules, that is, the substance of treaty obligations. Unlike other general texts, it does not attempt to spell out general rules on attribution; viz it does not provide any guidance on whose conduct is treated as conduct of a treaty party when it comes to breaches.[10] Nor does the Vienna Convention establish a general mechanism permitting authoritative decisions as to whether a treaty has indeed been breached; in the absence of special treaty rules, this remains a matter for auto-determination.[11] And finally, perhaps most conspicuously, the Vienna Convention does not categorize types of treaties with a view to identifying core aspects of obligations imposed by them: but for some brief references to the distinction between bilateral and multilateral treaties,[12] the Vienna Convention's approach is curiously undifferentiated. No attempt is made to distinguish between common types of agreements; there is no international law equivalent to the lengthy sets of residual rules governing particular types of agreements (sales, loans, exchanges, donations, etc), which are a key aspect of contract law rules in many domestic jurisdictions.[13] From the vantage point of the general law of treaties, each treaty is to be approached in its own right, on its own terms, and not categorized.[14] In other words, while supplying general rules on treaty formation, treaty interpretation, treaty suspension, and so on, the

---

[10] Contrast the approach adopted in the general rules on responsibility (below, II.3); and cf also Articles 7–8 VCLT, which lay down general rules on the representation of States in the conclusion of treaties. For brief comment on possible links between the two sets of rules, see Rosenne, *Breach of Treaty* (n 5) 58.

[11] Cf Articles 65 and 66 for fragments of a VCLT dispute settlement system.

[12] See, eg, Articles 40, 41, 55, 58 and 60 VCLT; and, for other differentiations, Articles 5 and 20(2) and (3) VCLT. As Hollis perceptively notes, only exceptionally does the general law of treaties 'differentiate treaties by their function. … The conventional approach is to conceive of the treaty as a single, uniform concept': D Hollis, 'Defining Treaties' in D Hollis (ed), *The Oxford Guide to Treaties* (OUP, 2012) 11, 36.

[13] See, eg, Articles 1582–2061 of the French Code Civil; ss 433–811 of the German Civil Code (BGB).

[14] Hollis, albeit considering other forms of differentiations between treaties, notes that while the treaty 'serve[d] as a sort of Swiss army knife for international law, … incorporat[ing] several tools within a single instrument', the 'standard constitutive definition describes only the unopened knife; it does not differentiate what treaties do or to what ends': Hollis, 'Defining Treaties' (n 12) 36.

general law of treaties has so far hardly attempted to standardize the substance of obligations arising under common types of treaties. As a consequence, international lawyers seeking to determine whether a treaty has been breached have to look to the particular instrument, whereas many domestic lawyers would look also to the applicable contract law.

3. Filling Gaps (continued): Treaty Breaches and the Law of State Responsibility

Second, to the extent that international law requires general rules on treaty breaches, the Vienna Convention drafters felt these need not be spelled out as part of the general law of treaties, because they were but a subset of an even broader category, that of breaches of international law or internationally wrongful acts. This broader category formed part of the general law of responsibility that would apply to breaches of treaty or custom. In fact, so firmly was this felt that the matter was never discussed in earnest, and when it arose during the ILC debates, in the early 1960s, the Commission summarily noted that the general law of responsibility in its (then novel) 'secondary variation'[15] was better suited to deal with 'the general principles governing the reparation to be made for breach of a treaty'.[16] As is well known, the process of working out those general principles – which 'should on the face of it [have] take[n] one summer's work'[17] – was to prove complex, eventually resulting in the 2001 Articles on State Responsibility. Yet the fundamental decision in favour of a unitary regime of responsibility – covering treaty breaches and other internationally wrongful acts – was never seriously questioned. In line with this, Articles 1, 2 and 12 of the ILC's 2001 text clarify that

---

[15] That is to say: 'the general conditions under international law for the State to be considered responsible for wrongful actions or omissions, and the legal consequences which flow therefrom' (ILC, Introductory Commentary to the Articles on State Responsibility, para 1). Pursuant to Roberto Ago, it was 'one thing to define a rule and the content of the obligation it imposes, and another to determine whether that obligation has been violated and what should be the consequence of the violation. Only the second aspect of the matter comes within the sphere of responsibility proper' (that is, responsibility in the 'secondary variation' understood by Ago and the ILC): Yearbook of the ILC (1970) vol II, Part 2, 306, para 66(c).

[16] Yearbook of the ILC (1966) vol II, 177.

[17] Cf R Higgins, *Problems and Process: International Law and How We Use It* (OUP, 1995) 148.

State responsibility is triggered by each and every breach of an international obligation, irrespective of that obligation's source.[18]

This approach has two implications. First, it further broadens the concept of responsibility and sets it apart from domestic concepts that do distinguish between breaches of agreements and breaches of other obligations. In its award in the *Rainbow Warrior* case, the Arbitral Tribunal noted summarily that 'in the field of international law there is no distinction between contractual and tortious responsibility'.[19] The ILC commentary to Article 12 ASR seems to go even further when suggesting that 'there is no room in international law for a distinction, such as is drawn by some legal systems, between the regime of responsibility for breach of a treaty and for breach of some other rule'.[20] In its secondary variation, responsibility was always going to be an omnibus concept, but comprising what in other legal systems would be referred to as liability *ex delicto* and *ex contractu*, it is of breathtaking scope.

Second, as part of its rules on wrongful conduct, the omnibus concept of responsibility offers at least some guidance on how to ascertain treaty breaches. It does so by laying down residual (secondary) rules that can be opted out of and that respect the special features of the special (primary)

---

[18] In the ILC's final text (n 1), this is no longer spelled out expressly, but it is read into Article 12 ASR which provides: 'There is a breach of an international obligation by a State when an act of that State is not in conformity with what is required of it by that obligation, *regardless of its origin* or character.' The ILC's commentary clarifies that the reference to 'origin' is meant to cover the sources of international law, incl. international treaties (paras 4–5). Draft article 17 of the ILC's first reading text on State responsibility (in Yearbook of the ILC (1976) vol II, 79) had been even clearer; it provided:

> 1. An act of a State which constitutes a breach of an international obligation is an internationally wrongful act regardless of the origin, whether customary, conventional or other, of that obligation.
> 2. The origin of the international obligation breached by a State does not affect the international responsibility arising from the internationally wrongful act of that State.

[19] *Rainbow Warrior*, RIAA XX, 215, at 251, para 75.

[20] ILC Articles (n 1) at 55. P Reuter agrees (*Droit des Traités*, 3rd edn, with P Cahier, PUF, 1995, at 170), as does I von Münch (*Das Völkerrechtliche Delikt* Keppler, 1963, at 136), but like the ILC, both merely assert the 'logic' of their unitary approach. The better view is that there would very well be 'room' in international law for a distinction between treaty-based and extra-conventional responsibility, but that international law has so far not developed it. For a similar assessment (and a detailed discussion), see the ILC's commentary to draft article 17 adopted on first reading, Yearbook of the ILC (1976) vol II, 79–87.

treaty rules.[21] Yet as treaty rules opt out rarely,[22] the residual framework of responsibility has assumed considerable prominence and fills at least some of the gaps left by the Vienna Convention. As international lawyers have fully internalized the ILC's State responsibility text, its main features can be dealt with summarily. They include the following:

- Responsibility is a broad notion that does not depend, at the level of the general rules, on fault or damage.[23]
- Responsibility is based on forms of 'public' conduct, while private conduct does not engage a State's international responsibility.[24]
- Just as in the general law of treaties, so the general law of responsibility would not meddle with the substance of obligations: this would be left to the primary rules[25] – that is, in the present case, specific treaties imposing obligations upon States, as interpreted and applied in line with the general law of treaties.[26]
- Notwithstanding the ILC's fascination with the primary-secondary divide, the text on responsibility contains default rules on a number of issues which verge on the primary: these include provisions on temporal law,[27] on defences/justifications ('circumstances excluding wrongfulness'),[28] and a rather ambitious (but surprisingly well received[29]) provision on complicity.[30] Whatever the rhetoric, the line between primary and secondary rules is not categorical.

---

21 See Article 55 ASR and further below, III.3.

22 For some examples, see CJ Tams, 'Unity and Diversity in the Law of State Responsibility' in A Zimmermann and R Hofmann (eds), *Unity and Diversity in International Law* (Duncker & Humblot, 2005) 437, 441–5.

23 See notably, Article 2 ASR and commentary thereto (n 1) 34–6.

24 See Articles 4–11 ASR and commentaries (n 1) 38–54.

25 On the term, and its pragmatic application, see E David, 'Primary and Secondary Rules' in J Crawford, A Pellet, and S Olleson (eds), *The Law of International Responsibility* (OUP, 2010) 29.

26 See general (introductory) commentary to the ILC's text (n 1) 31, paras 2–4; and further, para 2 of the introductory commentary to Part One, Chapter III (n 1) 55, where it is stated: 'In determining whether given conduct attributable to a State constitutes a breach of its international obligations, the principal focus will be on the primary obligation concerned … There is no such thing as a breach of an international obligation in the abstract.'

27 Articles 13–15 ASR and commentaries (n 1) 57–64.

28 Articles 20–27 ASR and commentaries (n 1) 71–86.

29 See the ICJ's judgment in *Application of the Convention on the Prevention and Punishment of the Crime of Genocide*, ICJ Rep 2007, 43, para 420 (where Article 16 ASR is said to 'reflec[t] a customary rule').

30 Article 16 ASR and commentary (n 1) 66–7.

These provisions establish a framework for the analysis of primary treaty obligations and shape important aspects of the international regime of treaty breaches. In the light of the ILC's fundamental decisions, any attributable instance of non-compliance with what is required by a treaty obligation amounts to a treaty breach; while fault and damage (unless required by the primary rule) do not need to be established. The ILC's text is important in that it puts forward influential provisions on attribution and on defences/ excuses, which inform judgments as to whether a particular instance of non-compliance entails responsibility. Finally, although more controversially, the ILC's text puts forward a rule against complicity in treaty breaches, which – within the limits of Article 16 ASR – broadens the circle of States that can bear some form of responsibility for treaty breaches. To the limited extent that international law regulates treaty breaches at the level of the general rules, it does so as part of the law of State responsibility.

* * *

International rules approach treaty breaches in a curious way. The notion of a treaty breach is not precisely defined, but is addressed as part of the more inclusive definition of an internationally wrongful act, which has proved useful but remains vague. While general regimes – of treaty law and responsibility – are decisive in other fields, when it comes to treaty breaches, international law remains shaped by particular treaty rules. Within the parameters set by the general rules of State responsibility, special (primary) rules are determinative, and international law remains at a relatively low level of standardization.

III. REMEDIES AND REDRESS

Matters are slightly different with respect to the consequences of treaty breaches and to the means of obtaining redress. In this field, general rules play a greater role, while special (primary) rules are not as dominant. That said, a distinction must be drawn between the two sets of general regimes addressed (the law of treaties and the law of responsibility) and between the rules on remedies on the one hand, and rules on obtaining redress on the other.

1. The General Law of Treaties: A Highly Selective Approach – Article 60 VCLT

Of the two sets of general rules, the general law of treaties is of lesser relevance. For the most part, this is a direct consequence of the strategic decisions described in the preceding section. As the Vienna Convention was not to duplicate or standardize primary treaty rules, and as questions of treaty breaches were 'outsourced' into the domain of responsibility, there was little scope for rules on remedies and redress. In line with this, the Vienna Convention addresses treaty breaches merely from one particular angle: it regulates the impact of a breach on the treaty relations between the parties. This it does by recognizing, in Article 60 VCLT,[31] that under certain conditions, a treaty breach by one party may permit another party to suspend or terminate the treaty in whole or in part.

Article 60 VCLT is one of the more intriguing provisions of the Convention; it puts forward a complex regime of great conceptual, but limited practical, relevance. As the provision has been analysed in some detail elsewhere,[32] it may suffice to outline its four main features:[33]

(i) As regards its outcome, Article 60 VCLT envisages two very narrowly defined options. It permits, under certain circumstances, the complete or partial suspension or termination of the *same* treaty that is said to have been violated by the prior breach. Conversely, Article 60 does not justify the suspension or termination of *other* treaties; it is intended to address problems 'within' one specific

---

[31] Other provisions of the Convention's long Part V (Invalidity, Suspension, Termination) could equally be invoked to justify suspension or withdrawal. However, as they typically refer back to the special treaty whose breach is alleged and do not provide for self-standing reactions to treaty breaches, they are left to one side here.

[32] See, eg, M Gomaa, *Suspension or Termination of Treaties for Grounds of Breach* (Martinus Nijhoff, 1996); FL Kirgis, 'Some Lingering Questions about Article 60 of the Vienna Convention on the Law of Treaties' (1989) 22 Cornell Intl LJ 549–73; R Pizillo Mazzeschi, 'Termination and Suspension of Treaties for Grounds of Breach' in B Simma and M Spinedi (eds), *United Nations Codification of State Responsibility* (Oceana, 1987) 57–94; DW Greig, 'Reciprocity, Proportionality, and the Law of Treaties' (1993–1994) 34 Virginia J Intl L 295–403; F Capotorti, 'L'Extinction et la Suspension des Traités' (1971-III) 134 Recueil des Cours de l'Académie de Droit International 417–587; E Schwelb, 'Termination or Suspension of a Treaty as a Consequence of its Breach' (1967) 7 Indian J Intl L 309–34; Simma, 'Reflections on Article 60 …' (n 5) 5–83; B Simma and CJ Tams, 'Commentary to Article 60' in O Corten and P Klein (eds), *The Vienna Convention on the Law of Treaties* (OUP, 2011) 1351; B Simma and CJ Tams, 'Reacting against Treaty Breaches' in D Hollis (ed), *The Oxford Guide to Treaties* (OUP, 2012) 576.

[33] The following draws heavily on Simma and Tams, 'Reacting against Treaty Breaches' (n 32) 576.

treaty relationship.[34] Pursuant to Article 72 VCLT, suspension is supposed to be temporary; it 'releases the parties between which the operation of the treaty is suspended from the obligation to perform the treaty in their mutual relations during the period of the suspension'. Termination, by contrast, has permanent effects; it 'releases the parties from any obligation further to perform the treaty' with effects *pro futuro* (Article 70). Contrary to what might be suggested by its title – 'Termination or suspension of the operation of a treaty …' – Article 60 deliberately limits the right of termination, which is available only with respect to bilateral treaties (Article 60(1)) or in the unlikely case of a collective decision by all treaty parties other than the wrongdoing State (Article 60(2)(a)), but *not* for individual responses to breaches of multilateral treaties (Article 60(2)(b) and (2)(c)). The exclusion of termination in the latter two provisions reflects the drafters' opinion that, in the case of multilateral treaties, the interest of third parties in the stability of treaty relations has to be taken into account.[35]

(ii) Suspension and termination are available only in response to a qualified treaty breach. Both presuppose a 'material breach' of the treaty, defined in Article 60(3) as '(*a*) a repudiation of the treaty not sanctioned by the present Convention; or (*b*) the violation of a provision essential to the accomplishment of the object or purpose of the treaty'. The latter definition in particular has been criticized because of its focus on the character of the obligation rather than the *intensity* or *gravity* of the breach.[36] Notwithstanding the precise formulation of the test, it is crucial to note that Article 60 restricts

---

[34] That said, within the framework of the same treaty, responding parties enjoy a wide discretion to choose which parts they wish to suspend, terminate or leave intact. Notably, the VCLT provisions on separability (Article 44(2)) do not apply: see the statement by H Waldock (Expert Consultant), in UN Doc A/CONF.39/11, 237 (para 40), and further Simma and Tams, 'Reacting against Treaty Breaches' (n 32) 585–6. The Vienna debates on the interplay between Articles 44 and 60 (which, at least initially, were controversial) are reproduced in UN Doc A/CONF.39/11, 229–34.

[35] See Yearbook of the ILC (1966) vol II, 255, para 7.

[36] This notably means that Article 60 does not permit responses against grave breaches of treaty provisions that are not essential. Conversely, trivial breaches of essential provisions can constitute material breaches under Article 60(3)(b). For critical comment, see Greig, 'Reciprocity …' (n 32) 342–3; P Malanczuk, *Akehurst's Modern Introduction to International Law* (7th edn, Routledge, 1997) 143; for further details, Simma and Tams, 'Reacting against Treaty Breaches' (n 32) 582–5.

all responses (including the suspension of a treaty). In fact, the Commission in drafting the provision 'was unanimous that the right to terminate or suspend must be limited to cases where the breach is of a serious character'.[37] As in other provisions of the Convention, the overarching concern seems to have been with the continuance and stability of treaty relations; hence responses releasing the party or parties from their obligations (if only temporarily) are not facilitated.

(iii) Article 60's most important contribution to subsequent debates lies in its attempt to regulate which parties to a treaty can react against a prior breach. Paragraph 2 of that provision is the best-preserved relic of Fitzmaurice's ambitious 'structural analysis' of international treaties that – drawing on the work of Triepel and others – sought to distinguish between reciprocal, absolute/objective and interdependent/integral treaty obligations.[38] While Fitzmaurice's classification scheme was not implemented comprehensively, it informs Article 60(2)'s regime of 'standing' to respond to breaches of multilateral treaties. Hence breaches of integral/interdependent obligations in the sense of Article 60(2)(c) VCLT entitle each and every party to a multilateral treaty to suspend the operation of the treaty, as – in line with Fitzmaurice's understanding – they are considered to be based on a concept of 'global reciprocity'.[39] Pursuant to Article 60(2)(b), States 'specially affected' by a breach can respond – the textbook example being a sending State affected by the breach, by the receiving State, of a multilateral obligation in the field of consular or diplomatic law.[40] By implication, breaches of absolute/objective obligations leave obligations of other parties unaffected and do not permit them to suspend, let alone terminate,

---

[37] Yearbook of the ILC (1966) vol II, 255, para 9.

[38] See notably, GG Fitzmaurice, Second Report on the Law of Treaties, Yearbook of the ILC (1957) vol II, 30–31, and 53–4, paras 115–126. For an analysis of Fitzmaurice's 'structural approach', see Simma, *Das Reziprozitätselement im Zustandekommen Völkerrechtlicher Verträge* (Duncker & Humblot, 1972); E Decaux, *La Réciprocité en Droit International* (LGDJ, 1980); Tams, *Enforcing Obligations* Erga Omnes *in International Law* (CUP, 2005) 48–63.

[39] LA Sicilianos, 'The Classification of Obligations and the Multilateral Dimension of the Relations of International Responsibility' (2002) 13 EJIL 1127, 1135. For details, see M Fitzmaurice and O Elias, *Contemporary Issues in the Law of Treaties* (Eleven Intl Pub, 2005) 158–64; Simma and Tams, 'Commentary to Article 60' (n 32) paras 38–9.

[40] See further, Simma and Tams, 'Commentary to Article 60' (n 32) paras 35–7.

the treaty: as noted by Fitzmaurice, the performance, by each State, of these obligations is in no way dependent on the corresponding performance by other States, and compliance does not result in any exchange of benefits.[41] As will be shown below,[42] the classification informing Article 60(2) was to influence the ILC's subsequent work on State responsibility, which to some extent retained Article 60's 'structural approach'.

It is worth noting that Article 60 itself qualifies the structural approach analysis by three ancillary rules: Article 60(1) VCLT clarifies that material breaches within bilateral treaties always affect the other party (even in the case of absolute/objective obligations). Paragraph 2(a) permits collective responses agreed on by all treaty parties (with the exception of the State responsible for the prior material breach). And Article 60(5) ensures that 'provisions relating to the protection of the human person contained in treaties of a humanitarian character, in particular to provisions prohibiting any form of reprisals against persons protected by such treaties', are not suspended or terminated. The latter provision, added only at the Vienna Conference, reinforces the concern with treaty stability.

(iv) Lastly, that same concern led drafters to subject the application of Article 60 to a cumbersome procedure. Article 60(1), (2)(b) and (2)(c) (ie, those provisions addressing individual responses) expressly provide that the responding State is entitled to *invoke* the prior breach *as a ground* for suspension or termination. This formula is intended to clarify that the legal effects of suspension or termination are only entailed according to the procedural rules of Articles 65 to 68 VCLT.[43] This is by no means a mere formality. Rather, Articles 65–68 envisage the notification of claims; the lapse of a three-month period during which other parties can protest; dispute resolution by a method chosen by the responding and protesting parties; and, failing their agreement on a mode of dispute resolution, a process of mandatory conciliation pursuant to VCLT Annex 1.[44] In short, over and above its substantive restrictions (material breach; standing; preference for suspension), Article 60 is

---

[41] See Fitzmaurice, Second Report on the Law of Treaties (n 38) 54, para 126.

[42] Below, III.2.b.

[43] Gomaa, *Suspension* (n 32) 98.

[44] For details, including on the rather dramatic debates surrounding the adoption of Articles 65 *et seq*, see IM Sinclair, *The Vienna Convention on the Law of Treaties* (2nd edn, Manchester UP, 1984) 226–33.

> placed in a 'procedural straightjacket' complicating the implementation of suspension and termination. Predictably, this procedure has not proved particularly popular. In fact there does not seem to be a single instance in which the cumbersome regime of Articles 65–68 has been applied – which in turn supports the view that (unlike Article 60's substantive aspects) the procedural conditions governing its invocation do not reflect customary international law.[45]

* * *

The short summary highlights the problems of Article 60 VCLT. In hindsight, the regime devised may well have been an over-ambitious attempt to 'civilize' inter-State relations. Restricting the availability of suspension and termination, Article 60 certainly helps preserve the stability of treaties. Yet by subjecting treaty suspension and termination to rather stringent conditions, the drafters inadvertently restricted Article 60's 'appeal' to States seeking to respond against another State's treaty breaches. Against that background, the absence of international practice based on Article 60 is indicative. It suggests that while enhancing our understanding of categories of treaty obligations, Article 60 is of limited practical relevance. This in turn corroborates the general assessment of the relevance of the Vienna Convention regime for assessing questions relating to remedies and redress. The major text on the law of treaties not only focuses on one narrow aspect of the broader problem; but insofar as it does address the matter fails to shape and guide international practice. As a consequence, international legal rules relating to remedies and

---

[45] In *Armed Activities on the Territory of the Congo (New Application: 2002) (DRC v Rwanda)*, the ICJ expressly noted that Article 66 (providing for compulsory conciliation) was not 'declaratory of customary international law' (ICJ Rep 2006, 6, para 125). In the *Racke Case*, which concerned the parallel problem whether responses based on the *clausula rebus sic stantibus* would require prior attempts at dispute settlement, the European Court of Justice adopted the same line of reasoning, holding that 'the specific procedural requirements there [ie, in Article 65 VCLT] laid down do not form part of customary international law' (*Racke GmbH and Co v Hauptzollamt Mainz*, Case C-162/96 [1998] ECR I-3655, paras 52–59). The view is controversial though: contrast notably *Gabčíkovo-Nagymaros Project* (ICJ Rep 1997, 7, para 109), where the ICJ noted that '[b]oth Parties agree that Articles 65 to 67 of the Vienna Convention on the Law of Treaties, if not codifying customary law, at least generally reflect customary international law and contain certain procedural principles which are based on an obligation to act in good faith'.

redress almost exclusively have to be sought outside the Vienna Convention regime.

2. Filling Gaps: The General Law of Responsibility

In the absence of relevant VCLT provisions, the general law of responsibility fills the main gaps. Especially as far as remedies are concerned (and to a lesser extent with respect to redress), the law of responsibility is of huge relevance and really shapes international law – subject only to the proviso that specific treaties can always 'opt out'.[46] The relevant provisions, applicable to treaty breaches and other wrongful acts alike (and thus foregoing any special regime applicable to breaches of agreements[47]) are well known and thus can be summarized briefly.

a) A highly influential code of remedies

Rules on remedies form the most influential part of the general regime of responsibility: from the beginning of the ILC's work, they have formed a core aspect of the ILC's clarification effort. And as specific treaties hardly ever opt out of remedies,[48] the ILC's residual rules setting out consequences of treaty breaches are of immense relevance. Drawing on centuries of diplomatic, arbitral and judicial practice, Part Two of the ILC's text lays down a general 'code of remedies' based on a handful of principles. These can be summarized in four propositions.[49]

First, the natural consequence of any breach is that the wrongdoing State must cease its wrongful conduct, if it is still ongoing.[50] Second, apart from cessation, consequences are essentially aimed at remedying

[46] Cf Article 55 ASR: 'These articles do not apply where and to the extent that the conditions for the existence of an internationally wrongful act or the content or implementation of the international responsibility of a State are governed by special rules of international law.'

[47] Cf *supra*, II.3.

[48] See below, III.3.a, for brief comment on the most prominent example.

[49] For a clear assessment, see R Higgins, 'Overview of Part Two of the Articles on State Responsibility' in J Crawford, A Pellet, and S Olleson (eds), *The Law of International Responsibility* (OUP, 2010) 537. The subsequent summary does not address the special regime of remedies considered to apply to qualified breaches of *jus cogens* obligations in the sense of Article 40 ASR. For details see the ILC's commentary to Article 41 ((n 1) 113–16); and further, CJ Tams and A Asteriti, '*Erga omnes, jus cogens*, and their Impact on the Law of Responsibility' in M Evans and P Koutrakos (eds), *The International Responsibility of the European Union* (Hart, 2013) 163.

[50] Article 30(a) ASR and commentary (n 1) 88–91.

past wrongs. The overarching principle is that of reparation,[51] which according to the well-known *Chorzow Factory* formula requires the responsible State to 'wipe out all the consequences' of its wrongful conduct.[52] Third, reparation is traditionally considered to take one (or a combination of) of three forms, whose availability depends on the type of breach in question:[53] restitution (re-establishment of the status quo ante); compensation (payment of indemnities); or satisfaction (in the case of non-material, or moral damage).[54] Of these, restitution is said to enjoy primacy as a legal concept, while compensation is probably the most relevant remedy in practice.[55] Fourth, in addition to these 'backward-oriented' remedies, the general law of State responsibility recognizes a duty to make guarantees and assurances of non-repetition in cases involving repetitive breaches of international law.[56] Unlike reparation, but similar to cessation, this duty, embraced by the International Court of Justice (ICJ) in its *LaGrand* judgment,[57] is future-oriented. It is, however, so far restricted to exceptional circumstances.

Designed in principle to apply to *all* internationally wrongful acts, irrespective of their source or content, the ILC's code of remedies is necessarily vague; concepts such as 'reparation' typically only gain meaning when applied to specific patterns of facts. Yet because of its vagueness, the ILC's general code seems to have stood the test of time. This explains its immense relevance to disputes about treaty breaches. Whenever a State considers its treaty rights to be affected, its response (protest, diplomatic claim, etc) will be couched in the language of the ILC's code of remedies, or at least take up its essence. While debates about whether a treaty has been breached will typically be conducted with reference to the terms of a particular treaty (ie, the primary rules), general concepts like reparation, cessation, compensation, and so on dominate discussions about available remedies. It seems difficult to think of any other question within the scope of the present inquiry in which general rules have greater relevance.

---

51 Articles 31 and 34 ASR and commentaries (n 1) 91–4, 95–6.

52 *Factory at Chorzow*, Merits, PCIJ Series A, No 10, at 47; *Factory at Chorzow*, Jurisdiction, PCIJ Series A, No 9, at 21.

53 Articles 34–7 ASR (n 1) 94–107.

54 *Factory at Chorzow*, Merits (n 52) 47.

55 See, eg, commentary to Article 36 ASR (n 1) 99, paras 2–3.

56 Article 30(b) ASR and commentary (n 1) 88–91.

57 *LaGrand*, ICJ Rep 1999, 9, paras 124–5.

b) Obtaining redress: controversial rules and their limited impact

The general regime of responsibility also addresses modalities of obtaining redress. However, this aspect of the general regime is rather rudimentary. For once, its focus is on inter-State means of implementing responsibility (thus offering nothing on enforcement by non-State actors,[58] whether international organizations, individuals or investors, or others). As regards the procedures of obtaining redress, the focus is on generally available forms of responses, which exist independently of treaty frameworks. This brings with it a second exclusion: the general law of responsibility provides no guidance on ways of obtaining redress that are peculiar to a particular treaty – such as institutionalized forms of dispute settlement within particular treaty regimes or forms of law enforcement or compliance control within international organizations. These factors restrict the practical relevance of the general law of responsibility insofar as it addresses questions of obtaining redress. Still, the ILC's text is relevant in two respects. First, it sets out general rules governing standing that define who can take (in the ILC's words) 'measures of a relatively formal character'[59] in response to a treaty breach. And second, it regulates one particular 'measure of a relatively formal character' – countermeasures – in more detail.

(i) The rules on *standing* are much discussed, but too often viewed as mysterious. In essence they are based on three fairly simple propositions. First, drawing on the structural analysis of treaty obligations laid down in Article 60(1) and (2) VCLT, Article 42 ASR confirms that States can respond to treaty breaches that affect them in an individual capacity: this is the case for obligations owed to them individually (eg, under bilateral treaties or multilateral

---

[58] In its introductory commentary to Part Three (addressing the invocation of responsibility), the ILC notes:

> Part Three is concerned with the implementation of State responsibility, ie with the entitlement of other States to invoke the international responsibility of the responsible State and with certain modalities of such invocation. The rights that other persons or entities may have arising from a breach of an international obligation are preserved by article 33, paragraph 2. ((n 1) 116)

Article 33(2) ASR provides that: 'This Part is without prejudice to any right, arising from the international responsibility of a State, which may accrue directly to any person or entity other than a State.'

[59] Commentary to Article 42 ASR (n 1) 117, para 2.

treaties requiring to be performed reciprocally).[60] In line with Article 60(2)(c) VCLT, and implementing the curious logic of global reciprocity,[61] the general law of responsibility recognizes a right of all parties to a treaty imposing integral obligations to respond to treaty breaches (Article 42(b)(ii) ASR).[62] All this follows the approach governing the suspension or termination of treaties in response to material breaches, which Article 42 ASR applies 'by analogy'.

Second, unlike Article 42, Article 48 ASR goes beyond the Vienna Convention *acquis*. In fact, it moves from the restrictive to the very liberal. Whereas the general law of treaties effectively excludes individual responses to treaty breaches affecting objective/absolute obligations,[63] the general law of responsibility – at least according to the ILC's approach[64] – recognizes a broadly formulated right of all treaty parties to respond to breaches of obligations 'owed to a group of States … , and … established for the protection of a collective interest of the group'.[65] As the ILC's commentary makes clear, 'collective interest treaties' are intended 'to foster a common interest, over and above any interests of the States concerned individually'.[66] By way of illustration, it refers to 'the environment or security of a region (eg a regional nuclear-free-zone treaty or a regional system for the protection of human rights)'.[67] With respect to all of these treaties, each and every treaty party is entitled to respond to a treaty breach and demand a cessation of ongoing treaty breaches and reparation in the interest of the main beneficiaries of the obligation.[68]

---

60 Article 42(a) and (b)(i) ASR. The link with Article 60 VCLT is acknowledged in para 4 of the commentary to that provision (n 1) 117.

61 Sicilianos, 'Classification of Obligations …' (n 39) 1135.

62 The provision only covers exceptional cases though: cf paras 13–15 of the commentary to Article 42 (n 1) 119.

63 *Supra*, III.1.

64 Article 48 is often considered to be an instance of progressive development: see para 12 of the commentary to Article 48 (n 1) 127 (with respect to Article 48(2)(b)); and further, J Crawford, 'Responsibility for Breaches of Communitarian Norms: An Appraisal of Article 48 of the ILC Articles on Responsibility' in D Erasmus-Khan et al (eds), *From Bilateralism to Community Interest: Essays in Honour of Judge Bruno Simma* (OUP, 2010) 221.

65 Article 48(1) ASR.

66 Para 7 of the commentary to Article 48 (n 1) 127.

67 Para 7 of the commentary to Article 48 (n 1) 127.

68 Article 48(2) ASR.

Third, while details of Articles 42 and 48 have been controversially discussed, their scope of application is hardly ever analysed – and if so, only with respect to one particular coercive means of seeking redress, namely countermeasures. For present purposes, a more fundamental point is relevant. It is important to reiterate that the rules of standing only apply to the formal invocation of responsibility. By implication, less formal forms of responding to treaty breaches are not governed by Articles 42 and 48, but are generally available. As the matter is often ignored, the relevant section of the ILC's commentary merits to be reproduced:

> A State does not invoke the responsibility of another State merely because it criticizes that State for a breach and calls for observance of the obligation, or even reserves its rights or protests. ... There is in general no requirement that a State which wishes to protest against a breach of international law by another State or remind it of its international responsibilities in respect of a treaty or other obligation by which they are both bound should establish any specific title or interest to do so. Such informal diplomatic contacts do not amount to the invocation of responsibility unless and until they involve specific claims by the State concerned, such as for compensation for a breach affecting it, or specific action such as the filing of an application before a competent international tribunal, or even the taking of countermeasures. In order to take such steps, ie to invoke responsibility in the sense of the articles, some more specific entitlement is needed.[69]

The statement, while made in the specific context of the invocation of responsibility, is important in that it affirms the need to distinguish between responses requiring some form of legal entitlement, and inherently permissible responses to treaty breaches.[70] It also suggests that only a State contemplating a formal and severe response would be required to establish a 'specific title or interest'.[71] The ILC's commentary refers to countermeasures, which involve the violation of the responding State's obligations, to formal diplomatic claims and (rather curiously, as the matter is surely one for the relevant dispute settlement regime to regulate) to the 'filing of an application before a competent international tribunal'.[72] Yet such formal responses are fairly rare. In most cases, treaty breaches prompt responses within the framework of 'informal diplomatic

[69] See para 2 of the commentary to Article 42 ASR (n 1) 117.

[70] The point is addressed in Simma and Tams, 'Reacting against Treaty Breaches' (n 32) 580.

[71] Para 2 of the commentary to Article 42 ASR (n 1) 117.

[72] Para 2 of the commentary to Article 42 ASR (n 1) 117.

contacts'.[73] As the ILC's statement usefully affirms, these – as well as other forms of unfriendly acts – fall below the threshold of gravity requiring legal regulation. Protests, expressions of concern, demarches, and so on are not subjected to any general restriction; they do not require the responding State to establish any legal entitlement, but are always available. This in turn restricts the practical impact of the ILC's text as far as means of obtaining redress for treaty breaches are concerned: not only does the ILC regime 'bypass' responses recognised in specific treaties (which do not depend on the general law of responsibility); what is more, it does not regulate non-formal forms of responding to breaches, which are generally permissible.

(ii) Countermeasures are the one means of obtaining redress that the general law of responsibility regulates in some detail. While countermeasures are a relatively rare phenomenon today, their legal regime (leaving aside controversies relating to third-party countermeasures in defence of collective interests[74]) is relatively settled – not the least because of the ILC's work on the matter.[75] In essence, the ILC's text affirms the traditional understanding of countermeasures as a flexible concept permitting the decentralized use of proportionate coercion against wrongful conduct. For present purposes, the differences between countermeasures and treaty law responses based on Article 60 VCLT are striking.

First, unlike responses based on Article 60 VCLT, countermeasures can be taken against any internationally wrongful act, including *any* breach of a treaty. There is no threshold requirement requiring a breach to be 'material'.[76] This means that, even within the field of treaty breaches, countermeasures have a much wider scope of application than responses based on Article 60.

Second, unlike treaty-based responses, States enjoy an extremely wide margin of discretion in choosing how to respond to treaty breaches via countermeasures. Their aim must be to 'induce the wrongdoing State to comply with its obligations under international law';[77] yet within those limits, responding States are free to

---

73 Para 2 of the commentary to Article 42 ASR (n 1) 117.

74 On which see Article 54 ASR with commentary (n 1) 137–9; and the discussion in Tams, *Enforcing Obligations* Erga Omnes (n 38) 198–247.

75 A succinct summary of the law can be found in J Crawford, *Brownlie's Principles of Public International Law* (8th edn, OUP, 2012) 585–9.

76 Contrast Article 60(2) VCLT discussed in III.1.

77 *Gabčíkovo* (n 45), para 85; Article 49(1) ASR.

calibrate their response: countermeasures thus need not be restricted to the non-performance of obligations *under the same treaty*.[78] A responding State can respond against treaty breaches notably by violating its obligations towards the targeted State under *other treaties*, or indeed under *general international law*. The law of countermeasures does not presuppose any nexus: to give just two examples, a breach of a bilateral treaty on customs cooperation may be met with economic sanctions violating World Trade Organization (WTO) law, just as violations of diplomatic immunity may prompt the freezing of assets.

Third, because of this flexibility, the general regime of responsibility contains broader exclusionary rules than Article 60(5) VCLT.[79] As clarified in Article 50 ASR, countermeasures do not justify the non-performance of obligations imposed by rules of *jus cogens* and cannot be employed to disrupt agreed modalities of dispute settlement or diplomatic relations.[80] More generally (though difficult to apply in practice), 'the effects of a countermeasure must be commensurate with the injury suffered';[81] in other words: countermeasures must be proportionate.[82] This indeed is a crucial limitation, which would seem necessary to keep countermeasures acceptable.

Finally, compared to the Vienna Convention rules on suspension and termination, the regime of countermeasures deliberately refrains from imposing far-reaching procedural preconditions akin to Articles 65–68 VCLT. To be sure, the responding State must give 'advance warning' and cannot resort to countermeasures pending institutionalized dispute settlement proceedings.[83] However, beyond

---

78 For a discussion of whether 'reciprocal countermeasures' should be subject to an autonomous regime, see J Crawford, Second Report on State Responsibility, UN Doc A/CN.4/498, at paras 327–9; and the separate opinion of Judge Simma in the *Macedonian-Greek* dispute before the ICJ: *Application of the Interim Accord of 13 September 1995 (the former Yugoslav Republic of Macedonia v Greece)*, ICJ Rep 2011, 695.

79 On which see *supra*, III.1.

80 Article 50 ASR with commentary (n 1) 131–4.

81 Article 51 ASR; and cf the ICJ's judgment in *Gabčíkovo* (n 45) paras 85–7.

82 For details, see R O'Keefe, 'Proportionality' in J Crawford, A Pellet, and S Olleson (eds), *The Law of International Responsibility* (OUP, 2010) 1157.

83 Article 52 ASR. Contrast the much more ambitious designs by the ILC's (then) Special Rapporteur Gaetano Arangio Ruiz, Fourth Report on State Responsibility, Yearbook of the ILC (1992) vol II, Part 1, 1; and ibid, Fifth

> these minimum requirements, the general law of responsibility deliberately refrains from making resort to countermeasures dependent on the prior exhaustion of dispute settlement procedures. Unlike in the field of treaty law, the Commission's concern when drafting the regime of countermeasures was to avoid the 'choking' of coercive responses.

* * *

When it comes to determining what amounts to a treaty breach, the general law of responsibility merely establishes a framework for analysis. With respect to remedies and forms of obtaining redress, the general regime is of much greater practical relevance. As regards redress, the ILC lays down residual rules, which can apply in the absence of specific provisions, and in that respect remain important. More importantly, the ILC's text takes the relevant decisions on remedies. To some extent, the greater relevance of general rules reflects the unwillingness of treaty drafters to formulate treaty-specific remedies, which simply leaves more room for general (default) rules. Conversely, the wide acceptance of a general code of remedies has relieved treaty drafters of the need to formulate treaty-specific remedies in each and every treaty. It is in the field of remedies that the legal regime governing treaty breaches and responses has progressed most towards the formulation of general standards.

3. Filling Gaps (continued): Special Treaty Regimes

As the general regime is of considerable reach and importance, special treaty rules on remedies and redress are not as dominant as they are with respect to identifying treaty breaches. Still, of course, specific treaties can opt out of, or clarify, the general regime, which is residual after all.[84] In assessing the relevance of such opt-out rules, it is necessary to distinguish between the field of remedies (where they are rare) and rules on obtaining redress (where special rules are common).

a) Remedies

With respect to remedies, treaties by and large do not provide for detailed and express rules. For the most part (though perhaps curiously) treaties

---

Report on State Responsibility, Yearbook of the ILC (1993) vol II, Part 1, 1 (proposals for draft Article 12 and a 'dispute settlement annex').

[84] Conceptually, this is unproblematic: both Article 60(4) VCLT and Article 55 ASR recognize the primacy of special (treaty) rules.

rarely expressly spell out the consequences of treaty breaches; hence the relevance of the general code of remedies. Some prominent treaty frameworks (such as regional human rights treaties[85]) mention particular remedies, but typically they are not construed to exclude the general regime.[86]

Of the major multilateral treaty frameworks, WTO law is the exception that proves the rule. Unlike other relevant treaties, the WTO Dispute Settlement Understanding (DSU) contains detailed provisions regarding remedies.[87] The relevant rules setting out the available remedies can be found in Articles 3.7 and 19.1 DSU. The general thrust of these provisions is that remedies are future-oriented. Article 3.7 stipulates that the first objective of the dispute settlement system is 'to secure the withdrawal of the measures concerned if these are found to be inconsistent with the provisions of any covered agreements'.[88]

Article 19.1 DSU clarifies that panels or the Appellate Body should recommend 'that the Member concerned bring the measure into conformity with that agreement'. WTO dispute settlement organs disagree on whether restitution and compensation (ie, the key remedies available under the general law of responsibility[89]) are completely excluded or available in exceptional cases.[90] What they agree on is that WTO remedies are decidedly future-oriented; they aim at re-establishing suitable conditions for trade. This stands in marked contrast to the general approach to reparation, which according to the oft-cited *Chorzow Factory*

---

[85] See, eg, Article 41 European Convention on Human Rights (ECHR, 1950) (mentioning 'just satisfaction'); or Article 63 of the Inter-American Convention of Human Rights (ACHR, 1969) and Article 46 of the Banjul Charter (1981) (both referring, amongst other things, to 'fair compensation').

[86] While the European Convention merely mentions 'just satisfaction', other treaties typically contain references to reparation or other remedies. More generally, through their jurisprudence, human rights courts and treaty bodies have developed a 'right to a remedy' of considerable specificity. See M Nowak, 'The Right of Victims of Gross Human Rights Violations to Reparation' in F Coomans et al (eds), *Rendering Justice to the Vulnerable: Liber Amicorum in Honour of Theo van Boven* (Kluwer Law International, 2003) 203, for a survey.

[87] The following discussion focuses on remedies available in the case of violation complaints, thus leaving to one side the somewhat different rules applicable to non-violation complaints and situation complaints. For details, sec M Trebilcock, R Howse, and A Eliason, *The Regulation of International Trade* (4th edn, Routledge, 2013) 215–16.

[88] Cf Article 3(7) DSU.

[89] See *supra*, III.2.

[90] See Trebilcock, Howse, and Eliason, *Regulation* (n 87) 205–6, and Tams, 'Unity …' (n 22) 447–9, for brief comment.

dictum requires responsible States to 'wipe out' all consequences of the wrongful act.[91]

b) Obtaining redress

While express clauses on remedies are rare, many treaties go to some length in spelling out procedures for redressing treaty breaches that go beyond (and are often much more refined than) general concepts such as countermeasures, protests, or treaty-based responses.[92] These treaty-based regimes are extremely diverse: while treaty drafters have shown little creativity in formulating remedies, they regularly use their imagination when negotiating mechanisms for obtaining redress, each of them tailor-made and fitting the demands of a particular treaty. The subsequent paragraphs can only hint at the most common categories of particular rules. Four types of special provisions stand out.

(i) Bi- and multilateral treaties often establish mechanisms of institutionalized dispute settlement: these can be regime-specific courts or tribunals with specialized jurisdiction (such as regional courts in fields such as human rights or economic integration, or the WTO dispute settlement organs), but also other treaty bodies (such as commissions, councils, conferences and meetings of parties, principal organs of international organizations, etc). Treaties that do not establish their 'own' institutions frequently rely on existing bodies (established by another treaty) as 'agencies' of dispute resolution – whether the ICJ under the system of compromissory clauses[93] or the Security Council in respect of treaties administered by the International Atomic Energy Agency (IAEA).[94] In fact, as the Vienna Convention regime deals with treaty breaches only in passing and as the law of responsibility addresses only generally available forms of redress, *any* response to a treaty breach that involves an international institution (whether as the body responding itself or as an impartial authority involved in a dispute settlement process instituted by another State) must be based on some form of particular procedure. Especially within multilateral treaty regimes, particular procedures are of central relevance and

---

[91] PCIJ Series A, No 10, at 47. Cf *supra*, III.2.a.

[92] Chinkin would seem to understate the relevance of these particular rules when noting that '[c]ertain agreements may provide for the parties' options in the case of breach': 'Nonperformance …' (n 3) 432.

[93] See Article 36(1) of the ICJ Statute (1946).

[94] See Article XII of the IAEA Statute (1956).

largely eclipse the generally available forms of redress recognized under the general regime of State responsibility.

(ii) Even where treaties do not establish institutions, they often expressly recognize the right of States to respond to treaty breaches in a particular manner. The right of self-defence under Article 51 UNC is but a prominent example of such expressly recognized responses to a qualified breach ('armed attack'). Early generations of multilateral cooperation treaties used to make express provision for a right to suspend treaty benefits in response to prior breaches:[95] these clauses are similar to Article 60 VCLT but typically not as over-regulated. More recently, conditionality clauses in the field of human rights have become quite common:[96] many development aid treaties today justify the suspension of development aid in response to serious human rights breaches;[97] similar approaches have been adopted under the Kyoto Protocol (1997) and the 1973 Convention on the International Trade in Endangered Species (CITES).[98] Just as with procedures involving treaty-based institutions, these responses are tailored to the demands of a particular treaty regime.

(iii) In addition, it may be briefly noted that a considerable number of treaties expressly regulate questions of standing. Notably, in a surprising number of instances, treaties expressly recognize a general right of each and every treaty party to react against a treaty breach: this is common under most human rights treaties,[99] but also

---

[95] See Article 35 of the 1957 Postal Convention (364 UNTS 3); and cf similar clauses in Article 8 of the 1923 Statute of the International Regime of Maritime Ports (58 LNTS 301); or Article 4, para 4 of the 1956 Multilateral Agreement of Non-Scheduled Air Services in Europe (310 UNTS 229.

[96] For details on the most prominent categories, see L Bartels, *Human Rights Conditionality in the EU's International Agreements* (OUP, 2005).

[97] See, eg, Articles 96 and 97 of the 2000 Cotonou Agreement between EU and ACP States (OJ 2000, L 317/3).

[98] A similar approach is followed under a number of multilateral agreements in the environmental field: thus the Kyoto Protocol and CITES, to give just two examples, envisage trade sanctions in response to treaty breaches. Admittedly, however, these treaty sanctions typically presuppose an institutional decision. For comment, see CJ Tams, 'Individual States as Guardians of Community Interests' in D Erasmus-Khan et al (eds), *From Bilateralism to Community Interest: Essays in Honour of Judge Bruno Simma* (OUP, 2011) 398–9.

[99] See, eg, (with differences of degree) the various provisions for inter-State complaints under human rights treaties (Article 33 ECHR, Article 45 ACHR, Article 47 Banjul Charter).

under conventions elaborated within the framework of the International Labour Organization,[100] treaties providing for regional economic integration (such as the Treaty on the Functioning of the European Union (TFEU)[101]), and the four 1949 Geneva Conventions.[102] In many instances, the general right of standing is linked to a particular enforcement mechanism (such as access to the Court of Justice of the European Union in inter-State proceedings under Article 259 TFEU); in others it is not linked to any particular means of obtaining redress (eg, under the 'ensure respect' clause of the Geneva Conventions). In very few cases are the express clauses actually used; most of them exist on the books only, as States only rarely rely on formal means of invoking another State's responsibility for breaches of collective interest obligations. Yet the existence of such liberal clauses suggests that a provision like Article 48 ASR (recognizing a broad right to invoke responsibility for breaches of public interest treaty obligations) is less dramatic or unusual than some of its critics suggest.[103]

(iv) Finally, as regards the generally available means of obtaining redress, it is worth noting that some treaties restrict or exclude the customary right to take countermeasures. This presupposes a functioning regime that provides for treaty-specific and effective mechanisms to address breaches; so it cannot lightly be assumed. Very rarely, treaties expressly declare 'their' treaty-specific responses to be exclusive: Article 344 TFEU (ex-Art 292 of the Treaty Establishing the European Community of *MOX Plant* fame) is an example in point,[104] Article 27(1) of the International Convention on the Settlement of Investment Disputes (ICSID, 1965) could be read to

---

100 Article 26 of the ILO Constitution.

101 Article 259 TFEU.

102 See Common Article 1 of the 1949 Geneva Conventions.

103 Analysing a broad sample of treaty clauses, F Voeffray rightly concludes that the idea of an *actio popularis* '*ne revêt … plus un caractère exceptionnel*' (*L'actio popularis – ou la défense de l'intérêt collectif devant les juridictions internationals* (Presses universitaires de France, 2004), at 383).

104 Article 344 TFEU provides: 'Member States undertake not to submit a dispute concerning the interpretation or application of the Treaties to any method of settlement other than those provided for therein.' See Case C-459/03, *Commission v Ireland (Mox Plant)*, 2006 ECR I-4635.

entail the same effect.[105] In the absence of express provisions, ambitious and effective dispute resolution systems could furthermore exclude 'archaic' responses like countermeasures implicitly. For example, the World Trade Organization's elaborate system of dispute resolution, which includes access to dispute settlement bodies and recognizes the right of member States to suspend treaty benefits on a reciprocal basis if negotiations have failed,[106] would be undermined if countermeasures under general international law were still available. Hence in the *Section 301* case, the Panel considered the DSU to 'prevent member States from unilaterally resolving their disputes in respect of WTO rights and obligations'.[107]

* * *

The examples highlight the importance of particular treaty rules. Their role may not be quite as crucial as in relation to the determination of breaches: international law could function on the basis of the general regime. And indeed, when it comes to remedies, most treaties are content to have the general remedies apply by default. But when it comes to means of obtaining redress, the general regime is not suited to provide guidance for a world of multilateral treaty regimes. Ambitious regimes for redressing treaty breaches have to be agreed at the level of specific treaties, and States regularly make use of that option.

IV. CONCLUDING THOUGHTS: A RESEARCH AGENDA

The preceding discussion indicates how and where international law seeks to regulate treaty breaches and responses thereto. The main findings can be summarized in four points.

---

105 Article 27(1) ICSID provides:

> No Contracting State shall give diplomatic protection, or bring an international claim, in respect of a dispute which one of its nationals and another Contracting State shall have consented to submit or shall have submitted to arbitration under this Convention, unless such other Contracting State shall have failed to abide by and comply with the award rendered in such dispute.

106 See Article 22 DSU.

107 *United States – Sections 301/310 of the Trade Act of 1974,* Panel Report of 22 December 1999, WT/DS/152/R, paras 7.35–7.46. For a discussion, see Trebilcock, Howse, and Eliason, *Regulation* (n 87) 213–14.

First, general rules of international law have no more than a modest impact on what amounts to a treaty breach. The law of State responsibility, and to a lesser extent the law of treaties, provides no more than a few simple tools designed to help interpret and apply provisions of particular treaties; and they affect the outcome of that process only in a limited way. In essence, notwithstanding decades of debates about general rules of treaty law and State responsibility, what amounts to a treaty breach remains a matter for the special (primary) treaty rules.

Second, as far as remedies are concerned, the general rules of treaty law and State responsibility are more prescriptive. While the concrete consequences triggered by a treaty breach depend on the type of wrong committed, the law of State responsibility clarifies which remedies are available. States retain the power to make choices (such as the possibility to opt for future-oriented remedies, as under WTO law), but the general regime takes relevant decisions – emphasizing the primacy of restitution, formulating a far-reaching principle of reparation aimed to facilitate a return to the status quo ante, and (more recently) recognizing the possibility of obtaining guarantees and assurances against repetition. The general law of treaties takes a more selective approach, focusing on the impact of breaches on the underlying treaty relationship. Agreed after lengthy debates, Article 60 VCLT privileges the stability of treaty relations by restricting the possibility of treaty suspension and termination. Yet practice has ignored the restrictions of this provision, which is best seen as an over-ambitious attempt to formulate a general rule.

Third, the general law of State responsibility formulates principles governing redress for treaty breaches. On balance, these leave States considerable room for responding – through informal means, but also by way of countermeasures, a private law enforcement mechanism that international law continues to accept. Notwithstanding their relative breadth, the general rules, however, remain ill-suited to more integrated treaty regimes: within these, States have long felt the need for more sophisticated forms of responses and made provision for reactions as diverse as collective sanctions, binding dispute resolution or other forms of compliance control. Designed to cover treaty breaches and other wrongful acts, the general law of State responsibility has little to say on such treaty-specific means of obtaining redress. Applicable across the board, the general regime fails to capture the diversity of responses against treaty breaches, especially in integrated treaty regimes.

Finally, all things considered, it is clear that the regime of treaty breaches and responses is a mix of general (meta-)rules and particular provisions: the existence of the former allows us to think of the international regime as a system; the latter permit variety and tailor-made solutions. What the preceding discussion highlights is that, in the normative mix, the general law of treaties plays a rather modest role. The central choices explaining this state of affairs may be briefly recalled: (i) the drafters' decision to address treaty breaches, their consequences, and the modalities for redressing them within the framework of responsibility (rather as part of a special regime of responsibility for treaty breaches); and (ii) their unwillingness to engage with the substance of treaty obligations, let alone formulate core obligations characteristic of common types of treaties. Both decisions were plausible at the time of drafting and remain plausible today. However, they limit the relevance of the Vienna Convention regime to an essential question of treaty law and practice and bear out Sir Ian Sinclair's more general observation that the Commission – when formulating the general law of treaties – opted against 'the broader canvas in order to concentrate on the domestic minutiae'.[108]

* * *

In addition to 'play[ing] an important rôle in both international law and foreign office practice',[109] treaty breaches and responses have been of interest to legal scholars for decades. Yet existing research focuses on selected issues while leaving others largely to the side. Given its limited practical relevance, Article 60 VCLT perhaps has rather been 'over-researched', just as the ILC's work, keenly followed by academic commentators, has yielded a wealth of research on specific aspects of State responsibility.[110] While questions of interpretation remain to be addressed, the preceding discussion suggests that there may be some virtue in exploring some of the 'broader canvas' issues which the present contribution has touched upon (dare one say 'canvassed'). Perhaps there is room for attempts at delineating categories of treaties, distinguished by their substantive content – perhaps resulting in common, residual, rules applicable to categories of treaties in fields such as investment protection, economic cooperation, boundary delimitation, etc? Perhaps, it might also be possible to distil general principles applicable to the enforcement of treaty rules, which go beyond Part Three of the ILC's Articles on State

---

108 Sinclair, *Vienna Convention* (n 44) 244 ('the Commission had deliberately decided to paint in the style of Pieter de Hooch rather than Titian or Verone').

109 Bilder, 'Breach of Treaty ...' (n 2) 193.

110 As James Crawford has noted, 'The [ILC] Articles have encoded the way in which we think about responsibility': J Crawford, 'The International Court of Justice and the Law of State Responsibility' in CJ Tams and J Sloan (eds), *The Development of International Law by the International Court of Justice* (OUP 2013) 71, at 81.

Responsibility? And finally, a serious engagement with the notion of treaty breach – situated in between the law of treaties and the law of State responsibility – could very well result in a clearer and more informed understanding of the interaction between these two major fields of international regulation. All this supposes a willingness to step back from 'the domestic minutiae' and look at 'the broader canvas'.[111] But after decades of often rather granulated debates about specific rules of treaty law and State responsibility, and thirteen years after the completion of the ILC's Articles on State Responsibility, this might be a refreshing change of perspective.

[111] Cf Sinclair, *Vienna Convention* (n 44) 244.

17. Succession to treaties and the inherent limits of international law

Andreas Zimmermann and James G. Devaney

I. INTRODUCTION

It is almost mandatory to start any chapter on State succession to treaties by reasserting that it is one of the most opaque areas of international law, lacking both a basis in consistent State practice[1] as well as satisfactory theoretical underpinnings.[2] Whilst this may be a mere statement of the obvious, today the basic point remains, namely that the law on State

[1] The International Law Commission (ILC) commented in 1974 that '[a] close examination of State practice afforded no convincing evidence of any general doctrine by reference to which the various problems of succession in respect of treaties could find their appropriate solution', Yearbook of the ILC (1974) vol II, Part I, para 51.

[2] A Hall, *A Treatise on International Law* (Higgins, 1924) 116, remarking that the subject of State succession generally is 'one upon which writers on international law are generally unsatisfactory. They are incomplete, and they tend to copy one another'; L Caflisch, 'The Law of State Succession Theoretical Observations' (1963) 10 Netherlands Intl L Rev 337, 337, remarking that 'the abundant judicial and diplomatic practice on State succession has always been – and still is – contradictory and obscure'; see also M Virally, Preface to Huu Tru Nguyen, *Quelques Problèmes de Succession d'États Concernant le Viet-Nam* (Établissements Émile Bruylant, 1970); see inter alia G Jellinek, *Allgemeine Staatslehre* (vol 1, O Häring, 1905) 278; W Fiedler, 'Die Konventionen zum Recht der Staatensukzession' Ein Beitrag der ILC zur Entwicklung eines 'Modern International Law' (1981) 24 GYIL 9, 9 ('one of the most difficult, confusing and among the least settled areas of international law' ['*eines der schwierigsten, unübersichtlichsten und mit am wenigsten geklärten Bereiche des Völkerrechts*']); J Weiss, 'Succession of States in Respect of Treaties Concluded by the European Communities' (1994) SEW 661, 670 ('still one of the least settled, almost chaotic areas of international law'); see also in the same vein the German Constitutional Court, BVerfGE vol 96, 68, 79 ('among the most disputed and least secure parts of international law' ['*einen der umstrittensten und unsichersten Teile des gesamten Völkerrechts*'] referring to A Verdross and B Simma, *Universelles Völkerrecht* (Duncker & Humblot, 1984) 608).

succession in relation to treaties is, to say the least, far from settled.[3] In fact, despite significant codification attempts undertaken by the international community in the 1970s, and the substantial body of literature on State succession generally, there continues to exist 'an almost total doctrinal schism'.[4] Today one might still get the impression that every 'international lawyer seeking a way out of this marshland is as likely as ever to be led into the centre of the miry bog itself'.[5]

With the impression that 'the more that is written on the subject, the less clear or coherent the whole becomes'[6] very much in mind, this contribution nevertheless undertakes the (Sisyphean) task to provide clarity and a straightforward analysis of this often vexing area of international law starting with an analysis of the very notion of State succession[7] before then turning to the historical development of the concept in relation to treaties.[8] Next, attention is turned to the Vienna Convention on Succession of States in Respect of Treaties 1978 (VCSST) and the extent to which the contents of this convention have been affirmed by State practice since its adoption in 1978 is examined.[9] Finally, the current state of the law on the matter will be considered before some potential avenues for possible reform and future development are explored.

---

3 Jennings has stated that the law of State succession '[i]s a subject which presents such a rich diversity of practice as to give some plausibility to a surprisingly varied range of theoretical analysis and doctrine', RY Jennings, 'General Course on Principles of International Law' (1967) Vol 121 Recueil des Cours de l'Académie de Droit International 437; Jellinek stated that there are very 'few points of international law as little clarified as the law of State succession', Jellinek, *Allgemeine Staatslehre* (n 2) 271; see also O Dörr, *Die Inkorporation als Tatbestand der Staatensukzession* (Duncker & Humblot, 1995) 21 and compare H Beemelmans, 'State Succession in International Law: Remarks on Recent Theory and State Praxis' (1997) 15 BU Intl LJ 71, 243, and K Doehring and G Ress, 'Diplomatische Immunität und Drittstaaten' (1999) 37 AVR 68.

4 MCR Craven, 'The Problem of State Succession and the Identity of States under International Law' (1998) 9 EJIL 142, 143.

5 T Maluwu, 'Succession to Treaties in Post-Independence Africa' (1992) AJICL 791; see also Udokang's statement in 1972 that the international law of State succession is no clearer than it was in the eighteenth, nineteenth and even the first half of the twentieth centuries still to some extent ringing true, O Udokang, *Succession of New States to International Treaties* (Oceana, 1972) 164.

6 Craven, 'The Problem of State Succession …' (n 4) 143.

7 See below at Section I.2 *et seq.*

8 See below at Section II *et seq.*

9 See below at Section IV *et seq.*

1. Uncertain Nature of the Current Rules on State Succession to Treaties

There are numerous factors which contribute to the uncertain nature of the current rules on State succession to treaties. First, State succession is inherently highly political given that whether a State is bound by a conventional obligation upon succession largely depends on recognition of that position as a successor State by other States.

Second, instances of State succession often occur in the wake of armed conflicts (such as was the case of the breakdown of the former Yugoslavia) which can separate successor States from legal counsel and from the archives in most cases located in the respective capital of its predecessor State (such as in the case of South Sudan). Successor States, which in many cases are uncertain of the law and the appropriate procedures to be followed, are then open to being manipulated by third States with vested interests in the approach to, and eventual outcome of, the incident of State succession.[10]

Third, due to the fact that the law on State succession (both in relation to treaties specifically and more generally) depends on instances of State succession, State practice is relatively sparse.

Fourth, there are a large number of actors who have a say in shaping the law in any given instance of State succession such as, apart from States, inter alia, depositaries of treaties[11] and human rights treaty bodies.[12]

Fifth, and perhaps the most significant contributing factor, is the, at least partially, ideology-driven attempt at codifying the law that resulted in the 1978 Vienna Convention on the Succession of States in Respect of Treaties.[13] From the outset, the limitations of the Vienna Convention were clear to the ILC. For instance, the Convention itself would not be binding on a successor State until it took specific steps to become itself a party to that Convention in one form or another. Even then, however, 'the

---

[10] A Boyle and J Crawford, *Annex A Opinion: Referendum on the Independence of Scotland – International Law Aspects* (Annex to Scotland Analysis: Devolution and the Implications of Scottish Independence; Presented to Parliament by the Secretary of State for Scotland by Command of Her Majesty, February 2013, www.official-documents.gov.uk, accessed 28 November 2013).

[11] See below at Section VII *et seq*.

[12] See below at Section V.3 *et seq*.

[13] Craven, 'The Problem of State Succession …' (n 4) 151; succession was specifically excluded from the scope of the Vienna Convention on the Law of Treaties by Article 73.

convention would not be binding upon it in respect of any act or fact which took place before the date on which it became a party'.[14] In addition, no other State would be bound by the Convention vis-à-vis a successor State until said new State had taken steps to become a party.[15] As such it was clear that the Convention itself was not (primarily) meant to regulate the law of State succession to treaties by way of binding treaty obligations, but rather sought to clarify, codify and progressively develop the law as a whole through attracting the accession of a significant number of States – a task only partly achieved.[16]

It remains unclear to what extent the VCSST has been successful in codifying or progressively developing the law on State succession regarding treaties. Thus far there are twenty-two parties to the Convention, only a handful more than the already small number required to bring the Convention into force.[17] The success of the Convention and to what extent its provisions have found support in State practice will be examined in greater detail below.[18] However, for now it is argued that rather than providing the intended clarification of customary law, the VCSST was undermined by ideological pressures exerted by States that had gained independence during decolonization who then exerted great pressure on the ILC to ensure the inclusion of a special regime for 'newly independent states' in the Convention.[19] Being drafted in the shadow of,

---

[14] Yearbook of the ILC (1981) vol II, Part II, 9.

[15] Ibid.

[16] Craven, 'The Problem of State Succession …' (n 4) 151; Yearbook of the ILC (1981) vol II, Part II, 9.

[17] United Nations Treaty Collection, Chapter XXIII, Law of Treaties, http://treaties.un.org/Pages/ViewDetails.aspx?src=TREATY&mtdsg_no=XXIII-2&chapter=23&lang=en, accessed 28 November 2013; M Craven, *The Decolonization of International Law: State Succession and the Law of Treaties* (OUP, 2009) 208, 'Many States', he reported, had regarded the Vienna Conference as 'altogether unimportant and not worth expenditure of public funds'; see also DP O'Connell, 'Reflections on the State Succession Convention' (1979) 39 ZaöRV 725, 726.

[18] See below at Section IV *et seq.*

[19] The International Law Commission was instructed to study the subject in light of 'the views of States which have achieved independence since the Second World War', indeed, '[t]he central theme running through the whole process of codification, of course, was the place assumed by decolonization within it. It was evident to many from the outset that there was an inevitable tension between the idea of seeking to codify and develop rules of succession to govern future cases of political transformation, at the same time as concentrating upon the particular experience of decolonization whose course was almost run', Craven, *The Decolonization of International Law* (n 17) 15 (quoting UNGA Res 1902

and under the influence of, decolonization ultimately meant that its provisions were of limited utility in the context of situations such as the break-up of the USSR and the former Yugoslavia – situations which it turned out were markedly distinct from decolonization.[20] In other words, whilst the Convention was significant in its time as an achievement of the decolonization process by which newly independent States were able to exert sufficient pressure to achieve this goal,[21] it consequently suffers from being a product of its time.

2. The Law of State Succession to Treaties: Why Bother?

There are a number of important factors which nevertheless justify the study of and research on the law of State succession to treaties. The first is that the law in this area seeks to regulate issues that go to the very heart of the international legal order. The underlying rationale of the law of State succession is that, since no new State can exist outside this legal order, it is necessary not only to regulate the creation and recognition of

---

(XVIII), 18 Nov 1963) and the definition of 'newly independent States' had 'been influenced by the application of the principle of self-determination which, according to the contemporary orthodoxy, meant that it was to be largely confined to former colonial dependencies', ibid. Newly independent State was a successor State 'the territory of which immediately before the date of the succession of States was a dependent territory for the international relations of which the predecessor State was responsible', Article 2(1)(f), 1978 Vienna Convention. The ILC stated that the dependent territories it envisaged were colonies, trusteeships, mandates and protectorates, Commentary to Draft Article 2, Yearbook of the ILC (1974) vol II, paras 6–7.

[20] Ibid; for criticism to this effect at the time, see I Sinclair, 'Some Reflections on the Vienna Convention on Succession of States in Respect of Treaties' in EJ Manner (ed), *Essays in Honour of Erik Castren: Celebrating his 75th Birthday, March 20, 1979* (Finnish Branch of the International Law Association, 1978) 181; O'Connell, 'Reflections …' (n 17) 728; Craven, *The Decolonization of International Law* (n 17) 15; eg, Reply of Republic of Hungary in the *Gabčíkovo-Nagymaros Project (Hungary/Slovakia)*, ICJ Rep 1997, 173, para 3.157 (asserting that the 1978 Convention 'is widely regarded as an unsuccessful exercise in international law-making and which does not correspond to subsequent practice').

[21] Craven, *The Decolonization of International Law* (n 17) 212; this stands alongside other achievements of decolonization that today are practically limited including use of force by liberation movements, internationalization of wars of national liberation (Article 1, para 4 Protocol Additional to the Geneva Conventions of 12 August 1949, and Relating to the Protection of Victims of International Armed Conflicts (Protocol I), 8 June 1977).

new States in international law but also to regulate alterations in the 'responsibility for the international relations of territory' to ensure the predictability and stability of the international legal order.[22]

Additionally, whilst the law in this area is undoubtedly highly politicized and context-specific, it remains the case that 'for certain cases general rules and practices can be identified that may serve as a guide for future cases related to succession, even if they may not prove truly determinative'.[23]

Finally, instances of succession tend to come in waves. Even today the law remains the subject of attention in international legal scholarship, as a result of recent instances of succession such as the recent emergence of South Sudan and other entities possibly on the cusp of succession of one form or another.

II. THE DEVELOPMENT OF THE LAW OF STATE SUCCESSION AND THE VCSST

1. Historical Background

State succession is far from a new phenomenon, having been a contentious international legal issue for hundreds of years.[24] As has just been mentioned, State practice suggests that instances of succession come in 'waves', some of the most prominent examples include the wave of State succession in the wake of World War I and the ensuing break-up of the Austro-Hungarian and Ottoman Empires, as well as the transformation of a number of States into the USSR.[25] Similarly, the process of decolonization after World War II saw the emergence of a significant number of States and had a remarkable impact on the law of State succession.[26]

---

[22] G Hafner and G Novak, 'State Succession in Respect of Treaties' in DB Hollis (ed), *The Oxford Guide to Treaties* (1st edn, OUP, 2012) 396.

[23] Ibid; Craven, *The Decolonization of International Law* (n 17) 2.

[24] See, eg, Grotius, *De jure belli et pacis,* lib II, cap ix, tit xii; see further DF Vagts, 'State Succession: The Codifiers' View' (1993) 33 Va J Intl L 275, 277 *et seq*.

[25] See generally A Zimmermann, *Staatennachfolge in Völkerrechtliche Verträge* (Springer, 2000) 81; DP O'Connell, *The Law of State Succession* (vol 5, CUP, 1956) 35.

[26] For a comprehensive overview, see Craven, *The Decolonization of International Law* (n 17); regarding the influence on the law of State succession in respect of treaties, see UN Conference on Succession of States in Respect of Treaties, First Session, Vienna, 4 April–6 May 1977, Official Records, vol 1:

Indeed, the 1978 VCSST emerged towards the very end of the decolonization process with the number of new States coming into existence thereafter dropping off for quite some years.[27] However, following a fairly stable period after the adoption of the Convention in 1978, a further wave came with the end of the Cold War which saw the breakdown of the USSR, the reunification of Germany, the dissolution of Czechoslovakia and the collapse of the Socialist Federal Republic of Yugoslavia. As a result, a subject which could have been seen of only academic interest after the end of decolonization all of a sudden became once more one of the most crucial issues in international law.

The most recent instance of State succession relates to the independence of South Sudan which was admitted to the United Nations (UN) as recently as 4 July 2011.[28] In addition, a number of other States have taken concrete steps which could potentially lead to succession of one form or another.[29]

One particularly noteworthy characteristic of the law of State succession to treaties is its inherently close association with the notion of the sovereign State. The State in international law, the centre of the international legal order ever since the Treaty of Westphalia in 1648, traditionally constituted the exclusive subject of international law and although this has changed somewhat in recent years, the inherently close relationship between the law of State succession and the concept of the State itself could be said to mark out the law in this area as being either somewhat 'traditional' or 'out-dated' depending on one's outlook on these matters. Yet even the law of State succession, an area of international law that was developed exclusively by States until recently, today faces issues that diverge from the traditional. For instance, in relation to the variety of actors in the field who could potentially have a say in shaping the law of State succession, some of the most influential, international organizations and human rights treaty bodies, are non-State

Summary Records of the Plenary Meetings and of the Meetings of the Committee of the Whole (A/CONF.80/16).

27 Hafner and Novak, 'State Succession …' (n 22) 397.

28 UN Doc A/RES/65308.

29 See, for instance, the situation regarding Kosovo, *Accordance with International Law of the Unilateral Declaration of Independence in Respect of Kosovo* (Advisory Opinion) 2010 General List No 141; and the Agreement between the United Kingdom Government and the Scottish Government on a Referendum on Independence for Scotland (Edinburgh 15 October 2012) http://webarchive.nationalarchives.gov.uk/20130109092234/http://www.number10.gov.uk/wp-content/uploads/2012/10/Agreement-final-for-signing.pdf, accessed 28 November 2013.

actors and as such challenge the traditionally State-centric nature of the law on the matter.

Whilst the law will undoubtedly face new challenges and will have to deal with different kinds of influences as the development of the law is increasingly influenced by actors other than States, it is unlikely that this area of international law will fundamentally change. Rather, it is more likely that current principles and doctrine will be adapted to accommodate these new influences instead of succumbing to them. And whilst it may be hoped that increased influence of non-State actors could in some way lead to clarification or increased coherence in the law; it is in fact hard to see how exactly introducing more actors into the interpretation process, each with their own motivations and agendas, could effectively contribute to clarifying the law. Indeed, evidence so far would suggest that further muddying of the water is a more likely result.

What is brought out by this development is that the law of State succession generally, and the norms governing State succession with regard to treaties specifically, have undergone more changes than those seen in other areas of international law, the current uncertain customary status of the 1978 VCSST being the most prominent proof of this.

2. Identity and State Continuity: A Preliminary yet Fundamental Question

Questions of succession to treaties are inextricably bound up with the issue of the identity of a State itself. When analysing issues of State succession it is thus necessary to consider the relationship between State succession on the one hand, and State continuity and identity on the other[30] – a question that is not infrequently overlooked in both State practice and academic writing. Since the law of State succession only comes into play if 'one State [is replaced] by another in the responsibility for the international relations of territory'[31] the law of State succession requires, leaving instances of cession of territory aside, a rupture in the personality of a State.[32] It is therefore fundamentally important to distinguish succession from instances of State identity and continuity,

---

[30] Boyle and Crawford, *Annex A Opinion* (n 10) para 17.

[31] VCSST Article 2(1)(b).

[32] A Zimmermann, 'The International Court of Justice and State Succession to Treaties: Avoiding Principled Answers to Questions of Principle' in CJ Tams and J Sloan (eds), *The Development of International Law by the International Court of Justice* (OUP, 2013) 54.

where treaty obligations continue to apply to the continuing State, albeit in its new form and with regard to a more limited territory.[33]

At the heart of the matter lies the question of how to define the distinction between State continuity and State succession. In other words, how is one to decide whether the predecessor State continues to exist with some changes to its territory and population or whether it has ceased to exist?[34] Whilst straightforward in theory, this distinction is problematic in practice due to the fact that no settled criteria exist to distinguish succession from continuity or identity.[35] Ultimately, 'the whole of the law of State succession depends on this distinction',[36] and as such is based on a notion itself strongly influenced by political considerations.

With regard to the distinction between succession and identity/continuity, State practice confirms that a mere change of territory or government will not affect continuity of States.[37] It is similarly a customary rule that belligerent occupation does not affect State continuity either.[38] By the same token, State practice also indicates that the 'submersion or disappearance' of the organs of the State in question over a substantial period of time will ultimately result in the extinction of that State, provided however (and crucially) that no unlawful act has brought about this submersion in line with the general principle of *ex injuria jus non oritur*.[39]

---

33 Ibid; Boyle and Crawford, *Annex A Opinion* (n 10) paras 18–20.

34 I Ziemele, 'Is the Distinction between State Continuity and State Succession Reality or Fiction? The Russian Federation, the Federal Republic of Yugoslavia and Germany' (2001) 1 BYIL 191, 215; Zimmermann, *Völkerrechtliche Verträge* (n 25) 66.

35 Zimmermann, '... Avoiding Principled Answers to Questions of Principle' (n 32) 54.

36 Ziemele, '... Reality or Fiction? ...' (n 34) 214: J Crawford, *The Creation of States in International Law* (Clarendon Press, 1979) 390.

37 See, for instance, the fact that the loss of former colonies did not bring the nature of the municipal territory into question.

38 V Avedian, 'State Identity, Continuity and Responsibility: The Ottoman Empire, the Republic of Turkey and the Armenian Genocide' (2012) 23 EJIL, 797, 800; KG Bühler, *State Succession and Membership in International Organizations: Legal Theories versus Political Pragmatism* (Kluwer Law International, 2001) 14.

39 Crawford, *Creation of States* (n 36) 417; Ziemele, '... Reality or Fiction? ...' (n 34) 217; after the breakdown of Yugoslavia Schachter even went so far as to say that there was a 'general presumption of continuity' with newly emerged States, O Schachter, 'State Succession: The Once and Future Law' (1993) 33 Va J Intl L 253, 259.

Beyond these basic points just how one is meant to gauge whether an entity can claim to be a continuation of the predecessor State remains by and large unsettled. Crawford has argued that a variation of the requirements for statehood might provide useful guidance when assessing whether a State continues to or has ceased to exist.[40] However, such modified criteria do not satisfactorily resolve all legal controversy surrounding State continuity.

In particular, it is important to note that the question in such cases is not about the *achievement* of statehood (which can, to a greater or lesser extent, be dealt with by the traditional rules on statehood by reference to criteria laid down in the 1933 Montevideo Convention on the Rights and Duties of States and reference to either the constitutive or declarative theories of recognition[41]) but rather whether the State in question has a valid claim to continue as *the same State* as the predecessor State.

Whilst the traditional rules for determining statehood and international personality are predicated on the basis of sovereign equality of States, who are presumed to possess a number of uniting and common characteristics, State continuity presumes that there are some inherent qualities of a State that distinguish it from other States. As such the issue of the identity of the State deals less with the form of statehood and more with the precise substance of the State in question.[42] It is these distinguishing qualities that any prospective continuator State must demonstrate in order to have its claim accepted.[43] In such cases, we are left trying to discern whether, for instance, the territory in question bears some sufficient resemblance to the previous State whose sovereignty had allegedly been previously extinguished. Whilst thinking in terms of identity more easily enables us to identify the precise substance of a particular State rather than the more rigid requirements employed in assessing Statehood and personality,[44] to what extent the use of this term moves us forward is

---

40 Ziemele, '… Reality or Fiction? …' (n 34) 215; Crawford, *Creation of States* (n 36) 400.

41 J Crawford, *Brownlie's Principles of Public International Law* (8th edn, OUP, 2012) 128 *et seq* and 143 *et seq.*

42 Craven, 'The Problem of State Succession …' (n 4) 162.

43 In other words '[i]dentity … presumes personality but is concerned with what is personal or exceptional in the nature of the subject. This can never be provided by reference to the traditional requirements of statehood', ibid.

44 M Craven, 'International Law of State Succession' 2 Intl LFD Intl 202, 203.

somewhat unclear since it remains extremely difficult to draw the distinction between these different concepts.[45]

State practice, as well as the jurisprudence of the International Court of Justice, seems to suggest that, in relation to the distinction between succession and identity, what often matters most is not objective facts, such as the size of territory or population, but rather to what extent the claim to continuation of identity was generally accepted by the international community as a whole, including international organizations.[46] To this extent recognition of a claim of continuity by third States would appear to be just as fundamental in relation to such continuity as it is to the creation of States.[47] International courts such as the International Court of Justice dealing with the matter tend to avoid addressing the identity of States in any definitive way unless claims of identity appear to have been generally accepted.[48]

Such a situation brings into question the utility of the law of State succession. One might wonder what purpose international law is serving if it can only oversee the categorization of acts of succession *ex post facto* whilst not offering guidance to those parties involved in the succession at the time. Put otherwise: is international law merely meant to retroactively legitimize or 'rationalize' a situation that has occurred? If

---

[45] Ziemele, '... Reality or Fiction? ...' (n 34) 218; see I Brownlie, *Principles of Public International Law* (Clarendon Press, 1998) 80.

[46] Zimmermann, '... Avoiding Principled Answers to Questions of Principle' (n 32) 57. Concerning the importance of recognition by the United Nations, see U Fastenrath, 'Recht der Staatensukzession' (1995) 35 Berichte der DGVR 9, 21.

[47] Caflisch, 'The Law of State Succession ...' (n 2) 344, 'the State preserves its identity, at least in international law, by virtue of a legal fiction, provided its competence *ratione loci* and *personae* remains essentially unaltered, and provided this state of affairs is acknowledged by the other States'.

[48] For example, the International Court of Justice in the recent *Germany v Italy* case simply took it for granted that the Federal Republic of Germany was identical to the German State responsible for violations of its international obligations before and during World War II, *Jurisdictional Immunities of the State (Germany v Italy: Greece Intervening)*, Judgment of 3 February 2012, www.icj-cij.org/docket/files/143/16883.pdf, accessed 28 November 2013; Zimmermann, '... Avoiding Principled Answers to Questions of Principle' (n 32) 55; see Zimmermann, *Völkerrechtliche Verträge* (n 25) 82 for further dicussion on status of Germany; see also the uncontested claim that the Russian Federation was the continuator of the USSR in *Case Concerning Application of the International Convention on the Elimination of All Forms of Racial Discrimination (Georgia v Russian Federation)* (Preliminary Objections) 2011, www.icj-cij.org/docket/files/140/16398.pdf, accessed 28 November 2013, para 105.

so, this would suggest that the main determining factors are in fact political and not legal ones and as such that perhaps the law of State succession is redundant. Such a position has been seriously put forward in the past. Schachter, for instance, eschewed talk of the law of State succession, instead referring to the *policy* of State succession as a means of ensuring the continuation of international law.[49]

Against the background of such claims, it is the task of international lawyers to make the law of greater use in this area by, in particular, confirming the existence and content of applicable rules of international law governing instances of State succession even if, for example, the instances of the dissolution of both the former Yugoslavia and that of the USSR indicate that the final decision as to whether third States accept a claim of identity or not is not always, to say the least, based on legal criteria.

III. STATE SUCCESSION TO TREATIES: THE FALSE DICHOTOMY OF UNIVERSAL SUCCESSION AND THE CONCEPT OF *TABULA RASA*

International legal scholarship on the law of State succession to treaties has traditionally been characterized by the dichotomy between the theories of universal succession and the 'clean slate' or *tabula rasa* theory.[50] The older of the theories, universal succession, in simple terms, consists of the idea that successor States automatically acquire the rights and liabilities (including treaty rights and obligations) of the predecessor State.[51] In contrast, the clean slate theory is a more recent development influenced by voluntarist approaches to international law which hold that the consent of any State is critical in order for it to become bound by international law.[52] As such, it is argued, a successor State is therefore not bound by any of the obligations of the predecessor State at the time

---

[49] Schachter, '… Once and Future Law' (n 39) 240; Craven, *The Decolonization of International Law* (n 17) 233.

[50] Hafner and Novak, 'State Succession …' (n 22) 401.

[51] This theory can be said to derive from Roman law and expounded in the works of Grotius (*De jure belli ac pacts*, II, ix, 10–12, xiv, 1, 10) Pufendorf (*De jure naturae et gentium libri octo* (1688, Oldfather and Oldfather tr, 1934) VIII, xii, 88) and Gentili (*De jure belli libri tres* (1612, Rofle tr, 1964) III, xxii).

[52] Cavaglieri, 'Règles Genérales du Droit de la Praix' (1928) 26 Receuil des Cours 311.

of secession or negotiated independence. However, the debate surrounding this binary distinction has long been regarded as being unhelpful and overly simplistic, with neither theory providing a satisfactory theoretical underpinning for the law of State succession in respect of treaties[53] nor being fully reflected in State practice.[54]

1. Universal Succession

On a theoretical level, the justification for imposing obligations on successor sovereign States without their consent is somewhat unclear to say the least, being based on unclear notions such as a communitarian interest in continuity of obligations.[55] A number of notable scholars have justified their position on this issue through reference to the alternative to continuity of treaty obligations, which according to them would be a more chaotic and unstable international legal system in which it would be more difficult to 'foster respect for the rule of law'.[56] In contrast, other scholars, also in favour of continuity, do not justify the value of continuity on the basis of value to the international community in a social sense, but rather take a more legalistic view, prioritizing 'stability of expectations'[57] and highlighting the opportunity costs States incur in binding themselves in international agreements.[58]

---

53 Craven, 'The Problem of State Succession ...' (n 4) 142 *et seqq.*

54 Ibid.

55 For discussion of this point, see Jennings, '... Principles of International Law' (n 3) 442 *et seq.*

56 See R Mullerson, 'New Developments in the Former USSR and Yugoslavia' (1993) 33 Va J Intl L 299, 303.

57 See for such a proposition, &Vagts, '... The Codifier's View' (n 24) 280–82.

58 The same sentiment was expressed by Crawford regarding the motivations behind State continuity, namely that 'the international community cannot allow the negation of the extensive body of legal relations built up over time. It cannot allow communities simply to opt out of obligations and responsibilities, even by so fundamental and difficult a process as dissolution of or secession from a State', J Crawford, *ASIL Proceedings* (ASIL, 1992) 21; Vagts, '... The Codifier's View' (n 24) 280–82; see also H Lauterpacht, 'Succession of States with Respect to Private Law Obligations' in E Lauterpacht (ed), *International Law Being the Collected Papers of Hersch Lauterpacht* (vol 3, CUP, 1977), the purpose of international law being 'to maintain the continuity of law, independent of the physical or legal death of the natural or juridical person concerned'.

2. *Tabula rasa*

On the other hand, aside from being somewhat of a misnomer when considering theories of succession,[59] the clean slate theory was very much a project born out of the process of decolonization, in light of which the universal succession to obligations of previous colonial powers was seen as completely irreconcilable. Such influence ultimately resulted in the inclusion of the special regime for newly independent States in the VCSST. However, outside the context of decolonization, surveys of contemporary practice indicate that the clean slate rule in its purest form was rarely applied and that the concept as a whole has fallen into relative *desuetudo*.[60] Even States gaining independence from colonial powers – the very situation for which Part III of the VCSST had been designed – tended to accept in practice at least some of the predecessor State's treaty obligations,[61] particularly those treaties relating to territory and watercourses.[62]

3. Assessment of the Dichotomy

Taken together, it is clear that in light of State practice neither theory is completely persuasive.[63] Rather, the task facing international legal scholarship as a result is determining a more useful starting point that more accurately reflects State practice to date.

---

[59] EG Bello, 'Reflections on Succession of States in the Light of the Vienna Convention on Succession of States with Respect of Treaties 1978' (1978) 23 GYIL 296.

[60] K Zemanek and TC Hartley, *The Legal Foundations of the International System: General Course on Public International Law* (Martinus Nijhoff, 1998) 84; see also Ziemele, '... Reality or Fiction? ...' (n 34) 219.

[61] International Law Association, Committee on State Succession to Treaties and Other Governmental Obligations, *The Effect of Independence on Treaties: A Handbook* (Stevens, 1965) 2; DP O'Connell, 'Independence and Succession to Treaties' 38 BYIL 84; Zimmermann, *Völkerrechtliche Verträge* (n 25) 147.

[62] On this distinction, recognized in Articles 11 and 12 of the 1978 Vienna Convention, see Craven, 'The Problem of State Succession ...' (n 4) 149; AD McNair, *The Law of Treaties* (Clarendon Press, 1961) 256; *Gabčíkovo-Nagymaros Project (Hungary/Slovakia)*, Judgment, ICJ Rep 1997, 7, para 123.

[63] M Helal, 'State Succession to Territorial Obligations: The Case of South Sudan and the 1959 Nile Waters Agreement', 26, http://works.bepress.com/mohamed_helal/1, accessed 26 July 2013, stating that this position is reflected in the fact none of the State practice with regard to the Nile riparians 'can be neatly categorized as falling within either of the two aforementioned theories of State succession. Rather, policies drew on elements of both theories, and were

IV. EXTENT OF AFFIRMATION OF THE RULES OF THE VCSST

Bearing this in mind, the following section will attempt to assess the extent to which the provisions of the VCSST have been affirmed by State practice since 1978, pointing out not only the (limited) number of those provisions which (either in 1978 or today) represent customary international law[64] but also the main points of contention in the law and making suggestions for reform where appropriate.

Previous thorough analyses of State practice suggest it is possible to speak of a taxonomy of instances of State succession.[65] This taxonomy consists of cases in which succession becomes an issue as a result of either (a) transfer of territory as provided for in Article 15 VCSST (such as the transfer of Alaska from Russia to the USA in 1867, the transfer of Alsace and Lorraine from France to Germany in 1871, the treaties following World War I (Versailles, St Germain and Trianon) and World War II (concerning Germany, Italy, Romania and Hungary), the transfer of West New Guinea from the Netherlands in 1962, the transfer of Walvis Bay from South Africa to Namibia in 1994 and the transfers of Hong Kong to China from Great Britain and Macao from Portugal to China in 1997 and 1999); (b) two different forms of unification of States, namely (i) the incorporation of one State into another (including the incorporation of the German Democratic Republic into the Federal Republic of Germany in 1990, historical examples include the incorporation of Texas into the USA in 1845 and Italian unification in 1860 amongst others), and (ii) a merger of two States to form a new State (including the 1958 merger of Egypt and Syria to form the United Arab Republic (UAR), the 1964 merger of Tanganyika and Zanzibar to form Tanzania and the merger of the Yemen Arab Republic and the State of the People's

---

essentially designed to give the governments of these newly independent States the flexibility to evaluate the contractual relations inherited from former colonial masters and to determine which of these treaties would devolve onto them'.

64 Zimmermann, *Völkerrechtliche Verträge* (n 25) 819 *et seq*; Craven, *The Decolonization of International Law* (n 17); Hafner and Novak, 'State Succession …' (n 22) 399.

65 Zimmermann, *Völkerrechtliche Verträge* (n 25) 221; Craven, *The Decolonization of International Law* (n 17); A Aust, *Modern Treaty Law and Practice* (CUP, 2007); Hafner and Novak, 'State Succession …' (n 22); J Klabbers and E Castrén-instituutti, *State Practice Regarding State Succession and Issues of Recognition: The Pilot Project of the Council of Europe* (Kluwer Law International, 1999).

Democratic Republic of Yemen to form modern day Yemen in 1990); (c) separation of one State from another to form a new State (including the separation of Eritrea from Ethiopia in 1993) and the separation of some States that had formed the USSR at the end of the Cold War, as well as more recently the separation of Montenegro (and possibly Kosovo if recognized as a State from Serbia); (d) the complete dissolution of one pre-existing State (including Czechoslovakia and the breakdown of Yugoslavia); and, finally, (e) the category of newly independent states created by the VCSST.

1. Transfer of Territory

Article 15 VCSST, under the heading of 'succession of part of a territory', sets out the 'moving boundary rule' by which, when a territory of one State becomes part of the territory of another, the treaties of the latter State become applicable to it, and the treaties of the former State cease being applicable. State practice, both before the adoption of the VCSST and ever since was consistent in relation to this rule and as such it can be considered to reflect customary international law.[66]

With regard to Hong Kong and Macao, the joint British–Chinese declaration of 1984, providing for the restoration of Chinese sovereignty over Hong Kong, stipulated that the application of Chinese treaties to Hong Kong would be decided by the Chinese Government. On the other hand, agreements to which China was not a party but which were implemented in Hong Kong could continue to be so implemented. In the case of multilateral treaties, the continued application of certain British treaties to Hong Kong after 1 July 1997, mainly in the field of human rights, was notified to the respective depository and no objection seems to have been encountered. No bilateral British treaties seem to have applied to Hong Kong after that date. Instead, treaties concluded by Hong Kong itself (as a subject of international law in its own right) have not lapsed by that date. Finally, Chinese treaties have only selectively been applied to Hong Kong after 1 July 1997. The practice with regard to Macao, as envisaged in the joint Chinese–Portuguese declaration of 1987, seems to be in line *mutatis mutandis* with the practice followed in the case of Hong Kong.

With regard to Walvis Bay, Namibia resumed control over this territory in 1994. Whilst the relevant treaty does not contain any explicit rules as

---

[66] Zimmermann, *Völkerrechtliche Verträge* (n 25) 823 and 449; Hafner and Novak, 'State Succession …' (n 22) 411.

to the fate of South African treaties previously applied to Walvis Bay, subsequent practice demonstrates that both parties have followed the rule embodied in Article 15 VCSST.[67]

On the whole, it might be said that the respective parties involved in a transfer of territory have either followed the moving boundary rule, or where they have purported to deviate from this rule, have received the required (explicit or implicit) approval by third States. The moving boundary rule thus constitutes perhaps one of the most settled and clear-cut aspects of the law of State succession with regard to treaties.

It may be suggested that States have followed the moving boundary rule as enshrined in Article 15 VCSST due to a combination of factors, including the fact that the same principle regarding the territorial scope of treaties to territory is also set out in Article 29 Vienna Convention on the Law of Treaties 1969 (VCLT),[68] that State practice was largely settled by 1978, and that, as such, Article 15 VCSST represented a codification proper of customary law as it then already stood (as opposed to a mere progressive development).

What can be derived from this is that the provisions of the VCSST that most closely codify existing State practice, and that are in line with the general parameters of treaty law, are those that are most effective and most often adhered to by States.

2. Unification of States

State practice evidences two main forms of unification of States, one specifically envisaged and one not envisaged as such by the VCSST.

3. Incorporation

The case of voluntary incorporation of one State into another was not anticipated nor provided for in the VCSST.[69] Neither Article 31 VCSST covering 'effects of uniting of States in respect of treaties in force at the

---

[67] Zimmermann, *Völkerrechtliche Verträge* (n 25) 447.

[68] Article 29 states that '[u]nless a different intention appears from the treaty or is otherwise established, a treaty is binding upon each party in respect of its entire territory'.

[69] See the admission on this point in Vagts, '... The Codifier's View' (n 24) 276; but see also Zimmermann, *Völkerrechtliche Verträge* (n 25) 244, 288, who suggests that, whilst Article 31 VCSST was meant to regulate all types of unification, separate and different rules of customary law apply in cases of incorporation.

date of the succession of States', nor Article 15 VCSST relating to 'succession in respect of part of territory' could be said to cover the type of situation where one State voluntarily agrees to give up its sovereignty and be incorporated into another. The reason for this is most likely that, at the time the VCSST was being drafted, it was hardly conceivable that a given population, in exercising its right of self-determination, would freely give up its own independent statehood. Yet, German reunification has proven this assumption to be wrong. It constitutes the most important case of a unification of two States by way of incorporation in recent times.

Article 11 of the 1990 Treaty of Unification (Einigungsvertrag) concluded between the Federal Republic of Germany and the German Democratic Republic (GDR) provided that, as a matter of principle, all treaties of the Federal Republic of Germany would extend to the territory of the former GDR, whereas Article 12 thereof provided that treaties of the GDR were to be the subject of individual negotiation with the relevant State parties. This again, to a greater or lesser extent, demonstrates the flexibility of the law of State succession with regard to treaties and its close interrelationship with general international law.

Almost all treaty partners of Germany subsequently accepted this position. An analysis demonstrates that the vast majority of those treaties entered into by the then GDR – with the notable exception of localized treaties – were considered by the respective treaty partners to have lapsed *ipso facto* with the extinction of the GDR and its absorption into the Federal Republic of Germany.[70] The German case would thus suggest that the model set out in Article 31 VCSST does not reflect customary international law when it comes to a unification of two States by way of absorption or incorporation and that, at the same time, a 'moving boundaries principle', *in extremis*, appears to apply.

4. Merger

In sharp contrast to a unification of two States by way of an incorporation, instances of merger of States were indeed envisaged by the VCSST and set out in its Article 31, paragraph 1 which provides that '[w]hen two

[70] Zimmermann, *Völkerrechtliche Verträge* (n 25) 264; see also the practice of the USA related to Germany in M Leich, 'Contemporary Practice of the United States Relating to International Law' (1991) 85 AJIL 539, who remarks that 'the delegations noted that most of the international agreements between the United States and the German Democratic Republic had expired in accordance with international law on October 3, 1990 with the unification of Germany'.

or more States unite to form one successor State, any treaty in force at the date of succession of States in respect of any of them continues in force in respect of the successor State'.[71] Article 31(2) however provides that Article 31(1) applies 'only in respect of the part of the territory of the successor State in respect of which the treaty was in force at the date of the succession of States'.[72] As such, Article 31(1) and (2) VCSST, when taken together, thus create a hardly manageable split treaty regime whereby existing treaty obligations potentially apply only to part of the successor territory, creating disparity of obligations and potentially divergent rights for individuals, should the obligations so provide.

In contradistinction to the practice followed by Germany, the unification of North and South Yemen in 1990 to form the Republic of Yemen largely followed the model provided for in Article 31 VCSST. In other words, unified Yemen seems to have considered that all treaties entered into by either of its two predecessor States continued to be in force. It might be also said, although not with complete certainty, that the territorial scope of application of such treaties was then limited to the territory to which it had previously been applied.

The split treaty regime underlying Article 31 VCSST has proved problematic in both theory and practice.[73] In fact, it is unclear why this system was adopted in the first place with the most likely answer being that most States participating in the codification effort considered the type of situation envisaged in Article 31 VCSST as largely unimportant and unlikely to occur sufficiently often in practice.[74] Indeed, this has proven to be not so far away from reality with only one instance of this form of succession occurring ever since the adoption of the VCSST in 1978. Furthermore, practice regarding the type of merger envisaged in Article 31 VCSST is scarce, Yemen being the sole example and the value of this practice as precedent is limited since the rationale behind the merger of these two States is unclear and the process of integration and

---

71 Unless as provided by Article 31(1)(a) and (b) the parties otherwise agree or it appears that doing so would be contrary to the object and purpose of the treaty in question.

72 Again unless, as Article 31(2)(a) provides, the successor State makes a declaration that the treaty applies to the whole of the territory, as provided for in (b) and (c), the parties to a bilateral or multilateral treaty agree otherwise.

73 For further details, see Zimmermann, *Völkerrechtliche Verträge* (n 25) 283–9.

74 HD Treviranus, 'Die Konvention der Vereinten Nationen über Staatensukzession bei Verträgen – Ergebnisse der Konferenz in Wien 1977 und 1978' (1979) 39 ZaöRV 259, 272; Zimmermann, *Völkerrechtliche Verträge* (n 25) 831.

succession is largely incoherent. Indeed, this incoherent approach has curtailed the relevance of this instance of succession for the further development of customary international law. Consequently, it is hard to discern whether a customary rule of international law in this respect exists or whether the law is still developing, any such development then, in any event, running counter to the fundamental principle underlying Article 29 VCLT.

5. Separation

In contrast to cases of the complete dissolution of a State, separation presupposes that one of the entities existing on the territory of the predecessor State continues its international legal personality and is, as such, identical, although in a limited geographical way, with that predecessor State. In such situations one of the central provisions of the VCSST applies, namely Article 34. It provides that where a part of a territory of a State separates to form a new State (crucially, not a 'newly independent state' in the sense of Part III of the VCSST which falls outside the scope of this provision):

> (a) any treaty in force at the date of the succession of States in respect of the entire territory of the predecessor State continues in force in respect of each successor State so formed, and (b) any treaty in force at the date of the succession of States in respect only of that part of the territory of the predecessor State which has become a successor State continues in force in respect of that successor State alone.

With regards to the predecessor State which continues to exist, Article 35 VCSST further provides that treaties already in force continue in force with regard to the remaining territory. As such the VCSST thereby adopts a continuity approach to treaty obligations.

During its codification efforts the ILC acknowledged that State practice in relation to this issue was not uniform, but nevertheless felt that it was sufficiently consistent to merit the inclusion of the principle of continuity in the Convention.[75] However, in practice, serious doubts have been cast upon this position as subsequent State practice has been, to say the least, far from consistent, and indeed so far from consistent in fact so as to bring the application of Article 34 VCSST to all cases of separation

---

[75] See Yearbook of the ILC (1974) vol II, Part I, 260–66.

into question. As a matter of fact, Article 34 VCSST might be seen merely as a codification as far as the dissolution of a State is concerned.[76]

However, with regard to separations where the predecessor State continues to exist the Convention was on significantly less firm ground, this provision only being included during the 1977/1978 Conference.[77] The result of this development is a somewhat mixed result of inconsistent State practice in instances of separation. Such cases of separation whereby part or parts of a State leave to form one or more separate independent States, whilst leaving the remaining territory as *the same* continuator State intact, are a prime example of the type of cases that most often raise issues of continuity and identity, the most important examples having been the break-up of the USSR, where the Russian Federation continues the legal personality of the USSR.

a) Break-up of the USSR

Given that the Russian Federation's claim to be identical with the USSR was, by and large, accepted, it automatically continued the treaty relations of the former USSR under the principle enshrined in Article 35 VCSST, unless such treaties were localized on the territory of one of the successor States of the Soviet Union. That result was almost unanimously accepted by the international community,[78] as well as by the International Court of Justice.[79] It ought to be also noted that Estonia, Latvia and Lithuania, which had been illegally annexed by the Soviet Union during World War II and which, as a result, returned to their previous sovereign identity after the collapse of the USSR in the early 1990s,[80] were accordingly (*not* being successor States of the USSR) not per se bound by the treaty obligations of the USSR. Belarus and Ukraine in turn were somewhat special cases, both possessing significant international legal personality, albeit in a limited form, prior to the breakdown of the USSR. As such they were parties to treaties in their own name and were both members of the United Nations. Accordingly they did continue to be

---

[76] Zimmermann, *Völkerrechtliche Verträge* (n 25) 429 *et seq.*

[77] Ibid, 217 *et seq.*

[78] A position that States generally accepted, see Klabbers and Castrén-instituutti, *State Practice* (n 65) 98 *et seq.*

[79] *Application of the International Convention on the Elimination of All Forms of Racial Discrimination (Georgia v Russian Federation)*, ICJ Reports 2008, Order of 15 October 2008, 353, 384.

[80] A Rasulov, 'Revisiting State Succession to Humanitarian Treaties: Is There a Case for Automaticity?' (2003) 14 EJIL 141, 145; Mullerson, 'New Developments …' (n 56) 308.

bound by those treaty obligations they themselves had entered into. Whilst with regard to the treaties of the USSR *mutatis mutandis*, the same rules did apply with regard to the other successor States of the Soviet Union, namely Armenia, Azerbaijan, Georgia, Moldavia, Kazakhstan, Kirgizstan, Tajikistan, Turkmenistan and Uzbekistan.

Those successor States did, however, not take the position that they were automatically bound by all treaties previously entered into by the Soviet Union.[81] The practice of third States is, at least when compared with the parallel practice in the two recent cases of a complete dissolution of a State such as Yugoslavia and Czechoslovakia, significantly less uniform. Accordingly, the break-up of the USSR constitutes a prime example of a certain lack of uniformity in State practice with the conflicting positions of the successor States to the USSR. Accordingly it continues to remain somewhat unclear to what extent the rules in Article 34 VCSST apply in such situations and to what extent these rules are declaratory of customary international law due to such inconsistent practice, but also due to the silence of the International Court of Justice on the matter.[82]

b) Independence of Eritrea

In 1993 Eritrea achieved independence from Ethiopia, separating to form an independent State and leaving Ethiopia as the continuator State. Importantly, in most cases Eritrea has *acceded* to treaties previously entered into by Ethiopia, instances of succession by Eritrea to both bilateral or multilateral treaties of Ethiopia being very rare.[83] Even those States, such as inter alia Germany, which in other cases had insisted on the continued application of the treaties of the respective predecessor State seem to have taken the position that the Ethiopian treaties have lapsed with regard to Eritrea which again raises the issue of a lack of

---

[81] Zimmermann, *Völkerrechtliche Verträge* (n 25) 377 *et seq*.

[82] *Gabčíkovo-Nagymaros Project* (n 62) 7, 68 ('The Court does not find it necessary for the purposes of the present case to enter into a discussion of whether or not Article 34 of the 1978 Convention reflects the state of customary international law').

[83] Zimmermann, *Völkerrechtliche Verträge* (n 25) 423. Indeed the only example of Eritrea becoming a State party by way of succession is the fourth Lomé Convention between the European Community and the African, Caribbean and Pacific Group of States (ACP) of 1989. On the contrary, the Georgetown Agreement of 1975 which constituted the ACP Group of States has been *acceded* to by Eritrea.

uniformity and coherence, third States taking an *'à la tête du client'* approach.

c) South Sudan

The most recent instance of State succession is the separation of South Sudan from Sudan, the former having been admitted to the United Nations on 4 July 2011.[84] Before achieving independence South Sudan had compiled a 'handbook' which addressed certain relevant issues of State succession.[85] Whilst the handbook took the (uncontroversial) position that Sudan would be the 'continuing state' and Southern Sudan would be a mere 'successor state',[86] when it came to the continuation of treaty obligations by South Sudan it was equivocal, appearing to claim that States are entitled to claim that they are not bound by any treaty obligations of the predecessor State (the clean slate principle). But also stated that 'based on recent state practice, the international community would likely expect an independent Southern Sudan to continue the Republic of Sudan's treaty obligations',[87] which once again hints at a largely wide freedom of action of successor States. The handbook further stated that '*in some instances*, new states must also deposit an instrument of *accession* with the appropriate treaty depository to affirm a commitment to be bound by a treaty's terms' – which suggests that the idea of automatic succession was not envisaged.[88] However, the handbook once again, perhaps deliberately, leaves open the question of when accession (rather than succession) is legally required or appropriate. The practice of South Sudan is thus, once again, evidence that there continues to be a lack of clear and unequivocal rules of treaty succession when it comes to instances of separation.

---

[84] UN Doc A/RES/65308.

[85] See Office of the President of the Government of Southern Sudan in Collaboration with the Public International Law & Policy Group, *South Sudan: A Guide to Critical Post-2011 Issues, Legal Handbook,* December 2009, accessed 21 May 2014 at www.scribd.com/doc/40343514/Southern-Sudan-a-guide-to-critical-post-2011-issues.

[86] Ibid.

[87] Ibid, the handbook set out examples to this effect including when: '(1) both parties agree otherwise, (2) the treaty is not relevant to the new state's territory, or (3) continuity would frustrate the treaty's object and purpose'.

[88] Ibid.

6. Dissolution

When it comes to cases of complete dissolution of a State, in contrast to a mere separation, State practice on the matter reveals that States, most notably in the context of the dissolution of Czechoslovakia and Yugoslavia, have more or less followed the procedure set out in Article 34 VCSST, State practice in this area being significantly more uniform than in cases of separation.[89] This said, even in cases of dissolution of States, the Secretary-General of the United Nations, when acting as depository of multilateral treaties, requires notification of succession to treaty obligations.[90] Further, in the case of bilateral treaties, 'negotiations tend to be the rule, leading to exchanges of notes including non-constitutive lists of treaties to remain in force, similar to cases of separation'.[91] In addition, the International Court of Justice in the *Bosnian Genocide* case, whilst leaving the issue of automatic succession expressly unanswered, found that Bosnia and Herzegovina could succeed to treaty obligations by way of a notification of succession. This may be taken as confirmation of the fact that such notification of succession serves as a means to succeed to a treaty, which under the VCSST was only meant to be relevant for newly independent States. However, as a result of the Court refusing to take a position on whether such succession was automatic or not, it remains unclear whether such notification, as such, is merely declaratory (because succession was automatic) or rather constitutive in nature (because succession was not automatic).[92]

---

[89] Ibid; Zimmermann, *Völkerrechtliche Verträge* (n 25) 367 *et seq*.

[90] See UN Office of Legal Affairs, *Summary of Practice of the Secretary-General as Depository of Multilateral Treaties* (UN, 1994), UN Doc ST/LEG/7/Rev. 1, 90, para 303

[91] Hafner and Novak, 'State Succession …' (n 22) 416. For an extensive analysis of third States' practice, see Zimmermann, *Völkerrechtliche Verträge* (n 25) 314 *et seq*, concerning Yugoslavia, and 337 *et seq*, concerning Czechoslovakia.

[92] See *Application of the Convention on the Prevention and Punishment of the Crime of Genocide (Bosnia and Herzegovina/Yugoslavia [Serbia and Montenegro])*, Provisonal Measures, ICJ Rep 1993, 3, para 25, and *Application of the Convention on the Prevention and Punishment of the Crime of Genocide (Bosnia and Herzegovina v Serbia and Montenegro)*, Judgment, ICJ Rep 2007, 43, para 20; see Zimmermann, '… Avoiding Principled Answers to Questions of Principle' (n 32).

a) Socialist Federal Republic of Yugoslavia

After the break-up of the former Yugoslavia which saw the independence of Slovenia, Croatia,[93] Bosnia and Herzegovina,[94] and the Former Yugoslav Republic of Macedonia,[95] the remaining part of the Socialist Federal Republic of Yugoslavia, namely the Federal Republic of Yugoslavia (consisting of Serbia and Montenegro), claimed the status of being a continuator State in relation to the Socialist Federal Republic of Yugoslavia.[96] However, this claim was neither generally accepted by the UN General Assembly nor by the UN Security Council, nor by the international community at large.[97]

Third States, as well as treaty bodies, have to a large extent, although not without exceptions, followed the approach underlying Article 34 VCSST with regard to all successor States of the former Yugoslavia, a result confirmed by an extensive survey of relevant State practice.[98] However, the value of this practice as a precedent is riddled with contradictions that somewhat undermine the value of the situation for the development of the law.[99] To give but one example, Croatia at different stages argued both against and in favour of automatic succession under Article 34 VCSST depending on different political aims, ultimately arguing in favour of it before the International Court of Justice.

b) Czechoslovakia

A further prominent example of the dissolution of States is provided by the break-up of Czechoslovakia. In that case an agreement was reached that on 1 January 1993 Czechoslovakia would cease to exist as a State and be replaced by two sovereign States, namely the Czech Republic and Slovakia. Both the Czech as well as the Slovak Republic have consistently taken the position that they have *ipso facto* succeeded to all

---

[93] Both States declaring independence on 29 June 1991 and being subsequently recognized by the EU by Opinion Number 7 of the Arbitration Commission of the Conference on Yugoslavia (Badinter Arbitration Committee), see 3 EJIL 1 (1992) 182 *et seq.*

[94] Declaring independence in November 1991 and being recognized as a State by the EU on 7 April 1992 and then admitted to the United Nations on 22 May 1992, see UNGA Res 46/237.

[95] Being admitted to the United Nations on 8 April 1993, see UNGA Res 47/225.

[96] See *Bosnian Genocide,* Provisional Measures, ICJ Rep 1993, 15.

[97] Zimmermann, *Völkerrechtliche Verträge* (n 25) 334 *et seq.*

[98] Ibid.

[99] See the fact that depositories' records have been described as 'devastated by incoherence', Rasulov, 'Revisiting State Succession ...' (n 80) 146.

bilateral and multilateral treaties of the Czech and Slovak Federal Republic (CSFR) unless they were localized on the territory of the respective other successor State. Third States have again largely shared that position.

The International Court of Justice in the *Gabčíkovo* case in turn left the question open as to whether Article 34 VCSST might now be considered to embody a rule of customary international law, since it considered the relevant treaty in the *Gabčíkovo* case to be of a localized nature. It was accordingly considered to have been inherited by the Slovak Republic regardless of whether there is by now universal succession in the case of a complete dismemberment of a State or not.

c) Conclusion

On the whole, it might be said, that whilst the principle of universal succession contained in Article 34 VCSST was by and large abided by in the cases of the complete dissolution of a State, namely the cases of Yugoslavia and the CSFR, it was not uniformly applied in separation cases such as the cases of the USSR and Eritrea. This confirms that when it comes to instances of separation the codification effort undertaken in 1978 by the VCSST, already then not supported by State practice, has not significantly contributed to a further development of customary law.

7. Newly Independent States

The concept of newly independent States, as discussed above, constitutes a notable achievement of the process of what has been described as the 'decolonization of international law'.[100] The influence of the decolonization movement can be seen, in particular, in the special inclusion of the regime for newly independent States such as former colonies in relation to succession to treaties as set out in Part III of the VCSST (Articles 16–30). As such, under Article 16 VCSST,[101] newly independent States

---

[100] See section 1.2 above. Influence of decolonization: 'At its first session in 1949 the ILC did not give priority to the topic of State succession. Yearbook of the ILC (1968) vol II, 213 [29]. At its 1962 session, however, prompted by UNGA resolution 1686 (XVI) of 18 December 1961, the ILC included on its priority list the topic of succession of States and governments', Hafner and Novak, 'State Succession …' (n 22) 401.

[101] Article 16 VCSST provides that '[a] newly independent State is not bound to maintain in force, or to become a party to, any treaty by reason only of the fact that at the date of the succession of States the treaty was in force in respect of the territory to which the succession of States relates'.

are not automatically bound by the treaty obligations of their predecessor States. However, Article 17 VCSST provides that such newly independent States, through notifications of succession, may voluntarily succeed to these obligations should they so choose.[102] In addition, Article 27 VCSST sets out that, providing the other States consent or can be deemed to have consented, a newly independent State may provisionally apply any multilateral treaty previously in force with regard to the predecessor State.[103]

In practice, newly independent States have, by and large, followed the regime set out in Articles 16, 17 and 27 of the VCSST and thus the customary status of these provisions could be said to have already crystallized at least since 1978. In fact, States followed a variation of this regime, commonly known as the Nyerere doctrine (so named after the first president of Tanzania who championed this doctrine), whereby newly independent States could renegotiate agreements in force by virtue of the predecessor State upon independence. In essence this 'pick and choose' doctrine essentially set out in the VCSST was also followed not only by the majority of newly independent States generally[104] but also, by and large,[105] by the few remaining former colonies which have gained independence since 1978.[106]

It is, however, important to note in order to evaluate the relevance of the codification effort undertaken in 1978 that the category of newly

---

[102] See Article 17(1) VCSST. However, it should be noted that this optional right is subject to paragraphs (2) and (3) which provide that newly independent States may only do so to the extent that their succession would not be contrary to the object and purpose of the treaty or substantially alter the treaty relations established by the treaty, and in the case of some treaties the consent of all parties to the treaty may be required.

[103] Article 27(1) VCSST states that 'If, at the date of the succession of States, a multilateral treaty was in force in respect of the territory to which the succession of States relates and the newly independent State gives notice of its intention that the treaty should be applied provisionally in respect of its territory, that treaty shall apply provisionally between the newly independent State and any party which expressly so agrees or by reason of its conduct is to be considered as having so agreed'.

[104] Hafner and Novak, 'State Succession …' (n 22) 409; Zimmermann, *Völkerrechtliche Verträge* (n 25) 830; Hafner and Novak, 'State Succession …' (n 22) 410.

[105] One exception is the special case of Namibia, see Zimmermann, *Völkerrechtliche Verträge* (n 25) 233–44.

[106] Ibid, 232–3, see Belize, Brunei, Dominica, Kiribati, Micronesia, Palau, the Solomon Islands, Zimbabwe, St Christopher and Nevis, St Lucia, St Vincent and the Grenadines and Tuvalu.

independent States has retained very little of its practical relevance post-decolonization.[107] Inter alia, in 1999, the International Law Commission did not employ the term 'newly independent State' in its draft articles on the nationality of natural persons in relation to the succession of States.[108]

V. SPECIFIC FORMS OF TREATIES

Contemporary international law in relation to State succession to treaties differentiates not only between the different forms of succession but also between different types of treaties in question.[109] Such obligations that a successor State automatically succeeds to can be conceived, to use Jennings's terminology, as 'the necessary working capital of international jural relationships that a new State needs at the outset'.[110] Whilst this category of obligations is by no means uncontroversial, it can be said with some confidence that there are some treaty rights and obligations which make up the 'working capital' that any successor State necessarily inherits.

1. Border Treaties

The first category which, perhaps, is the least controversial is that of treaties relating to borders between States. Already State practice up to the drafting of the VCSST, Article 11 VCSST itself,[111] but also more recently (after 1990) confirms that a succession of States does not, as such, affect a boundary established by a treaty. In fact, the International Court of Justice in the *Temple at Preah Vihear* and *Frontier Dispute*

[107] O'Connell, 'Reflections …' (n 17) 726; O'Connell had stated that he was 'unrepentantly doubtful about the merits of codification, which can only arrest the historical development of the law and encapsulate it within a particular time frame and a particular ideological milieu', ibid; Craven, *The Decolonization of International Law* (n 17) 93; Hafner and Novak, 'State Succession …' (n 22) 410.

[108] International Law Commission, *Articles on Nationality of Natural Persons in Relation to the Succession of States (With Commentaries)*, 3 April 1999, Supplement No. 10 (A/54/10).

[109] Hafner and Novak, 'State Succession …' (n 22) 399.

[110] Jennings, '… Principles of International Law' (n 3) 442.

[111] Article 11(1) of the VCSST provides that 'succession of States does not as such affect … a boundary established by a treaty or … obligations and rights established by a treaty and relating to the regime of a boundary'.

cases, noting that the underlying aim of automatic succession to treaties was to 'achieve stability and finality' declared this to form part of customary international law.[112] This is even true where, like in the case of treaties of the GDR, the respective successor State does not, as a matter of principle, succeed to the treaties of its predecessor State.[113]

This may be explained by the fact that the international community has a primordial interest in the stability of boundaries; an interest also reflected in Article 62(2)(a) VCLT.

2. Other Forms of Localized Treaties

Consistent recent State practice also demonstrates that other forms of localized treaties including territorial treaties and watercourse treaties are similarly subject to automatic succession. Generally, all parties to territorial treaty regimes, as well as third States, again have a common interest in seeing their continuation, and this was reflected by the fact that both parties in the *Gabčíkovo* case believed Article 12 VCSST to represent customary international law.[114] In accepting this position as such, and instead contesting whether the particular treaty regime in question could be clarified as a territorial agreement for the purposes of Article 12 VCSST, it was clear that international law was sufficiently settled to enable the International Court of Justice to pronounce on this issue, finding the treaty regime unaffected by State succession and Article 12 VCSST to be declaratory of customary international law.[115] As such, in the case of State succession the treaty regime established for the territory in question will continue to apply automatically between the successor State and the respective other contracting parties.

3. Human Rights and International Humanitarian Law Treaties

In relation to human rights treaties[116] it has been argued that the obligations contained in the main human rights treaties automatically and

---

[112] *Case Concerning the Temple of Preah Vihear (Cambodia v Thailand)*, Merits, Judgment, ICJ Rep 1962 (15 June), 6, 34; *Frontier Dispute*, Judgment, ICJ Rep 1986, 554, 567.

[113] Zimmermann, *Völkerrechtliche Verträge* (n 25) 482 *et seq.*

[114] Craven, *The Decolonization of International Law* (n 17) 248.

[115] *Gabčíkovo-Nagymaros Project* (n 62) para 123.

[116] Defined broadly as those treaties encompassing international human rights law and international humanitarian law, see Rasulov, 'Revisiting State Succession …' (n 80) 144.

thus without any need for notification, and in line with a perceived 'humanization' of international law,[117] bind any successor State; moreover, that such obligations are effectively unaffected by State succession.[118] Additionally, both the International Committee of the Red Cross (ICRC) and the Security Council, seem to have taken the position that in cases of both separations and complete dismemberments the respective successor States also remain bound by the 1949 Geneva Conventions and, where applicable, the 1977 Additional Protocols thereto.[119]

This position has also been advocated by international legal scholars, a number of judges in cases before the International Court of Justice,[120] as well as by the Human Rights Committee and other human rights treaty bodies.[121] For instance, Judge Shahabuddeen argued that the nature of human rights treaties themselves warrant that they ought not to be affected by an instance of State succession, placing emphasis on the humanitarian object and purpose of such treaties and the gap in protection that would be left were such obligations to not automatically bind successor States, and that such a gap in protection would be incompatible with the aims and purposes of such treaties, namely the protection of individuals and human rights.[122] In addition the International Criminal Tribunal for the former Yugoslavia, in the *Čelebići* case, found that Bosnia and Herzegovina automatically succeeded to the Geneva Conventions under customary international law 'as this type of convention

---

117 AA Cançado Trindade, *International Law for Humankind: Towards a New* jus gentium (Martinus Nijhoff, 2010).

118 See, for instance, MT Kamminga, 'State Succession in Respect of Human Rights Treaties' (1996) 7(4) EJIL 469–84; Mullerson, 'New Developments …' (n 56).

119 Kamminga, '… Human Rights Treaties' (n 118) 473.

120 See, for instance, the separate opinion of Judge Weeramantry in *Bosnian Genocide Case*, Preliminary Objections, ICJ Rep 1993, 654–5 and the separate opinion of Judge Shahabuddeen in ibid, 634.

121 HRC General Comment No 26, UN Doc A/53/40, 4.

122 Separate opinion of Judge Shahabuddeen in *Bosnian Genocide Case* (n 120) 636–7, Shahabuddeen stated that 'to effectuate its object and purpose, the Convention would fall to be construed as implying the expression of a unilateral undertaking by each party to the Convention to treat successor States as continuing as from independence any status which the predecessor State had as a party to the Convention. The necessary consensual bond is completed when the successor State decides to avail itself of the undertaking by regarding itself as a party to the treaty.' See also the separate opinion of Judge Weeramantry in ibid, 646.

entails automatic succession'.[123] Similarly, the Eritrea Ethiopia Claims Commission held that '[t]reaty succession may happen automatically for certain types of treaties'.[124]

However, despite support from a number of international legal scholars,[125] neither the support of successor States since the end of the Cold War nor human rights bodies provide unequivocal support for the development of a rule of automatic succession with respect to humanitarian treaties.[126] A survey of practice shows that only a limited number of States have consistently *succeeded* to humanitarian law treaties whilst others such as, for example, Armenia, Azerbaijan, Moldova, Uzbekistan and Georgia had chosen to instead *accede* to those treaties.[127] Such instances of accession significantly undermine, or at least put into question, the proposition that succession occurs automatically to human rights treaties.[128]

In practice, the principle of consent has proved resilient and States have jealously guarded their right to 'pick and choose' which obligations

---

[123] *Čelebići Case (Prosecutor v Mucić et al)* [2001] ICTY Case No IT-96-21-A [111]–[113].

[124] Eritrea Ethiopia Claims Commission, Partial Award, Prisoners of War, Ethiopia's Claim 4 (*The Federal Democratic Republic of Ethiopia v The State of Eritrea*), The Hague, 1 July 2003 [24].

[125] See, for instance, Kamminga, '… Human Rights Treaties' (n 118); B Simma, *From Bilateralism to Community Interest in International Law* (Martinus Nijhoff, 1994); and M Shaw, 'State Succession Revisited' (1996) 5 FYIL.

[126] See the International Law Association (ILA) Report which also noted that the date of succession for those States who indeed succeed was the date of notification, not the date of independence, suggesting that succession in these circumstances was not automatic but more akin to accession, ILA, *Rapport Final sur la Succession en Matière de Traités,* 70 ILA Rep, New Delhi Conference (2002) 619; Craven, *The Decolonization of International Law* (n 17) 253.

[127] Thus, in the case of the Genocide Convention of 1948, Slovenia, Bosnia-Herzegovina, the Czech Republic and Slovakia all notified the depositary of their succession, whilst Armenia, Moldova, Georgia and Azerbaijan all chose to accede to the Convention, ILA, *Rapport Final sur la Succession en Matière de Traités,* (n 126) 619 ; ibid shows that, by way of example, with regard to the Genocide Convention of 1948 Slovenia, Bosnia-Herzegovina, the Czech Republic and Slovakia all deposited notes of succession compared to Armenia, Moldova, Georgia and Azerbaijan who deposited notes of accession; Rasulov, 'Revisiting State Succession …' (n 80) 159.

[128] Zimmermann, '… Avoiding Principled Answers to Questions of Principle' (n 32) 62.

they should be bound by, resisting any moves towards being automatically bound even when it comes to humanitarian treaties.[129] Such inconsistent practice has prevented the development of customary law towards a principle of automatic succession for human rights treaties and has cast doubt upon the normative status of pronouncements of human rights treaty bodies and their potential to influence the development of international law.[130] What is more, it raises the question as to the relevance of and potentially the hierarchy between the practice of various actors such as States, international courts, and tribunals, as well as treaty organs which may be perceived as an ongoing development not only in the field of the law of State succession but international law generally.

VI. SPECIFIC QUESTIONS WITH REGARD TO TREATY SUCCESSION

1. Unilateral Declarations and Devolution Agreements

In addition to the customary rules of international law on the succession of States to treaties and the treaty regime for those States party to the VCSST, States often seek to regulate succession to treaty obligations through either an agreement between a successor and predecessor State as to what treaty obligations they believe to retain legal force as a result of State succession, or through the successor State unilaterally issuing a declaration setting out which treaty obligations it believes apply to it as a result of succession.

However, Article 8 VCSST provides that a devolution agreement between a predecessor and successor State has no legal effect on any other State, and similarly Article 9(1) VCSST provides that no unilateral declaration by a State, subject to applicable rules of customary law, can as such have any legal effect on a third State, such as another State party to a multilateral treaty, for instance. The practice of, inter alia, the United Nations Secretary-General as depository confirms this position.[131] As such, unless the other State explicitly consents, can be said to have acquiesced, or otherwise implied its consent, neither a devolution agreement nor a unilateral declaration can have, in line with the *pacta tertiis* principle, any legal effect on any other State as such. This stands in line

---

[129] See ILA, *Rapport Final sur la Succession en Matière de Traités* (n 126) 574.

[130] See ibid, 620.

[131] See, eg, UN, *Summary of Practice* (n 90)

with general principles of international law such as the *pacta tertiis nec nocent* rule and the principle of *res inter alios acta*. Despite this lack of legal effect on other States, unilateral declaration and devolution agreements, due to their commonplace nature, are significant in contemporary international law in that they signal intent to succeed or accede to certain treaties and do not deny automatic succession to some treaties.[132]

2. Time Element in Treaty Succession

Whilst the exact determination of the time of the succession might sometimes be difficult to determine especially where the relevant developments are stretched over time, it might be said, with sufficient confirmation by State practice, that any declaration of succession, if made, has a retroactive effect to the moment in which the succession took place.[133] Further, the International Court of Justice has addressed this issue in the *Bosnian Genocide* case in which Bosnia had claimed that it had become a party to the 1948 Genocide Convention at the moment of independence.[134] The Court stated that Bosnia's succession had taken effect 'since the beginning of the conflict'.[135] Consequently, in the *Croatian Genocide* case, Croatia's status as a party to the Genocide Convention at all times remained unchallenged.[136] As such, questions arise as to the fairness of this retroactivity and the limits that exist with regard to this retroactivity.[137]

---

[132] Aust, *Modern Treaty Law* (n 65) 305.

[133] See, eg, UN, *Summary of Practice* (n 90) 87; La pratique de la suisse dépositaire de traités internationaux multilatéraux en matière de succession d'Etats, CAHDI (93) 14, para 4, where it is stated: '*l'expression du consentement à être lié par le traité rétroagit à la date d'indépendance de l'Etat successeur*', and La pratique de la suisse dépositaire de traités internationaux multilatéraux en matière de succession d'Etats, CAHDI (94) 8, para 2: '*puisqu'il s'agit d'une succession, celle-ci devrait normalement ne pas prendre effet à la date de la notification, mais rétroagir à la date où le nouvel Etat a acquis une existence internationale*'; Zimmermann, '... Avoiding Principled Answers to Questions of Principle' (n 32) 66.

[134] *Application of the Convention on the Prevention and Punishment of the Crime of Genocide*, Preliminary Objections, Judgment, ICJ Reports 1996, 595, para 34.

[135] Ibid.

[136] Ibid.

[137] For some critical considerations in this regard, see the statement made by the USA during the work of the ILC leading to the adoption of the ILC Draft for the 1978 Convention, USA, Yearbook of the ILC (1974) vol II, Part I, 56.

VII. CONCLUDING REMARKS AND FURTHER RESEARCH QUESTIONS

Given that State succession with regard to treaties cuts across all fields of international law, States remain hesitant to ratify *any* convention on treaty succession regardless of its contents given they cannot envisage in advance the possible consequences of such ratification. Furthermore, all treaty-based norms related to State succession do, unlike other codification treaties such as the Vienna Convention on the Law of Treaties which are applied on a daily basis, possess merely potential importance, as they only become relevant in possible future instances of State succession. Thus, States may not easily appreciate the benefits of ratifying a treaty codifying rules pertaining to State succession.

In addition, the rather technical issues of State succession are not of major political importance given that any codification convention in the field will de facto be only applied to future successor States. What is more, the rule on treaty succession will also only be applied in fragile situations involving difficult political and territorial questions where the impact of rules of international law is, to say the least, generally limited. Given these inherent limitations, one might not be surprised that so far only twenty-two States have expressed their consent to be bound by the VCSST. Still, it is worth noting that amongst those States there are a large number of States most concerned and, in particular, successor States such as Bosnia-Herzegovina, Dominica, Croatia, the Former Yugoslav Republic of Macedonia, Slovenia, Ukraine, the Seychelles, the Slovak Republic and even Estonia (though it is not a successor State).

Some thirty-five years after the adoption of the 1978 VCSST it is unlikely that (at least a significant number of) other States will follow. It is also worth noting that the 1983 Vienna Convention on Succession of States in Respect of State Property, Archives, and Debts has not entered into force yet as so far there are only seven ratifications. As such, it is therefore not surprising that both the ILC and the General Assembly opted in 1999 to merely adopt a resolution of the General Assembly recommending certain practices when it came to codifying the rules of State practice concerning the nationality of natural persons.[138]

On the whole, it seems that, as far as the law on State succession is concerned, the codification efforts *stricto sensu* must be said to not have

---

[138] See UNGA Res 54/112, A/RES/54/112, 2 February 2000 and UNGA Res 55/153, A/RES/55/153, 30 January 2001.

achieved a great deal of success. It seems that there is little chance to further 'refine' the law on the matter by way of a renewed codification effort.

Furthermore, it also seems that both successor and third States tend to prefer ad hoc political solutions rather than fixed and somewhat rigid rules. And indeed, in most situations such political solutions can be seen as constituting a relatively unproblematic way of resolving State succession-related issues that arise. These ad hoc solutions, in turn, however, further increase the uncertain nature of the rules on treaty succession which, in turn, then lead to an even further increase in pragmatic political solutions.

Such ad hoc solutions are inherently self-serving as each actor (naturally) seeks to promote their own interests. These divergent interpretations of the law prevent the law gaining any kind of value for States involved in succession who seek guidance, and by the same token also prevent the development of customary international law in this regard, and importantly, have also dissuaded the International Court of Justice so far from making any substantive pronouncements on controversial aspects of the law of State succession to treaties.

It thus seems that the law is at least somewhat relegated to the role of *ex post facto* categorizing, explaining and rationalizing solutions which have been agreed politically, rather than guiding or shaping the orderly transition of States in international law in relation to treaties concluded by a predecessor State.

As far as research on the matter is concerned, there are several issues to be addressed. For one, access to primary material as far as treaty succession is concerned is often fiendishly difficult to access and scarce in nature. To give but one example, in order to investigate and analyse the State practice of South Sudan as to its succession to bilateral treaties previously entered into by Sudan, one would not only have to have access to the list of such treaties by which South Sudan remains bound but also to discover whether South Sudan and the respective other party or parties have taken the position that the succession to such treaties, if ever, has taken place automatically (a possible exchange of notes on the matter than being of a mere declaratory nature), or whether, instead, the parties were of the view that succession deepened on the exchange of notes being of a constitutive character. Yet, in order to decide the matter, one would have to have access to the specific wording of such notes, not only seeing the list of treaties currently in force and the date of their entry into force with regard to South Sudan. Yet, the official website of the South Sudanese Ministry of Foreign Affairs does not even contain a list of treaties, let alone a link to the official gazette of the country. As such, one would have to analyse, one by one, State practice of third States which is, if not impossible, per se limited to those few States which publicly provide information on the matter either through the internet or in their official gazettes (the latter being available in some very few libraries throughout the world anyhow).

This in turn leads in many instances, a limited number of exceptions aside, to many authors almost exclusively focusing on depositary practice. However, this approach, in focusing on secondary sources, to a large extent disregards State practice proper. Those limitations regarding access to primary material in turn frequently leads to various authors using the very same information. Accordingly, if one were to undertake serious empirical research on the state of the law one would have to undertake research on the ground. Trying to, for instance, gain access to archives and treaty lists, however, is difficult to achieve given the sensitivities of the underlying questions which, as mentioned, go to the heart of issues such as statehood.

In any case, apart from analysing the law as it currently stands on the matter as such, one ought to also address in more detail the interrelationship between State succession to treaties and the general law of treaties and consider whether rules such as the *clausula rebus sic stantibus* or similar general concepts may be relevant.

More theoretically, it would be also necessary to further analyse the role of the various entities such as States, international organizations, treaty bodies, and international courts and tribunals coping with an instance of State succession. To determine whether, with regard to the law of State succession to treaties, the degree of influence by non-State actors on the law is as important as it is in other areas such as human rights, or whether the law of State succession continues to constitute a more traditional, State-oriented area of international law.

Finally, taking into account the fact that the codification effort leading to the 1978 VCSST, whilst having been strongly influenced by the process of decolonization, may be called a belated one, it might be worth analysing the general and indeed fundamental question whether such general and abstract codifications in the form of a treaty instrument continue to constitute today an appropriate instrument to develop the law or whether it is better to opt for other instruments such as 'guiding principles' or mere 'recommendations'.

18. Treaties and armed conflict

*Yaël Ronen**

I. INTRODUCTION

The relationship between treaty relations and armed conflict is far from settled. Their coincidence seems self-evident, with treaties regulating inter-State relations, and the laws of armed conflict traditionally regulating inter-State armed conflict. Not surprisingly, the notion of war as anathema to treaty relations originally led interest in the topic to focus on the compatibility of treaty relations with the occurrence of armed conflict.[1] New issues emerged, however, with the expansion of both treaty law and the laws of armed conflict, in particular the loss of the perceived exclusivity of States as participants in the international legal arena. First, non-international armed conflict has become a dominant phenomenon and has been increasingly regulated by international law. Second, while treaties are still concluded by definition between States or intergovernmental organizations, they no longer regulate only inter-State relations.[2] Consequently, the points of contact between treaties and armed conflict have grown in number and complexity.

The present chapter considers various areas of intersection between treaties and armed conflict. Armed conflict is considered both as a legal and as a factual phenomenon, and treaties are examined both as a general category and in the context of particular self-contained regimes. Section 2 addresses the role of armed conflict in the termination, withdrawal or suspension of treaties. Subsequent sections consider aspects in the relationship between armed conflict and treaties that are premised on the continuing existence of treaties. Section 3 focuses on armed conflict as a normative phenomenon and considers the relationship between the laws of armed conflict and norm-setting treaty regimes. This section notes not only the effect of armed conflict on treaties but also the converse, namely

* I am grateful to Yael Naggan for excellent assistance in research.

[1] R Rank, 'Modern War and the Validity of Treaties' (1952–1953) 38 Cornell L Q 321.

[2] The same is largely true for international law more generally. In view of the focus of this book, only treaty law will be considered directly.

the effect of certain treaty regimes on the laws of armed conflict. Section 4 concerns the effect of armed conflict on the content of treaty obligations. Section 5 considers the effect of international armed conflict on the territorial scope of application, an issue that has arisen specifically with respect to human rights treaties.

II. ARMED CONFLICT AS A GROUND FOR TERMINATION OR SUSPENSION OF TREATIES

1. Background

Termination and suspension of treaties are generally regulated by the Vienna Convention on the Law of Treaties (VCLT).[3] However, the Convention deliberately avoids regulation of the effect of armed conflict on treaties, with Article 73 stating that the Convention 'shall not prejudge any question that may arise in regard to a treaty … from the outbreak of hostilities between States'. This choice of the International Law Commission (ILC) when drafting the treaty reflected its position that 'the outbreak of hostilities between states must be considered as an entirely abnormal condition, and that the rules governing its legal consequences should not be regarded as forming part of the general rules of international law applicable in the normal relations between states'.[4]

Until the end of the Second World War, the effect of armed conflict on treaties had attracted only limited doctrinal interest.[5] Jurisprudential analysis, principally by domestic courts, was inconclusive.[6] With the emergence of modern armed conflict, characterized by the informality of both inception and termination of hostilities, the legal effect of armed conflict on treaties (as opposed to its practical effect) has become even more difficult to ascertain.[7] Three attempts have been made to codify the

---

[3] Vienna Convention on the Law of Treaties (adopted 23 May 1969, entered into force 27 January 1980) 1155 UNTS 331, Articles 54–67.

[4] ILC, 'Draft Articles on the Law of Treaties with Commentaries', Ybk of the International Law Commission, 1966, vol. II, commentary (2) to Draft Article 69 (later adopted as VCLT Article 73).

[5] For a literature review, see ILC, 'The Effect of Armed Conflict on Treaties: An Examination of Practice and Doctrine, Memorandum by the Secretariat' (1 February 2005) UN Doc A/CN.4/550, para 8.

[6] CM Chinkin, 'Crisis and the Performance of International Agreements: The Outbreak of War in Perspective' (1980) 7 Yale J of World Public Order 177, 190.

[7] ILC, 'The Effect of Armed Conflict on Treaties …' (n 5) para 4.

topic during the twentieth century, by the Institute of International Law in 1912, by the Harvard Research on the Law of Treaties in 1935[8] and again by the Institute of International Law in 1985.[9] Yet the effect of armed conflict on treaties remained a problematic issue. A fourth attempt at establishing a legal framework was undertaken by the ILC in 2004, and it is the focus of this section.

Doctrine on the effect of armed conflict on treaties has been divided,[10] with three main views having been put forward at various periods and regions. The traditional view was that the outbreak of war *ipso facto* abrogates all treaties.[11] This doctrine was based on the combined notions that war is a complete rupture of international relations, whereas treaties represent the most refined form of such relations. The very continued existence of international treaties was therefore irreconcilable with a state of war. This view, held principally by European States, was gradually abandoned as insufficiently nuanced, and incompatible with practice, which is much less sweeping.[12] There has also been little support for the converse view, according to which war permits all treaties to continue in existence, either in full force or in a state of suspension.[13]

A third view, which originated in the US and the UK but has gained ground also in the practice of European States, is that war terminates some treaties, suspends others and leaves others unaffected. A similar doctrine was adopted by the former Soviet Union.[14] Although this view grew to be prevalent, differences existed regarding the grounds on which

---

[8] Chinkin, 'Crisis and the Performance …' (n 6) 192–3.

[9] Institute of International Law, 'The Effects of Armed Conflicts on Treaties', 1985, accessed 14 May 2014 at www.idi-iil.org/idiE/resolutionsE/1985_hel_03_en.PDF.

[10] Research in International Law under the Auspices of the Faculty of the Harvard Law School, Drafts of Conventions Prepared for the Codification of International Law, 'Article 35, Effect of War' (1935) 29 The American J Intl L Supplement: Research in International Law 1183.

[11] CJB Hurst, 'The Effect of War on Treaties' (1921) 2 British Ybk of Intl L 37, 39.

[12] Rousseau, *Droit International Public* (vol I, 1971) 218–19, para 195, cited in ILC, 'First Report on the Effects of Armed Conflicts on Treaties, by Mr Ian Brownlie, Special Rapporteur' (21 April 2005) UN Doc A/CN.4/552, para 37; Lauterpacht and Oppenheim (7th edn, 1948) cited ibid, para 11.

[13] A view adopted, with some qualification, by the Institute of International Law in 1912, Editorial Comment, 'Effects of War upon Treaties and International Conventions: A Project Adopted by the Institute of International Law at its Session in Christiania, in August, 1912' (1913) 7 AJIL 149.

[14] JF Triska and RM Slusser, *The Theory, Law, and Policy of Soviet Treaties* (Stanford UP, 1962) 168–9.

a treaty was held to be terminated, suspended or unaffected. For example, American doctrine looked for the intention of the parties as to the effect of war when that intention was clear,[15] but otherwise policy was determined on the basis of compatibility of a treaty with national policy.[16] The untenability of this approach is self-evident, as it purports to leave each State free to determine unilaterally the validity of its treaties. In contrast, Soviet policy, outwardly similar to that of Western States, rested not so much on doctrine regarding the normative effect of armed conflict on treaties but rather on the fundamental changes of circumstances which accompany an armed conflict.[17]

Views nonetheless coalesced round two standards for determining which treaties were terminated or suspended. According to one standard, the validity of a treaty depends on its subject matter classification. This standard has not found favour with States[18] despite being convenient to apply. A second standard was the intention of the parties at the time of formulating the treaty. Being subjective, this standard is more difficult to apply effectively, particularly in situations of profound discord, but has gained acceptance, inter alia on the ground that it derives from the application of VCLT Articles 31–32.[19] The two standards are, of course, not entirely distinct, since the object and purpose of the treaty (reflected in its classification) are underpinned by the intention of the parties.

Until the end of the Second World War, the question of the status of treaties arose mostly in the aftermath of wars, when it was deemed necessary to determine in peace treaties whether pre-war treaties needed to be revived in order to be valid. Practice varied among States and over time. A study of US practice, for example, did not reveal a single treaty which the US could be said to have definitely regarded as terminated as a result of war. It was common practice for economic and humanitarian treaties to return to full effectiveness without any act of revival, but with respect to political multilateral treaties the matter was less clear. Bilateral

---

[15] SH McIntyre, *Legal Effect of World War II on Treaties of the United States* (Martinus Nijhoff, 1958) 357.

[16] Ibid, 356; ILC, 'The Effect of Armed Conflict on Treaties …' (n 5) para 11.

[17] Triska and Slusser, *Soviet Treaties* (n 14) 170–71.

[18] McIntyre, *Treaties of the United States* (n 15) 16; ILC, 'Second Report on the Effects of Armed Conflicts on Treaties by Mr Ian Brownlie, Special Rapporteur (16 June 2006) UN Doc A/CN.4/570, para 35.

[19] ILC, 'First Report on the Effects of Armed Conflicts on Treaties, by Mr Lucius Caflisch, Special Rapporteur (22 March 2010) UN Doc A/CN.4/627, paras 44–6.

treaties appear to have been impaired more than multilateral ones, being generally regarded as at least suspended, with exceptions for provisions regarding private interests of individuals.[20] The effect of armed conflict on treaties of Western European States has generally been more treaty-destructive than in the US (and the UK), but these States have also gradually toed the Anglo-American line.[21] The paucity of treaties to which the Soviet Union was party in the wake of the Second World War rendered the entire issue of little interest or significance in the Eastern bloc.[22]

Practice from the period subsequent to the termination of the Second World War[23] is even less conclusive. In the few instances where treaties have been suspended or terminated, there is no indication that this has occurred on the basis of a distinct doctrine regarding the normative effect of armed conflict on treaties, rather than due to practical difficulties resulting from the existence of armed conflict that feed into established doctrines of treaty law regarding termination, suspension or withdrawal from treaties.[24]

Against this backdrop of divided doctrine and ambiguous practice, the ILC has undertaken in 2004 a study of the topic, with a view to advancing understanding of it and to updating a doctrine which has been elaborated largely for another age.[25] In 2011 it adopted a set of a Draft Articles on the Effect of Armed Conflict on Treaties ('Draft Articles').[26] It recommended that the General Assembly consider the elaboration of a convention on the basis of the Draft Articles, a matter that is scheduled to be examined in the General Assembly's 69th session (2014).[27] The Draft Articles cannot be regarded as codification of customary law, but constitute an important stage in the progressive development of international law, reflecting a preference for legal stability and continuity.[28] This section provides an overview of the Draft Articles, focusing

---

20 McIntyre, *Treaties of the United States* (n 15) 350–55.

21 Ibid, 50.

22 Triska and Slusser, *Soviet Treaties* (n 14) 168–72.

23 ILC, 'The Effect of Armed Conflict on Treaties …' (n 5) paras 82–119.

24 VCLT Articles 61, 62.

25 ILC, 'The Effect of Armed Conflict on Treaties …' (n 5) para 164.

26 ILC, 'Draft Articles on the Effects of Armed Conflicts on Treaties (with Commentaries)' (2011) UN Doc A/66/10.

27 UNGA Res 66/99 (9 December 2011) UN Doc A/RES/66/99, paras 3, 4.

28 ILC, 'Draft Articles on the Effects of Armed Conflicts on Treaties, with Commentaries' (n 26), Commentary to Article 1, para 5.

particularly on issues where the Draft Articles depart from the VCLT's scheme.

The Draft Articles adopt the prevalent approach, according to which termination, withdrawal or suspension of a treaty does not occur *ipso facto* upon the existence of an armed conflict but is essentially a matter of interpretation. Given that the Draft Articles do not provide for any automatic consequence or even any sweeping presumption regarding the impact of armed conflict on the status of treaties, it is not surprising that the ILC adopted very broad definitions of both the terms 'treaties' and 'armed conflict'. The definition of treaty is taken from the VCLT, making no formal distinction between bilateral and multilateral treaties. This is in line with practice relating to armed conflict: if in the past multilateral treaties were viewed as more resilient to armed conflict than bilateral ones, experience since the Second World War indicates an increased resilience of bilateral treaties as well.[29] The particular characteristics of the treaty may nonetheless be a factor in the determination whether a treaty is susceptible to termination, withdrawal or suspension.[30]

The same inclusive approach was adopted with respect to the definition of armed conflict for the purpose of the Draft Articles. Armed conflict is defined broadly, following the jurisprudence of the International Tribunal for the Former Yugoslavia, namely that an armed conflict exists whenever there is a resort to armed force between States or protracted armed violence between governmental authorities and organized armed groups.[31] The very inclusion of non-international armed conflict introduces a significant element of progressive development of international law,[32] and has been subjected to criticism by States.[33] The Draft Articles exclude from their scope conflicts between non-governmental organized armed groups.[34] Although such a conflict may also affect a State, it

---

29 ILC, 'The Effect of Armed Conflict on Treaties …' (n 5) paras 151–2.

30 Draft Article 6(a) lists 'the number of parties to the treaty' as an indicative factor in that determination.

31 *Prosecutor v Tadić* (Appeals Chamber, Decision on the Defence Motion for Interlocutory Appeal on Jurisdiction) ICTY-94-1 (2 October 1995), para 70.

32 ILC, 'Third Report on the Effects of Armed Conflicts on Treaties, by Mr Ian Brownlie, Special Rapporteur' (1 March 2007) UN Doc A/CN.4/578, paras 12–15; ILC, 'Effects of Armed Conflicts on Treaties, Note on Draft Article 5 and the Annex to the Draft Articles, by Mr Lucius Caflisch, Special Rapporteur' (18 May 2011) UN Doc A/CN.4/645, para 6.

33 ILC, '… Note on Draft Article 5 and the Annex to the Draft Articles' (n 32).

34 ILC, 'First Report on the Effects of Armed Conflicts on Treaties, by Mr Lucius Caflisch …' (n 19) para 21.

would likely constitute a factual circumstance pertinent to the implementation of the treaty rather than a normative element affecting the status of the treaty.

2. Indicia for Susceptibility to Termination, Withdrawal or Suspension

The Draft Articles explicitly reject the approach according to which armed conflict *ipso facto* terminates or suspends the operation of treaties. Where the treaty itself contains provisions on its operation in situations of armed conflict, these provisions apply.[35] Otherwise, the general rules of treaty interpretation are to be applied in order to establish whether the treaty is susceptible to termination, withdrawal or suspension in the event of an armed conflict.[36] To this extent, the ILC Draft Articles resemble the scheme of the VCLT, according to which a treaty that is silent on the matter is not subject to suspension or withdrawal unless it is established that the parties intended to admit the possibility of denunciation or withdrawal, or that such a possibility is implied by the nature of the treaty.[37] The Draft Articles do not expressly mention the parties' intention. However, they call for application of '[t]he rules of international law on treaty interpretation', which themselves accommodate the intention of the parties.[38] In other words, the Draft Articles should not be read as purporting to introduce new parameters for treaty interpretation with respect to its susceptibility to termination, withdrawal or suspension.

However, the Draft Articles make an important departure from the scheme of the VCLT by proposing that whether a treaty is susceptible to termination, withdrawal or suspension as a result of armed conflict is a matter not only of treaty interpretation but also of other factors that are external to the treaty. Draft Article 6 provides for two sets of indicia. The first set, in Draft Article 6(a), lists in addition to 'the nature of the treaty, its subject matter, object and purpose, content', also 'the number of parties to the treaty'. The significance of the object and purpose of the treaty in establishing its susceptibility to termination, withdrawal or suspension is evident in Draft Article 7, which refers to an indicative list of treaties which continue in operation despite the onset of an armed

---

[35] Draft Article 5.
[36] Draft Articles 3–5.
[37] VCLT Articles 54, 56.
[38] ILC, 'Draft Articles on the Effects of Armed Conflicts on Treaties (with Commentaries)' (n 26) Commentary (3) to Article 5.

conflict, and which appears as an annex to the Draft Articles.[39] This list reflects the underlying foundation of the Draft Articles, which is to favour continuity and stability,[40] and creates a rebuttable presumption of continuity. This presumption parallels that in VCLT Article 56, which places on the party wishing to suspend or withdraw from a treaty the onus of establishing that it has the right to do so. The indicative list of treaties that remain operative is based on State practice, particularly that of the US.[41] It includes treaties on the laws of armed conflict; treaties declaring, creating or regulating a permanent regime or status or related permanent rights, including treaties establishing or modifying land and maritime boundaries; multilateral law-making treaties; treaties on international criminal justice; treaties of friendship, commerce and navigation and agreements concerning private rights; treaties for the international protection of human rights; treaties relating to the international protection of the environment; treaties relating to international watercourses and related installations and facilities; treaties relating to aquifers and related installations and facilities; treaties which are constituent instruments of international organizations; treaties relating to the international settlement of disputes by peaceful means, including resort to conciliation, mediation, arbitration and judicial settlement; and treaties relating to diplomatic and consular relations. Admittedly, Draft Articles 6(a) and 7 do not digress greatly from the scheme of the VCLT, since they largely overlap with Draft Article 5, which echoes the general rules of treaty interpretation.

The more significant departure from the VCLT rules on the interpretation of treaties, which allow the consideration of factors intrinsic to the treaty being interpreted, can be found in Draft Article 6(b), which lists as potentially relevant factors 'the characteristics of the armed conflict, such as its territorial extent, its scale and intensity, its duration and, in the case of non-international armed conflict, also the degree of outside involvement'. These are factual factors, entirely external to the treaty itself and subsequent to it. The Draft Articles acknowledge that the extent or duration of the conflict may create conditions that make performance of the treaty impossible and that undermine the trust of the parties (to the

---

[39] Ibid, Article 7 and annex.

[40] ILC, 'Draft Report of the International Law Commission on the Work of its 60th Session' (5 May–6 June and 7 July–8 August 2008) UN Doc A/CN/4/L/732/Add.2, Chapter V Effects of Armed Conflicts on Treaties, Addendum, Commentary 5 to Article 1.

[41] ILC, 'Draft Articles on the Effects of Armed Conflicts on Treaties (with Commentaries)' (n 26) Commentary (4) to annex.

conflict and the treaty).[42] Draft Article 6(b) thus reflects the notion that whether a treaty is susceptible to termination, withdrawal or suspension is context-dependent, and specifically conflict-dependent. This clearly departs from the VCLT scheme, which is based on the assumption that a treaty is either susceptible to termination, withdrawal or suspension, or it is not; but that this is an objective characteristic of the treaty itself (even if difficult to ascertain), rather than a consequence of specific circumstances subsequent to its conclusion.

3. Relationship to VCLT Grounds of Termination, Withdrawal or Suspension

One of the vexing questions relating to the existence of a legal doctrine on the effect of armed conflict on treaties is the relationship between such doctrine and grounds under the law of treaties that regulate the termination, withdrawal from, or suspension of, treaties. Such grounds include material breach, a supervening impossibility of performance of the treaty, and a fundamental change of circumstances.

None of these grounds of termination, withdrawal or suspension, provided for in the VCLT,[43] is necessarily triggered by armed conflict, although armed conflict may constitute a factual circumstance leading to their applicability. Thus, while armed conflict is a normative factor under the ILC Draft Articles, it is merely a factual circumstance under the VCLT grounds of termination, withdrawal or suspension. The principal requirement for the invocation of all three grounds is that the change claimed by the State party has a fundamental impact on the obligations under the treaty. Such a change would undermine the accomplishment of the object or purpose of the treaty[44] in the case of a breach; make the obligations impossible to perform due to the disappearance or destruction of an object indispensable for the execution of the treaty;[45] or radically transform their extent.[46] Clearly, not every armed conflict fulfils these requirements. Certainly the applicability of the laws of armed conflict is insufficient grounds for termination, withdrawal or suspension of a treaty under the narrow interpretation of VCLT Article 61 on impossibility of performance, which focuses on physical absence of objects rather than on

---

42 ILC, 'First Report on the Effects of Armed Conflicts on Treaties, by Mr Lucius Caflisch …' (n 19) para 43.

43 VCLT Articles 60–62.

44 VCLT Article 60(3)(b).

45 VCLT Article 61(1).

46 VCLT Article 62(1)(b).

legal regimes.[47] Similarly, the existence of an armed conflict does not, by itself, meet the rigorous requirements of VCLT Article 62,[48] although the change in political atmosphere accompanying an armed conflict between parties to a treaty may constitute a fundamental change of circumstances for the purposes of certain treaties. Another condition for the applicability of any of the three VCLT grounds for termination, withdrawal or suspension is that a party to a treaty cannot invoke them if the change that it relies on is the result of its own breach of an international obligation toward the other party to the treaty. This requirement is echoed in the Draft Articles, which stipulate that an aggressor State may not terminate or withdraw from a treaty, or suspend its operation, as a consequence of an armed conflict that results from its own act of aggression, if the effect would benefit that State.[49] In summary, the existence of an armed conflict which triggers the simultaneous applicability of both the VCLT grounds and the doctrine considered here is possible but not inevitable.

The Draft Articles note that they are without prejudice to such grounds for termination, withdrawal or suspension.[50] A problem nonetheless would arise if the same conditions lead to conflicting outcomes under the different doctrines. Whether this is the case with respect to the effect of armed conflict on treaties is unclear. The main doubt concerns the question whether termination, withdrawal or suspension is automatic or merely invocable. Under the VCLT, termination, withdrawal or suspension are not automatic and are subject to consent (albeit tacit) and dispute settlement in case of objection.[51] During the ILC's deliberations on the Draft Articles, the question whether termination, withdrawal or suspension should be subject to consent remained controversial until a relatively late stage. It was accepted that a State invoking armed conflict as grounds for termination, withdrawal or suspension must notify the other parties to the treaty of its intention to act upon such grounds; but there were reservations as to whether other parties may object, and whether a dispute on the matter should be submitted to a dispute settlement mechanism. It was the view of the first Special Rapporteur on the topic that the VCLT Article 65 scheme is not helpful in a case of armed

---

47 *Gabčíkovo-Nagymaros Project (Hungary/Slovakia)*, Judgment, ICJ Rep 1997, 7, [103].

48 Chinkin, 'Crisis and the Performance ...' (n 6) 189.

49 Draft Article 15.

50 Draft Article 18.

51 VCLT Article 65; O Corten and P Klein, *The Vienna Conventions on the Law of Treaties: A Commentary* (OUP, 2011) 1485.

conflict, for two main reasons. First, in case of armed conflict, the *cause* of the termination or suspension is not the breach of the treaty but considerations of necessity dictated by the circumstances of the armed conflict. Furthermore, it is reasonably clear that the policy choice between termination and suspension is driven by elements of security. The case of armed conflict thus falls outside the paradigm of termination or suspension recognized in the VCLT. Second, in the circumstances of an armed conflict, the significance of peaceful settlement as a procedural safeguard is reduced if not eliminated[52] and cannot be assumed to be a practical measure. In view of these differences, Special Rapporteur Brownlie proposed a scheme of detailed notification but excluded any machinery for compulsory settlement of disputes.

Had the approach advocated by Special Rapporteur Brownlie been adopted, a situation where armed conflict triggers both the doctrine presently under consideration and the VCLT grounds might have resulted in directly conflicting consequences, namely an obligation to settle disputes in case of objection under the latter but not under the former. This conflict was largely removed when at a late stage the ILC Draft Articles were revised to include a provision on the right of notified States parties to the treaty to object to a notification of termination, withdrawal or suspension, as well as an obligation to seek a solution through peaceful means. The provisions are more flexible than those of VCLT Article 65 in that they do not set a rigid timetable but refer to objection 'within a reasonable time', accommodating the constraints on diplomatic action during armed conflict.[53] Moreover, in practice, States invoking the VCLT grounds for termination, withdrawal or suspension rarely follow the procedure in Article 65.[54] Consequently, the normative distinctions between the doctrines persist, although they might be less significant than may appear at first sight.

---

[52] ILC, 'Fourth Report on the Effects of Armed Conflicts on Treaties, by Mr Ian Brownlie, Special Rapporteur, Procedure for Suspension and Termination' (14 November 2007) UN Doc A/CN.4/589, paras 28–9.

[53] ILC, 'Draft Articles on Responsibility of States for Internationally Wrongful Acts, with Commentaries (2001)', Ybk of the International Law Commission, 2001, vol. II, 26, UN Doc A/56/10, Draft Article 9.

[54] Corten and Klein, *The Vienna Conventions on the Law of Treaties* (n 51) 1489.

III. THE RELATIONSHIP BETWEEN THE LAWS OF ARMED CONFLICT AND TREATIES SETTING NORMATIVE REGIMES

This section follows the previous section in that it pertains to treaties which continue applying under their own terms even in the event of armed conflict. Where these treaties establish normative regimes rather than a set of contractual obligations, their applicability simultaneously with the laws of armed conflict may give rise to conflict of norms. This section examines the relationship between the laws of armed conflict and such treaty regimes, a matter which has brought to the forefront a discussion of potential conflicts with human rights treaties, and, with less force, with treaties on environmental protection. Both regimes differ from other self-contained regimes in that they establish non-reciprocal obligations. The singling out of human rights treaties is further justified by the fact that they regulate in part the same relations as those which the laws of armed conflict purport to regulate (namely between a State and individuals), albeit on a different conceptual basis, that of rights (rather than the principle of humanity).[55] This overlap in subject matter would suggest a particularly high potential for conflict between norms.

Traditionally, the laws of armed conflict and human rights treaties had been considered to apply in a mutually exclusive fashion.[56] The latter applied in peacetime, while the former applied in times of armed conflict. A similar view was held regarding treaties for environmental protection.[57] In addition, human rights treaties applied within a State while the laws of armed conflict applied to the conduct of a State outside its territory. According to these views, where the laws of armed conflict apply, they displace the other regime.[58] However, this dichotomy has eroded with

---

[55] C Droege, 'The Interplay between International Humanitarian Law and International Human Rights Law in Situations of Armed Conflict' (2007) 40(2) Isr L Rev 310, 312–13.

[56] J Crawford, *Brownlie's Principles of Public International Law* (OUP, 2012) 653–4.

[57] *Legality of the Threat or Use of Nuclear Weapons*, Advisory Opinion, ICJ Rep 1996, 226 [28].

[58] For Israel's position, see: United Nations Committee on Economic, Social and Cultural Rights, 'Israel's Replies to List of Issues to be Taken Up in Connection with the Consideration of Israel's Third Periodic Report Concerning Articles 1 to 15 of the International Covenant on Economic, Social, and Cultural Rights' (September 2011) UN Doc E/C.12/ISR/Q/3/Add. 1, response to question 2:

time, inter alia as international human rights treaties have grown to be regarded as establishing a universally applicable regime, including in situations of both international and non-international armed conflict. The International Court on Justice (ICJ) has expressly held that the protection of the International Covenant on Civil and Political Rights (ICCPR)[59] does not cease applying in times of war.[60] This view is supported by the overwhelming weight of international legal opinion and State practice.[61] Similarly, the ICJ has rejected the notion that environmental treaties are displaced by the laws of armed conflict.[62] Consequently, the question arises as to how to reconcile the applicability of these treaty regimes with the laws of armed conflict.

> Israel recognizes that there is a profound connection between Human Rights Law and the Law of Armed Conflict, and that there may well be a convergence between these two bodies of law in some respects. However, in the current state of international law and State practice worldwide, it is Israel's view that these two systems-of-law, which are codified in separate instruments, nevertheless remain distinct and apply in different circumstances.

The US, generally regarded as holding a similar view, has recently somewhat softened its position: See UN Human Rights Commission, 'Consideration of Reports Submitted by States Parties under Article 40 of the Covenant, Fourth Periodic Report, United States of America' (22 May 2012) UN Doc CCPR/C/USA/4, paras 506–7, in which the US notes that:

> Under the doctrine of lex specialis, the applicable rules for the protection of individuals and conduct of hostilities in armed conflict are typically found in international humanitarian law … In this context, it is important to bear in mind that international human rights law and the law of armed conflict are in many respects complementary and mutually reinforcing.

For further analysis, see M Milanovic, 'US Fourth ICCPR Report, IHRL and IHL' (*EJIL: Talk!*, 19 January 2012, accessed 27 November 2012 at www.ejiltalk.org/us-fourth-iccpr-report-ihrl-and-ihl/.

[59] International Covenant on Civil and Political Rights (adopted 16 December 1966, entered into force 23 March 1976) 999 UNTS 171.

[60] *Legality of the Threat or Use of Nuclear Weapons* (n 57) [25].

[61] FJ Hampson, 'The Relationship between International Humanitarian Law and Human Rights Law from the Perspective of a Human Rights Treaty Body' (2008) 90 Intl Rev of the Red Cross 549, 550. For a review of international practice, see Droege, '… Situations of Armed Conflict' (n 55) 314–17.

[62] The Court was of the view that the issue is not whether the treaties relating to the protection of the environment are or are not applicable during an armed conflict, but rather whether the obligations

> stemming from these treaties were intended to be obligations of total restraint during military conflict: *Legality of the Threat or Use of Nuclear Weapons* (n 57) [30]. By implication, it responded negatively to the non-issue.

According to the ICJ, insofar as concerns rights which are regulated by both the laws of armed conflict and international human rights treaties, the principle *lex specialis derogat legi generali* applies, with the laws of armed conflict constituting the special law.[63] However, the effect of this rule is uncertain. In the *Nuclear Weapons* advisory opinion the ICJ relied on it to interpret ICCPR Article 6 *in light of* the laws of armed conflict. In the *Wall* advisory opinion the ICJ again claimed to utilize the *lex specialis* rule,[64] whereby it proceeded to simply *apply both* the laws of armed conflict and human rights law, introducing a new and unexplained effect of the *lex specialis* rule. In short, while the interpretative principle of *lex specialis* is said to regulate the relationship between the laws of armed conflict and other legal regimes, the very meaning of the rule is ambiguous.[65] It could mean either the *application* of a general standard in a given circumstance, or its *modification, overruling or setting aside*. The first case is sometimes seen as not a situation of normative conflict at all but is taken to involve the *simultaneous* application of the special and the general standard. Thus, only the latter case (of modification etc.) is thought to involve the application of a genuine *lex specialis*.[66]

Moreover, the *Nuclear Weapons* advisory opinion illustrates that the laws of armed conflict are not necessarily the special law, and indeed, determining which law is special and which is general is a conundrum of applying the *lex specialis* rule.[67] With respect to the relationship between the laws of armed conflict and treaties protecting the environment, the ICJ stated that '[s]tates must take environmental considerations into account when assessing what is necessary and proportionate in the pursuit of legitimate military objectives'.[68] In other words, environmental treaties constitute special law that serve to interpret the general standards of necessity and proportionality, in the same manner as the laws of armed conflict constitute *lex specialis* in applying the standard of 'arbitrarily'

---

63 *The Legal Consequences of the Construction of a Wall in the Occupied Palestinian Territory*, Advisory Opinion, ICJ Rep 2004, 136, [106]; *Legality of the Threat or Use of Nuclear Weapons* (n 57) [25]; *Case Concerning Armed Activity on the Territory of the Congo (Democratic Republic of the Congo v Uganda)*, Judgment, ICJ Rep 2005, 168, [216–20].

64 *The Legal Consequences of the Construction of a Wall* (n 63).

65 ILC, 'Fragmentation of International Law: Difficulties Arising from the Diversification and Expansion of International Law, Report of the Study Group of the International Law Commission, Finalized by Martti Koskenniemi' (13 April 2006) UN Doc A/CN.4/L.682, paras 94–7.

66 Ibid, para 88.

67 Ibid, para 96.

68 *Legality of the Threat or Use of Nuclear Weapons* (n 57) [30].

under ICCPR Article 6. To be clear, of interest here are constraints not already within the laws of armed conflict that aim to protect the environment, such as Additional Protocol 1 of 1977 to the Geneva Conventions of 1949, Article 35(3),[69] which prohibits the employment of 'methods or means of warfare which are intended, or may be expected, to cause widespread, long-term and severe damage to the natural environment'; or the Convention of 18 May 1977 on the Prohibition of Military or Any Other Hostile Use of Environmental Modification Techniques, Article 1,[70] which prohibits the use of weapons which have 'widespread, long-lasting or severe effects' on the environment. These provisions constitute part of the laws of armed conflict, regardless of whether they are incorporated within instruments dedicated to the laws of armed conflict or otherwise. Rather, the question is whether norms that have been established independently of the laws of armed conflict apply simultaneously with the laws of armed conflict so that they affect the application of standards within that law. Yet after stating that 'the existing international law relating to the protection and safeguarding of the environment ... indicates important environmental factors that are properly to be taken into account in the context of the implementation of the principles and rules of the law applicable in armed conflict',[71] the ICJ reached what appears to be a contradictory conclusion, namely that 'the most directly relevant applicable law governing the question of which it was seised, is ... the law applicable in armed conflict which regulates the conduct of hostilities',[72] implying that the laws of armed conflict constitute the special law in comparison with environmental treaty law.

It appears that no general conclusion can be drawn regarding the relationship between the laws of armed conflict and other legal regimes.[73] The applicability of the *lex specialis* rule in situations of armed conflict does not dictate *a priori* precedence to any body of law, and the matter is

---

69 Protocol Additional to the Geneva Conventions of 12 August 1949, and relating to the Protection of Victims of International Armed Conflicts (Protocol I), 8 June 1977, 1125 UNTS 3.

70 Convention on the Prohibition of Military or Any Other Hostile Use of Environmental Modification Techniques (10 December 1976, entered into force 5 October 1978) 1108 UNTS 151.

71 *Legality of the Threat or Use of Nuclear Weapons* (n 57) [33].

72 Ibid, [34]. Notably, the Court did not mention the term '*lex specialis*' in this context.

73 ILC, 'Conclusions of the Work of the Study Group on the Fragmentation of International Law: Difficulties Arising from the Diversification and Expansion of International Law (2006)', Ybk of the International Law Commission, 2006, vol. II, conclusion 6.

entirely context-dependent.[74] Consequently, while general intuition might suggest that the effect of armed conflict is to diminish State obligations under other bodies of law, it may well be that these other bodies feed into the interpretation of the laws of armed conflict, constraining States' freedom of action rather than expanding it.

IV. ARMED CONFLICT AS A GROUND FOR MODIFYING TREATY OBLIGATIONS

Even where the continued existence or applicability of a treaty during armed conflict is not disputed, the existence of armed conflict – as a fact, rather than as a legal regime considered in the previous section – may constitute grounds for modification of the extent of obligations under the treaty. Provisions envisaging modifications in view of armed conflict are again particularly relevant in treaties on protection of the environment and on human rights.

Certain environmental protection treaties specifically envisage the modification of the obligations they create in situations of armed conflict. Such provisions characteristically concern exemption from liability for damage caused due to an act of armed conflict.[75] Although the laws of

---

[74] ILC, 'Fragmentation of International Law: Difficulties Arising from the Diversification and Expansion of International Law' (n 65) paras 119–20.

[75] OECD Convention on Third Party Liability in the Field of Nuclear Energy (adopted 29 July 1960, entered into force 1 April 1968) 956 UNTS 251, Article 9 ('The operator shall not be liable for damage caused by a nuclear incident directly due to an act of armed conflict, hostilities, civil war, insurrection or, except in so far as the legislation of the Contracting Party in whose territory his nuclear installation is situated may provide to the contrary, a grave natural disaster of an exceptional character'); Vienna Convention on Civil Liability for Nuclear Damage (adopted 21 May 1963, entered into force 12 November 1977) 1063 UNTS 265, Article IV(3)(a) ('No liability under this Convention shall attach to an operator for nuclear damage caused by a nuclear incident directly due to an act of armed conflict, hostilities, civil war or insurrection'); International Convention on Civil Liability for Oil Pollution Damage (adopted 29 November 1969, entered into force 19 June 1975) 973 UNTS 3, Article III(2) ('No liability for pollution damage shall attach to the owner [of a ship at the time of an any occurrence which causes pollution damage] if he proves that the damage [caused by oil which has escaped or been discharged from the ship]: (a) resulted from an act of war, hostilities, civil war, insurrection or a natural phenomenon of an exceptional, inevitable and irresistible character'); Convention on Civil Liability for Oil Pollution Damage Resulting from Exploration for and Exploitation of Seabed Mineral Resources Civil

armed conflict themselves exclude liability for lawful acts of armed conflict,[76] the scope of the provisions cited here is wider, as they extend, for example, also to non-international conflict. Moreover, there are provisions on other modifications. For example, the International Convention for the High Seas Fisheries of the North Pacific Ocean stipulates that:

> [i]n any decision or recommendation [of the Commission regarding abstention from fishing and conservation measures] allowances shall be made for the effect of strikes, wars, or exceptional economic or biological conditions which may have introduced temporary declines in or suspension of productivity, exploitation, or management of the stock of fish concerned.[77]

Modification of some human rights treaties in light of armed conflict is regulated by derogation clauses. Such clauses exist in the ICCPR, the European Convention on Human Rights (ECHR),[78] and the American

---

Liability (adopted 1 May 1977, not in force) 16 ILM 1451, Article 3(3) ('No liability for pollution damage shall attach to the operator if he proves that the damage resulted from an act of war, hostilities, civil war, insurrection, or a natural phenomenon of an exceptional, inevitable and irresistible character'); International Convention on the Establishment of an International Fund for Compensation for Oil Pollution Damage (adopted 18 December 1971, entered into force 16 October 1978) 1110 UNTS 57, Article 4(2)(a) ('The Fund shall incur no obligation under the preceding paragraph if: (a) it proves that the pollution damage resulted from an act of war, hostilities, civil war or insurrection or was caused by oil which has escaped or been discharged from a warship or other ship owned or operated by a State and used, at the time of the incident, only on Government non-commercial service'); Convention on the Regulation of Antarctic Mineral Resource Activities (adopted 2 June 1988, not in force) 27 ILM 868, Article 8(4)(b) ('An Operator shall not be liable pursuant to paragraph 2 above if it proves that the damage has been caused directly by, and to the extent that it has been caused directly by: ... b) armed conflict, should it occur notwithstanding the Antarctic Treaty, or an act of terrorism directed against the activities of the Operator, against which no reasonable precautionary measures could have been effective').

[76] Hague Convention (IV) Respecting the Laws and Customs of War on Land and its Annex: Regulations Concerning the Laws and Customs of War on Land (adopted 18 October 1907, entered into force 26 January 1910) Martens Nouveau Recueil (ser 3) 461, Article 3.

[77] International Convention (with Annex and Protocol) for the High Seas Fisheries of the North Pacific Ocean (adopted 9 May 1952, entered into force 1 March 1955) 205 UNTS 65, Article IV(2).

[78] European Convention on Human Rights and Fundamental Freedoms (adopted 4 November 1950, entered into force 3 September 1953) 213 UNTS 222.

Convention on Human Rights (ACHR).[79] These clauses define the conditions under which States may suspend in part certain guarantees provided for in the treaties, in order to respond to an emergency which threatens the life of a nation, as well as the limits on such suspension.[80] Only the ECHR and ACHR expressly mention 'war', but armed conflict is the paradigmatic phenomenon covered by all three instruments,[81] which allow derogation in case of a 'public emergency which threatens the life of the nation' (ICCPR and ECHR) or 'emergency that threatens the independence or security of a State Party' (ACHR). At the same time, not every armed conflict necessarily meets this description. The condition of 'threatening the life of the nation' has been interpreted as 'a threat to the organised life of the community of which the State is composed'.[82] Thus, the situation in which derogation clauses are likely to be invocable is that of armed conflict (or less grave situations, namely of disturbances, riots and other violence which does not amount to armed conflict) within the territory of a State. If the armed conflict is outside national territory, the organized life of the nation is less likely to be directly at threat. Indeed, with respect to the ECHR, 'war' as such has never been invoked as grounds for derogation; the need to counter terrorist violence, on the other hand, has often been so cited.[83]

Even if an armed conflict does not reach the level of emergency which triggers the right to derogate, it may still permit States to limit their human rights or environmental obligations, in accordance with ordinary limitation clauses, which allow restrictions on most rights. Protected interests that are particularly likely to be affected by armed conflict are public order[84] and national security.[85] It should be noted that the effect of

---

[79] American Convention on Human Rights (adopted 22 November 1969, entered into force 18 July 1978) 1144 UNTS 123.

[80] ICCPR Article 4, ECHR Article 15, ACHR Article 27.

[81] UNCHR 'General Comment No 29: States of Emergency (Article 4)' (31 August 2001) UN Doc CCPR/C/21/Rev.1/Add.11, para 3; D Harris, M O'Boyle, E Bates, and C Buckley, *Law of the European Convention on Human Rights* (OUP, 2009) 625.

[82] *Lawless v Ireland (No 3)*, (1961) 1 EHRR 15, para 28.

[83] Harris et al, *Law of the ECHR* (n 81) 625.

[84] Hampson, '… Human Rights Treaty Body' (n 61) 560; Harris et al, *Law of the ECHR* (n 81) 620.

[85] Eg, provisions allowing limitations on obligations to provide information in order to protect national security: Convention on the Protection and Use of Transboundary Watercourses and International Lakes (adopted 17 March 1992, entered into force 6 October 1996) 1936 UNTS 269, Article 8 ('The provisions of this Convention shall not affect the rights or the obligations of Parties in

armed conflict is not synonymous with pursuit of 'national security' interests, which may be wider or narrower depending on the circumstances.

There are other interests that may justify limitations on State's obligations (or relaxation of prohibitions), which the occurrence of armed conflict may affect. For example, armed conflict may generate famine, which may be grounds for modification of obligations.[86] Some treaties refer more generally to the possibility of exceptional circumstances justifying derogations, within which armed conflict may fall,[87] or, even

---

accordance with their national legal systems and applicable supranational regulations to protect information related to … national security') and similarly Convention on the Protection of the Marine Environment of the Baltic Sea Area (adopted 1992, entered into force 17 January 2000) 2099 UNTS 197, Article 18(1) ('The provisions of this Convention shall not affect the right or obligation of any Contracting Party under its national law and applicable supra-national regulation to protect … national security') and similarly Convention on Cooperation for the Protection and Sustainable Use of the Danube River (adopted 29 June 1994, entered into force 22 October 1998) OJ L342 (40) (12 December 1997), Article 12(5).

[86] African Convention on the Conservation of Nature and Natural Resources (OAU) (adopted 16 June 1969, entered into force 31 March 1976) 1001 UNTS 3, Article XVII(2) ('The provisions of this Convention shall not prevent Contracting States: (a) in time of famine; … to enact measures contrary to the provisions of the Convention, provided their application is precisely defined in respect of aim, time and place').

[87] Convention on the Conservation of Migratory Species of Wild Animals (adopted 23 June 1979, entered into force 1 November 1983) 1651 UNTS 333, Article III(5)(d); Convention on the Conservation of European Wildlife and Natural Habitats (adopted 19 September 1979, entered into force 1 June 1982) ETS No 104, Article 9(1) (' Each Contracting Party may make exceptions from the provisions of Articles 4, 5, 6, 7 [regarding the obligation to adopt measures to protect wild flora and fauna] and from the prohibition of the use of the means mentioned in Article 8 provided that there is no other satisfactory solution and that the exception will not be detrimental to the survival of the population concerned: … in the interests of public health and safety, air safety or other overriding public interests'); Convention on Wetlands of International Importance, especially as Waterfowl Habitat (adopted 2 February 1971, entered into force 21 December 1975) 996 UNTS 245, Article 2(5) ('Any Contracting Party shall have the right to add to the List further wetlands situated within its territory, to extend the boundaries of those wetlands already included by it in the List, or, because of its urgent national interests, to delete or restrict the boundaries of wetlands already included by it in the List').

more leniently, qualify the obligation in the first place so as to accommodate unspecified constraints.[88] Notably, however, armed conflict as such is neither a necessary nor a sufficient condition for the applicability of such limitations.

V. THE EFFECT OF ARMED CONFLICT ON THE TERRITORIAL SCOPE OF TREATY APPLICATION

The territorial scope of treaty application is not a matter which can be simply stated in terms of the intention of the parties or of a presumption as to their intentions.[89] While the VCLT clarifies that treaties apply within the entire territory of a State,[90] it is silent on the extraterritorial applicability of treaties, noting that such applicability cannot be established by reference merely to the intention of the parties. Beyond express stipulation in a treaty, various factors may come into play in determining a treaty's territorial application. This section examines armed conflict as such a factor, which by extending the territorial reach of State action outside its territory triggers a corresponding extraterritorial extension of treaty obligations.

This issue may be pertinent to any treaty the subject matter of which does not in itself imply extraterritorial effect. However, it is considered in this chapter specifically with respect to human rights treaties, an issue which has been at the forefront of scholarly debate, international jurisprudence and practice.[91] Human rights treaties were originally designed to apply in the relations of a State within its own population; they were therefore, in distinction from every other area of international law,

---

[88] International Covenant on Economic, Social and Cultural Rights (adopted 16 December 1966, entered into force 3 January 1976) 993 UNTS 3, Articles 2(1), 4.

[89] 'Draft Articles on the Law of Treaties with Commentaries' (n 4) commentary 5 to Draft Article 25 (later adopted as VCLT Article 29).

[90] See on this M Milanovic, 'The Spatial Dimension: Treaties and Territory', chapter 7 in this handbook.

[91] In the last decade alone, the following monographs have been published that are dedicated to the matter, not to mention an abundance of articles: M Milanovic, *Extraterritorial Application of Human Rights Treaties: Law, Principles and Policy* (OUP, 2011); F Coomans and MT Kamminga, *Extraterritorial Application of Human Rights Treaties* (Intersentia, 2004); K Da Costa, *The Extraterritorial Application of Selected Human Rights Treaties* (Brill, 2012); M Gondek, *The Reach of Human Rights in a Globalising World: Extraterritorial Application of Human Rights Treaties* (Intersentia, 2009).

perceived from the outset as applicable only within a State's territory. Their extension geographically and personally to individuals present outside a State's territory is ostensibly a mere application of an established legal formula – jurisdiction, to new facts – the exercise by States of various levels of personal and territorial control outside their territory. In fact this brings about a qualitative change, namely the extension of States' obligations outside their territory.

The extraterritorial applicability of human rights treaties is not necessarily an armed conflict-related issue. A State may be subject to human rights obligations beyond its borders outside the context of armed conflict,[92] while involvement in armed conflict does not necessarily trigger extraterritorial obligations (clearly not when the armed conflict takes place within the territory of a single State, and arguably not even in every case of international armed conflict, since the applicability of human rights law during hostilities is an open question). Nonetheless, in practice the paradigmatic situation in which obligations of human rights treaties apply extraterritorially is indeed that of an armed conflict extending across borders, and accordingly this specific point of contact between armed conflict and treaty obligations will be examined.

Human rights treaties typically give rise to obligations when States exercise 'jurisdiction', a term distinct from sovereignty or territorial control. Consensus seems to grow that it connotes a measure of control over territory or over persons;[93] what level of control remains highly controversial. Armed conflict is a likely circumstance in which a State may find itself in a position to exercise control over persons outside its territory and thus affect their rights.[94] Interestingly, however, the one situation with respect to which it can be said with confidence that the extraterritorial applicability of human rights treaties is agreed upon is belligerent occupation, a situation regulated first and foremost by the laws of armed conflict. This view was held by the ICJ in the *Wall* advisory opinion and in *Congo v Uganda*,[95] and had been endorsed even

---

[92] UNCHR 'General Comment No 31 [80]: The Nature of the General Legal Obligation Imposed on States Parties to the Covenant' (26 May 2004) UN Doc CCPR/C/21/Rev.1/Add.13, para 10; UNCHR, *Lopez Burgos v Uruguay*, Communication No R.12/52 (6 June 1979) UN Doc Supp No 40 (A/36/40) 176 (1981).

[93] *Al-Skeini v UK* App no 55721/07 (ECtHR, 7 July 2011).

[94] Extraterritorial territorial control may exist when a State leases territory, eg, the US's position in Guantanamo Bay.

[95] *The Legal Consequences of the Construction of a Wall* (n 63) [108]–[111]; *Democratic Republic of the Congo v Uganda* (n 63) [219].

earlier (albeit in different terms) by the European Court of Human Rights.[96] It should be clarified that it is not the existence of occupation as a *legal* phenomenon which triggers the applicability of human rights treaties; rather, the *exercise of effective control* to a degree which gives rise to the applicability of the laws of belligerent occupation that also triggers the applicability of human rights treaties.[97] Belligerent occupation is defined by the non-consensual exercise by a State of effective control over non-sovereign territory. Effective control over territory is the most demanding standard of control; it is therefore tempting to argue that where it exists for the purpose of establishing the existence of occupation, it should also establish jurisdiction for the purpose of applicability of human rights treaties.

The notion that 'effective control' has an identical meaning for both the laws of occupation and international human rights law is attractive in its simplicity. However, it may be too simplistic, for a number of reasons. First, occupation is an inter-State relationship; it relates to the fundamental existence of the ordering units of international law, States, which are defined by their territoriality. It is therefore only natural that the definition of occupation is intimately linked with issues of territorial control. In contrast, human rights doctrine is person-centered, where territory as such is not of particular significance. Inferring jurisdiction for the purpose of human rights obligations from the existence of effective control may therefore be either too restrictive or too broad an inference. An area may be under sufficient control of a State to be regarded as occupied, but the occupying power's position may be still challenged in a manner which in practice prevents it from discharging some of its responsibilities under human rights treaties. Territorial control that establishes occupation might therefore be insufficient for the discharge of all

---

[96] *Loizidou v Turkey* (Merits) ECHR 1996–VI 2216. Even Israel, one of the two main opponents to the extraterritorial applicability of international human rights law as a matter of principle, has conceded in the practice of its supreme court, that international human rights law, including human rights treaties, apply in the West Bank, which it regards as governed by the laws of occupation. See, eg, HCJ 3239/02 *Marab v IDF Commander in the West Bank*, ILDC 15 (IL 2003) para 41 to President Barak's judgment, referring to the ICCPR with respect to standards of detention which should be upheld in the West Bank, official translation accessed 15 May 2014 at http://elyon1.court.gov.il/files_eng/02/390/032/A04/02032390.a04.pdf.

[97] *Al-Skeini v UK* (n 93).

or some of a State's human rights obligations.[98] A converse cause for doubt as to the conflation of the concept of 'effective control' for the purpose of the law of occupation with the same concept in the context of human rights treaties, operating in the converse manner, is that the types of obligations under the law of occupation and under international human rights treaties differ and therefore require different thresholds for applicability. The law of occupation is based on absolute obligations. The threshold for its applicability is correspondingly high. In contrast, international human rights law is based on the application of standards, for balancing conflicting interests. It is accordingly more flexible and can accommodate a variety of degrees of the extent of a State's control. Correspondingly, a lower threshold of control might suffice to trigger its applicability.[99]

While these considerations operate in opposite directions, they do not, of course, offset each other. In conclusion, 'jurisdiction' for the purpose of human rights law might not be identical to 'effective control' for the purpose of the laws of occupation. This attenuates the link between armed conflict and applicability of human rights treaties.

VI. OPEN QUESTIONS: A RESEARCH AGENDA

Each of the sections above presents a different type of link between armed conflict and treaties. Within each, various issues remain unexplored. The VCLT is silent on the effect of armed conflict on treaties, while the ILC Draft Articles are silent on the relationship between the framework they propose and the VCLT termination and suspension grounds. This relationship remains an important question in the study of the effect of armed conflict on treaties. A similar issue of the relationship between doctrines which is not explored in this non-exhaustive chapter is the role of armed conflict with respect to secondary rules of State responsibility regarding circumstances precluding wrongfulness, such as force majeure (in which case a non-international armed conflict in which

---

[98] The practicability – and advisability – of imposing human rights obligations extraterritorially is evidently questionable in so far as concerns positive obligations. Milanovic, *Extraterritorial Application of Human Rights Treaties* (n 91) 207–28.

[99] Droege, '... Situations of Armed Conflict' (n 55) 332.

a government is not involved might become of particular interest)[100] and necessity.[101]

Another underexplored issue is the relationship between the laws of armed conflict and human rights treaties and the extraterritorial applicability of human rights obligations in situations of a non-international conflict that take place across borders. All these issues require the attention of international law scholars and are likely to shape a future agenda for research.

---

[100] The Permanent Court of International Justice has addressed the matter summarily, stating: '*Force Majeure* – it cannot be maintained that the war itself, despite its grave economic consequences, affected the legal obligations of the contracts between the Serbian Government and the French bond holders. The economic dislocations caused by the war did not release the debtor State, although they may present equities which doubtless will receive appropriate consideration in the negotiations', *Case Concerning Payment of Various Serbian Loans Issued in France, France v Kingdom of the Serbs, Croats and Slovenes* (Judgment) PCIJ Rep Series A No 20 (12 July 1929), 39–40.

[101] ILC, 'Draft Articles on Responsibility of States for Internationally Wrongful Acts, with Commentaries' (n 53) Draft Articles 23, 25.

PART V

EXPANSIONS

19. Treaties and international organizations: Uneasy analogies

Philippa Webb

I. INTRODUCTION

The expansion of activities that States undertake in a collective manner has led to the increasing use and creation of international organizations (IOs). These IOs, in turn, have become parties to a rising number of treaties. The United Nations (UN) is a party to 1500 treaties listed in the United Nations Treaty Series (UNTS) database.[1] The European Union (EU) is a party to over 2000 agreements.[2] Classic treaties involve relationships between entities, such as host State agreements between States and IOs and cooperation agreements between IOs. An emerging trend is for IOs to become parties to substantive law-making treaties on, for example, the law of the sea and human rights. The IO may be a party to a treaty in addition to its member States or it may extend the effects of the treaty to its member States. It may be a party to a 'mixed agreement'

[1] http://treaties.un.org/, accessed 1 May 2014. These range from VCLT-IO to Exchange of Notes between the Government of the United Kingdom of Great Britain and Northern Ireland and the United Nations Interim Administration Mission in Kosovo (UNMIK) Concerning the Transfer of Mr Luan Goçi to the Jurisdiction of the United Kingdom of Great Britain and Northern Ireland. Not all treaties concluded by IOs are registered in the UNTS database. The obligation to register treaties with the Secretariat in Article 102(1) of the 1945 United Nations Charter does not apply to international organizations, but only to 'any Member of the United Nations'. See also UN Doc A/Res/97(I) (1946) and UN Doc A/Res/52/153 (1997).

[2] www.consilium.europa.eu/policies/agreements, accessed 1 May 2014. Brolmann notes that this database may be over-inclusive from the perspective of the formal law of treaties: C Brolmann, 'The 1986 Vienna Convention on the Law of Treaties: The History of Draft Article 36*bis*' in J Klabbers (ed), *Essays on the Law of Treaties: A Collection of Essays in Honour of Bert Vierdag* (Martinus Nijhoff, 1998) 127, fn 21.

that covers a field that partly belongs to the competence of the organization and partly to that of its member States.[3]

The law of treaties as applied to IOs gives rise to uneasy analogies with the law applicable in an inter-State context. The current legal framework does not seem to have kept pace with the dynamic participation of IOs in all aspects of international life. There is a tension between treating IOs in the same way as States and accommodating their specific characteristics.[4] After a brief introduction to the two Vienna Conventions, this chapter explores this tension through the concepts of sovereignty/competence, equality and the attribution of responsibility.

II. THE TWO VIENNA CONVENTIONS ON THE LAW OF TREATIES

The International Law Commission (ILC) set out to draft a convention that would codify the 'entire subject of the law of treaties', including agreements between States and IOs and between two or more IOs.[5] Encountering strong opposition within both the ILC and the UN General Assembly to this 'equal treatment' of States and organizations, the draft of the 1969 Vienna Convention on the Law of Treaties (VCLT) was expressly limited to inter-State treaties.[6] The project of drafting a treaty that would address IOs and their special characteristics was recommended by States at the 1969 Vienna Conference and shortly afterwards was expressly mandated by the General Assembly.[7]

The essence of the problem was summed up by Paul Reuter, the ILC Special Rapporteur for the topic:

---

[3] HG Schermers and NM Blokker, *International Institutional Law* (4th edn, Martinus Nijhoff, 2011) 1129.

[4] Cf Tomuschat's view that despite the fact IOs lack 'flesh and blood' (territory and population), in some sectors 'their status is exactly the same as that of States' and 'the rules of international responsibility pertain to that class of rules': C Tomuschat, 'The International Responsibility of the European Union' in E Cannizzaro (ed), *The EU as an Actor in International Relations* (Kluwer Law International, 2002) 177, 178.

[5] S Rosenne, *The Law of Treaties: A Guide to the Legislative History of the Vienna Convention* (AW Sijthoff, 1970) 44–5.

[6] Ibid, 41–6.

[7] Official Records of the Vienna Conference on the Law of Treaties, Resolution Relating to Article 1 of the Vienna Convention on the Law of Treaties, at 178–9 (proposed by Sweden, adopted 85 votes in favour, no votes against, with 13 abstentions). UNGA Res 2501 (XXIV) (1969).

> International organizations are neither sovereign nor equal; all their powers are strictly at the service of their member states; it is the function they assume that justifies and circumscribes their activities and their very being. It is therefore necessary to establish to what extent this difference in the basis of the rule requires that the rule be modified, or at least rendered more flexible, in respect of international organizations.[8]

Some minor concessions to the special features of IOs were made in the 1986 Vienna Convention on the Law of Treaties between States and International Organizations or between International Organizations (VCLT-IO). For example, IOs undertake an 'act of formal confirmation' not 'ratification' (Article 14). Interestingly, this distinction did not reflect the existing international practice as most treaties open to IOs use the term 'ratification' for both States and organizations.[9] In Article 45 on the loss of a right to invoke a ground for invalidating, terminating, withdrawing from or suspending the operation of a treaty, a State may lose that right if it *acquiesced* through its conduct in the validity of the treaty whereas an organization loses the corresponding right through *renunciation* by reason of conduct of the competent organ.[10] A possible rationale for this difference is that an IO's acquiescence is more complicated than a State's to establish.[11]

Ultimately, however, the two Vienna Conventions are almost identical, which belies the different capacities and power dynamics between States and IOs. The 1986 diplomatic conference that adopted the VCLT-IO rejected all the substantive changes suggested by the ILC and favoured consistency with the VCLT over adapting the law to the special features of IOs.[12] As Gaja says, the text of the VCLT-IO 'gives the reader a strong feeling of *déjà vu*'.[13]

---

[8] Yearbook of the ILC (1977) vol II, Part One, 120, para 6.

[9] P Manin, 'The European Communities and the Vienna Convention on the Law of Treaties between States and International Organizations or between International Organizations' (1987) 24 Common Market L Rev 457, 468. See, eg, 1985 Vienna Convention for the Protection of the Ozone Layer, Article 13; cf 1982 UN Convention on the Law of the Sea (UNCLOS), Annex IX, Article 3, which uses 'instrument of formal confirmation'.

[10] VCLT-IO, Article 45(1)(b); cf Article 45(2)(c).

[11] G Gaja, 'A "New" Vienna Convention on Treaties between States and International Organizations or between International Organizations: A Critical Commentary' (1987) 58 BYIL 253, 259.

[12] Ibid, 254.

[13] Ibid, 253. The first 72 Articles of each Convention share the same numbering.

III. SOVEREIGNTY AND COMPETENCE

Each State enjoys sovereignty, which is based on its territory.[14] An IO has no territory; it has 'competence' not sovereignty, which is delimited by its functions. As the International Court of Justice (ICJ) has stated:

> international organizations … do not, unlike States, possess a general competence. International organizations are governed by the 'principle of speciality', that is to say, they are invested by the States which create them with powers, the limits of which are a function of the common interests whose promotion those States entrust to them.[15]

The difference between unlimited sovereignty and functionally limited competence defines the treaty relationship between States and IOs, and can create uncertainty as to the extent an IO can act in its own name or bind its member States.

1. Capacity to Conclude Treaties

A key substantive difference between States and IOs is the existence of the capacity to conclude agreements. Whereas all States possess the capacity to conclude treaties (VCLT, Article 6), the equivalent capacity of an IO 'is governed by the rules of that organization' (VCLT-IO, Article 6). For some IOs, treaty-making capacity is expressly conferred in their constituent instruments, but for other IOs it will only be implied.[16] Occasionally, the capacity of an IO to become a party to a treaty is recognized in the text of a treaty itself, as has been done with respect to the European Community (EC).[17]

The diversity of IOs has led the ICJ to be cautious in establishing a blanket rule. It has recognized the treaty-making capacity of 'at least *certain* international organizations'.[18] It has spoken of the UN being the

---

[14] VCLT-IO, Article 29 provides that 'a treaty between one or more States and one or more international organizations is binding upon each State party *in respect of its entire territory*' (emphasis added). Of course, the jurisdiction of a State can be extraterritorial in certain circumstances: M Milanovic, *Extra-territorial Application of Human Rights Treaties* (OUP, 2011).

[15] *Legality of the Use by a State of Nuclear Weapons in Armed Conflicts*, Advisory Opinion, ICJ Rep 1996, 78, para 25.

[16] UN, *Treaty Handbook* (UN, 2006) 27.

[17] Ibid.

[18] Emphasis added. *Reparation for Injuries Suffered in the Service of the United Nations*, Advisory Opinion, ICJ Rep 1949, 174, 178–9.

'supreme international organization', yet the Court also observes that the UN's legal personality, rights and duties fall short of that of a State.[19] The UN enjoys '*a large measure* of international personality',[20] not the full measure accorded to States.

The VCLT-IO essentially leaves it to each IO to 'chart their present and future needs'[21] in this regard and only implicitly recognizes that international law lays down the principle of the treaty-making capacity of IOs.[22] The preamble confirms the functional basis for treaty-making capacity, stating that IOs 'possess the capacity to conclude treaties which is necessary for the exercise of their functions and the fulfilment of their purposes'.[23]

Once an IO's treaty-making capacity has been established, there is the question of which organ is competent to conclude the agreement. Although there is a great variety of forms of government and State structures, there is general agreement on which officials and organs are competent to conclude treaties. There is much less certainty as to the competent organ of an IO, reflecting the narrower conception of the powers of an organization as opposed to a State. The diversity of practice is illustrated by agreements on privileges and immunities (APICs).[24] APICs have been made between an IO's organ and its members,[25] have been concluded between members and then approved by the organization's plenary body[26] or have excluded the organization altogether.[27] The APIC of the International Criminal Court (ICC) was negotiated by the ICC Preparatory Commission (a body serviced by the UN), adopted

---

19 Ibid, 179.

20 Ibid, emphasis added.

21 N Sybesma-Knol, 'The New Law of Treaties: The Codification of the Law of Treaties Concluded between States and International Organizations or between Two or More International Organizations' (1985) 15 Georgia J Intl CL 425, 443.

22 The Commentary acknowledges that views were divided on this point: Yearbook of the ILC (1982) vol II, Part 2, 24.

23 Gaja, 'A "New" Vienna Convention …' (n 11) 261, fn 31 (citing similar wording in a proposal submitted by the delegations of Czechoslovakia, the German Democratic Republic and the Ukrainian SSR).

24 Schermers and Blokker, *International Institutional Law* (n 3) 1135.

25 Convention on the Privileges and Immunities of the League of Arab States, approved by the Council on 10 May 1953.

26 1946 General Convention on Privileges and Immunities of the UN, 1 UNTS 115.

27 See the 1949 Agreement on the Privileges and Immunities of the Council of Europe, 250 UNTS 14.

by the Assembly of States Parties (composed of States parties and separate to the Court) and then opened by signature by all States, whether or not parties to the 1998 ICC Statute.[28] The default position is to entrust the conclusion of an agreement to the plenary body, but some organizations delegate specific tasks to the exclusive competence of certain organs. In the UN, the Security Council has primary competence for peace and security and the Secretary-General on administrative matters.[29]

In sum, the increasing participation of IOs in treaty-making has not been matched by a general recognition of their treaty-making capacity. Determining the capacity of an IO entails specific analysis of its rules, functions and structure.

2. Creating Treaty Obligations for States

The gap between 'State sovereignty' and 'IO competence' is illustrated by the question of whether treaties involving IOs can create obligations for third States, including the member States.[30] This is one area where the VCLT could not provide guidance, and it was the issue that aroused the 'most comment, controversy and difficulty, both in and outside the Commission'.[31]

During the negotiations on the VCLT-IO, the ILC drafted Article 36*bis*, which would have extended the effects of treaties entered into by IOs to their member States.[32] The ILC was influenced by the example of the (then) European Economic Community (EEC), which is competent under international law to conclude treaties that bind its institutions and its

---

[28] Schermers and Blokker, *International Institutional Law* (n 3) 1136. ICC-ASP/1/3 (Part II-E).

[29] The UN Office of Legal Affairs has said that '[a]s a matter of general policy' formal agreements are not concluded by organs, such as the UN Secretariat, without express authorization from the General Assembly or 'other competent deliberative organs'. It drew a contrast with informal, non-binding 'memoranda of understanding': [1981] UNJY 149.

[30] This is different to the question whether the responsibility of an IO for breaches of treaty obligations in relation to third parties may be attributed to its members (discussed below). For much more on treaties and third parties, see Proelss (in this volume).

[31] Yearbook of the ILC (1982) (n 22) 43.

[32] It would have required the consent of the contracting parties to the treaty; the unanimous agreement of the member States to be bound by the said provisions of the treaty; and the consent of member States must have been brought to the knowledge of States and organizations that participated in the negotiation of the treaty.

member States; it also gives guarantees to non-member States that they assent to and accept by entering into treaty relations with the EEC.[33]

Article 36*bis*, however, proved too controversial at the 1986 Vienna Diplomatic Conference and it was not accepted.[34] At least four views existed, illustrating the diverse perspectives on the sovereignty/competence analogy. One view was that Article 36*bis* was unnecessary because the provisions on the effects of treaties for third States should also apply to member States (Articles 35 and 36). These provisions refer to States giving consent to specific, existing provisions; moreover, there is 'some incongruity' in considering member States as 'third States' when often the IO only acts under the direct control of its members.[35] A second view held by many States was that the issue would not be governed by the VCLT-IO and there was no need for the provision. The Soviet Union took the strong view that member States should only be bound by a treaty concluded by an IO if they give their express, ad hoc consent.[36] Finally, IOs participating in the conference objected to Article 36*bis* because they feared the proposed wording was too restrictive.[37]

In the end, the question was left unresolved. Article 74(3) VCLT-IO was introduced as a saving clause, stating that the provisions of the Convention 'shall not prejudge any question that may arise in regard to the establishment of obligations and rights for States members of an international organization under a treaty to which that organization is a party'. The 1973 *Institut de droit international* resolution also evaded this question.[38] Both the resolution and VCLT-IO, Article 74(3) give a

---

[33] 1957 Treaty Establishing the European Communities, 297 UNTS 3, Article 228(2). See P Manin, 'L'Article 228, Paragraphe 2 du Traité CEE' in P-H Teitgen (ed), *Etudes de Droit des Communautés Européennes (Mélanges Offerts à Pierre-Henri Teitgen)* (Pedone, 1984).

[34] Tomuschat, '... International Responsibility ...' (n 4) 207; Brolmann, 'The 1986 Vienna Convention ...' (n 2)127.

[35] Gaja, 'A "New" Vienna Convention ...' (n 11) 264. See also Tomuschat, '... International Responsibility ...' (n 4) 211.

[36] Manin, 'The European Communities and the Vienna Convention ...' (n 9) 469.

[37] Ibid.

[38] 1973 *Institut de droit international* Resolution, Section V (an agreement concluded lawfully by an IO binds it but is 'without prejudice to any obligation that may arise from such agreement for Member States either under the relevant rules of the Organization or under any general rule of international law').

disappointing non-answer to the long-debated question of the effects of treaties for member States of an IO.[39]

A step further than creating treaty obligations for member States would be for an IO actually to impose a treaty on a State. A potential example in this regard is the establishment of the Special Tribunal for Lebanon (STL). In Resolution 1757 (2007), the Security Council decided that:

> acting under Chapter VII of the Charter of the United Nations, that the provisions of the annexed document [the Agreement between the United Nations and the Lebanese Republic on the establishment of a Special Tribunal for Lebanon], including its attachment [the Statute of the STL] … shall enter into force on 10 June 2007, unless the Government of Lebanon has provided notification under Article 19(1) of the annexed document before that date.[40]

In the event, the Lebanese Government faced domestic political obstacles and could not provide the notification that 'the requirement for entry into force ha[d] been complied with'.[41] The annexed document and the Statute thus entered into force on 10 June 2007 under the authority of the Security Council, thereby establishing the STL.

The STL defence counsel challenged the legality of the STL,[42] contending that Resolution 1757 unilaterally imposed a treaty on Lebanon in violation of the law of treaties, including the VCLT-IO.[43] The prosecution did not assert that a Security Council Resolution had the capacity to impose a treaty by substituting its resolution for Lebanon's consent. Rather, the prosecution claimed that Resolution 1757 allowed for two methods of establishing the STL: (1) through an international agreement between the UN and Lebanon pursuant to the written notification of the Lebanese Government; (2) absent such notification, by a measure pursuant to Article 41 of Chapter VII of the Charter, under the

---

[39] Cf the opposite phenomenon, the question of whether member States may impose legal obligations on an IO through a treaty, analysed in Tomuschat, '… International Responsibility …' (n 4).

[40] UNSC Res 1757 (2007), para 1(a). See also Brolmann, 'The 1986 Vienna Convention …' (n 2) 26.

[41] Article 19(1) of the Agreement.

[42] *Prosecutor v Ayyash et al*, Case No STL-11-01/PT/TC, Defence Motions Challenging the Legality of the Tribunal, 4–9 May 2012.

[43] *Prosecutor v Ayyash et al*, Case No STL-11-01/PT/TC, The Corrected Version of the Defence for Mr Hussein Hassan Oneissi's Motion Challenging the Legality of the Tribunal, 10 May 2012, 1, paras 36, 38, 80–102 (noting that even if the Convention has not entered into force, the UN is a party and its provisions constitute customary international law).

Security Council's authority to maintain international peace and security.[44] In the prosecution's view, the second method was lawfully applied in this case.[45] In July 2012, the judges of the STL issued their decision on the jurisdictional and legality of the Tribunal. The Trial Chamber held that Resolution 1757 was the sole basis for establishing the STL; the *provisions* of the draft Agreement entered into force through the Resolution rather than the draft Agreement itself.[46] Lebanon's sovereignty was not violated because the Security Council did not unilaterally impose a treaty on Lebanon, but integrated the provisions of the intended agreement into its Resolution.[47] The Appeals Chamber unanimously agreed with the Trial Chamber.[48]

3. Mixed Agreements

When the subject matter of a treaty relates to the competences of both the IO and its member States, the full and effective discharge of the obligations may require it to be a 'mixed agreement' jointly concluded by the organization and its members.[49] Since all States enjoy sovereign equality and *plénitude des pouvoirs*, there is no equivalent to mixed agreements in the inter-State context.

There is inconsistent practice on the conclusion of mixed agreements, which vary depending on the content of the agreement and the respective spheres of competence of the IO and the member States. Defining these areas of competence is not straightforward and may involve political sensitivities. In the practice relating to the EU, its competence is not

---

[44] *Prosecutor v Ayyash et al*, Case No STL-11-01/PT/TC, Prosecution Consolidated Response, 6 June 2012, paras 23–6.

[45] See also the expert opinion of Professor Dan Sarooshi, who observes that there is nothing to prevent the Council from deciding to adopt an agreement as a measure under Chapter VII. Nonetheless, the 'legal basis of the establishment of the STL is not *per se* the agreement, but the exercise by the Security Council of its Chapter VII powers', *Prosecutor v Ayyash et al*, Case No STL-11-01/PT/TC, Annex C Expert Opinion of Professor Dan Sarooshi, 6 June 2012, paras 57–9.

[46] *Prosecutor v Ayyash et al*, STL-11-01/PT/TC, Trial Chamber, 27 July 2012, paras 46–7.

[47] Ibid, para 61.

[48] The Appeals Chamber also held, Judge Baragwanath dissenting, that the Trial Chamber was correct in stating that it lacked the authority to review a Security Council Resolution. *Prosecutor v Ayyash et al*, STL-11-01/PT/AC/AR90.1, Appeals Chamber, 24 October 2012.

[49] T Rensmann, 'International Organizations or Institutions, External Relations and Cooperation' in R Wolfrum (ed), MPEPIL (2012) para 23.

always clearly attributed[50] and even when it is clear, member States may resent their exclusion from the agreement or insist on concluding an unnecessary mixed agreement.[51] clear division of competences at the time of the conclusion of an agreement may become more blurred over time.[52] The European Court of Justice (ECJ) has stated that mixed agreements have to be assessed with regard to the 'essential objective rather than the terms of individual clauses of an altogether subsidiary or ancillary nature'.[53] The ECJ has held, for example, with respect to the participation of the EC and member States in the World Trade Organization, that the EC has exclusive competence in the field of trade in goods and in cross-border services not involving the travel of people, but as to all other trade in services there is mixed competence.[54]

Sometimes an IO and its member States may conclude a mixed agreement with third parties in order to avoid taking a decision on competence. Such practice creates uncertainty for third parties and third States have insisted on including a provision in some UN conventions that any organization becoming party to the convention declare the extent of its competence in its instrument of ratification.[55] Regardless of such a declaration, the interests of third parties generally will be protected. The VCLT-IO provides that an IO may not invoke the violation of its internal rules on competence to conclude treaties in relation to third States or organizations unless it was manifest that the IO acted in violation of a rule of fundamental importance.[56]

Another layer of complexity is added when an IO joins a treaty, but only some of its member States become parties. This can hamper the operation of the treaty unless the other contracting parties accept that the treaty will only operate in relation to those member States that are also

---

[50] The ECJ has held that some powers may be implied by other treaty provisions and by measures adopted by the EU: *Commission v Council*, Case No 22/70 (*ERTA case*) [1971] ECR 274.

[51] Schermers and Blokker, *International Institutional Law* (n 3) 1131.

[52] Ibid. See, eg, Opinion 1/08, 30 November 2009, [2009] ECR I-11129, where the ECJ clarified the division of competences under the trade policy.

[53] Opinion 1/78 [1979] ECR 2917.

[54] Opinion 1/94 [1994] ECR I-5267.

[55] Schermers and Blokker, *International Institutional Law* (n 3) 1133. Such clauses are in practice directed to the EU. See, eg, UNCLOS and the 1992 UN Convention on Biological Diversity, Article 34(3).

[56] VCLT-IO, Article 46(2) and (3).

parties to the treaty and only partially apply to other members, in accordance with the competence of the IO.[57]

The UN Convention on the Law of the Sea (UNCLOS) demonstrates some of the challenges of concluding mixed agreements. States insisted on including Article 2 of Annex IX, which restricts the participation of IOs in two ways: (1) an IO could only sign the Convention if a majority of its member States were also signatories; (2) at the time of signature, an IO must make a declaration specifying the matters governed by UNCLOS in respect of which competence has been transferred to that IO by its member States which are signatories, and the nature and extent of that competence.[58] These restrictions represent a breakdown of the analogy between IOs and States; IOs are not treated as equal actors, but are closely associated with (and limited by) the participation of their member States.

4. IOs and Law-Making Treaties

As IOs take on activities traditionally reserved to States, either on their own or jointly with their members, they may have to become parties to law-making conventions.[59] The participation of the EC in UNCLOS is a prime example. Other law-making treaties, however, have not yet properly included IOs in their legal frameworks.[60]

---

[57] Schermers and Blokker, *International Institutional Law* (n 3) 1134, citing the example of Euratom and the United States.

[58] The EC signed on 7 December 1984 and gave its act of formal confirmation on 1 April 1998.

[59] Schermers and Blokker, *International Institutional Law* (n 3) 1141. An IO does not become bound to a treaty simply by virtue of its member States being a party. The ECJ held that the EU was not a party to the 1973 International Convention for the Prevention of Pollution from Ships (MARPOL) even though all EU member States are parties: Case C-308/06 *The Queen, on the application of International Association of Independent Tank Owners (Intertanko) and Others v Secretary of State for Transport* [2008] ECR I-4057. See also the uncertainties created by the EU's assumption from member States of authority over international investment policy: *Oostergal and Laurentius v Slovak Republic*, UNCITRAL Ad Hoc Arbitration (23 April 2012).

[60] The ICJ has recognized that as subjects of international law IOs are bound to the treaties to which they adhere: *Interpretation of the Agreement of 25 March 1951 between the WHO and Egypt*, Advisory Opinion, ICJ Rep 1980, para 37.

The EU is in the process of becoming a party to the 1950 European Convention on Human Rights (ECHR).[61] Its accession to the ECHR is required under Article 6 of the 2007 Treaty of Lisbon and foreseen by Article 59 of the ECHR, as amended by Protocol 14 in 2004. At present the ECHR and its Court do not formally apply to EU acts, but all EU member States have an obligation to respect the ECHR even when they are applying or implementing EU law. This 'divergence' in the application of the ECHR may be rectified by the EU, as such, becoming a party.[62] The laws and actions of the EU itself will be subject to the same judicial scrutiny as those of the 47 States of the Council of Europe. Negotiations for the accession began in 2010 and they have highlighted a variety of institutional issues that are raised by an organization joining a law-making treaty.[63] For example, should the EU have its own judge on the European Court of Human Rights (ECtHR) and, if so, should that judge only be allowed to vote on EU matters? Should the EU become a member of the Committee of Ministers that supervises the implementation of the ECtHR's judgments? What should be the priority between the ECJ and the ECtHR when applications are brought against the EU? Should it be possible for the EU to exclude its foreign and security policy from the jurisdiction of the ECtHR in the same way as it does from the ECJ's jurisdiction? Such questions are difficult and rather technical. For some issues the position of the EU will be similar to that of a State party to the ECHR, but for others choices will have to be made as to when the veil of the EU will be pierced and what special arrangements are needed to take into account specific features of EU law.[64] If and when the EU accedes to the ECHR, it may open the way to other IOs becoming parties; many complaints before the ECtHR involve the acts of such organizations.[65]

---

[61] It is already a party to numerous general economic treaties, particularly commodity agreements.

[62] COE, 'EU Accession to the European Convention on Human Rights', www.coe.int/what-we-do/human-rights/eu-accession-to-the-convention, accessed 1 July 2012.

[63] For a longer list, see Schermers and Blokker, *International Institutional Law* (n 3) 1143.

[64] Ibid. On the issue of the prior involvement of the ECJ where an application to the ECtHR alleges that a provision of EU law is incompatible with the Convention, the presidents of each Court have issued a joint statement advocating a flexible procedure with the ECJ internal review preceding the ECtHR external review: ECtHR Press Release no 75, 27 June 2011.

[65] See, eg, Eurocontrol, the European Patent Organization, the European Space Agency, the International Criminal Tribunal for the Former Yugoslavia, the

The International Committee for the Red Cross has for decades urged the UN to ensure the application of the core international humanitarian law treaties by forces under its command.[66] The UN Office of Legal Affairs (OLA) has maintained that the 1949 Geneva Conventions contain many obligations that can only be discharged by the exercise of juridical and administrative powers that the UN does not possess, such as the authority to exercise criminal jurisdiction over members of the military personnel of a peacekeeping force or administrative competence relating to territorial sovereignty. In OLA's view, the UN 'is unable to fulfil obligations which for their execution require the exercise of powers not granted to the Organization, and therefore cannot accede to the Conventions'.[67] The compromise has been for the UN Secretary-General to issue a bulletin on the observance by UN forces of international humanitarian law, which sets out selected obligations but falls far short of the UN becoming a party to the Geneva Conventions.[68] Similarly, when Serbia complained about UNMIK's failure to comply with the Hague Convention for the Protection of Cultural Property in the Event of Armed Conflict, OLA advised that the Convention was not applicable as such, but the UN was willing to apply 'the relevant provisions to the extent of their applicability in the circumstances'.[69]

There is evidently a 'disconnect' between the substantive tasks being carried out by IOs and their accountability under law-making conventions. International organizations accepting to comply with a truncated list of obligations is an unsatisfactory solution. A more coherent approach to law-making treaties is called for, which will allow IOs to become full parties while recognizing the limits of their competence.

IV. EQUALITY

The sovereign equality of States, despite the differences in their territories, populations, political and legal systems, economics and cultures, is

---

Iran-US Claims Tribunal and NATO: Schermers and Blokker, *International Institutional Law* (n 3) 1145.

66 U Palwankar, 'Applicability of International Humanitarian Law to United Nations Peace-Keeping Forces' (1993) 294 Intl Rev Red Cross.

67 Memorandum of the UN OLA, 15 June 1972, (1972) UNJY 153 (cited in Schermers and Blokker, *International Institutional Law* (n 3) 1142).

68 ST/SGB/1999/13.

69 [2004] UNJY 350.

a fundamental principle of international law.[70] Obviously, no such principle of equality exists between States and IOs; it also does not exist between IOs.[71] IOs may have near-universal membership (UN) or only a handful of members (Mekong River Commission); they might have extensive competences and binding powers (EU) or very limited functions (International Copper Study Group);[72] they might be clearly established as an international organization (Organisation for Economic Co-operation and Development (OECD)), or their status may be implicit (International Energy Agency (IEA)).[73] Inequality thus cuts along two axes: between States and organizations, and among organizations themselves.

The inequality between States and IOs was apparent at the 1986 conference to adopt the VCLT-IO. The IOs invited to the conference could participate in public and private meetings, submit substantive proposals and contribute to consensus, but they could not participate in the General Committee or Drafting Committee, cast a vote or prevent consensus from being formed.[74] Ratifications of the VCLT-IO by organizations do not count towards the 35 necessary for entry into force.[75] This reflects the view that the enactment of general rules of international law

---

[70] UN Charter, Article 2(1).

[71] Schermers and Blokker, *International Institutional Law* (n 3) 22.

[72] Examples taken from ibid; K Schmalenbach, 'International Organizations or Institutions, General Aspects' in R Wolfrum (ed), MPEPIL (2012) paras 12–18.

[73] The IEA is an interesting example. It was created through two instruments. The first was an OECD Council decision establishing the IEA as an 'autonomous body within the framework' of the OECD (15 November 1974). The second was an 'Agreement on an International Energy Program' (signed 18 November 1974), which provided that a program would be carried out through an 'autonomous agency' of the OECD. The language usually used by States that the parties 'hereby establish an international organization to be known as …' does not appear in either instrument. Nonetheless, the IEA considers itself an international organization and is recognized by other bodies (such as the United Nations Framework Convention on Climate Change (UNFCCC)) as an international organization separate to the OECD. See R Scott, *The History of the International Energy Agency 1974–1994* (OECD/IEA, 1994) Vol I, Chapter II.

[74] UNGA Res 40/76 (1985), Annex 1 Draft Rules of Procedure, Rule 60. The organizations that participated were those that had 'traditionally been invited to participate as observers at legal codification conferences convened under the auspices of the United Nations' (UNGA Res 39/86 (1984), para 2(e)). Schermers and Blokker indicate that 18 organizations participated (*International Institutional Law* (n 3) 1141).

[75] VCLT-IO, Article 85(1).

should depend on States alone.[76] The inequality of States and IOs as agents in the development of international law is confirmed in Article 53, which defines a peremptory norm as 'a norm accepted and recognized by the international community *of States* as a whole …'.[77] This implies that resolutions and actions of IOs that could be cited as evidence of the development of a *jus cogens* norm should be viewed as evidence of the views of member States and not the IO itself.[78]

1. Rules of the Organization

A specific way in which States and IOs are treated differently in the law of treaties is that the 'rules of the organization' are not the equivalent of State internal law. The notion of State internal law in the VCLT could not be transposed to the VCLT-IO due to the great diversity of organizations and the need to respect their special circumstances.[79] Moreover, the rules of the organization play a larger role in the VCLT-IO as compared to references to internal law in the VCLT.[80] This is partly because the rules, especially the constituent instrument, form the *lex specialis* that governs relations between an IO and its member States.[81]

The ILC decided that the relevant rules 'means, in particular, the constituent instruments, decisions and resolutions adopted in accordance with them, and established practice of the organization'.[82] The reference to practice is not typical of a treaty definition of 'rules' and builds in an evolutionary aspect to the law of the VCLT-IO. The ILC Commentary acknowledges that 'the question how far practice can play a creative part … cannot be answered uniformly for all international organizations'.[83] The relationship between 'rules' and State internal law will have to be

---

[76] Manin, 'The European Communities and the Vienna Convention …' (n 9) 460.

[77] Emphasis added.

[78] Manin, 'The European Communities and the Vienna Convention …' (n 9) 480–81 (using the EEC as an example).

[79] Yearbook of the ILC (1982) (n 22) 23–4.

[80] Reference to the 'rules of the organization' appears in Articles 7(3)(b), 35, 36(2), 37(3), 39(2) and 65(4) without corresponding reference to a State's internal law.

[81] See VCLT-IO, preambular para 13.

[82] VCLT-IO, Article 2(1)(j).

[83] Yearbook of the ILC (1982) (n 22) 24. See also *Institut de droit international*, Rome Resolution: The Application of the Rules of the General International Law of Treaties to International Agreements Concluded by International Organizations, Rapporteur René-Jean Dupuy (1973), Section II: 'Any

worked out through the practice of IOs and States and the case law of national and international courts.

2. Host State Agreements

An important category of treaties between States and IOs is the host State agreement, which typically concerns the status, privileges, immunities and activities of the organization or its organ, its premises, its staff and delegations in the territory of the host State. It may be a single, comprehensive treaty or an agreement in the form of an exchange of letters.[84]

No general treaty in force governs the relationship between host States and IOs. The Vienna Convention on the Representation of States in their Relations with International Organizations of a Universal Character was adopted in 1975 (1975 Vienna Convention), but faced opposition from host States who felt their interests were insufficiently protected and has not entered into force.[85] IOs cannot be parties to the Convention,[86] which limits its potential impact on the actual practice in host State relations. The slow uptake by States of the 1975 Vienna Convention led the ILC to discontinue its work on codifying the status, privileges and immunities of IOs, their officials and experts.[87] As a result, the law relating to host State relations is ad hoc; it depends on the host State agreement, other relevant agreements (eg, on privileges and immunities) as well as domestic law.

---

international organization may conclude agreements in accordance with its own relevant rules and with the general practice in the field'.

[84] See, eg, for the ICJ and the Netherlands: Letter from the President of the International Court of Justice to the Minister for Foreign Affairs of the Netherlands, 26 June 1946; Letter from the Minister for Foreign Affairs of the Netherlands to the President of the International Court of Justice, 26 June 1946; Letter from the Minister for Foreign Affairs of the Netherlands to the President of the International Court of Justice, 26 February 1971.

[85] It has 34 parties and requires 35 to enter into force. There have been no new ratifications since 2008. The major host States (US, the Netherlands, Switzerland, France, Austria) are not even signatories to the Convention.

[86] 1975 Vienna Convention, Articles 86–88. Article 90 provides that after the entry into force of the Convention, 'the competent organ of an international organization of a universal character may adopt a decision to implement the relevant provisions of the Convention'.

[87] Yearbook of the ILC (1992) vol II, Part 2, paras 359–62.

This stands in contrast to the way inter-State diplomatic and consular relations are governed by a single, almost universally ratified treaty.[88]

The basic inequality between States and IOs is manifested in particular ways in the relationship between an IO and its host State. If the host State is also a member State of the IO, it may occasionally have a conflict of interest. For example, the Netherlands had a dispute with the International Criminal Court (ICC) and the other member States over whether it should continue to pay the Court's six million euro annual rent after the expiry of the lease.[89] While the other member States sought to avoid increases in the regular budget, the Netherlands felt it had fulfilled its duty as host State by providing space for the past 10 years rent-free.

Host State agreements invariably provide that the IO is under a general obligation to respect the law of the host State. The question of applicable law can become complicated when other States come into the equation. One example is the IEA, which is based in France but rents its office space from the Australian Embassy.[90] Given the sovereign equality between Australia and France, the IEA is unable to request the Australian Government to comply with French health and safety standards.

Agreements also tend to oblige the host State to respect the inviolability of the IO's buildings and archives, to grant immunity from legal process and from taxation of its income and assets[91] and to admit onto its territory persons who have been invited by the IO. The actual fulfilment of these obligations may need to be discussed on a case-by-base basis, as the host State is torn between its domestic political priorities and its obligations under the host State agreement. In 1988, the US refused to issue a visa to Chairman Arafat of the Palestine Liberation Organization after he was invited to address the UN General Assembly, forcing the UN to reconvene in Geneva.[92] The Netherlands has generally allowed persons onto its territory who had been invited by the various international courts,

---

88 Vienna Convention on Diplomatic Relations of 1961, the Vienna Convention on Consular Relations of 1963. J Herbst, 'International Organizations or Institutions, Headquarters' in R Wolfrum (ed), MPEPIL (2012) para 14.

89 Lauren Comiteau, www.rnw.nl/international-justice/article/icc-rent-free-now, accessed 1 May 2014.

90 Ingrid Barnsley, former Acting Chief Legal Counsel of the IEA, July 2012 (interview with author).

91 Schermers and Blokker, *International Institutional Law* (n 3) 1083.

92 Ibid.

even when these persons were included on an EU 'blacklist' or had an outstanding arrest warrant.[93]

3. Relationship Agreements between IOs

Inequality also subsists in agreements between IOs. The vast majority of such agreements are bilateral.[94] Unlike in inter-State treaties, the delineation of the respective rights and duties does not proceed on the assumption of equality or the expectation of reciprocity. Agreements may be quite one-sided. For instance, under the 2004 Negotiated Relationship Agreement between the ICC and the UN, the ICC is expected to report to the UN, but not vice versa.[95] According to the 1947 agreement between the UN and the International Civil Aviation Organization (ICAO), the General Assembly has a right to veto ICAO membership applications from States that fought against UN member States during the Second World War.[96]

According to Article 115(b) of the ICC Statute (which was negotiated under the auspices of the UN, but to which the UN is not a party), a source of the ICC's budget is funds provided by the UN, subject to the approval of the General Assembly, in particular in relation to expenses incurred due to referrals by the Security Council. In practice, however, the UN has not provided funding in relation to the referrals made to the ICC by the Security Council.[97] This has been a point of contention in the UN–ICC relationship[98] that will have to be resolved through 'institutional

---

[93] Ibid. See also the attendance of the then Prosecutor-General of Djibouti during ICJ hearings in the *Certain Questions of Mutual Assistance in Criminal Matters Case*, ICJ Reports 2008.

[94] Schermers and Blokker, *International Institutional Law* (n 3) 1126. An example of a multilateral agreement is the Regulations for the UN Joint Staff Pension Fund (UNGA Res 248(III)), which is adhered to by organizations such as the ICC and IAEA.

[95] The one caveat is that the ICC reports 'if it deems it appropriate': Article 6 ICC-UN Relationship Agreement.

[96] Schermers and Blokker, *International Institutional Law* (n 3) 1090.

[97] UNSC Res 1593 (2005) para 7:

> [r]ecognizes that none of the expenses incurred in connection with the referral including expenses related to investigations or prosecutions in connection with that referral, shall be borne by the United Nations and that such costs shall be borne by the parties to the Rome Statute and those States that wish to contribute voluntarily.

[98] UNSC Res 1593 (Darfur, Sudan) and 1970 (Libya) have both included a paragraph recognizing that:

dialogue'[99] (on an unequal footing) since there is no provision for dispute settlement between the two bodies.

4. Dispute Settlement

The inequality between States and IOs is thrown into stark relief by treaty provisions on dispute settlement. This was the only topic apart from the final clauses on which there had to be a vote within the Committee of the Whole during the 1986 conference on the VCLT-IO.[100]

In the inter-State context, VCLT, Article 66 addresses two types of disputes. Disputes regarding the application or interpretation of the *jus cogens* provisions are submitted to the ICJ under its contentious jurisdiction unless the parties agree to arbitration. Disputes regarding other provisions, namely invalidity, termination or suspension of treaties, may initiate a procedure set out in the Annex by submitting a request to the UN Secretary-General.

For the VCLT-IO, disputes regarding provisions other than those concerning *jus cogens* norms are subject to the same special procedure as the VCLT; any party, whether a State or IO, may send the request to the UN Secretary-General.[101] The situation regarding *jus cogens* norms is considerably more complex. The fact that only States may be parties to contentious disputes before the ICJ (Article 34 of the 1945 ICJ Statute) prevents the transposition of the equivalent provisions of the VCLT.

A complicated series of options is proposed. The simplest scenario is where the dispute over the VCLT-IO provisions on *jus cogens* involves only States, they may submit it to the ICJ's contentious jurisdiction. However, if the dispute arises between a State party and an international organization, a variety of steps may be taken. The State party to the dispute may request the organization party to the dispute (if authorized under Article 96 of the UN Charter) to request an advisory opinion from the ICJ; the organization (if authorized under the Charter) may request an

---

> none of the expenses incurred in connection with the referral, including expenses related to investigations or prosecutions in connection with that referral, shall be borne by the United Nations and that such costs shall be borne by the parties to the Rome Statute and those States that wish to contribute voluntarily.

Many ICC States parties view this as having to exonerate the UN from the cost of activity ordered by the Security Council.

99 Resolution ICC-ASP/10/Res.4 (2011).

100 Gaja, 'A "New" Vienna Convention …' (n 11) 266.

101 VCLT-IO, Article 66(4).

advisory opinion from the ICJ; the organization (if not authorized under the Charter) may through a UN member State request an authorized organ to ask for an advisory opinion; if the request for an advisory opinion is not granted, any party may submit the dispute to arbitration in accordance with the procedure set out in the Annex; or all the parties may agree to submit the dispute to an arbitration procedure, including one specified in the Annex.[102] One can see a strange interaction at work: organizations authorized under Article 96 of the Charter to request advisory opinions are actually the most powerful in this context. States must channel their requests through such organizations. Yet, unauthorized organizations are in the weakest position, and must rely on a member State to represent their interests to an authorized organization.[103]

The advisory opinion route taken in the VCLT-IO is an imperfect substitute for the ICJ's contentious procedure available in inter-State disputes.[104] First, the formulation of a request for an advisory opinion will be crucial: the way it is phrased can have a powerful influence on the Court's answer.[105] It will be the requesting organization technically that formulates the question, but the reality is that it will be drafted and negotiated by member States. Second, if the dispute is between an IO and a State, the organization will not be able to participate on equal terms. It will not have a right to appoint a judge ad hoc, whereas a State may appoint a judge ad hoc if there is not already a judge of its nationality on

---

[102] VCLT-IO, Article 66(2) and (3).

[103] This scenario becomes even more ridiculous if the dispute is between an unauthorized organization and an authorized UN organization, with the latter organization controlling whether a request is made to the ICJ.

[104] In 2005, the ICJ amended Article 43 of its Rules of Court to establish a mechanism to enable IOs to submit observations on conventions that they are party to that are at issue in contentious disputes before the Court. In practice IOs decline to comment (see, eg, the various cases involving the Pact of Bogota in which the Organization of American States (OAS) has declined to comment).

[105] In the *Accordance with International Law of the Unilateral Declaration of Independence in Respect of Kosovo*, Advisory Opinion, ICJ Rep 2008, the ICJ observed that the General Assembly had asked for its opinion on whether or not the declaration of independence is in accordance with international law, *not* the legal consequences of that declaration. The request from the Assembly 'does not ask whether or not Kosovo has achieved statehood. Nor does it ask about the validity or legal effects of the recognition of Kosovo by those States which have recognized it as an independent State' (para 51).

the bench.[106] Finally, the advisory opinion procedure is not binding on the parties under the ICJ Statute, unlike the judgments in inter-State cases.[107] To address this anomaly, Article 66(2)(e) VCLT-IO provides that the opinion 'shall be accepted as decisive by all the parties to the dispute concerned'.

The inequality between States and IOs in the dispute settlement provisions of the VCLT-IO means that in most cases the default position will be arbitration.[108]

V. ATTRIBUTION OF RESPONSIBILITY FOR TREATY BREACHES

The non-sovereign and unequal status of IOs is vividly illustrated by the question of attributing responsibility for treaty breaches by an organization to its member States.[109] In line with the general approach taken in international law, this matter is not regulated in the Vienna Convention(s), but addressed as part of the rules on responsibility.[110]

The baseline is that membership of an international organization *as such* does not entail international responsibility for member States, whether concurrent or subsidiary, when the organization commits an internationally wrongful act, such as the breach of a treaty obligation.[111]

---

[106] ICJ Statute, Article 31(3). See, eg, *Advisory Opinion on Western Sahara*, ICJ Rep 1975, 12 (Judge ad hoc appointed for Morocco). States do not choose to exercise this right in all advisory proceedings.

[107] ICJ Statute, Article 59.

[108] See, eg, the *Applicability of the Obligation to Arbitrate under Section 21 of the United Nations Headquarters Agreement of 26 June 1947*, Advisory Opinion, ICJ Rep 1988 (ICJ holding that the US as a party to the UN Headquarters Agreement was under an obligation to enter into arbitration with the UN).

[109] The question of attribution of responsibility between IOs is not addressed here. It is covered by the DARIO, see, eg, Article 18. For analysis of the different but closely related question of attribution of *conduct* to an IO (especially the UN), see A Tzanakopoulos, *Disobeying the Security Council* (OUP, 2011) chp 2.

[110] As the Arbitral Tribunal in *Rainbow Warrior* noted, 'in the field of international law there is no distinction between contractual and tortious responsibility' (*'Rainbow Warrior' Case*, RIAA XX (1990), 215, 251). For more on this, see Tams (in this volume).

[111] *Institut de droit international*, Lisbon Resolution: The Legal Consequences for Member States of the Non-Fulfilment by International Organizations of their Obligations towards Third Parties, Rapporteur Rosalyn Higgins (1995), Article 6. This position attracts wide consensus in legal scholarship:

The question of what more is needed has not yet been clearly answered. The ILC Draft Articles on the Responsibility of International Organizations (DARIO) attempt to establish general rules,[112] whereas the ECtHR has taken a contextual, case-by-case approach.

The analogy with the allocation of responsibility in an inter-State context is hard to maintain. International organizations have limited competence, limited funds (usually provided in large part by their members), no territory, no population for creating material resources.[113] As Tzanakopoulos has pointed out, the ILC transformed the exceptional nature of derivative responsibility[114] into a general rule in DARIO, without paying sufficient attention to the difference in the operation of IOs: organizations act almost exclusively through their member States while States rarely act through other States.[115] This chapter will focus on the ILC's idea of 'circumvention of responsibility' in Articles 61 and 17, which has no equivalent in the ILC Articles on the Responsibility of States for Internationally Wrongful Acts (ARSIWA). Many other sections of DARIO do, however, duplicate the ARSIWA, which can also cause tensions and contradictions.[116]

What is at stake in the attribution of responsibility between IOs and States? Allocating responsibility for the breach of treaty obligations is essential to international cooperation. If there is a low threshold for a member State to be held responsible for the treaty breach of an organization, it may discourage States from becoming members and entrusting tasks to IOs. However, an unrealistically high threshold may

---

J d'Aspremont, 'Abuse of the Legal Personality of International Organizations and the Responsibility of Member States' (2007) Intl Org L Rev 91, 95.

[112] Subject to Article 64 on *lex specialis*, which may include rules of the organization applicable to the relations between an international organization and its members.

[113] M Hartwig, 'International Organizations or Institutions, Responsibility and Liability' in R Wolfrum (ed), MPEPIL (2012) para 25.

[114] That is, responsibility for conduct attributable to another subject of international law.

[115] Tzanakopoulos, *Disobeying* (n 109) 47.

[116] See the critical perspective of a senior UN Secretariat official in D Shraga, 'ILC Draft Articles on Responsibility of International Organizations: The Interplay between the Practice and the Rule' (2011) ASIL Proceedings. See also Article 21 of DARIO, which provides that 'self-defence' is a circumstance precluding the wrongfulness of an act of an international organization, whereas Article 51of the Charter limits self-defence to armed attacks against States. The general rule on IO responsibility for member States is in Article 62 of DARIO.

encourage the abuse of rights by member States[117] and provide a disincentive for the IO to engage in risky activities, such as peace-keeping.

Article 61 of DARIO concerns the circumvention of international obligations of a member State of an IO:

1. A State member of an international organization incurs international responsibility if, by taking advantage of the fact that the organization has competence in relation to the subject-matter of one of the State's international obligations, it circumvents that obligation *by causing the organization to commit an act that*, if committed by the State, would have constituted a breach of the obligation.
2. Paragraph 1 applies whether or not the act in question is internationally wrongful for the international organization.[118]

This Article establishes a test that requires the member State to possess the intent to avoid compliance with an obligation and a relationship of causation.[119] This is a high standard as compared to tests used in the ILC Rapporteur's previous drafts such as 'prompting'[120] the organization to commit the act or even the mere conferral of competence to the organization by a member State.[121] Quite apart from the challenge of proving intent, it is hard to imagine when an individual member State can *cause* the organizations to commit a breach of a treaty obligation. Paasivirta points out that EU member States are hardly ever in a position to 'prompt' (let alone 'cause') the EU to act because the right of initiative belongs exclusively to the European Commission in most areas of EU

---

[117] *Institut de droit international*, Lisbon Resolution: The Legal Consequences for Member States of the Non-Fulfilment by International Organizations of their Obligations towards Third Parties, Rapporteur Rosalyn Higgins (1995), Article 5(b).

[118] Emphasis added. If the act of the international organization is wrongful and caused by the member State, there could be an overlap between the cases covered in this Article and those in Articles 58 (aid or assistance by a State), 59 (direction and control exercised by a State) and 60 (coercion by a State). The ILC points out that this is not problematic 'because it would only imply the existence of a plurality of bases for holding the State responsible': ILC, Draft Articles on the Responsibility of IOs, with Commentaries (2011) 95. Those Articles are largely duplicative of the ILC Articles on State Responsibility.

[119] The Commentary clarifies that the existence of an intention to avoid compliance is implied in the use of the term 'circumvention': ILC, Draft Articles on the Responsibility of IOs, with Commentaries (2011) 93.

[120] Article 60(1) in the 2009 ILC Report (A/64/10, 2009) 163.

[121] See Article 28 of the 2007 ILC Report, (A/62/10, 2007) 194.

legislation.[122] Thus, a member State 'causing' the EU to commit an act within the meaning of Article 61 is illusory. It seems that Article 61 would only be applied in the context of small organizations with limited membership and a decision-making structure that allows domination by one member State.[123]

D'Aspremont argues that when a member State has 'effective and overwhelming' control over the decision-making process of an international organization, it must be held jointly or concurrently responsible for international law violations that involve decisions of that organization.[124] This appears to set a lower threshold than Article 61 of DARIO because d'Aspremont does not require causation. Nonetheless, the test of 'effective *and* overwhelming control' goes well beyond the 'effective control' test for attribution of conduct to States established by the case law of the ICJ and reflected in ARSIWA.[125] D'Aspremont admits that his test would be difficult to prove, given that the tools used by member States in exercising such control are not easy to identify.[126] It would probably only apply to IOs dominated by a few major donor States that benefit from weighted voting.[127]

In a series of cases, the ECtHR has upheld the principle that a member State may be held responsible for a treaty breach by an IO, but it has not found any violations on the facts.[128] Although the ECtHR has made clear

---

[122] E Paasivirta, 'Responsibility of a Member State of an International Organization: Where Will it End? Comments on Article 60 of the ILC Draft on the Responsibility of International Organizations' (2010) 7 Intl Org L Rev 49, 60.

[123] Ibid, 61.

[124] d'Aspremont, 'Abuse of the Legal Personality …' (n 111) 93.

[125] *Application of the Convention on the Prevention and Punishment of the Crime of Genocide (Bosnia and Herzegovina v Serbia and Montenegro)* ICJ Rep 2007, paras 403–5; cf *Prosecutor v Tadic*, Case No. IT-94-1-A (1999) (using the 'overall control' test). ARSIWA, Article 8.

[126] d'Aspremont, 'Abuse of the Legal Personality …' (n 111)116–17.

[127] However, even if IOs with weighted voting, it may be that the practice is always to take decisions by consensus (as in the IEA), which makes the degree of control being exercised by a State very hard to quantify.

[128] *Waite and Kennedy v Germany* (ECHR, Judgment of 18 February 1999) 1999-I, 410, para 67 (on the question of the immunity of the European State Agency in relation to employment claims). The Court held that the 'essence of the applicant's "right to a court" under the Convention had not been impaired', 412, para 73. *Bosphorus Hava Yollary Turizm ve Ticaret Anonim Sirketi v Ireland* (ECHR, Judgment of 30 June 2005) 2005-VI, 157–8, para 154 (the implementation of an EC Regulation enforcing UN sanctions). The Court found that Ireland was not responsible because the relevant rights were protected within the EC 'in a manner which can be considered at least equivalent to that for which the

that the mere transfer of competence by a State to an organization does *not* absolve it of its responsibility under the ECHR in the areas covered by the transfer, the Court has not specified the test for incurring that responsibility. It would appear that a member State would not easily be held responsible, especially where there has been an effort to make available alternative and 'equivalent' means for satisfying ECHR requirements within the international organization.[129]

The mirror of Article 61 – the circumvention by an IO of international obligations through decisions and authorizations addressed to members – appears in Article 17 of DARIO:

> 1. An international organization incurs international responsibility if it circumvents one of its international obligations by *adopting a decision binding member States or international organizations to commit an act* that would be internationally wrongful if committed by the former organization.
> 2. An international organization incurs international responsibility if it circumvents one of its international obligations by *authorizing member States or international organizations to commit an act that would be internationally wrongful if committed by the former organization* and the act in question is committed *because of that* authorization.
> 3. Paragraphs 1 and 2 apply whether or not the act in question is internationally wrongful for the member States or international organizations to which the decision or authorization is addressed.[130]

As with Article 61, proof of intent is implied by the term 'circumvention'.[131] Causation, however, is only required in Article 17(2) where the organization authorizes its members to commit an internationally wrongful act. In Article 17(1), at the moment of adopting the binding decision the organization is held responsible – thus allowing the third party that would be injured to seek a remedy – even though an internationally wrongful act has not yet been committed. The rationale is that the international organization would have to refrain from placing its members in the 'uncomfortable position' of either infringing their obligations

---

Convention provides', 158, para 155. *Gasparini v Italy and Belgium* App no 10750/03 (ECHR, Decision of 12 May 2009) (two employees of NATO alleged the inadequacy of the settlement procedure concerning employment disputes with NATO). The Court found the obligation to ensure 'equivalent protection' to that under the ECHR mechanism was not breached because the NATO procedure was not tainted with 'manifest insufficiency'.

129 Paasivirta, 'Responsibility of a Member State …' (n 122) 56.

130 Emphasis added.

131 ILC, DARIO, with commentaries (2011), 41.

under the binding decision or causing the international responsibility of the organization.[132] This rationale nonetheless produces the odd result that the promulgation of a binding decision leads to IO responsibility for an 'act' that may never occur. The ILC emphasizes that the decision must be binding to fall within Article 17(1). If members have some discretion to take an alternative course which does not imply circumvention, responsibility could arise for the organization only if circumvention actually occurs, as stated in Article 17(2).[133]

Situations arising under Article 17(2) – responsibility through authorization of an act – will require careful contextual analysis of the scope of the authorization and the causal relationship between it and the breach. While the authorizing IO would be responsible if it requested, albeit implicitly, the commission of an act that would represent a circumvention of one of its obligations, that organization would clearly not be responsible for any other breach that the member State or IO to which the authorization is addressed might commit. The UN has noted that the cumulative conditions in Article 17, especially the requirement that the decision imputing responsibility to the IO must be in circumvention of its international obligation, 'makes its application in the realities of international organization[s] highly unlikely'.[134]

The UN is constantly navigating the relationship between authorization and responsibility in its peacekeeping operations. This can be seen in a letter from the UN Secretary-General to the Prime Minister of Rwanda in 1996:

> insofar as 'Opération Turquoise' is concerned, although that operation was 'authorized' by the Security Council, the operation itself was under national command and control and was not a United Nations operation. The United Nations is, therefore, not internationally responsible for acts and omissions that might be attributable to 'Opération Turquoise'.[135]

The ECtHR has attributed to the UN the acts of a UN-authorized operation, the International Security Force in Kosovo (KFOR), which was conducted under regional command and control, on the grounds that the Security Council had 'delegated' its powers to the operation and had

[132] Ibid.

[133] Ibid.

[134] *Responsibility of International Organizations: Comments and Observations Received from International Organizations* (UN Doc A/CN.4/637/Add.1 2011) 22.

[135] ILC, DARIO, with commentaries (2011), 42.

'ultimate authority and control'.[136] From the UN's perspective, the Court disregarded the test of 'effective command and control' that 'for over six decades has guided the UN and Member States in matters of attribution'.[137] In its practice, the UN has refused to entertain claims against military operations not under its direct command and control, notwithstanding that they were authorized by the Security Council.[138] The ECtHR decisions create uncertainty as to where responsibility lies in peacekeeping operations, and may deter the UN from engaging in such operations. At the same time, the finding of responsibility may encourage the UN to put better controls in place during such operations.

The fact that an IO has limited competence – in contrast to the sovereignty of a State – complicates the question of attribution for ultra vires acts. On one view, all ultra vires acts by definition cannot be qualified as the act of the organization.[139] However, the ICJ has held that the UN assumes responsibility for ultra vires acts of its organs or individuals acting as its agents; the violation of the internal distribution of powers does not absolve the organization of responsibility.[140] This is reflected in Article 8 of DARIO, which closely follows Article 7 of ARSIWA. While this parallel provision may not sufficiently take into account the limited competence of IOs, it does provide better protection for third parties who may be injured by an ultra vires act.

The uncertainty surrounding the attribution of responsibility between IOs and member States does not only concern the allocation of responsibility, but also the legal *consequences* of joint or concurrent responsibility. As observed above, States and IOs have unequal access to dispute settlement by the ICJ. In a dispute over shared responsibility, the responsibility of the organization will be part of the 'very subject matter' and will require the appearance of the organization before Court, which is not possible under Article 34 of the ICJ Statute. Thus, the dispute

---

[136] *Behrami & Behrami v France*; and *Saramati v France, Germany and Norway* (ECtHR, 2 May 2007); *Kasumaj v Greece* App no 6974/05 (ECHR, 5 July 2007); *Gajic v Germany* App no 31446/02 (ECHR, 28 August 2008); *Beric v Bosnia and Herzegovina* App no 36357/04 (ECHR, 16 October 2007).

[137] *Responsibility of International Organizations* (n 134) para 9.

[138] Ibid, para 10.

[139] Hartwig, 'International Organizations …' (n 113) para 19.

[140] *Certain Expenses of the United Nations (Article 17, paragraph 2, of the Charter)*, Advisory Opinion, ICJ Rep 1962, 169; *Difference Relating to Immunity from Legal Process of a Special Rapporteur of the Commission on Human Rights*, Advisory Opinion, ICJ Rep 1999, 62, para 66.

would be dismissed for the absence of a necessary third party,[141] leaving only the circuitous and non-binding advisory opinion route. If the dispute is brought before national courts, it is likely to be dismissed on the basis of the entitlement of the member State and/or the organization to immunity.[142] In a recent case, the Dutch Supreme Court held the UN was immune from claims that it was responsible, at least in part, for failing to prevent the 1995 genocide at Srebrenica.[143] The UN's usual practice is to invoke its immunity in such cases, but to pay *ex gratia* lump sum compensation for injury or damage caused by its agents.[144]

The attribution and allocation of responsibility for treaty breaches between IOs and their member States is a complex area. It is probable that the general rules established in the DARIO will only apply to a subset of IOs with limited members. The rules for bodies like the UN and EU are likely to continue to be developed through practice in national, regional and international courts.

VI. CONCLUSION

More than six decades ago in the *Reparations* advisory opinion, the ICJ observed:[145]

> The subjects of law in any legal system are not necessarily identical in their nature or in the extent of their rights, and their nature depends upon the needs of the community. Throughout its history, the development of international law has been influenced by the requirements of international life, and the progressive increase in the collective activities of States has already given rise

---

[141] *East Timor (Portugal v Australia)*, ICJ Rep 1995, 90. d'Aspremont, 'Abuse of the Legal Personality …' (n 112) 117.

[142] d'Aspremont, 'Abuse of the Legal Personality …' (n 111) 117. Even if there is no immunity from jurisdiction, the entitlement to immunity for enforcement is generally broader.

[143] *Stichting Mothers of Srebrenica*, Supreme Court, 13 April 2012. The Hague Court of Appeal in the same case had pointed out that the claimants could sue the Netherlands or the individual perpetrators of the genocide: *Stichting Mothers of Srebrenica*, Appeal Court of The Hague, 30 March 2010.

[144] [1965] UNJY 41; cf the UN's reluctance to accept blame or to make an *ex gratia* payment for the cholera outbreak introduced in Haiti by UN peacekeepers. In cases where a payment is made, the UN may require the signing of a release and may reserve the right to seek reimbursement from a State [2010] UNJY 521–2. See also UNGA Res 52/247.

[145] *Reparations*, Advisory Opinion (n 18) 178.

> to instances of action upon the international plane by certain entities which are not States.

Numerous IOs have been created and entrusted with functions to meet the 'requirements of international law', but this has not developed in parallel with a satisfactory legal framework for attributing responsibility and settling disputes. This legal framework is likely to develop through practice rather than codification, at least in the medium term. It will probably be driven by the practice of the highly active and relatively powerful IOs, such as the UN and EU, and the judicial bodies attached to each of these institutions. With a view to greater clarity, scholarship can play an important role in describing, assessing and, perhaps, influencing international practice. In that process, engagement with the following questions would seem particularly important:

1. Should IOs be assimilated to States for the purpose of the law of treaties or should their special characteristics be emphasized?
2. How can equality in dispute settlement between States and IOs and between IOs be enhanced?
3. How should the law on treaties strike a balance between an IO as a forum for and association of States and as an independent actor and party to a treaty?
4. What should be the general rule governing the ability of an IO to impose treaty obligations on third parties? Should the rule differentiate between member States and non-member States?
5. Should IOs that facilitated and participated in the conclusion of treaties also be parties to such treaties? If the treaty creates a new IO or organ, should the participating organization be represented in the new body?
6. Should there be a general rule on which organs of an IO are competent to conclude treaties? If so, what criteria should be applied?
7. Should IOs be allowed to adhere to universal or regional conventions on human rights? Indeed, should IOs be required to adhere to such conventions because they have human rights obligations?[146]
8. What is the role of practice in interpreting the VCLT-IO and the 'rules of the organization'?

---

[146] On the human rights obligations of the UN, see G Verdirame, *The UN and Human Rights: Who Guards the Guardians?* (OUP, 2011). See also G Acquaviva, 'Human Rights Violations before International Tribunals: Reflections on Responsibility of International Organizations' (2007) 20 LJIL 613.

9. How does the Security Council's Chapter VII power relate to the general principles regarding the treaty-making capacity of IOs?
10. In what circumstances should we 'pierce the veil' in determining responsibility for treaty breaches by IOs? What role, if any, should immunity of the IO or State play?

20. Treaty law and multinational enterprises: More than internationalized contracts?

Markos Karavias

I. INTRODUCTION

The relationship between international law and the multinational enterprise (MNE)[1] has always been uneasy. MNEs, private legal entities operating across national boundaries and wielding staggering economic power, do not readily square with a State-centric perception of international law. Faced with the emergence of the multinational corporate phenomenon throughout the second half of the twentieth century, international law doctrine struck an ambivalent position, most aptly summarized in the *Barcelona Traction* judgment. There, the ICJ stressed that 'international law is called upon to recognize institutions of municipal law that have an important and extensive role in the international field. This does not necessarily imply drawing an analogy between its own institutions and those of municipal law'.[2] A similar assessment of the situation was later made in the third US Restatement of Foreign Relations Law, according to which 'the multinational enterprise or corporation ... is an established feature of international economic life, but it has not yet achieved special status in international law or in domestic legal systems'.[3]

---

[1] The term 'multinational enterprise' has been employed in international law literature interchangeably with the term 'transnational corporation'. According to the definition offered by Vernon and quoted by Vagts, a multinational enterprise refers to a 'cluster of corporations of diverse nationality joined together by ties of common ownership and responsive to a common management strategy'. D Vagts, 'The Multinational Enterprise: A New Challenge for Transnational Law (1969–70) 83 Harvard L Rev 740. On the role of MNEs in the global economy, see P Malanczuk, 'Multinational Enterprises and Treaty-Making' in V Gowlland-Debbas (ed), *Multilateral Treaty-Making* (Martinus Nijhoff, 2000) 47–52.

[2] *Barcelona Traction, Light and Power Company, Limited*, ICJ Rep 1970, 33, a dictum reprised in *Ahmadou Sadio Diallo*, ICJ Rep 2010 [104].

[3] *Restatement (Third)* Vol 1 (1987) 126.

The root of this ambivalence resides perhaps in the actual workings of these enterprises, which grow ever more complex.[4] Yet, some argue that exactly because MNEs 'are engaged in vast and complex international operations, which involve them in manifold contracts with different governments … the problem of their international status cannot be so simply dismissed'.[5] In other words, the modalities of MNEs' operations militate both for and against weaving them into the fabric of public international law.

Some decades ago, the direct application of international law to MNEs in the field of investment law would either be brushed aside as a problematic proposition[6] or excoriated as a neo-colonialist effort to grant MNEs an international status and ultimately to wrest the substance of sovereignty from the State.[7] Following the end of the Cold War, the question of the status of MNEs under international law resurfaced in the light of sensational instances of corporate misconduct linked with gross human rights abuses and environmental disasters. Most prominently, the allegations leveled by the Ogoni people against Royal Dutch Shell sparked protracted litigation under the 1789 Alien Tort Statute before American courts, which culminated in the *Kiobel* judgment of the United States Supreme Court.[8] Calls for the international regulation of MNEs' conduct have proliferated in the hope that the submission of corporations to international law would act as a more credible deterrent, thus inducing their compliance with fundamental rules of the international legal order.[9] Nowadays, submitting MNEs to international law appears to some both feasible and desirable. In the words of Clapham, 'the point [where corporations are not only treated as partners, but as having responsibilities under the international law of human rights] is nearer than usually

---

4 D Carreau, *Droit International Public* (Pedone, 1986) 30–31.

5 CN Okeke, *Controversial Subjects of Contemporary International Law* (Rotterdam University Press, 1974) 207.

6 See F Rigaux, 'Des Dieux et des Héros: Réflexions sur une Sentence Arbitrale' (1978) 67 *Revue Critique de Droit International Privé* 445.

7 See DA Ijalaye, *The Extension of Corporate Personality in International Law* (Brill, 1978) 148.

8 *Kiobel v Royal Dutch Petroleum Co.*, 133 S.Ct. 1664 (2013). On the Alien Tort Statute litigation saga, see generally G Fletcher, *Tort Liability for Human Rights Abuses* (Hart, 2008); M Koebele, *Corporate Responsibility under the Alien Tort Statute* (Martinus Nijhoff, 2009).

9 See D Kinley and J Tadaki, 'From Talk to Walk: The Emergence of Human Rights Responsibilities for Corporations at International Law' (2004) Virginia J Intl L 938.

imagined. In fact, many of us imagine we are already there'.[10] Topographical similes aside, this proposition highlights a change of mind leading us away from the alleged incompatibility between public international law and private corporate entities. Yet, the ways international law chooses to include MNEs within its regulatory ambit remain contested.

II. MNES AS SUBJECTS OF INTERNATIONAL LAW

Discussions on the status of MNEs under international law invariably start off with an investigation into the international legal personality of these entities. To affirm the international legal personality of an MNE is seen as the necessary *laissez-passer* into the realm of international law. Yet, this way of framing the question bypasses a more fundamental question, namely that of the applicability of international law to MNEs.

Confronted with this question, lawyers tend to refer to the *Jurisdiction of the Courts of Danzig* advisory opinion, where the Permanent Court of International Justice (PCIJ) held that 'it cannot be disputed that the very object of an international agreement, according to the intention of the contracting Parties, may be the adoption of some definite rules creating individual rights and obligations and enforceable by the national courts'.[11] Of course, this dictum does not speak to the creation of international rights and obligations for legal persons; yet, it is viewed as a jurisprudential alchemist's stone with the capacity to transmute non-State actors into addressees of international legal rules.[12] Still, it is not unambiguously clear that the intention of the PCIJ was to recast the then prevalent State-centric international law doctrine in postulating that international treaties granted rights or imposed obligations directly on individuals or other legal entities.

According to Anzilotti, the Court simply declared in this statement that a treaty could not create individual rights, but could oblige the parties to incorporate rules, whose content was defined in the treaty itself, that

---

[10] A Clapham, *Human Rights Obligations of Non-State Actors* (OUP, 2006) 270.

[11] *Jurisdiction of the Courts of Danzig*, Advisory Opinion, PCIJ 1928 Series B, No 15, 17–18.

[12] See PK Menon, 'The International Personality of Individuals under International Law' (1992) 1 Journal of Transnational Law and Policy 164.

subsequently created individual rights in the municipal system.[13] Lauterpacht espoused a much wider reading of the opinion, according to which treaties, if the parties so intended, applied directly to individuals.[14] This reading corresponded, in Lauterpacht's view, to the then gradually evolving consensus that 'there is nothing in international law which is fundamentally opposed to individuals and other legal persons becoming subjects of international rights and duties, ie subjects of international law'.[15]

A revisiting of the opinion reveals that the PCIJ was preoccupied with the narrower question of whether the provisions of an agreement between Poland and the Free City of Danzig (Beamtenabkommen) did produce rights and obligations for Danzig railway officials when transposed into the 'contract of service' between the Polish Railways Administration and the Danzig officials, in other words as part of the contract governing their terms of service.[16] According to the Court, the object of the Beamtenabkommen was to create a special legal regime governing the relations between the Polish Railways Administration and the Danzig officials.[17] Furthermore, the provisions of the Beamtenabkommen should not be construed in a manner which would make the applicability of these provisions dependent on their incorporation into a Polish Regulation.[18] One could thus suggest that the Court recognized the applicability of international law to individuals, yet not under the heading of the direct application of treaties to individuals. The Court accepted that the creation of a *special legal regime* governing the employment of Danzig officials necessitated its insulation from national legislation. The parties to the Beamtenabkommen essentially agreed on the substantive content of a model contract and the transposition of this content into an actual contract. Via this form of *renvoi*, States were free to create rights and obligations for individuals under international law.

Today, it is generally accepted that international law is applicable to entities other than States. In its *Reparation for Injuries* advisory opinion, the ICJ dissociated sovereignty from international legal personality in

---

13 D Anzilotti, *Cours de Droit International* (Recueil Sirey, 1929) 407–8; cf A McNair, *The Law of Treaties* (Clarendon Press, 1961) 338.

14 H Lauterpacht, *The Development of International Law by the Permanent Court of International Justice* (Longmans, Green and Company 1934) 510.

15 H Lauterpacht, *Private Law Sources and Analogies of International Law* (Longmans, Green and Company, 1927) 79.

16 *Jurisdiction of the Courts of Danzig* (n 11) 17.

17 Ibid, 18.

18 Ibid, 20.

holding that 'the subjects of law in any legal order are not necessarily identical in their nature and extent of their rights ... their nature depends upon the needs of the community'.[19] In other words, international law may bind entities which, unlike States, do not have a general competence to act on the international plane, but whose legal competence to act is circumscribed by the function they are called upon to fulfill.[20] O'Connell summed up this proposition by postulating that international law 'may select different entities and endow them with different legal functions'.[21] Thus, international law does not systemically exclude corporations from its ambit and there is nothing in international law which hinders States from freely consenting to confer rights or impose obligations upon legal persons.

An affirmation of the potential applicability of international law to corporations speaks volumes as to the structure of international law, yet it is silent on the actual measure of their international legal personality. According to the standard definition of a subject of international law, the latter is an entity capable of possessing rights and duties under international law and having the capacity to maintain its rights by making international claims.[22] Still, the truth of the matter is that international law does not contain a written rule setting out the criteria of subjectivity.

Whereas there is unanimity in accepting States and international organizations as subjects of international law, the situation differs as regards MNEs. It has been suggested that they have not been categorically recognized as possessing international legal personality[23] or that 'in principle' private corporate bodies do not have such personality.[24] Shaw argues that the question of international personality of transnational corporations remains an open one.[25] It appears that the objections or affirmations voiced regarding the personality of corporations proceed

---

[19] *Reparation for Injuries Suffered in the Service of the United Nations*, Advisory Opinion, ICJ Rep 1949, 174.

[20] Cf RY Jennings, 'General Course on Principles of International Law' (1967) 121 RCADI 348, according to whom 'the inquiry is now always into function; for once the theoretical possibility of international personality in entities other than States is conceded, there is no other useful approach'.

[21] DP O'Connell, *International Law* (2nd edn, Stevens, 1970) 80.

[22] See *Reparation for Injuries*, (n 19) 179.

[23] N Castell and C Derycke, 'Les Entreprises' in H Ascensio, E Decaux and A Pellet (eds), *Droit International Penal* (Pedone, 2000) 155.

[24] I Brownlie, *Principles of Public International Law* (7th edn, OUP, 2008) 65.

[25] M Shaw, *International Law* (6th edn, CUP, 2008) 250.

from tactical rather than doctrinal quarters.[26] As Lowe has incisively argued '[corporations] have some characteristics in common with States, the archetypal subjects of international law, and some characteristics in common with human beings, the archetypal objects of international law, and they should be recognized as entities *sui generis*' concluding that '[a]t this stage of development of international law the classification of corporations must be a matter of choice'.[27]

III. MNES AS ADDRESSEES OF INTERNATIONAL TREATY LAW

It has nowadays become commonplace to argue that States should employ international treaty law to regulate the activities of MNEs and curb the nefarious consequences of the operation of large corporate groups on human well-being and the environment.[28] Interestingly, this argument has a dual connotation. First, that international law is suited to the needs of regulating corporate operations and, second, that such regulation should take the form of an international treaty. Still, this ignores the fact that ever since World War II, States have been skeptical about, if not hostile to, the idea of utilizing international law to regulate corporate activities – with the notable exception of international rules governing the treatment of foreign investors – the obvious reason being that corporate activities were perceived as a challenge to State sovereignty.[29]

This does not mean that international treaties are without application to corporations, yet the medium of international treaty law has been employed to confer rights on corporations, rather than create binding obligations thereon. The most telling example is the 1950 European Convention of Human Rights (ECHR), under whose Article 34 legal persons are recognized as beneficiaries of human rights protection. They may, in their capacity as 'non-governmental organizations … claiming to be the victim of a violation by one of the … Parties of the rights

---

[26] P Daillier and A Pellet (eds), *Droit International Public* (8th edn, LGDJ, 2009) 715.

[27] V Lowe, 'Corporations as International Actors and International Law Makers' (2004) Italian Ybk Intl L 24, 26.

[28] Kinley and Tadaki, 'From Talk to Walk …' (n 9) 935–6; cf J Zerk, *Multinationals and Corporate Social Responsibility* (CUP, 2006) 297–8.

[29] M Sornarajah, *The International Law on Foreign Investment* (2nd edn, CUP, 2004) 4–5.

guaranteed by the Convention[,] lodge individual applications with the Court'. This protection offered to corporations was later incorporated expressly into European human rights. According to Article 1 of the 1952 First Protocol to the ECHR, the right to protection of property is conferred on 'every natural or legal person'. Moreover, in a string of judgments, which stand out as testament to the dynamic – and one might suggest creative – take of Strasbourg judges on the ECHR text, corporations have been recognized as beneficiaries of the right to respect of private life,[30] and as entitled to receive monetary compensation for non-pecuniary losses under Article 41 ECHR.[31] In other words, the corporation may not have a soul to damn and a body to kick, but it has a soul to be taken care of. Naturally, this anthropomorphic approach to 'corporate human rights', an oxymoron, finds its inherent limit in the nature of specific human rights themselves. The prohibition of torture normatively speaks to the inviolability of the human body and psyche, and would thus constitute a normative bar to the recognition of corporations as rights holders under, for example, Article 3 ECHR or the 1984 Convention Against Torture.

The flipside of the coin, namely the establishment of treaty law obligations binding directly on corporations is admittedly more complex. Suffice here to deal with the conundrum of MNEs and human rights. Human rights are traditionally concerned with the relationship between individuals and power.[32] Such power has come to be associated on the international level with the sovereign State. Consequently, international human rights have been perceived as intending to safeguard the rights and freedoms of individuals against arbitrary State action.[33]

The suggestion that human rights norms target corporate action is based on a two-fold argument relating to the formulation and scope of human rights norms. Admittedly, the abstract formulation of human rights provisions does not necessarily bar application to corporations, since the relevant rules do not *expressis verbis* target State action. Human

---

[30] In *Colas Est*, the European Court of Human Rights held that a legal regime allowing raids of corporate premises without a court warrant violated the company's right to respect for its registered office, branches or other business premises under Article 8 ECHR. ECtHR, *Societe Colas Est v France*, Application no 3797/97 (2002) [40–41].

[31] ECtHR, *Comingersoll SA v Portugal*, Application no 35382 (2000) [36].

[32] P Wachsmann, *Les Droits de l'Homme* (3rd edn, Dalloz, 1999) 3.

[33] See T Buergenthal, 'International Human Rights in an Historical Perspective' in J Symonides (ed), *Human Rights: Concepts and Standards* (Ashgate, 2000) 3.

rights either ban certain conduct or recognize a certain liberty, yet they do so by focusing on the right holder, as opposed to naming the obligation bearer. This of course is only logical given that at the time human rights treaties were drafted, the threat to the enjoyment of human rights was perceived as emanating from the State apparatus.[34] As to the scope of human rights, it is argued that, in the wake of liberalization and the retreat of the State from public functions, MNEs wield such power that their conduct poses a threat to the enjoyment of human rights and for that reason corporations should be recognized as addressees of international human rights treaties.[35] Essentially, corporations – the argument goes – are assuming State-like characteristics as far as their functions and their economic power are concerned.

The argument that human rights treaties bind corporate bodies has not found its way into the case law of human rights treaty bodies.[36] On the contrary, the State has retained its key position as the sole addressee of human rights norms. As the European Court of Human Rights (ECtHR) has noted, 'the State cannot completely absolve itself of its responsibility by delegating its obligations in this sphere to private bodies or individuals … [on the contrary] the State [remains] under a duty to exercise supervision and control over private psychiatric institutions'.[37] In a case regarding the operation of a private law foundation tasked with administering a compensation scheme agreed upon by Germany and Poland, the ECtHR held that the acts of said foundation engaged the responsibility of Poland since 'the exercise of State powers which affects Convention rights and freedoms raises an issue of State responsibility regardless of the form in which these powers happen to be exercised, be it for instance by a body whose activities are regulated by private law'.[38]

---

[34] See R Provost, *International Human Rights and Humanitarian Law* (CUP, 2004) 63. More specifically in respect of the ECHR, see A Drzemczewski, 'The European Human Rights Convention and Relations between Private Parties' (1979) 2 Netherlands Intl L Rev 168.

[35] S Joseph, 'Taming the Leviathans' (1999) 46 Netherlands Intl L Rev 173–4.

[36] According to the UNSC Special Representative on Business and Human Rights, 'the [human rights] treaties do not address direct corporate legal responsibilities explicitly, while the commentaries of the treaty bodies on the subject are ambiguous.' (19 February 2007) UN Doc A/HRC/4/35 [41].

[37] ECtHR, *Storck v Germany*, App no 61603/00 (2005) [93].

[38] ECtHR, *Wós v Poland* App no 22860/02 (2006) [72]. Cf Article 5 of the Articles on the Responsibility of States for Internationally Wrongful Acts (2001) UN Doc A/56/10.

A similar conclusion has been reached by the Human Rights Committee, which states in its General Comment No 31 that:

> the positive obligations on State Parties to ensure Covenant rights will only be fully discharged if individuals are protected by the State, not just against violations of Covenant rights by its agents, but also against acts committed by private persons or entities that would impair the enjoyment of Covenant rights in so far as they are amenable to application between persons or entities.[39]

Finally, the idea that the State shoulders positive obligations to protect the rights of individuals vis-à-vis the operation of corporate groups is not only found in the context of civil and political rights, but also in that of economic, social and cultural rights. Thus, the UN Committee on Economic, Social and Cultural Rights has noted that the right to food and the right to the highest attainable standard of health impose an obligation on the State to take appropriate measures with a view to ensuring that activities of the private business sector are in conformity with these two rights.[40]

It is clear that human rights treaty bodies adhere to a traditional view, according to which human rights may only be violated by action or omission attributable to the State. Yet, the gradual withdrawal of the State from what is perceived as part of the public sphere would imply the withdrawal of the protection afforded by human rights guarantees. Human rights treaty bodies have upheld that privatization does not absolve the State of its responsibility for human rights violations arising out of the conduct of corporate entities to which it has delegated any of its functions.[41] The reinterpretation of human rights to incorporate an *obligation to protect* human rights in the relationships between individuals and corporations should be seen as serving a remedial function: it extends human rights protection to the fault line of the public–private realm where the actions of corporate actors cause State sovereignty to erode.

One could argue that essentially corporations are 'left off the hook', granted leeway to operate in disregard of internationally recognized

---

[39] HRC, 'General Comment No 31: The Nature of the General Legal Obligation Imposed on States Parties to the Covenant' (26 May 2004) CCPR/C/21/Rev.1/Add.13 [8].

[40] CESCR, 'General Comment No 12: The Right to Adequate Food' (12 May 1999) UN Doc E/C.12/1999/5 [15]; CESCR, 'General Comment No 14: The Right to the Highest Attainable Standard of Health' (11 August 2000) UN Doc E/C.12/2000/4 [51].

[41] See *Storck v Germany* (n 37).

human rights. According to this zero-sum logic, corporations are either direct addressees of international human rights law or nothing at all. Still, this logic distorts legal reality. It is true that the rise of the modern corporate phenomenon has not led to the recognition of the corporation as an obligor under international human rights treaty law. Still, via the doctrine of the *obligation to protect* international treaty law becomes relevant for corporate actors. Through the dynamic interpretation of human rights guarantees States parties to the relevant treaties assume the obligation to regulate corporate activities on the basis of their domestic law to the extent that these activities impinge on the enjoyment of human rights.

IV. MNES AS PARTIES TO INTERNATIONALIZED CONTRACTS WITH STATES

Contractual agreements between States and private corporations do not call international law into application, in the sense that corporations are in principle devoid of international legal personality and therefore lack the requisite capacity to conclude agreements governed by international law.[42] Still, following World War II, and especially from the 1960s onwards, there has been a shift both in doctrine and practice, suggesting that certain categories of contracts between States and corporations are not wholly excluded from the regulatory ambit of international law.[43] These contracts have been classified in literature as *State* or *internationalized contracts*. Apart from the identity of the contracting parties, the key feature of this category of legal acts appears to be the fact that they are not wholly submitted to the law of the contracting State or some other State. Rather, these contracts have been *internationalized* via the use of various legal tools.

[42] According to an oft quoted dictum of the PCIJ, '[a]ny contract which is not a contract between sovereign states in their capacity as subjects of public international law is based on the municipal law of some country'. *Serbian Loans,* PCIJ 1929 Series A, No 20/21, 41.

[43] FA Mann writing as early as 1944 argued for the application of international law to contracts lacking an express choice-of-law clause if the contract 'is so rooted in international law as to render it impossible to assume that the parties intended to be governed by a national system of law'. FA Mann, 'The Law Governing State Contracts' (1944) 21 British Ybk Intl L 21.

The justification for the internationalization of contracts was provided by 'the requirements of international intercourse'.[44] Contracts have become a stable legal vehicle for financial and investment activities on the international legal plane. States and corporations entering into contracts establish a set of rights and obligations in force for the duration of the contract, whose observance depends on the goodwill and co-operation of the parties. Yet, one should not lose sight of the fact that one of the parties is a sovereign State, embodying, and tasked with safeguarding, the collective interest of its citizens, whereas the corporation is interested in furthering its own profit-oriented goals. The State thus retains a 'predominant concern and responsibility for the territory and people over which its sovereignty extends. The State regulates activities in such agreements in the general interest of the public. The public interest … authorizes the governmental authority to undertake certain unilateral powers: to suspend, vary or rescind the contract'.[45] Contracting with a State under that State's law necessarily means facing the risk of a unilateral change in the law impacting on the operation of the contractual arrangement. It has been predominantly this risk that corporations sought to counteract via the internationalization of the contract. At the same time, States by consenting to such internationalization have aimed at luring in foreign investment, while safeguarding a measure of freedom of action.[46]

As stated above, the internationalization of contracts has come about in various guises. Contracts between States and corporations have included stabilization clauses with the effect of freeze-framing the host State's legal regime at the time of the conclusion of the contract and immunizing the latter from any change in the law.[47] Admittedly, it is within the sovereign prerogative of States to amend or repeal national legislation, in a manner contrary to the contractual arrangement, yet the inclusion of a

---

44 FA Mann, 'The Proper Law of Contracts Concluded by International Persons' (1959) 35 British Ybk Intl L 46. Cf C Leben, 'Retour sur la Notion de Contrat d'Etat et sur le Droit Applicable à Celui-ci' in *Mélanges Offerts à Hubert Thierry* (Pedone, 1998) 252.

45 AFM Maniruzzaman, 'State Contracts with Aliens: The Question of Unilateral Change by the State in Contemporary International Law' (1992) 9 J Intl Arbitration 144.

46 See Sornarajah, *Foreign Investment* (n 29) 68–9.

47 For an initial assessment of the operation of stabilization clauses, see P Weil, 'Les Clauses de Stabilisation ou d'Intangibilité Insérées dans les Accords de Développement Économique' in *Mélanges Offerts a Charles Rousseau* (Pedone, 1974) 301–28. See more generally R Dolzer and C Schreuer, *Principles of International Investment Law* (2nd edn, OUP, 2012) 82–5.

stabilization clause aims at rendering the contracting State liable for damages in case national legislation impacts upon the operation of the contract.[48]

Another technique of internationalization has been the inclusion into the contract of a choice-of-law clause either excluding the application of the domestic legislation of the State or coupling the applicability of domestic legislation with a reference to international law at large or to general principles of (international) law. The idea here is that international law, as a hierarchically superior set of rules, should trump domestic legislation in cases of normative conflicts.[49]

The debate on the internationalization of contracts found its initial high tide in the *Texaco Calasiatic* arbitral award[50] regarding the nationalization by Libya of several petroleum concessions held by two American companies. The award expressly accepted the possibility of internationalization, noting that '[c]ontracts between States and private persons can, under certain conditions come within the ambit of a particular and new branch of international law: The international law of contracts'.[51] An internationalization of the contract came about in the following three cases: (a) when the contract referred to 'general principles of law' as the applicable law; (b) when it contained an arbitration clause; and (c) when the contract had the character of an 'economic development agreement'.[52]

The critique voiced against the internationalization of contracts as envisaged in *Texaco* revolved predominantly around questions of legal personality. The crux of the matter lay in the capacity of States to enter into contracts governed by international law with entities lacking international legal personality. According to Cohen-Jonathan, nothing in international law prevented the State from elevating its contracting partner to the level of international law for the needs of the contractual arrangement. The corporation would then enjoy a limited measure of functional international legal personality, closely associated with the performance of the contract, that would not produce any legal effects

---

[48] See N David 'Les Clause de Stabilité dans les Contrats Pétroliers. Questions d'un Praticien' (1986) 113 *Journal de Droit International* 94.

[49] RY Jennings, 'State Contracts and International Law' (1961) 37 British Ybk Intl L 162.

[50] *Texaco Overseas Petroleum Company and California Asiatic Oil Company v The Government of the Libyan Arab Republic* (19 January 1977), reprinted in (1978) 17 *International Legal Materials* 1. [English translation].

[51] Ibid, [32].

[52] Ibid, [40–45].

vis-à-vis third States not privy to the contract.[53] On the other end of the spectrum, Rigaux suggested that this proposition rested on circular reasoning. The corporation derived its international personality from entering into a contract governed by international law, yet in order for it to be able in the first place to enter such a contract it should already enjoy a measure of international personality under international law.[54] Relevant to the personality debate was the question of party autonomy to choose international law as the applicable law despite the fact that one of the parties lacked international legal personality. According to the view taken by Sole Arbitrator Dupuy in *Texaco Calasiatic*, international law itself allowed for such party autonomy.[55]

Yet, even at the time *Texaco Calasiatic* was decided the debates on the personality of corporations were giving way to considerations regarding the actual implications of grounding State contracts into the international legal order. One of the driving forces behind this shift of focus was the changing landscape of the international law on foreign investment,[56] and more specifically the rapid growth of the institution of mixed arbitration spurred on by the conclusion of innumerable investment treaties, both multilateral and bilateral.

One of the revolutionary aspects of investment treaties is the introduction of a right of action by a foreign investor to seek damages for a violation of the investment contract before an arbitral tribunal.[57] Contracting investors do not thus depend on the willingness of their home States to espouse their claim and exercise diplomatic protection, but they retain an independent right to initiate investor–State arbitration seeking redress in their own name vis-à-vis the host State.[58] The majority of bilateral investment treaties (BITs) now contain provisions expressing the

---

[53] G Cohen-Jonathan, 'L'Arbitrage *Texaco Calasiatic* Contre Gouvernement Libyen' (1977) 23 Annuaire Français de Droit International 458. A similar opinion was voiced prior to the handing down of *Texaco Calasiatic* by I Seidl-Hohenveldern, 'The Theory of Quasi-International and Partly International Agreements' (1975) Revue Belge de Droit International 570.

[54] Rigaux, 'Des Dieux et des Héros …' (n 6) 445.

[55] *Texaco* (n 50) [35].

[56] A Fatouros, 'International Law and the Internationalized Contract' (1980) 74 AJIL 141.

[57] See more generally, S Schill, *The Multilateralization of International Investment Law* (CUP, 2009) 249–61.

[58] Mixed arbitration should not be considered an evolution of the concept of diplomatic protection, but as an alternative thereto. See C Tams and A Tzanakopoulos, '*Barcelona Traction* at 40: The ICJ as an Agent of Legal Development' (2010) 23 Leiden JIL 790.

consent on the part of the contracting States to submit disputes to arbitration administered by the International Center for the Settlement of Investment Disputes (ICSID), for the benefit of nationals of the other State party to the treaty, provided both States are parties to the 1965 ICSID Convention.[59] They also offer arbitration administered by other institutional actors (eg, the Permanent Court of Arbitration) or ad hoc. Similar provisions are present in multilateral treaties, such as Article 1122 of the 1992 North American Free Trade Agreement and Article 26 of the 1994 Energy Charter Treaty, which express the offer of States parties to arbitrate under ICSID, an offer to be taken up by investors who are nationals of other States parties to the aforementioned treaties.

A second noteworthy aspect of investment treaties relates to their choice-of-law provisions. At the outset, one needs to underline the fact that all major investment law instruments recognize the principle of party autonomy, that is, the freedom of contracting parties to choose the law applicable to their contractual relationship.[60] Thus, it rests with the State and the contracting corporation to explicitly choose the applicable law to the contract by inserting a choice-of-law provision. Parties may choose to submit their contract exclusively to host State law, or the law of a third State or international law. Yet, practice indicates that the choice of a single body of law is not preferred.[61] Parties tend to opt for a combined choice of the host State's law and international law as the law governing the contractual relations. Irrespective of the choice made, if this choice is explicit, arbitrators are obliged to respect it.

As contracting parties are free to choose the applicable law, they are also free not to make such choice. In this case, the choice-of-law provision included in a multilateral or bilateral investment treaty may provide the applicable law. Notably, Article 42(1) of the ICSID Convention reads that any tribunal operating under ICSID rules:

> shall decide a dispute in accordance with such rules of law as may be agreed by the parties. In the absence of such agreement, the Tribunal shall apply the

---

[59] See A Lowenfeld, *International Economic Law* (2nd edn, OUP, 2008) 570.

[60] See T Begic, *Applicable Law in International Investment Disputes* (Eleven, 2005) 13–15.

[61] Ibid, 15–18. Specifically, as regards the choice of international law as the exclusive applicable law, it has been argued that this is 'not advisable. The contacts of the investment activity to various technical provisions of the host State's law would make such a formula impractical.' C Schreuer, L Malintoppi, A Reinisch and A Sinclair (eds), *The ICSID Convention: A Commentary* (2nd edn, CUP, 2009) 562.

> law of the Contracting State party to the dispute (including its rules on the conflicts of laws) and such rules of international law as may be applicable.

Equally, a number of BITs contain choice-of-law clauses the majority of which incorporate references to the BIT itself, the law of the State party to the dispute, and the rules and principles of international law.[62]

Of course, the choice-of-law provision included in a BIT or a multilateral investment treaty may come into play even if the contract expressly contains a choice-of-law provision itself. This may well be the case, when the investor seizes an arbitral tribunal arguing that the wrongful conduct of the contracting State amounts to a breach of the BIT itself.[63] In other words, the dispute is no longer exclusively contractual in nature, but calls an international treaty into application. As the ad hoc Committee held in the annulment decision in *Vivendi*:

> [a] state may breach a treaty without breaching the contract, and vice versa … In accordance with this general principle (which is declaratory of general international law), whether there has been a breach of the BIT and whether there has been a breach of contract are different questions. Each of these claims will be determined by reference to its own proper or applicable law – in the case of the BIT, by international law; in the case of the [contract], by the proper law of the contract.[64]

The Committee went on to add that:

> where the essential basis of a claim brought before an international tribunal is a breach of contract, the tribunal will give effect to any valid choice of forum clause in the contract … [Where] the fundamental basis of the claim is a treaty laying down an independent standard by which the conduct of parties is to be judged, the existence of an exclusive jurisdiction clause in a contract between the claimant and the respondent state … cannot operate as a bar to the application of the treaty standard.[65]

---

[62] Schreuer et al, *The ICSID Convention* (n 61) 576.

[63] The investor in such a case would invoke a breach of a substantive rule of international law or of an 'umbrella clause' included in the respective BIT. An umbrella clause is a provision that guarantees the observance of obligations assumed by the host State vis-à-vis the investor. On the divergent jurisprudence concerning the legal consequences of umbrella clauses, see Dolzer and Schreuer, *Investment Law* (n 47) 166–78.

[64] *Compañía de Aguas del Aconquija SA and Compagnie Générale des Eaux/Vivendi Universal v Argentine Republic*, Decision on Annulment (3 July 2002) [95–6].

[65] Ibid, [98] and [101].

Arbitral tribunals have in turn applied international law as the law governing the merits of the dispute in all of these cases, that is: (1) when international law forms part of the law expressly chosen by the parties;[66] (2) when international law constitutes an implied choice of law in the absence of a choice of law by the parties;[67] and (3) when the applicable choice-of-law provisions do not derive from the contract but from an investment treaty.[68] A close analysis of the function international law fulfills when applied to the merits of a dispute falls outside the confines of the present analysis.[69] What has now become clear is that there exist no doctrinal or structural barriers to applying international law to investment disputes between States and corporations. In the words of the ad hoc Committee in *Wena Hotels v Egypt* annulment decision:

> More recently … a more pragmatic and less doctrinaire approach has emerged, allowing for the application of both domestic law and international law if the specific facts of the dispute so justifies. It is no longer the case of one prevailing over the other and excluding it altogether. Rather, both sources have a role to play.[70]

The introduction of the private right of action and the applicability of international law to investment disputes have recast the traditional debate about the position of corporations under international law as contracting parties with States. The main objection to the envelopment of the corporation into the international legal order was the fact that it lacked legal personality and therefore that it could not enter into an agreement governed by international law. The objection would perhaps retain its validity in the theoretical case where a corporation and a State entered into a freestanding contractual arrangement, which lacked any point of contact with international law. Yet, the impact of investment treaties has been such that investment contracts between States and corporations will in principle find an anchor in international law. As Weil has noted:

> [c]onsidered not very long ago in some quarters to be a theoretical fantasy, the theory of the internationalization of investment relations can no longer be questioned: not only must disputes arising out of foreign private investments

---

66 Cf *AGIP v Congo*, Award (30 November 1979) [80–83].

67 Cf *Autopista* v *Venezuela*, Award (23 September 2003) [207].

68 Cf *Goetz v Burundi*, Award (10 February 1999) [94].

69 See Schreuer et al, *The ICSID Convention* (n 61) 617–30.

70 *Wena Hotels* v *Egypt*, Decision on Annulment (5 February 2002) [116].

be settled by international arbitration; they must also be resolved on the basis of international law.[71]

The justification for internationalization of contracts does not reside any longer solely in practical expediency but in the expressed consent of States in investment law agreements to allow corporations to submit themselves to and invoke international law rules.

V. MNES AS PARTIES TO INTERNATIONALIZED FUNCTIONAL CONTRACTS WITH INTERNATIONAL ORGANIZATIONS

The proliferation of international organizations since 1945 across a variety of fields has given rise to a multitude of contractual arrangements between these organizations and private corporations. International practice appears too inchoate to allow for an exhaustive classification of the contracts entered into by international organizations and corporations. Yet, the tripartite classification of contracts proposed by Batiffol may serve as a convenient starting point.[72] The first category encompasses auxiliary contracts, incidental to the operation of international organizations, which are as a rule submitted to a given municipal legal order. Examples of this category are maintenance, procurement and insurance contracts. The choice of municipal law in this respect reflects ordinary commercial practice. The second category comprises employment contracts. It is generally accepted that the internal law of the organization acting as an employer governs the employment relationship between organization and international civil servant.[73] The third category consists of contracts entered into by international organizations in direct implementation of their functions as set forth in their constituent instruments, and in this sense such contracts may be termed 'functional

---

[71] P Weil, 'The State, the Foreign Investor, and International Law: The No Longer Stormy Relationship of a *Ménage À Trois*' (2000) 15 ICSID Review 412.

[72] H Batiffol and P Lagarde, 2 *Droit International Privé* (7th edn, LGDJ, 1983) 282–6.

[73] CF Amerasinghe, *Principles of Institutional Law of International Organizations*, (2nd edn, CUP, 2005) 279; HG Schermers and N Blokker, *International Institutional Law* (4th edn, Martinus Nijhoff, 2003) 379.

contracts'.[74] The applicable law to these contracts is in principle municipal law.[75]

Overall, the classification offered by Batiffol suggests that contracts between international organizations and private corporations are not internationalized in the same way as State contracts. Nonetheless, a certain type of contract seems to escape this classification scheme as the circumstances under which it is concluded hint towards its direct submission to international law. The contract in question is the exploration for polymetallic nodules contract concluded between the International Seabed Authority (ISA)[76] and respective contractors.

1. The Contract for Exploration for Polymetallic Nodules

The exploration for polymetallic nodules constitutes an activity in the 'Area' (ie, the seabed and subsoil beyond national jurisdiction), thus falling within the scope of Section 3 of Part XI of the 1982 United Nations Convention on the Law of the Sea (UNCLOS), namely Articles 150–155 UNCLOS. According to Article 153(2) UNCLOS, 'Activities in the Area shall be carried out …: (b) in association with the Authority [ISA] by State Parties, or state enterprises or natural or juridical persons which possess the nationality of States Parties or are effectively controlled by them or their nationals, when sponsored by such States …'. According to Article 153(3) UNCLOS, activities in the Area undertaken by any of the aforementioned entities are to be carried out on the basis of a contract between the ISA and the contractor in question. Thus, the conclusion of a contract is a necessary condition of the exploration for polymetallic nodules.

---

[74] K Zemanek, *Vertragsrecht der International Organisationen* (Springer, 1957) 52.

[75] CW Jenks, *The Proper Law of International Organisations* (Stevens, 1962) 151.

[76] The ISA came into existence on 16 November 1994, as a result of the entry into force of the UNCLOS on the same date. Article 176 UNCLOS grants the ISA 'international legal personality and such legal capacity as may be necessary for the exercise of its functions and the fulfillment of its purposes'. This express recognition of the international legal personality of the ISA is noteworthy since '[t]he explicit conferment of international legal personality on intergovernmental organizations has for a long time remained the exception rather than the rule'. P Sands and P Klein, *Bowett's Law of International Institutions* (5th edn, Sweet & Maxwell, 2001) 470.

2. The Contract as Secondary Law of the ISA

Articles 160(2)(f)(ii) and 162(2)(o)(ii), construed in conjunction with Annex III, Article 17 UNCLOS expressly provide for the legislative mandate of the ISA, in discharge of which the ISA adopted in July 2000 the Regulations on Prospecting and Exploration for Polymetallic Nodules (hereafter Regulations).[77] The Regulations are of paramount significance since they set in motion the scheme laid out in the UNCLOS, enabling the ISA to enter into contracts for exploration with eligible contractors. The Regulations essentially mirror the substance and language of Annex III UNCLOS, the rationale being that contractors would 'have only one piece of reference material … and [would] therefore have no need to refer to the Convention or its Annexes'.[78] The Regulations are not legally independent from the UNCLOS, which in establishing the legislative mandate of the ISA serves as the fountainhead of the Regulations' validity. Thus, the Regulations constitute part of the secondary law enacted by the ISA and, by extension, of international law.[79]

The Regulations, like other instruments of a technical nature promulgated by international organizations, produce effects beyond the organization's internal legal order, as they seek to govern the relationship between the ISA and third entities wishing to engage in exploration activities. What is more, the Regulations are indispensable for the application of respective provisions of the UNCLOS, and therefore they have binding force. Indeed, according to Article 153(1) UNCLOS, any activities carried out in the Area must conform inter alia to the relevant Regulations. The binding force of the Regulations may furthermore be deduced from the ISA's central legislative role in establishing a regime for the Area and its resources.

Yet, the system of exploration encompasses a plurality of potential contractors, be they States, private corporations or natural persons. It is obvious that not all contractors can become parties to the UNCLOS or members of the ISA. Thus, the necessary condition of conducting

---

77 (4 October 2000) Doc ISBA 6/A/18, reproduced in (2000) 16 *International Organizations and the Law of the Sea Documentary Yearbook* 426.

78 Doc LOS/PCN/SCN.3/WP.6/Rev.1, reproduced in R Platzöder, 6 *The Law of the Sea Documents: 1983–1989* (1990) 425, 426.

79 According to the International Tribunal for the Law of the Sea (ITLOS) Seabed Disputes Chamber, there exists a 'close connection' between the UNCLOS and the Regulations. See ITLOS Seabed Disputes Chamber, *Responsibilities and Obligations of States Sponsoring Persons and Entities with Respect to Activities in the Area* (Advisory Opinion) [1 February 2011] [60].

exploration activities in the Area is the conclusion of a contract with the ISA. It is through the incorporation of the Regulations into the contract for exploration that their binding force takes effect vis-à-vis all contractors. Such incorporation takes place via the use of standardized clauses. The Regulations set out in the form of Annexes the Contract for Exploration[80] and the Standard Clauses for the Exploration Contract[81] (hereafter Standard Clauses). The Standard Clauses, in turn, transpose the content of the UNCLOS provisions and the Regulations into the contractual arrangement, thus interlinking the UNCLOS with the secondary law enacted by the ISA and the contract for exploration. According to Standard Clause 1.3, the Standard Clauses must be interpreted and applied together with the UNCLOS and the 1994 UNCLOS Implementation Agreement as a single instrument. Furthermore, according to Standard Clause 1.2, terms and phrases defined in the Regulations shall have the same meaning when mentioned in the Standard Clauses. These provisions seek to prevent any fragmentation of the legal regime for seabed exploration through variations in interpretation. Concluding, the ISA has opted for the standardization of the contractual arrangement in order to 'clarify the relationship between the contract and the Regulations and [ensure] that contract terms are uniform among contractors'.[82]

3. The Law Applicable to the Contract

The choice-of-law provision of the contract for exploration, namely Standard Clause 27.1, reads: 'This contract shall be governed by the terms of this contract, the rules, regulations and procedures of the Authority [ISA], Part XI of the Conventions, the Agreement and other rules of international law not incompatible with the Convention.' Yet, the Standard Clauses are to be read as a single instrument with UNCLOS, which includes an express choice-of-law provision in regard of the contract for exploration. According to Annex III, Article 21(1) UNCLOS, 'The contract shall be governed by the terms of the contract, the rules,

---

[80] Doc ISBA 6/A/18, Annex 3, Contract for Exploration, reproduced in (2000) 16 International Organizations and the Law of the Sea Documentary Yearbook 456–7.

[81] Doc ISBA 6/A/18, Annex 4, Standard Clauses for Exploration Contract, ibid 458 *et seq*.

[82] Chairman of the Legal and Technical Commission, Statement to the Council of 23 March 1998, reproduced in MW Lodge, 'International Seabed Authority's Regulations on Prospecting and Exploration for Polymetallic Nodules in the Area' (2002) 20 J Energy and Natural Resources L 279.

regulations and procedures of the Authority, Part XI and other rules of international law not incompatible with this Convention.'

The ordinary meaning of the terms used in Annex III, Article 21(1) UNCLOS affirms the applicability of international law to the contract for exploration.[83] This view is vindicated by the negotiating history of the provisions. Turning to the *travaux préparatoires*, participants of the UNCLOS conference were in agreement that international law was the law applicable to the exploration contract. The phrases 'terms of contract', 'rules, regulations and procedures of the Authority' and 'Part XI' formed part of the initial Proposal submitted by Group 77 to the First Committee during the Second Session.[84] The Chairman of the Negotiating Group I stated: 'I included the rules of international law not incompatible with the present convention as the law applicable to the contract.'[85] The formulation of the provision, coupled with a lack of any heated debate, proves that the applicability of international law to the exploration contract never came into question during the UNCLOS conference.

The choice-of-law provision of the contract for exploration is striking in a number of ways. First, it provides for an *express* choice of international law, departing from the practice of international organizations not to include a provision on the applicable law when contracting with private parties.[86] Second, the omission of any reference to municipal law in the contract for exploration logically results in its insulation from municipal law.

More significantly, the express choice of international law as the law governing the contract neutralizes 'party autonomy' in opting for a choice-of-law provision. States, in adopting UNCLOS, granted the ISA capacity to enter into contracts with private corporations. At the same time, States agreed that these contracts are subject to international law. Thus the ISA would be acting ultra vires the UNCLOS if it concluded a

---

[83] G Sacerdoti, 'State Contracts and International Law: A Reappraisal' (1986–87) Italian Ybk Intl L 38, affirming the submission of the contracts between the Authority and corporations to international law by virtue of Annex III, Article 21(1) UNCLOS.

[84] Text on the Conditions for Exploration and Exploitation prepared by Group 77, Doc A/CONF.62/C.1/L.7, III *Official Records of the Third United Nations Conference on the Law of the Sea* (hereafter *Official Records*) 172, 173.

[85] Report by the Chairman of the Negotiating Group I, Doc A/CONF.62/L.35, XI *Official Records* 86, 90.

[86] T Rensmann, 'Internationale Organisationen im Privatrechtsverkehr' (1998) 36 Archiv des Völkerrechts 334.

contract for exploration with a corporation and submitted it to a municipal law.

Consenting by virtue of treaty law to grant corporations the required legal capacity to enter into agreements governed by international law, States have recognized as valid and effective the submission of the contract for exploration to international law. Therefore, reprising the words of Jennings, UNCLOS provides for 'a point of contact with international law whereby [the choice of international law as the applicable law becomes] an obligation existing in and effective in international law'.[87]

The internationalization of the exploration contract also corresponds to practical needs. The international organization does not have a legal order comparable to those of States, to which the contract could be submitted. Furthermore, the internationalization of the contract serves the purpose of safeguarding the independent function of the organization.[88] Finally, it prevents the legal fragmentation of the exploration system, which would emerge if each contract were submitted to the municipal law of the sponsoring State party.

4. The Responsibility of the Contracting Corporation for Breach of Contract

The international law character of the exploration contract can be further gleaned from the nature of the responsibility incurred by the contractor in case of breach of contract attributed to it. According to Standard Clause 16.1, the contractor shall be 'liable for the actual amount of any damage ... arising out of its acts or omissions ...'. In order to ascertain the normative content of the term 'liable' one needs to revert to the Regulations, in accordance with Standard Clause 1.2, which provides that '[t]erms and phrases defined in the Regulations shall have the same meaning in these standard clauses'. Still, the Regulations provide for a further *renvoi*, positing in Regulation 30 that '[r]esponsibility and liability of the contractor shall be in accordance with the Convention'. Annex III, Article 22 UNCLOS establishes that the 'contractor shall have responsibility or liability for any damage arising out of wrongful acts while conducting activities in the Area'. The corporation may only conduct activities in the Area on the basis of a contract. Consequently, a

---

[87] Jennings, 'State Contracts ...' (n 49) 178.

[88] N Valticos, 'Les Contrats Conclus par les Organisations Internationales avec des Personnes Privées' (1997) 57/I Annuaire de l'Institut de Droit International 9.

corporation may incur 'responsibility or liability' only for violating its contractual undertakings.

The key to interpreting Article 22 UNCLOS is keeping in mind that it applies to all contractors, whether States or corporations.[89] The formulation of the provision supports such a reading. Moreover, at no point during the negotiations was it suggested that the nature of the responsibility of the contractor depended on whether it was a State, a state enterprise, a private corporation or a natural person. The interpretation of Annex III, Article 22 UNCLOS that seems to best accord with the spirit of the Convention is that contractors' responsibility for wrongful breaches of contract is responsibility under international law, since the contract itself is governed exclusively by international law.[90] At the same time, States are not obliged to transpose the Regulations of the ISA in their municipal legal orders.[91] Thus, a violation of the contractual terms amounts to a violation of international law. To suggest that the contractor is responsible under municipal law would lead to the following absurdity: in case of a State engaging in activities in the Area on the basis of a contract, the State would retain the prerogative to pass municipal legislation exonerating itself from responsibility as a contractor. Furthermore, responsibility under municipal law implies that the responsibility of each contractor would be judged against the yardstick of the rules of its sponsoring State, thus fragmenting the regime set up by the UNCLOS.

The 'responsibility and liability' of the contractor for a wrongful act in breach of the contract has to be distinguished from the responsibility of the State resulting from its failure to ensure that the sponsored contractor abides by the contract. As noted by the ITLOS Seabed Disputes Chamber:

> the main liability for a wrongful act committed in the conduct of the contractor's operations or in the exercise of the Authority's powers and functions rests with the contractor and the Authority, respectively, rather than with the sponsoring State. In the view of the Chamber, this reflects the distribution of responsibilities for deep seabed mining activities between the contractor, the Authority and the sponsoring State.[92]

---

89 R Wolfrum, *Die Internationalisierung Staatsfreier Räume* (Springer, 1984) 521.

90 *Responsibilities and Obligations* (n 79) [67], where it is stated that '"responsibility" has the same meaning as in the ILC Articles on State Responsibility'.

91 Wolfrum, *Staatsfreier Räume* (n 89) 524.

92 *Responsibilities and Obligations Advisory Opinion* (n 79) [200].

The Chamber went on to conclude that 'the liability of the sponsoring State arises from its own failure to carry out its responsibilities, whereas the contractor's liability arises from its own non-compliance. Both forms of liability exist in parallel'.[93]

5. Dispute Settlement Provisions

The international law character of the exploration contract may finally be deduced from the characterization of the dispute arising from its operation as international. While there exists no fixed criterion to discern the international character of a dispute, one can rely on a combination of a personal criterion, focusing on the entities granted access to international dispute settlement, as well as a material criterion, which concerns the law to be applied to the dispute.[94]

The UNCLOS expressly grants corporations a right of access to an international tribunal in order to enforce their rights deriving from the contract for exploration. According to Article 187(c), the jurisdiction of the Seabed Disputes Chamber extends to disputes between parties to a contract in respect of the interpretation or application thereof. The Chamber's extended jurisdiction *ratione personae* is exceptional, since corporations can act both as plaintiffs and defendants. Article 188(2)(a) UNCLOS expressly stipulates that 'any party to the dispute' may seek recourse before an international tribunal should a dispute arise. Therefore, one may envisage a situation where the ISA seeks recourse before an international tribunal against a contracting corporation.

Article 187(c) UNCLOS has to be read in conjunction with Article 188(2)(a) UNCLOS, which provides that such disputes 'shall be submitted, at the request of any party to the dispute, to binding commercial arbitration, unless the parties otherwise agree'. UNCLOS appears to establish a rebuttable presumption that contractual disputes be submitted to commercial arbitration. Yet, this freedom to choose a forum is limited by virtue of the same provision, which stipulates that any dispute involving the interpretation of UNCLOS provisions regarding activities in the Area has to be referred to the Seabed Disputes Chamber for an interlocutory ruling. According to Article 188(2)(b) UNCLOS, the arbitral tribunal has to render its award in conformity with the ruling of the Chamber. As to the scope of the 'ruling' exception, it is probable that the

---

[93] Ibid, [201].

[94] See CF Amerasinghe, *Jurisdiction of International Tribunals* (CUP, 2003) 4–9.

dispute will in principle involve the interpretation of UNCLOS provisions, since the substance of the contractual arrangement has been set forth first in the UNCLOS and its Annexes and then transposed into the secondary law of the ISA.

Finally, as to the applicable law to the dispute, which determines inter alia the rules that apply to the interpretation of the agreement and the consequences of its breach, Article 293 UNLCOS states in clear terms that 'a court or tribunal having jurisdiction under this section shall apply this Convention and other rules of international law compatible with this Convention'. This provision precludes the application of any municipal rules to the dispute. Such a strict reading of the provision is in accord with the negotiating history of the provision. It was argued during the UNCLOS drafting debates that along with international law rules, 'any other applicable law' should be included in the text, yet the proposal was dropped due to objections regarding the applicability of any rules other than those of international law to the dispute.[95]

6. The Internationalization of the Contract for Exploration

It becomes apparent that the contract for exploration for polymetallic nodules under the UNCLOS constitutes an exceptional case of *internationalization* of a contract between an international organization and a private corporation. The contract becomes internationalized via its overall submission to international law as regards the applicable law to the contract, the responsibility that arises from a wrongful act in breach of the contract, and the applicable law in the context of dispute settlement.

VI. EXPANSIONS: AN AGENDA FOR RESEARCH

No hard and fast rule can be devised to describe the forms and methods adopted by international law to entangle MNEs in its ambit due to the hybrid nature of these entities. Corporations may assume a position similar to that of the individual insofar as they enjoy a measure of human rights protection under an international treaty. At the same time they may act as contracting partners to States and international organizations. In the wake of liberalization, States may choose to delegate the exercise of certain functions to corporations, which have been traditionally been seen

---

95 See A/CONF.62/Background Paper 1, Article 16, reproduced in R Platzöder, 12 *Third United Nations Conference on the Law of the Sea: Documents* (Oceana, 1987) 194, 201.

as forming part of the substance of sovereignty. MNEs thus exercise various functions and ultimately their functions serve as the yardstick against which the extent of their participation in the international legal process should be measured.

MNEs' functional polymorphy generates a further methodological difficulty for international law. International legal rules have in principle a 'nexus to the concept of the State', whereas the emergence of new rules involves an 'abstraction of the particular characteristics of the States in question'.[96] In other words, the 'conceptual structure of international law [attaches] rights and duties to the category "state"'.[97] Therefore, the affirmation of the applicability of international law to corporations should not be taken to mean that by way of analogy international law applies to corporations in a wholesale manner. International legal rules, when they are not created to deal with MNEs as such, have to be 'transliterated' when they apply in the corporate context.

Discussions on the application of international law to MNEs focus mostly on their role as contracting partners of States and international organizations, which is natural given that the latter employ the legal vehicle of a contract to entrust corporations with a given function. What is of paramount significance is the changing landscape within which these contracts are concluded. Contracts in the field of investment law or the law of the sea do not operate in a legal no-man's-land suspended between domestic and international law. On the contrary, the international legal order is increasingly building up a normative structure, within which such contracts are embedded. It might be suggested that the *Jurisdiction of the Courts of Danzig* advisory opinion is much more relevant to this point than to the direct application of treaties to non-State entities. The PCIJ was faced with the creation of a legal regime on the basis of international law regarding the employment of Danzig railway officials, which took effect via the transposition of international law to the 'contract of service' of these officials. In a way, the opinion seems to foreshadow the mode of operation of investment law and the law of the sea. States set down the framework of a playing field, within which they may then establish contractual arrangements with private entities. Still, even within this playing field legal clarity and certainty are wanting. One may single out two issues that have generated significant controversy in the jurisprudence of investment arbitral tribunals and that constitute areas

---

[96] A Bleckann, 'Article 2(1)' in B Simma (ed), *The Charter of the United Nations* (OUP, 1994) 87.

[97] P Allott, 'State Responsibility and the Unmaking of International Law' (1998) 29 Harvard J Intl L 14.

where future research is required, namely the legal effect of 'umbrella clauses' and the nature of the responsibility assumed by the host State when found in breach of an investment contract.

One of the most intriguing aspects of international investment law to which increasing attention is being paid is its interaction with the international law of human rights. As argued above, corporations are not obligors under the latter, yet the expansive reach of human rights is affecting corporate operations. Human rights have been invoked by host States as a defense precluding the wrongfulness of conduct in breach of the contract. Nonetheless, arbitral tribunals have been somewhat reluctant to enter the fray. In *Siemens*, Argentina claimed that 'the human rights so incorporated in the Constitution would be disregarded by recognizing the property rights asserted by the Claimant given the social and economic conditions of Argentina'.[98] The Tribunal dodged this submission by holding that 'without the benefit of further elaboration and substantiation by the parties, it is not an argument that, *prima facie*, bears any relationship to the merits of this case'.[99] In *Sempra*, Argentina invoked a 'state of necessity', in the sense that the preservation of the constitutional order, including respect for the human rights guarantees enshrined in the 1969 American Convention on Human Rights, justified a breach of the investor's rights.[100] Once more, the arbitral tribunal shied away from considering the argument in full, suggesting that 'the constitutional order was not on the verge of collapse, as evidenced by ... the orderly constitutional transition that carried the country through five different Presidencies ...'.[101] The reluctance of the tribunals may be justified on the basis of their limited jurisdiction and the perceived 'private' character of the disputes at hand. But the question on the relationship and interaction between international investment law and international human rights law, especially in their treaty form, remains.

A step further in the direction of the integration between investment law and human rights would be the inclusion of provisions in a BIT upholding certain fundamental principles or barring certain conduct in violation of international *ordre public*, which the competent tribunal would then be called upon to apply. The idea is not that far-fetched. Non-investment concerns forming part of the international *ordre public* have been brought to bear in the context of investment proceedings.

---

98 *Siemens v The Argentine Republic*, Award (6 February 2007) [75].

99 Ibid, [79].

100 *Sempra Energy International v The Argentine Republic*, Award (28 September 2007) [331].

101 Ibid, [332].

Thus, in *World Duty Free v Kenya* the Tribunal found that a contract for the construction, maintenance and operation of a duty-free complex had been procured by corruption. According to its reasoning, 'in light of the domestic laws and international conventions relating to corruption, and in light of the decisions taken in this matter by courts and arbitral tribunals, this Tribunal is convinced that bribery is contrary to the international public policy of most, if not all, States ... Thus, claims based on contracts of corruption or on contracts obtained by corruption cannot be upheld by this Arbitral Tribunal'.[102]

Concluding, one may suggest that human rights considerations are becoming increasingly relevant for corporate conduct. At the same time, those considerations are gradually beginning to enter the realm of international investment law. It is this synergy that potentially opens up vistas for future research.

[102] *World Duty Free v Kenya*, Award (4 October 2006) [157].

21. Treaties and individuals: Of beneficiaries, duty-bearers, users, and participants

Ilias Plakokefalos

I. INTRODUCTION

The place of the individual in the international legal order is a controversial and complex issue. The debates around the position international law adopts, or should adopt, regarding the individual have taken many shapes and forms over the years. It is true that most steps that have been taken towards the inclusion of the individual in the international legal order can be traced in treaty law. It is equally true that there has not been a consistent stance of international law towards the identification of a place for the individual. The individual may be seen – and is primarily seen – as a *beneficiary* of international law since he or she is accorded protection (either directly or indirectly) through a number of instruments. They may also been seen – more recently – as *users* of international law. Broadly speaking the former term denotes an individual being granted a 'mere benefit' by international law, in particular by means of an international treaty, while the latter signifies the creation of a 'substantive (legally enforceable) right'.[1] Whether in the future the individual will also be treated as a *participant*, that is, as an actor rather than a recipient of benefits or substantive rights, remains to be seen. Before going into the substance of these terms, and of the role of the individual in the law of treaties, a few preliminary steps are required in order to delineate the topic.

First, this chapter will only deal with individuals and not with groups of individuals (eg, NGOs or rebel groups) or corporate actors.[2] The analysis will be focused on the individual person, and on their relationship with and position in the law of treaties. Second, the chapter will not confine itself to an analysis of the position of the individual strictly

[1] See further sections IV and V below. See, for a similar distinction recently, A Roberts, 'Clash of Paradigms: Actors and Analogies Shaping the Investment Treaty System' (2013) 107 AJIL 45, 60.

[2] On corporate actors, see the chapter by M Karavias in this *Handbook*.

within the law of treaties, solely looking at what the Vienna Convention on the Law of Treaties (VCLT)[3] has to say on the topic. It will also incorporate an analysis of the position of the individual within a number of special treaty regimes.

The following section of this chapter (II) addresses the discussion in international law on subjects and international legal personality. It demonstrates that while an appraisal of this discussion is essential in order to proceed to the analysis of the position of the individual in the law of treaties, there is nothing that prevents a study of the position of the individual in a manner that is detached from the debate on the doctrine of subjects. The next section (III) is devoted to determining the position of the individual according to the law of treaties *sensu stricto* (ie, the VCLT and relevant customary law). There is little – if any – material on the topic. However, the doctrine of subjects of international law is informed by the practice adopted – among other things – in specific international treaties and special treaty regimes, which are discussed in subsequent sections. Moreover, the doctrine of subjects forms the starting point for any discussion of the individual.[4] At the same time it provides for a conceptual basis for the analysis that follows. So the issue of subjects will be discussed at the outset, in order to provide the necessary background, and will then be taken up at the end of this chapter as a possible topic for further research.

The next step (section IV) is to trace the route of the individual within international law from beneficiary to user to participant. The individual as beneficiary is studied first, focusing on the variations of such a position of the individual in the various treaty regimes under international law. A similar exercise is then undertaken with respect to the individual as user (section V). The concluding section (VI) seeks to set a research agenda for the future, focusing on the individual as a participant in treaties, on the relationship between the place of the individual in the law of treaties on the one hand and the individual within treaties on the other, and on the bearing that the developments regarding the position of the individual with respect to treaties may have on the doctrine of subjects and legal personality.

---

[3] Vienna Convention on the Law of Treaties (adopted 23 May 1969, entered into force 27 January 1980) 1155 UNTS 331.

[4] Most treatises on the issue do involve at least a preliminary discussion of the issue of subjecthood. The examples range from J Spiropoulos, 'L'Individu et le Droit International' (1929) 30 *Recueil des Cours de l'Académie de Droit International* 191 to K Parlett, *The Individual in the International Legal System: Continuity and Change in International Law* (CUP, 2011).

II. SUBJECTHOOD, LEGAL PERSONALITY, AND THE LEGAL 'CAPACITY' OF INDIVIDUALS

All law regulates human behaviour, and international law is no exception.[5] Individuals are at the epicenter of international law as they are at the epicenter of municipal law. This may be harder to witness in international law than it is in municipal law; yet, a closer look reveals that during the twentieth century many international treaties have been concluded with an eye on the individual. The rise of human rights treaties is an obvious example. Even before the rise of human rights, however, international humanitarian law gave special attention to the individual.[6] International environmental law was also initially geared towards the individual, albeit in a broad manner and not in the sense of according it rights or imposing on it duties.[7] International economic law has offered numerous examples of a special focus on the individual as well.[8] In all these canonical areas of international law we find instruments that provide, with infinite variations in scope and content, for the protection of the individual. This is in line with the more general trend that has been traced in modern international law: that of an 'inward trend' in the directionality of norms.[9] Next to 'outward-looking' international obligations, which seek to regulate the conduct of States as between themselves

[5] H Kelsen, 'Théorie Générale du Droit International Public, Problèmes Choisis' (1932) 42 RCADI 117, 145–6.

[6] Early humanitarian treaties did not confer any rights on the individual but they had provisions that sought to protect them, see, for instance, Hague Convention IV Respecting the Laws and Customs of War on Land (adopted 18 October 1907, entered into force 26 January 1910) 25 CTS 277.

[7] The first collective declaration of States pertaining to international environmental law, the Stockholm Declaration of 1972, was clearly anthropocentric. This can be clearly seen from its full title, Stockholm Declaration on the Human Environment, UN Doc. A/Conf.48/4 and Corr.1, 1972. As environmental awareness grew, less anthropocentric approaches were followed (see, eg, Rio Declaration on Environment and Development, UN Doc. A/Conf.151/5/Rev.1, 1992). This does not mean that the individual stopped being at the center of very important treaties, such as the Åarhus Convention, Convention on Access to Information, Public Participation in Decision-Making and Access to Justice in Environmental Matters (adopted 25 June 1998, entered into force 30 October 2001) 2161 UNTS 450.

[8] Even though international economic law is, admittedly, focused more on legal rather than natural persons.

[9] See A Tzanakopoulos, 'Domestic Courts in International Law: The International Judicial Function of National Courts' (2011) 34 Loyola of LA Intl and Comp L Rev 133, 138–42, with further references.

and on the international plane exclusively, many modern international obligations are actually 'inward looking', requiring the State to take particular conduct within the domestic legal order.[10] Such inward looking norms are most likely to be seen as 'benefitting' individuals, and as susceptible of being 'used' by them, in an attempt to control the exercise of State power.[11] In the final analysis, all law is addressed to individuals, though sometimes mediated through a legal entity, be it the State, the international organization, a corporation, and the like.

The Permanent Court of International Justice (PCIJ) authoritatively indicated that States may conclude treaties that confer rights directly to individuals. In its advisory opinion on the *Jurisdiction of the Courts of Danzig*[12] the PCIJ held that:

> [i]t cannot be disputed that the very object of an international agreement, according to the intention of the contracting parties, may be the adoption by the Parties of some definite rules creating individual rights and obligations and enforceable by the national courts.[13]

Despite the controversy surrounding the case, the opinion serves as a clear indication that, no matter what the prevailing doctrine on subjects holds, States are free to conclude treaties that do indeed create rights and obligations for individuals. Individuals thus have the legal capacity to enjoy rights and incur obligations and, moreover, to seek enforcement of those rights, if a treaty so allows. The extent of the rights and obligations will also be dictated by the treaty.

It was the PCIJ that also made clear the distinction between benefitting the individual by bestowing rights upon it, and enabling it to have recourse to a procedure (judicial or otherwise) in order to enforce these rights. It observed that 'it is scarcely necessary to point out that the capacity to possess civil rights does not necessarily imply the capacity to exercise those rights oneself'.[14]

---

[10] See ibid.

[11] See, eg, Roberts, 'Clash of Paradigms …' (n 1) 45–6:

[12] *Jurisdiction of the Courts of Danzig (Pecuniary Claims of Danzig Railway Officials who have Passed into the Polish Service, Against the Polish Railways Administration)*, PCIJ 1928 Series B, No 15, 17–18.

[13] Ibid.

[14] *Peter Pázmány University*, Judgment, PCIJ 1933 Series A/B, No 61 at 231. See further below, sections IV and V.

The literature on the position of individuals in international law takes usually – if not always – as its starting point the doctrine of subjects.[15] This can be easily explained. Before discussing the individual in public international law, one must first position the individual within the system. States are the paradigmatic subjects of international law. Any other entity, including individuals, is not self-evidently a subject of that law. The idea that the individual is a subject of international law is certainly not novel. In one sense, it formed a reaction by part of the literature to the hardcore positivist views on international law of the early twentieth century. Anzilotti was vehemently opposed to any idea that the individual could be a subject of international law.[16] Kelsen and Lauterpacht both objected to this strict approach, despite coming at it from different angles. Kelsen claimed that individuals are both authorized and obligated by international law, albeit indirectly.[17] Lauterpacht for his part stated that 'there has been an increasing realization that the direct subjection of individuals to the rule of international law is an essential condition of the strengthening of the ethical basis of international law'.[18]

Despite, or perhaps because of, the wealth of literature on the topic[19] there is no uniform definition of the concept of subjecthood and no clear

---

[15] See Spiropoulos, 'L'Individu …' (n 4); A Orakhelashvilli, 'The Position of the Individual in International Law' (2000–1) 31 Cal W Intl L 241–76; E Roucounas, 'Facteurs Privés et Droit International Public' (2002) 299 Recueil des Cours 23, 23–40; A Bianchi, 'The Fight for Inclusion: Non-State Actors and International Law' in U Fastenrath, R Geiger, DE Khan, A Paulus, S von Schorlemer and C Vedder (eds), *From Bilateralism to Community Interest: Essays in Honour of Brunno Simma* (OUP, 2011) 40.

[16] D Anzilotti, *Corso di Diritto Internazionale* (Vol 1, Cedam Padova, 1955) 113.

[17] H Kelsen, *Pure Theory of Law* (M Knight tr, The Lawbook Exchange Ltd, 2009/University of California Press, 1967) 325.

[18] H Lauterpacht, 'The Subjects of the Law of Nations' (1947) 63 LQR 438, 526–7.

[19] See among many others the works cited in (n 2) and (n 15) above, as well as, eg, PK Menon, 'The Subjects of Modern International Law' (1990) 3 Hague Ybk Intl L 30–86; B Cheng, 'Introduction to Subjects of International Law' in M Bedjaoui (ed), *International Law: Achievements and Prospects* (Martinus Nijhoff, 1991) 23–40; the essays in R Hofmann (ed), *Non-State Actors as New Subjects of International Law* (Duncker & Humblot, 1998); the essays in T Skouteris and A Vermeer-Künzli (eds), *The Protection of the Individual in International Law: Essays in Honour of John Dugard* (CUP, 2007); R MacCorquodale, 'The Individual and the International Legal System' in A Bianchi (ed), *Non-State Actors and International Law* (Ashgate, 2009) 121–46 as well as the many references therein.

picture of its relationship with the (cognate) concept of international legal personality. According to the prevailing view, the terms 'subject' and 'international legal personality' denote the same thing and may be used interchangeably.[20] There is also the view that subjects of international law are actors that possess all attributes of legal personality (ie, they can bear obligations and enjoy rights, they can pursue these rights internationally in their own name, they can be held responsible for breaches of their obligations, and they can participate in law making).[21]

Regardless of the correct view on the definition of these concepts, a third concept may be used to connect those of subjects and international legal personality: the concept of 'capacity'. Capacity is a concept that may be employed to give content to the concepts of both subjecthood and international legal personality. The International Court of Justice (ICJ) defined the international legal person in terms of its capacity to possess rights and obligations and to bring corresponding claims at the international level.[22] Similarly, both editions of the *Max Planck Encyclopedia of International Law* define legal personality in terms of the capacities the actor in question possesses.[23] Capacity then seems to inform the content of the notions of both subjecthood and international legal personality. In other words, it is the range of any given entity's capacity (ie, the attributes of international legal personality the entity possesses) that will determine whether that entity is a subject or not, and to what extent. Therefore, the question whether an individual is a subject or whether an individual possesses legal personality is unhelpful and misleading. Rather, the crucial point is the extent of the legal capacity the individual may be endowed with under international law and, specifically, for the purposes of this chapter, under certain treaty regimes. This allows one to discuss the legal capacity of individuals under treaty law without having to determine whether the individual is a 'subject' or has 'international legal personality'. One reading of the *Reparation for Injuries* advisory opinion, which refers to an entity (the UN) possessing 'a large measure of international legal personality', may be seen as supporting this position. The notion of international legal personality (and thus of

---

[20] H Mosler, 'Subjects of International Law' in R Bernhard (dir), *Max Planck Encyclopedia of International Law* (Martinus Nijhoff 1984) 442, 443.

[21] Lauterpacht, 'The Subjects ...' (n 18) 438.

[22] *Reparations for Injuries Suffered in the Services of the United Nations*, ICJ Rep 1949, 174, 177–9.

[23] Mosler, 'Subjects of International Law' (n 20) 442; C Walter, 'Subjects of International Law' in R Wolfrum (dir), *Max Planck Encyclopedia of International Law* (OUP, 2012) accessed 24 February 2013 at www.mpepil.com.

subjecthood) is presented in the opinion as a relative notion, in the sense that the more attributes of international legal personality one has, the more of a subject one is. The extent of one's 'subjecthood', 'legal personality', or – better – 'capacity' will further depend on the particular treaty regime within which an entity operates: for example, an individual may not be a subject in general international law, but may be so within the context of the European Convention of Human Rights,[24] or a particular bilateral investment treaty (BIT), or the Convention on the Settlement of Investment Disputes between States and Nationals of Other States (ICSID).[25]

This detachment of capacity from subjecthood and legal personality has the advantage of sidestepping the rather dated discussion on whether capacity needs to satisfy some minimum requirements as to content in order to lead to the establishment of personality.[26] However, one crucial distinction must be reiterated. In keeping with the idea of (variable) capacity, there is a difference between the capacity to hold rights and the capacity to enforce those rights before judicial, quasi-judicial, or administrative bodies, national or international. Rights of individuals not coupled with the capacity of such individuals to seek enforcement of said rights in their own name can be further divided into two categories. On the one hand these (individually unenforceable) rights can be purely aspirational, such as the right to a healthy life in harmony with nature as enshrined in Principle 1 of the Rio Declaration,[27] or the rather elusive concept of the right to food.[28] On the other hand, they may be rights that, in order to be enforced, must be taken up by a State, usually the State of

---

[24] European Convention for the Protection of Human Rrights and Fundamental Freedoms (adopted 2 November 1950, entered into force 3 September 1953) 87 UNTS 103.

[25] Convention on the Settlement of Investment Disputes between States and Nationals of Other States (adopted 18 March 1965, entered into force 14 October 1966) 575 UNTS 159. See, eg, A Tzanakopoulos, 'Denunciation of the ICSID Convention under the General International Law of Treaties' in R Hofmann and CJ Tams (eds), *International Investment Law and General International Law: From Clinical Isolation to Systemic Integration?* (Nomos, 2011) 75, 89 with further references.

[26] Mosler, 'Subjects of International Law' (n 20).

[27] Rio Declaration (n 7).

[28] On the right to food, see *Report by the Special Rapporteur on the Right to Food, Olivier de Schutter*, 14 January 2013, A/HRC/22/50/Add.3.

nationality of the individual, through the mechanism of diplomatic protection.[29]

The issue, therefore, turns, inevitably, to the scope of the capacity individuals are endowed with under treaty regimes. In examining the scope of an individual's capacity within specific treaty regimes, we can determine whether the individual is merely affected by the law as: a 'reflex', that is, the individual is meant simply as a 'beneficiary' of the regime (the scope of the individual's legal capacity merely extends to being accorded individually unenforceable rights) or, similarly, the regime imposes duties on the individual; as a 'user' (the scope of legal capacity extends to being able to bring claims at the international level); or as a 'participant' (the scope of legal capacity allows the individual to be a treaty party).

To sum up, the point of departure for this chapter is that individuals may have different capacities to act in various circumstances and under various international legal regimes (or canonical areas). The analysis that follows looks at the capacities individuals have been endowed with by means of international treaties. In this way, a differentiation between the individual as a beneficiary or duty bearer, the individual as a user, and the individual as a potential participant will be reflected more accurately.

III. CAPACITY OF INDIVIDUALS UNDER THE GENERAL LAW OF TREATIES

The customary law of treaties, as reflected in part in the Vienna Convention on the Law of Treaties of 1969, does not permit individuals to enter into treaties with States. This is a capacity that is reserved for States, at least under the terms of the VCLT, or to international organizations to the extent that the Vienna Convention on the Law of Treaties between States and International Organizations 1986 reflects customary law and the constitutive instrument of the relevant international organization so allows. Individuals are still able to enter into

---

[29] On diplomatic protection, see Articles on Diplomatic Protection, *Official Records of the General Assembly, Sixty-First Session, Supplement No. 10* (A/61/10). See also, *Avena and Other Mexican Nationals (Mexico v United States of America)*, ICJ Rep 2004, 12; *LaGrand Case (Germany v United States of America)*, ICJ Rep 2001, 466.

agreements with States, under general international law or under specialized treaty regimes,[30] which are sometimes called 'transnational contracts' or are given other designations, but which do not constitute treaties under general international law.[31]

The general law of treaties does not directly accord any other capacity to individuals. Whatever references are made to individuals, and whatever capacities are accorded to them, are in their guise as representatives of States, and are thus subsumed in the capacity accorded to the State. An obvious example is Article 7 VCLT, which provides for the individuals who have the capacity to represent a State for the purposes of concluding a treaty.[32]

However, the general law of treaties, and the VCLT in particular, are still important with respect to the position of the individual in relation to the law of treaties. Even though they do not accord individuals any capacities directly, they perform an 'enabling' function: by not prohibiting the allocation of rights under treaties to entities other than States, they confirm that treaties may be used to accord legal capacity to individuals. In fact this is as close to explicit as it gets in the VCLT: Article 60(5) disapplies the general right of States to terminate or suspend a treaty for material breach in the case of provisions 'relating to the protection of the human person contained in treaties of humanitarian character, in particular to provisions prohibiting any form of reprisals against persons protected by such treaties'.[33]

While the VCLT denies individuals the capacity of being a 'third party',[34] the provision of Article 60(5) seems to elevate them to quasi-third parties,[35] in the sense that treaties of a humanitarian character bestow on individuals something akin to 'acquired rights', that is, rights that cannot be retracted as a response to a serious breach of the treaty by another State. This can be coupled with the protection offered by Article 60(1)–(3), which makes it very difficult for States to terminate or withdraw on account of breach from treaties which are not meant to be

---

[30] See section V below regarding the provisions of the UN Convention on the Law of the Sea on prospecting in the 'Area'.

[31] See section VI below regarding these 'transnational contracts'.

[32] See also Articles 1(c) and 8 VCLT.

[33] See generally B Simma and CJ Tams, 'Article 60: Convention of 1969' in O Corten and P Klein (eds), *The Vienna Conventions on the Law of Treaties: A Commentary* (OUP, 2011) 1351, 1366–8, paras 42–7.

[34] The term being reserved to States, see Article 1(h) and section 4 VCLT.

[35] See also C Chinkin, *Third Parties in International Law* (Clarendon Press, 1993) 13–15, 120 seq.

operating in 'bilateral constellations' – that is, primarily treaties which involve human rights 'pledges', rights pledged to those within the jurisdiction of the State assuming the relevant obligations.[36]

States are then free, under the law of treaties, to accord individuals whatever legal capacity they wish to, by means of treaties between them, even if they are less free to retract rights or benefits already bestowed.[37] Depending on the capacity that such treaty regimes accord to individuals, the latter may be qualified as mere 'beneficiaries', as actual 'users', and perhaps even as 'participants': not only of the specialized treaty regime, but even of the law of treaties itself, as we shall come to see. These issues are now taken up in turn.

IV. REFLEXES: THE INDIVIDUAL AS BENEFICIARY AND DUTY BEARER

1. Beneficiaries

The conclusion of human rights treaties in the last 60 to 70 years did not introduce any technical novelties regarding the position of the individual in international law. It was the sheer number and scope of human rights treaties that made all the difference. On the global level, the International Covenant on Civil and Political Rights[38] (ICCPR), the International Covenant on Economic Social and Cultural Rights[39] (ICESCR), the Convention on the Elimination of Racial Discrimination[40] (CERD), the Convention on the Rights of the Child,[41] and the Convention on the Elimination of Discrimination Against Women[42] (CEDAW) are fine examples of an ever increasing number of instruments that accord benefits to the

---

[36] See Simma and Tams, 'Article 60 …' (n 32) 1367–8, para 45.

[37] But see Chinkin, *Third Parties* (n 34) 121–2.

[38] International Covenant on Civil and Political Rights (adopted 16 December 1966, entered into force 23 March 1976) 999 UNTS 171.

[39] International Covenant on Economic Social and Cultural Rights (adopted 19 December 1966, entered into force 3 January 1976) 993 UNTS 3.

[40] International Convention on the Elimination of All Forms of Racial Discrimination (adopted 21 December 1965, entered into force 4 January 1969) 660 UNTS 195.

[41] Convention on the Rights of the Child (adopted 20 November 1989, entered into force 2 September 1990)1577 UNTS 3.

[42] Convention on the Elimination of All Forms of Discrimination Against Women (adopted 18 December 1979, entered into force 3 September 1981) 1249 UNTS 13.

individual. On the regional level, the European Convention on Human Rights and Fundamental Freedoms[43] (ECHR), the American Convention on Human Rights[44] (ACHR), and the African Charter on Human Rights and People's Rights[45] also create a number of rights that strengthen the protection of the individual.

The legal capacity of the individual differs according to the precise terms of each of the aforementioned instruments. This serves as a reminder of the position taken in this chapter that it is capacity that determines the exact position of the individual. For example, at the danger of stating the obvious, an individual has to be a woman to benefit from CEDAW or a child to benefit from the Convention on the Rights of the Child. Capacity then is accorded by some of these instruments to specific individuals only. Other treaties, like the ICCPR, award certain capacities to *all* individuals within the jurisdiction of the parties. Finally, the scope or extent of the legal capacity accorded by these instruments also differs (on which point, see further section V). But in the first instance, what is clear is that individuals are the beneficiaries of the obligations assumed by States through the relevant treaties.

The protection of aliens, which pre-dates human rights instruments, has also been translated into treaties that accord benefits to the specific individuals making 'investments' in States other than their State of nationality, that is, 'foreign investors'.[46] The customary rules of protection of aliens have spurred significant litigation before international tribunals concerning individuals. Both PCIJ and ICJ decisions have dealt with the protection of aliens.[47] Bilateral investment treaties as well as inter-State trade agreements have provided for a more detailed and precise layer of protection of the individual concerning their economic

---

43 European Convention for the Protection of Human Rights and Fundamental Freedoms (adopted 2 November 1950, entered into force 3 September 1953) 87 UNTS 103.

44 American Convention on Human Rights (adopted 22 November 1969, entered into force 18 July 1980) 1144 UNTS 331.

45 African Charter on Human Rights and People's Rights (adopted 27 June 1981, entered into force 21 October 1986) 21 ILM 58.

46 AL Marriott, 'Bilateral Investment Treaty Arbitration in the Early 21st Century' in MA Fernández-Ballesteros and D Arias (eds), *Liber Amicorum Bernando Cremades* (La Ley, 2010) 807; R Dolzer and C Schreuer, *Principles of International Investment Law* (OUP, 2012) 1–4.

47 There is ample case law on this issue ranging from *Mavrommatis Palestine Concessions*, Judgment, PCIJ 1924 Series A, No 2 to *Ahmadou Sadio Diallo (Republic of Guinea v Democratic Republic of Congo)*, ICJ Rep 2010, 639.

activities in the host States. It must be stressed that there is nothing in most bilateral investment treaties that denies protection to individual persons.[48] Granted, these treaties are usually concluded with the corporate actor in mind, yet it is clear that individual persons may (and do) also benefit from them as long as they qualify as 'investors'.

In international environmental law there have been increasing efforts so as to offer protection to individuals regarding the degradation of the environment. Besides broad, aspirational provisions,[49] there have been a limited number of instruments that do indeed bestow benefits or rights on individuals. The most striking example is the Åarhus Convention,[50] which puts the individual center stage regarding its procedural rights in decision-making processes on environmental matters. Besides environmental treaties, environmental protection has become increasingly prominent in human rights instruments. The European Social Charter, for example, includes a provision on the right to a healthy working environment.[51] This right has been used to tackle broader environmental issues that are connected with the working environment.[52] The applicants in the *Marangopoulos Foundation* complaint, for example, did not limit themselves to claims constrained by the contours of Articles 2(4) and 3 of the European Social Charter. Instead, they made broader claims regarding the inadequacy of environmental assessments and of monitoring conducted by the government in the whole region,[53] and regarding the impact of the choice of lignite in the energy sector.[54] Nevertheless, it must be admitted that regarding the actual level of protection environmental treaties could

---

[48] PM Dupuy, 'Unification Rather than Fragmentation of International Law? The Case of International Investment Law and Human Rights Law' in PM Dupuy, F Francioni and EU Petersmann, *Human Rights in International Investment Law and Arbitration* (OUP, 2009) 45.

[49] See (n 27).

[50] Convention on Access to Information, Public Participation in Decision-Making and Access to Justice in Environmental Matters (adopted 25 June 1998, entered into force 30 October 2001) 2161 UNTS 450.

[51] European Social Charter (adopted 3 May 1996, entered into force 1 July 1999) 163 CTS, Articles 2(4) and 3.

[52] *Marangopoulos Foundation for Human Rights (MFHR) v Greece*, Complaint No. 30/2005.

[53] Ibid, para 29.

[54] Ibid, paras 33–6.

possibly accord individuals more 'focused' – as opposed to 'aspirational' – rights than they currently do.[55]

International humanitarian law (IHL) is, along with human rights, the domain which has the protection of the individual at the very core of most of its rules. The difference from human rights is that most of humanitarian law provisions are not framed as endowing the individual with rights.[56] They are framed as obligations upon States to protect individuals, without a corresponding individual right necessarily being conferred to the individuals themselves.[57] A number of exceptions, however, can be found in the third and fourth Geneva Conventions.[58] These pertain to procedural rights of protected persons, such as the right to petition or the right to a fair and regular trial.[59] The same is true for the Additional Protocols to the Conventions.[60]

Finally, the International Labour Organization (ILO), whose work is rarely mentioned in this connection,[61] places great emphasis on the individual in most of its conventions. Still, like the conventions on humanitarian law, most ILO instruments impose obligations on States to take appropriate measures for the protection of workers and the abolition of forced and child labour. In some instruments, however, there are clearly defined rights of workers. In the Convention Concerning the Application of the Principles of the Right to Organize and to Bargain Collectively, for example, it is stipulated that the workers shall enjoy adequate protection against anti-union discrimination.[62] Still, while most conventions do not confer individual rights in the sense that Article 36(2)

---

55 There is significant literature on this topic. For a recent account, see A Boyle, 'Human Rights and the Environment: Where Next?' (2012) 23(3) EJIL 613.

56 Parlett, *The Individual in the International Legal System* (n 4) 178–83.

57 Ibid.

58 Geneva Convention III Relative to the Treatment of Prisoners of War (adopted 12 August 1949, entered into force 21 October 1950) 75 UNTS 135; Geneva Convention IV Relative to the Protection of Civilian Persons in Time of War (adopted 12 August 1949, entered into force 21 October 1950) 75 UNTS 287.

59 Parlett, *The Individual in the International Legal System* (n 4) 183.

60 Ibid, 189–90.

61 The ILO has adopted 189 Conventions and 202 Recommendations so far. This body of work is extremely significant.

62 Convention Concerning the Application of the Principles of the Right to Organize and to Bargain Collectively (No. 98) (adopted 1 July 1949, entered into force 18 July 1951) 96 UNTS 257.

of the Vienna Convention on Consular Relations[63] was found to do in *LaGrand*,[64] they seek in any event to protect the individual in a diverse range of situations relating to work conditions.

Overall, since the end of the Second World War there has been a significant body of conventions that seek to protect the individual. This is done by imposing obligations upon States parties to adopt certain conduct with respect to individuals within their jurisdiction, which may sometimes result in bestowing the individual with an individual right (irrespective of whether this can be pursued in the individual's own name at the international level). Human rights instruments most clearly result in such accordance of individual rights. The presence of the State, however, cannot be underestimated. The body of rights as they emerge from the conventions is heavily controlled by States, either through the choice of subject matter or through the choice of scope of application of the relevant instruments, geographical or otherwise.

2. Duty Bearers

Besides benefitting from protection that treaties afford them, individuals also bear obligations under international treaty law. The Nuremberg tribunals marked a very important point in the treatment of the individual in international law.[65] The trials established that an individual might be personally responsible under international law for a number of international crimes. Even before Nuremberg, international law envisaged the criminal responsibility of the individual for particular crimes such as piracy.[66] It was only after Nuremberg, however, that specific treaty arrangements provided for the individual criminal responsibility.

---

[63] Vienna Convention on Consular Relations (adopted 22 April 1963, entered into force 19 March 1967) 596 UNTS 261.

[64] See (n 29).

[65] On the importance of the Nuremberg Tribunals, see K Parlett, 'The Individual and Structural Change in the International Legal System'(2012) 1(3) Cambridge J Intl and Comp L 60, 71.

[66] It has been questioned in the past whether piracy was indeed an international crime, as Spiropoulos among others claims, see Spiropoulos, 'L'Individu …' (n 4), 229. An alternative view is that the crime of piracy merely gave states universal jurisdiction to prosecute it under their own laws against piracy, see Lauterpacht, 'The Subjects …' (n 18) 441–2.

First of all, the Geneva Conventions[67] and their Additional Protocols[68] lay the ground for the responsibility of individuals under international criminal law. Common Article 3 provides for the prohibition of a number of acts against members of armed forces that have laid down their arms and those who are placed *hors de combat* due to wounds, sickness, or detention. Moreover, Articles 50 of the first Geneva Convention, 51 of the second, 130 of the third, and 147 of the fourth define the grave breaches against persons protected by each of the Conventions; Articles 49 of the first Convention, 10 of the second, 129 of the third, and 146 of the fourth provide that the High Contracting Parties are under an obligation to enact legislation so as to provide penal sanctions for the persons that commit such grave breaches. Alternatively, the parties shall extradite these persons to another party. Apart from the Geneva Conventions, the Genocide Convention also provides, as its title suggests (Convention on the Prevention and Punishment of the Crime of Genocide), that genocide is a crime under international law that the contracting parties are under an obligation to prevent and punish.[69]

These examples show that it is clear and well established that individuals also have the capacity to bear obligations under international criminal law. The interesting point in the case of international criminal law is that the capacity to have rights/bear obligations and the capacity to bring a claim in the enforcement of these rights or to be prosecuted for violation of the obligation at the international level may not be found in

---

[67] Geneva Convention I for the Amelioration of the Condition of the Wounded and Sick in Armed Forces in the Field (adopted 12 August 1949, entered into force 21 October 1950) 75 UNTS 31; Geneva Convention II for the Amelioration of the Condition of the Wounded, Sick and Shipwrecked Members of Armed Forces at Sea (adopted 12 August 1949, entered into force 21 October 1950) 75 UNTS 85; Geneva Convention III Relative to the Treatment of Prisoners of War (adopted 12 August 1949, entered into force 21 October 1950) 75 UNTS 135; Geneva Convention IV Relative to the Protection of Civilian Persons in Time of War (adopted 12 August 1949, entered into force 21 October 1950) 75 UNTS 287.

[68] Protocol I Additional to the Geneva Convention of 12 August 1949 and Relating to the Protection of Victims of International Armed Conflicts (adopted 8 June 1977, entered into force 7 December 1978) 1125 UNTS 3; Protocol II Additional to the Geneva Convention of 12 August 1949 and Relating to the Protection of Victims of Non-International Armed Conflicts (adopted 8 June 1977, entered into force 7 December 1978) 1125 UNTS 606.

[69] Convention on the Prevention and Punishment of the Crime of Genocide (adopted 1 January 1948, entered into force 12 January 1951) 78 UNTS 277, Article 2.

the same convention. The crime of genocide or the grave breaches as defined in the Geneva Conventions were envisaged as crimes that would be prosecuted under national law. The reappearance of the individual on the international criminal justice scene, after Nuremberg, took place in quite an unorthodox manner. In the early 1990s, the United Nations Security Council established two ad hoc international criminal tribunals, for the crimes committed in former Yugoslavia (ICTY) and for those committed in Rwanda (ICTR).[70] The statutes of both tribunals establish individual criminal responsibility.[71] The ICTY statute stipulates that the tribunal has power to prosecute persons that have committed grave breaches of the Geneva Conventions, the crime of genocide, violations of the laws and customs of war, and crimes against humanity.[72] The ICTR statute on the other hand posits that the tribunal may prosecute the crime of genocide, crimes against humanity, and breaches of Common Article 3 of the Geneva Conventions.[73]

It is clear that the Statutes of the Tribunals make direct reference to the Geneva Conventions, establishing an international judicial process for the prosecution of the crimes stipulated therein. The Statutes also make reference to the crime of genocide using the definition and phraseology of, but without making direct reference to, the Genocide Convention. A similar pattern is followed in the Statute of the International Criminal Court (ICC). The ICC is the first permanent court with jurisdiction to administer international criminal justice, and was founded by the Treaty of Rome in 1998.[74] Articles 6–8 of the Statute posit that the ICC has jurisdiction to prosecute the crime of genocide, crimes against humanity, war crimes, and the crime of aggression. Again, Article 8, in defining war crimes, makes explicit reference to the grave breaches as defined in the Geneva Conventions. While human rights instruments may provide both for the capacity to hold rights and for the capacity to seek enforcement of those rights in the same instrument or in protocols to that instrument, international criminal law has developed in a different way. International

---

70 UNSC Resolution 827, S/RES/827 of 25 May 1993; Resolution 955, S/RES/955 of 8 November 1994.

71 ICTY Statute accessed 24 February 2013 at www.icty.org/x/file/Legal%20Library/Statute/statute_sept09_en.pdf, Article 7 ICTY; ICTR Statute, accessed 24 February 2013 at www.unictr.org/Portals/0/English/Legal/Statute/2010.pdf, Article 6 ICTR.

72 ICTY Statute, Articles 2, 3, 4 and 5.

73 ICTR Statute, Articles 2, 3 and 4.

74 Rome Statute of the International Criminal Court (adopted 17 July 1998, entered into force 1 July 2002) 2187 UNTS 3.

crimes have been codified in or created through treaties different from those that provide for the prosecution of these crimes at the international level. The statutes of the international criminal tribunals have drawn directly from such former treaties in order to substantiate the tribunals' jurisdiction *rationae materiae*.[75]

V. THE INDIVIDUAL AS USER

It is mainly human rights treaties that have championed the capacity of the individual to bring international claims in its own name against a State before an international court or treaty body. As stated, the capacity to hold rights does not necessarily go hand-in-hand with the capacity to enforce these rights at the international level. This is confirmed by the fact that not all treaties which endow the individual with one type of capacity (to hold rights) also endow it with the other (to bring an international claim). However, most human rights instruments do contain a process for seeking international enforcement of the rights therein guaranteed. This process may sometimes involve recourse before an international court or tribunal, or it may also take the form of a complaints process before human rights treaty bodies that do not qualify as judicial organs.

As far as judicial procedures are concerned, the ECHR, most prominently, offers the full range of capacities to individuals to pursue their human rights claims against the member States of the Council of Europe.[76] The American Convention on Human Rights also accords individuals a right to recourse before the Inter-American Court of Human Rights,[77] as does the Protocol to the African Charter that establishes an African Court of Human and People's Rights.[78] It must be noted, however, that individuals were not accorded access to these tribunals directly and unequivocally from the outset. Rather, this happened through

---

75 The statutes also draw from custom but this falls outside the scope of this chapter.

76 Protocol No. 11 to the Convention for the Protection of Human Rights and Fundamental Freedoms, Restructuring the Control Machinery Established Thereby (adopted 11 May 1994, entered into force 1 November 1998) ETS No.5.

77 Rules of the Court accessed 24 February 2013 at www.corteidh.or.cr/reglamento.cfm, Article 25.

78 Protocol to the African Charter on Human and People's Rights on the Establishment of an African Court on Human and People's Rights (adopted 9 June 1998, entered into force 25 January 2004) OAU Doc. OAU/LEG/EXP/AFCHR/PROT (III) Article 5(3).

a long, incremental process that involved the adoption of additional protocols,[79] or the exercise of judicial activism,[80] or both. Even so, the States parties to these conventions retain some powers as to the proceedings.[81]

Turning to human rights treaty bodies, the Human Rights Committee of the ICCPR can hear individual claims and provide an opinion.[82] Similar proceedings exist for the Committee for the Elimination of All Forms of Racial Discrimination.[83] The optional protocol to the ICESCR also breaks new ground in providing for an individual complaint procedure relating to the economic, social, and cultural rights protected by that Covenant.[84]

Bilateral investment treaties also normally allow individuals who qualify as investors to bring claims against host States in various arbitral fora. However, since it is corporations that usually take advantage both of the protection and the corresponding right to bring claims, the majority of awards concern disputes between States and corporate entities rather than individuals.

International environmental law does not offer individuals any similar avenues for recourse before international bodies. However, the phenomenon of bringing what can be termed 'essentially environmental claims' before human rights courts is not unknown. In these claims, individuals seek to rely on human rights provisions in order to protect what is in essence an interest or a right that is in the instance more closely

---

[79] See AA Cançado Trindade, *The Access of Individuals to International Justice* (OUP, 2011) 37–47.

[80] Ibid.

[81] Especially in the context of the American and African Conventions, see Articles 25 and 5 of the Rules of the Court and the Protocol to the Convention respectively.

[82] 1966 Optional Protocol to the 1966 International Covenant on Civil and Political Rights (adopted 16 December 1966, entered into force 23 March 1976) 999 UNTS 171.

[83] CERD, Article14.

[84] Optional Protocol to the International Covenant on Economic, Social and Cultural Rights, A/RES/63/117, adopted on 10 December 2008. The Protocol entered into force on 5 May 2013. See also Provisional Rules of Procedure under the Optional Protocol to the International Covenant on Economic, Social and Cultural Rights, adopted by the Committee at its forty-ninth session (12–13 November 2012), E/C.12/49/3.

connected to environmental factors than to human rights pure and simple.[85]

The discrepancy between the capacity to hold rights under international environmental law and the capacity to exercise these rights on the international level should not be exaggerated. It is the nature and content of the rights enjoyed by individuals under international environmental law that makes a difference. Broad, aspirational environmental protection would be hard to translate into an internationally enforceable right, especially given the fact that, unlike human rights or investment protection, environmental values and rules are rather more recent.[86] Moreover, most environmental problems are more easily resolved through concerted action among States rather than by way of individual enforcement.[87] In contrast to environmental values, and closer to human rights, concrete protection of investors in a bilateral setting also more easily lends itself to judicial dispute settlement.

On a more general note, there is an effort, mainly by scholars but also in practice, to see that environmental values or investment protection are dressed up in a human rights gown. Indeed, there are increasing efforts to address the protection and preservation of the environment not only as a collective goal, but also as the '*fait generateur*' of individual environmental rights.[88] Similarly, there has been an effort to read rights of

---

[85] See, for example, *Lopez Ostra v Spain*, Decision of 9 December 1994, Series A No 303, 53, para 24; *Tatar v Romania*, Requete No. 67021/01, 06/07/2009. On the jurisprudence of the Court on environmental matters, see L Loucaides, 'Environmental Protection Through the Jurisprudence of the European Convention on Human Rights' (2005) 75 BYBIL 249. Investment law has also been used by applicants in order to further environmental claims, either directly or incidentally, see J Viñuales, 'Foreign Investment and the Environment in International Law: An Ambiguous Relationship' (2009) 80(1) BYBIL 244.

[86] See (n 7).

[87] Environmental law has mainly evolved through multilateral environmental agreements (MEAs) that do not include an option for enforcement through individual recourse to courts. MEAs typically impose obligations on states, coupled with reporting and implementation criteria, which are often reviewed by the bodies of the relevant agreements. While some instruments contain provisions for the participation of the public in environmental decision making (see, eg, Convention on Environmental Impact Assessment in a Transboundary Context (adopted 25 February 1991, entered into force 10 September 1997) 1989 UNTS 309), these are the exception rather than the rule.

[88] See (n 85).

investors under international law as human rights.[89] Human rights come into investor-State disputes on the other end of the spectrum as well. That is, States have started bringing 'human rights defences' against investor claims.[90] This could lead to broader protection of either the investor or the State in terms of both substance and procedure. The investor's rights would not be limited to property-related rights but could extend to a right to private life, for example.[91] Similarly, the State would be in a position to defend its conduct on the basis that it was complying with its obligations to protect human rights. In much the same vein, some human rights could be read broadly enough so as to incorporate aspects of environmental protection.[92] In terms of procedure, protection of the environment could be 'incorporated' in a human rights agenda that can find its way before courts such as the European Court of Human Rights (ECtHR). The same is true for investors' rights in cases where bringing a claim before an arbitral tribunal would not be possible or desirable for the claimant. This tendency to read environmental protection or investor protection in human rights could indeed have a broadening effect on the content of human rights, investor rights, or on the scope of environmental protection. So it could be said that the 'model' of international human rights protection is being 'rolled out' in other areas of international law, gradually transforming the individual from a mere beneficiary to an actual user of international treaty law.

In any event, the discrepancy between holding a right and having the capacity to bring an international claim regarding that right is still generally visible in international law. Most procedures that involve individuals are controlled either by States or by inter-State bodies, and the outcome of complaints procedures rarely has a direct effect. States remain the principal players in the enforcement game. Nevertheless, the progress achieved over the past 40 years in terms of access of individuals to international justice is remarkable. Given the incremental nature of

---

[89] See M Karavias in this *Handbook*; EU Petersmann, 'Human Rights and International Economic Law' (2012) 4(2) *Trade Law and Development* 283, 297–300.

[90] B Simma, 'Foreign Investment Arbitration: A Place for Human Rights?' (2011) 60 ICLQ 573; N Klein, 'Human Rights and International Investment Law: Investment Protection as Human Right?' (2012) 4(1) Goettingen J Intl L 200.

[91] Of course, this is of no great practical importance where the investor is an individual. The individual in this case would benefit from the human rights protection anyway but not in his capacity as an investor. On the human rights benefits of corporations, see M Karavias, in this *Handbook*.

[92] See (n 85).

that progress, there is reason to believe that such access will continue to expand. It seems that the capacity to enforce rights will grow both in terms of substance (more rights will be internationally 'actionable') and in terms of process (more fora will be available to hear individual complaints).

Treaties, then, may create not mere benefits for individuals, but substantive rights which can be claimed on the international level. In being given the capacity to claim in its own name, the individual is upgraded from a mere beneficiary to an actual user of the treaty (regime), employing the treaty to achieve protection of rights at the international level. But such capacity to claim internationally is not necessary for the individual to be seen as a user of treaties: the same can be said even if the treaty does not allow for claims to be brought by the individual on the international level. First, States do not restrict the reach of international law to the international level. They create rights and processes that individuals can directly enjoy on the domestic level. Second, individuals themselves become more assertive of their rights, again on the domestic level. This apparent evolution, however slow, uneven, or haphazard it may be, brings the individual closer to the epicenter of international law.

Indeed, treaties may allow individuals to 'use' them domestically: this is the case when, for example, a treaty establishes an 'individual' right even if it does not allow for an international claim to be brought by the protected individual. Such rights, the ICJ confirmed, are accorded by Article 36(2) of the Vienna Convention on Consular Relations,[93] as well as probably by other treaties not usually regarded as establishing rights of individuals. The right can then be invoked before the domestic court, and the individual can use it to control governmental action. Taking this thought further, the many 'inward-looking' obligations that States assume by means of concluding treaties may be seen as giving individuals a basis on which to challenge governmental conduct, even regulatory conduct.[94] Inter-State treaties then are used by the individual to challenge State conduct by requesting judicial review under domestic public law.[95] This is of course subject, to a large extent, to the peculiar regulation of the domestic legal system regarding the 'domestication' of international law,[96] but the position in international law is clear: a treaty, even if not a

[93] *LaGrand* and *Avena* (n 28).

[94] See Tzanakopoulos, 'Domestic Courts in International Law ...' (n 9) 138–42 with further references.

[95] Cf Roberts, 'Clash of Paradigms ...' (n 1) 45–6 for a similar thought.

[96] See Tzanakopoulos, 'Domestic Courts in International Law ...' (n 9) 147–50 for further analysis.

'rights' treaty, may actually grant individual rights which require implementation at the domestic level. The individual thus should be able, at least under international law, to use it domestically.

There are examples of treaty regimes where States have clearly provided for individuals to be able to use the treaty on the domestic level. The Åarhus Convention on Access to Information, Public Participation in Decision-Making and Access to Justice in Environmental Matters is a good example.[97] The Convention defines the 'public' as meaning any natural or legal person.[98] Under Article 4, it envisages that the public can request and obtain information on environmental matters. Article 6 posits that the public may participate in the decision-making process through the submission of comments. Finally, Article 9 provides for access to justice: if any person considers that they did not receive the information they requested or that they were not allowed to participate under the provisions of the treaty, they have a right of review of the relevant decisions either before a court or another independent body established by law.

The Convention on Civil Liability for Oil Pollution (CLC) and the related Fund Convention[99] are two other examples where the individual may actually use international law on the domestic level. The CLC provides that the owner of a ship that causes oil pollution damage shall provide compensation.[100] While there is no direct reference to who can be a claimant, the preamble and Articles 1(2) and 3(4) make it clear that the claimant can be an individual. The individual is mentioned also in the Fund Convention, which provides for an additional layer of compensation in case the shipowner cannot fulfill the obligation to compensate under the CLC. Article 4(1) posits that the Fund shall provide compensation to 'any person suffering pollution damage if such person has been unable to obtain full and adequate compensation'. These conventions envisage a

---

[97] For an analysis of the convention, see M Fitzmaurice, 'Note on the Participation of Civil Society in Environmental Matters: The 1998 Åarhus Convention on Access to Information, Public Participation and Access to Justice in Environmental Matters' (2010) 4 Human Rights and Intl L Discourse 47.

[98] Article 2(4).

[99] International Convention on Civil Liability for Oil Pollution Damage (adopted 27 November 1992, entered into force 30 May 1996) 973 UNTS 3; Protocol of 1992 to Amend the International Convention on the Establishment of an International Fund for Oil Pollution Damage, 1971, (adopted 27 November 1992, entered into force 30 May 1996) 1110 UNTS 57, IMO, LEG/CONF.16 of 2 December 1992.

[100] CLC Article 3.

direct claim by the individual against the shipowner or the Fund.[101] Further, they also provide for access to justice through an obligation on States parties to establish the jurisdiction of their domestic courts to hear cases arising within the ambit of the conventions.[102]

These instruments go beyond the granting of rights to individuals. They engage them in the domestic decision-making processes as fully as possible or they provide them with access to compensation if they are victims of environmental damage. To some extent they do away with the intermediary steps that involve the presence of the State and they allow international law to be directly used by the individual. Of course it is still States that are under the obligation to provide for the framework in which these rights will be exercised.[103] Still, these provisions confer a capacity on the individual to use international law against the State, and even against other individuals.

There are also subtle ways for individuals to employ treaty law as a defence. Recently, a Greek court of first instance was faced with a situation where number of immigrants escaped from a detention center. The conditions in the detention were truly appalling, and the immigrants were actually in fear of their health and lives. All of them were later apprehended. They were charged with the crime of 'escape' under Greek criminal law. They pleaded in defence that the conditions of their detention were so appalling as to violate a number of rights guaranteed under the ECHR. The Court, in a striking decision, in effect accepted that ECHR rights may be entered as criminal law defences.[104]

Use of treaty law, and indeed use of the law of treaties, may actually occur in an even more subtle manner: the law of treaties in and of itself does not, as we saw, accord any specific capacities to the individual – at

---

[101] Fund Convention, Article 4; see also IOPC Fund, Claims Manual, Edn 2008, 17, accessed 24 February 2013 at www.iopcfunds.org/uploads/tx_iopcpublications/2008_claims_manual_e.pdf.

[102] CLC Article 9(2); Fund Convention, Article 7(2).

[103] This is obvious not only from Article 9(2) of the CLC which provides that contracting parties shall ensure that their courts have jurisdiction. Contracting parties shall also, for example, control the procedure of issuing an insurance certificate for the shipowner (Article 7). The Fund Convention provides, for instance, that contracting parties shall recognize the Fund as a legal person (Article 2(2)) and also that the contributions to the Fund are made through the contracting parties (Article 10(1)).

[104] See A Tzanakopoulos, 'Greek Court Acquits Immigrants who Escaped Appalling Detaining Conditions' 12 January 2013, EJIL: Talk! Report accessed 24 February 2013 at www.ejiltalk.org/immigrants-who-escaped-appalling-detention-conditions-acquitted/.

most it leaves States free to do so through the treaties they conclude.[105] However, individuals may use the law of treaties itself before international and domestic courts in order to determine the existence, scope, and content of treaty obligations allegedly binding on States and applicable to the facts of the case before the court. In this connection, individuals may use the parts of the law of treaties regarding, for example, intertemporal law, treaty conclusion, the rules of interpretation, and even reservations. A clear example of the latter instance could be the *Belilos* case before the ECtHR:[106] where the individual has access to a court (individual or domestic) and an international treaty obligation is at play on the facts, the individual will be able to use the law of treaties to argue about the character of a particular 'statement' of the State, to establish that it is a reservation, and to discuss its effects on the obligation binding on the State under the relevant treaty.

VI. BEYOND USERS? INDIVIDUALS AS PARTICIPANTS

The preceding section mapped out the ways in which the individual appears in the international legal order in relation to international treaties. The individual has the capacity to hold rights and to bear obligations and also has the capacity to bring claims, as well as to be prosecuted before international courts, tribunals, and treaty bodies. These capacities are not concurrent. They rather occur in a 'mix-and-match' fashion according to the specific treaty regimes. This happens because all of these capacities are filtered through the activities of the States. States and not individuals conclude treaties and decide upon the rights conferred on individuals. States and not individuals set up international courts that have jurisdiction to hear cases brought by individuals. What is more, States do not provide for general rights, obligations, or procedures for individuals. They set up treaty regimes with a specific scope of application *rationae personae* and *rationae materiae*. Similarly, the courts that may entertain claims by individuals are limited by their statutes or their constitutive treaties. To sum up, there is no international law of treaties applicable to individuals in general, as there is no international court with general jurisdiction that can entertain cases brought by or against individuals.

---

105 See section III above.

106 *Belilos v Switzerland* (10328/83) [1988] ECHR 4 (29 April 1988).

This lack of cohesion regarding the place of individuals in international law leaves them either included in or excluded from the ambit of rights, obligations, and processes, depending on the particular treaty regime. States determine such inclusion or exclusion.[107] There are, however, signs that this pattern is not settled. In a number of situations, as we saw, individuals are upgraded from mere beneficiaries to users of international treaty law, and indeed so even on the domestic level. Could it be that we are now moving beyond the individual as a user, to a stage where the individual will be seen as a fully-fledged participant in international treaty law?

There have been voices in the literature that suggest that the individual should not be seen any longer as an actor that simply bears a number of capacities depending on treaty law. Roucounas has suggested that under the UN Convention on the Law of the Sea[108] the individual, among other actors, has become a user of that body of law.[109] The existence of a – largely undefined – category of 'users of the sea' was affirmed by the International Tribunal for the Law of the Sea (ITLOS) Seabed Disputes Chamber. In its advisory opinion, the Chamber stated that among the parties that can bring a claim before it are the 'users of the sea'.[110] Perhaps Roucounas can be interpreted to mean that, as a user of the sea, the individual should become a participant in the law of the sea, at least in its treaty aspect.

Higgins has used the term 'participants in the international legal system'; in this she included individuals.[111] Higgins distanced herself from the mainstream literature claiming that:

---

[107] This terminology is borrowed from Bianchi's paper on individuals ('The Fight for Inclusion …' (n 15)). Inclusion means inclusion of an entity in the system as a subject/actor, see p 46.

[108] United Nations Convention on the Law of the Sea (adopted 10 December 1982, entered into force 16 November 1994) 1834 UNTS 397.

[109] Roucounas, 'Facteurs Privés…' (n 15). See also E Roucounas, 'Effectiveness of International Law for the Users of the Sea' (2004–2005) VIII/IX Cursors Erumediterraneos Bancaja de Derecho Internacional 869. Roucounas does not define what a user in the law of the sea is. He states, however, that the users can be private or public as well as real or fictitious and generally he refers to a user as anything, from the ship and its crew to the State, see ibid at 872.

[110] ITLOS Seabed Disputes Chamber, *Responsibilities and Obligations of States Sponsoring Persons and Entities with Respect to Activities in the Area*, Advisory Opinion,) accessed 24 February 2013 at www.itlos.org/fileadmin/itlos/documents/cases/case_no_17/adv_op_010211.pdf, para 179.

[111] R Higgins, *Problems and Process: International Law and How We Use It* (Clarendon Press, 1994) 50.

> the notion of 'subjects' and 'objects' has no credible reality, and, in my view, no functional purpose. We have created an intellectual prison of our own choosing and then declared it to be an unalterable constraint.[112]

DP O'Connell wrote, almost 60 years ago, that '[t]he individual as the end of community is a *member* of the community, and a member has status: he is not an object'.[113] What O'Connell points out is that the individual is in fact a member of the international community. He contends that '[i]f personality is no more than a sum of capacities, then he (the individual) is a person in international law, though his capacities may be different from and less in number and substance than the capacities of a State'.[114]

These authors make some far-reaching statements, and yet they do not offer any definite answers. How is the individual transformed from a mere beneficiary of treaty law to a user, and beyond that to a participant or a 'member of the community'?

As far as users are concerned, section V demonstrated that States control to what extent they will allow use of treaty regimes by individuals, whether at the international or the domestic level. But individuals also play a role in pushing for the evolution of their own status as users by seeking to employ inward looking treaty norms to challenge and control governmental action. Much the same applies perhaps for the notion of participants: the Åarhus Convention seems to have allowed individuals to become participants in decision-making processes regarding environmental matters.

Another area of law where the individual can be seen as a participant is international investment law. First, the individual must be a party to a transnational contract with a host State. To the extent that the contract is governed – wholly or partly – by international law,[115] the individual can be seen as participating in the international legal order.[116] This is certainly not the place to analyse the thorny question of 'internationalized contracts', that is, contracts between States and individuals subject to international law; however, a few remarks are in order. There are two

---

112 Ibid, 49.

113 DP O'Connell, *International Law* (2nd edn, Stevens & Sons, 1970) 108.

114 Ibid.

115 On this point, see the chapter by Karavias in this *Handbook*.

116 Charles Leben considers the individual as a limited subject of international law in the field of international investment law, if there is a clause in the internationalized contract that grants access to an international tribunal, see C Leben, 'La Théorie du Contrat D'État e L'Évolution du Droit International des Investissements' (2003) 302 RCADI 197, 309.

main strands in the literature regarding the existence of internationalized contracts. According to one view, internationalized contracts do not exist. They are merely a theoretical device invented so as to ensure protection to the investor without due regard to the interests of the host State.[117] It is clear that if this view is followed, the individual cannot be seen as a participant. According to the prevailing view, however, the contract can indeed be internationalized if there is a choice of law provision indicating international law as the governing law of the contract.[118] In this case, both parties – the individual and the State – assume obligations under international law. The breach of international obligations, even by an individual, entails necessarily the individual's *international* responsibility. A contract, an (internationalized) agreement, thus elevates the individual from a user to a fully-fledged participant in the international legal system.

This capacity of the individual (to participate) is, however, marginally exercised. It is corporate entities and not individuals that nowadays conclude most internationalized (mostly investment/concession) contracts.[119] If the fact that there are rather few instances where international law is the only law governing the contract is also taken into account, it seems that the role of individuals as participants is indeed minimal.

While the individual as participant is a rather exceptional phenomenon, it signifies that the next step, the next upgrade, is possible using the traditional devices of treaty law: States may grant even more capacities to individuals, and individuals may seek to use treaties to claim or consolidate such capacities.

---

[117] M Sornarajah, *The International Law on Foreign Investment* (3rd edn, CUP, 2010) 289–99.

[118] On this point, see, FA Mann, 'The Law Governing State Contracts' (1944) 21 BYBIL 11; P Weil, 'Droit International et Contract D'Etat' in *Mélanges Offerts á Paul Reuter: le Droit International, Unité et Diversité* (Pedone, 1981) 549; Leben, 'La Théorie du Contrat D'État …' (n 114) 252–63. It is indeed rare that parties to such contracts choose international law as the exclusive governing law. More often than not they opt for the law of the host state in combination with generally applicable principles of international law, see Sornarajah, *Foreign Investment* (n 115) 278. The default provision of the ICSID Convention (Article 42) also opts for a mixed body of law governing the contract: the law of the host state and such rules of international law as may be applicable.

[119] Sornarajah, *Foreign Investment* (n 115) 60.

VII. CONCLUSION: AN AGENDA FOR RESEARCH

This chapter has explored the position of the individual in the law of treaties. The first claim of the chapter is that there is no need to enter into a discussion of the concept of personality of the individual in the international legal order. It is more accurate to see the individual as endowed with different capacities: a capacity to hold rights and to enforce these rights, a capacity to bear obligations, and so forth. After a brief look into the role of the individual in the VCLT, the chapter examined the individual as a beneficiary and a bearer of obligations, as a user, and finally as a participant. The practice in the law of treaties leads to the conclusion that States often endow individuals with rights (and with the capacity to enforce those rights) while at the same time the individual can be a bearer of international obligations (usually under international criminal or international humanitarian law). These aspects of the role of the individual in the law of treaties are rather unproblematic, despite the slow development of the law in most of these areas.

More interesting, and therefore more problematic, are two other roles of the individual. The individual has used international law either directly, when endowed by States with the power to bring claims in international fora, or indirectly, when invoking international treaty law before domestic courts. While there are some moves that suggest that more and more international fora will be open to the individual, the second way the individual uses international law is more subtle and, possibly, less controlled by States.

The individual as a participant, on the other hand, appears more in the scholarly debate than in the practice of international law. This may change in the future, but for the time being is more of a fascinating theoretical possibility than concrete reality.

The matter of the individual as 'user' of and 'participant' in treaty law certainly requires more attention and analysis; a number of questions remain. Is there a real tension between States that wish to keep the individual under their control and the individual that seeks to escape that control? Could it be that States have conceded what is absolutely necessary (eg, direct access to regional human rights courts) but they safeguard their primacy under any other aspect of international law? Or could it be that we are witnessing the first signs of wider individual participation, dictated by, among other things, the realities of a highly interconnected international legal order? All these questions merit closer attention and analysis. They constitute an agenda for future research regarding the individual in international treaty law.

Index

This index lists aspects of treaty law addressed in the preceding chapters. As the whole book is about *the law of treaties* and much of its about the *Vienna Conventions* governing aspects of that law, those terms are not referenced. The same holds true for names of cases.